The Abnormal Personality

Robert W. White received both his undergraduate and graduate training at Harvard University and has spent more than thirty years there in a range of capacities: Chairman of the Department of Social Relations, Director of the Harvard Psychological Clinic, and Professor of Clinical Psychology. During this time Dr. White has been distinguished for his many contributions to the fields of clinical psychology and personality. He is now Emeritus Professor at Harvard University and devotes his professional efforts to scholarly writing.

Norman F. Watt received his undergraduate education at Northwestern University and his graduate training at The Ohio State University. He then served as NIMH post-doctoral research fellow at the Federal Institute of Technology in Zurich, Switzerland. He taught for seven years in the Department of Social Relations at Harvard University as Assistant Professor and Lecturer in Clinical Psychology, and then served on the faculty of the University of Massachusetts at Amherst for eight years, as Associate Professor, Professor, and finally Chairperson in the Psychology Department. Presently, Dr. Watt is Professor of Clinical Psychology at the University of Denver. He is known primarily for his longitudinal research in schizophrenia and for chairing the Risk Research Consortium of investigators in that field.

The Abnormal Personality

Robert W. White
Professor Emeritus, Harvard University

Norman F. Watt
Professor, University of Denver

5th edition

John Wiley & Sons
New York   Chichester   Brisbane   Toronto

Photo Research by Flavia Rando-Picturebook
Photo Editor, Stella Kupferberg

Library of Congress Cataloging in Publication Data:

White, Robert Winthrop.
    The abnormal personality.

    Bibliography: p.
    Includes indexes.
    1. Psychology, Pathological.   2. Psychotherapy.
I. Watt, Norman F., joint author.   II. Title.   [DNLM:
1. Mental disorders.   2. Psychopathology.   3. Psychotherapy.   WM100 W587a]

RC454.W488   1981   157   80-22055
ISBN 0-471-04599-3

Printed in the United States of America

10 9 8 7 6 5 4 3 2 1

Preface

The first four editions of *The Abnormal Personality* were published in 1948, 1956, 1964, and 1973. In many respects this fifth edition shows its relation to the earlier ones. We have retained the basic organization, the once-novel practice of integrating case histories in the textual discussion, the informal expository style, and the emphasis on psychodynamic conceptions of personality and abnormal functioning. A textbook that is published in five separate decades must, however, change quite substantially to be responsive to new developments in the mental health disciplines. Chapter headings are similar to those in the fourth edition, but what appears under them is in most cases different, with long sections that are wholly new.

Abnormal psychology—and indeed our whole society—has undergone revolutionary changes since the first publication of this text. At that time, mental hospitals were largely custodial, research on the biological bases of human behavior was in doldrums, shock treatments were just coming into prominent use, group methods of psychological treatment looked like dubious shortcuts, and mental health received only feeble public interest and financial support. The chief breakthrough for abnormal psychology was the psychoanalytic treatment of the neuroses, with the light this cast on personal development and unconscious motivation. The most dramatic happening in the intervening years was the revolution in public attitudes whereby mental health became a popular cause and a community responsibility. Concurrently, mental hospitals began to be transformed into therapeutic milieus and more recently were phased out in large part, to be replaced by community mental health centers and outpatient facilities. Shock treatment was perfected but then substantially displaced by tranquilizing and antidepressant drugs. Biological research leaped forward, especially with respect to behavioral genetics and the biochemistry of the brain. Group psychotherapy expanded widely, behavioral treatments and family therapy rose to established places, and the generality of the medical or disease model, so long traditional in explaining abnormal behavior, was effectively challenged. Psychoanalytic thinking moved toward ego psychology and produced among other things the socially oriented concept of ego identity, and the cumbersome analytic technique began to give way to innovations branching out in all directions. Being faithful children of their own times, the earlier editions chronicled those developments and reflected the shifting tides of theory. So too does this one.

The past does not change, but our historical introduction illustrates the principle that each age rewrites history to emphasize present concerns. Understandably, there is more change evident in our rewriting of recent history than of ancient history. We have kept the same five case studies for the clinical introduction as in the fourth edition; three of them were new then, and two of the subjects were not born when the first edition went to press. For the first time, the opening section of that chapter introduces students to the problem of classification, and in particular to the most recent revision of *The Diagnostic and Statistical Manual of Mental Disorders* (1980). This acknowledges that the process of naming what we see is an inextricable part of understanding what we see.

The next three chapters pursue the theme of adaptation. The adaptive process is first presented descriptively, then related to fundamental principles of learning and cognitive organization. The chapter on the development and organization of personality offers an account of normal growth while showing at each point how development can go astray. A whole chapter is devoted to the subject of anxiety and defense, examining the special effects of anxiety on the learning process and developing the concept of protectively burdened personalities. To the extent that disordered behavior represents faulty adaptive habits, these three chapters provide a foundation for its understanding.

The neuroses are rechristened "anxiety disorders," and they are presented not as diseases, with sharp distinction between symptom and underlying cause, but as miscarriages in meeting the difficulties of living. More attention than ever before is devoted in this chapter and throughout the book to biological advances in research, theory, and clinical practice. Two chapters on psychological treatment follow immediately. We count it an educational blunder to postpone treatment to the end of the book, as if description of disorders were a goal in itself regardless of what can be done about them. The chief methods of treatment, including behavior therapy, were developed for anxiety disorders, even though wider applications have later been discovered. Dealing with the subject at this point is therefore historically appropriate; it is also of service in directing attention to possible treatment for each of the disorders discussed in subsequent chapters. Much of the new writing in these two chapters reflects the trend to break with established traditions in delivering clinical service.

The chapter on psychophysiological disorders comes next, much sooner than in previous editions, largely because of our growing recognition that these disorders have much in common with anxiety disorders. The new research on life stress especially emphasizes the importance of social context in determining bodily dysfunction. The next three chapters dealing with conduct disorders, drug dependence, and sexual disorders also exemplify with special force the social embeddedness of abnormal behavior. Many of these troubles have in common the acting out, rather than the suppression, of certain impulses, and they share the theme of conflict with the law. Crime and drug use have received much public exposure in recent years, causing alarm and increased effort in both research and treatment. All the sexual disorders have come out of the closet, so to speak, demanding attention and fresh perspectives. We have concentrated particularly on the biological foundations of sexual behavior and considered the subject in the light of recent changes in sexual, social, and political consciousness.

The three chapters on the psychoses and brain disorders rely more heavily on medical models of disease and present a great deal of new research, some of it quite technical, on genetics, biochemistry, diagnosis, premorbid development, treatment, and outcome. These serious disorders have come to be regarded in longitudinal perspective for good reason. The advances in brain physiology, if not yet a breakthrough, seem to be headed in that hopeful direction.

The last two chapters give special focus to the social dimensions of disordered behavior, first with specific reference to mental retardation and then more generally to the problems of community mental health. The 1960s may be regarded as the decade of enlightenment about the causes of mental retardation, and the 1970s have exposed several possible cures, so we have featured some exciting new developments in the treatment and prevention of retardation. The decade of the 1970s was also a period of testing, disillusionment, and rethinking of the promises of the community mental health movement. The last chapter evaluates this development with special attention to crisis intervention, mental health consultation, services for children and other underserved groups, parent education, and prevention, which may become the watchword for mental health in the 1980s. Part of the work in a community mental health system must be done by professionally trained people, but they cannot do it all. They can be effective only in a favorable climate of public opinion, which is reflected in the facilities provided, volunteer service, public and private financial support, and dedication to a social order conducive to sound human growth.

Our purpose in this book is to write about abnormal people in a way that will be valuable and interesting to students new to the subject. A first course in abnormal psychology is not intended to train specialists. Its goal is more general: it should provide students with the opportunity to whet their interest, expand their horizons, register a certain body of new facts, and relate what they learn to the rest of their knowledge about humankind. The value of a course in abnormal psychology is not limited to those who plan to become professional workers with troubled people. We try here to present the subject in such a way as to emphasize its usefulness to all students of human nature.

The most obvious change in this edition that will be noticed immediately by those who have used the book before is the presence of illustrations. The first four editions contained very few graphic illustrations and no photographs. Each chapter of this edition is illustrated with fine art and several photographs carefully selected to highlight important points in the text. Many chapters also contain graphic illustrations. There are even a few cartoons that make a point. We feel that the illustrations enhance the pedagogical value as well as the interest of the book, and we look forward to the reactions of teachers and students.

It is a pleasure to express our gratitude to Dr. Donald Peterson, Professor Joachim Meyer, Dr. Gloria Leon, and Dr. Margaret Riggs for permitting us to use their case material. Special thanks are also due to Drs. Andrew Crider, David Ricks, Brendan Maher, and Sid Glassman, who read and criticized various sections of the book. We are indebted to Dr. Richard Lewine for the exhaustive glossary of terms in this volume and for the accompanying resource manual. Ted Grubb and Mark Kirchhofer prepared the companion booklet of test questions.

Close observers will have noticed that this edition is published by John Wiley & Sons, not by Ronald Press, which published the first four editions. A part of the bargain for us in the purchase of Ronald by Wiley was the capable staff of production specialists at Wiley who have given us their time and their talents. We wish to acknowledge, in particular, the extraordinary skill of Rosemary Wellner in copy editing, of Stella Kupferberg in photograph selection and art work, and of Rosie Hirsch in production management. Lori Morris, Miriam Navarro, and Connie Rende also deserve our thanks for their services, as does Jack Burton, the Psychology Editor whose name is seldom seen in neon lights though his editorial products are read all over the country and around the world. Only authors can adequately appreciate how much we owe to Linda Wilbanks, Diana Scriver, and Debra Karas for their secretarial and administrative services. And finally we wish to thank Helga Watt for her conscientious proofreading of every word in this text. Our debt to the hundreds of thousands of students and teachers who have read, criticized, and enjoyed the book over the years goes without saying.

ROBERT W. WHITE
NORMAN F. WATT

Marlborough, New Hampshire
Englewood, Colorado
July, 1980

viii

Contents

4. Development and Organization of Personality   113

5. Anxiety and Defense   159

6. Anxiety Disorders   187

7. Psychological Treatment: Individual Methods   225

16. Mental Retardation   605

17. Community Mental Health   647

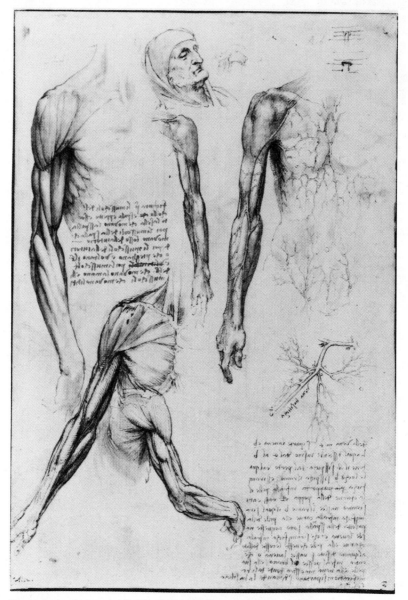

Drawings by Leonardo da Vinci. Royal Library, Windsor Castle.
Reproduced by gracious permission of Her Majesty Queen Elizabeth II.

I
Historical Introduction: Origins of Abnormal Psychology

Abnormal psychology was once considered a remote province of knowledge, explored only by a few specialists. As such it played no more than a minor part in our thinking about human nature. Today it contributes richly to the training of professional workers, especially psychiatrists, psychologists, social workers, teachers, and ministers, whose duties bring them in frequent contact with troubled people. More than this, it occupies a respected place among general college courses, for it is seen to be capable of making a significant contribution to all thinking about human problems and the human quest for a better way of life. Abnormal personalities are not mysteriously set apart from the normal. Their various peculiarities are often simply exaggerations of what is to be found in every human being; their problems may represent unfortunate outcomes of processes we all use in seeking to lead our lives. They are therefore well suited to enlarge our understanding of personal development as a whole. If we know what can go wrong with adaptive behavior, we are the wiser in making it go right.

When we set ourselves to examine the field of abnormal psychology we can proceed in two ways. We can look into the history of the subject and discover how it came to be what it is today. This method offers distinct advantages over an immediate plunge into facts and current problems. Science generally advances in a disorderly fashion. At any given moment the greatest activity occurs at three or four isolated points, the location of which is determined by temporary urgency, by newly discovered techniques, or even by fashion. It is easy to get lost in the details and preoccupations of current research, and the best protection against doing so is to anchor our study firmly in the framework of history. By turning up the facts in the same order in which they confronted past investigators one can better appreciate the really basic difficulties that tend to impede understanding, and one can more readily keep the whole subject in place in the larger context of human affairs. On the other hand we could begin our study in a quite different way: by making a clinical survey of the facts that constitute the subject matter of abnormal psychology. We could examine a series of cases illustrating the kinds of things we will be studying in more systematic form throughout the book. The clinical method has the advantage of realistic vividness and of proceeding in the right direction from fact to theory. The advantages of each method are in fact so great that in this book we use them both. This chapter contains an *historical introduction* to abnormal psychology; the next one provides a *clinical introduction*.

THE SUBJECT MATTER OF ABNORMAL PSYCHOLOGY

The province of abnormal psychology can be roughly described as the study of *maladaptive personal reactions* to life and its circumstances. When we say *maladaptive* we have in mind people whose lives in some way go astray, so that they find themselves frustrated, unhappy, anxious, baffled in their deepest desires, misfits in their society; or, in the most serious instances, people who get so badly out of touch with surrounding life that we call them insane. When we say that the disorder lies in *personal reactions* we intend to limit the field more closely by excluding what may be called the external reasons for frustration and sorrow. Accidents, bereavements, ill health, war and other disasters, unemployment and poverty, lack of opportunities, unfair social barriers, and a hundred other external circumstances may stand in the way of happy and effective living. These obstacles are tremendously important, but it is not the task of psychology to study them in their own right. They are already claimed for other fields of knowledge such as medicine, public health, and especially the various social sciences. To all of these circumstances, however, the individual makes a personal reaction. Even to a disease affecting one's own body each person reacts in a way that is peculiar to oneself. It is at this point, where the personal reaction begins, that we cross into the province of psychology, and we reach the subprovince of abnormal psychology when we concentrate on personal reactions that are more or less persistently maladaptive.

Let us take the example of unemployment. A man may become unemployed through no fault of his own, purely as a result of economic forces over which he has no control. This external circumstance evokes in him some kind of personal reaction. The professional task of the social scientist is to understand the economic forces that brought about the unemployment; that of the psychologist begins with the personal reaction. Unemployed people react to their misfortune in various ways. Many of these ways it would not occur to us to call disordered or abnormal. Unhappiness and discouragement, indignation and bitterness, seem well justified by the circumstances. Attempts to understand the situation and to change it by organized action appear well adapted to the problem as it stands. Certain people, however, behave in more extreme and peculiar ways. One man may take the blame entirely on himself, declaring that his misfortune is a well-deserved punishment for his own sin and worthlessness. Another may believe that his former employers formed a conspiracy to throw him out of work and are even now trying to poison his food and take his life. A third may become extremely shy, hiding from his neighbors even when they too are unemployed, convinced that everyone holds him in contempt because he is no longer able to support his family. Still another may decide on an act of violence such as shooting the President. These people, we say, are acting in a peculiar fashion. Their personal reactions are highly unlikely to deal with their problem of unemployment in an effective way. Their behavior seems only to make matters worse.

In the simplest possible terms, we experience ourselves as having various needs, desires, and intentions and as being surrounded by a world of people and things that have their own laws of being, sometimes, but not always, hospitable to what we want. *Adaptive* behavior consists of interacting with this world so as to maximize the benefits it contains for us and minimize the harms. This implies being able to appraise reality correctly, to guide and control our own behavior sufficiently, and to arrive at actions that represent a good compromise between desire and reality. Behavior is *maladaptive* when it is not warranted by existing circumstances and when it is poorly designed to achieve desired results. Abnormal psychology is the study of these disordered and disproportionate personal reactions.

EVOLUTION OF ATTITUDES TOWARD DISORDERED PEOPLE

If one undertook today to make a list of maladaptive personal reactions bothersome enough to suggest the need for psychological help, the result would be

3

a bulky catalogue. In the course of time we have learned to see in this light a great many forms of behavior that were earlier viewed as moral problems belonging in the realm of volition. If people were unhappy, anxious, and irritable, if they were unduly boastful and self-centered, if they did not get along well with their family and friends, if they wasted time and took to drink or drugs, they were likely to be censured and told to mend their ways. The idea that such difficulties in living might be strongly rooted, resistant to change, and in need of scientific study and professional help has had widespread acceptance only in recent years. This attitude has made its way into the history of abnormal psychology only in the course of the present century.

Quite the opposite is the case with the severer forms of mental affliction. Here we can observe a distinct evolution of attitudes in Western society from medieval to modern times. Insanity is described in some of the earliest scientific writings. The insane, with their obvious unfitness to take care of themselves and their inconvenience and occasional danger to others, have always managed to establish some kind of claim on public attention. The early history of abnormal psychology is thus the history of attempts to understand insanity.

For the most part this history is a discouraging tale of isolated observations that never grew into a body of tested knowledge. The Greek physician Hippocrates, somewhere around 460 B.C., did his best to bring insanity into the fold of medicine by pronouncing it a disease of the brain and treating it like other diseases. In the writings of the great medical practitioners from Galen in the second century to Weyer in the sixteenth, and of the great observers of human nature such as Vives and Montaigne, one finds many shrewd observations on the nature of insanity, much sympathy for the lot of its victims, and a disposition to seek humane methods to restore tranquility of mind. Indeed, the history of mental disorders reveals many surprising anticipations of what we now like to regard as modern attitudes and modern discoveries. But these prophetic voices of the past cried in a wilderness of public indifference. The mentally disordered might be seen as objects of charity, they might be treated as social outcasts, they might even be actively persecuted. But they were not viewed by people at large as constituting a scientific problem that might slowly yield its secrets to painstaking impersonal study. Nor did the social and economic conditions exist that make the sustained investigation of such a problem possible.

The Insane as Objects of Charity

Recent historical studies have dispelled an earlier stereotype that throughout the Middle Ages and up to the middle of the eighteenth century the insane were either totally neglected or actively persecuted. During the Middle Ages Christianity spread throughout Western Europe, bringing with it "the Christian duty of charity towards the poor or sick of any description."

The provision of care for the distressed appears on the scene almost as soon as the Christian missionaries had succeeded in securing a stable foothold in new lands, and

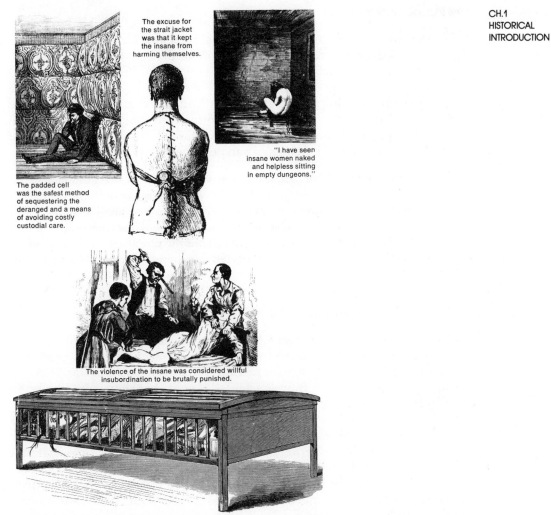

The excuse for the strait jacket was that it kept the insane from harming themselves.

The padded cell was the safest method of sequestering the deranged and a means of avoiding costly custodial care.

"I have seen insane women naked and helpless sitting in empty dungeons."

The violence of the insane was considered willful insubordination to be brutally punished.

Insane woman confined to "crib" in New York State institution, 1882.

Examples of brutal attempts to cope with mental illness in earlier times

the provision of such care tended to secure their success in converting the local people. The Church was responsible for extending and developing hospitals well beyond anything known in classical times. Almshouses and charitable hospitals were established for the aged, the sick, and the poor. The mentally ill, as can be seen from the literature of the times, were often described as sick and we can assume that many such persons who were not cared for by their families were extended help and protection in such institutions (Maher & Maher, 1981, in press).

Special quarters for the mentally ill began to be attached to hospitals during the fourteenth century, and an asylum especially for these patients was built in Valencia in 1409.

5

The Insane as Social Outcasts

When they were not fortunate enough to find such havens, the mentally disordered were likely to be treated as outcasts and hardly distinguished from criminals. The community felt responsible for them only to the extent of preventing them from troubling others. Some of the less troublesome wandered about the countryside, begging and stealing their food and finding shelter in barns and pigsties. Others were thrown into prison where, side by side with criminals, they lived amid revolting filth, often chained, always at the mercy of their keepers. In 1785 a French physician described the situation as follows:

> Thousands of deranged are locked up in prisons without anyone's thinking of administering the slightest remedy; the half-deranged are mixed with the completely insane, the furious with the quiet; some are in chains, others are free in the prison; finally, unless nature comes to their rescue and cures them, the term of their misery is that of their mortal days, and unfortunately in the meantime the illness but increases instead of diminishing (Colombier, cited in Zilboorg & Henry, 1941, p. 316).

The Insane as Possessed by Demons

Possession by evil spirits has had a long history as an explanation of behavior that is peculiar and unreasonable. Confronted by such behavior, people in simpler times found it easy to assume that a malignant demon was directing the lunatic behavior either from outside or from within the victim's body. In the fifteenth and sixteenth centuries this belief reached an extreme development in the institution of witchcraft. During this period a substantial number of people were accused and tried as witches, sometimes tortured to obtain confessions, and if found guilty were publicly burned. What gave the witchcraft trials their peculiar ferocity was the belief that the accused person had surrendered to the devil and made a solemn pact to do his evil work. For someone to be possessed was thus not merely a personal misfortune; it put the whole community in great moral danger.

Many older sources imply that during these centuries huge numbers of people were condemned and killed. Recent historical research (Spanos, 1978; Maher & Maher, 1981, in press) cautions us not to take these reports literally. Witch burnings occurred, but they were never a standard way of dealing with mentally disordered people. The most celebrated American example, the Salem witchcraft trials of 1692, in which twenty people were condemned to death, was a late outburst of a dying belief. Up to that time sentences for witchcraft had been rare in New England, and during the trials there was much sharp public criticism of the "Salem superstition." Within a year Judge Samuel Sewall, who had sentenced the alleged witches, completely changed his mind and stood in church while the minister read to the congregation his confession of error and remorse.

The Insane as Sick People

Lasting improvement in the lot of the mentally disordered came only when the insights of Hippocrates and Galen were revived and insanity was accepted as a challenge to the physician. Pinel, a prominent figure in this movement, declared that "the mentally sick, far from being guilty people deserving of punishment, are sick people whose miserable state deserves all the consideration that is due to suffering humanity. One should try with the most simple methods to restore their reason" (Pinel, cited in Zilboorg & Henry, 1941, pp. 323–324). As this insight began to gain ground, efforts were made to segregate the mentally sick in asylums where they could be under strictly medical supervision. This was likely to mean better care for the patients, and it gave the doctors a chance to build up a greater knowledge of mental illness.

For a long time, however, the perception of the insane as sick people did not much relieve them of harsh treatment. The most prominent obstacle to restoring their reason was their own violence, resistance, and lack of control. A physician in charge of a ward, like a teacher in charge of an outrageously rebellious class, had to achieve some measure of order and quiet before it was possible to do anything useful. According to one authority of the day:

> Discipline, threats, fetters, and blows are needed as much as medical treatment. Truly nothing is more necessary and more effective for the recovery of these people than forcing them to respect and fear intimidation. By this method, the mind, held back by restraint, is induced to give up its arrogance and wild ideas and it soon becomes meek and orderly. This is why maniacs often recover much sooner if they are treated with torture and torments in a hovel instead of with medicaments (Willis, cited in Zilboorg & Henry, 1941, p. 261).

Even the great American pioneer in psychiatry, Benjamin Rush, who in other respects advanced the cause of humane treatment, described in 1812 "terrifying modes of punishment" for refractory patients, recommending "pouring cold water under the sleeve, so that it may descend into the armpits and down the trunk of the body," or, if this failed, deprivation of food and threats of death (Rush, p. 180).

Psychiatric writings well into the nineteenth century showed a preoccupation with establishing control. The patients must be subjugated, made submissive, accustomed to "unconditional obedience" to the physician's authority, even if this called for rough treatment and severe punishment. Only on this basis, it was reasoned, could one start measures sympathetically designed to restore reason (Kraepelin, 1917/1962). We may well wonder whether the initial severity created favorable conditions for the subsequent restoring of reason.

Pinel's Reforms

Philippe Pinel (1745–1826) is probably the best remembered of those who approached the problem with more sympathy and more courage. Pinel was a physician and scholar who lived most of his life in Paris, who gradually centered his interest on mental disorders, and who found a golden opportunity to carry out his progressive ideas when in the first years of the Revolution he was made physician-in-chief at the Bicêtre, a hospital chiefly populated by the mentally deranged. He was convinced that the violence that so impressed others was largely a result of keeping patients under restraint. He therefore proposed to remove the chains and fetters that bound most of the patients. This required permission from the Commune, and the president came in person to talk with the patients and assure himself that no political enemies were concealed among them. Greeted by shouts and the clanking of chains, with his attempts at conversation answered only by curses and execrations, the president is reported to have asked Pinel, "Citizen, are you mad yourself, that you would unchain such beasts?" To this Pinel replied, "It is my conviction that these mentally ill are intractable only because they are deprived of fresh air and of their liberty" (Semelaigne, 1930, p. 41). Permission was granted, and Pinel proceeded with his experiment. In some cases no great benefits resulted, yet there were numerous instances where patients previously considered dangerous and completely unmanageable became calm and reasonable when released from restraint and treated with kindness. Some who had been incarcerated half a lifetime were shortly discharged from the hosptial with their health

Pinel removing the chains of the mental patients. History may have credited the wrong person for this landmark achievement in the history of mental health: Spanos (1978) claims the credit belongs to one of Pinel's assistants.

restored. But above all Pinel showed beyond any doubt that a large mental hospital could be safely and beneficially managed with a minimum of mechanical restraint.

This was Pinel's most dramatic action, but it was only the beginning of the reforms that laid a foundation for the psychiatry of the future. Soon after the experiments at the Bicêtre he was transferred to the larger Salpêtrière hospital where he applied himself to a huge task of reorganization. He began to train attendants so that they should be something better than guards, and he tried to give the patients the benefit of comfort and a healthful routine. Of enduring importance was his introduction of the psychiatric case history and the systematic keeping of records. This arose from his habit of observing patients closely and taking careful notes. Before his time it often happened that no one remembered when or for what cause a patient had entered the hospital. Obviously it was impossible to build up a sound knowledge of mental disorders until Pinel's custom of making records became an established practice. Only in a well-regulated hospital, moreover, could methods of treatment properly be explored, different methods compared, and results followed and verified. Pinel himself completed in 1801 a treatise on the nature and treatment of mental disorders, based largely on his own hospital experience. In the introduction he portrays the new role of the physician as he himself enacted it.

> The habit of living constantly in the midst of the insane, of studying their habits, their different personalities, the objects of their pleasures or their dislikes, the advantage of following the course of their alienation day and night during the various seasons of the year, the art of directing them without effort and sparing them excitement and grumbling, the gift of being able to assume at the right time a tone of kindness or of authority, of being able to subdue them by force if methods of kindness fail, the constant picture of all the phenomena of mental alienation, and finally the functions of supervision itself—the combination of all these must give an intelligent and zealous man an immense number of facts and minute details usually lacking in the narrow-minded physician unless he has taken a special interest during fleeting visits to asylums (Pinel, 1801, p. 15).

This was indeed the dawn of a new day both for the mentally disordered and for people's whole understanding of their own natures.

The ideas behind Pinel's reforms began to spread slowly through the Western world. At last the public mind was beginning to be ready to receive them. In England William Tuke, a wealthy Quaker merchant, founded in 1796 the York Retreat where amid quiet country surroundings kind and gentle methods of treatment were put into effect. In the United States several hospitals were opened early in the nineteenth century to embody the new humane principles: the Friends' Asylum at Philadelphia in 1817, McLean Hospital in Massachusetts in 1818, Bloomingdale in New York in 1822, and the Hartford Retreat in 1824. On the medical side not enough was known to go beyond keeping the patients in the best possible physical condition, but results were

Treatment of the mentally ill in this country became more humane early in this century, but custodial management did not really constitute effective treatment. Notice the attendant here reading a book instead of attending to the patients as human beings.

sought through psychological measures known in those days as *moral treatment* (Bockoven, 1963). As far as possible, the patients were engaged in normal conversation and treated with respect. An atmosphere of kindness and serious purpose was maintained; patients were encouraged to act according to these standards. The physical environment was kept pleasant and beautiful, with opportunities for recreation and interesting things to do. Moral treatment might be described as a combination of good influences and gentle persuasion. It was a humane idea that sometimes produced good results.

These centers of enlightenment did not quickly put an end to policies of restraint. Naturally it was slow work to secure reforms that entailed greater expense, but it is surprising to realize the force of opposition within the medical profession itself. When Gardiner Hill, around 1840, was fighting to promote the policy of nonrestraint and demonstrating in his own Lincoln Asylum that the plan really worked, other British medical practitioners pronounced it the "wild scheme of a philanthropic visionary," indeed "a breaking of the sixth commandment," and asserted that "restraint forms the very basis on which the sound treatment of lunatics is founded" (Bromberg, 1937, p. 105). Not until 1850 could it be reported that nonrestraint was generally accepted.

10

The Insane as Public Charges: State Hospitals

The pioneer mental hospitals, privately supported, could by no means meet existing needs. To meet these needs it was necessary to enlist public funds, and this presently became a major crusade. By 1840 there were fourteen mental hospitals in the United States capable of accommodating altogether something like 2500 patients. But the census of the same year showed over 17,000 insane, of whom scarcely more than 5000 were supported as public charges (Deutsch, 1937). The great mass of the mentally ill were still without benefit of treatment, public support, or proper accommodations. The correction of this state of affairs was one of the many reform movements that spread through the country toward the middle of the last century. It was set in motion largely by Dorothea L. Dix, a Massachusetts schoolteacher who on her own initiative began to investigate the almshouses, jails, and private homes where the pauper insane were kept. In 1843 she presented to the Massachusetts legislature a memorial describing in detail what she had seen: insane persons "confined in cages, closets, cellars, stalls, pens . . . chained, naked, beaten with rods, and lashed into obedience" (Dix, 1843, p. 4). The success of her petition marked the beginning of a long, remarkably effective career. Miss Dix personally investigated conditions throughout the United States, presenting reports and arguing with state legislators, until she had become the chief moving force in the founding or enlarging of more than thirty state hospitals. She afterwards extended her activities to Scotland and England, and her tours of inspection in most of the countries of Europe carried her influence still farther afield. Few people today remember how much the modern system of state hospitals owes to this indomitable worker. Her influence was in no small measure responsible for the trend revealed in the following figures. In 1840 the mental hospitals of the United States housed 2561 patients—14 percent of the estimated number of insane in the country. Half a century later, in 1890, the mental hospitals housed 74,028 patients—69 percent of the insane in the country (Deutsch, 1937). The neglected lunatic of previous centuries at last stood a good chance of finding proper shelter, food, and medical attention.

The Mental Hygiene Movement

By 1900 the care of mental patients had greatly improved, but there was still much to be accomplished. A vivid picture of conditions in that year can be found in the autobiography of Clifford W. Beers, who later inaugurated the mental hygiene movement. As a young man of twenty-four, recently graduated from college, Beers became depressed, attempted suicide, and for the next two years saw the inside of three different mental hospitals from the point of view of a patient. After returning to health he wrote the story of his illness in *A Mind That Found Itself* (1908), a book destined to achieve a tremendous influence toward the understanding of mental disorders. Beers admitted that

11

he was a difficult patient. During the latter part of his illness he was elated, arrogant, dictatorial, doubtless exceedingly irritating to those in charge, and inclined at times to create rather violent scenes. Considering this, and comparing his treatment with what was meted out in earlier centuries, his care was a model of patience and forbearance, yet he was choked and thrown to the floor, kicked and spat on, kept tightly clad in a cold cell, bound painfully tight in a straitjacket, and treated with childish displays of temper by the attendants, as when his holiday dinner was snatched away because he dallied over it. It is perhaps not surprising that the attendants displayed shortcomings; the first training school for mental nurses in this country was then not quite twenty years old, and the practice of hiring untrained guards was still widespread. On the doctors' part, what we miss is not so much a lack of humanity as a lack of insight and of that attitude that makes it possible not to be irritated by the patient's refractory behavior. In small and useless ways Beers was thwarted and thereby infuriated. His clothes were withheld, he was denied pencil and paper, and once he was even forbidden to collect some harmless corncobs that happened to strike his fancy. Moreover, there was practically no attempt to study his mental processes or to understand how the illness came about. "It was upon the gradual but sure improvement in my physical condition," Beers wrote, "that the doctors were relying for my eventual return to normality" (Beers, 1931, p. 73).

Beers and his book became the agents of another forward stride in the evolution of attitudes toward disordered personal behavior. In 1909 Beers established the National Committee for Mental Hygiene, later expanded to international dimensions, having in view three main purposes: (1) to alter the widespread popular belief that mental disorders were incurable and that they carried a stigma of disgrace, (2) to improve those conditions in mental hospitals that Beers's own experiences brought so clearly into the open, and (3) to encourage the early recognition and prevention of mental disorders through the establishment of child guidance clinics designed to study and treat problems of behavior before they grew to more serious proportions. The response to these intended enlightenments seemed at first very slow. Mentally disordered people continued to be regarded as baffling and sinister, best handled by removal from the community and consignment to the care of specialists. Hospitals were given better support, but not enough; child guidance clinics were opened, but not in sufficient number; and funds for research continued to run in a trickle compared to those available for the study of other human ailments. Even as late as 1950 most supporters of mental health still regarded their movement as the Cinderella of the medical world. Few would have predicted the abrupt change of status that was about to take place.

Community Mental Health

No doubt it was simply the final stage of an evolution that had long been under way, but when the change came in the 1950s it went forward with revolutionary speed. Mental health sprang into the position of a major public concern. All at once it became the object of large government programs, substantial financial support, and enthusiastic volunteer service in the community. Social historians have the intriguing task of explaining this burst of interest and relating it to other contemporary social movements. The resulting state of affairs would perhaps strike Pinel, Tuke, and Miss Dix like a dream come true, but it should be noticed that the revolution went far beyond their goals and in certain respects entailed a change of direction. When the Joint Commission on Mental Illness and Health, authorized by Congress in 1955, submitted after long study its final report in 1961, it discouraged further building of mental hospitals and recommended instead that major support be thrown to the establishment of community mental health clinics. The objective was set at "one fully staffed, full-time mental health clinic available to each 100,000 of population" (Joint Commission on Mental Illness and Health,

The crusades of Dorothea Dix and others succeeded in terminating the physical abuse of mental patients in this country, but the dehumanizing effects of isolation and inactivity continued to be seen until the trend toward deinstitutionalization took hold in the 1970s. In some institutions scenes like this can still be seen.

1961, p. xiv). Obviously it will take a long time to reach such a goal, but the number of community mental health centers has increased rapidly, and this pattern of health care presently commands substantial public approval.

Implicit in this plan is recognition that maladaptive personal behavior is embedded in the community and should be treated there as far as possible. The mental hospital continues to have its use for acute and severe disorders requiring specialized or extended treatment, but it is no longer a remote institution into which people are shunted as soon as their behavior becomes bothersome to others. The ideal of community mental health is to have available, at a single center close to home, the whole spectrum of resources that can be brought to bear to alleviate disordered behavior, including emergency services, outpatient facilities, consultation, social service, family counseling, and preventive measures to the extent that these are discovered possible. Any plan of this type requires strong community support. It implies acceptance of mental health as at least in part a responsibility of the community, not just a job for doctors. There is work here for the citizen as well as the specialist.

MENTAL DISORDERS CONSIDERED AS DISEASES OF THE BRAIN

In the early stages of scientific study progress consists largely in ordering and classifying the facts. Not until this preliminary step has been accomplished is it possible to develop hypotheses and put them to any kind of crucial test. Because of the absence of hospitals, records, and facilities for observation, the study of mental disorders lingered long in the first stage. During the twenty-three centuries from Hippocrates to Pinel there were thousands of attempts to make a satisfactory classification. But Pinel himself, when writing his treatise in 1801, felt that the time was not yet ripe for sharp distinctions and clearly defined categories. He preserved only the little that was common to the earlier attempts and contented himself with distinguishing four large groups: mania, melancholia, dementia, and idiocy.

With the establishment of hospitals and the taking of systematic records, a wealth of facts began to accumulate. Examples of insanity became available in large numbers. To understand this rich experience, to arrange and organize the facts in some intelligible fashion, became for the curious scientist an increasingly urgent problem. But the difficulties proved at once to be enormous. "Mental disease," Pinel remarked, "appears greatly to tax the attention of good observers because it presents itself to us as a mixture of incoherence and confusion" (1801, p. 1). By their very nature the phenomena seemed to defy understanding. Moreover, the really good observer was likely to be baffled by the wide range of individual differences. "When one has seen many insane people," wrote one of Pinel's contemporaries, "one can recognize that there are as many differences among them as there are personalities among individuals whose minds are healthy. It is therefore really difficult to make up classes

14

of diseases which would not prove fictitious" (Foděré, 1817, cited in Zilboorg & Henry, 1941, p. 392).

The Medical Model

Hippocrates had been convinced that mental disorders were diseases of the brain. After many intervening interpretations, such as demon possession and moral inferiority, this view returned to prominence during the nineteenth century. The underlying causes of mental disorder were to be looked for in conditions affecting the central nervous system. This way of viewing the problem was strictly in accord with the outlook of medical science that constantly sought to establish the bodily conditions and tissue changes responsible for illness. Representative of the trend was the German psychiatrist Griesinger (1817-1868) who recognized no distinction between neurology and psychology and who considered a diagnosis valid only when it specified a physiological cause. In France the same tendency was illustrated by Magnan (1835-1916) who gave his most careful attention to disorders associated with very obvious conditions such as alcoholic intoxication, paralysis, and the changes accompanying childbirth. In 1857 a major treatise was published by the French psychiatrist Morel (1809-1873) whose thinking was organized around the theory of degeneration: briefly stated, that mental disease was the result of hereditary neural weakness. These workers and many others who accepted their premises believed that when the brain and the human constitution revealed their secrets the riddles of mental disorder would be solved.

At first thought it might seem that this way of looking at it would give help to the problems of classification. But we must remember that until late in the nineteenth century very little was known about the brain and the human constitution. Only the gross anatomical divisions of the nervous system—cerebral hemispheres, cerebellum, medulla oblongata, spinal cord, and peripheral nerves—were known in the first half of the nineteenth century. More precise localization of functions began only in 1861 with Broca's discovery of a center controlling speech. The mapping of cortical areas was accomplished between 1870 and 1900, but is still a matter of some dispute. Of similarly recent date is our knowledge of microscopic structure. Not until 1889 did improved microscopy disclose the existence of the synapse, thereby showing that each nerve cell and its fibers formed an anatomically separate unit. Thus before 1900 only the very grossest abnormalities of brain structure could have been perceived. Griesinger, Magnan, Morel, and their followers had little sound knowledge at their disposal. Their confidence in brain pathology was based more on faith than on facts, and was reasoned out by analogy with the rest of medical practice.

In time, however, the medical model led to important discoveries. According to this model, each separate disease had a characteristic *beginning*, a typical *course*, and a typical *outcome*. Each disease, furthermore, was represented

15

not by a single symptom but by a typical pattern of symptoms or *symptom-complex*, which might vary in detail from one case to another yet still signify a common underlying disorder. If one could show that certain symptoms frequently occurred together, that they made their first appearance in some fairly regular way, that they ran a typical course that led to a typical outcome, then one was probably well on the way toward isolating a specific disease produced by a specific condition of the brain. Let us examine this method in action, choosing what is probably its greatest triumph.

The Discovery of General Paresis

One of the most creditable chapters in the modern history of medicine was the discovery of general paresis. This disorder, alternatively called *dementia paralytica* or *general paralysis*, was first clearly described in 1798 by Haslam, who noticed among patients at the Bethlehem Hospital a frequent association of delusions of grandeur, dementia, and progressive paralysis. Haslam was unable to carry his observations further than this; he simply recognized a common association of symptoms, a *symptom-complex*, and thus set apart certain patients from the undifferentiated mass of the insane. He characterized these patients as follows:

> Speech is defective, the corners of the mouth are drawn down, the arms and legs are more or less deprived of their voluntary movements, and in the majority of patients memory is materially weakened. These patients as a rule fail to recognize their condition. So weak that they can hardly keep on their legs, they still maintain they are extremely strong and capable of the greatest deeds (Haslam, 1798, p. 259).

A few years later, in 1805, a French physician, Esquirol, who later succeeded Pinel at the Salpêtrière, observed that patients having this symptom-complex never recovered, deterioration and paralysis progressed fairly rapidly to a fatal outcome. Esquirol thus called attention to a typical *course* and a typical *outcome*. It is worth noting that such observations, necessarily extending over a period of time, could scarcely have been made except under the conditions of hospital care and record keeping that Pinel had only lately established in Paris.

As experience increased, so that reliance could be placed on statistics, it became clear that general paresis occurred in men about three times as often as in women. The *time of onset* was found to be rarely earlier than the age of thirty or later than fifty. The *mode of onset* proved particularly baffling. Attempts to reconstruct the patient's history generally showed an insidious beginning marked at first by barely perceptible abnormalities of behavior. Only after a period of time did this behavior come to be sharply at variance with the patient's previous mode of living.

The identification of the organic disorder proceeded slowly at first, handicapped by the prevailing ignorance of brain structure and brain function. In the first half of the century post-mortem examination of paretic brains showed

brain and to be able whenever a disorder occurs to infer the seat and extent of the morbid changes that have caused it (Kraepelin, 1917/1962, p. 125).

Kraepelin brought to this task a genius for combination and classification. His work was carried out in large hospitals, with large numbers of patients, and with extensive hospital records—a proper culmination of Pinel's reforms. He was in tune with the objective scientific trend of his times. The work of Pasteur and Lister had prepared the way for the understanding and mastery of infectious diseases. Remarkable triumphs in clinical medicine were occurring all around him; within a short space of time a great many varieties of bodily disease had been isolated and clearly defined. The growing resources of the physiological laboratory were constantly at his disposal and he followed with keen interest all developments along this line. As a result his conception of the possible bodily aspects of mental disorder was not confined to brain conditions as such. He was aware of the possible effects of metabolic changes and of improper bodily economy, and he was impressed by the newly discovered functions of the thyroid gland, which exerted such a dramatic influence on both physical and mental growth.

Thus oriented and equipped, Kraepelin studied large numbers of case histories. He examined not only the story of each illness and its course while the patient was in the hospital but also the history of the patient's previous life, and he followed the histories of patients who were discharged from the hospital. In this way he was able to establish regularities concerning the symptoms and course of disease. Discounting individual variations, he sorted out what was common to numerous cases and arrived at classifications. Working along these lines, he came to the conclusion that in addition to the entities already recognized there were two major mental diseases: *manic-depressive psychosis* and *dementia praecox* (now generally called *schizophrenia*).

Manic-Depressive Psychosis

In forming the first of these two disease entities Kraepelin drew together the excited, elated conditions (mania) and the melancholy, depressed states (depression), showing that in a great many cases these moods succeeded each other in the same patient. He was impressed that the moods, although so opposite in content, both represented excessively strong expressions of affect. In the manic state the patients were overactive, talkative, strangers to fatigue, full of happy thoughts and buoyant plans. In the depressed condition they tended to be silent and passive, showing no initiative and dwelling in sad recollections and dark forebodings. In neither state were their thoughts in good touch with reality. One and the same patient would talk of fabulous riches when manic and of a criminally negligent penniless state when depressed. They were singularly unresponsive to social influence; helpers soon discovered that it was as useless to try to slow down a manic patient as it was to cheer up a depressed one. These patients were surely mentally disordered, but Kraepelin observed that there was no lasting intellectual impairment—no dementia—and that during their well periods they appeared wholly normal.

Kraepelin believed that he had isolated a symptom-complex having a typical beginning, course, and outcome. The heart of the symptom-complex was the excessive moods and their abrupt changes; there were no signs of deterioration such as defects in walking, speech, and memory. The onset was sudden rather than gradual; the course was periodic instead of steadily progressive; the outcome was spontaneous recovery, though with some likelihood of future recurrence. Each of these points emphasized the fundamental difference between manic-depressive psychosis and general paresis. But the final step for the perfect demonstration of a disease entity could not yet be taken. The conditions in brain and body that caused the disorder were still a matter of speculation. There was evidence that an hereditary disposition played some part, but this could hardly be a complete explanation. It was plausible to suggest an irregularity in metabolic functions, but this could not be conclusively demonstrated.

In spite of this uncertainty, the manic-depressive category has stood up well. Kraepelin's careful work had brought an important insight to the understanding of mental disorders. We see in Chapter 14 that his category continues to be used and is the subject of intensive research.

Dementia Praecox (Schizophrenia)

Dementia praecox represented an even larger synthesis of previously described disorders. Included in it were patients whose behavior was eccentric, others who sat in silent withdrawal, others who resisted all attempts at care and conversation, others who constantly proclaimed themselves victims of persecution, others who expressed bizarre ideas and fantasies, and a good many who talked what seemed to be complete nonsense; occasionally there would be episodes of violent behavior. The unity in all this was not immediately apparent, but Kraepelin believed he had detected several regularities: an early onset, a flattening of affect, and progress in the direction of incurable dementia. It was true that dementia praecox started earlier, often in adolescence or the twenties, than manic-depressive disorders which commonly appeared in the thirties and forties, and general paresis, which might not show until the fifties. And it appeared to be true that as dementia praecox patients grew older in the hospital they suffered increasing intellectual deterioration. Speculating again about a possible cause, Kraepelin suggested that the sex glands might be at fault, producing an unfavorable chemical state that affected the nervous system. He justified this guess by pointing out frequent associations between onset and changes in sexual function: the changes of puberty, menstrual irregularities, and childbirth.

This great synthesis did not fare as well as the manic-depressive one. It was presently criticized by the Swiss psychiatrist Bleuler, who believed that in describing the symptom-complex Kraepelin had not chosen the most important regularities. He declared that the alleged dementia of older patients could be distinguished from true dementia as exhibited by patients with organic brain disease. He also challenged Kraepelin's idea about the universality of flat affect. This, like the supposed dementia, was actually a kind of apathy characteristic of patients who had been in the hospital a long time. In earlier stages there was often a marked show of affect, including anxiety, panic, sadness, anger, with sometimes rapid alternations among conflicting feelings.

Bleuler looked elsewhere for the distinguishing marks of the disorder. He believed that the central feature was disturbance in the manner of thinking, in what he called in the language of the day the "associational processes." The patients suffered from a loosening of connections among their ideas, a weakening of attention, an inability to maintain a mental set that would confer continuity. Their ideas and conversation therefore seemed to wander incoherently, with as little sensible connection as the images in a dream. Bleuler called this *autistic* thinking, in contrast to *realistic* thinking, which was under the discipline of logic and circumstances. Considering Kraepelin's label misleading, he called the disorder *schizophrenia* ("split mind"), referring to the splitting up of the associational processes and the lack of integrated functioning. But Bleuler remained a little uncertain about his own theory. He sometimes referred to "the group of schizophrenias" as if there might be several different disorders.

Bleuler's term was generally adopted, and on the whole his point of view prevailed. But schizophrenia continued to be a puzzle. As Klerman sees it:

> The period subsequent to Bleuler, from about 1910 to 1950, was marked by theoretical acrimony and limited therapeutic success, although most psychiatrists in both Europe and North America quickly accepted Bleuler's criteria for defining the syndrome. Many unsuccessful attempts were made to find biological causes via searches for anatomical defects in the brain or various toxins elsewhere in the body fluids. . . . The efforts using available biological techniques were failures. Not only did cures not materialize, but just getting out of the hospital was an achievement if not a miracle. Eighty per cent of patients admitted to public mental hospitals were never discharged (Klerman, 1978, pp. 99–121).

It is worth pointing out that the biological view of a disorder accomplishes nothing in the way of treatment so long as the cause is hypothetical and has not actually been discovered. In an historical study Bockoven has shown that rates of recovery at mental hospitals declined during the nineteenth century while the view was gaining ground that mental patients were suffering from brain disorder (Bockoven, 1963). As Clifford Beers had observed, the typical mental hospital around 1900 was simply a place of custody where little was done beyond keeping patients in good physical condition. It is possible that therapeutic leverage was weakened by thinking of patients merely as medical problems instead of as burdened people who might profit from personal inter-

21

est, encouragement, and interesting occupations in a sympathetic environment.

In historical perspective, however, it is clear that the medical model of mental disorders made great progress through the work on general paresis and the observations and theories of Kraepelin and Bleuler. If this way of thinking ran into doldrums, it was because biological science was not sufficiently advanced. The physiology and biochemistry of the nervous system have proved to be enormously complex. Nothing as simple as gross destruction of brain tissue, nothing as unitary as metabolic irregularity or faultily working sex glands, is likely to be the sole villain in either major mental disorder. But this does not discredit the biological point of view. In the second half of the present century biological and biochemical research began to pick up speed and presently justified, as we see in later chapters, the continued use of the medical model in thinking about mental disorders.

BEGINNINGS OF PSYCHOPATHOLOGY: THE STUDY OF HYSTERIA

The Psychological Model

The history of psychopathology followed a different route from that of the medical model. This alternative way of looking at maladaptive personal reactions was not a product of the mental hospitals, and the patients who were studied were not as drastically disordered. Many of them belonged in a category not at all clearly defined that came to be called *neurosis*. In some cases the symptoms did not seem to reflect any plausible defects in the nervous system, but they sometimes bore a convincing relation to the patients' thoughts, feelings, and strivings. We can speak of *psychopathology* when ideas or other psychological processes appear to be responsible for maladaptive behavior. Pathology means the science of disease processes; psychopathology deals with those disorders that have their origin in psychological processes instead of in tissue or chemical dysfunction.

Is it really possible to assign such a part to mental processes? Early investigators thought it doubtful, and tried their best to explain what they observed in physical terms. But a winding trail of evidence eventually brought the conviction that what people believed and wanted could affect their bodies and push their behavior into maladaptive paths. Gradually there emerged what we have today: a psychological model of maladaptive personal reactions, based on current knowledge of learning, cognition, and motivation, that can stand in contrast to the medical model.

Mesmer and Hypnotism

The psychological model won its way into modern thought through the study of hysteria. In the early stages this study was much assisted by the use of hypnotism, which itself offered an interesting trial ground for the psychological point of view. Hypnotism first became widely known through the activities of Franz Anton Mesmer (1733–1815), a Viennese physician who discovered that he could cure various ailments by applying magnets to the afflicted parts of the patient's body. Presently he made the further discovery that the magnets were unnecessary; the same results could be obtained through the touch of his hands. By analogy with the action of magnets he christened this influence *animal magnetism*, and he considered it a strictly physical process. An invisible fluid, he supposed, passed between him and the patient, influencing the patient's body in a distinctive fashion. Shortly before the French Revolution Mesmer moved his practice to Paris, where he was soon immensely successful. His methods became highly theatrical. Groups of patients sat around a *baquet* (tub) grasping iron rods. To sounds of soft music Mesmer in a lilac robe then entered the room and magnetized the *baquet*. Typically the patients responded with violent fits and convulsions, from which they recovered with their symptoms much improved.

These dramatic procedures brought charges that Mesmer was a charlatan. A commission of distinguished scientists was appointed to investigate his claims. The commissioners made a number of careful experiments that contradicted the theory of animal magnetism. They showed that the phenomena supposed to be produced by magnetism occurred only if the patient knew he or she was being magnetized, and they drew the conclusion that the demonstrable effects were obtained through "the excitement of the imagination." At that time this conclusion had the effect of discrediting Mesmer, but it was actually an alternative hypothesis for explaining the observed facts. One of Mesmer's pupils aptly put the question: "If Mesmer had no other secret than that he was able to make the imagination exert an effective influence upon health, would he not still be a wonder worker?" (Janet, 1925, p. 161).

Mesmer has been called the father of hypnotism, which for many years was called mesmerism. But it was actually one of his followers, Puységur (1751–1825), who hit on the phenomena today considered most characteristic. Disliking the violent crises provoked by Mesmer, he preferred to induce a quiet, sleeplike state that he believed could be equally beneficial to health. This state was produced merely by encouraging relaxation and repeatedly stating that sleep would follow. The resulting hypnotic state was not quite the same as sleep. The hypnotized person could answer questions, converse, and in some cases move around actively without awakening. Good subjects were remarkably responsive to whatever was suggested. Parts of the body could be temporarily paralyzed and made insensitive to touch and pain. Subjects could be made to hear and see whatever the hypnotist proposed, and they would enact little dramas according to his direction. Some of these curious phenomena were valuable in effecting cures. Symptoms could be made to disappear by suggestion in the hypnotic state, and the improvement might be maintained when the patient awakened, generally with no recollection of what had occurred during sleep. Much repetition and several sessions were usually re-

23

quired to produce a lasting result, but success was frequent enough so that during the second half of the nineteenth century hypnotic clinics flourished in various parts of the Western world. Hypnotism had its day as the popular treatment for nervous disorders.

The notion of animal magnetism, a physical force, died slowly. In the search for alternative explanations the most distinctive concept to emerge was the psychological one of *suggestion*. In a technical sense suggestion means a specific form of influence different from conveying information, reasoning, persuading, exhorting, and commanding, all of which appeal to us at the ordinary alert level of mental functioning. Suggestion, it was hypothesized, worked at a subconscious level. Much was made of the notion, called *ideomotor action* by William James, that ideas tend to go straight over into appropriate action if other considerations do not interfere. The relaxed hypnotic state came to be understood as one in which other considerations were silenced, criticism laid aside, and trustful compliance made total. Under these circumstances ideas proposed by the hypnotist affected the patient's behavior just as if they had started in the patient's mind.

Charcot's Study of Hysteria

The reported therapeutic successes of hypnotism become less surprising if we make the assumption that considerable numbers of the patients who sought this treatment suffered from the form of disorder known as *hysteria*. This disorder, known even to the ancients, manifests itself in a large variety of symptoms many with an outward resemblance to organic diseases. Prominent in nineteenth-century descriptions of hysteria are such symptoms as partial or total blindness, impairments of hearing, and paralyses of hands, arms, legs, even a whole side of the body, usually accompanied by anaesthesia of the same parts. Symptoms of this kind could easily be interpreted as results of local injury to the nervous system. Occasionally patients would have convulsive attacks ("hysterical fits") that resembled epileptic convulsions, and it was not uncommon to find gaps and peculiarities in memory suggestive of possible brain disorder. In retrospect it can be seen that if hypnotism cured nothing but hysteria it might still gain the reputation of curing almost anything.

In 1878 several severely incapacitated hysterical patients came to the attention of J. M. Charcot, a distinguished neurologist in Paris. Charcot himself had never practiced hypnotism, but some of his assistants at the hospital became interested in the subject and experimented with the patients. One day they showed their chief some remarkable facts. Before his eyes they demonstrated that by means of hypnotism it was possible to produce artificially all the typical bodily symptoms of hysteria, and afterwards to remove them again. By hypnotic suggestion a patient's perfectly healthy arm could be rendered paralyzed and anaesthetic; Charcot himself, examining the patient, could not tell the difference between this and a natural hysterical paralysis

24

with anaesthesia, except that it disappeared on further suggestion. The whole array of hysterical symptoms could be brought into and put out of existence at whatever speed and in whatever form one chose. How could the nervous system do it?

Challenged by this discovery, Charcot set to work to investigate hysterical symptoms. Clearly they were not caused by local injury to the nervous system. He tried to discover how the symptoms started, and found that the circumstances were often peculiar. One patient, for instance, was in a street accident during which, so he thought, a carriage ran over his legs. At the hospital both legs remained paralyzed for months, but as a matter of fact the carriage had not even touched the patient. A young girl stepped lightly out of bed one morning only to find her left leg paralyzed in a rigid clubfoot position. Charcot examined many such cases: the initial circumstances were never sufficient to account for the symptom. The disappearance of symptoms also occurred in a strange fashion. Sometimes a paralysis would end abruptly during a moment of emotional excitement. Sometimes it could be removed by hypnotic suggestion. Charcot discovered that Mesmer's claims were partly justified: the young girl with the clubfoot paralysis was cured after a strenuous series of hypnotic sessions (Charcot, 1890). Again it appeared that symptoms were capable of migration. Paralysis might shift spontaneously from one side of the body to the other. One of the most startling discoveries was that the hysterical symptom might cease to operate when the patient was inattentive or asleep. Janet, a student of Charcot's, told of a man paralyzed in both legs who was addicted to walking in his sleep. He often climbed out on the roof and had to be rescued by the attendants with extreme care because his legs became totally paralyzed the moment he was awakened (Janet, 1920).

Probably the most significant of Charcot's discoveries was that hysterical symptoms often made what we might call anatomical nonsense. Sometimes a patient would have a paralyzed hand with anaesthesia that stopped at the wrist, thus including roughly the area that would be covered by a glove. Such an anaesthesia is anatomically impossible in the sense that no conceivable nerve injury could produce it. The arm is supplied by three main nerve trunks extending down into the hand. Injury to any one would involve only part of the hand and would affect part of the arm as well. Injury to the center in which the three paths join would produce an anaesthesia including the whole arm and shoulder. The glove anaesthesia therefore is a perfect example of anatomical nonsense that strikes the final blow at a neurological hypothesis for hysteria.

How, then, does a glove anaesthesia come into existence? We can see that there is an oddly mental character to this seemingly physical symptom. The area of anaesthesia corresponds to the idea one has of the hand as an anatomical unit. The first patient's paralysis likewise corresponds to an idea he had that a carriage ran over his legs. But we must beware of jumping to the conclusion that these patients are simply putting on a conscious act. Mental ori-

25

Much of the early interest in psychiatry centered on Charcot's dramatic demonstrations of the effects of hypnosis and what they revealed about the psychology of hysteria.

gins do not necessarily mean conscious or voluntary origins. That patients often had no conscious idea about their symptoms was testified in many ways. Sometimes examinations revealed an area of anaesthesia, or perhaps even a blindness of one eye, of which up to that moment the patient had been totally unaware. The most telling fact, however, that absolved hysterical patients from conscious deception, was that sometimes the symptoms made perfect anatomical sense. There were cases, for example, clearly hysterical and curable by suggestion, in which paralysis of the entire right side was accompanied by disturbances of speech. One certainly could not suppose that in 1880 clinical patients of slight education had an idea about the location of the speech centers in the left cerebral hemisphere and the control by this hemisphere of the right side of the body.

Janet's Conceptualization

Charcot left the problem at this point. The symptoms of hysteria were mental, yet not wholly mental; they were psychological, yet mixed up in a puzzling way with bodily processes. The attempt to capture this paradoxical quality in a theory was made by Pierre Janet, who during the 1890s began to publish his acute observations of neurotic patients. Janet was fascinated especially by changes of memory in hysteria, and he described with great care the phenomenon of *somnambulism*, in which the patient's memory seemed to be curiously divided. The patient would act for a time under the complete dominance of a single set of ideas, with no recollection of the rest of his experience or sometimes even of his identity. Janet's classic example was the case of Irene, a young woman whose memory was normal except that she had forgotten the recent death of her mother. Every so often, suddenly becoming oblivious to everything around her, she would act out with vivid gestures and frantic expressions of grief the harrowing scene at her mother's deathbed; equally suddenly she would go on calmly doing whatever she had been doing before, with the dramatic interlude completely forgotten. Janet was particularly impressed by the forgetting. "Things happen as if an idea, a partial system of thoughts, emancipated itself, became independent, and developed itself on its own account," he wrote. "The result is, on the one hand, that it develops far too much, and, on the other hand, that consciousness appears no longer to control it" (Janet, 1920, p. 28).

To understand such facts Janet adopted the concept of *dissociation*. This concept was designed to account for the pathological separation between systems of ideas that normally would interpenetrate and influence one another. In hysteria, as Janet conceived of it, the personality lost some of its normal organization. Certain systems fell out of the hierarchy, so to speak, and escaped from the governing influence of the self. Janet believed that the concept of dissociation applied equally to the bodily symptoms of hysteria. If a patient was unable to walk it was because the organized system of images and sensations that functioned during walking had become dissociated from the rest of the personality. Charcot's patient who believed himself run over by the carriage had a dissociated idea that his legs were paralyzed, and this idea, simply because it was dissociated, became overdeveloped—like Irene's drama of grief—and actually controlled the motility of his legs. Dissociation occurred not only to systems of memories but to natural subsystems of the neural mechanism.

True to the confusingly mixed character of hysterical symptoms, Janet's explanation hovered between the medical and the psychological. He allowed that dissociation was more likely to occur in people who were fatigued, anxious, and worn out by their problems. He implied that the splitting off of a system of ideas might serve to avoid unbearable pain or a conflict of irreconcilable motives. This put him on the edge not only of a psychological explanation but of a psychodynamic one, in which systems of ideas were driven apart, so to speak, by the force of conflicting urges. But it impressed Janet that dissociation occurred importantly only in certain patients, those customarily classified as hysterics. Other people cannot split up their memories and neuromuscular systems, no matter how strong the inducements. Janet dealt with this difficulty by the further hypothesis of an hereditary weakness or *constitutional vulnerability*. Hysterics, he concluded, were burdened by an innate tendency

27

toward dissociation, a weakness of capacity to maintain the organization of self under conditions of stress. It fitted this interpretation that hysterics were often described, apart from their symptoms, as impulsive, childlike, self-dramatizing people who tended to lose themselves in each passing experience.

Janet's thinking was not confined to hysteria. He was a careful observer of another large class of so-called "nervous disorders," characterized by irrational fears, obsessive ideas, and compulsive actions or rituals that often interfered greatly with patients' lives. As people, these patients made a decidedly different impression from hysterics. Far from forgetting the unpleasant, their minds were full of ruminations, doubts, conflicts, anxieties, and attempts to solve everything intellectually. Janet called this whole category of neurosis by the name of *psychasthenia*, and he postulated behind it a constitutional vulnerability of an entirely different kind. In this way he made a classification for the chief "nervous disorders"—the *neuroses*—much as Kraepelin had done for the more severe mental disorders—the *psychoses*.

Breuer and Freud's Theory of Abreaction

A different way of looking at hysterical symptoms had been developed in the meantime by a Viennese physician, Joseph Breuer, who shortly enlisted the collaboration of a younger colleague, Sigmund Freud. From 1880 to 1882 Breuer had under treatment a curious and difficult case of hysteria. The patient, a girl in her early twenties, was bedridden for several months with a long array of symptoms. Both legs and the right arm were paralyzed, sight and hearing were impaired, the neck muscles were uncomfortably contracted, there was a persistent nervous cough, and at times speech became difficult. Besides these largely somatic afflictions there were frequent alterations of mental state: confusions and a dreamy condition that Breuer called "absence." During her periods of "absence" the girl often mumbled to herself as if her thoughts were busy. Breuer took note of her words and later, during hypnotic sessions, repeatedly gave them back to her. In this way she was led to reveal the fantasies that occupied her in her dreamy states. When she had unburdened herself of these fantasies she felt relieved, and awakened from the hypnosis temporarily much improved.

Presently Breuer discovered that under certain circumstances a symptom might be permanently removed. If during hypnosis the patient could remember the situation in which the symptom began, and if the accompanying emotion was freely and fully expressed, the symptom would disappear for good. Breuer found that the paralysis of the right arm had its origin during a painful period when the patient was nursing her father through his protracted last illness. One evening she dozed off at her father's bedside and had a nightmare: a huge black snake was attacking her father and she tried in vain to fend it off with her right arm. She awoke terrified, freed her arm that was over the back of the chair, and hastily suppressed her feelings lest her father perceive her

28

Sigmund Freud's consulting chamber at Bergasse 19. The artifacts seen here show not only the psychoanalytic couch, but also the memorabilia reflecting Freud's immersion in anthropology, mythology, and history.

fear. When the patient not only recalled this forgotten incident but also experienced fully the emotion she had so forcibly suppressed, her paralysis disappeared for good (Breuer & Freud, 1936).

In the course of time this patient was completely cured. The process was always the same: recovery during hypnosis of some drastic incident in which emotion had been suppressed, full and dramatic expression of the emotion, permanent disappearance of the symptom that had been laid down on that occasion. The release of suppressed emotion—of "strangulated affect"—was the core of Breuer's discovery, and received the name of *abreaction*. Reviewing this case some years later, Freud (1910) set forth the theory in the following words.

> . . . We are forced to the conclusion that the patient fell ill because the emotion developed in the pathogenic situation was prevented from escaping normally, and that the essence of the sickness lies in the fact that the imprisoned emotions undergo a series of abnormal changes. In part they are preserved as a lasting charge and as a source of constant disturbance in psychical life; in part they undergo a change into unusual bodily innervations and inhibitions which present themselves as the physical symptoms of the case.
>
> You see that we are in a fair way to arrive at a purely psychological theory of hysteria, in which we assign the first rank to the affective processes (pp. 30–31).

29

This theory was not only more purely psychological but also more psychodynamic than the one proposed by Janet. The dissociation of memories and bodily movements from conscious control was interpreted always in dynamic
terms—in terms of a conflict of forces between emotions pushing for expression and other motives pushing them back. The personality did not, in this interpretation, fall apart; it was pushed apart by strong conflicting forces. Every
symptom expressed conflict and became intelligible when the circumstances of
conflict could be recovered.

FREUD'S BASIC DISCOVERIES

After his study of the Breuer case it seemed clear to Freud that hysteria could
be cured by the release of pent-up emotion. The therapeutic problem was to
secure abreaction so that the energy of strangulated feelings might come to
normal expression instead of "spilling over" into bodily symptoms. Abreaction, however, could not take place without recall of the original pathogenic
situations, and these seemed often to be completely forgotten. In the Breuer
case it was necessary to enlist the aid of hypnosis in order to bring forward the
crucial memories. Freud began to use this method with his neurotic patients,
but he soon became discontented with hypnotism. Many patients were insus-
ceptible to hypnosis, and even with good subjects the results seemed uncertain
and transient. Freud began to look elsewhere for a technique of abreaction.

The Method of Free Association

At first glance the method he chose seems hardly a method at all. Instead of
requiring the patient to talk about some particular subject, Freud asked him
"to abandon himself to a process of *free association*, i.e., to say whatever came
into his head while ceasing to give any conscious direction to his thoughts"
(1927, p. 25). Patients were told that they must report all that occurred to
them, resisting any temptation to choose among their thoughts. Their only
obligation was to communicate everything in the order of its occurrence and
to make no attempt to supervise the course of their associations in the interests
of logic, decency, or conventionality. To the extent that patients could actually do this, Freud reasoned, their thoughts would be guided by the imprisoned
feelings that needed abreaction, and the entrance of these feelings into conscious experience would be hastened.

It was perhaps unfortunate to call this process "*free* association." It is free
from many conventional restraints, but it is not free in the sense of being an
idle wandering of fancy. Freud himself declared that "free association is not
really free." In the first place, all the associations have to be communicated to
a listener. The reveries have to be made public, which at once brings into play
all of one's desires to make sense, to be logical, and to put up a good front.

30

Under these circumstances it is by no means an easy matter to tell everything that drifts through one's head. In the second place, the patient is suffering from a neurosis and has come to the physician to be cured. This circumstance dominates the whole situation and exerts an influence on the course of the associations even when the patient makes no conscious attempt to control them. Freud probably put the matter too strongly when he claimed that nothing will occur to the patient that is not somehow related to the neurosis. But the therapeutic purpose is always present and constitutes the most consistent factor influencing the train of thought.

Resistance and Repression

The adoption of free association led to Freud's next discovery. His patients found it impossible to obey the fundamental rule of telling everything.

> The patient tries in every way to escape its requirements. First he will declare that he cannot think of anything, then that so much comes to his mind that it is impossible to seize on anything definite. Then we discover with no slight displeasure that he has yielded to this or that critical objection, for he betrays himself by the long pauses which he allows to occur in his speaking. He then confesses that he really cannot bring himself to this, that he is ashamed to; he prefers to let this motive get the upper hand over his promise. He may say that he did think of something but that it concerns someone else and is for that reason exempt. Or he says that what he just thought of is really too trivial, too stupid, and too foolish. I surely could not have meant that he should take such thoughts into account. Thus it goes, with untold variations, in the face of which we continually reiterate that "telling everything" really means telling everything (1920, pp. 249–250).

If driven from these simpler tactics the patients found more complicated ways of resisting the fundamental rule. They might embark on elaborate arguments about the theory and soundness of the procedure. They might show an eager curiosity to be instructed in such a way that they might practice it alone in the privacy of their own rooms. They might even begin to act out toward the physician various anxious and hostile feelings set off by the task of associating. In countless ways Freud's patients showed a strong resistance against telling everything.

Resistance does not go on forever. In the course of time a patient, perhaps after hours of circling around the topic, becomes able to bring forth memories and painful feelings about some earlier event in life. Often the patient is surprised that an experience now so clearly recalled has been so long forgotten. It was on these observations that Freud based his theory of repression. Strong forces evidently prevented the patient from remembering certain emotionally charged experiences. Freud reasoned that these same forces, which now opposed the entry of the forgotten ideas into consciousness, must have been responsible for their original banishment. He called this original process *repression*, and considered it to be attested by the observed facts of resistance.

31

Anxiety and Defense

Freud next asked himself why such a process should occur. He came to the conclusion that repression was a device whereby the personality is protected from unbearable pain. In all his cases it appeared, after the forgotten material had been recovered, that in the original situation a wish had been aroused that conflicted sharply with the person's other desires, especially with what Freud called "ethical, aesthetic, and personal pretensions." Absorbed at first in studying the banished urges as they crept back into consciousness, Freud gradually turned his attention to the forces in personality that were responsible for the banishment. His interest became centered on defensive activities. With the same sensitivity that had enabled him to infer the existence of unconscious wishes, he now began to understand the unwitting evasive tactics whereby patients protected themselves from mental pain.

In 1926 Freud published an important work, *Inhibition, Symptoms and Anxiety* (Bunker, trans., 1936), in which he assigned to *anxiety* the central place in the theory of neurosis. Repression, he concluded, is one of several *defense mechanisms* directed against the emergence of impulses that would carry with them unbearable anxiety. If urges were merely at odds with adult ethical, aesthetic, and personal pretensions, the conflict would not require such drastic measures. The urges responsible for neurosis represented a greater danger, portending disaster and evoking panic. This suggested that the conflicts had first occurred in early childhood, when fear of parental punishment, desertion, and loss of love can easily be of panic proportions. Freud thus arrived at a much needed clarification of his theory: he now saw neurosis as the outcome of attempts to avoid severe anxiety through the use of desperate and primitive defense mechanisms such as repression, mechanisms that prevented a later discriminating solution of the conflict. The resistance observed during treatment could now be understood as a fight against the emergence of anxiety. Abreaction of imprisoned emotions was not a correct statement of the goal of treatment. The crucial thing was to bring into awareness the anxiety that had become associated with certain urges, so that its force could be reduced.

Freud called his method of treatment *psychoanalysis*. As the method evolved it came to require a great deal of time. The analyst's part was a relatively passive one. Patients were allowed to bring forth essential memories and feelings at their own slow pace, while physicians limited their activities to pointing out resistances and indicating possible connections among remembered events. Freud's belief that neurosis had its roots in early childhood added to the length of treatment. Recall of the initial pathological events seemed to happen only when a long chain of recovered memories led the way to them. Even with five appointments a week a thorough psychoanalysis was likely to require as much as three years, sometimes even more. To be psychoanalyzed represented an enormous commitment of time and money, but Freud was convinced that no other method could cure a neurosis in a lasting way.

The Importance of Sexual Strivings

While he was still concentrating on the nature of suppressed wishes, Freud convinced himself that neurotic misery was closely linked to sexual needs. Particularly in cases where fatigue was a prominent complaint—a variety of neurosis called *neurasthenia*—he found grave disturbances in the patient's current sexual life. In his own words: "The more I enquired into such disturbances (bearing in mind that all men conceal the truth in these matters) and the more adept I became at persisting in my interrogations in spite of denials at the beginning, the more regularly did pathogenic factors from sexual life disclose themselves, until there seemed to me little to prevent the assumption of their general occurrence" (Freud, 1924, p. 273). This much he obtained from direct inquiry, but the use of free association presently led to discoveries far more startling. In patients with all varieties of neurosis, including hysteria and the obsessive-compulsive states, the same thing happened again and again: the associations led back into the patient's past until "experiences were finally reached which belonged to his infancy and concerned his sexual life; and this was so even when an ordinary emotion, not of a sexual kind, had led to the outbreak of the disease. Without taking into account these sexual traumas of childhood it was impossible to explain the symptoms, comprehend their determination, or prevent their return. After this, the unique significance of sexual experiences in the aetiology of the psychoneuroses seemed incontestably established" (Freud, 1924, p. 275).

The words just quoted were written in 1905, the same year in which Freud produced his monograph, *Three Contributions to the Theory of Sex*. In 1905 the ideas advanced in his monograph were considered extremely radical and were quite generally met by shocked repugnance. The claims to which Freud was led by the free associations and recollections of his patients can be summarized in the following statements. (1) The sexual need is active in infancy and to a lesser extent throughout childhood. (2) It is more diffuse in its nature than the adult need, consisting of a variety of "partial impulses" not strongly dominated by genital excitation, showing itself in such actions as thumbsucking, display of the naked body, inquisitiveness about the bodies of others, masturbation, pleasures connected with anal excretion or retention, and anything else that yielded pleasurable stimulation of sensitive or erogenous zones of the body. (3) The sexual need is not innately attached to any particular objects, with the choice accomplished by learning; in childhood, therefore, members of the family and playmates of either sex may become its objects. (4) It is subject to an active campaign of adult disapproval that tends to encourage repression. (5) The childhood history of sexual experiences, fantasies, and repressions exerts a powerful effect on sexual behavior following the strengthening of the urge at puberty. Both the methods of satisfaction and the object choices must be revised if the person is going to advance to a normal adult sexual life.

From these ideas Freud went on to a massive generalization, the *libido theory*, in which he gave sexuality the predominant position among human energies and attributed to it a regulating role in the whole course of development. This arbitrary step led to discord in the psychoanalytic movement. Fortunately, it also led to the careful observation of other motives likely to become sources of anxiety. Alfred Adler, for instance, heard a different theme in the free associations of neurotic patients. Everywhere he noticed the subtle workings of a striving to dominate, degrade, and triumph over others. He came to believe that the ruling motive in neurosis was a *striving for superiority*, directed, however, toward dominating the household by being ill. Adler was convinced that at heart the patients felt weak and inadequate: they suffered from anxious *feelings of inferiority* for which illness was an attempt at *compensation*. "The exemptions and privileges of illness and suffering give the patient a substitute for his original hazardous goal of superiority" (Adler, 1929, p. 33). Karen Horney, who also started with Freud's methods, attached special importance to *aggression*, an urge that in early childhood becomes easily linked with anxiety because of its effects on parents. Even more than sex, Horney believed, aggressive behavior begets anger and hostility in parents that awaken great fears in the child and may precipitate disastrous defensive measures, so that future assertiveness is paralyzed (1937, ch. 4).

These formulations enlarged the range of motives that had to be considered important not only in neurosis but in all human behavior. They unseated sex from the conceptual throne on which Freud had put it, but they did not cancel his shrewd observations of the extensive part played by sexual strivings in human life. Nor did they supplant the idea that anxiety is the core of the problem of neurosis.

Psychodynamics

Pathways of discovery often start in unexpected places and proceed through strange twists and turns. What began as a search for a better way of treating neurotic patients led Freud in the end to a radically changed view of human nature. The picture that emerged differed greatly from the conventional one of Freud's time. The conscious self, with its pride, its declared values, and its civilized virtues, began to look like a shaky superstructure beneath which surged the instinctual drives, the satisfaction of which Freud interpreted as the true goal of living. Freud came to see the conscious self as largely a system of defenses, distortions, and self-deceptions. It came into existence through the child's training for acceptable civilized behavior as this was understood by the parents and the surrounding culture. In neurotic patients the plan for socialization had conspicuously miscarried. The anxiety generated by training had produced so great a constriction of instinctual urges as to be incompatible with health. But instincts could not be wholly suppressed, and their clamor for outlets could be detected not only in neurotic symptoms but in dreams, fantasies, inadvertent behavior, errors, and slips of the tongue.

34

Because of this emphasis on forces—motives and wishes—Freud's theory of personality is called *psychodynamic*. Few theories of behavior dispense altogether with motivational concepts such as drive, but other schools of thought give relatively greater prominence to learning, perceptions, and intellectual development. Freud's interest was drawn to the forces; his genius lay in penetrating the conscious level and disclosing beneath it the play of wishes, anxieties, and defenses. It was here, he reasoned, that one confronted the true springs of behavior, the forces that under certain circumstances produced neurosis but were in any event the authentic causes of all behavior.

Psychodynamic theory, first in Freud's version and then in the thinking of other workers, was destined for a large career. One did not have to share Freud's views on the centrality of sex or the falsity of the conscious self to see that what we do and think expresses desires and wishes much more than had previously been supposed. Before long the new insights were being extended to an increasingly wide range of problems. The psychodynamic element was sought in delinquency, criminal behavior, chronic alcoholism and other drug addictions, sexual deviations, possibly even in the psychoses, and certainly in many aspects of everyday life. In an alcoholic, for instance, one might look not just for an hereditary susceptibility but for an otherwise frustrated wish to be a more confident, assertive person, for an urge to spite a demanding spouse, for a need to escape burdensome responsibility, possibly even for an unwitting determination to injure and destroy oneself; coming to terms with these problems might be essential for a cure. The psychodynamic point of view signifies a sophisticated awareness of the striving aspect of behavior in all its complexities, conflicts, and disguises.

The importance and wide range of Freud's ideas make him a monumental figure in modern intellectual history. His own writings touched on anthropology, history, the study of religion, and the psychodynamic analysis of works of art. His influence spread widely into the social sciences and humanities, having an especially marked effect on literature. He contributed to a revolution in child training and in attitudes toward sex. It is never safe to attribute revolutions to one person; they must be in the air, so to speak, before individual voices are truly heeded. But the widespread current interest in openness and warmth in human relations, in authenticity of feelings, and in breaking down the hypocrisies, evasions, and subtle cruelties that result from inept socialization, is in harmony with Freud's outlook and probably owes a great deal to his influence.

MEDICAL AND PSYCHOLOGICAL MODELS

Study of the history of abnormal psychology has introduced us to two different ways of understanding maladaptive personal behavior. Each has its own history and traditions; each is supported by a large body of observations; each

represents the work of many minds attempting to find explanations and construct appropriate theories. The medical model rests squarely on the concept
of disease and calls for finding correlates in the nervous system and its biochemical environment. The psychological model rests on motives, feelings,
and adaptive habits; it calls for finding causes in conflicts, inappropriate
learnings, and defenses against anxiety. As we have seen, the two models were
developed for different kinds of maladaptive behavior. The medical model
was built mainly from study of the psychoses, whereas the psychological model
developed out of attempts to treat the neuroses. From this circumstance alone
we should be on guard against the idea that one model is right, the other
wrong. Both are needed to understand the full range of maladaptive personal
behavior.

This solution is simple in the abstract, but applying it judiciously is not always easy. In some research literature, battle lines are drawn between the two
theories. This is partly a matter of intellectual preference. To some workers a
biochemical explanation seems more solid and satisfying; to others a psychological interpretation feels more congenial and convincing. Unfortunately the
conflict has been sharpened by professional rivalries. The medical model is
taken to justify the idea that all treatment should be under the direction of
physicians. The psychological model allows that people with psychological instead of medical training, especially psychologists and social workers, could be
fully responsible for various types of treatment. With these problems intrud-
ing, some of the literature reflects a competitive spirit that makes it hard to be
fair about the facts.

A more legitimate difficulty lies in the facts themselves. There are pure
cases of medical disorder and pure cases of psychological disorder, but most
cases are likely to require elements from each model. Indeed, as Masserman
(1979) has pointed out, the understanding of individual patients must always
be a far more complicated matter than is suggested by these abstract models.
To grasp what is contributing to a patient's complaint one has to consider the
possibility of genetic defects, physical constitutions, current organic disorders,
personal history, recent emotional upsets, and current stress. And it is advisable, before deciding on a plan of treatment, to estimate such possible assets
as intelligence, talents, adaptive versatility, and a supporting environment.
Proper understanding requires a careful unscrambling of these interacting influences. Abnormal psychology is no field for simplistic and doctrinaire modes
of thought. As part of the study of human behavior, it challenges us at every
point to deal intelligently with a subject matter that is inherently complex.

SUGGESTIONS FOR FURTHER READING

The historical development of abnormal psychology has been the subject in recent
years of considerable research. The best introduction to this work will be found in two

chapters by Maher & Maher in G. Kimble and K. Schlesinger (Eds.), *History of Modern Psychology* (1981, in press). The survey carries the story from earliest times to the present. Students who wish to examine the care and treatment of disordered persons as an aspect of American social history will be intrigued with an older book by A. Deutsch, *The Mentally Ill in America* (1937) and a newer one by J. S. Bockoven, *Moral Treatment in Community Mental Health* (1972). Clifford Beers' autobiography, *A Mind That Found Itself* (1908), still retains its value and fascination not only as the fountainhead of the mental health movement but also as a description of the mental state of a person temporarily insane.

The development of the disease concept of mental disorders from Pinel to Kraepelin and Bleuler is described in detail by G. Zilboorg in certain chapters of *A History of Medical Psychology* (1967).

Two chapters in R. E. Fancher's interestingly written *Pioneers of Psychology* (1979), one on Mesmer and the early hypnotists and one on Freud, provide background on the evolution of psychopathology. No one has ever equalled Janet in the art of cinical description: *The Major Symptoms of Hysteria* (1920). Although this work is in several respects out of date, it conjures up the excitement that originally surrounded the study of this disorder when it was an outstanding medical mystery and leaves the reader's mind full of memorable cases. Freud's own introduction to his work is still the most satisfactory: *A General Introduction to Psychoanalysis* (1919) and *New Introductory Lectures on Psychoanalysis* (1933), both available as paperbacks. A systematic presentation of Adler's work, mainly in selections from his writing, is to be found in H. L. & R. R. Ansbacher's *The Individual Psychology of Alfred Adler* (1956); this, too, is available in paperback.

The Gross Clinic by Thomas Eakins. Property of Jefferson Medical
College of Thomas Jefferson University.

2
Clinical Introduction:
Examples of Disordered Personalities

INTRODUCTION TO THE CASES

In Chapter 1 the field of abnormal psychology was described as the study of maladaptive personal reactions to life and its circumstances. We will now pursue this study by examining some representative examples. What does it mean to be psychologically disordered? How does it feel, and how does this feeling express itself in behavior? What are the symptoms? What sense can be made out of persistent maladaptive behavior, and how can its causes be untangled? The answers to these questions are complicated, and they become more difficult because here, as in any aspect of personality, we must allow for a wide range of individual differences. Maladaptive reactions occur in people and it is important to look at them in their natural habitat. Case histories,

39

moreover, are the chief element in the foundation of fact on which abnormal psychology was historically built.

This chapter consists mainly of a description of five examples. It will be useful, however, to have a short prelude on varieties of disorder. Here we gather up the topics discussed in Chapter 1 and provide a rough framework for everything that follows.

Varieties of Disorder

Over the last twenty years a detailed and elaborate scheme for the description of mental disorders has come into existence. The scheme was prepared by a series of committees of The American Psychiatric Association. Published in 1952, revised in 1968, it is now in its third edition under the title *Diagnostic and Statistical Manual of Mental Disorders* (American Psychiatric Association, 1980), familiarly known as DSM-III. There has been a startling growth in the number of categories recognized: 60 in 1952, 145 in 1968, 230 in 1980. Before the reader assumes that we now know all about 230 varieties of mental disorder, we should point out that the scheme is intended to be strictly descriptive. There are no necessary implications about causes, outcomes, or treatments. Its purpose is to describe comprehensively what clinical workers observe in their work, and thus establish criteria for a common language and more accurate communication. In a realm where labels have often been applied in inconsistent ways, this is potentially a valuable contribution.

Among those who prefer the psychological to the medical model the reception of DSM-III has been lukewarm. In their effort to be comprehensive, the authors of the manual at first swept under the heading of mental disorders such items as parent-child problems, insomnia, and problems of identity that certainly do not fit what most people understand by that title. Schacht and Nathan (1977) have criticized the scheme on this ground, and Garmezy (1978) has selected children's reading disabilities from the list to show the damaging consequences, for both theory and practice, of implying that these problems are actually mental disorders. It is plain, however, that "mental disorders" in the title of DSM-III is a historical accident and should not be taken literally. While we must guard against harmful consequences of an inappropriate term, the intention of the scheme is merely to order and classify clinical observations, not to imply anything final about origins and treatment.

A few workers go further and deplore any tendency to multiply diagnostic labels. They quote the American psychiatrist Adolph Meyer who once said: 'We understand this case; we don't need any diagnosis" (R. Watson, 1951). Szasz in particular has argued that hanging the label of an alleged disease on someone may cut short the effort at understanding and lead to unwarranted steps, such as commitment to a mental hospital, which may not be in the person's best interests (Szasz, 1966). As we see in our clinical examples, diagnostic labels have not always played a helpful part in finding out what was the matter.

Table 2-1 Main Headings: Diagnostic and Statistical Manual of Mental Disorders (DSM-III)

1. Disorders Usually First Evident in Infancy, Childhood, or Adolescence
2. Organic Mental Disorders
3. Substance Use Disorders
4. Schizophrenic Disorders
5. Paranoid Disorders
6. Psychotic Disorders Not Elsewhere Classified
7. Affective Disorders
8. Anxiety Disorders
9. Somatoform Disorders
10. Dissociative Disorders
11. Psychosexual Disorders
12. Factitious Disorders
13. Disorders of Impulse Control Not Elsewhere Classified
14. Adjustment Disorder
15. Psychological Factors Affecting Physical Condition
16. Conditions Not Attributable to a Mental Disorder
17. Personality Disorders

Source: American Psychiatric Association, 1980.

The main headings of DSM-III are given in Table 2-1. A quick reading of the list will reveal a number of categories we became familiar with in the last chapter. It will also disclose leftover categories ("not elsewhere classified") that testify to the difficulty of finding consistent places for everything that clinicians observe. Finally, there are concessions to the psychological model: category 16 acknowledges that many clinical problems are not properly described as mental disorders, and category 17, treated as a separate axis, makes room for a variety of enduring traits that do not necessarily become serious problems. The scheme thus moves a little away from its medical ancestry.

We will discuss those categories most important for what follows in this book.

Disorders Usually First Evident in Infancy, Childhood, and Adolescence (1).
This category is of great importance; it includes mental retardation, conduct disorders, childhood anxieties, eating disturbances, and other deviations from normal development. In this book we do not take up childhood disorders separately, but scatter them through the chapters to which they most appropriately belong.

Organic Mental Disorders (2). This category covers disorders in which abnormal organic conditions play the decisive part. In the last chapter this kind of illness was illustrated by general paresis; the fourth case in the present chap-

41

ter provides another example. In such cases injury to the brain or abnormality in its biochemical environment is directly related to psychological symptoms. Included are some mental and behavorial consequences of excessive concentrations of alcohol and other drugs; for example, the DT's (*delirium tremens*) that sometimes follow extreme alcoholic intoxication.

Substance Use Disorders (3).   Here are listed the problems of excessive use and addiction connected with alcohol, barbiturates, cocaine, amphetamines, hallucinatory drugs, and other substances that produce marked alterations in behavior. Not shirking controversy, the authors of DSM-III have included marijuana and tobacco in the list.

Schizophrenic Disorders (4).   This heading includes the various forms of abnormal behavior and thought that led Kraepelin and Bleuler to postulate a large disease entity.

Paranoid Disorders (5).   Making a separate heading for paranoid disorders allows for a pattern sometimes encountered in which there is an excessively hostile, suspicious, blaming attitude toward others without further signs of loss of contact with reality.

Affective Disorders (7).   This is the currently preferred name for Kraepelin's manic-depressive psychosis.

Anxiety Disorders (8, 9, 10, 12).   A radical innovation in DSM-III is the abolition of the category of neurosis. The phobic and obsessive-compulsive forms are now classified as anxiety disorders, in harmony with Freud's view of their origin in anxiety. Hysteria, however, is broken down into three headings. Somatoform disorders are those seemingly real, if not always quite real, bodily symptoms like anaesthesias and paralyses that so impressed Charcot and the hypnotists. Dissociative disorders include the memory gaps, losses of identity, and other fragmentations of consciousness that were central to Janet's theories of hysteria. The term "factitious disorders" is used to designate symptoms that are under voluntary control and that seem to be produced merely to assume the role of a sick person. In a descriptive scheme these widely different patterns no doubt deserve separate headings. We need not lament the dropping from this list of *neurosis*, which was never an apt technical term, implying as it did that something was wrong with the nerves. But in Chapter 6 we have hysteria under the title of Anxiety Disorders, believing that it, too, has a special relation to anxiety. And in view of long historical use we cannot suppose that "neurosis" and "neurotic" will quickly drop from our vocabulary.

Psychosexual Disorders (11).   The chief contents of this category which we explore in Chapter 11, are disorders of gender identity, disorders of sexual aim such as voyeurism, and disorders of sexual performance like impotence and frigidity.

Conditions Not Attributable to a Mental Disorder (16). This heading is far from being a scrapheap of small leftovers. It contains a fairly large proportion of the complaints that come to the attention of clinical workers. Its subheadings include antisocial behavior, marital problems, parent-child difficulties, child abuse, and problems connected with occupation. Although the main heading can hardly be praised as explicit, it at least reserves a place for many difficulties of living that nowadays lead large numbers of people to look for psychological help.

Personality Disorders (17). The disorders placed under this heading are "pervasive personality traits" that are "exhibited in a wide range of important social and personal contexts." These traits, deeply ingrained and inflexible, cause "either impairment in adaptive functioning or subjective distress." Examples are a grandiose sense of self-importance that tends to antagonize everybody, or, in contrast, a shy, self-effacing modesty with avoidance of most human contacts. Possession of such a trait is certainly not literally a sign of mental disorder, but it can lead to great difficulties in living. In Chapters 3 to 5 we examine such qualities as products of learning and interpret them in accord with a psychological model.

The Student's Attitude Toward Abnormality

Throughout history mentally disordered people have been viewed with suspicion and dread. This attitude lies deeply embedded in our cultural tradition, and few are wholly exempt from its subtle influence. In the past students were sometimes warned that abnormal psychology might upset them. More recently there has been a sharp change in the cultural attitude. Community mental health has become a major social objective, and helping patients is a popular field for volunteer work. This is a great step forward, but psychological disorders and persistent maladaptive behavior present real difficulties to sympathetic understanding. People who do not behave in ways that seem sensible or talk in a coherent, responsive fashion are always disconcerting.

There is an experience reported so often by medical students that we might facetiously refer to it as "medical students' disease." This consists of feeling vividly in themselves all the symptoms they are studying in their textbooks: distinct palpitations when they are studying disorders of the heart, ticklings of the throat and labored breathing when they read about respiratory diseases, curious pains in the abdomen when they examine pictures of gastrointestinal ailments. Students of abnormal psychology should not be alarmed if they, too, have numerous attacks of "medical students' disease" while reading about disordered behavior. Every type of disorder has much about it that can be dupli-

43

Being a mental health worker requires not only intelligence and skill, but also deep human commitment and an unusual capacity for empathy.

cated in the experience of healthy people, though it occurs in healthy people with less prominence and disproportion. As a matter of fact, it is most unsatisfactory to be immune to "medical students' disease." A touch of the ailment is a sign that one is really opening oneself to the subject, trying to grasp it and feel it instead of just reading about it.

While suffering this affliction, the student should not forget the comforting thought that abnormal psychology deals predominantly with inferior and unsuccessful forms of adaptive behavior. It thus tends to draw a picture that exaggerates failure and helplessness at the expense of successful self-direction. Most people are not helpless. Constructive activities are possible for them whereby they overcome at least some of the difficulties in their path. No doubt there should be a book that classifies the chief varieties of heroism, fortitude, and creative problem-solving, and contains case histories of magnificent behavior under severe stress in shipwrecks and fires, on dangerous missions, on flights to the moon. But our subject here is maladaptive behavior, and we must not stray from it.

1. AN ADOLESCENT MALADJUSTMENT: WALTER LILLY

Our first example is a high school boy of 15 bearing the fictitious name of Walter Lilly (Peterson, 1968). The boy had caused alarm at school by walking out of his physical education class in an acutely disturbed state. The school's social worker described him as "hysterical and shaking all over," "incoherent and rambling in his talk," "agitated, depressed," and admitting to "ruminations about suicide," all of which suggested that he might be on the verge of a serious breakdown. Some months earlier Walter had several times left the physical education class to appear in the principal's office weeping copiously, and talks with the social worker had been instituted, but Walter's mother had requested that these talks be stopped. Seriously alarmed by the new turn of events, the school authorities now decided that Walter should see a clinical psychologist and told the parents that their son would be suspended if they did not agree. The situation confronting the clinical psychologist thus consisted of a badly disturbed adolescent boy, a resistive father and mother, and school authorities who had in effect forced the family to seek psychological treatment. Although far from ideal, this tangle of human relations is typical of clinical problems. Inevitably the person designated as the patient is part of a social system.

The clinical psychologist, meeting his new client in the waiting room, sees before him a large, plump youngster who immediately begins to shake with sobs. The father, who has brought Walter in, urges him to stop crying, but his tears are still flowing when he reaches the psychologist's office. The following dialogue ensues.

E   (EXAMINER). Walter, what's wrong?
C   (CLIENT). I'm scared I'm going to die.
E   Afraid you're going to die.
C   I think my heart's not right.
E   It isn't working right?
C   (Sniffs.) I'm scared to go anywhere.
E   Mm hm.
C   (Sniffs.) I want to get better like I used to be. (Cries continuously.) Last month I was so good.
E   You were feeling better then.
C   I wasn't scared. My heart was beating all right. I went and did things. . . .
E   Yes . . .
C   Now I'm scared. . . . I'm scared I'm going to die, and I don't want to die (sobs) because I . . . want to grow up and get a job (sobs). . . .
E   And have a reasonably happy life. Sure you do. Of course you do. . . . What sorts of things happen to your heart that make you think it isn't right?
C   It beats slow. And I'm scared to go to bed at night because I'm afraid I won't get up in the morning.
E   Afraid you won't be able to wake up at all.
C   (Sniffs, sobs.) Oh God . . . I've been this way all this month.
E   Have you?
C   Scared (cries) . . . get all light feeling in my head, a funny feeling like I'm going to fall over when I get nervous.
E   Just dizzy . . . and you think you just might not be able to stand up at all.
C   And I want to get better and have fun.

45

E Sure you do.

C (Sobs.) Everybody's been so good to me . . .

E Everybody's good to you, but you're still just as scared as you ever were, aren't you?

C (Sniffs.)

E What sorts of things go through your mind that frighten you so? What sorts of things are you thinking of?

C (Sniffs.) That I'll have a heart attack or something. You think you see people they go uptown and they fall over on the street you know . . . and things.

E You read about it or you hear about it. . . .

C Yes. . . .

E You think this might happen to you.

C I don't want to die.

E Of course you don't want to die.

On first reading, the psychologist's contribution to this dialogue may seem less than brilliant, but it is well adapted to the circumstances. Repeating what the subject has said is a way of recognizing his feelings and giving him assurance that he is understood, which at the outset is the most important thing to accomplish. Walter is not reproached for crying; his fear of heart failure is not ridiculed; he is given no reassurances, which at this point would sound false; he is simply encouraged to tell his story. From what Walter says it is evident that anxiety—being scared—is the focus of his difficulty, and that his dread is capable of mounting to panic. To be afraid of going out and doing things, of sleeping at night, and of the physical education class clearly qualifies as disordered personal behavior rather than response to actual danger. But this is something for the examiner to notice, not for the client to be told.

As the interview continues, Walter describes his fear of the neighbors, two old people for whom he sometimes does chores. These neighbors, he is sure, look at him "like I'm no good," in spite of his efforts to please them. He goes on to tell, with renewed tears, of the death two years before of the grandmother who had lived in adjoining quarters. "Ever since my grandma died I've been no good," he sobs; "she'd help me, and she'd be right there when I needed her." At school he had one somewhat colorless friend, shy like himself, with whom he feels comfortable, but the rest of the children fill him with fear. He reports that they make fun of him, spread stories about him, laugh at his awkwardness in physical education, play practical jokes on him, and sometimes demand money that he does not dare refuse them. Evidently he is treated as an easy mark and cannot think of any way to improve his position. These remarks indicate that the feeling of being no good has become pervasive for Walter, especially since the death of the one person who was able to assuage it. He is helpless and hopeless. Asked much later in the interview what he would wish for if he had three wishes, he says, with renewed tears: "To have some friends, and to be myself again, the way I was, and to have a grandma that cares for me."

Are we dealing here with a disease or with accumulated difficulties of living? There is, of course, a "symptom" in the form of heart trouble, and it would be irresponsible not to have a physical examination. The results are negative; the functioning of Walter's heart proves to be entirely normal. This permits the interpretation that heart disease is simply an idea on which the boy has seized to account for his dreadful feelings of acute anxiety and impending disaster. Do we then call anxiety his "symptom"? If so, it is not a symptom in the same sense as chronic anxiety arising, for instance, from overactivity of the thyroid gland. Walter is anxious because he feels no good, because nobody respects him, nobody accepts him, nobody any longer gives him a kind look. This is not a disease. It arises from difficulties in living, and it takes an acute form when acquired patterns of behavior become wholly unworkable. Readers should ponder how they would feel if they saw their personal world as hostile and belittling as the one described by Walter. The anxiety appears less inappropriate in the light of Walter's belief that he has lost all possibility of being loved and valued.

But we have not yet considered the parents. Walter himself makes a remark late in the first interview that suggests a different pattern of interactions at home.

> c   At home I get real mad. I have a bad mouth. I mean I get . . . angry and
> I scream off and say bad words. I know I shouldn't do that. . . . I get too
> many things in my head and I have to scream off. And at school I don't
> say a word to anybody. I just let them pick on me.

That he often behaved this way at home was confirmed by his father, who came for an interview a few days later directly from his job as a construction worker. Mr. Lilly said that he never hit Walter—"he's just too pitiful"—but that he sometimes got mad with the boy, especially when he "kept the whole family up half the night a-crying and a-moaning." What happened, the examiner asked, when Walter took to screaming off? With a nervous laugh, the father said, "Well, to tell you the truth, I guess we always give in . . . so's we won't bother the neighbors. They're sort of old, and I don't think they appreciate the noise."

Mr. Lilly was also asked about Walter's reaction to his grandmother, to which he replied that "she spoiled him rotten." This subject was amplified in an interview that was requested with Mrs. Lilly.

> E   So then, how did she and Walter get along? I mean, how did she treat
> Walter that made her such a special person to him?
> c   I don't know how to tell you this.
> E   Well, do the best you can.

47

C   Well, as we know, and as you have said, he was spoiled. We'd correct him, and Grandma, she . . . she'd say it wasn't the right thing to do, and she'd almost cry, so. . . .

E   Would she?

C   Yes. . . . Oh, I've seen the time where, well, we did, we had to have her in our home after she broke her hip . . . and, when I tried to correct Walter, she'd cry. I'll tell you. . . .

E   It must have been a very. . . .

C   It was rough, I'll tell you, it's been a rough life. I don't advise anyone to do it.

E   It must have been difficult for you. You were caught right between, weren't you?

C   Well, yes. . . .

E   Suppose Walter should do something that you thought he ought to be corrected about, and you tried to do it, and then, if I understand it, Walter would go running to Grandma. . . .

C   Right, that's right.

E   And she would protect him . . . and cry.

C   Yes. . . .

E   And say, "There, Walter, everything will be fine."

C   Yes. . . .

E   And don't you touch him. . . .

C   Yes. . . .

E   And would you correct him or wouldn't you? How would that turn out? Who won, Grandma or you?

C   Well, I imagine Grandma did . . . just to keep the peace, I think, Grandma did.

E   So Walter really wouldn't get corrected.

C   Right.

The psychologist next visited the school, hoping not only to secure information but also to enlist cooperation in whatever program of treatment he decided to adopt. He learned that Walter had scored below average on a standard intelligence test and was doing barely passing schoolwork; there was no reason to hope that academic excellence could become a compensatory source of self-esteem. The physical education teacher confirmed the picture of the boy as physically awkward and as the butt of jeers and pranks by his schoolmates. It came out that Walter had cried and asked to be excused from a shop class in which the boys got a little rough, and had been allowed to take an art course instead. The teachers agreed that he never showed anger at school and seemed to be afraid of almost everything.

With this much information the psychologist felt able to take a first step toward treatment. Whatever the historical origins and full meaning of Walter's behavior might be, his crying at school had the effect of getting him excused from unpleasant situations, and his lamentations and screaming off at home yielded him both parental attention and his own way in matters of dispute. This gave the psychologist a chance to apply elementary learning principles and to try to extinguish the behavior by removing its reinforcements. To do so required the cooperation of the school authorities, who were asked to pay no attention to Walter's crying and to excuse him from nothing on account of it. The psychologist himself in his meetings with Walter looked out the window whenever there was sniffing and sobbing, offering attention and response only when these accompaniments were absent. The parents likewise took part, attempting to carry out the following instruction:

> Don't scold him, don't argue with him, don't do a blooming thing when he cries. Just go on about your business. Pay no attention to him at all. But if he does anything else—nearly anything at all that a fifteen-year-old boy should do or talk about—then you talk to him. Show him you're interested in that.

Appealingly simple as this procedure sounds, we must not forget that Walter was suffering from acute anxiety. His behavior was not just a tactic to obtain results, and extinguishing it would be unlikely to remove his real distress. The psychologist therefore began at the same time a program designed to reduce the intensity of the anxiety attacks. This program, called "desensitization," is described more fully in a later chapter. In essence it involves developing a state of deep physical relaxation and calmness, then encouraging the client to imagine a series of scenes leading up to those that have previously set off anxiety. The procedure is designed to reduce anxiety by introducing feared stimuli vividly but in a safe situation with no harmful results (extinction). When sufficiently trained in this procedure a person can sometimes be allowed to practice it alone between visits to the therapist. Eight meetings and a certain amount of practice between times were devoted to this device for modifying behavior.

These two different lines of attack on Walter's problems brought results that were modestly favorable. From school it was reported that he had not cried for several weeks, certainly a real gain, but that he continued to play a passive and ineffectual part both in class and with other children. At home he had stopped moaning and had taken some enjoyable trips with his parents, but his father reported an increase in angry behavior: "He may be an angel in school, but he's getting to be a hellion around home." In his sessions with the psychologist, crying had disappeared and his fear that he was going to die was substantially reduced. "Once in a while I still feel like something might be wrong with my heart," he said, "but I don't really believe that any more and it don't bother me like it used to." He no longer thought that the neighbors considered him no good, and his reply was more forward-looking when he was again asked to think of three wishes: "a car, good grades, and to be happier."

Walter was definitely better; he had successfully emerged from the acute crisis. If contacts with the client had ceased at this point, the psychologist would have been justified in listing the case as improved.

We must not, however, be too quick to congratulate ourselves about a result of this kind. Walter had been relatively well until the last month before his acute attack at school. Has he simply been returned to that state, without substantial change in his difficulties in living? It is a gain, possibly lasting, that his immediate environment has stopped rewarding his childish tactics of crying and screaming, but this does not guarantee that he will adopt more mature strategies and discover new grounds for self-esteem. So long as he remains passive at school and angrily demanding at home there is still a risk that he will feel no good to the point of once more becoming acutely scared. How far to go in treating a case is always a difficult decision. One can never hope to forestall all possible problems. The best course is to weigh on the one hand the likelihood of being able to produce specific beneficent changes, and on the other the costs of doing so, reckoned in terms of the time, effort, patience, and insight of all concerned.

In Walter's case it was decided to attempt two further changes, one in his interactions with his father, the other in his behavior toward other adolescents. To expedite the first change, son and father were seen together for an hour each week. Talking things over among themselves, the three were gradually able to discern a pattern in those exchanges that caused friction and angry outbursts. The trouble would begin when Walter made a demand, like going to look for a second-hand car, that Mr. Lilly felt obliged to refuse. Walter would then increase his insistence, become irritatingly nagging, and finally shout, curse, and scream off at his father, who in turn became angry, occasionally to the point of striking his son. But then the father would feel guilty about his outburst and "make it up" to Walter by doing what had been demanded in the first place. Once this pattern was clearly perceived, somewhat to the surprise of both participants who did not realize what they had been doing, a program could be planned that was more compatible with self-respect on both sides. The psychologist proposed that when Walter made an insistent demand Mr. Lilly should decide at once whether he could meet it. If he could not, his decision would stand and he would pay no attention to Walter's nagging and tantrums, never changing his mind on their account. For his part, Walter should accept such decisions quietly and try to refrain from nagging. Needless to say, neither party found it easy to carry out these proposals. Arguments continued to arise, emotions to boil, and tempers to explode. But there was an encouraging reduction in the frequency of angry exchanges until at last a whole month went by without them. Son and father were learning how to keep out of a trap that was painful to them both.

When two people are involved in unsatisfactory interactions it is sometimes useful, as in this case, to see them together. This was impossible, however, with Walter's peers, on whose time the psychologist had no claim. The most

that could be expected in dealing with this problem was that Walter might
change his behavior sufficiently to elicit a different kind of response from the
other children. Attention was first paid to his giving money when it was demanded. The psychologist made use of dramatic dialogue to encourage Walter to take a stronger line with the juvenile thieves.

E   What would you do? Suppose I come up and say, "Hey, Lilly, how much
money you got?" What would you do?

C   Probably give you a quarter (laughs).

E   Oh, come on now, what would you say instead? Suppose I come up and
say, "Hey, Lilly, how much money you got?"

C   I haven't got any.

E   What would he say then?

C   He'd probably say, "You're a liar," and then I have to show him what
I've got in my pockets, and then he'll go away if I really don't have any,
but first I got to show him. If I don't do it, one time he ripped my pocket
off. He did it once.

E   Did he?

C   Yes, I should have smacked him down, should have hit him real hard
(laughs).

E   Yes, or at least do something or say something besides just letting him
have the money. Let's try it. "Hey, Lilly, how much money you got?"

C   Nothing. I haven't got any money.

E   You're lying. Show me.

C   (Laughs.) Yes, I'll show you.

E   That's what you do, isn't it. You just go ahead and show him. Try something else. "Go ahead, show me."

C   (Laughs.) Get lost (very weakly laughs).

E   There you go. Fine. But put some feeling in it this time. GET LOST!

C   Get lost!

E   That's a little better. What would he do then? What is it you said that. . . .

C   He'd probably walk off, like he did with the other kids. Maybe not.

E   But the chances of his walking off are at least as good as if you just let
him have the money. Let's try it again. "Listen, you're lying, you got
some money. Show me. . . ."

C   *Get lost!*

E   That's better. Still not too convincing, but that's better.

The psychologist here tries simple *persuasion*, which can sometimes be used
effectively in treatment. In this case, persuasion is directed toward changing a
specific kind of behavior, and coaching is supplied by the psychologist who
provides models of more assertive replies. It is to be anticipated, of course,
that Walter will have great difficulty behaving this way in real situations, but
the chances of success are at least a little raised by his having seen the possibili-

51

ty of greater assertion, rehearsed it, and presumably felt some desire to be able to report at a future interview that he had carried it out.

The extent to which Walter had been intimidated by his peers is revealed in a conversation that took place after he had taken a job as a stockboy at a grocery store.

C There's one guy at work that makes me awful nervous. I don't know. He's kind of quiet . . . something about him.

E You feel uncomfortable when he's around.

C Mm hm. Of course, maybe I should talk to him. . . . I don't know.

E Tell me some more about that.

C Well, he talks to everybody but me, and I figure, well, if you're going to be like that I can be snobby . . . I can stick my head up in the air and not talk. I don't know why he's that way.

E You feel he's sort of. . . .

C Independent. . . .

E Leaving you out deliberately?

C Yes. And you hate to see that. When he talks to somebody else and there you are and he won't say a word to you. But I do my job . . . I don't worry about him.

E What would happen . . . suppose . . . what would happen if you just came in and said Hi! and just started talking about something. What do you think he'd do?

C I don't know. Who would talk first, me or him?

E You.

C Oh. . . .

E What would happen?

C He'd probably talk. I don't know. . . . I don't know if I could do that. . . .

E Well, I know this would be hard for you, but suppose you talked to him anyway. What's the worst thing that could happen?

C Nothing. I can't really think of anything bad that could happen.

The psychologist guessed that Walter, in spite of his expressed doubts, would be able to take this small step, and therefore assigned it as "homework for next week." Walter took the necessary initiative and discovered that the other boy was willing to talk. This boy's silence, it came out later, was a response to Walter's apparent aloofness and suspicion—a good example on both sides of the self-defeating tactics created by social anxiety. Walter's small victory at the grocery store did not, unfortunately, lead to large triumphs in social confidence. Progress in this direction was slow; problems remained in his affectional relationships with others and in his evaluation of himself. He has a better chance to grow than he had before—this is all one can say, but it is enough to justify the effort put into psychological treatment.

Our first example illustrates a number of points. Description of Walter Lilly's behavior requires several of the headings in DSM-III: *anxiety disorder* represented by his panics, *factitious disorder* as shown in his "heart attacks," *personality disorders* as exhibited in the traits of avoidance, dependence, and demandingness, and *parent–child disorders*, a category that for Walter necessarily includes the grandmother. The descriptive tags alone do not say much, but the therapist discovers how they fit together. This he accomplishes by a great deal of sympathetic listening, and he does not force his own ideas prematurely on the client. He then begins to employ techniques of behavior modification based on applying basic principles of learning: extinction, counterconditioning, and control of reinforcement contingencies. In addition, he draws on the historic method of persuasion, in which the subject's positive feeling toward the therapist inspires greater initiative in undertaking new kinds of behavior. But he does not confine himself to a one-to-one relation. The parents are drawn in and attempts made to modify their behavior, sometimes simply by giving advice, sometimes in joint meetings that exemplify family interactions. A portion of the wider community becomes involved through enlisting the aid of the school authorities. These extensions of the program of treatment are typical of contemporary practice in community mental health centers. In Walter's case the choice of procedures is not doctrinaire. Each step is taken because it seems likely to produce a specific beneficent change. The results show the value of this practical eclecticism.

Walter's trouble is clearly more psychological than medical. It represents a failure to outgrow childish demandingness at home and timid submissiveness at school, which together as he grows older create an increasingly unworkable pattern of living, painfully deficient in securing acceptance and building self-esteem. The steps taken to help Walter are most aptly described as re-educative, and their goal is a resumption of blocked personal growth.

2. AN ADOLESCENT MENTAL BREAKDOWN: KATHI HERMANN

Our next example is a German girl who entered a mental hospital at the age of 18. From this circumstance alone one might assume that Kathi Hermann suffered from a definite disease and that her troubles would have little resemblance to Walter Lilly's. We will soon see, however, that Kathi was deeply involved in adolescent difficulties of living. If disease is present it must be deduced from her ways of handling these problems, not looked for as a thing apart. When Walter Lilly had the acute attack of anxiety that brought him to psychological treatment, there was the possibility that he would become disorganized to a degree that could be called "breakdown," but this did not happen. Events took a different course for Kathi, and our main task is to try to discover why they did so.

Childhood History

Kathi was an illegitimate child whose mother elected to have her, keep her, and bring her up. She was a lively, breast-fed baby, "normally defiant" during the second and third years, described at two-and-a-half by a family friend as "already a real personality." It was unfortunate that this household consisted only of mother and child: when the mother was sick, as happened more than once, the child had to be bundled off to a home. Furthermore, from the age of five Kathi had an orthopedic difficulty that kept her in bed at a hospital for prolonged periods. These bouts continued after she entered school, but presently the trouble was corrected without residual handicap.

The picture of Kathi as a schoolgirl, given by her mother and herself, suggests vitality and forcefulness. From the start she got along well. Teachers' reports described her as a leader of her class to whom the other children paid heed. "Because I was respected by my classmates," Kathi said, "probably because I had the biggest mouth, I quickly found my way back into the school rut after the hospital stays." For a while she preferred boys as companions, finding it more fun to climb trees than to play with dolls. Her studies went well, and her artistic interests, stressed by the school, were strong, having gotten a good start during her periods as an invalid. Her mother recounted that she began painting early, played the main part in a children's movie, and sang a lot on the radio. One looks in vain for evidence of abnormality in Kathi's reported history from 7 to 13. That she was a bit of a tomboy is not unusual, and on the whole she sounds active, talented, socially competent, in good contact with her surroundings.

Beginning of Adolescent Rebellion

Trouble began, however, after puberty when she encountered the two common problems of sex and independence. To understand her difficulties with these problems we have to be better acquainted with her mother, who was so much the central feature of her childhood existence. When the mother brought Kathi to the mental hospital, she impressed the examiner unfavorably. "She gave the history in somewhat long-winded and gossipy fashion, and repeatedly referred to her numerous connections with people of high standing such as professors, doctors, well-known conductors and pianists." The mother's membership in such circles proved to be more a matter of aspiration than of fact. Starting from a strict middle-class upbringing, she had made for herself by creditable hard work a position in the administrative department of a professional organization, where she had frequent contact with professional people without being one of them. According to her daughter she was much wrapped up in this work and talked about it constantly, but not in a way that showed much empathy for its human aspects. Her attitude toward her child appeared to be a combination of spoiling, protectiveness, intrusive dominance, and a need for close companionship. Kathi said that her mother had often interfered with her friendships, driving away those companions who were not the "kind of people" she wanted around her daughter. When the hospital interviewer asked the mother about the sources of her information about her daughter, she replied that "of course" she always read Kathi's letters and diaries.

Establishing independence from such a parent, especially without the help that might have been afforded by a father and siblings, was bound to be more than commonly difficult. The evolution began for Kathi when at 14 she was sent for a few months to France. This exile was necessitated by the mother's entrance into a mental hospital following the breakup of an eight-year affair she had been having with an engineering inspector. Arrangements were made for Kathi to live with a French family and go to a private school with a curriculum much like the one she attended at home. Her substitute mother in the French family, she later told her doctor, turned out to be "peculiar": allegedly a lesbian, she had a large number of male friends. At all events, Madame undertook to loosen the hold of Kathi's mother. She encouraged the girl to abandon her neat and clean ways in favor of sloppy dress, and she indignantly declared that mothers had no right to burden their children with their own love affairs and business problems. Kathi cried a good deal over her mother's illness and their separation, but Madame's influence was timely and set in motion a cool new look at the mother–daughter relation. At school she simultaneously confronted the problem of sex. She saw girls being pushed into a corner and half undressed by boys, but she was careful not to get involved in such scenes.

Forces of rebellion had been mobilized, and conflicts with her mother grew more and more frequent after her return to Germany. Her need for companions of her own age became greater, but now, she told her doctor, her efforts were blocked by the presence at school of a strong exclusive clique that she understood to be engaged in drug orgies and other activities bordering on the criminal. In her loneliness she attached herself to a boy friend with whom she held agreeable philosophical discussions and who told her a great deal about the clique. The boy's heart was elsewhere however, and when they parted she took an overdose of pills. In retrospect she said that she had not really meant to kill herself, but to see what it is like to be near death, part of her desire to get to know and experience everything. For months after this she suffered from a succession of physical, very likely psychophysiological ailments, and her schoolwork went to pieces. A male teacher took an interest, tried to help her, sought like Madame to loosen the mother–daughter tie, and exchanged affectionate caresses with her. Later she found out, so she claimed, that this teacher was really a homosexual and had had relations with her former boy friend.

At this point the reader will have noticed what seems to be an excessive preoccupation with the theme of homosexuality. Bearing in mind that the history was given retrospectively when Kathi was in the mental hospital, we do not know just when she arrived at those interpretations, but they seem always to say than an observed heterosexual activity is not real, that the actor is in truth homosexually inclined. But in describing her relation to the unfriendly clique she seemed to be recounting what she had experienced at the time. She felt that the clique was actively persecuting her. A former member who had been dropped warned her that this would happen. She even received anonymous telephone calls saying that she was likely to be kidnapped. Her mother became so alarmed by these calls that she notified the police. One day Kathi could not find anyone to give her a ride home from school. At last she asked a girl she did not know, and as she sat down in the car she noticed that the cars of other classmates and clique-members, standing behind them, were making strange, inexplicable movements. Retrospectively she wondered whether this persecution had originated with the girl for whom her boy friend had deserted her.

The idea of being persecuted—the paranoid theme—is so common in the psychoses that its appearance in an adolescent's ruminations always causes alarm. But persecution, like homosexuality, is a real fact in the world, and one must not jump too quickly to diagnostic conclusions. What Kathi reports on these subjects is not impossible, though it may seem improbable; further evidence would be needed before deciding that her testing of reality had broken down. In a way the most disquieting element in her story is her apparent misperception of the cars standing behind her. When the perceptual process itself is disturbed, there is added reason to fear that a schizophrenic breakdown is in the making.

A Beatnik Chapter

Perhaps to get her away from the apparently unfriendly atmosphere at school, Kathi, now almost 16, was sent for a term to a fashionable boarding school in Holland. At first she thought the other girls too prim, but soon she found a friend in Hanneke, who introduced her to quite a different world. Following her friend's example she began stealing at school, and soon she was taken to the country home where Hanneke's alcoholic and promiscuous mother maintained a gambling establishment. Here she became attached to a young man with a prison record, had sexual relations with him, and kept up a correspondence for some time after her return to Germany. Her mother was horrified to find her daughter turned into "an unkempt beatnik," "terribly fat, addicted, smoking," running around in skirts and sweaters that were far too tight and announcing that she found them sexy. Quarrels immediately began about going out alone at night. Further friction arose because of Kathi's new role at school as a fountain of sexual enlightenment. Fearing a scandal, the mother took her out of school and shipped her off to a German boarding school. Kathi described herself as being at this point "sick of everything" and as having "lost all respect."

Kathi was disappointed in the boarding school, where she did not find avenues to adventure of the sort provided by Hanneke. The girls, she decided, were all promiscuous and the older teachers were lesbians. Studies no longer interested her and she soon had to repeat a grade. But the struggle to disengage from mother continued, transferred to the medium of letters. In the mother's view, the letters she received were "sassy" and always demanded money. In the daughter's view, the letters she received were "nasty" and full of insults to her Dutch boy friend. At home for Christmas during the year in which she was 16, Kathi talked in a way that friends described as "disconnected and contradictory." One evening, becoming furious, she seized a bread knife and threatened to kill her mother; then, because mother would not stop screaming, beat her black and blue. Thereafter Kathi had the upper hand in quarrels. Her mother learned to "keep her mouth shut in order to have peace." But the victory was oddly marred. "I consider it weakness that she is not able to handle me," said Kathi, as if, much as she wanted to rebel, she had not realized that there would be no one to help her control her impulses.

A Paradoxical Half Year

Kathi's career at boarding school ended abruptly when she was heard saying publicly that one of the teachers was a lesbian. As other girls had said the same thing, the mother angrily demanded of the school that they, too, should be dismissed. Possibly this maternal support was helpful to Kathi, who now returned home to enter a public school. During the next three months she appeared to her mother normal and calm, and by hard study she completed the requirements for the German equivalent of a high school diploma. She immediately entered a women's technical school where she felt "very much at home," and "finally found a nice group" to which she attached herself "without any misgivings." Taking just these facts we might hopefully conclude that the crisis of adolescent rebellion had passed. She had subdued her mother without losing a kind of basic backing, had found the support of congenial friends, and could once more organize her life in effective patterns. Unfortunately this prognosis is too optimistic. Four months after starting technical school, still just short of her eighteenth birthday, she entered the mental hospital.

Apparently the struggle for independence was only in abeyance. Kathi wrote in her diary that she was beginning to feel restless again. She had a transient sexual affair with a medical student that may not have been without its problems. At all events there were fresh outbursts against mother, in one of which she threw a cup of tea in her mother's face. During a visit they both made to a relative, Kathi became extremely excited, broke a lot of things in the kitchen, called her mother a whore and used similarly degrading language about her when talking to family friends. She was so violent that a physician was consulted and sedatives prescribed. On the morning before hospitaliza-

57

tion Kathi again went into uncontrollable rage, accusing her mother of ruining her life. The mother, well aware of her daughter's capacity for violence, may have been in fear of her own life when she sought the services of the hospital.

Behavior and Treatment at the Hospital

Kathi slipped easily into the role of a patient under observation. Making lively talk with other patients on the ward and dramatically recounting her adventures, she even converted it into a star role. The history she gave to the psychiatrist was animated and vivid, and she laughed off those episodes that had caused disquiet as if they had been merely gags. This behavior can be viewed as an attempt to treat lightly a threatening situation and not be overwhelmed, but it was carried to extremes. The interviewer was impressed by a lack of correspondence between the flippant, giggling, excited narration and the emotions that must have accompanied the original events; the affect being shown was inappropriate to the content being described. Furthermore, the disconnected and wandering fashion in which the story was told suggested serious disorganization. It was judged that Kathi first needed calming down, and this was successfully accomplished by means of tranquilizing drugs. A tentative diagnosis of schizophrenia was entered in the books, but with the note that much observation would be required to make it firm. Arrangements were then made for Kathi to be discharged not to go home to her mother but to live in the family of a professor of psychiatry near the technical school that she would continue to attend. In view of the repeated deadlocks in the mother–daughter relation, separation was deemed the safest and most practical step. How the plan worked out is for the future to tell.

On the Nature of the Disorder

Although Kathi Hermann and Walter Lilly are decidedly different people, there are certain similarities in their adolescent difficulties. Both have trouble in separating themselves sufficiently from parental influence and establishing successful relations with other young people. It is not hard to empathize with Kathi's struggles. In large part they are the universal ones of adolescence, and she is in tune with her times in wanting sexual freedom, in seeking to broaden and deepen the range of experience, even in choosing Hesse as her favorite author. She seems to have more than ordinary difficulty with sexual identity, as shown in her preoccupation with homosexuality; this would expectably add to the other burdens of adolescence. But her main themes—rebellious aggression and loneliness—are central problems for this phase of life. Kathi occasionally wrote poetry and stories. Her verses describing a screaming rage could come only from personal experience, as could her account, originally written in the first person, of a rebel who turns on his foe. This character, unable to "stand the pain any more," attacked his self-righteous torturers "in hellish joy"—"to

58

see them tremble before him in cold, panicky fear, in terrible horror, gratified every drop of blood in his boiling veins." Doubtless she also knew the aftermath of this eruption, when her character "for a long time fell mute, twisted in endless pain." Her verses on loneliness sound equally poignant and personal. Wherever she goes she is doomed to loneliness, "alone in the currents of this world." In vain she tries to communicate and find her way back to a lost feeling of familiarity and belonging.

> I am a stranger in my own world,
> And nobody understands
> that I want to come back again.
> Nobody understands my words.

Because her feelings are so vivid and easily grasped, it is tempting to give Kathi's disorder a purely psychodynamic explanation. She is unable to escape from the trap of a dominant, intrusive mother who has also been her sole source of security. This engenders enormous rage, so great that it spills over into her relations with contemporaries, making her suspicious and accusatory and thus further obstructing her escape from mother. Finally the rage breaks through in acts of violence, freedom is sought impulsively in ways and with companions ill-chosen, and judgment itself is shattered by the force of passion. According to this interpretation it is not necessary to speak of a disease. Instead of being schizophrenic, Kathi is a victim of unusual adolescent stress and is temporarily disorganized by it. Perhaps she is no more seriously disturbed than Walter Lilly, who had fits of crying and screaming and who was mistrustful of other adolescents, except that she is more of a fighter and therefore dangerous to her mother.

This explanation is appealingly simple, but we must not pass lightly over the question of disorganization. Are we to consider Kathi's stress sufficient cause to make any adolescent go temporarily berserk, or must we assume a vulnerability to disorganization that causes her to go to pieces where a steadier person would have found a more workable solution? Her disconnected talk, inappropriate affect, shrill giggling, and silliness at the hospital, taken together with the apparent perceptual distortion in the incident of the cars, suggested the kind of disorganization characteristic of severe schizophrenics. It is possible, therefore, that Kathi was born vulnerable to schizophrenic breakdown under stress.

To decide between these two interpretations is formidably difficult. Even with much more information—with extended observation and refined tests—it would be hard to come to a firm decision. The problem lies in what we might call the interwoven nature of personality: constitutional proclivities, acquired habits, and the stresses of events are in continual interaction, making it extraordinarily difficult to unravel the separate strands. In their uncertainty the hospital staff was probably wise to make allowance for both possibilities.

Separation from the mother might be expected to reduce aggression; continuing in school might provide the chance to feel at home with contemporaries; maintenance doses of tranquilizers might control the tendency to excited disorganization; and living under a watchful professional eye might result in timely changes of program if these proved to be desirable.

3. CHRONIC MULTIPLE DISORDERS: BENTON CHILD

As a contrast to the relatively young cases thus far described, we take next the example of a 40-year-old man who has been in and out of a mental hospital four times during the last seven years. He seems not to have profited greatly from these visits, although his condition has slightly improved. The case of Benton Child is not unusual. Hospital records abound with similar stories of people burdened by chronic complaints who reach bad moments that bring them in for shelter and treatment, who improve enough to be discharged, but who then cannot make a go of their lives outside and presently reappear at the hospital. In such cases the problem of diagnosis can be baffling. What is really wrong with the patient? Do the complaints arise from unusual difficulties in living? Do they point to habitual adaptive strategies that are proving unworkable in the face of current problems? Or are the patient's problems compounded by real handicaps or by distorted perceptions suggestive of mental disorders? It is no simple matter, as we will see, to intervene beneficially in the lives of such chronically troubled people.

Family Background and Childhood

Benton Child was the sole offspring of an oddly matched couple. His mother's family, the Bentons, lived in a small community where they owned and operated a manufacturing business. The mother, graduate of a teacher's college and a two-your business course, served as secretary in the family's business and largely directed it after her father's death. The father, Roy Child, a high school graduate, was factory manager at the time he married the boss's daughter. The two seem to have been far apart in personal qualities. The father showed little interest in management, which he left more and more to his wife; at the age of 50 he stopped working altogether, and spent most of his time at home watching his health with great care. The mother not only continued to run the business but also held numerous offices in community organizations. So slight was the father's part in the family business that after his wife's death some of the Benton relatives criticized him for making a will in favor of his son instead of returning the Benton money to those who made it.

When Benton Child was born, both parents were in their thirties. This circumstance, his wife later told the doctor, was important for his development: his parents were too old to give him love and companionship, though generous in meeting his material needs. As regards material needs he could, as the hospital history records it, "get anything he wanted; he just went to his mother and asked for it and she would give it to him." Such indulgence does not necessarily signify love. It may be the easiest way for a busy mother to keep a child from being a bother. But the mother was also inclined to be overprotective. When Benton had trouble adapting to school she declared that he was "too good to play with the other children." It is probably not by chance that the father makes no appearance in these recollections. His influence at home may have been as small as his influence at work.

Benton does not remember disliking school when he first entered at the age of 6, but a little later he was sometimes "beaten up by other kids" and came to fear them. By the time he reached high school, where he was an "average" student, things were going better; he recalls that he "enjoyed dramatics and was a good singer." After graduation he attended a nearby small college for a year, where he "didn't flunk out, but didn't do well and dropped out." This ended his educational career, and at 19 he went into the family business, where he was carried on the payroll even when he chose to take somewhat liberal time off from work.

Young Manhood: Increasing Difficulties

At about this time he met his future wife Deborah, and they were married two years later when both were 21. For several years the marriage appeared to be stable and satisfactory. The couple lived in a company-owned house with utilities provided. Benton's job was secure, and income was increased by Deborah's holding a job of her own in a nearby village. Although sexual relations had begun before marriage, there were no children for five years. But this relatively easy existence presently came to an end. During the next eight years two sons and two daughters were born. According to his wife's report, Benton was pleased to have her pregnant, but after the birth of each child he felt resentment at the inevitable loss of her attention. In the midst of this period of rapid family growth the Benton factory was seriously damaged by fire, and it was decided to wind up the business rather than attempt rebuilding. Benton was thus suddenly thrown on the job market and obliged to maintain his own home. After trying another line that proved uncongenial he was taken on by the company for which Deborah worked. His work was fairly mechanical, but it called for attention and care, and he set a high standard of perfection in performing it. These several circumstances made his life more difficult, and he met the stress by increasing his once moderate use of alcohol to the point where he was often losing time from work. Describing their home life later to the hospital social worker, Deborah allowed that between her job and her children she had little time to be a good homemaker or an attentive wife. In order to reduce her own worries and responsibilities she had shifted from secretarial work to running a machine; "the doctor says it's the best medicine for me—at the end of the day I leave it."

61

Mounting difficulties of living form part of the picture thus drawn, but these cannot be considered unusual. Raising four children in economic circumstances that require both parents to work is bound to be stressful, but most couples accomplish it without requiring the services of a mental hospital. In Benton's case, we can assume an established expectation that things will be easy. As a child his demands on his mother were quickly met, and for a time in early adulthood he was spared the full responsibilities of worker, father, and householder. A person with a history of this kind may experience average demands as excessively burdensome. The history taken at the hospital suggests, however, another possible contribution to Benton's difficulties. The record shows a series of ailments starting long before the period of stress. As a child Benton reportedly had low blood pressure and spells of weakness and dizziness. At 14 there was a curious episode when for ten days he was unable to walk; one is reminded of the hysterical paralyses described by Charcot and Janet. At 17 he suffered from "spells" of some kind that were diagnosed as mild epileptic attacks; as a consequence he took anticonvulsant medicine for several years until finally a more specific diagnostic test, an electroencephalogram, proved normal and discredited the original diagnosis. Physical complaints continued during the more stressful years. At 28 he complained of nervousness for which his doctor prescribed a tranquilizing drug. This prescription continued next year when he asked for treatment for "an icy burning feeling in his arm," and he has been on one or another tranquilizer ever since. When he was 32 he complained of "sinking spells," periods of weakness and vagueness that might occur even when he was sitting in a chair. Three years later he consulted a doctor again, this time because of nervousness, depression, and irritable rages; he was given a different tranquilizer. It is easy to write off these chronic complaints as reflections of tension and anxiety, but there is also the possibility of a constitutional burden. The theme of "low spells" is sufficiently recurrent to suggest a trait of low energy that might well encourage the passive dependent style permitted by his early surroundings.

Trouble in the Child family was deepened when Benton began to accuse his wife of unfaithfulness. This started after the birth of the second child, a year before his favored position in the family business came to an end. One of the evidences he used was the five-year interval before the first child was born. Being of Roman Catholic faith, the couple had not used contraceptives; Benton reasoned that he must be infertile, hence none of the children could be his own. That he chose this dubious interpretation reflects rather seriously on his judgment, but he became increasingly obsessed by the subject and used it to generate quarrels. Deborah denied the accusations. At first, they were not true, she later told the hospital authorities, but after three years of Benton's pestering she decided that she might as well have the pleasure for which she was being blamed, and began an affair. This was easily managed because husband and wife worked on different shifts, but eventually Deborah and her friend were involved in a minor boating accident under circumstances that confirmed Benton's suspicions. He began at once to go around with a 19-year-old girl whom he often brought to the house, and he complained in public about his wife's wretched cooking and housekeeping as well as her infidelity. During drinking bouts he became increasingly argumentative, quarrelsome, and hard to handle.

First Hospitalization

As a consequence of one of his alcoholic episodes, occurring when he was 35, Benton arrived at the state hospital. One evening he lay on the floor drunk, complaining of difficulty in breathing, but occasionally sitting up and cursing wildly. Deborah called a neighbor to help get him up, but he fought off the neighbor. She then called a doctor who after trying in vain to get him to take a sedative signed an emergency commitment form and called the police to take him to the hospital. The reader may feel that the specific incident hardly warrants commitment to a mental hospital. But there were four children in the house, and with the husband's behavior irrational and tending toward violence, something had to be done. In a community with limited mental health resources the hospital and the jail are the only alternatives.

The first commitment was of short duration. Nervous and shaky for two days, Benton quickly calmed down; by the third day he was talking rationally with other patients and asking to leave. He was allowed to visit home the first weekend, then to stay a week, and was finally discharged after 17 days, with advice to attend aftercare clinics provided by the hospital. The diagnosis entered in the hospital record was "*psychoneurosis, anxiety neurosis.*" Tranquilizing drugs were the only recorded attempt at treatment.

Second Hospitalization

More than two years elapsed before the second admission to the state hospital. In the meantime the relation between Benton and Deborah steadily deteriorated. In addition to periods of heavy drinking, Benton was now having mood cycles varying from tense and anxious to low and depressed. When tense he talked a great deal, exhausting his wife with an increasing flow of accusations. When low he seemed inaccessible and despairing, so that Deborah began to wonder about a risk of suicide. He stopped working and was at home all the time. Deborah found his behavior increasingly intolerable, began threatening to leave him, and finally had him evicted from the house. He retired to his parents' house, where he soon made himself unwelcome and wanted to return home, but Deborah agreed to this only on condition that he consult a psychiatrist. She said afterwards that at this point she no longer felt any affection for Benton, who had become "just an object" to her, a highly problematical object. To the psychiatrist Benton presented a picture of weakness. He complained that his legs were weak, and that he sometimes felt dizzy while driving; he had been trying to build himself up by exercises and inspirational books.

63

When a physical examination disclosed no grounds for the complaints, the psychiatrist, agreeing to see him every two weeks, recorded the diagnosis of *"personality trait disturbance, passive–aggressive, inadequate, immature."*

Before the new treatment could start, Benton's behavior at home became acutely alarming to his wife and upsetting to the children. At times silently withdrawn, he would at other times yell, scream, and throw himself on the floor. So a friend was prevailed on to take him to the state hospital on a voluntary admission, a procedure he readily complied with. His recovery on this occasion did not proceed as rapidly as before. He was full of complaints, some of them physical, like cold hands and feet, some of them centered on restlessness and worry, but the admitting physician noted a basic mood of depression and indifference that continued without change for at least 10 days. This time he was given antidepressant medication that did not, however, produce much improvement in his mood, and he was started in group psychotherapy, where it was noticed that he sought the most comfortable chair, smoked continuously, and took no part in the conversations. Deborah made it clear that she did not want him at home until "he's all well," and she urged him to "open up and talk to the doctors about the 'real you.'" As a voluntary patient, however, Benton had the right to request release, and he did so after two months, announcing his intention to live with his parents and return to his job. This time the recorded diagnosis was *"psychoneurosis, anxiety neurosis, with alcoholism, multiple somatic complaints, bizarre behavioral reactions, and depression."*

Third and Fourth Hospitalizations

The events of the next three years can be briefly summarized. A month after discharge Benton again entered the hospital, having intentionally taken an overdose of his current medication. In explanation of this act he said, "I just can't seem to function out there." He had felt weak, he failed to find a job, and then his mother had become seriously ill. His third stay at the hospital lasted three months, during the course of which his mother died. He continued to feel inadequate and depressed, but the staff judged him to be "using the hospital as a shelter" and benefiting little from it, so his request was granted to leave and to live with his father. This proved to be a disaster. Two days later he was back, "afraid of everything, can't make decisions, can't get along with father, can't sleep." This time Benton remained in the hospital for nine months. He improved slowly, became calmer, took more interest in other patients, and worked regularly in the hospital bakery. He was presently allowed to go home to his wife for weekends. Difficult at first, these visits progressively got better; he began repainting the interior of the house and made himself so welcome that Deborah agreed to take him back. The hospital diagnosis at discharge, as if to leave no stone unturned, was *"schizophrenia, latent type."*

Information obtained from his visits to the aftercare clinics shows that for the next two years, to the present, he is doing all right. He returned to his job at his former place of employment, where Deborah was presently laid off, making him the sole breadwinner. His use of alcohol has stayed within bounds, his tranquilizer keeps him comfortable, and he and Deborah are getting along much better. It is too soon to conclude that his troubles are over or that his improvement will be permanent, but his condition at last report represents a distinct gain over the behavior and states of mind that caused him to become a hospital patient.

Psychological Interpretation

The reader, after receiving this much information, may still be left wondering what went wrong with Benton Child and why he made at least a partial improvement. The official diagnoses are cast as far as possible in the traditional language of mental disorder, although the range—psychoneurosis, alcoholism, depression, schizophrenia—is too broad to be of much help. But the physicians include also a variety of terms that refer to learned traits and adaptive strategies, terms such as passive-aggressive, inadequate, and immature. The case presents a confusion of physical complaints, difficulties in living, and peculiarities of judgment—a situation that is not uncommon in the study of abnormal behavior. How much sense can we hope to make of it?

We can start with Deborah's account of her husband's personality. She sees him as immature and inadequate, and she blames this on spoiling by his mother. "Even today," she said at one point, "if he wants a new car or new clothes he merely asks his mother and she gets them for him." This dependence is carried over into the marriage relation. "His trouble is that he thinks I'm his mother. I have to make all the decisions. He leans on me. He never has made a decision in all his life." Deborah admits that her own personality is somewhat complementary: "I'm too domineering, everything has to go my way." One can imagine those two people drawn together at 19 because of this fit between their patterns of dominance and submission and because Benton perceived in Deborah a wife who would take care of him as had his mother. Unfortunately, this expectation prevented Benton from advancing to the point of being able to take care of anyone else, either his wife or his children. "He thinks he loves his children," said Deborah, "but he doesn't want them around." When he comes home "he wants the children to eat and be put to bed. He has never cuddled or loved them when they were small." Benton's dependence leads inevitably to resentment when his wife gives attention to the children instead of taking care of him. It leads him to respond like a child to a frustrating mother, with tantrums and depression rather than modulated attempts at compromise. During his fourth hospital stay Benton expressed agreement with this picture of himself: "I've never really grown up." His subsequent improvement can be attributed in part to his recognition that he had come to a dead end. Bereft of his mother, unable to get along with his father, too anxious and helpless to live alone, his only chance of leaving the hospital was to patch things up with Deborah and commend himself by such helpful actions as repainting the house. It remains to be seen whether this motive is strong enough to maintain a workable marriage relation.

There is a marked similarity between the pattern of Benton's marriage and that of his parents. His mother was the dominant member of the household, and his father, retiring early and fussing over his health, set a poor example of effectiveness. The hypothesis suggests itself that Benton's feeble enactment of the masculine role was copied from his father, a simple consequence of identification with the most available model. This explanation, however, cannot stand alone. Identification is not an automatic process that requires sons to copy fathers. There are plentiful instances in which the son of an ineffective father has rejected the model, taken pleasure in being the better man, and identified with some strong figure such as a maternal grandfather who, like Benton's, was successful in life. The likeness between father and son in this case could equally suggest that Benton had inherited his father's genetic make-up and was living with a handicap of low energy, lack of zest, and frequent fatigue. With our present knowledge it is difficult to disentangle the contributions made by constitution and by learning to any given pattern of life; it is unwise, however, to assume that all the influence comes from one source.

Benton's conviction of inadequacy was of long standing and included doubts about his sexual prowess. Going over his history with a doctor during his fourth hospitalization, he expressed the feeling that he was "not much of a man." He had "always felt" that his penis was unusually small. We can speculate that the first comparison might have been made with his father, but what he actually recollected was verification of this smallness by his schoolmates. He had had homosexual experiences in boyhood and again more recently. It was for these reasons that he believed his children were not his own, and in fact he became temporarily impotent after the fourth child was born. His reasoning exemplifies the pervasiveness of self-doubt. Instead of taking his wife's pregnancies as welcome proof of his manhood, he assumed that Deborah must have become unsatisfied and unfaithful. A deeply rooted conviction of inferiority can play havoc with the testing of reality.

Effects on the Patient's Children

What was happening meanwhile to the children in this troubled family? How did they fare in an atmosphere of parental friction and paternal instability? Shortly before Benton's first hospitalization Deborah became acutely worried about the two older children, young Benton and Milly, 12 and 10 years old. Both were given to uncontrollable outbursts of temper, and the boy especially alarmed his mother by throwing himself on the floor and screaming, a pattern the origin of which is not far to seek. Deborah was also afraid that the children's schoolwork was suffering, so on the advice of her doctor she arranged to have them visit a child guidance clinic. The children were seen at the clinic, their abilities were tested, and communication was opened with the school about young Benton's learning difficulties, which were judged to be minor and easily manageable. According to subsequent reports both children were doing well in spite of the troubles at home. Milly tended to be her mother's lieutenant in the family and began to show something of Deborah's manipulative dominance, thus coping successfully with social life at school. Young Benton did well in basketball, found in the teacher-coach a person to admire and emulate, and entered high school with firm plans to become a teacher of physical education and athletic coach. In this new framework of his existence there was no room for screaming fits on the floor. Nothing could better illustrate the point just made that sons do not have to copy their fathers. Young Benton was fortunate to find a worthy identification figure away from home, but it was not just luck. Copying an athlete occurs most readily in someone who has started to become an athlete. Recalling the father's early low blood pressure, his dizziness, his being beaten up by kids at school, and his episode of apparent paralysis at 14, it seems likely that the son is physically more vigorous and can therefore use a model who would have had no meaning for the father.

Comments on Treatment

At the age of 40 Benton Child has had a great deal of private and public health care. He has been to many doctors for many complaints, and he has spent more than a year of his life at a state mental hospital. What has all this accomplished for him? The most consistent theme in his treatment seems to be to give him drugs. He has had anticonvulsant medication for nonexistent epilepsy, antidepressant drugs that failed to elevate his mood, and continuous prescriptions of tranquilizers that may in fact have lessened his anxiety and tension. He and Deborah have spent many hours giving his history to the hospital staff, and there is a notation at one point that he talks about his problems without getting benefit from it. Group psychotherapy has been tried without observable effect, and the hospital has provided occupations that gave him some sense of usefulness. But all of this, representing a good deal of professional effort, seems to have left him just about where he was before, and his improved attitude at home can be attributed more to his having no other way out than to insights and new behavior generated by his treatment.

In contrast to the case of Walter Lilly, there seems to have been no direct and concentrated attack on Benton's life problems. No intensive effort was made to change the behaviors, such as demandingness, tantrums, accusations, and avoidance of decisions, that led to trouble, or to build up in specific ways the confidence that might enable him to take realistic initiative and raise his sense of competence. In all probability such efforts would have taken longer than they did with a youth like Walter Lilly, and they might not have worked at all. Benton's behavior had become deeply rooted, his sense of defeat more

67

pervasive; and he had built alcoholic escape into his life pattern in a way that might have defeated all therapeutic intervention. Nevertheless, the reader will surely feel that a more concentrated attempt should have been made to deal directly with Benton's problematical behavior and feelings. Why did everyone skate around the edges, rely on drugs, use only group therapy, and avoid the central issue of maladaptive personal behavior? Should we not expect them to do better?

Undoubtedly we should, but it is only fair to ask: Who are "they?" These events took place not in a favored community with large medical resources but in the far more typical surroundings where doctors are in short supply and overworked, community mental health facilities hardly exist, and the state hospital, the chief resource, is chronically understaffed. Walter Lilly was a lucky boy to have the large amount of time and personal attention that helped him to resume his growth. There was no one in the state mental hospital who had this amount of time to give to Benton Child. Even if the staff were larger so that intensive work could be done with selected cases, would Benton be a likely choice? Limited resources must be directed to the most promising cases, and it is doubtful that Benton, at his age, with his passivity and depressed attitude, his lack of sparkle and low initiative, and his history regarding alcohol, would have appeared in this light. Should the staff then be further enlarged so that there is time for all? The obstacle to such a plan is the taxpayers. Mental health care is exceedingly expensive, and a sudden doubling of the state hospital budget would require a substantial increase in the tax rate. If you are a taxpayer or expect soon to become one you will see that the problem is not simple. But when we say that "they" did not do very well in the case of Benton Child we should refer not only to the professional staff, which perhaps did all it had time for, but also to the taxpayers, who allowed the patient only such limited care as they thought they could afford.

4. A PROGRESSIVE BRAIN DISEASE: MARTHA OTTENBY

Our fourth example, drawn from the work of Goldstein and Katz (1937), is the case of a woman, fifty-six years old, who suffers from a degenerative disease of the brain. Martha Ottenby led a contented though rather uneventful life up to the age of fifty-four. At that point her husband and friends began to notice peculiar changes in her behavior, changes that steadily increased until it became necessary to send her to a mental hospital. She was found to have a rare brain disease for which no cure is known, and which is almost certain to bring about her death within a few years. In the meantime, however, she lives pleasantly enough in the hospital, unaware that her mind is disordered and that her recovery is impossible. To the student of abnormal psychology such cases offer an unusual opportunity to learn about the functions of the brain. By examining the evolution of symptoms, and by noticing the results of mental tests, we can construct a picture of the functions performed by those areas of the brain that have been injured by disease.

Nature of the Organic Disorder

It will be easier to understand this case if we first consider the nature of the patient's brain disorder. Martha Ottenby is diagnosed as having *Pick's disease*, a quite rare degenerative disorder that nevertheless has been of special interest to neurologists because it acts selectively on the frontal lobes of the cortex and spreads only later to other areas. The cause of this condition is as yet unknown. There is some evidence that it runs in families, but in many cases, including the present one, a search of the family history reveals no other victims. Evidence for an infectious origin is altogether lacking. The time of onset is almost always in later middle life, suggesting that Pick's disease may be connected with aging and may be considered a premature aging of certain parts of the cerebral cortex. At all events, when a post-mortem examination of the brain is made, a marked atrophy of the cortex, especially of the frontal lobes, is found. In the affected areas the gray and white matter appears shrunken and of an abnormal color. Microscopic examination reveals that many nerve cells have disappeared, while those that remain show characteristic alterations of a degenerative type. The cortex seems to be undergoing a process of decay.

While it is undoubtedly proper to conceive of Pick's disease in this way, we must remember that the decay goes well beyond what is normal, even in very old people. We must also remember its highly localized character, confined to the cerebral cortex and in most cases still further limited, at least in the earlier stages, to the frontal lobes. Except for her brain disorder, Martha Ottenby is anything but decayed; she is not even old for her years. Her hair is gray, but she is a plump, ruddy woman with a strong healthy pulse, satisfactory blood pressure, normal reflexes, and every indication of sound physical health. Only one physical examination gives conclusive evidence of abnormality. This is a procedure known as the air encephalogram. It is performed by introducing air under slight pressure into the brain cavity, then taking X rays to show how the air has distributed itself among the tissues. Martha Ottenby's air encephalogram revealed a great deal of air congregated over the frontal lobes, especially at the frontal poles, indicating that the cortical tissue was considerably shrunken in these areas. This was as decisive evidence for Pick's disease as could be obtained by methods then available.

It is like telling a story backwards to give the final diagnosis before relating the history of the case. In the present instance, we are justified by the extra profit to be derived from studying the history and the earliest symptoms when we know the nature of the underlying brain disorder. We now return to chronological order and see what can be gleaned from the patient's past life.

Personal History

Martha Ottenby was born in Sweden, where she grew up a jolly, sociable, active child of average intelligence. So far as could be ascertained, none of her grandparents, neither of her parents, and none of her five brothers and sisters, ever showed signs of mental disorder. Martha became a dressmaker at the age of twenty, and soon earned the reputation of a skillful worker. When thirty-two she came to the United States; at the late age of forty she married. This last event was not entirely happy, inasmuch as the husband shortly lost his money and ran into debt; moreover, in his discouragement he occasionally resorted to alcohol and came home badly intoxicated. To keep the household going, Martha continued her work as a dressmaker. It was hard to earn enough in this way, so that she was constantly worried about the precarious financial situation. But in spite of these difficulties Martha's life was not without its satisfactions. Except when marred by alcoholic episodes the marriage was happy and the atmosphere of the home pleasant. Martha was a neat housekeeper. She enjoyed her home and this made her able to be patient with her husband's difficulties and her own.

Earliest Symptoms

The earliest symptom of Martha's disorder was an apparently trifling matter: on several occasions she allowed food to burn on the stove. Her husband, having been married to her for fourteen years, was astonished at these lapses from her usual domestic efficiency. It seemed as if she were growing a little forgetful, so that when she momentarily turned away from her cooking it slipped out of her mind. Before long it became apparent that in several other ways her behavior was changing. She felt tired a good deal of the time, and had to lie down often during the day. Sometimes she was bothered by mild headache. Her interest in dressmaking began to diminish; she sat at home and spent most of her time reading weekly magazines. Presently her husband noticed another curious sign of forgetfulness: Martha read the same stories over and over without any loss of interest, apparently not realizing that she had read them several times before. Her standards of physical appearance declined; the neat, trimly dressed Martha began to look sloppy and untidy. If her attention was called to some carelessness in her personal appearance, she would become very angry. On the whole her mood was a little sad, in noticeable contrast to her previous cheerful disposition.

At about this point in her illness her brother died. Her reaction to this loss revealed clearly that her mind was becoming disordered. She kept imagining that she saw her brother outside and would run into the street to talk with him, sometimes forgetting that she was not fully dressed. If questioned, she knew that her brother was dead, but a short time later she would again be convinced that she saw him. She told of long conversations with the brother during his last illness, all of which the husband knew could not have occurred. At times she even launched into an actual conversation just as if her brother were making a call.

Her mental confusion became increasingly obvious and difficult. She herself began to feel "all mixed up," and she was confused about the identity of people around her, though continuing to recognize her husband, her sister, and her dog. Bizarre thoughts came to her mind. Faulty perceptions occurred: she saw a strange cat cross the street with legs all over its body, and she imagined that it would progress by rolling rather than by walking. At this point it was decided to take her to the hospital.

Behavior at the Hospital

On arrival at the hospital, Martha's sadness increased to a point of real distress. She fancied that a cat had come along with her, had died, and now lay behind her bed. Her brother was still much on her mind. She believed that he had been in the ward and had made a disturbance there; at other times she saw him in the street and cried because he was being sent away hungry. These unhappy imaginings soon gave place to a more cheerful mood. She occupied herself with reading and without the least trace of self-consciousness would sing loudly as she read.

In the course of time she settled down to a cheerful, quiet, orderly way of life. She was generally to be found sitting on a bench, arms folded, a smiling expression on her face, attentive to what was going on around her. Visitors were greeted with smiles and friendly gestures, but no further conversation would follow unless it were prompted by the other person. She was cordial to the doctors and nurses, although unable to remember their names. When engaged in conversation she showed animated interest. The form and structure of her speech was not in the least impaired; the only difficulty was a tendency to slip into Swedish, her mother-tongue, and it seemed impossible to make her understand that the hospital staff was not familiar with this language. She spent a good deal of time knitting in the workroom, performing her work with interest and skill.

When called upon for an interview, or when given tests, Martha became uneasy. She gave quick, brief answers, waiting anxiously to see whether they met the requirements. Suitable questioning revealed various defects in her mental processes. She continued to report strange ideas, hallucinations, and delusions, chiefly centered around her brother. She was badly mixed up about her age, her recent history, when she was married, when she came to the United States, how long she had been at the hospital. She could not give her home address correctly, and stated that she lived with her children whose names she gave; these proved, however, to be the names of her brothers and sisters, for Martha had no children of her own. Along with these striking defects of memory there could be observed a marked lack of initiative. Although friendly, Martha started no conversations. She never asked for things nor began enterprises on her own account. It did not occur to her to wash herself, although she did so willingly enough if the nurse took her to the washroom. When she grew sleepy in the evening, she lay down fully dressed unless told to undress herself.

At first glance it is hard to make sense out of these mental changes. At one moment we seem to see a person hopelessly confused about the most elementary matters: her age, her address, her brother's recent death. The next mo-

71

ment we observe someone behaving in alert, friendly fashion, helping in the ward, knitting in the workroom, able to perform simple arithmetic problems. Just what is wrong in such a case? Is it possible to describe the mental changes in such a way as to make them intelligible?

Comparison with Previous Cases

In the three cases already discussed we attempted to understand disordered behavior by thinking of it as mainly misdirected adaptive behavior. In each case the person had encountered serious difficulties in living and had not developed successful ways of meeting the problems. There was no reason to suppose that the brain was, so to speak, out of order. Unskillful patterns of living can be acquired by intact brains as easily as skillful ones if favored by the conditions under which learning takes place. Walter Lilly might be accused of not using his head when he fails to speak to a fellow worker and concludes that the other boy does not like him, but it is anxiety that produces this result, not an inability to grasp the point once it is shown him. In Martha Ottenby's case it is possible to discern personal problems. The delusion that she lived with her children suggests the fulfillment of a wish denied in her actual life. The centering of her thoughts around her dead brother points to an unusual dependence on this brother and need for his supporting presence. Presumably her husband was a problem to her at least part of the time. But although these difficulties are discernible, we do not get the least impression that Martha became ill on their account or that her illness represents a strategy designed to solve them. Her trouble has no consistent personal meaning and serves no personal purpose. The disorder began in the brain tissues, not in the strategy of adaptation that the brain learns to carry out.

These examples serve to illustrate the distinction made in Chapter 1 between medical and psychological models. The medical model, as it might have been employed by Kraepelin, applies well to the case of Martha Ottenby, whose condition is the result of a disease. The examination of behavior and the analysis of mental changes has in her case the purpose of guiding the investigator to a correct diagnosis of conditions in her brain tissues. If a method of curing or preventing Pick's disease is found, it will undoubtedly have to do with chemical or metabolic conditions in the brain. The investigator can afford to overlook Martha's problems about children and about her brother except insofar as the expression of these problems displays mental deterioration. The disease concept applied in the wrong place leads to diagnostic blunders that keep people from receiving psychological help that may be much needed. Equal folly results from misplaced application of the psychological model. The investigator hunts relentlessly for personal conflicts and fails to see the evidence for a brain condition or other bodily ailment that could be arrested or cured. A good therapist must be equally alert to the signs of bodily disorder and the indications of emotional disorder, no matter how obscure and elusive these signs may be.

Reduction of Behavior to the Immediate and Concrete

In Martha's case, we want to make intelligible the behavior and mental changes brought about by her illness. What has the destruction of frontal lobe tissue done to her? As a first attempt at analyzing the changes one is apt to inspect the record and find out what mental functions seem to be impaired. Language is undisturbed, but grave weakness is found in the sphere of memory. Loss of interest and initiative played a prominent part in the description, and there were also changes of mood with evidence of a lowered capacity to control emotional expression. This analysis forms a natural starting point, but we must be very careful not to treat these various mental functions as if they were separate faculties of the mind. Are we right in saying that memory, as a whole, is weakened, and that interest and initiative have declined? Let us look again at the patient's behavior, this time with a careful eye for those small details that best serve to clarify a case.

One day the patient was asked to lead the way to the workroom, situated on an upper floor of the hospital. She went directly to the door of the ward and turned to the nurse to unlock it. Given the key she opened the door, locked it behind her, returned the key to the nurse, rang for the elevator and entered it on its arrival. When let out at the proper floor she went straight to the workroom and sat down at her usual place, asking the supervisor for her knitting. Thus far she behaved without hesitation, even with vivacity. When asked almost at once to put away her work and accompany the doctor, she became bewildered and obeyed only after much urging. At this point an experiment was made. The patient was stopped a short distance from the elevator and led a little way along a corridor. Since the ground plan of the various floors was identical, this corridor corresponded to the one the patient would take on her own floor to reach her sleeping room. She now walked straight along the corridor and turned into the room corresponding to her sleeping room. Naturally she was perplexed to find herself in a strange room, but the most curious outcome of the experiment was that even after being told she was on the wrong floor she could not understand how the mistake had come about and was quite unable to find her way to the proper floor.

This sample of behavior deserves our most careful attention. It is not correct to say that the patient has lost the use of her memory. She remembers the way to the workroom, remembers that the ward door is locked and that it must be locked again behind her, remembers her place in the workroom and the knitting in which she was engaged. Memory images arise appropriately when they are necessary to carry out a definite task. Similarly, once a specific task has been instituted she shows no impairment of interest and initiative. Yet the patient would never have started for the workroom of her own accord, and when interrupted in the course of her return she became completely disoriented as to the different floors. In practice she could follow the complicated route perfectly well, but when asked to describe it — to think of it in the abstract — she became altogether confused. She seems to fail when it is necessary to deal with experience abstractly, in her mind, without immediate perceptual promptings.

The hint that we get by examining this piece of behavior can be strengthened by looking at some other samples. Martha is asked about the season of the year, but she cannot tell what season it is. When the form of inquiry is changed to whether it is warm or cold, she answers that it is warm, referring, however, to the temperature of the room. Only when she looks out the window and sees snow does she decide that it is a cold season and agrees that it must be winter. She is given a test performed in the following manner: the experimenter makes a little design by laying small sticks on the table, then breaks it up and asks her to reproduce the design. Martha succeeds or fails in this test, not according to the complexity of the pattern or the number of sticks used, but according to the possibility of perceiving the design as a concrete and familiar object. Thus she succeeds in reproducing designs that remind her of a flag, a roof, a window, and even a letter of the alphabet, but she fails with quite simple designs when they do not resemble an object.

When we consider the various peculiarities of Martha Ottenby's behavior, it appears that she performs with relative success in concrete situations or when dealing with immediate impressions. Her trouble seems to come in dealing with any kind of abstraction. She is unable to stand apart from the immediate properties of the situation or to resist the behavior it invites. She reproduces designs when they remind her of concrete objects, but not when they seem like abstract figures. She reacts correctly to the temperature of the room and to the sight of snow outside, but has a struggle to relate these facts to the relatively abstract idea of winter. She finds her way successfully, but cannot tell anyone how she did it and is hopelessly lost if the sequence of her actions is interrupted. What strikes us most about Martha's behavior is *immediacy* and *specificity*. It is governed by concrete impressions and present circumstances, by sight of corridor and snow, by the impression that somebody walking on the street is her brother. These immediate impressions exert such a powerful force on the patient that she cannot resist them or detach herself from their influence. It can be shown, by questioning, that she knows her brother is dead: she has not forgotten this fact. Yet when she sees someone who resembles him she surrenders so fully to this impression that for the moment she does forget not only that he is dead but that she herself is not properly dressed to run out on the street. This is what is meant by saying that her behavior is reduced to an immediate and concrete level. She has not lost memory, interest, initiative, or imagination as such; she has lost the power to use these processes in other than wholly concrete fashion.

We thus learn a great deal from Martha Ottenby, even though it is impossible to cure her. As students of the brain we learn that there is probably an intimate relation between the frontal lobes and the capacity to transcend the immediate and the concrete. As students of mental processes, we obtain an enriched picture of what is meant by such transcendence. Even in ordinary acts it is necessary to detach oneself from immediate experiences, whether they arise from outside or from one's own thoughts. When we see a person who reminds us vividly of a former friend, we detach ourselves from the immediate force of this impression long enough to remember whether the friend is alive or dead, where we were accustomed to see the friend, whether it is at all likely that the person might now be here. It is also often necessary to give an account of one's actions "in the abstract," that is, while not actually performing them. We can tell someone how to get from one place to another, without ourselves actually traversing the route. We can return to an interrupted task, picture it as a whole, and continue from where we left off, without having to go back to the beginning. These accomplishments seem commonplace enough, but Martha Ottenby's plight serves to remind us of their importance. Transcendence of the immediate and concrete seems to depend on an intact cerebral cortex.

5. A PERSISTENT BUT UNSUCCESSFUL CRIMINAL CAREER: BERT WHIPLEY

The man who will serve as our final example differs in certain respects from the previous cases. As a youth he rebelled against authority and for a dozen years conducted a losing battle with the forces of law and order. Economic circumstances played a part in shaping his criminal career, but as we look into his history we find many instances of misguided, self-defeating behavior, making him a singularly ineffective criminal, and subsequent events confirmed his liability to serious mental disorder.

Example of a Bungled Crime

Our subject, whom we call Bert Whipley, comes to professional attention because of a remarkable series of events that occurred one weekend during the summer when he was twenty-three. Early one Saturday morning, having completed his sentence on several charges involving larceny of cars and burglary, he was given his release from the State Reformatory. His sister was waiting to take him home. On the way they stopped to call on a young married woman with whom they were both well acquainted. Before his imprisonment Bert and this young woman had spent considerable time together, with a rather one-sided result; she fell in love with him, but his emotions remained somewhat confused. During his stay at the Reformatory she expressed her devotion by visits and frequent letters. On this particular Saturday she declared herself eager to leave her husband and suggested that she and Bert go together to a distant part of the country where they might both find jobs and start a new life. Bert's replies were evasive and noncommittal. After the call he and his sister drove home to join their parents and several brothers and sisters; the

75

Whipleys were a very large family. The rest of the day was spent contentedly enough, but by evening Bert felt restless and tired of talk, so he made a solitary round of several bars. Next day, a hot summer Sunday, the whole family went to a lake to swim and did not return until late afternoon. Toward dusk Bert wandered off by himself, found a car parked with the keys in it, and drove away on a main road leading out of the city.

He had gone about seven miles when he became aware of a car overtaking him and heard the challenging sound of its horn. Terrified, he put on all possible speed and swung out to pass the car ahead. He was approaching a curve around which another car suddenly burst into view. To avoid a collision Bert swerved off the road, coming to a jolting stop in a potato field. The pursuing car turned in after him and he immediately gave himself up to the men who stepped out. Almost at once he discovered that these men were not police officers, as he had supposed; they were the owners of the potato field returning to their farmhouse. But it was too late to escape. In the first breath he had admitted stealing the car, and he was turned over to the police.

This time Bert Whipley was sentenced to State Prison, but while awaiting transfer he managed to escape from the county jail, located downtown in his home city. To avoid detection before darkness fell, he slipped into a nearby moving picture theater where he sat trembling and shaking every time someone came down the aisle. Driven out by his own restlessness before dark, he made his way along the main street of the city hoping to reach a safe place where he could telephone to a friend to bring him a different suit of clothes. Caution demanded that he go by side streets and back alleys, but he wandered for half a mile along the central thoroughfare until he was picked up by the police. He received an addition to his sentence and landed in State Prison with four to six years staring him in the face.

What is the explanation of this curiously self-defeating behavior? When we consider all the circumstances it is not surprising that he turned again to crime. There was very little to induce him to "go straight." His previous experience with job hunting consisted mainly of having doors slammed in his face, and now, stigmatized as a convict, his chances were even poorer. His home was crowded and noisy; we can already judge from his behavior on that first evening that he found it disagreeable and irritating. It was much easier, skilled as he was in burglary, to fill his pockets quickly and go far away with his devoted girl friend. Burglary was his purpose when he stole the car and began the ill-fated drive that ended in a potato field.

That he preferred such a course to the miserable prospect of job hunting is easily understood, but what are we to make of his failure to carry out his criminal program? Judging from the criminal's point of view he could hardly have made a worse mess of it. Quite without justification he assumed that a car behind him on the road was in pursuit; he lost his nerve, wrecked the stolen car, and surrendered himself to civilians who had not the slightest intention of punishing him. Later he escaped from jail but concealed his whereabouts so poorly that it was an easy matter for the police to find him. He wants to be a criminal but he virtually brings about his own punishment, an inconsistency that points to severe difficulty of some kind.

Examination of the Patient in Prison

Suppose we visit the prison and look first at the prisoner's record. He made his first appearance in court at the age of seven, charged with "malicious mischief"—breaking windows in a school building. At fourteen he was arrested on various charges of stealing and was sentenced to the State Reform School. When he left reform school he went to another state where he was soon in its reformatory on charges of burglary and larceny. After serving his sentence there he returned to his native state, resumed burglary and larceny, and earned himself a long sentence in the State Reformatory. During nine years, up to the age of twenty-three, he was at liberty in the community for only twenty-two months. No self-respecting criminal would have any patience with such a record. Bert Whipley must have bungled many an enterprise before the episode with which we are familiar.

When we turn to the prisoner himself we find a mild-mannered young man of rather slight build and a somewhat anxious but intelligent expression. His general intelligence, as measured by various tests, is equal to that of the average college student. Serious literary interests appear in his conversation: besides good current literature he is reading Montaigne's *Essays*, and he tells us that his favorite book is Dostoevski's *Crime and Punishment*. We discover that he has served as librarian at the Reformatory and that he is remarkably skilled in certain lines of craftsmanship. At any sign of interest in his work, however, he becomes self-critical and pronounces his efforts entirely worthless. This attitude of self-contempt proves pervasive. If we ask him about himself he quotes the opinions of the prison authorities to the effect that he is lazy, stubborn, disinclined to take courses and improve himself, unwilling even to learn a trade; and he does not seem to entertain any different opinion of his own. He tells somewhat guardedly about his various crimes, admitting that he has often been careless, thus contributing to his own capture. When he plans a burglary it never occurs to him that he might fail, but he becomes tremendously excited when carrying out his carelessly laid plans and is not unlikely to leave some telltale clue. Further study of Bert Whipley shows that in spite of his criminal behavior he has an unusual familiarity with feelings of guilt; in tests of imagination he produces two odd but pertinent stories. In one of these the principal character, having just completed a long prison sentence, gazes contentedly from a window that has no bars, but then in some inexplicable manner falls out the window to his death. In the other story the hero cheats on a school examination, but suffers untold torment and agony until he confesses to the authorities. When we compare these themes with Dostoevski's *Crime and Punishment*, which describes a guilty conscience with such extraordinary

77

detail and culminates in a similar voluntary confession, we can hardly doubt that our subject is no stranger to the experience of guilt.

The Pattern of Contributing Causes

How are we to understand the personality and the self-defeating existence of this young man potentially so gifted? Like anyone else he has been exposed to cultural pressures designed to encourage stable, persistent, socially acceptable behavior. In spite of this he has become an habitual criminal with a propensity for getting caught. Our inquiry resolves itself into two questions: (1) how did the criminal tendencies, the persistent stealing, become fixated at the expense of stable socialized living; and (2) why does he fail in his criminal enterprises, losing his cunning at the critical moment so that he practically exposes himself to capture and punishment?

As might be expected, the answers are not simple. Several factors make their contribution. Some part is played by chronic environmental stress: poverty, unemployment, poor neighborhood influences, tempestuous scenes in the home. But the crucial influences are those attributable to modes of personal adjustment acquired during childhood and adolescence. In order to understand our subject's contemptuous attitude toward society, and his equally contemptuous attitude toward himself, we have to examine the history of the learning process whereby these attitudes were established.

The Whipley family circle contains many examples of psychological disorder. Bert's father has recently been committed to the State Hospital because of chronic alcoholism and some suspicion of mental disorder. His uncle has been in mental hospitals several times and was finally committed for life to an institution for the criminally insane. An older brother has a record of delinquency and drunkenness. Two sisters have had severe breakdowns, requiring psychiatric treatment. In the past this loading of the family history with psychological disorders would have been assumed to indicate hereditary instability. More aware today of the importance of learning, we jump less quickly to such a conclusion, bearing in mind that the presence of even one disordered person in the household can create an unusual environmental pressure for the other members. While it is possible that Bert's alcoholic father transmitted some weakness through the channels of heredity, it is certain, as we will see, that he influenced his offspring directly and powerfully through the avenues of learning. Much can be explained by examining the atmosphere in which Bert grew up and noticing the patterns of reward and punishment he received. This at all events is the proper starting point, even if in the end there are grounds for assuming innate vulnerability.

Attitudes Encouraged by the Parents.   Bert's father was in a respected line of skilled work, not only practicing but teaching his skill. Rather suddenly the demand for this type of work ceased. Thwarted and angry, the father was at home a great deal, used alcohol excessively, and literally terrified the household by his outbursts of furious rage. He tried to teach Bert, but lost his temper on the spot if there was any hitch in the learning. Gradually Bert became his scapegoat, receiving torrents of sarcasm, criticism, and abuse. Everything the son tried to do was made a subject of ridicule by the father. The mother, an easygoing homemaker, tried to soften the quarrels, but her influence was small. She was indulgent to Bert when his father was not around. If he balked at household chores, she did them herself rather than make her son's lot harder. Sometimes when the parents had noisy and violent scenes, the neighbors would advise Mrs. Whipley to separate from her husband, but when he returned sober, tearfully apologizing, she always took him back. Bert grew up with a rankling sense of injustice. In front of callers, Mr. Whipley posed as the ideal loving parent, but the door would hardly be closed before he turned on his family to heap them with abuse. He posed as a religious man but slandered the church in private. He was brutal to his wife but was always taken back. So far as his father was concerned, Bert could see no justice in the family world.

Throughout his childhood and early adolescence, therefore, Bert's self-respect was steadily battered down by his father's ridicule and criticism. Neither parent offered real encouragement to stable and responsible behavior. Bert was in a state of chronic suppressed anger, nursing a sense of injustice, filled with contempt for law, order and good behavior, as hypocritically preached by his father. His parents unwittingly trained him into a pattern of domestic behavior that consisted of criticizing his father whenever possible, dodging the father's anger, and coming around for a hand-out from his mother.

Attitudes Encouraged by Neighborhood Companions. Meanwhile poverty brought the family into a neighborhood where Bert found many of his companions occupied with petty larceny. There were "good" boys and "bad" boys in the neighborhood, but it was among the bad ones that Bert began to find life most rewarding. Among these new friends he discovered a way of proving himself a "big guy" and commanding respect. He assisted two older fellows in stealing a car, in return for which he was allowed to go on a joyride that included pursuit by a police car and successful escape. He soon became an expert, organizing his own joyrides. The experience held a peculiar fascination for him because he found esteem and a sense of triumph, while at the same time hurling defiance and contempt at the symbols of law and order. He became a great fellow in a delinquent gang and his criminal career was fast established. In reform schools and jails he later met many unrepentant criminals who taught him that people who work for a living are "suckers," and who instructed him in the techniques of an easier way to get along. At the same time he began to find a curious satisfaction with prison life. When released, he experienced distinct uneasiness and anxiety.

The facts thus far discussed explain the strength of Bert Whipley's criminal tendencies. To put the whole matter in a nutshell: he was exposed to a system

79

of rewards and punishments that discouraged every attempt at stable, social-ized behavior and that generated an unusually strong satisfaction in criminal enterprises. What is not yet explained is the failure of Bert's crimes, his fre-quent capture and long imprisonments, together with the self-contempt and feelings of guilt we found prominent in his personality. If it were merely a question of frequent capture, we might suppose that, being not very stable, he went to pieces under stress and lost his cunning because of excitement. This explanation, however, would ignore his guilt feelings, his careless planning, and the almost gratuitous exposure of himself to arrest. It appears that crime and punishment have a highly personal meaning to Bert Whipley, the under-standing of which takes us again into his history.

An Early Experience of Guilt. When Bert was four years old he was jealous of his baby brother. This situation is a peculiarly difficult one for a small child to handle. He feels anger toward his new rival and resentment against his faithless parents, but if he shows any of this hostility he only makes matters worse by antagonizing his parents. Bert was sick with a contagious disease, and his parents warned him to keep away from the smaller child. While his parents were out he lured the baby into his room and played with him for some time. Soon the brother was sick, and Bert's position deteriorated: the parents paid more attention than ever to the baby. His resentment rising, Bert's next act was unequivocally hostile. When no one was looking he slipped into the baby's room and set fire to the curtains so that the room filled with smoke and the baby began to cough. Fortunately the flames did not spread, but a few days later the baby's condition grew worse and he died. Bert received no punishment for his hostile action, but he was well aware of his parents' grief. Believing that he had killed the brother, he was left with a heavy load of guilt. For months afterwards he was haunted by a voice that seemed to ring in his ears saying "Put it out, put it out," and he would run to his mother scream-ing with terror. Ten years later he still sometimes heard the voice and experi-enced the rising panic. Nineteen years later he related the unforgotten inci-dent with distinct signs of distress.

Presumably a single event must be of catastrophic proportions to leave an indelible mark on personality. The tendency of this particular experience would be to make Bert liable to guilt feelings—to considering himself evil and deserving of punishment. Such feelings would expectably creep up on him precisely at those moments when he was engaged in criminal activity. We do not know whether or not the effects of this incident were reinforced by other early guilt-producing situations, but the whole problem was kept alive during later childhood because of his stormy family life, the constant battering of his self-respect, his burning resentment, and the wonderful satisfaction he pres-ently discovered in delinquent behavior. Successful crime had once caused him untold misery and terror, the terror that comes to a child who believes that his parents can never love him again. However strong his present motives toward delinquency, each criminal act had the power to call up some part of that misery and terror. His criminal accomplishments were thus repeatedly undermined by ancient feelings of guilt.

The Attraction of Prison

It might seem that dread of imprisonment would have had more effect than it did in curbing Bert's antisocial urges. Being in prison, however, was in many ways an adaptive solution for his difficulties in living. The restrictions and indignities of prison life served as a chronic punishment, kept guilt feelings in abeyance, and permitted him the satisfaction of griping about his unfair lot. His impaired sence of initiative was small handicap in an environment that allowed little initiative, and his sense of worthlessness was lulled by the postponement of real life tests. Prison afforded provision—food, shelter, rest, a chance to read—such as his mother had tried to provide for him in the stormy home. Life within prison walls was too congruent with many of his needs to act as an effective deterrent to criminal behavior. Of course it was not wholly satisfactory; when inside, he yearned for freedom, for the companionship of

Prison may have suited Bert Whipley's needs, but the dehumanizing atmosphere would frustrate and stultify most people psychologically.

women, and for the chance to do what he pleased. But was there a danger that if he stepped forth to freedom he would, like the character in his story, fall unaccountably to his death?

Subsequent Events

That this was no idle symbol soon became apparent. After serving three years of his sentence Bert was released from State Prison on parole. It was a time when jobs were readily obtainable; furthermore, his parole officer was relatively sympathetic, and arrangements were made for Bert to receive psychological help. Conditions seemed as favorable as they would ever be for life outside. Almost at once things began to go wrong. Bert found it impossible to keep jobs; fatigue, illness, or mistrust of the employers put a quick end to each attempt. He found it impossible to observe the conditions of his parole, especially regarding the frequenting of bars. He began to be quarrelsome and created disturbances, becoming increasingly convinced that the people around him were evil and dangerous. Two months after his release from prison he became seriously confused and disoriented as to the time of day. While in this state he was arrested for picking a senseless quarrel. He was committed to a mental hospital where he remained for the next seven months.

This disastrous outcome casts additional light on his difficulties. The speed with which he passed into a confused and agitated state suggests an unusual weakness in organization. When studied in prison he had described anxiety at the time of previous releases, when he had to decide what to do and where to go instead of following an imposed routine. At the time of discharge he had shown uncommon uneasiness about directions for reaching offices to which he was supposed to report. He did not feel equal to the jobs he undertook or to the human relations they entailed. Apparently he faced life outside with a deep conviction that he could not cope with it, and he showed little capacity to endure even ordinary frustrations. These characteristics unfortunately did not change. More than twenty years later his history was still repeating itself. Once more we find him looking for casual employment, drinking heavily, creating a disturbance, showing signs of deep confusion, and being again committed to a mental hospital.

Classification of the Disorder

The case of Benton Child has prepared us for difficulties in classifying disordered behavior. Bert Whipley does nothing to clarify the problem. Part of his behavior belongs under the heading of *delinquency*, and the official diagnosis at the prison was *psychopathic personality*. This label is generally applied when the following characteristics are present: habitual delinquent behavior, a marked lack of moral scruples, insensitivity to the rights of others, and a generally erratic and purposeless way of living. This state of affairs differs from *anxiety disorder* in that the underlying difficulties, whatever they may be, display themselves in overt behavior directed against society. Instead of being felt as internal, in the form of unhappiness and symptoms of various kinds, the troublesome tendencies are turned into overt action of a delinquent or criminal sort. Whipley corresponds in several respects to the typical *sociopathic personality*, but on one point the prison diagnosis must be considered wrong. It is highly characteristic of the sociopath that he or she feels no guilt or remorse. In respect to the rights of others—the victims of his stealing, for example—Whipley is quite free from self-reproach, but as we have seen he is heavily weighted with a much less appropriate feeling of guilt that originated in his early childhood. In this one respect, then, his condition resembles *anxiety disorder* instead of *sociopathic personality*. It seems proper to say that he started with an early childhood anxiety disorder and that his later experiences then turned him forcibly toward delinquency without entirely obliterating the effects of the earlier condition.

More has to be added, however, to cover the breakdowns that led Whipley into the mental hospital. The confused, disoriented, agitated state that preceded his commitments is typical neither of *anxiety disorders* nor of sociopathic personality; it gives ground for a diagnosis of *psychosis*. Taking into account the mistrustful attitude toward others, a good first guess would be *schizophrenia, paranoid type*, but further evidence, including a marked progression from an excited to a depressed mood, led the hospital staffs to settle on the diagnosis of *manic-depressive psychosis*. In either case there is reason to assume some genetic contribution to his difficulties, though this would hardly be more than a relatively nonspecific vulnerability to disorganization and extreme moods. The picture that forms itself is of a person of less than average capability to hold together under stress having the misfortune of a turbulent history containing more than average amounts of stress. The strategies arrived at to deal with this imbalance—crime and capture, prison life, alcohol—provided no training in the direction of a normal way of life.

Thus when we ask what is wrong with Bert Whipley we find ourselves trying to untwist a tangle of influences that resulted in a lot of things being wrong. This makes him a good "textbook case," more typical of disordered personalities than an example who neatly fits one diagnostic category or has one sharply circumscribed problem. But what are the implications for treatment? The attempts made to help him with problems of everyday living when he was on parole were a failure. In the mental hospital his acute symptoms were brought under control but his way of living remained unchanged. Where else and how else would it be possible to intervene usefully, bearing in mind the possible genetic tendency to mood swings, the powerful allure of alcohol, the restless impatience that blocks holding a job, the negative value attached to work? By the time Bert Whipley was twenty-six the discouragements to stable living had come to outweigh any encouragements likely to be within the power of professional helpers. It would be better to meet such a case much earlier in life, when competition with destructive influences would have had more chance of

83

success, But such timely meetings rarely take place unless the community's mental health services are unusually well developed.

CONCLUSION

In this clinical survey we have examined five representative examples of disordered behavior. We have seen five very different personalities, and we have looked at a wide range of burdens and difficulties in living. Is there any order in this diversity? Can we do more than explain single cases? Can we find out how the difficulties of life make one person maladjusted, another anxious, another delinquent, another psychotic, while another passes through comparable vicissitudes without impairment to psychological health? That is the task of abnormal psychology: to bring order, system, and understanding into facts as diverse as those described in this chapter. Obviously, the possibility of curing disorders, still more of preventing them, depends on our being able to perceive them as expressions of general lawful processes. This requires that they be seen in relation to normal development, which forms the essential background for any systematic study of disordered behavior.

SUGGESTIONS FOR FURTHER READING

Two collections of case studies illustrating all the main varieties of disordered behavior have been published by A. Burton & R. E. Harris, *Case Histories in Clinical and Abnormal Psychology* (1947) and *Clinical Studies of Personality* (1955). Another two-volume work is *Case Studies in Childhood Emotional Disabilities*, edited by George E. Gardner, Vol. I (1953), Vol. II (1956). A case study that has become a classic is that of a delinquent by C. R. Shaw, *The Jack Roller* (1930).

Of special value to the student who wants to try interpreting case materials is a book by H. Weinberg & A. W. Hire, *A Case Book in Abnormal Psychology* (1956), which consists of detailed clinical case reports with practically no interpretative comments.

Valuable for understanding is the study of the experience of disordered people as they reported it. An illuminating collection of firsthand accounts has been made by B. Kaplan, *The Inner World of Mental Illness* (1963), which includes the autobiography of a deluded schizophrenic patient, L. Percy King. Further material of this kind is to be found in C. Landis & F. A. Mettler, *Varieties of Psychopathological Experience* (1964), and in V. W. Grant, *This is Mental Illness* (1963).

Case studies of people more or less normal or but slightly maladjusted are to be found in R. W. White's *Lives in Progress* (3rd ed., 1975); in H. E. Jones's *Development in Adolescence* (1943); and in Lois B. Murphy's *Personality in Young Children*, Vol. II (1956).

84

First Infant School in Green Street (ca. 1825). Museum of The City
of New York and The Metropolitan Museum of Art, Edward Arnold
Collection.

3

The Adaptive Process

Through history and through clinical examples we have seen that abnormal psychology covers a diverse subject matter. Some forms of disordered personal behavior lend themselves to interpretation as diseases, fitting the mode of thinking that prevails in medical practice. Other forms are better described as consequences of experience, as misdirected attempts to meet the difficulties of living. Many cases, of course, represent a combination of the two, but the underlying causes are so different that they require separate study. In this book we take up first the problems historically called psychogenic. They are of psychological origin, by which we mean that they arise out of the adaptive process whereby from childhood onward we learn how to deal with and live with our surroundings.

More is at stake in studying the adaptive process than finding out how to treat anxiety or modify a piece of undesirable behavior. Psychological treatment may not require uncovering the whole history of learnings that led up to the present complaint. Much better than treatment, however, is prevention, and progress toward prevention depends on understanding how adaptive behavior can go astray at any level of development. In guiding one's own behavior, in bringing up children, in giving counsel to younger people, in working for conditions in the community and in the larger society that will be conducive to fuller personal development, it is essential to have a background of knowledge about the growth of personality. This means knowledge of normal as well as abnormal outcomes, workable as well as unworkable patterns, and it implies recognizing the special hazards that go with different stages of growth.

MEANING OF ADAPTATION

Like other words in everyday use, *adaptation* is often encumbered by unwarranted implications. All too commonly it is considered a one-way process instead of an interaction between a person and the environment. It is then made to imply that all change must take place within the person who must conform to the expectations of others and to the prevailing demands of the social order. This view ignores the part played by people in changing their material and social surroundings so as to make the environment more hospitable to human needs. Sometimes the misunderstanding is innocent, but it easily lends itself to political use by those who want to force conformity on others.

Another common misunderstanding is to define adaptation not as a process but as an end-state such as happiness, contentment, or peace of mind. The well-adjusted person, according to this view, is happy, confident, buoyant, and unburdened by problems. Unwittingly, this notion ignores the tragic aspects of human experience and implies that all problems can be happily solved. There is nothing in the concept of adaptation that warrants blithe illusions about reality. In some circumstances the best possible outcome may still entail discouragement, sorrow, and enduring frustration.

Still another implication that on closer scrutiny proves misleading is the linking of adaptation exclusively with change. It is true, of course, that change is constantly occurring. Every step in development calls for something new; change must go on from day to day and from period to period through a person's life. In many situations, however, the adaptive problem is to resist distractions that would provide a welcome change, in order to stick to the task at hand. This can be a large problem for people whose livelihood depends on uninteresting, monotonous work. It is present also to those who love their work but must put in long hours of reading, study, research, practice, or rehearsal to do it well. Children find the requirement of persistence a hard one, as we see when it is lifted during recess periods or after school. What is needed for successful adaptation is a happy combination of flexibility to change and strength to persist.

The adaptive process represents the struggle of a person to come to terms with the environment. It implies a constant interaction between the person and the surroundings, each making demands on the other. Sometimes a mutually satisfactory bargain can be struck between these demands, or at least a bargain that is not unbearable for either side. When it becomes difficult to strike such a bargain we can most clearly discern the hampering part played by disordered personal reactions.

MAIN FEATURES OF ADAPTIVE STRATEGY

Dealing with the problems of living requires attending to several things at the same time. Confronted by a crisis, we need to understand it, we need to keep from being too badly upset by it, and we need to do something about it. These three aspects of adaptive strategy can be stated more formally as follows: What we do is likely to be successful to the extent that (1) *adequate relevant information* can be brought to bear, (2) *affect* can be kept *supportive* rather than disorganizing, and (3) *competent action* can be discerned and attempted (White, 1974). These have to be managed all at once, though with differences of emphasis depending on the character of the problem. Putting the aspects of adaptive behavior into words may suggest that they are more conscious and calculated than is actually the case. The strategies implicit in behavior may be almost wholly unwitting, but we can understand them better with this analysis in mind.

Adequate Relevant Information

Much as we may admire forthright action in the face of difficulties, this can be a disastrous strategy if there is a shortage of relevant information. Taking plenty of time to size up a situation is common in both animal and human behavior. If we decide to put out food for hungry winter birds we may be disappointed at first by their hesitant acceptance of our hospitality, forgetting that they know nothing of our kindness and survive only through constant alertness to possible danger. Similarly, when children are placed in a new situation it is good strategy for them to look things over carefully before committing themselves to action. This is illustrated in studies of preschool children made by Lois Murphy in Topeka (1962). The children were observed in such novel situations as coming to the research center for the first time to take psychological tests, or attending an outdoor party at the psychologist's home. A few of the children blundered right ahead as if confident that everything would be all right; another few clung to their mothers and tried to turn their backs on the

In strange situations a youngster experiences mixed emotions that may paralyze organized behavior. This boy obviously enjoys this one, but with some reservations.

A toddler usually studies new situations very carefully before taking action.

novel scene. The rest, staying cautiously close to their mothers at first, inspected the situation intently, and did not venture forth until they had completed their survey. Preschool children are usually too inexperienced to understand in advance what is involved in such situations. It is therefore adaptive to begin by trying to build up relevant information.

In a study of adult behavior under stress, Hamburg and Adams (1967) were impressed by the prominence of seeking and using information. The point is well illustrated by parents whose sick child receives the diagnosis of leukemia with short life expectancy. Enduring this painful crisis is helped by collecting relevant information. The parents, feeling that they may have been at fault, are relieved to learn that earlier reporting of the illness would not have changed the prognosis. Their bewilderment is reduced by gathering information on how they should behave toward the child during the time that remains. Sometimes an educated parent will zealously search the current medical literature looking for hints of new treatment that may have escaped the doctor's attention. The doctor struggling to keep up with reports of medical research also illustrates the adaptive importance of securing adequate relevant information.

Affect Supportive Instead of Disruptive

A second main aspect of adaptive strategy is to avoid or control feelings likely to disrupt behavior and to strengthen those that support it. We are subject to a variety of emotions that are capable of getting out of hand in the sense that they can disrupt or paralyze organized behavior. There are situations in which fear, anger, despair, grief, and excitement are clearly appropriate, but if they become too intense they may interfere seriously with adaptive efforts. This possibility is recognized in everyday speech by such common phrases as wildly excited, too angry to speak, paralyzed with fright, consumed by grief, and crushed by despair. The preschool children in the Topeka study were indeed sometimes paralyzed with fright. This caused them to be speechless, immovable, and so rejective of proffered objects and social overtures that they could neither increase their information nor discover possible lines of action.

Grief has been the object of considerable study since the publication of a paper by Lindemann in 1944. Bereavement usually involves extensive changes in the survivor's pattern of life. As Lindemann puts it, the bereaved person "is surprised to find how large a part of his customary activity was done in some meaningful relationship to the deceased and has now lost its significance." The crisis can ultimately be met only by developing new directions of interest and action, but acute grief—with its apathy, indecision, and burdensome physical accompaniments—tends to obstruct this development. Time is required to recover from bereavement. Time also plays an important part in recovery from accidents or illness that leaves a person with substantial permanent handicap. Studying a group of hospital patients in this situation, Hamburg and Adams (1967) noticed a number of instances in which the patients were at first relatively cheerful but disinclined to talk about or think about the future. Later they began to consider seriously the restricted lives they would have to live, and at that point their mood changed to one of depression. The adaptive process of seeking relevant information could go forward only at the speed at which the patient could tolerate the despair aroused by thinking about the diminished future.

Possibilities for Competent Action

Situations are stressful when we are unable to produce relevant and expectably effective actions. Even a situation as dangerous as space flight does not overwhelm the well-trained astronaut who knows what to do in almost any emergency. When people seek advice on personal problems it is because they do not know what to do next; they have exhausted their available repertory without finding an acceptable solution. For the Topeka children, the discovery of a channel for competent action was often a turning point in the adaptive process. When they saw among the proferred materials something they knew how to handle, like beads to string or blocks with which to build, they could leave their mothers' sides and become immersed in action. This step did not always lead further: one child spent the whole time at the party building with blocks in a corner of the garage. But action tends to allay anxiety, increase a sense of competence, and thus lead to less constricted behavior.

The discovery that something can be done played a significant part in the recent revolution of public attitudes toward mental health. Parents of mentally retarded children, for example, used to feel that their burden simply had to be borne as patiently as possible. Today they are likely to be members of associations for the mentally retarded engaged in providing kindergartens for younger children, pressing for special assistance for those of school age, and developing sheltered workshops for retarded adults. Taking action in this way is beneficial not only to the mentally retarded, whose prospects for maximal development have been greatly improved, but also to the parents, who need no longer suffer in silence and who get the support of other parents with the same problem.

Analysis of Two Examples

Understanding can be increased by making a closer analysis of specific adaptive tasks. To this end we select two familiar problems that are often met successfully but that sometimes become the occasion for disordered personal reactions.

Transition from School to College.   The problems of the first year of college will serve as one example. When freshmen arrive on the campus they are in many ways prepared by past experience to fit comfortably into their new life, but will rarely be able to make the transition without distinct efforts toward adaptation. In several respects they qualify as maladjusted until they can accomplish certain new steps in growth. For one thing they are quite likely to be strangers in the material environment. They have to learn a new local geography so that they can find their way around. They must also learn new routines and schedules, and it is often true that they must take suddenly increased responsibility for managing their lives. Perhaps for the first time they must do their own shopping, handle their own money, watch over their own health, and plan their work to meet deadlines a week or even a month ahead. Many

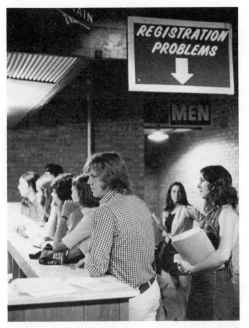

It is natural to feel strange and a little isolated when making such a major transition as the one to college.

study problems turn out to be difficulties in reaching this higher level of self-management. Similarly, freshmen must learn to interact with new people whose backgrounds may differ widely from their own, whose histories they have not shared, whose interests they must discover. Often there are feelings of loneliness and isolation until progress can be made in the new social field. The strength of such feelings is attested by the joy that is experienced on finding someone who comes from one's own county or who shares a favorite hobby. Part of the freshman problem can be summarized by saying that they have lost their habituated familiarity with the objects and people of their home environment and have to develop relevant information about what is expected and what can be done in the college community.

In making the transition it is not always easy to control disruptive emotions. Many freshmen are assailed by sadness at being separated from home and familiar surroundings. They may feel a little like crying and may suffer at times from acute homesickness. Another not uncommon feeling is a certain anxiety over one's prospects of making the grade in the new enterprise. This anxiety may be experienced as a diffuse but lasting discomfort or it may be focussed on social activity or scholastic exercises, particularly exams. To the extent that sadness and anxiety obtrude themselves disruptively they are likely to have a further poor effect: these are feelings one has been taught to suppress as much as possible, and their reappearance seems like a childish weakness. The emo-

93

tions thus add insult to injury. But perhaps the most troublesome emotion is anger, usually experienced in the more subdued form of an indiscriminate dislike for the new surroundings and the new people. The college community is making one feel frustrated—what is more natural than to feel resentment toward the source of frustration? Yet this feeling, too, is not wholly acceptable. Presumably it conflicts with a desire to like the place and do well there; certainly it creates an obstacle to wholehearted attempts at adaptation.

Difficulty may also be experienced in mobilizing supportive feelings such as interest and enthusiasm. Freshmen must arrive at what we may call a new economy of happiness. In their previous lives they have probably worked out some kind of balance between joys and sorrows, satisfactions and frustrations; a balance sufficiently favorable so that their lives have seemed worthwhile and valuable. To some extent they will have found their lines of excellence, maintained a basis of security, made some kind of rewarding place in society. This balance is now temporarily upset, and it can be restored only in the course of time. Freshmen often experience a sharp and painful drop in prestige. As seniors in high school they may have attained local eminence as athletes, debaters, editors, actors, and officers of organizations. At college they are jolted down again to the youngest level of society. The freshman learns to interact smoothly enough with the new environment but may nevertheless feel discontented, unable to find a living wage of happiness in a life so lacking in personal distinction. Sometimes a visit to the old school—a return to the scene of former triumphs—will give a sudden boost of spirit, but a permanent new equilibrium can be reached only by finding sources of satisfaction, prestigeful or of other kinds, appropriate to the life of the present and future. Many students eventually find college far more satisfying than anything they have known before, but they mostly report that it took them time to make this discovery, to "find themselves." Building an economy of happiness in a new situation takes energy and patience.

Obviously the situation calls for new competent actions, but these may not be instantly discovered. When conditions are difficult, there is a tendency toward regression; that is, a tendency to fall back on forms of behavior that were satisfying earlier in life but have since been outgrown. A high school debating hero, for example, may come to college realizing that his new companions will not want to hear about his former triumphs, but if he meets hard sledding in his attempts to find common grounds of new interest he may discover, to his own consternation, that he is proudly telling about the three-state cup won by his debating team, that he is talking in his platform voice, or that he has reverted to a juvenile self-confidence in pronouncing judgments. His awareness of what is needed may not prevent him from slipping back a few steps to earlier modes of adjustment. Sometimes regression reaches further into the past. Bewilderment in the new scene may reinstate a dependent attitude in a person lately quite competent who now expects someone to take care of everything, or asks for guidance in matters that are not really difficult. Loss of one's most recent adjustive habits tends to throw one back on earlier ways of behaving just at the moment when new behavior is most needed. There is competition between the new and the old, and sometimes the old displays a disconcerting tenacity.

The transition from school to college is not a crisis that occurs suddenly. When challenges to adaptation can be anticipated, strategies can be set in motion beforehand. This is illustrated in a study by Silber and others (1961) of high school students getting ready to enter college in the fall. The subjects were chosen because they showed a high level of competence in the important aspects of adolescent life and could be expected to face with confidence the important step before them. They were not immune to anxiety, but they tried as best they could to deal with the transition in advance. Increased information about college life was sought by writing to their college, visiting the campus, and talking with college students and graduates among their acquaintances. Anxiety was controlled by reflecting that worry is normal, that nearly everyone entering college feels uneasy, that one need not aspire to overwhelming success right away; and by recalling success in previous transitions such as the one from junior to senior high schools. With respect to competent action, many of the students sought practice in advance, a sort of rehearsal for college life. They began to read books considered to be at the college level. They worked unusually hard at term papers, anticipating that this type of work would be of great importance in college courses. They became interested in buying their own clothes and in budgeting their time. Looking for summer jobs, they tended to reject those usually occupied by high school kids, like baby-sitting and mowing lawns; they preferred work identified with adult status and sought competition with adults on equal terms. These anticipatory actions helped reduce the changes actually required when college opened in the fall.

It is easy to imagine the opposite of these competent strategies: anxiety and apathy, trying not to think about college, clinging to already familiar forms of satisfaction. Implicit in the study are useful hints for counselors. Telling an anxious student not to worry—trying to influence the student's total attitude—may be less effective than pointing out some of the specific anticipatory actions not in themselves unduly awesome, that tend to reduce the magnitude of the step to be taken.

Staying in College: Sophomore Slump. Our second example illustrates the problem of adaptation when the main requirement is not for change but for endurance. The freshman, let us say, makes a successful transition to college, so that everyone who cares is pleased with the progress. But a time may come when the excitement of novelty diminishes, when studying is felt as an increasingly wearisome grind, when efficiency breaks down and time seems to be more wasted than used. The student may feel anxious and guilty about this slump in performance, but faces the even stronger feelings of boredom and restlessness that make it impossible to reverse the trend. Troubles of this kind may happen at any time, but they occur often enough during the second year

95

to be nicknamed "sophomore slump." Not everyone has this experience, though a good many are aware of it in mild degree. But for some students there is a real crisis: habits of work collapse; social life loses its savor; feelings of worthlessness and boredom become disturbing; and the trouble may end by flunking out, leaving school, or (in extreme but not frequent instances) by a real mental breakdown. The student feels unable to secure adequate relevant information about what is happening, affects are predominantly disruptive and the economy of happiness destroyed, and attempts at competent action have the character of restless blind stabs in the dark.

Although it is always necessary to allow for wide ranges of individual differences, we can perhaps recognize a common central theme in the loss of happiness. The glow of early success loses its warming power. The student has proved equal to college studies and to keeping afloat in college life. Parents and teachers back at school have had their expectations fulfilled. But these motives are not enough to sustain those repeated acts of initiative, planning, and self-discipline that are necessary for success at the college level. Earlier motives of pleasing parents and teachers and proving that you can get high marks have to be superseded by something that is more in accord with mature adulthood. The student's education must become meaningful for his or her own life. This may come about easily if college studies prove intrinsically interesting and an inclination is felt to have some part in intellectual activities. It may come about naturally if studies have a clear relevance to an attractive vocation. When actions are subordinated to strong interests and cherished personal goals, we are able to resist distractions and endure frustrations in order to perform them. Very likely, however, students will not yet know what they want to do with their lives and may not feel that studies have much bearing on the future. There are no rewards in a struggle that seems pointless.

We must be careful at this point to avoid assuming that everyone ought to adjust to college. The student in sophomore slump, wasting time and seemingly going to pieces, may be trying to carry out a rebellion against a kind of life that is not at the moment valuable for his or her personal growth. It may be more important to take a job or to try something highly adventurous, proving worth and finding interests in action instead of in studies. Students are sometimes well advised to drop out of college for a while, deciding later whether they want to return. This may be the most effective way to quiet disruptive affects, permit the student to secure more adequate self-information, and open new channels for competent action that may restore the economy of happiness to an acceptable balance (Hirsch & Keniston, 1970).

RELEVANT PRINCIPLES OF LEARNING

Up to this point we have discussed the adaptive process in everyday language, using familiar human examples. The behavior shown in these examples is not unusually complex as compared, for instance, with the clinical cases in the last chapter. Adequate description, however, required using such ideas as self-esteem, the economy of happiness, interest, imagination, and planning — concepts that are familiar in human experience but not easy to capture in a scientific system.

To reach a more fundamental conceptualization let us look at the adaptive process from a different angle. For many years, since Pavlov's momentous work on conditional responses, experimental psychologists have been investigating learning and trying to establish its basic principles. In the interests of scientific control, much of this work was done with animal subjects or with relatively simple human learning situations. Partly on this account the resulting principles did not at first seem useful for understanding clinical problems. During the 1960s, however, the chasm between laboratory and clinic was spanned by a rapidly growing demonstration that anxious behavior, in particular, could be understood and treated through a deliberate application of basic principles of learning derived originally from animal experiments. These behavioral principles are clearly relevant to abnormal human behavior and therefore deserve careful consideration.

Conditioned Response

The conditioned response was discovered in the early years of the twentieth century by the Russian physiologist Ivan Pavlov. The basic experiment, in which a hungry dog is fed just after the sounding of a bell and gradually comes to salivate to this signal alone, is described in every textbook of psychology. It may be hard today to recapture the excitement originally created by this now familiar experiment. The association of ideas had long occupied a position of prominence as a theory of human mental life, and the demonstration that something similar went on in animal behavior — the association of the bell with food — strengthened a belief that the essence of the learning process had at last been discovered. To the early behaviorists, conditioning became the key to learning and thus to most of the secrets of behavior. The central idea, of course, was not new. Pavlov's contribution lay in developing a laboratory situation in which the critical variable — the response to a stimulus — could be isolated and accurately measured. On this basis was built a whole program of experiments to study the characteristics of conditioned responses (Ban, 1964).

Pavlov's basic experiment demonstrated that an originally unconnected stimulus could acquire the power to set off a response simply by being present along with the natural stimulus for that response — in this case food in the mouth. The sound of a bell or buzzer, the ticking of a metronome, a flash of light could serve equally well, and other responses, such as withdrawal from pain, could be conditioned to a wide range of stimuli. If we think of learning as the picking up of signals for what is going to happen, the conditioned response experiments provide an appropriate paradigm. When one stimulus oc-

97

curs repeatedly with another, it is likely that they are connected in the real world. The dog salivating at the sound of the bell was responding appropriately to the reality created by the experiments in which bell and feeding were made to happen together. But the mechanism is not foolproof; it does not preclude the occasional formulation of a conditioned response to a stimulus that is not actually relevant.

This possibility becomes greater when conditioned responses are formed quickly. It has been shown that when pain or danger are involved, evoking an anxiety response, it takes only a small number of occurrences to establish conditioned responses. The conditioned stimuli that thus gain the power to elicit anxiety may be almost anything that is present at the time of fright, regardless of relevance. Learning under conditions of fright tends to be global and indiscriminate, especially in early childhood. The conditioning of anxiety responses thus provides a believable origin for the irrational fears that sometimes plague people even in adult life. If a young child is terrified by witnessing an accident, anxiety may be displayed subsequently in connection with the scene itself, with the neighborhood, with streets, with ambulance sirens, with red lights on top of cars, or with white coats as seen on the medical attendants who stepped out of the ambulance. Under certain circumstances conditioned responses of this type may persist into adult life, their origins forgotten, so that an otherwise composed person may experience extremely unpleasant anxiety at the sight of waiters in white coats or a school band in white uniforms. We undoubtedly oversimplify the matter by saying that all seemingly irrational fears are handed straight down from early childhood frights with no intervening development, but the conditioning experiments certainly suggest how some of these fears get started.

Generalization

Adaptive imperfection may result also from the process of generalization. In one of his experiments Pavlov used a metronome beat of a certain frequency to establish a conditioned salivary response. He then noticed that salivation followed the sound of the metronome set at entirely different frequencies. Generalization of the conditioned stimulus can be said to occur when stimuli bearing some resemblance to the original one also acquire the power to elicit the response.

The point was illustrated in an often cited experiment by Watson and Rayner (1920) on the conditioning of fear reactions. A year-old child called Albert, who reached out and played with everything that was put before him, including a pet white rat, was experimentally conditioned to fear the rat. This was accomplished by pairing the showing of the rat with a natural fear stimulus, the loud unpleasant sound made by striking a steel bar. Five combined presentations were enough to establish a strong fear response to the rat alone. Tests were then made with other objects put in front of Albert. Fear responses occurred to a rabbit, a dog, and a light-colored fur coat; a milder response was made to some partly wrapped cotton wool; no uneasiness was aroused by the boy's blocks, with which he played with his customary vigor. He also played as usual with the experimenters' hair, oblivious of the dirty trick they had played on him by striking the steel bar in the first place. The generalization of the fear reaction was apparently determined by visual similarity to the furry white rat.

Another route for generalization was demonstrated by Diven (1937) in an experiment with adult human subjects. After somewhat awesome preparations with attachment of wires to various parts of the subject's body and mention of electrical circuits, the experiment proceeded with a form of word association test. The subject was instructed to give a series of associations to each word in the list, continuing until asked to stop. The stop signal was called at twelve seconds. In the word list there was a repeating element: six times the word *red* occurred, followed by the word *barn*. After associating to *barn* for twelve seconds, the subject was given a startling and somewhat painful electric shock through electrodes on the ankle. On completion of the word list, a time interval was introduced, after which the whole procedure was repeated except that no electric shocks were given.

Anxiety was measured by means of the galvanic skin response (GSR), which indicates crudely the amount of sweat produced on the palm of the hand. Toward the end of the first session and throughout the second, the largest GSR's occurred on the word *barn*—the actual signal for the shock—but significantly above-average responses accompanied three other classes of words. These were (1) the word *red*, which always preceded *barn*, (2) the word, whatever it might be, that followed *barn*, and (3) all words in the list having a distinctly rural association, such as "hay," "plow," "pasture," "sheep," in contrast to urban words like "pavement," "subway," "streetcar." The anxiety reaction spread thus to other signals related to the original signal either by *contiguity in time* (preceding or following it), or by *meaning* (belonging in the same area of experience, in this case the country). One subject, a foreigner, showed attachment of GSR's to the preceding and following words but none to the rural words. It was found afterwards that because of imperfect knowledge of English he had failed to catch the meaning of the word *barn*. In the great majority of the other subjects the meaningful associations of this word were utilized as channels of generalization.

Even more surprising than this result was the finding that the same generalization occurred when the subjects failed to realize consciously that *barn* was the actual signal. Of the fifty-two subjects who took part in the experiment, twenty-one were unable to say what word preceded the shock. This seems less remarkable when we remember that the shock was separated from *barn* by twelve seconds during which the subject gave a chain of word associations. It appeared, however, that failure to recognize *barn* consciously did not in any way prevent the attachment of anxiety to the rural words. The signal character of *barn* was somehow apprehended, but the subject was not aware of this and could not report it. In a later repetition of Diven's experiment, it appeared that generalization spread more widely, on the average, when the connection between signal word and shock was not consciously perceived (Lacey, Smith, & Green, 1955).

Extinction

Of special importance for the understanding of abnormal behavior is the manner in which conditioned responses are unlearned. We are not doomed to repeat forever the responses we first learn, nor are we permanently enslaved to irrelevant stimuli picked up through contiguity or generalization. Experimental extinction was demonstrated by Pavlov simply by failing to reinforce the conditioned response. When the sound of the bell was no longer followed by food in the mouth, the salivary response eventually disappeared. Time was required to produce this result, and traces of the conditioned response were retained even when it appeared to have faded out. Sometimes it reappeared briefly after an interval of time, and it could be quickly brought back to full strength by a much smaller number of reinforcements than were needed for the original learning. But to all intents and purposes conditioned responses dropped out of the behavioral repertoire when the conditioned stimulus was no longer followed by the unconditioned one.

Among its numerous services, extinction contributes to the making of finer discriminations and thus helps to undo the effects of generalization and of irrelevant cues. Pavlov's dogs first learned to salivate to any frequency of metronome sounds, but when only one frequency was followed by food the conditioned response to all other frequencies was extinguished and the dogs became accurate in discriminating the critical frequency. In like fashion a child starting with a generalized fear of white coats might discover that they sometimes occur in benign circumstances without frightening results, and might presently come to discriminate between benign white coats and those worn by the shot-giving pediatrician and mouth-probing dentist, in whose presence a certain anxiety may continue to be reinforced.

Described in this way, extinction sounds like a perfect mechanism for ridding us of all responses that do not correspond to current actualities. Let Albert have a few exposures to the white rat without sound from the steel bar and he will soon rejoice once more in the rat's company. Unfortunately, conditioned fear reactions are more quickly formed than they are extinguished. Albert's fear was learned in five repetitions; many more would probably be required to extinguish it.

The possibility of using extinction as a means of overcoming children's fears was shown in the somewhat analogous case of three-year-old Peter described in 1924 by M. C. Jones. This child had somehow acquired a strong fear of furry animals and furry objects, a fear that seemed to center on rabbits. The fear was removed by a carefully planned program of extinction and of counter-conditioning—associating the rabbit with pleasant circumstances. A pet rabbit was gradually introduced to Peter's presence, at first in a cage at a distance, when he was enjoying a pleasant meal, or had the company of fearless playmates. On successive occasions the cage could be brought nearer without frightening Peter; then the rabbit could be released into the room; finally the boy touched and played with the rabbit in normal childlike fashion. It will be noticed that if done badly this procedure might have had a disastrous result. Bringing the rabbit too near too soon would have caused panic and possibly formed a connection between anxiety and eating. Skill and good timing were required to effect the unlearning of the phobia.

The conditioned response in Pavlov's sense applies most directly to abnormal behavior having to do with emotional reactions. Irrational fears, guilt, angers, and jealousies play a considerable part in maladaptive personal behavior, and the concept of extinction is needed to understand how they can be unlearned.

Operant Conditioning

Another kind of conditioning, important in both animal and human learning, leads not to picking up signals but to the gradual shaping of responses. It is illustrated by Thorndike's historic experiments in which hungry cats were placed in cages and left to find out how to unlatch the door that stood between them and the food dish on the outside. As the cats could not fathom the mechanical principles used by the designer of the doors, they went through a variety of poorly directed clawings and bitings some one of which eventually caused the door to swing open. The principle was established that those random responses that opened the door and allowed the cat to reach the food were more likely to occur on a second trial, still more likely on a third, and so on until the cat used the correct action at once and escaped without delay. Thorndike formulated this principle as the *law of effect,* according to which the pleasure or satisfaction of eating the food strengthened (reinforced) the responses that had just preceded attainment of this goal. In more technical language, a reinforcing event strengthens any response it follows. Reinforcement in this sense is a formula that has great explanatory power in understanding how animals and children pick up sequences of behavior that are instrumental in securing what they want and avoiding what they fear.

This way of learning is to be distinguished from the conditioned responses of Pavlov's experiments. It is not a question of attaching signals to a strong unconditioned response that itself remains unchanged. What is involved is the strengthening of a response that already exists in the animal's repertory but is not strong enough to emerge early in the effort to escape from the cage. Skinner (1953) uses the term *operant* to describe classes of behavior that exist in an animal's repertory: "the term emphasizes the fact that the behavior operates

101

upon the environment to generate consequences." "In the Pavlovian experiment," he continues, "a reinforcer is paired with a stimulus; whereas in operant behavior it is contingent on a response. Operant reinforcement is therefore a separate process and requires a separate analysis." He refers to the law of effect as *operant conditioning* and to the learning shown in Thorndike's experiments as an increase through reinforcement of the probability that a certain class of operants will occur.

In animal experiments Skinner has shown that by means of operant conditioning it is possible to shape behavior into forms that seem remote from the original repertory. The experimenter, of course, has to start from things the animal already tends to do, but by supplying a reward such as food at precisely the right moment he can gradually reinforce a chosen response, and by taking advantage of the natural variability of behavior he can selectively reinforce those versions of the chosen response that are closest to the new pattern he wants to produce. This is illustrated in teaching a pigeon to peck at a particular spot on the wall of the experimental box. When the learning is complete the pigeon pecks the spot and thus secures the food reward as quickly and expertly as a human being buying candy from a slot machine. But this result is produced by successfully reinforcing bits of behavior that merely tend in the direction of the final peformance. Skinner describes the procedure as follows:

> We first give the bird food when it turns slightly in the direction of the spot from any part of the cage. This increases the frequency of such behavior. We then withhold reinforcements until a slight movement is made toward the spot. This again alters the general distribution of behavior without producing a new unit. We contin-

Operant conditioning techniques have shaped these pigeon's pecking behavior. Similar procedures were used to train pigeons during World War II to guide offensive missiles to their targets.

ue by reinforcing positions successively closer to the spot, then by reinforcing only when the head is moved slightly forward, and finally only when the beak actually makes contact with the spot. We may reach this final response in a remarkably short time. A hungry bird, well adapted to the situation and to the food tray, can usually be brought to respond in this way in two or three minutes. . . .

Operant conditioning shapes hehavior as a sculptor shapes a lump of clay. Although at some point the sculptor seems to have produced an entirely novel object, we can always follow the process back to the original undifferentiated lump (1953, pp. 91-92).

This is all very well for pigeons, one may protest, but does it really apply to human behavior? And there is likely to be vehemence in the protest because people do not like to think of themselves as lumps of clay that can be shaped according to a sculptor's whim. Visions come to mind of a brutal totalitarian state using an educational program based on operant conditioning to reduce its citizens to subservience, though this is at odds with Skinner's own vision as represented in his novel, *Walden Two*, which has its setting in a utopian enclave benignly conditioned toward humanitarian and cultural goals (1952). But we should hesitate to reject our kinship with pigeons, cats, and dogs, even though our larger brains and linguistic capacities introduce much that these creatures do not have. The following experiment by Ayllon and Haughton (1964) shows that under certain circumstances human behavior is influenced in the same direct way by immediate reinforcement and extinction. Two women who had been in a mental hospital for more than three years spent most of their time talking about their somatic complaints—their shot nerves, sleeplessness, aches, pains, and chronic ailments. It was decided to extinguish this talk by paying no attention to it, turning a deaf ear, while showing attentive interest to whatever more appropriate conversation the patients initiated. Under this regime, extended over many days, the frequency of talk about somatic complaints was greatly reduced. To complete the demonstration that the reinforcement program was responsible, the procedure was reversed and the patients were rewarded with attentive interest to their somatic talk, with the result that it soon increased threefold. Then the conditions were changed again, and over another stretch of time the two patients responded to the staff's lack of interest by almost never mentioning their bodily condition.

In such instances it seems natural to say that behavior is shaped by operant conditioning. But Skinner's analogy of the lump of clay is not quite legitimate. Unlike clay, pigeons and people are living organisms, and this characteristic must be included if learning situations are adequately described. The behavior of the pigeons could be shaped because the birds were hungry and wanted food. Shaping would not have occurred if the rewards were of no interest to pigeons. Similarly, the two patients changed the content of their talk because the staff's favor was important to them. They would not have done so for people who meant nothing in their lives. Thus behavior is not shaped in a me-

103

chanical fashion by environmental contingencies, as Skinner maintains; these provide the grounds on which the needs or intentions of living organisms are carried out (Rychlak, 1977). This change, based on more accurate description, brings operant conditioning and the concept of reinforcement into harmony with the idea expressed at the beginning of this chapter that human adaptive behavior implies a constant interaction between person and surroundings, each making demands on the other.

Skinner points out that the concept of operant conditioning helps to understand not only the acquisition of behavior but also its maintenance. On this subject he writes as follows:

> Operant conditioning continues to be effective even where there is no further change which can be spoken of as acquisition or even as improvement in skill. Behavior continues to have consequences and these continue to be important. If consequences are not forthcoming, extinction occurs. When we come to consider the behavior of the organism in all the complexity of its everyday life, we need to be constantly alert to the prevailing reinforcements which maintain its behavior. We may, indeed, have little interest in how that behavior was first acquired. Our concern is only with its present probability of occurrence, which can be understood only through an examination of current contingencies of reinforcement. This is an aspect of reinforcement which is scarcely ever dealt with in classical treatments of learning (1953, p. 98).

This idea is clearly relevant to our behavior in everyday life. Certain regularities in our living, like doing our work each day or seeking familiar sources of amusement, would come to a stop if they did not yield our customary security and satisfactions. With little difficulty we give up our habit of going to the art cinema if the films cease to entertain us. When the same idea is applied to understanding clinical problems, it invites a search not into the patient's past but into the current circumstances that may be serving to reinforce and thus maintain the abnormal behavior. In making a diagnosis the therapist, according to Peterson, should ask the following questions:

> What, in specific detail, is the nature of the problem behavior? What is the person doing, overtly or covertly, which he or someone else defines as problematic and hence changeworthy behavior? What are the antecedents, both internal and external, of the problem behavior and what conditions are in effect at the time the behavior occurs? What are the consequences of the problem behavior? In particular, what reinforcing events, immediate as well as distant, appear to perpetuate the behavior under study? What changes might be made in the antecedents, concomitants, or consequences of behavior to effect desired changes? (1968, p. 57).

In the case of Walter Lilly, described in the previous chapter, both the school authorities and the parents were so worried by the boy's symptoms that they fussed over him, excused him from unpleasant requirements, and allowed him to stay at home, thus rewarding him for complaining about his fears. These

reinforcement contingencies were gradually changed, and although there was
much more to be done to complete the boy's treatment, this application of operant conditioning was valuable in getting things started.

In human instances of operant conditioning the reinforcement can take a variety of forms. Children's behavior can be strengthened by rewards of food, but they are responsive also to reinforcements of a more social character such as attentive interest, approval, and evidences of esteem. These social rewards first acquire their power in early childhood, when the child's satisfactions and sense of security are largely mediated by adult caretakers. In the relative helplessness of infancy, attracting attentive interest becomes a necessary condition for most forms of satisfaction. This provides a believable origin for the value of social rewards, but in accord with Skinner's view of the maintenance of behavior this value would be extinguished if it were merely historical. Attentive interest, for instance, must have continuing meaning, apart from its earlier connection with satisfactions if it is to serve as a reinforcement in shaping and maintaining current behavior. Human behavior is capable of being reinforced by a wide range of social consequences. Although strict behaviorists sometimes shy away from the concept of motivation because of certain past misuses, it is legitimate to say that human beings have a wide range of motives that make them susceptible to reinforcement.

Cognitive Organization

The principles of learning thus far discussed are clearly of great importance in understanding human behavior, both normal and abnormal. But human beings are complex creatures whose behavior becomes elaborately patterned and whose transactions with their surroundings involve more than is commonly implied by stimulus and response. As we saw earlier in the chapter, successful adaptation requires securing adequate information. This often calls for a substantial amount of information processing before responses are possible. Present stimulating conditions have to be worked over in the light of past experience. We are aware of this internal activity when we reflect on experience, think out problems, and weigh different courses of action, but cognitive organization must be postulated for a wider range of processes than those of which we are aware.

Even the behavior of animals often requires the concept of cognitive organization. In his memorable studies of chimpanzees made during the second decade of this century, Köhler found it necessary to assume processes that in human experience we would call insight — a sudden new perception of a problem that shows us how it works. Chimpanzees do not pronounce the syllables "Ah-ha!" or shout "Eureka, I have found it!" but they sometimes act in a way to which these vocalizations would be appropriate. The animals were able to discover, for instance, that the gap between the floor and a high suspended banana could be closed by building a three-story tower of empty boxes. They were able to solve the problem of reaching a distant banana by fitting one stick into the hollow end of another to make a long pole. Particularly striking about these learnings was their suddenness: immobility and sullen staring gave place aburptly to coordinated actions that carried out the animal's new plan with relative efficiency (Köhler, 1925). It is hard to make sense of this without speaking of a cognitive field in which there can be both organization and reorganization, a field relevant to needs and one that controls the pattern in which behavior will unfold. Of similar import were the researches of Tolman (1932) with rats. Even these relatively lowly animals could be seen in conflict situations hesitating, wavering, looking from left to right, exhibiting "vicarious trial-and-error" prior to action. If an animal looks before it leaps we can hardly avoid attributing a function to the looking, a process that yields information about the feasibility of the leap. Tolman spoke of a *cognitive map*: incoming impressions, as he put it, are "worked over and elaborated into a tentative map indicating routes and paths and environmental relationships" (Tolman, 1948). Human beings need much more complicated cognitive maps, helping them to steer not only in physical but also in social space.

In recent years there has been a strong growth of research on cognitive development in children. A monumental figure in this tradition is the Swiss philosopher-psychologist Jean Piaget, who has taken infinite pains to find out how children come to understand the world around them. This learning is not a matter of passive registration; it is accomplished by an active process of investigation. Piaget emphasizes the inherent activity by referring constantly to the child's "construction" of reality (Piaget, 1954). He shows that even an idea like the permanent existence of objects, which seems to adults so central to all thought, is constructed by children through exploratory play. Piaget's subjects, even when less than a year old, did not let a novel object just sit there, but within the limits of their repertory of behavior explored it, tested it out, and discovered what it could be made to do. In this way children construct a cognitive map of the physical world, learning what effects different objects are likely to have on them, and how objects are related to one another.

Social Learning

Children's understanding of the family circle and of human relations in general is likewise a process of construction out of experience. The social cognitive map must include what effects it is possible to have on what people, under what circumstances, and what effects other people are likely to have on oneself. The idea of internal organization becomes especially necessary for understanding these more complex learnings. What is today called *social learning theory* goes beyond traditional ideas of conditioning to include processes, actually a good deal more efficient, whereby we learn to understand and interact with other people.

Part of the construction of social cognitive maps can be accomplished by observing the interactions of other people and by listening to what they say.

Ordinary conversation around the dinner table provides a child with a fund of impressions about human nature, all the more so if the adults are given to gossip. There is also television, and there are books. The listener, the watcher, and the reader can be considered passive only in the sense that they are sitting still. Information input contributes to cognitive organization when it is met by mental activity—when it is received with interested attention, construed in the light of previous experience, and thus effectively worked into the body of knowledge that guides future behavior.

Learning by observation is difficult to explain without reference to internal organization. Commenting on a series of laboratory experiments on imitation, Bandura and Walters (1963) point out that "when a model is provided, patterns of behavior are typically acquired in large segments or in their entirety rather than through a slow, gradual process based on differential reinforcement" (p. 106). A child is capable of copying an admired adult's gait, tone of voice, expressive movements, and specific acts all at once, without being reinforced, like Skinner's pigeons, for a long series of approximations. Furthermore, a number of experiments have shown that reinforcement can be vicarious instead of actual. The degree to which nursery school children copy

Children usually model their behavior, their values, and their identity after their parents.

aggressive behavior shown in a film is influenced by the aggressive character's fate, by whether the behavior yields rewards or punishments (Bandura & Ross, 1963). Observed behavior can be grasped as a whole, not only in its form but in its consequences, a feat of cognitive organization that spares us pain and speeds the growth of social behavior.

The copying of models has been assigned considerable importance in the growth of personality. In psychoanalytic writings the process is called *identification*. Observing the models around them, children from time to time find a person they want to be like, and copy that person as best they can. Identification is defined by Bronfenbrenner as "a motivated attempt to resemble a specific other person" (Bronfenbrenner, 1960). Erikson points out that identification with a model can accomplish a synthesis of desires and capacities that have not before found appropriate channels. "When such synthesis succeeds," he writes, " a most surprising coagulation of constitutional, temperamental, and learned reactions may produce exuberance of growth and unexpected accomplishment" (Erikson, 1963). Parents and other family members are important objects of identification, but, as we saw in the case of Benton Child, children may be unimpressed by these models and want to be like people outside the family circle. Benton himself seems to have copied his ineffectual father, and for a time the resulting faults reappeared in his son. But young Benton presently discovered in the teacher-coach at school someone he wanted much more to be like, and growth and unexpected accomplishment rapidly followed.

Careful study of life histories provides evidence that identification is common and important in individual development. Such study shows also that for most people not one but several identifications have occurred and have been synthesized by a further process of internal organization into a workable whole. When we remark that a young person exhibits the best traits of both parents—or it may be the worst traits—we are recognizing this organization. A person's identity, says Erikson, "develops out of a gradual integration of all identifications," patterned "in order to make a unique and a reasonably coherent whole" (1963, p. 207). This can be a highly adaptive outcome. But the case of Bert Whipley, whose environment provided so few models of stable behavior and who was drawn to those engaged in lawbreaking, reminds us that identifications may have a part in disordered behavior.

Another topic studied by social learning theorists is called *locus of control*. People differ in the extent to which they attribute their behavior to forces within themselves, as compared to outside sources. In the language of social learning theory, Rotter describes this variable as follows:

When a reinforcement is perceived by the subject as following some action of his own but not being entirely contingent upon his action, then, in our culture, it is typically perceived as the result of luck, chance, fate, as under the control of powerful others, or as unpredictable because of the great complexity of forces surrounding him. . . . we have labeled this a belief in *external control*. If the person perceives that the event is contingent upon his own behavior or his own relatively permanent characteristics, we have termed this a belief in *internal control* (Rotter, 1966, p. 1).

Rotter devised a scale to measure this difference. The scale consisted of propositions, to which subjects could express their degree of agreement, ranging from those that emphasize luck, chance, and powerful external influences ("Getting a good job depends mainly on being at the right place at the right time") to those that imply considerable control over outcomes ("Becoming a success is a matter of hard work"). Subsequent research has shown that people do indeed differ on locus of control, that the differences are fairly stable, and that a person's attitude has the character of a general disposition, applying to a variety of situations. Surveying a number of studies, Phares concludes that those who believe in internal control make "greater efforts at coping with or attaining mastery over their environments" and that they accomplish this through "superior cognitive processing" (1976, p. 78). They make more attempts to acquire information, retain it better, and organize it more effectively. It is further characteristic of internals, on the average, that they are more successful at resisting influence and more aware of their capacities for choice and decision. We might expect that these several qualities would lead to successful adaptation. In a review of the evidence, Lefcourt (1976) finds reason to believe that an external control orientation is more common among psychologically disordered people. Feeling helplesss to influence one's surroundings is not conducive to effective adaptation.

The theoretical language used by students of cognitive processes and by social learning theorists is likely to be somewhat different, but they are at one in recognizing the importance of internal organization. We respond not just to incoming stimuli but to what we make of them. And what we make of them depends on how we perceive them in relation to relevant past experience, how we place them on our cognitive maps, and how we construe them according to present need.

THE HUMAN FIELD OF COGNITION AND ACTION

The scope of the cognitive field is enormously enlarged by human powers of abstraction and symbolic representation. An immense extension of the horizon results from the capacity to talk about and think about things that are not immediately present. Solomon Asch describes this in the following words:

> Men live in a field that extends into a distant past and into a far future; the past and the future are to them present realities to which they must constantly orient themselves; they think in terms of days, seasons, and epochs, of good and bad times. . . . Because they can look forward and backward and perceive casual relations, because they can anticipate the consequences of their actions in the future and view their relation to the past, their immediate needs exist in a field of other needs, present and future. Because they consciously relate the past with the future, they are capable of

109

representing their goals to themselves, to aspire to fulfill them, to test them in imagination, and to plan their steps with a purpose.

An integral part of man's extended horizon is the kind of object he becomes to himself. In the same way that he apprehends differentiated objects and their properties he becomes aware of himself as an individual with a specific character and fate; he becomes *self*-conscious. . . . Because he is conscious of himself and capable of reflecting on his experiences, he also takes up an attitude to himself and takes measures to control his own actions and tendencies. The consequence of having a self is that he takes his stand in the world as a person (1952, pp. 120–122).

A further consequence of "having a self" is having a sense of the characteristics of that self and a feeling of its worth. As we saw in the clinical introduction, and as we will see in the following chapters, self-esteem is a highly important ingredient of well-being. Chronically low self-esteem can have damaging side effects like Benton Child's doubt about the paternity of his children or Bert Whipley's inability to take pride in his craftsmanship. One of the commonest complaints of people seeking psychological help is low or damaged self-esteem, and an improvement in this respect is one of the most common outcomes of successful treatment.

To understand behavior in the expanded world of human experience it is necessary to employ concepts capable of representing orientation toward the future. The term *proaction*, in contrast to *reaction*, has been proposed by Henry Murray to signify behavior that is steered by the anticipation of future goals and satisfactions. Under the heading of proactive behavior Murray puts such processes as the making of plans, the imagining of future possibilities, and the execution of serial steps that lead to distant goals—steps that are not necessarily rewarding in themselves (Murray, 1953). But even if we consider much shorter segments of behavior there is reason to give prominence to the future-oriented concept of *plan*. This concept is made central in a theoretical discussion of learning by Miller, Galanter, and Pribram (1960), who show that even so simple an act as hammering a nail into place can be understood only in terms of a plan. The action is initiated and its course guided by a plan to produce a certain result; it ends when that result is attained. Proaction and planning were illustrated earlier in the chapter in the behavior of competent high school seniors getting ready for the transition to college. Human behavior cannot be fully comprehended without such concepts (Rychlak, 1977).

In this chapter we have studied the learning processes whereby from childhood onward we find out how to deal with and live with our surroundings. We spoke of the adaptive process as an interaction between person and environment, each making demands on the other. The outcome at any given moment is a bargain or compromise between these demands. Adaptive strategy is likely to be more satisfactory to the person when adequate relevant information can be brought to bear, when affect can be kept supportive instead of disorganizing, and when ways can be found to take competent action. Human beings, we have seen, are enormously resourceful in processing information, managing emotions, and developing new patterns of behavior. But this resourceful-ness does not guarantee that all will come out well. The same learning proc-esses that produce good adaptation may lead in less favorable circumstances to problems, distress, and disorganized behavior. There are certain problems in development that seem to be especially fraught with maladaptive possibil-ities. To these we turn in the next chapter.

SUGGESTIONS FOR FURTHER READING

In Lois Murphy's *The Widening World of Childhood* (1962) will be found a mine of information about children's powers and methods of coping with the environment. Strategies of adaptation are discussed by R. W. White in *The Enterprise of Living*, 2nd ed., 1976.

Principles of learning are staple fare in most elementary textbooks of psychology. Readers who want further enlightenment on learning in general will find it in H. W. Stevenson's book, *Children's Learning* (1972), an excellent review of the whole subject. The original classic on operant conditioning is B. F. Skinner's *Science and Human Nature* (1953). Imitation and vicarious learning are added to simpler pictures of con-ditioning by A. Bandura & R. H. Walters in *Social Learning and Personality Develop-ment* (1963). On imitation and identification, including recent research, there is *Imi-tation: A Developmental Perspective* by R. Yando, V. Seitz & E. Zigler (1978). The cognitive side of learning is presented in a lucid and cogent style by J. H. Flavell in *Cognitive Development* (1977). Two books that came out at the same time give satis-factory coverage of the interesting topic of locus of control: E. J. Phares, *Locus of Con-trol in Personality* (1976) and H. M. Lefcourt, *Locus of Control: Current Trends in Theory and Research* (1976).

The relation of learning theory to personality is well summarized in Chapter 11 of C. S. Hall & G. Lindzey's *Theories of Personality* (2nd ed., 1968). Its value in clinical work is discerningly set forth by D. E. Peterson, *The Clinical Study of Social Behavior* (1968). J. H. Rychlak has written a book called *The Psychology of Rigorous Human-ism* (1977). This is a difficult book, philosophical and theoretical, but it will repay careful study, especially for those who feel that natural science accounts of behavior tend to miss or misrepresent important aspects of human beings.

Republican Automatons (1920) by George Grosz. Collection, The Museum of Modern Art, New York. Advisory Committee Fund.

4
Development
and
Organization
of Personality

If people who feel the need of psychological help always complained of a neatly circumscribed trouble, like being afraid to cross streets, their treatment could be a straightforward application of the simplest learning principles described in the last chapter. Often, however, the complaint is not narrowly limited. The troubled person says, "I don't know who I am," "I don't feel right with people," or "I can't find anything that interests me." These global complaints are doubtless the result of learning, but favorable change through relearning is not likely to be simple. The complaint almost certainly involves several aspects of the person's life that may well form an organized pattern. When patterns have to be changed, the helping process will require more talk and more time. The organization of personality must be understood before appropriate steps can be taken toward betterment.

For this reason we devote this chapter to the development and organization of personality. Growth is a continuous process. It does not pass through sharply separated steps, divide itself into neat chapters, and move toward maturity one aspect at a time. But we cannot describe it lucidly by talking about everything at once, and there is justification for the idea that the most important problems have their critical periods at different times of life. In this chapter we therefore follow a rough chronology of significant developmental problems, considering them as phases of growth that are normally traversed without mishap but that sometimes give rise to lasting difficulties of living.

To study development implies a belief that early experience has an influence on later behavior. The case of Walter Lilly in Chapter 2 showed the importance of examining the present situation, with a view to discerning the strictly contemporary rewards and reinforcements that may be holding some piece of abnormal behavior in place. But it was also true that Walter kept responding submissively to other boys when this was working to his disadvantage, and that he continued his noisily demanding tactics at home when his grandmother was no longer present to assure their success. There is a certain inertia in strategies that at some point in life have served us well. We do not easily give them up when pressed by new and different circumstances. They may lead us, moreover, to make choices that significantly affect the course of further development. Without the help he received, Walter Lilly might have continued indefinitely taking no social initiative, thus unwittingly choosing an isolated pattern of life. In this sense early experience tends to make a continuous contribution to the growth and organization of personality.

DEPENDENCE AND DEPRIVATION

Childhood Dependence

Children begin life in a state of virtually complete helplessness. Discomforts are removed and gratifications provided almost entirely through the actions of caretakers. Outside of restless activity and the very important act of crying, there is not much that infants can do about their troubles. In the early months, life revolves around hunger and its satisfaction. With feedings are associated many additional sources of pleasure: stimulation of the mouth; the agreeable acts of sucking and swallowing; being picked up, rocked, and cuddled.

To start from such helplessness may seem a liability in view of the independence that will be expected when infants reach adulthood, make their way in the world, and themselves become caretakers. Should we not try to hurry babies out of their dependence and start them promptly on the long climb?

Recent thought and research have gone strongly against this prescription. Two studies in particular became cornerstones of the idea that a dependent relation with the mother was conducive to health and development. Ribble (1941, 1943) collected evidence in a children's hospital that babies prosper better when given plentiful mothering; that is, when they are held, patted, cuddled, rocked, and given a surplus of loving attention beyond the strict necessities of daily care. Babies thus treated showed stronger respiration, firmer sucking and swallowing, better digestion, and superior physical development. Shortly afterwards, Spitz (1945) made a comparative study of children reared in a foundling home and children reared by their mothers in the nursery of a penal institution. The foundling home was a good one, but one adult had to take care of seven or more children with little time to spare. Spitz found that rate of mortality and susceptibility to illness were higher in the foundling home, motor and language development were retarded, and signs of distress, such as screaming and odd repetitive behavior, were more common. He gave the name "hospitalism" to the pattern of defects observed among the foundling children, and he argued that a close bond with the mother fostered security and confidence in the child. A few years later the argument was clinched in

Establishing a warm affectional bond between parents and baby is an essential requirement for healthy psychological development of the baby (and of the parents).

a monograph by Bowlby (1952) that had a powerful influence on childrearing and on institutional practice. Today it is generally accepted that a strong attachment to caretakers, even though the relation is a dependent one, provides "a secure base or haven" that is advantageous for future development (Mussen, Conger, & Kagan, 1979).

Effects of Early Deprivation

This view of the value of attachment leads one to ask what happens to children who do not receive adequate mothering. Do the effects persist, so that the damage can be considered permanent? An early study by Goldfarb (1955) indicated that the consequences could be lasting and serious. Fifteen children brought up in institutions to the age of three were carefully matched with fifteen whose early years had been spent in the more favorable climate of foster homes. Tested and examined at about 12 years of age, the two groups proved to be significantly different in several respects. The institutional children were behind on various tests of intellectual ability, their speech was less well developed, they were rated lower on friendly contact with examining adults, and in an experimental game they more often broke the rules without signs of guilt.

This picture of impaired development received support from experiments with a variety of animals. Chickens, kittens, puppies, and chimpanzees showed developmental deficits when reared under conditions that prevented normal mothering.

Particularly pertinent are the experiments made by Harlow (1958) in which baby monkeys were provided with mechanical mother surrogates. The artificial mothers, made of cloth or of wire, provided abundant milk through a conveniently placed nipple, emitted bodily warmth, and were set in positions suitable for clinging; in all these respects, they were designed to be good mothers. Harlow was able to show, in the first place, that clinging and contact are of great importance for satisfaction and security. To a baby monkey a cloth mother is far more acceptable than one made of wire. In the second place, observing the animals' development into adulthood, he showed that the mechanically reared monkeys remained almost completely unresponsive to other monkeys, so much so that very few of the females produced offspring and only one was observed to try to nurse her young. The central deprivation to which they had been exposed, that of interaction with a living member of the species, resulted in a permanent incapacity for social response (Harlow & Harlow, 1961). But in further experiments it was possible to show that the mother was not the sole source of this social development. Motherless infants raised in groups of four, or raised in separate cages but allowed a daily period of play together, showed normal social and sexual development, permitting the conclusion that "opportunity for infant–infant interaction may compensate for lack of mothering" (Harlow & Harlow, 1962). Some form of early warm and friendly contact seems essential to keep the monkey from developing into a surly, suspicious adult.

The animal experiments, of course, represent more extreme deprivations than those suffered by institutional children. A finding by Provence and Lipton (1962) shows that when institution-reared children are adopted into families they make "dramatic gains" in development, although it was still possible to detect "residual impairments of mild to severe degree in capacity for forming emotional relationships," and in certain other aspects of growth, including impulse control and imaginative play. The abundant research that has now been done on this topic, according to Clarke and Clarke (1976) who review it, suggests an even more cautious interpretation. Intellectual deficits, at least, can be largely compensated by later improvements in the environment or by timely intervention. There is still evidence, however, that difficulty with emotional relationships may be lasting (Rutter, 1970).

Adaptive and Maladaptive Possibilities

Establishing a firm bond between child and caretakers should be the chief task of the first year of life. When successful, this results in what Erikson (1963) calls a "*basic sense of trust*." Eventually, however, the dependence of this period must be outgrown. Adequate behavior in adulthood requires a large capacity for independence in making decisions, carrying enterprises forward, meeting responsibilities, and taking care of others. But we must be careful not to exaggerate the needful level of independence. Throughout life we are necessarily dependent to some extent on those around us. Under conditions of stress and sickness we legitimately become more so, and during old age there is a further decline in the appropriateness of trying to be self-sufficient. Dependence need not be rooted out as if it were inherently evil. The adaptive goal is a flexibility that makes it possible to be dependent — and to be independent — in appropriate relation to circumstances.

One maladaptive possibility is what we might call *compulsive self-sufficiency*, a tendency to be independent without much regard for circumstances. The lost motorist who will not ask the way stands as a cartoon for this devotion to self-sufficiency. Familiar to hospital nurses are patients who want to do everything themselves, resisting care and even imperiling their recovery by refusing to relax and rest. Equally familiar to youth workers are young delinquents who reject all help because of a determination to be beholden to no one. Similarly disconcerting are the elderly who insist on taking walks and going shopping alone when they can no longer reliably remember the way back. In these and other ways, compulsive self-sufficiency can stand in the way of receiving help when it is available, appropriate, and necessary for better adaptation.

The opposite maladaptive possibility is shown when *dependent tendencies*

117

"DON'T BE SO DAMNED IMPATIENT AND HELPLESS! JUST READ THE COMPASS. WE'LL FIND IT FOR SURE IF WE DRIVE AROUND A FEW MORE TIMES."

The compulsively self-sufficient person is often as poorly adapted to life situations as extremely dependent people are.

persist at a strength that is unlikely to receive favorable response. A perfect example was provided in Chapter 2 by Benton Child, who through parental indulgence developed an expectation of easy provision and who thus could not deal with the responsibilities of being a husband, father, and family provider. Friendships sometimes perish because one partner demands an exorbitant share of attention and support. In marital discord a common complaint is the charge, often made by both parties, that the spouse is not being sufficiently helpful. Mutual relations are apt to become difficult when dependent hungers get in the way.

These maladaptive patterns probably do not owe their existence to what happened during the first year of life. They represent strategies developed over time that at some period have been highly successful. The simplest hypothesis would be that because of circumstances—such as Benton Child's spoiling parents—these strategies have been strongly reinforced and thus made resistant to change. But there is often more to it: the trait in question is related to other aspects of personality. In Child's case there was congruence between his dependent behavior and his temperamental passivity. Dependence may become connected with power, a means of forcing people to be attentive and helpful. Compulsive independence may be involved in separating oneself from disliked parents, in affirming one's image of self-made success, or in fighting off the fear of old age. Maladaptive patterns are often reinforced in more than one way, which makes it easier to understand their persistence in inappropriate circumstances.

EARLY GROWTH OF COMPETENCE

Exploratory Play

Careful observation shows that even from the beginning there is another side to the infant besides passive dependence. Very early there are signs of spontaneous activity, taking such forms as following and fixating with the eyes or exploring and experimenting with the hands. The nature of this activity becomes clearer toward the middle of the first year, when manipulation becomes an absorbing occupation. By the time they are a year old, children may be spending as much as five or six hours of their waking days in exploratory play that is not related to the hungers, pains, and anxieties that still require the mother's ministrations. They develop their repertory of actions by manipulating all objects within reach; they test in playful babbling their power to make various kinds of sound; and they learn about the properties of their own bodies by successive attempts to sit up, crawl, and take steps in an upright position. This kind of activity appears to be self-rewarding, and its biological function seems to lie in learning about the properties of things and what can be done with them—in other words, in becoming competent to deal with the environment (White, 1959).

The zest for active exploration presently invades the sphere of the mother's ministrations. It is discovered that water can be dribbled from the wet washcloth onto the floor, that milk will spread in an interesting way over a flat surface, that utensils produce a gratifying series of sounds when banged or thrown from the high chair. David Levy (1955) selects what he calls "the battle of the spoon" to illustrate the nature of such actions and their relation to being

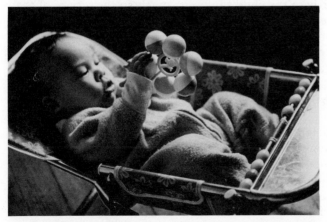

Babies become acquainted with the world by exploring and manipulating objects with their mouths and their hands. Do you think any feature of this toy will escape the youngster's attention?

mothered. One day the child seizes the spoon and undertakes to load it and steer it into its mouth. As the spoon is likely at first to miss its target and to reach some other part of the face upside down, the maneuver is far from resulting in a more efficient intake of food; but the child may continue it insistently, resisting the mother's attempts to recapture her maternal role. Levy points out that the behavior cannot be classed as aggressive; it is not done to annoy the mother, however surely it may produce this result when she thinks about cleaning up. It is part of an urge to do things autonomously, to control the environment as much as possible through one's own initiative. The most important reward in children's explorations lies in the feeling of efficacy that comes from producing an intended result through expended effort. This is something no mother can bestow.

During the second and third years of life children emerge rapidly from their early condition of helplessness. One of the major advances is learning to walk. This makes it possible to explore the house and yard, to venture into the street, and sometimes to escape from parental supervision. Particularly important is the increased mastery of speech, permitting children to name objects, form concepts, issue commands, grasp more fully what is said to them. In due course they discover the powerful properties of the word "no" and begin to test the extent to which they can resist and control the human part of their environment. These experiments usher in a time that has often been called the period of two-year-old negativism. When the child begins to issue or resist commands, there is a direct confrontation of wills, a clear-cut problem of who is going to prevail. The child, as Stern (1930) expressed it, now "realizes himself as a living entity, as one complete center of power; he wishes to affirm himself, his existence, his importance, and to increase it." The parents, too, have something to affirm, partly in the child's interest, partly in the service of their own pride. Today we regard as harsh the old-fashioned advice that at this point in life it is necessary to "break the child's will" and "show who is boss," but no experienced parent will suppose it possible to give the child's urges toward competence a totally free rein.

Competence and Self-Esteem

The attainment of competence thus begins in playful exploration and experimentation with one's physical and human surroundings. The process continues to be important through all stages of development (White, 1960). It becomes less random and playful as the needed skills turn into intentional goals, but older children and adolescents can be deeply absorbed in mastering athletic skills, acquiring social abilities, and learning to drive a car, and adults, too, can be heavily concerned with problems of competence. Indeed, competence may become more important over time because of its close connection with self-esteem.

There can be no doubt that self-esteem is affected by the income of esteem received from others. There can also be no doubt that a good many kinds of excellence have to be socially defined before children can have any way of judging success or failure. But we must not suppose that self-esteem is wholly a matter of esteem income—that no coin can ever be minted within. When an act comes out as intended, a person experiences a *feeling of efficacy*, of having effectively influenced the environment. This feeling feeds into the person's *sense of competence*, the more general experience of being a competent person who can produce desired effects. And sense of competence is a vital root of self-esteem. Silverberg (1952) put the matter strongly:

> Throughout life self-esteem has these two sources: an inner source, the degree of effectiveness of one's own activity; and an external source, the opinions of others about oneself. Both are important, but the former is the steadier and more dependable one. Unhappy and insecure is the man who, lacking an adequate inner source for self-esteem, must depend for this almost wholly upon external sources. It is the condition seen by the psychotherapist almost universally among his patients (p. 29).

What conditions can be considered conducive to the development of a strong sense of competence and hence to well-founded self-esteem? The answer proposed by Stallibrass (1979) for preschool children's play groups will put us on the right track. Play groups are most successful when there is abundant space, indoors and outdoors, and a good supply of materials likely to evoke the children's motor and creative interests. Under these favorable circumstances, which minimize crowding and competition for materials, the children occupy themselves for long periods with little adult supervision. The adult's role consists of occasional umpiring and occasional help, but Stallibrass points out that activities need rarely be suggested and that rewards beyond a few appreciative words are superfluous. Action in the service of efficacy is spontaneous and self-rewarding.

Ideal conditions, of course, are not usually possible. In depressed environments the natural flowering described here may be crushed almost from the start (Connolly & Bruner, 1974). But it is probably a sound conclusion that the growth of a sense of competence is best supported when children's initiatives are allowed to go forward as far as is practicable and safe, when they are coached in things they want to learn, and when whatever they do well receives appreciation. Giving this appreciation requires in the adults a generous spirit, free from envy and hostility, ready to respect another's performance—a spirit not always easy to maintain through the wear and tear of dealing with children.

How a sense of competence develops will undoubtedly prove to be far more complex than these descriptions imply. The growth history may be different in the physical, social, and intellectual spheres. When observation and measurement are made more exact, further subdivisions will probably suggest them-

121

selves. The relation between the child's intrinsic feelings of efficacy and the surrounding social input seems likely to be intricate. Promising research in these directions has been reported by Harter and associates (Harter, 1978).

Maladaptive Possibilities

When we think of the obstacles to developing a strong sense of competence we may find it hard to believe that anyone can have too much. But *overconfidence* is a not unknown human characteristic that can interfere seriously with adaptive behavior. A combination of high natural abilities, unusual opportunities, and exceptional social rewards may lead to an overconfidence and conceit that somehow escape the trimming down commonly provided by circumstances and other people. A college senior, apple of his parents' eyes, intelligent, articulate, handsome, and popular, was defeated for an important class office, his first serious failure. For a few days he was depressed, thought about suicide, and blamed his parents for not preparing him for frustration. Fortunately the absurdity of these reactions presently dawned on him, and he emerged from the experience a little sadder but wiser and more realistic about himself. Extreme conceit persisting in adult life is usually to be regarded not as simple overconfidence but as a defensive reaction to anxiety along lines we will study in the next chapter.

The opposite maladaptive possibility has been called historically an *inferiority complex*. As mentioned in the first chapter, this concept was introduced by Alfred Adler, who gave it an important place in his theory of anxiety disorders. It refers not merely to being inferior, which most of us are in a good many respects. It deserves to be considered a *complex* only when the person continually makes unfavorable comparisons between self and others, covering far more lines of excellence than any one individual could hope to carry. For example, a young man at a party hears someone tell a story well, he wishes he might possess this excellence and laments his inferiority as a storyteller. The next moment someone else entertains with a song, and he feels miserable that he cannot do likewise. Then dancing starts, and he has a chance to deplore his mediocrity at that. A single evening will provide him with an opportunity to feel inferior in a dozen ways. But it is not these dozen inferiorities that trouble him. It is rather the overall fact that he does not have sufficient competence anywhere to form a nucleus of self-esteem and satisfy the self as a whole. If he could find some real excellence of his own, he would be willing to forego distinction in storytelling, singing, and dancing.

Normal self-esteem is dependent on only a small range of excellencies. Failure in many areas may mean little if it is compensated by success in just one area. As Allport (1943) observed, "Only in terms of ego-psychology can we account for such fluid compensation. Mental health and happiness . . . depends upon the *person* finding some area of success *somewhere*. The *ego* must be satisfied."

122

Adler traced the origin of the inferiority complex to early family life and to belittlement of the small child's attempts to be efficacious. Too strenuous a put-down program by parents or by older siblings makes it difficult for children to feel that their desires can have appreciable influence. Other circumstances contribute to inferiority feelings: low energy, handicaps, poor health, limited capacity, prejudice, a deprived environment. But it is also true, as we saw in the case of Benton Child, that adult sense of competence can be blunted by too quick provision for every need and too complete protection from every difficulty. At all events, inferiority feelings interfere badly with taking initiative and with feeling contentment in human relations.

DISCIPLINE AND SELF-CONTROL

During the second and third years children increasingly run afoul of the law. At this stage of life the law is represented by parental expectations and discipline. Children discover that there are many restrictions on freedom. They must not order parents around or be rude to visitors. There are also things that they are supposed to do, such as sharing toys with other children and putting away the playthings that a busy day has scattered all over the house and

Asserting one's will forcefully is an important part of establishing self-control and autonomy.

123

yard. The world proves to be full of strange moral hazards, and one must learn how to accommodate one's desires to the often mysterious requirements of the social order.

The learning problem involves internalizing a set of restrictions that either control one's impulses or require behavior not dictated by them. An urge to hit another child must be controlled, the behavior of sharing toys must be produced. Demands for these accomplishments come originally from parents, and the extent to which they will be internalized depends on the relation between child and parents. In simplest terms, the sacrifices of self-control may be worthwhile if they please people you want to please; they may not seem so to children who do not like or trust their parents. In an influential analysis in social learning terms, Bandura and Walters (1963, ch. 4) showed how self-control was influenced both by direct parental rewards and by copying parental models.

The problem of discipline should not be seen simply as a struggle between the child's desires and the parents' restrictions. What the parents require is not a complete suppression of impulses; they ask rather that impulses be guided into socially acceptable channels. As Murray (1938) has pointed out, cultural and parental prescriptions can usually be described as "time-place-mode-object formulas which are allowed or insisted upon for the expression of individual needs."

> A child is allowed to play during the day but not at night (time). He may defecate in the toilet but not on the floor (place). He may push other children but not hit them with a mallet (mode). He may ask his father but not a stranger in the street for money (object). No need has to be inhibited permanently. If an individual is of the right age and chooses the permitted time, the permitted place, the permitted mode and the permitted object, he can objectify any one of his needs (p. 136).

Children are asked to pattern their behavior in ways that may seem at first difficult and frustrating, but the culture does not require the complete surrender of fundamental desires. In the end it is no hardship to use the toilet if one is available or to give up playing in the street if there are other places to play.

These considerations are necessary in order to grasp the true nature of the growth problem when discipline and control are the issues. There is almost always something for children to do if they are able and willing to do it. The crucial point here is willingness: can children pattern their behavior in expected ways without damage to sense of competence and hence to self-esteem? Here we must remember that, resistant as they may be to constraint, children want to grow up. Erikson (1963) points out that meeting a parental requirement can be a matter not of surrender but of pride in accomplishment. In a study of child development made in a situation where many parents believed in maximum permissiveness, it was observed that the children often insisted on feeding themselves, dressing themselves, and using the toilet in adult fashion before the parents had taken steps toward training (Chess, Thomas, & Birch,

124

1959). Becoming socialized entails sacrifices, but it is not entirely a bad bargain. Prosocial behavior can connect with important impulses and can contribute to a sense of competence. Reviewing studies that extend throughout childhood, Mussen and Eisenberg-Berg (1977) notice impressive and consistent individual differences in children's acquisition of prosocial tendencies. These differences are shaped by the character of socializing experiences as well as by certain traits in the children.

Maladaptive Possibilities

Departures from a normal course of development are most likely to occur when parental training takes the form either of *coercive discipline* or of *lax indulgence*. Substantial experimental evidence exists for the different effects of these parental attitudes (Becker, 1964).

Coercive methods of discipline do not encourage children's positive interest in becoming socialized. Whether they are tricked into obedience by clever parental devices, ridiculed and made to feel shame, or threatened with painful and terrifying punishments, they will have a sense of being forced and there will be little willingness in the response. They are left with no middle ground between a hopeless fight and unconditional surrender.

The effects of coercive discipline can be conveniently grouped into two patterns. One solution can best be described as *anxious conformity*. Desires and resentments are suppressed, and the person becomes a model of cleanliness, goodness, sharing, and all-around propriety. If these traits persist into later life they may create an outwardly good adjustment to society and its requirements, but behavior will lack spontaneity and confidence, and the person will be ill-prepared when the environment begins to make conflicting demands. There is also the danger, so memorably disclosed in the study of authoritarian personality by Adorno and others (1950), that rigidly conventional behavior will go with self-righteousness and aggressive blaming of other people and outgroups.

The other consequence of coercive discipline is an enduring *resentment against demands*, an essentially negative attitude even when overt resistance is impossible. In extreme cases the person becomes a compulsive nonconformist, doing everything in a way that obviously differs from social expectations. In less extreme cases, perhaps with some outward conformity, rebellion will leak out in irritating ways like missing appointments or keeping everyone waiting. This guerrilla warfare against demands, often unwitting and compulsive, has little resemblance to nonconformity and criticism of the social order arrived at later through mature judgment. Indeed, it may interfere with such purposes: the person cannot brook the demands made to participate in organized social action.

In recent years cultural values in the United States have swung significantly away from coercive attitudes. For a while, at least, permissiveness became the

125

magic word in mental health advice on childrearing. But permissiveness, especially in parents unsure of their values, often degenerated into *lax indulgence*. Under such a regime few serious demands were made; children were not required to pick up toys, inhibit aggression, help at home, or even be present at regular meal hours. Permissiveness was sometimes carried to the point at which adult friends hated to call at the house, knowing that the atmosphere would be too child-centered for serious conversation. The effect of such laxity is to delay the growth of control: children are given too little incentive to master impulses, so they remain longer their victim. This is a handicap in any situation involving others. It makes trouble for the child in play group or nursery school, still more so during regular schooling when increasing amounts of control and organization become necessary. There is reason to suppose that excessive indulgence, with consequent lack of training for serious application and work, has contributed to the frequency of running away, experimenting with impulses, seeking unusual experiences, using drugs, and feeling confused and lost in the world. If coercive discipline tends to make people "uptight," unlimited indulgence may have made some of them uncomfortably "downloose."

AGGRESSION AND ITS MANAGEMENT

As used in this book, *aggression* refers to tendencies that aim at injury and destruction. When fully conscious, such tendencies are accompanied by feelings of anger and hate. Prompt arousal of aggression undoubtedly has survival value in precarious, competitive conditions of life, but for civilized living our endowment in this respect seems all too strong. Many worthy enterprises have been ruined by the intrusion of our angry, destructive, and hateful inclinations, and we have not run up a good historical record for living peaceably together.

Nature of Aggression

The pattern of rage emerges in infancy as a general struggling and vigorous flailing of the arms and legs. The situations that most clearly evoke this response involve interference with activities and a restriction of movement, as in dressing or changing the diapers; and the child's movements, although not yet directed at an object, are of some service in getting rid of the restriction. In the second half of the first year, the child's manipulative activities, in themselves exploratory rather than aggressive, may lead at times to frustration and pain. An animal too roughly explored, for instance, may act in self-defense; and the child, perhaps after being consoled, may try rather insistently to repeat the rough treatment. During the second year of life, there is clear emergence of acts with an aggressive intent. Striking and kicking may be "carried out with a mischievous facial expression and with clear signs of enjoyment. . . .

 126

Finally the child clearly realizes that what he does *hurts*. The child has experienced pain and discomfort from aggression directed toward him, and he now connects his inner experience with his own overt activity. This usually takes place during the third year of life" (Mittelmann, 1954, pp. 161–262). It is now possible to speak of truly aggressive, hostile behavior.

In childhood, aggression manifests itself in relatively crude forms such as angry outbursts and tantrums. The tantrum is a forceful method of securing what one wants, but it meets with decreasing success as the months go by and the child grows more capable. The restrictive force comes from the mother, who discovers that if she does not curb tantrums in her child she will have to curb them in herself. This illustrates the difficulty of the educative process, but children are entitled to help in controlling their explosive outbursts. No child enjoys being in a temper. The violent force of the urge may even arouse anxiety. What children want is not to be angry but to remove the cause of frustration. In the course of time they will be able to learn that frustrations can be better removed if anger is controlled sufficiently to permit coherent and perceptive action. One learns, for instance, that losing one's temper in an argument makes one both ridiculous and ineffective. Young children are ready enough to express aggression, but they are also soon able to realize that they get better results by controlling it. On this, parents and teachers can build.

It soon happens, however, that aggression is caught up in more complex patterns, and these create far greater adjustive difficulties. Children's daily social experiences, taking place mostly within the family circle, occur with people on whom they are dependent, whom they love, but who make demands

Fighting releases a head of emotional steam, but it is also an attempt to change frustrating circumstances. It is important to teach children not only self-control, but also more competent ways of dealing with frustration.

that arouse aggressive feelings. Parents meet needs and give affection but also exert pressure toward socialization. One of the things that complicates human relationships even in the earliest years is the alternation of love and hate that we call *ambivalence*. The objects of love and aggression are the same; at times they call out these conflicting feelings practically at the same moment. Children soon discover that there can be no easy solution to this problem. If anger, complaints, and criticism are expressed too freely they are likely to invite return expressions of hostility and to imperil future harmony. Frustration begets aggression but aggression may bring about a disastrous loss of security and esteem. Thus aggression is always potentially present in the family circle as an added complication to the other problems of emotional growth.

The problem of adjusting loves and hates within the family circle is well illustrated in the example of sibling rivalry. With the birth of a new sibling, the older child has to accept a reduction in parental attention. The baby is seen enjoying privileges of dependence that the older one is in the process of outgrowing. Inevitably jealousy and hostile impulses are experienced, but aggressive behavior does not remove the frustration nor win back the parents' love. The birth of a younger sibling sometimes upsets a child badly, as we saw in the case of Bert Whipley in Chapter 2. It takes time to discover possible rewards in the role of the bigger child who perhaps helps with the baby's care but in any event is esteemed for being more mature.

AGGRESSION AND COMPETENCE

There is a reciprocal relation between aggression and competence. A situation with which one is competent to deal need not be more than momentarily frustrating. Much has been written about the desirability of expressing aggression instead of bottling it up in continuously simmering resentment. There may be a certain relief in so doing, but more valuable than blowing off a head of emotional steam is to produce some real change in the frustrating circumstances. Clinical workers often encounter situations, like that described in Chapter 2 between Walter Lilly and his father, in which a parent and child repeatedly arrive at an angry impasse that neither of them really wants. Clearly it would be absurd to encourage Walter and his father to ventilate their aggression, which is what they do anyway. What must be learned is a more competent way of dealing with the situation, so that the impasse is avoided and the anger is not constantly refueled. Sometimes an angry parent, given a wise tip on how better to handle an infuriating child, comes to the next appointment with a report of success, a restored sense of competence, and not a trace of remaining anger.

In the residential treatment of emotionally disturbed children, in whom aggression is often a stubborn problem, it has been found valuable to stress not just self-control but the discovery of more competent ways of dealing with frustrations. More effective, according to Trieschman, Whittaker, and Brendtro (1969), than trying to stop a piece of aggressive behavior is to propose alternative behavior that to some degree expresses the child's feelings but in a way is less disruptive and self-defeating. A child can be taught, for instance, "a way to ask to join a game instead of stealing the ball." Trieschman has made a study of tantrums, showing how at each stage the child even in fury tries to maintain some effect on the environment and accomplish some kind of purpose. The angry child's wild alternatives, such as "either fix it or I'll smash it," can be countered with a more reasonable proposal to try to fix it or else replace it. Naturally such maneuvers do not work on every occasion, but in the course of time the steady pressure to find more modulated, more effective ways of dealing with frustration is heeded, and the need to blow one's top is thereby reduced.

Maladaptive Possibilities

Successful management of aggression implies a flexible system of controls and outlets. Crude manifestations, like crude perceptions, give place to discerning ways of dealing with frustration, and it is an especially happy outcome when anger is channeled toward social evils about which something constructive can be accomplished. A flexible system of controls and outlets is most easily attained when the child begins development in an atmosphere that is tolerant but firm on the subject of aggression. Maladjustive possibilities lie in too wide a divergence in either direction: when little attempt is made to curb aggression, or when the attempt is so strenuous that no outlets are left for reducing the tension.

Inadequate curbing of aggression can obviously lead to serious maladaptive consequences. In thinking about them we must include not only the aggressor but the victims of aggression. Recently there has been rising interest in so-called "battered children"—children who have received crude violence at home—who prove more numerous than previously supposed. Instances of wife-beating are similarly not hard to find in clinical and social records. Many blows have been dealt people through their property and their sentiments by seemingly senseless vandalism. Juvenile delinquency and crime leave behind them a trail of consequences decidedly maladaptive for the victims. And it cannot be supposed that an uncontrolled tendency to blow one's top is conducive to congenial social living.

Aggressive and delinquent behavior should not, of course, be attributed to family influence alone. The following case is neither new nor rare (Evans, 1954). A boy is brought up in a large family in desperate financial straits. He is given rough treatment by older siblings, receives scant affection from his harassed mother, is early turned out into the streets of a badly organized neighborhood. The family has a bad reputation with the police, and he is treated roughly in that quarter. He thus grows up in an environment where aggression

129

is curbed only by other aggressions, where the obvious avenue to security lies in being more toughly aggressive than the other person, where at the same time serious frustrations constantly mobilize his hostility to a maximum. In situations of this kind, which appear frequently in the history of delinquents and criminals, poor control of aggression is by no means the only problem. It is true, nevertheless, that when other frustrations are severe the failure of family and neighborhood control over aggression leaves wide open an outlet that can have serious maladaptive consequences for both the individual and society. On slum streets, according to those who have lived there, aggression in the form of fighting is given active social encouragement rather than control (Lewis, 1961; Brown, 1965).

The maladaptive consequences that result for the aggressor from hostility openly expressed often take the form of punishment, rejection, and restraint. Even in the milder form of badly controlled temper there are consequences of rejection and social isolation that narrow the possibilities for adaptive growth.

Too strenuous curbing of aggression has a different series of consequences. The most obvious pattern is that of a person who can never openly express aggression nor even become aware of hostile feelings. Such people show serious blocks in asserting themselves even in the most legitimate fashion. They must avoid aggression by such wide margin, so to speak, that they cannot express any desires with which it might be remotely connected. We can scarcely assume that hostility is dead in these people; we must therefore suppose that it is aroused but somehow spends itself internally. Perhaps the internal reaction brings about a kind of self-hate and feeling of unworthiness, or perhaps the anger is bottled up with no outlet except a chronic raising of the blood pressure or some other physiological effect. Neither consequence is compatible with good adjustment or good health. Horney (1937) described the "vicious circle" that is likely to operate when aggression is too heavily suppressed. Children who have to stifle their hostility find themselves placed all too often in a weak position. They cannot defend themselves or demand justice. An unfair punishment has to be accepted, favoritism toward a sibling has to be overlooked or taken as a true sign of one's worthlessness. Such children simply must put up with it when others encroach on their rights and wishes, thus allowing others to do this more and more. A feeling that one is a weak, helpless person in a hostile world results.

If suppression is a little less drastic there may be room for chronic feelings of resentment. Blocked angry impulses are sometimes capable of changing their objects and aims and emerging in a kind of delayed action. Suppose that a man's ire is aroused at work when his boss unjustly criticizes him. He says nothing, but when he gets home he kicks open the front door, yells at the dog, criticizes his wife's cooking, decides to attend a political rally that is aiming to throw the incumbent party out of power, and goes to bed and dreams that he knocked a heavier opponent out of the ring. The postponements and ramifications of aggression are many and subtle. Nursery school teachers know the

130

sight of angry and distressed children throwing things around, breaking toys, hitting other children, not because of anything that happened in school but because of chronic frustration at home. Black writers, having endured the lifelong frustration of social injustice, provide the strongest testimony to the destructive effects of chronic anger and resentment on every aspect of personal development (Wright, 1940; Baldwin, 1955; Grier and Cobbs, 1968).

Chronic resentment can be woven into a pattern of personality that is partially successful, though with maladaptive costs. This pattern has been described as a *derogatory style* (White, 1976) characterized by finding fault with just about everything and everybody. The person so disposed seems selectively aware of ineptitude, deception, self-seeking, and corruption in the surrounding world. Such a person's conversation is filled with criticisms, sometimes well-supported with information. This strategy serves the purpose of representing oneself as a shrewd person who cannot be fooled. It accommodates a steady flow of resentment and at the same time may intimidate others, who fear that they themselves will later be described in derogatory fashion. The maladaptive cost becomes apparent in closer human relations. The derogatory style does not invite trustful friendships; people find it hard to love someone whose chief output is belittlement. Accommodating so much aggression in one's adaptive style creates the risk of personal isolation.

In discussing authoritarian personality we have already mentioned the pattern of highly controlled, conventional behavior with an outlet of open aggression toward outgroups. The targets are pictured as enemies or as moral inferiors toward whom hostility is appropriate. This outward channeling of aggression is unfortunately assisted by a variety of societal devices that tend to legitimatize violence (Sanford & Comstock, 1971).

MENTAL DEVELOPMENT AND EDUCATION

As we advance to developmental problems that come to a peak further along in children's lives, we assume that the new experiences of later childhood and adolescence provide opportunities to learn new behavior and unlearn inappropriate old behavior. In the spirit of ideas advanced by Sullivan (1953), we picture the child's enlarging world as offering a chance to correct those residues of family training that may have been harmful. Being at school and mingling with other children bring new kinds of experience: studying, competition, group memberships, and cooperation. These enlarging situations do not necessarily make for a corresponding enlargement of personality, but they give this a chance to happen.

Competence During the School Years

Children's sense of competence and self-esteem are strongly affected by their experience in the family circle. Occasionally they are so blasted by criticism and ridicule that children can no longer trust their own experience of competence. Usually the balance between encouragement and discouragement is more favorable to self-esteem. In any event an important chapter in establishing self-esteem has already been written before a child leaves the bosom of the family.

A whole new arena opens when children venture outside, particularly when they go to school. In the worlds of school and playground they find an opportunity for a new deal in the estimation of competence. In the schoolroom there are new tasks, new challenges to competence, and children soon come to realize that these tasks have ultimate significance in the grown-up world, which gives them, as Erikson (1953) expresses it, "a token sense of participation in the world of adults" (p. 212). Perhaps this participation can be sensed most easily in learning to master tools and produce useful objects, but the "three R's," if at first a little abstract, can soon be appreciated as part of the equipment needed to take part in adult affairs. At its best the school serves to develop and maintain in the child what Erikson calls *"a sense of industry* and a positive identification with those who *know* things and know how to *do* things" (p. 214). This opens a prospect on new kinds of excellence that put pressure especially on mental competence or intelligence. Being good at schoolwork, finding oneself comfortably effective in the operations required by one's lessons, becomes a bastion of self-esteem for part of the pupils, while for others the wearisome daily grind produces a general sense of inadequacy in this sphere.

There is also the playground, where the experience of competence depends on a different repertory of effective actions. Strength, agility, and good coordination are important foundations of self-esteem in this sphere, with qualities more socially colored, such as assertiveness and humor, coming in as important adjuncts. In direct comparison with others of the same age, children must prove themselves worthy of respect because they handle themselves well in the games and banter of the group. It is a sharp strain for many children when they pass from the atmosphere of a child-centered home into the competitive realities of even a friendly play group. They must now show what they have in the way of physical prowess, courage, manipulative skill, outgoing friendliness, all in direct comparison with other children of their age. The penalties for failure are humiliation, ridicule, rejection from the group. Even the last is probably a less basic threat than rejection from parental love, but is is nonetheless an acute threat.

As children grow they meet an increasing array of situations that put competence to the test. Experiences of competence and incompetence become differentiated with respect to different spheres of activity. A girl proves particularly competent, let us say, in walking and running, not as good in building with blocks or handling small objects, decidedly poor in drawing, writing, and other fine coordinations. The ratio of success and failure is different in each sphere, and if the experiences of competence continue in a fairly consistent fashion there will eventually be differences in the confidence with which each sphere is approached. The girl of our illustration, entering a new school, will run buoyantly to the playground, confident that she can deal with whatever she may encounter, but she will enter the crafts room somewhat dubiously and will take up penmanship with a weary feeling that she is never any good at this kind of stuff. Children show decided differences in overall level of confidence, but they also typically differentiate their competence in different spheres, and this tendency increases with age. In the normal course of growth self-esteem is nourished more and more from one's better spheres of competence, injured less and less by one's poorer spheres.

School Phobia

The child's long educational journey starts with a single step, that of getting to school. For many children this step awakens anxiety. It means exchanging the familiar satisfactions of home for a place full of other children and of adults whose friendliness and ability to keep things in order are unknown. To the child's eyes there are real dangers, and some degree of uneasiness is appropriate. Time is required to discover that the new environment can be endured, possibly even enjoyed.

Occasionally the anxiety released by the prospect of school is too great to be managed. The child becomes unable to remain at school without the mother's constant presence, or wakes up in the morning with pain and nausea that expresses dread of going at all. Often the parents and the school authorities, fearing the consequences of panic, agree to postpone school attendance for the time being; but the results are no better when the attempt is resumed.

In an early study it was discerned that the children's fear centered on separation from the mother (Waldfogel, Coolidge, & Hahn, 1957). This was transparently evident in children who would go to school only if their mothers accompanied them and remained there. From this we might deduce that school phobia would occur in highly dependent children, but Eisenberg (1958) showed that the mothers were often highly dependent on the children and were equally anxious about the separation, feeling bereft of their maternal role. The situation was complicated by the mothers' unwitting communication of their anxiety by tremulous gestures and reassurances given in a quavering voice. To think of school phobia as a disorder located in the child is usually wrong; the trouble is in the child–family unit (Rodin, 1967), and can be considered a form of mutual separation anxiety. Its correction can be aided by a variety of methods for extinguishing the child's anxiety, but joint work with child and parents is central to success (Schafer & Millman, 1977).

Overachievement and Underachievement

All teachers are aware that some pupils do not perform at the level of their capabilities. There are children, obviously bright if one assesses the quality of

133

their mischief or of their competence on the playground, who seem never to direct appreciable energy to a school lesson; there are also children who slave at every assigned task and at great cost produce a good performance. For research purposes, potential is measured by intelligence tests and achievement by school grades. Underachievement is thus defined as school grades well below intelligence scores, and overachievement as school grades well above. The latter possibility is not paradoxical when we bear in mind that intelligence tests do not really measure a fixed innate potential (Hunt, 1961; McClelland, 1973). At most they suggest current capacity to do schoolwork, but this is enough for the present purpose. We deduce that both overachievement and underachievement have to do with motivation, perhaps also with expectations that emanate from parents and teachers.

In the beginning, children presumably do not have a strong intrinsic interest in their education. Schooling is presented to them first as an adult requirement. Much of the art of teaching consists of awakening an intrinsic interest in the work, but this is never uniformly successful, and in any event there are constraints and irksome requirements at school, so that the opening of a new term is rarely felt to be an occasion for rejoicing or the final session a day of mourning. In many families college and even graduate school have become passionate family requirements, so that higher education may continue to be felt as something that is done to please the adult world. This relation between schooling and adult requirements provides an important clue to the motivational aspects of both overachievement and underachievement.

Doing poorly in school affects both children and parents. Both may be indifferent to school success, in which case children may find the effort not worth the small rewards. But if the parents do care, and their children do not care about pleasing them, failing in school can be a tempting way to disappoint them. Very likely the children are not conscious of moving toward such an outcome; they know only that the discomforts of studying seem insuperable. The ensuing displeasure at home does not change the behavior when in their hearts the children do not want to give their parents pleasure. A similar situation may exist with teachers who are sensed to be indifferent or hostile; there is underlying satisfaction in showing them that they cannot teach. Research on academic underachievement repeatedly shows that the problem can be related to a negative attitude toward adults.

Overachievement is expectably connected with a family situation in which academic excellence is held to be of supreme importance. It implies also a willingness on the part of the child to fulfill this expectation, indeed a zeal to do so in order to stand high in parental favor. The achievement regime may be successful if the child's capacities are equal to the strain. But working at or beyond the limit of capacities means vast and continuous application. Other aspects of development may lag behind, and eventually there may be a surge of rebellion against the Spartan straight-A regime, or there may be deep inferiority feelings over not quite equalling the parental aspirations. Often

134

enough the phenomenon of sophomore slump, discussed in Chapter 3, occurs in overachievers who have come to wonder if the effort is really worthwhile.

Dropping Out of School

At the present time about a quarter of the students in American high schools drop out without receiving a diploma. In comparison with earlier times this is a small proportion. Dropping out used to be considered a sensible move on the part of a person who found no interest in high school studies. It meant assuming adult responsibilities more promptly, and it did not preclude later vocational success. Recently, however, because of changed attitudes in the job market, dropping out has come to be considered a serious problem. Technological changes have reduced the proportion of jobs requiring little thought or skill, and a high school diploma is regarded as the minimum requirement for all but the lowest grades of occupation. Dropping out of high school now puts people in a vocational trap: the range of jobs for which they can ever qualify is severely limited. It is significant that many current dropouts say that they plan to get a diploma later by night classes or correspondence courses.

On the basis of several studies Schreiber (1968) has drawn a composite portrait intended to portray the average high school dropout. Two factors are typically involved: a negative attitude toward studies and a lack of social involvement at school. Limited aptitude for school work as shown in below-average scores on intelligence tests plays some part, but is usually not in itself the decisive factor. Performance has been poor and attitude apathetic for some time, so that schoolwork yields nothing better than feelings of incompetence and inferiority. There is little participation in extracurricular activities and little sense of belonging in high school society; most of the dropout's friends are already out of school. Presumably such a student has not made a favorable impression on the teachers and may be known chiefly as a disciplinary problem. To the dropout school is both boring and unfriendly, hardly an environment in which one wants to stay. Unfortunately the decision made at 16 may be much regretted in later years, when applications for jobs are turned down because they are not supported by the magical diploma. Otherwise dropping out, especially from schools of poorer quality, might often be judged a sensible move.

Ability and Interest

In contrast to these several maladaptive possibilities, life at school may prove to be conducive to strong growth. This is especially likely when ability can be well utilized and interest aroused. A difference obviously exists between the sense of competence that comes from doing something well and the experience of interest that makes one want to engage in certain kinds of activity for their own sake. A child who is simply proud of mastering difficult lessons on electronics has a different experience from one who finds electronics utterly fasci-

135

nating and wants to learn more and more. But these two experiences—of competence and of intrinsic interest—often go together, and they have somewhat the same effect on development. Whether the inclination is for sports, for craftsmanship, for school studies, for music, for art, for managing others, it can serve as a point of integration in personality.

The integrative action can be pictured as follows. The person now has a reliable line along which it is possible to function with growing mastery and pleasure. In the sphere of excellence the person repeatedly enjoys the experience of competence and thus provides self-esteem with a strong inner source. Ability is fairly likely to bring social as well as intrinsic rewards, and development can then be guided by an efficient selective principle. Confidence of esteem in one area allows one to discard the skills and roles that offer less promise. Moreover, the interest suggests the groups and companions whose esteem will be felt most valuable. A boy with a scientific interest, for example, no longer has to care about every "bunch" in his high school, or even about the "leading crowd"; he needs only the shared interest and esteem of the hi-fi nuts or the budding nuclear physicists. If he goes to college he will probably know what subjects he most wants to study, and he may shortly discover a group of like-minded companions who will become his chief social circle. Even his vocational problems will be solved in advance so long as there are opportunities in the line dictated by his central cluster of competence and interest. There is obvious danger of a one-sided development when a particular interest is so strong that it consumes most of a person's energies. But even this outcome may compare favorably with the vocational indecisions of people who have never been engrossed in this way, who know neither what they are especially good for nor what especially turns them on. Vocational guidance in these cases is directed toward trying to clarify both points.

SOCIAL DEVELOPMENT: RELATIONS WITH GROUPS

Prominent at one time in mental health teaching was the idea that children's interactions with one another were of outstanding importance for development. When the influence of parents was made suspect by Freud and his followers, when conventional ideas about the family began to crumble, group participation seemed the only flawless prescription for healthy growth. Parents hoped that developmental magic would be worked by thrusting children early and often into the company of their peers. Then groups themselves came under study, and it was quickly apparent that their promptings toward growth did not exempt them from important maladaptive possibilities.

Becoming a member of a group is capable of enlarging and enriching an individual's life. Membership can yield security and warmth, welcomed by anyone but especially by children whose families do not provide these qualities. It can yield an increased sense of competence: the group can deal with situations in which the individual would be helpless. The group provides stimulation, conversation, and things to do, making life more interesting. It can teach skills, provide models, be a source of information. It can create a feeling of companionship that leads members to seek each other's company, whether for serious enterprises or for loitering on street corners.

On the other hand, membership in a group is bound to entail certain restrictions. The individual is no longer free to follow whim and impulse. A member's initiative may be submerged because the group decides on something different. The group defines a number of possible *roles* and helps individuals find the ones they are best fitted to play. A boy who aspires in baseball to play third base may find himself relegated to right field or even forced to be water-boy. The group provides a set of *norms*, indicating by approval or disapproval the behavior that will be accepted. These roles and norms constitute a framework—a structure of expectations—into which the individual must fit in order to maintain membership.

Children begin their group experience with little understanding of what is involved. They learn about roles and norms through slowly accumulating experience. Groups between six and nine, in the early part of what Sullivan (1953) called the *juvenile era*, are only crudely structured. The children's social sensitivities are likewise crude, and not much can be learned beyond competition and primitive cooperation. At about nine, group self-management becomes a possibility with an increasing definition of roles and norms. Informal games, played for fun without intrusion of adult constraints, are especially educative with respect to the necessity for roles and norms; even fun cannot go on entirely without them. During adolescence the company of other adolescents is decidedly helpful in becoming independent of parents. Rebellion, whether quiet or noisy, carries the risk of loneliness, but peer groups can take over the function of providing support.

Participating with others provides the means of developing, one way or another, one's sense of interpersonal competence. It permits discovery of the influence one can have and wants to have on other people. This does not imply seeking power for its own sake, nor is it limited to competition, argument, or other unfriendly relations. Satisfaction can be found in having an effect on others by making them laugh, telling something that awakens interest, contributing a useful idea to a discussion, providing reassurance, expressing love and respect and eliciting like expressions from others. These benign ways of affecting people yield a feeling that the human environment is responsive instead of formidable.

All these consequences are predicated on successful and satisfying experiences in peer relations. Peer society, however, is a natural phenomenon, not a device set up to promote growth. Groups at school, well run by an adult supervisor, may sometimes achieve an atmosphere that is highly favorable to growth, but spontaneous groups of children or adolescents, dedicated not at all to developmental goals, may work in quite the opposite fashion. They can

137

Playing with peers provides the opportunity to develop interpersonal competence and to learn how to influence other people. Besides that, it is fun.

be cruel in rejecting a member who is slow, clumsy, or not "on the ball" in group activities. They can seize on handicaps, peculiarities of appearance, class status, religious and ethnic differences, and use them as grounds for psychological ostracism if not outright expulsion. They can intimidate those who object to the way things are done, buying conformity with the threat of ridicule or physical violence. When a few tyrants are in control of a group they can stifle initiative with as much force as an authoritarian parent. In some circumstances group participation can have a destructive effect on individual members.

Maladaptive Possibilities

In a rough way we can distinguish two general maladaptive possibilities in the realm of group relations: (1) *social isolation*, in which the person does not sufficiently receive the educative benefits of membership in groups; and (2) *social enslavement*, in which the person has learned to respond so automatically to the expectations of everyone else that no stable sense of self, no real ego-identity, is able to develop.

Social Isolation.   Many forces may conspire to prevent a child from entering readily into groups. Fragile physique or unusual sensitiveness may be handicaps from the start, predisposing one to shy, tense withdrawal from the normal bruisings of child society. Geographical isolation may get the child off to a poor start regarding social experience. A serious obstacle is offered by parental overprotection. Perhaps the parents apprehensively interfere with the child's social contacts or try to create a too perfect environment at home. Children who are accustomed to whine for their own way or to demand it aggressively will react badly to the give and take of the group and probably suffer rejection. On the other side of the picture, the difficulty may lie less with the individual than with the available groups. The first group may be dominated by children with bullying tendencies who enjoy making the newcomer miserable. Or it may be that after an auspicious beginning the child discovers rejection because of belonging to a different class, race, nationality, or religion from the majority in the neighborhood. When parents move a great deal, children will experience a certain feeling of rejection merely because they are newcomers who must be assimilated to already existing groups.

When circumstances pile up to hinder satisfying membership in the more available groups, it sometimes happens that the difficulty is solved by searching out or even bringing together a small and special group with congenial interests. In such cases the child is not isolated from other human beings, though still perhaps ill at ease in large and boisterous groups.

In the event that this avenue is not open, an attitude toward others develops that can best be described as evasive. The child is unable to satisfy needs for companionship, unable also to experience competence in having desired effects on others. This was well illustrated in our clinical introduction by Walter Lilly, who could not resist requests for money and who dared not speak to a taciturn, perhaps equally shy, fellow worker. Social interaction in such a case becomes an area of helpless incompetence in which the initiative always comes from others and one has to endure whatever they please to put forth. Opposition is foredoomed, argument is hopeless, even a friendly overture means doing what the other person wants. Under these circumstances social interactions yield neither pleasure nor self-respect. Attempts will be made to avoid them, but as this is very difficult, resentment builds up against other people, who are experienced as intrusive and annoying. This resentment still further blocks the desire for social contact.

When these circumstances prevail, the person tends to remain shy, retiring, homebound, limited in interests to things that can be done alone. The give and take of group relations are not learned; convivial good fellowship is not experienced. Children may compensate in fantasy for the lack of expanded selfhood that comes from human interactions at their best, but they will never feel quite certain of their actual position in the social organism. Certain developments will be harder, especially those that depend on separation from parental support. Without the compensating support of age-mates at adolescence, there will be less confidence in separating from parental supervision and opinions and in carrying out a mature sexual adjustment. Unless in the meantime a person has developed exceptional talents that create a special relation with others, it is hard to avoid feeling progressively isolated and insignificant.

Sometimes the situation is met by an attempt at reversal. Instead of admitting frustrated social inclinations and rejection, the person develops a role of contemptuous independence. Such people reject the very idea of membership in stupid, commonplace groups with their plebeian interests and petty politics. They tend to inflate themselves into important personages who can achieve great things if not hampered by the mob or by the interference of friends. They try to pump up in themselves the feeling of strength and importance that actually comes most readily through social memberships. With exceptional talent such a person may accomplish something, but the usual fate is essential isolation, ineffectiveness, and bitter resentment.

Social Enslavement.
Another path along which social development can go astray is excessive conformity to the expectations of others. The person who travels too far in this direction comes to guide behavior entirely by what other people want or expect. It is impossible to make suggestions or express wishes unless these are sure to please the people immediately present. People who depend heavily on group affiliation may become unusually skillful at playing the right role in the right place. They grow expert in meeting the expectations of each company they happen to be in, and they never err by telling the sex joke, the Scotch joke, the joke on the President, the joke on the party out of power, to the wrong audience. This sensitivity to what will please others has the effect of pleasing others and is therefore judged by them to be evidence of remarkable social adjustment. Never troublesome to others, such a person is not in danger of criticism or rejection. And these seem to be the dangers this behavior is intended to avoid.

Social enslavement is favored by various circumstances. To some extent it can be absorbed directly from parents: discrepancies between parents' well-mannered behavior toward other adults and the things they say about them in private must often strike the child as meaning that the parents are afraid of other people. When children are forced prematurely into group activities, when their social careers are pushed by their parents rather than by their own motives, interaction may become a chore best dealt with by falling in with what the other children want. If entrance into groups proves difficult, the child may undertake to buy his or her way by deference and docility. If the child's social hunger is particularly acute, as is sometimes the case when rejection is experienced in the family circle and a new source of security is needed, it will be difficult for the child to run the slightest risk of not being accepted.

People whose social interactions have developed in this way are characterized by David Riesman (1950) as *other-directed:* their contemporaries are the source of direction, and they become adept at "paying close attention to the signals from others" (p. 18). The initiation of their behavior comes from friends and from the mass media, and may be subject to changes of fashion.

The maladjustment that underlies excessive conformity comes to light most clearly when the person is faced by conflicting expectations. This is particularly likely to happen in such times as the present, when social standards and values are changing. Inherent contradiction exists among some of our long-cherished values: for example, between considerate love and competitive success. With such conflicting norms in the background, it is all the more likely that the groups available to any one person will uphold contradictory values. When socially enslaved people are forced to decide which of two group values they will espouse as their own, they are likely to feel confused and bewildered. No stable inner pattern, no integrated self, can serve as a point of reference. They must announce their true colors, but they have none. The core of the maladjustment lies in the fact that they have leaned on social judgments and have not brought their own desires, peculiarities, and sense of competence into their self-conceptions. The self-picture is diffused and fails in its integrative function.

SOCIAL DEVELOPMENT: INTIMATE RELATIONS

Interacting with others in groups is an important educative experience, but it does not offer a complete curriculum in social development. One attribute of maturity is to be capable of sustaining and enjoying intimate relations with one's spouse and closest friends. Behavior in groups, which is relatively public behavior, does not provide the conditions that are essential for the growth of intimacy. These conditions can be met only in what we may call a private relationship between two people, one in which confidences can be exchanged and secret aspirations shared. In later childhood most children seek a closer, more personal relationship with someone who can be considered a special friend or chum. Important new developments in social interaction get under way.

Because these developments are apt to appear at a time when puberty is not far away, and because later an intimate relationship is often also a sexual one, it is sometimes supposed that the friendships of the years from ten to thirteen can be attributed to the burgeoning sexual need. The full significance of these relationships is overlooked, however, if we think of them as solely erotic, especially if, because they typically start between children of the same sex, we regard them simply as a disturbance on the way to heterosexual adjustment. Close friendships between children play a highly constructive part in the growth and integration of personality. They strengthen the understanding of oneself and others, and they lay important foundations for appeciative, loving relationships in later life.

In their early stages close friendships may engage but a small part of the child's feelings. Helene Deutsch (1944) pointed out that girls between 10 and 12, as part of the process of breaking away from dependence on parents, develop a strong need for secrecy. To surround her person with secrecy, the girl needs a partner, and she is apt to find one in another girl like herself in age

Intimate friendship with youngsters of one's own sex typically develops in early adolescence before much interest in the opposite sex arises.

and interests, "with whom she giggles and titters, with whom she locks herself
up in her room, to whom she confides her secrets." Some of these secrets may
have to do with the sexual facts of life, but Deutsch's studies indicate that "expression of intense tenderness between girls is not found at this time, and mutual masturbation almost never occurs under normal circumstances." The
close relationship serves the purpose of ego development rather than erotic
satisfaction. Guilt is lessened by sharing supposedly guilty secrets; support is
obtained in the process of emancipation from adult control; above all, "identification with a similar being can strengthen the young girl's consciousness
that she is an independent ego." "The positive aspects of such friendships are
paramount," Deutsch concludes, "and lack of them is a serious loss in this period of life" (pp. 13, 27).

A unique part is played by close friendships in discovering and defining the
self. From the competitions and compromises that occupy juvenile groups one
may emerge with a fairly clear sense of one's social competence and reputation
for prowess, but the more private aspects of experience can be defined and
corrected only in an intimate relationship. Here it is possible to speak of things
that one would not disclose to the world at large, to consider new dimensions
of personal worth besides those that receive group approval. Here it is possible, for example, to speak of the fears one has endured and combatted to meet
a group standard; great relief and strengthening may follow the discovery that
the other person, too, has been fearful in situations externally well met. Here
also it is possible to mention one's hopes and aspirations for the future and
thus to secure some social reflection on what has previously been private—but
perhaps not wildly fantastic. When in adolescence the desire for intimacy

shifts to a member of the opposite sex, the goal of self-definition still plays a prominent part. In Erikson's words, "to a considerable extent adolescent love is an attempt to arrive at a definition of one's identity by projecting one's diffused ego images on one another and by seeing them thus reflected and gradually clarified. This is why many a youth would rather converse, and settle matters of mutual identification, than embrace" (1963, p. 228).

In the course of time, very often before the shift of interest to a person of the opposite sex, youthful friendships become charged with strong emotional meanings, and it is through this that they perform their most important service for development. This topic has been most fully expounded by Sullivan (1953), who attributed to the close friendships of preadolescence the power to correct various faults in the child's previous social growth. The relation takes on a new meaning: the friend's interests and happiness assume an importance equal to one's own. With a chum the child "begins to develop a real sensitivity to what matters to another person; and this is not in the sense of 'what should I do to get what I want,' but instead 'what should I do to contribute to the happiness or to support the prestige and feeling of worthwhileness of my chum' " (p. 245). Research on children's understanding of friendship, according to Damon (1977), reveals the emergence at about 12 or 13 of the idea that more is involved than joint activity; "friends must assume one another's burdens and troubles, thereby showing active caring for the other" (p. 147). This interest can properly be called love, even when no overt sexual element is discernible. It involves wanting to understand the other person, wanting to encourage and give help, wanting to share interests, all of which maximizes the chances that true mutuality will emerge. In friendships of this kind an injured self-respect, battered in the competitions of group life, can be brought back to health; a new sense of worth can be nourished by the friend's appreciative concern. Fortunate experiences of this sort pave the way for the mutual affectionate relationships of adult life.

Maladaptive Possibilities

It is as true of friendships as it is of groups that their effect on development is not always constructive. Sometimes one of the partners dominates or exploits the other. Sometimes the overtures from one side are not answered by real interest or understanding. Perhaps the need for intimacy in one partner evokes only a need for erotic experience from the other. Rebuffs in forming intimate relationships may produce wariness, reserve, and a tendency to shut in one's private concerns. Sometimes, on the other hand, a friendship will prosper so warmly that jealousy is aroused when either of the partners takes an interest in someone else. The consequences may be painful and may discourage f attempts at closeness; in such cases, however, the person may well h enced developmental benefits before the relation came to grief

Even though the going is not always smooth, it is a mist out of a major pathway toward maturity. Someti workers make a policy of breaking up pairs of children so that they will mingle more widely in the group. Presumably in some cases the children continue their friendship in secret, thus learning the valuable lesson that adult ineptitude need not spoil their growth. Otherwise they can only assume that there is something wicked about intimacy, which will certainly hinder their progress toward emotional maturity. It is a common complaint among young people that they have lots of acquaintances but no real friends. On this account they feel lonely, but they also feel a little like strangers to themselves, for they have not had enough chances to find out, through intimate interaction, what they are really like.

SEXUAL DEVELOPMENT

Sexual development comes to a conspicuous peak at puberty, when there is a rapid increase in the sensitivity of the genital organs. This alone, with its novel interests and urgent impulses, might be a considerable adaptive problem, but the underlying growth plan does not allow the young person to concentrate on one thing at a time. Simultaneously there is a physical growth spurt that fairly quickly produces adult stature, with the changed relation this implies to surrounding adults. There is likewise a mental growth spurt that facilitates an expansion of interest to adult concerns and a power of abstract thinking that may lead to lively argument. Sexuality is only one of several developments that move into higher gear at puberty. Small wonder that it is often mixed up with rebellion, independence, self-respect, and the achievement of identity.

As a further possible difficulty, the sexuality that flowers at puberty already has a long history.

Early Childhood Sexuality

One of Freud's most important contributions was the discovery that sexual needs are active throughout childhood. As we saw in Chapter 1, Freud called attention to many aspects of child behavior that should clearly be called sexual, even when allowance is made for the fact that genital maturity and power of procreation have not been reached. The most indisputable example is mas-
~rbation, which is almost universally practiced by children of both sexes,
᠁lly with increasing interest during the fourth and fifth years. Growing
ᵣₑᵤt of this is curiosity about the sexual organs and the anatomical dif-
developᵧₑen the sexes. This may lead to experimentation with other chil-
behaviorᵣₜ for information from adults. Sexual excitation is undoubt-
᠁rentiated from other forms of pleasant bodily stimulation
᠁herty when the special excitability of the genital organs
Nevertheless we would overlook crucial problems of
᠁ny the presence of sexual elements in childhood

144

For the child to bring sexual activities into line with adult expectations is an early and difficult problem of adaptation. In the past our culture was generally hostile to childhood sexuality. Requests for sexual enlightenment were condemned as dirty and disgusting, and masturbation, widely believed to produce disastrous consequences, was suppressed by coercion and dire threats. These attitudes have been gradually replaced by a tolerant disregard of childhood sexuality, now regarded as harmless, and even by encouragement on the part of parents determined to avoid the warping consequences of repression. But in large segments of our society children are still asked to constrain sexual impulses to a degree that may invest them with strong negative feelings. The sexuality of puberty may thus be burdened by attitudes already strongly established.

A second consequence of childhood history is more controversial. Freud came to believe that a child's sexual feelings first became attached to the members of the family. From the recollections of patients he postulated that at about the age of five boys typically developed an erotic attachment to their mothers with a corresponding jealousy and fear of their fathers. This was the *Oedipus complex*, named from the tragedy of Sophocles in which Oedipus unwittingly kills his father and marries his mother. The parallel complex for girls, love of father and jealous fear of mother, is sometimes called the *Electra complex.* Adaptive progress through this first involvement in the "eternal triangle" consisted, for the boy, in renouncing the mother as a sexual object and identifying with the father's prohibitions and values, thus laying a foundation for conscience. The girl progressed in the same way with a reversal of characters. Mishaps in this process, Freud believed, were the principal cause of anxiety disorders.

For giving this one situation such a central place in development, and for describing it in such adult sexual terms, Freud has been severely criticized, for instance, by psychoanalysts Horney (1939) and Alexander (1953), by psychologist Murphy (1947), and by sociologist Bossard (1953). Sexual feeling is no doubt a natural accompaniment of affectionate relations, especially when these include caresses and other bodily contacts. But in the normal course of growth these relatively mild attachments to family members are not likely to interfere with the new requirement at puberty that love objects be sought outside the family. Only when family attachments are unusually strong—probably for dependent and other reasons besides sex—are they likely to interfere with the next phase of sexual development.

Sex Roles and Imitation

After about the third year of life, sexual behavior can no longer be adequately described in terms of drive and satisfactions. Children become aware of their sexual identity. One of the terms in the Stanford-Binet Intelligence Test for age three is the question: "Are you a little boy or a little girl?" The majority of three-year-olds answer correctly, and some of the brighter ones are contemp-

145

tuous of such a foolish question. Sexual identity is soon discovered to imply a good many aspects of behavior having hardly anything to do with anatomy or bodily pleasure. The child gradually learns a complete sex role. In the older tradition, being a girl means playing with dolls, being clean and pretty, helping mother around the house; being a boy means not playing with dolls, liking rough and tumble and outdoor adventure, and helping father with outside chores. These traditional sex role expectations are today under severe criticism. Their relation to biologically determined differences seems slight, and their social function of promoting an ultimate division of labor between the sexes appears to be badly overdone. Even so, the conception of masculine and feminine roles, including many aspects of behavior, is deeply rooted in our culture, and most children are unlikely to escape its impact.

In learning his or her sex role the child is likely to make use of the most available models: father and mother. Copying the behavior of models is the easiest way, especially in the beginning, of acquiring social roles and other patterns of social behavior. It can happen, however, that the appropriate model is in some way compromised, so that the parent of the opposite sex appears more worthy of imitation. The daughter of a steady, affectionate father and an irresponsible, alcoholic mother may reject the feminine role and prefer to take father as her model. The son of a steady, affectionate mother and an irresponsible, alcoholic father may see nothing worth emulating in the masculine role. These reversals in the copying of sex roles do not necessarily interfere with later sexual behavior, which is affected by many other influences. But they occur with what looks like more than chance frequency in clinical cases in which there is marked disturbance in sexual functioning.

In the course of time sexual development tends to be still more closely related to other aspects of personality. Although some young people at puberty make immediate attempts at fulfillment with partners, many adolescents cannot treat sexuality in this purely physical way. Thinking of intercourse as a personal relation, they do not want to hasten into it without confidence that they can deal with the attendant emotions. In a study of American middle class and working class high school boys Offer (1969) described the reluctance of these boys, at least before senior year, to become seriously involved with girls; they preferred to delay intercourse until, as some of them said, "we can handle it." Time was needed to establish confidence, social skills, self-respect, and a willingness to risk proving one's worth as a loveworthy person. Like other strands of development, sexuality is apt to be importantly woven into personality as a whole.

A revolution in attitudes toward sex has been moving along in our society since the 1920s and has culminated today, for many people, in a highly tolerant outlook. In this view, sex should be encouraged and enjoyed. Adolescents, rather than their parents, should be fully responsible for their own erotic development. The most extreme proponents of this outlook regard sex as a simple pleasure to be enjoyed in a spirit of play and fun whenever two people are

Young adolescents frequently express their affection for members of the opposite sex awkwardly at first, for example, by teasing. Notice the affirmation expressed in their eyes, however.

so inclined. To others the fun theory separates sex too sharply from the rest of personality, and overlooks its larger possibilities. When sex forms part of an intimate relation that is expected to last, at least for a time, it becomes an expression of personal closeness that greatly enriches the relation and that may live up to rhapsodical literary descriptions of deep love. We would be short-sighted not to realize that sex is thus capable of enlarging into something much greater than physical satisfaction.

Maladaptive Possibilities

One maladaptive consequence of its long childhood history occurs when *sex is strongly associated with negative feelings*. Although this was more common in the recent past than it is today, we cannot assume that repressive training does not persist in many parts of society. If parental training and cultural attitudes are strongly negative, sex is likely to become connected with feelings of guilt, disgust, and inferiority. When sexual feeling is suppressed and denied because it implies something shameful and dirty, the chances of progress at puberty are sharply reduced. The consequence may be a general inhibition of sexual interest and behavior. In extreme cases the person never dares to venture into an erotic relationship. More commonly the interference is less complete, but sex can be experienced only as something shameful and demeaning; its power to deepen love and strengthen relationships is thus thrown away. In cases of impotence, frigidity, and failure to work out a mutually satisfactory physical relation, a background of this kind is common.

Another maladaptive possibility can be described as *compulsive promiscuity*. The compulsive element is most evident when sex is used not just for itself

147

but to serve some other need that is of great urgency. A young woman, for instance, who has long felt unpopular and rejected, may find in the temporary closeness of the sexual embrace an acceptance so much needed that it must be sought again and again. A young man who has considered himself weak and submissive may discover that sexual excitement makes him both dominant and potent, and he becomes hooked on reaffirming these virtues. In such cases sex is being used to prove something, but the proof does not generalize to non-sexual situations and must be constantly repeated. Because of this compulsiveness there is little room to be considerate of the partner, little scope for choosing partners sensibly, and a danger of getting into undesirable situations that might easily have been foreseen.

The natural, open, untrammeled attitude toward sex that has become more common today seems generally favorable to growth, but not all problems of sexual development vanish so easily. College counselors find their services in demand by students who believe in and practice maximum sexual freedom. Even when sexual encounters are physically successful, which is not always to be expected when the partners are relatively inexperienced, they may not lead to the anticipated feelings of satisfaction. Expected feelings may be slow to appear, or unexpected ones may be troubling. A close relation calls for outgrowing childlike attitudes toward love objects—jealousy, demandingness, dependence, petulance—and sexual intercourse does not accomplish this by magic. Furthermore, sexual freedom, like any other doctrine, can degenerate into a rigid demand. Clinical reports are appearing in which the person undertook early intercourse to save face with experienced peers or out of a sense of duty to parents who extolled its virtues. When sexuality is prompted by these external pressures instead of by inner need and readiness, it may fail altogether to contribute to personal growth.

SELF AND EGO IDENTITY

The Concept of Self

Central in each of our lives is the experience of being one person, the same from day to day. Readily as we may analyze ourselves to perceive different aspects, different needs, and indeed qualities that undergo considerable change, we return to the fact that all these are part of one person leading an individual life. The basic unity of the organism is most clearly reflected in the idea of self. Without this idea, we could easily slight the ways in which our various tendencies are patterned to make that organism live and grow. The concept of self provides the key to the organization of personality.

A unifying concept becomes particularly valuable when we want to take account of constructive and long-range behavior. The setting of distant goals, the discharging of obligations, the making and keeping of promises, the taking of initiative and persisting against obstacles, the struggle to live up to

148

ideals, the whole forward movement whereby a person becomes an independent, effective, and at the same time reliable human being—all this activity implies a very high degree of organization. It implies a hierarchy of tendencies so ordered that the ones affirmed to be of the most importance are given right of way over the less important. To say that this hierarchy takes shape in the interests of the *self*, and that things are more important or less important to a *self*, seems at present the most satisfactory way to conceptualize the whole subject.

In careful historical and theoretical work one would not be justified in using *self* and *ego* interchangeably. But we need not insist on the distinction in considering *ego identity*, which for our purposes here might as well have been called *self identity*.

Ego Identity

The interaction between self and social environment is captured by Erikson (1963) in the concept of ego identity. This expression signifies a sense of being a distinct individual in one's own right within a social framework. It includes one's self as a continuous, active personal being; and it also includes one's self as a meaningful part of the surrounding human group. As Erikson puts it:

> It is the identity of something in the individual's core with an essential aspect of a group's inner coherence which is under consideration here: for the young individual must learn to be most like himself where he means most to others—those others, to be sure, who have come to mean most to him. The term identity expresses such a mutual relation in that it connotes both a persistent sameness within oneself (self-sameness) and a persistent sharing of some kind of essential character with others (1959, p. 109).

The sense of identity is strengthened by the progressive mastery of useful actions such as walking, talking, reading, or carpentry. These are experienced as achievements by the child, and their value is further affirmed by consistent recognition on the part of adults. But their value for ego identity depends on their being relevant to adult reality; they open the way to a feeling of partnership in a larger world—to the feeling that one has a place and function in the world.

The process of identification plays an important part in this growth. "Ego Identity," says Erikson, "develops out of a gradual integration of all identifications," patterned "in order to make a unique and a reasonably coherent whole." Erikson regards adolescence as the most decisive period in the growth of ego identity, when the time is first ripe for establishing a firm sense of oneself in adult perspective.

In a study of college students based on interviews, Marcia (1966) describes four types of what he calls *identity status*. Students in the first category, *identity foreclosure*, seem never to have had doubts about who they are; the values of home and the opportunities ahead are sufficiently congenial to be accepted without struggle as a basis for living. In the next status, *identity diffusion*, are students who are relatively adrift and uncommitted but not especially worried about it; lack of a sense of identity does not create a feeling of crisis. Marcia calls the third status *moratorium*: the subjects are uncommitted with respect to values and life plans, but feel that they must discover themselves before the end of college and are working hard at it. The fourth status, *identity achievement*, represents arrival at firm commitments to occupations and values; unlike the first group, this commitment has been achieved after a period of diffusion, crisis, and struggle. In a rough way these descriptions represent a range of normally adaptive solutions to the problems of identity in late adolescence. They may even occur in sequence. A study by Perry (1970) shows a fairly regular progression during the college years. At the start, values and truth itself seem absolute; learning means discovering the right answers. Then comes recognition of the relativity of values, the wide range of what have been considered right and wrong answers in different times and circumstances. This can be disconcerting, suggesting that nothing is any better than anything else. If the students continue to grapple seriously with the problem, they finally recognize the necessity for responsible personal choice and commitment, reaching decisions as to what is worth working for in their time and circumstances.

Maladaptive Possibilities

Because the sense of self is actively present, starting early, throughout the course of development, many maladaptive possibilities discussed in this chapter can be seen as having a deleterious effect on identity. This is conspicuously true of feelings of incompetence and inferiority, with their injurious consequences for self-respect. It is true also of social isolation, and notably true of social enslavement, in which responding to the expectations of other people largely swamps recognition of one's own preferences and powers of initiative. Perhaps the maladaptive possibilities connected with identity should consist of a summary of all that has gone before. But in the recent literature much attention has been paid to a phenomenon common in our time in which *identity diffusion* is the central complaint. "I don't know who I am" is the sentence often chosen to represent this condition, from which we learn that knowing "who I am"—having ego identity—is an essential aspect of an organized, purposeful, satisfying sense of living. People who complain of not knowing who they are will probably amplify the description by saying that their lives seem meaningless, that what they are doing is without point for the future, that nothing is really important or useful, and that existence is zestless and boring. There is more to this than a sense of personal inadequacy or a depressed mood. These people cannot see how they can fit into the world, so to speak, as the world they know about is now constituted; no valuable interaction can be discerned. "I don't know who I am" is expanded into "I don't know who I can be in the world as I have experienced it."

An interesting example of identity diffusion is provided by a group of college dropouts studied by Hirsch and Keniston (1970). Subjects were chosen who were in good academic standing and financially unpressed, but who were dropping voluntarily out of Yale College. The decision to leave school was not hasty or impulsive; it involved much thought, pain, often self-reproach, and it was made only when staying became wholly unbearable. The authors regard dropping out not as a disorder or weakness but as a possibly wise adaptive step when the student's developmental necessities are not in phase with what is offered by the college environment. The students suffered from a work paralysis that had been going on for some time. Their time perspective had collapsed, especially regarding future orientation, so that they felt themselves living in a disconnected present. They described their existence as having become hollow, empty, meaningless; even social life seemed a bore; and the possibility of really living seemed to exist only away from the academic environment. Self-reproach assailed them for not going through college as so many others do; this entailed a changed conception of themselves and a search for a new self in a more congenial environment. Intensive interviews with these subjects disclosed acute difficulties, not usually overt, in relation to parents, especially to fathers. More than others, the dropouts had formed identifications with the fathers as strong and worthy models, had responded to college requirements as to those of their fathers, but had become belatedly disillusioned about their fathers, whose faults and weaknesses they had at last begun to understand. Identification with father played such a large part in their own identity that when it failed there was not enough left to prevent confusion. It is as is the student said, "If I cannot be my worthy father's worthy college son, because my father is not worthy, then who am I?" Search for a new self had become an urgent problem, and for the time being, at least, college could not be felt as the proper place for it.

The results of this study are illuminating, but they must be taken to represent only one of several different ways in which ego identity can become problematically diffused. Another avenue to weak identity is offered by social enslavement and the other-directed attitude already described. Furthermore, the finding of identity is made harder when occupations are seen as forbiddingly impersonal, perhaps even as morally compromised, and when society is subject to major criticism. Many young people today have trouble picturing a significant life in traditional occupational slots and do not want to make themselves part of a technological system with so many destructive consequences. Ego identity depends on a successful relation between the individual and society. Its difficulties may lie on both sides.

GENERATIVITY

One of the most essential aspects of adult living is taking care of the people on whom the continuing of human existence depends. This means primarily the care of the young, the nurturing of those creatures now small and relatively helpless who will grow up to be the next generation of adults. Under civilized conditions this care includes an extended education and the provision of many facilities for well-rounded development. Caring thus extends to the institutions that contribute to youthful development and guidance. Allport (1961) described this aspect of maturity as *extension of the sense of self*. It is shown when the welfare of another person or of a valued cause becomes as important as one's own welfare; "better said, the welfare of another is *identical* with one's own" (p. 283). Erikson (1963) proposes the word *generativity*, which is "primarily the concern in establishing and guiding the next generation." He adds that "mature man needs to be needed," emphasizing the mutuality that is inherent in caring and being the object of care (p. 266).

On the long path toward becoming a caring adult, boys are almost at once handicapped: they are often discouraged from playing with dolls. If they learn

Guiding children in recreational activities is an important part of adult development, giving expression to generativity needs, as well as a significant socialization experience for children.

a traditional version of the male sex role they may be still further crippled in developing their caretaking talents, understanding that such things belong in the province of women. But the care of animal pets is not prohibted, nor is the care of property. It is traditionally the boys who mow the lawn and help repair the house. The nurturing of younger siblings might seem to offer perfect training, but here the situation is so complicated by jealousy and rivalry that the caretaking spirit is easily smothered and the behavior, if it occurs at all, is only a wearisome duty. Cherishing the feelings and self-respect of others struggles forth again in the friendships of late childhood and early adolescence. Even these harbingers of adult caring do not receive unqualified social support, being often discouraged, as we saw, in favor of group activities.

Nurturant tendencies are thus likely to have a checkered history, more so for boys than for girls. They are not likely to show to best advantage during late adolescence, when personal growth and ego identity are understandably matters of great concern. They are more strongly called forth when there is commitment to an occupation and when there is a spouse and children standing in need of care. At this point, failure to mobilize generativity has a variety of maladaptive consequences.

Maladaptive Possibilities

Continuing dependent tendencies offers one of the gravest obstacles to becoming a caretaker. This was shrewdly described by a college girl whose roommate had suffered a devastating family tragedy. She responded warmly to her roommate's sorrow and bewilderment, trying her best to be a sympathetic and helpful listener. After a while, however, she became aware of an unwelcome resentment; why must she always hear the other girl's problems when she so much wanted help with her own? A frequent theme in clinical histories, especially those involving marital difficulties, is continuing childlike dependence of husband on wife, wife on husband, sometimes even of parents on children. Being inappropriate to the actual demands of adult life, these needs are constantly thwarted. The resulting anger and hostility effectively destroy the generous spirit of caring.

Enduring self-centeredness can also stand in the way of generativity. College students chronically complain that many of their teachers are not interested in teaching them or in knowing them as persons. Often the complaint is justified: the teacher, an expert immersed in some branch of knowledge, is in fact preoccupied with research, publications, and intellectual career, and has not advanced to the point of wanting to share interests with younger people. The generativity that such teachers possess is not evoked by teaching; it is restricted to what they call "their own work" where they can more nearly follow their inclinations.

It should be allowed, however, that the balance can tip too far in the opposite direction, so that caring for others swallows up the possibility of having

153

any life of one's own. There are college teachers who devote themselves gener-
ously to their students, giving time, appreciative criticism, and encouragement in abundance, but producing no work of their own; perhaps in the end
they become less stimulating mentors. The problem occurs most typically in
women who become completely engrossed in caring for their children and
making a home, only to discover a mounting resentful tension over abandon-
ing their other interests and talents. It is also possible for nurturant tendencies
to get out of hand in occupations centered on helping people. Psychotherapists and social workers are sometimes made painfully aware that their desire
to be helpful has been exploited by their clients, and that they have failed to
use the possibly less sympathetic techniques that would actually have been
more effective.

LIFE PATTERNS: WORKABLE AND UNWORKABLE

In this chapter we have passed in review a series of problems in development
stretching from early infancy to young adulthood. In each case we have indicated successful ways of dealing with the problem, but we have also considered
the maladaptive consequences arising from a less successful handling. This account shows that difficulties in living exist in great number and variety. The
person who travels the whole pathway of growth without picking up a single
maladaptive tendency appears an improbable fiction. But it is necessary to
think of personality as an organization rather than an additive collection of
traits, maladaptive or otherwise. It is also necessary to bear in mind the enormous variety of external conditions amid which different people lead their
lives. We cannot talk about maladaptive tendencies without considering the
circumstances that make them maladaptive; what goes in one situation will
not go in another. The most pertinent question to ask about the consequences
of a given developmental history is whether or not the person has achieved a
workable pattern for living the particular life that is open to him or her.

Take the question of dependence in an adult male: the example of Benton
Child naturally springs to mind. Benton did not outgrow the dependent tendencies fostered by his protected and indulged childhood, but when he married Deborah, who was full of initiative and liked to dominate, it looked for a
while as if a workable pattern had been achieved. There are plenty of instances of successful marriages based on a dominant–dependent relation between wife and husband. In the Childs' case, however, the pattern soon proved
to be unworkable. The force of Benton's dependence, the immaturity of his
petulant demandingness, and his failure to assume minimum family responsibilities, made the burden of family life too one-sided for his wife to bear. No
hopeful signs appeared of gains in self-confidence or of nascent generativity.
Strife ensued, stress developed, alcohol was enlisted, and Benton's behavior
became disordered to a degree that led to the mental hospital.

From the contents of this chapter a generalized picture of good adaptation and psychological soundness could be constructed. A person who fitted the picture would have managed to avoid, or at least to escape from, all the maladaptive possibilities we have described. But this is not quite the way to think about adaptive excellence. There are great individual differences in what suits a person and in what different life situations require. Good adaptation has widely different meanings for performing artists, short order cooks, engineers, social workers—one could go on endlessly. Certain maladaptive qualities are fatal in some life patterns but do not much matter in others. Thus being a well-adapted person does not mean having a list of abstract traits with high scores on all. It means achieving and maintaining a workable relation between one's individual self and one's available life situations.

SUGGESTIONS FOR FURTHER READING

The topics examined in this chapter are discussed at greater length and with fuller illustration by R. W. White in a book called *The Enterprise of Living* (1976); Chapters 9–17 are especially relevant. Erikson, in the second edition of his important work, *Childhood and Society* (1963), and again in *Youth: Identity and Crisis* (1968) develops the idea of ego identity, which serves to relate the concept of self to the individual's place and function in society. Noteworthy contributions to the theory of social development are to be found in H. S. Sullivan's recorded lectures, *The Interpersonal Theory of Psychiatry* (1953); see especially Chapters 12–18.

The development of personality interpreted strictly in terms of social learning will be found in A. Bandura's *Social Learning Theory* (1977). Included are such topics as modeling, self-reinforcement, cognitive control, and an efficacy theory of action.

The name of John Bowlby occupies a prominent place in current thinking about dependence and attachment in young children. See especially J. Bowlby, *Maternal Care and Mental Health* (1951); M. D. Ainsworth et al., *Deprivation of Maternal Care: A Reassessment of Its Effects* (1966); both published in one volume (Schocken Books, 1966). The psychoanalytic view of dependence and its place in development is discussed in detail by H. Parens & L. J. Saul, *Dependence in Man: A Psychoanalytic Study* (1971).

Arguments for the importance in development of an urge toward competence are given by R. S. Woodworth, *Dynamics of Behavior* (1958), Chapters 4, 5; and by R. W. White, "Motivation Reconsidered: The Concept of Competence," *Psychological Review*, 1959, 66, pp. 297–333. Alfred Adler's ideas, including the inferiority complex, can be gathered most readily from the survey of his works, with extensive excerpts, by H. L. Ansbacher & R. R. Ansbacher, *The Individual Psychology of Alfred Adler* (1956).

The topic of aggression is interestingly surveyed in a book by R. N. Johnson, *Aggression in Man and Animals* (1972). H. A. Hornstein's book, *Cruelty and Kindness: A*

New Look at Aggression and Altruism (1976), pleasingly written, covers much ground and affords valuable insights.

Social development receives an organized and useful survey in H. R. Schaffer's *The Growth of Sociability* (1971). A good guide to the study of self is provided by K. J. Gergen, *The Concept of Self* (1971), an unusually clear, concise treatment. Two recent books on sexual development will be found especially valuable: J. H. Gagnon's *Human Sexualities* (1977), which includes information on trends, changing values, and stress points in current attitudes; and B. L. Forisha, *Sex Roles and Personal Awareness* (1978), which is especially strong on the origin and nature of sex roles.

The Castle of the Pyreness by René Magritte, Private Collection, New York, New York © ADAGP.

5
Anxiety and Defense

In the last chapter we described a variety of ways in which development can go astray. These possibilities are called maladaptive because they interfere with the flexibility that is needed to meet the problems of living. Excessive dependence, for instance, as well as compulsive independence, make it impossible to adapt one's behavior to the usual events of life in which it is sometimes appropriate to lean on others and sometimes necessary to act decisively on one's own. Similarly, social isolation and social enslavement, if either is carried to excess, may prevent developing a true sociability that leaves room for other aspects of personal growth. Maladaptive tendencies restrict the path of development and thus prevent a full flowering of personality.

159

The maladaptive possibilities described in the last chapter are not at all uncommon. Few readers can have finished the chapter without mild attacks of "medical students' disease." But the presence of maladaptive qualities at any one time does not mean that they will be there forever. Being learned in the first place, they are subject to relearning. Most people are aware of having "outgrown" certain traits that had led to unrewarding consequences. Some will recall voluntarily discarding such a trait and making a conscious effort to be different. We know all too little about self-corrective processes of this kind, but they must occur frequently. We do know, however, that change is sometimes difficult and that many people today seek professional help for such problems as dependence, competence, social adjustment, ego identity, and general depression. They ask for help in changing maladaptive patterns that resist change in spite of unwelcome consequences.

Thus far we have attributed the stubbornness of these patterns to overlearning. They represent strategies that have previously worked well, that have been reinforced by successful results and perhaps by encouragement and praise. Being a charmingly dependent small child and thus becoming the parents' favorite is a hard position to abandon when greater maturity is eventually required. Further difficulty in changing a piece of maladaptive behavior comes from its relation to other aspects of personality. If a young man has become proficient with a derogatory style, his mind stored with instances of outrageous human failings, his pride nourished by a sense of penetrating shrewdness, his security protected by keeping others a little afraid of him, he has a lot to lose by changing. Perhaps he has become aware of his own deficiencies in showing appreciation and eliciting love, but real changes in these directions may feel like threats to pride and security. Overlearned strategies do not usually stand alone. They are integrated into complex patterns and may serve several purposes. This increases their resistance to change.

Still more serious is the influence of anxiety. As we saw in the historical introduction, the study and treatment of the neuroses led to the conclusion that anxiety was the central problem in these disorders. Anxiety played a special part in their childhood origins and in their later elaborations. It was also the villain in treatment: change was laboriously slow because of the anxiety it evoked. Clearly we must examine anxiety and its effects on behavior.

THE ANXIETY REACTION

In a book of large historical significance, William McDougall (1908) catalogued the chief human instincts, emphasizing those shared with other animals. McDougall believed that each instinct when aroused carried with it a characteristic emotional experience. His list began with "the instinct of flight and the emotion of fear." He gave them this priority because of their power to interrupt and take precedence over other activities. Once aroused, fear "haunts the mind; it comes back alike in dreams and waking life, bringing with it vivid memories of the terrifying impression. It is thus the great inhibitor of action, both present action and future action, and becomes in primitive societies the great agent of social discipline through which men are led to the habit of control of the egoistic impulses" (p. 57). McDougall's vocabulary is old-fashioned, but he dealt with the place of anxiety in human affairs and in the growth of personality—problems that have lost none of their importance.

A second historical milestone is the work of Walter Cannon (1929) on the bodily accompaniments of emotional reactions. Studying fear and rage in animals, Cannon discovered a pattern of bodily reactions favorable to strenuous emergency behavior like flight or fighting. The pattern was activated by the sympathetic division of the autonomic nervous system; heart rate, respiration, blood sugar concentration, and other processes were quickly altered to favor violent exertion. These arrangements, clearly of value to creatures living in the wild, are not always as appropriate in civilized human existence. Imagined dangers or risks about which nothing immediate can be done may keep bodily systems as well as the mind in a state of lasting upset.

A third monument we owe to Emilio Mira (1943), psychiatrist to the Republican Army during the war in Spain. Mira differentiated several stages in

This is part of a time-honored circumcision rite among the Mandingo tribe in Africa. The threatening figure in the backround appears from the surrounding trees, dressed in red straw, wielding a knife and stick. In primitive societies fear is the great agent of social discipline.

161

the course of the fear reaction. He showed that mild anxiety was often experienced as constructive because it focused one's attention and increased efficiency. A small amount of risk is often felt as a stimulus and challenge that causes us to extend ourselves. People caught in sudden emergencies sometimes recall with amazement how promptly they thought of things to do and how energetically they behaved. If the danger is somewhat greater, or perhaps merely less definite in location, activity will begin to be limited and possible danger situations given a wide margin. One can picture the change by thinking of the slower steps and more attentive observation displayed by a person on foot who finds the ground suddenly marshy, or the cautious driving of a motorist who discovers the road is slippery. With continuing threat, the struggle to maintain control will prove increasingly costly, demanding extreme concentration and meticulousness.

Up to this point the presence of danger usefully restricts behavior. Attention is concentrated on possible sources of threat; spontaneity is lost; certain features of behavior are exaggerated to maintain safety and control. As danger mounts, however, control becomes increasingly difficult. Consciousness becomes occupied incessantly with the danger. Bodily signs of anxiety break out; tremor, restlessness, fast-beating heart, quickened breathing become oppressive. Thought and judgment deteriorate, actions are erratic and poorly controlled, and there is an unpleasant feeling of losing one's mental balance. A panic-stricken person, scarcely aware of what goes on, may rush wildly about, laughing, shouting, crying in rapid succession. These reactions sometimes lasted many days in soldiers exposed to prolonged fire. In some cases a stuporous and comatose state follows the peak of panic. Carried too far, intense fear thus ends in a complete breakdown of ordered behavior.

The Experience of Panic

Everyone knows what fear feels like when experienced in slight or moderate intensities. Few people, however, can remember the full force of their childhood panics, and few still, even those who have been in great danger, can report the contents of acute anxiety in adult life. If we are to appreciate the role of anxiety in maladaptive behavior, we must realize the overwhelming nature of the experience of panic. The following excerpts describe a severe attack in a 36-year-old writer and teacher, William Ellery Leonard (1927). Leonard was standing on a bluff looking out over a quiet lake, having left his walking companion in the woods behind. Painful recent events, the suicide of his wife for which most of the community held him to blame, had been causing mounting apprehension and waves of anxiety. As a small child he had narrowly escaped being run down by a locomotive, and this gave special significance to a train that passed along the opposite shore of the lake and brought the panic to its climax.

I stand looking out over the silent and vacant water, in the blue midday. I feel a sinking loneliness, an uneasy, a weird isolation. I take off my hat; I mop my head; I fan my face. Sinking . . . isolation . . . diffused premonitions of horror. "Charlie" . . . no answer. The minutes pass. "Charlie, Charlie" . . . louder . . . and no answer. I am alone, alone, in the universe. Oh, to be home . . . home. "Charlie." Then on the tracks from behind Eagle Heights and the woods across the lake comes a freight-train, blowing its whistle. Instantaneously diffused premonitions become acute panic. The cabin of that locomotive *feels* right over my head, as if about to engulf me. I am obsessed with a *feeling* as of a big circle, hogshead, cistern-hole, or what not, in air just in front of me. The train *feels* as if it were about to rush over me. In reality it chugs on. I race back and forth on the embankment. I say to myself (and aloud): "It is half a mile across the lake—it can't touch you, it can't; it can't run you down—half a mile across the lake."—And I keep looking to *make sure*, so intensely in contradiction to what the eye sees is the testimony of the *feeling* of that cabin over my head, of that strange huge circle hovering at me. . . .

Meanwhile the freight chugs on toward Middleton. I rush back and forth on the bluffs. "My God, won't that train go; my God, won't that train go away!" I smash a wooden box to pieces, board by board, against my knee to occupy myself against panic. I am intermittently still shrieking, "Charlie, Charlie." I am all the while mad with the terror and despair of being so far from home and parents. I am running around and around in a circle shrieking, when Charlie emerges from the woods (pp. 304–307).

It should be added that this experience of panic was so intense and unbearable that it was almost immediately forgotten. Leonard remembered only that he had had some sort of attack on the bluff. The full memory was gradually recovered more than ten years later during states of relaxation induced to promote recall.

Effects of Anxiety on Performance

People who perform in public confirm Mira's findings that a little anxiety, a touch of excitement, sharpens attention and improves performance, but a little more may produce unwelcome disruption like forgetting lines or playing wrong notes. Students giving a report before a group are sometimes dismayed to hear themselves uttering a badly jumbled version of what they had in mind. At a crucial moment in an athletic contest errors may occur that would never have happened during practice. Beyond a light stage, anxiety tends to disrupt skilled performance. At more advanced levels, as in severe stage fright, the interference with organized activity becomes painfully evident.

Educational achievement is unfavorably affected by anxiety. There has been considerable research on this problem. Anxiety can be measured in specific situations, such as when taking an exam, by physiological measures like heart rate and blood pressure or by behavioral signs like restlessness and distractibility. It can also be measured as a relatively constant trait: the Taylor Anxiety Scale, for instance, yields an inventory of life situations reported by subjects that make them feel anxious (Taylor, 1953). Subjects with high anxiety, as measured by this scale, are less confident, less adventuresome, and more

163

self-disparaging than subjects with low anxiety, and they are less favorably regarded by friends and teachers (Sarason et al., 1960; Cowen et al., 1965). Reviewing a large body of research, Gaudry and Spielberger (1971) conclude that "the overwhelming weight of evidence consistently points to a negative relation between anxiety and various measures of learning and academic achievement" (p. 77). In school systems where much weight is placed on a small number of examinations, students prone to anxiety may never be estimated at their true ability.

RECOVERY FROM FRIGHTENING EXPERIENCES

If human beings were perfectly designed to lead their lives under the civilized conditions they have invented, there would be no occasion for them to study abnormal psychology. Unfortunately we are not perfectly designed, certainly not for these conditions; we are here through having passed the acid test of survival in crude surroundings with only small beginnings of control over our environment. That we are so easily frightened suggests emotional endowments appropriate in the distant past but now likely to interfere with the most effective working of the adaptive process.

As we saw in Chapter 1, anxiety eventually came to occupy a central place in the understanding of neurosis. We are prone to these disorders because the fear reaction tends to freeze the adaptive process and make it inflexible in certain respects. To the extent that psychological treatment deals with changing these inflexibilities, its central task is the reduction of anxieties that are no longer appropriate to real dangers.

Relearning After Fright

The inflexibilities to which fear gives rise can best be understood by examining what is involved in recovering from frightening experiences. Following a fright, the overwhelming impulse is simply to avoid the whole frightening situation. Perhaps the danger is so great that no other response is possible. Very often, however, the danger was only momentary (like a motor accident) or is such that, given a second chance, the person could really cope with it. Furthermore, many dangers occur in the pursuit of vital interests that the person cannot sacrifice. The pilot whose plane crashes cannot afford to give up flying as a livelihood. Active children do not want to surrender explorations and adventures because on one occasion they have been frightened. Pride may be involved: the person is ashamed to continue being afraid. One has to come to terms with the circumstance of having been frightened. It means *renewed contact* with the threat, a new *appraisal* of its threatening character, and *new actions* to cope with it. It means, in short, new learning in the face of a strong motive to avoid new learning.

164

Obviously this is a precarious learning situation. It can easily happen that the dictates of safety will prevail, in which case avoidance will continue, the appraisal of danger will not be altered, and extinction cannot take place. Several investigators of animal behavior have reported great difficulty in extinguishing responses that were first made to avoid shock or some other fearsome stimulus. In one experiment, for example, rats badly frustrated and punished in a discrimination problem continued indefinitely to make a fixed response, thus never discovering that punishment could be avoided by a more varied repertory (Maier, 1949). In another study, dogs learned in a few trials how to avoid a severely painful electric shock, then continued to make the avoidance response through as many as 650 trials unreinforced by further shocks (Solomon & Wynne, 1954). These observations give the impression that avoidance responses have been built into the animals' behavior with a firmness that defies the usual modification by new experience. Precisely the same impression is conveyed by human anxiety disorders. William Ellery Leonard, frightened as a child by a locomotive, years later experiences an overwhelming urge to flee from a locomotive that is half a mile away across a lake, and becomes panic-stricken when he cannot do so. Bert Whipley as an adult continues to punish himself for the fancied childhood crime of killing his baby brother. Behavior learned in the service of avoiding anxiety seems endowed with peculiar and often quite damaging persistence. Mowrer (1950) refers to this as the *neurotic paradox*, "the paradox of behavior which is at one and the same time self-perpetuating and self-defeating."

> Common sense holds that a normal, sensible man, or even a beast to the limits of his intelligence, will weigh and balance the consequences of his acts: if the net effect is favorable, the action producing it will be perpetuated; and if the net effect is unfavorable, the action producing it will be inhibited, abandoned. In neurosis, however, one sees actions which have predominantly unfavorable consequences; yet they persist over a period of months, years, or a lifetime. Small wonder, then, that common sense has abjured responsibility in such matters and has assigned them to the realm of the miraculous . . . (p. 487).

Animal Experiments

The persistence of maladaptive behavior seems less miraculous in the light of the unfavorable learning situation created by fright. Safety is involved: it is nip and tuck whether there will be new learning or a renewed attack of anxiety that will make future new learning all the more difficult. The whole problem is beautifully illustrated in Masserman's (1946) studies of experimental neurosis in cats, studies that include the process of recovery. We give a few examples.

Masserman's cats were trained to depress a switch that first set off a bell or light signal and then dropped a pellet of food into a food box. When this habit was well learned, the cat was subjected to a sudden air blast at the moment of

165

feeding; this was repeated on several occasions until avoidant behavior became well established. Various procedures were then adopted to study the process of recovery. Three of these are of particular interest here.

1. Solution of the conflict between fear and hunger was *forced* by placing the hungry cat in the cage and slowly pushing it toward the food box by means of a movable partition. All animals reached a state bordering on panic as they approached the scene of former air blasts. Some, on seeing the food in the box, dove at it desperately and managed to eat; this put them on the way to recovery. Others became wildly panic-stricken, ate nothing, and left the situation in a state far worse than before.

2. Another method, called *retraining*, consisted of petting, stroking, and feeding the cat by hand when it was replaced in the experimental cage. Under this treatment the cat gradually calmed down and by slow degrees recovered the possibility of feeding from the box and depressing the switch. It even learned to tolerate the air blast and eat in spite of it. But if the process were rushed and the signals and air blast reintroduced too soon, the cat was thrown back into its anxious condition and further efforts at retraining were less effective. This procedure represents a combination of extinction and counter-conditioning—connecting the cage with pleasurable, relaxing stimulation to counteract the fear response.

3. The third method, *spontaneous working-through*, called for putting the hungry cat in the cage and leaving it entirely to its own devices. This procedure illustrates particularly well the fine balance between fear and the hunger driven urge to overcome fear. At first the animal ignored the switch, even refusing to eat a pellet of food placed on it. As hours went by, however, the cat became increasingly restive and would approach the switch, touching it very gently. The first time the switch was depressed sufficiently to set off the bell or light signal, the cat would hastily retreat and make no effort to secure the pellet in the food box. After a while, growing bolder, it would depress the switch freely and feed without signs of alarm. Reintroduction of the air blast somewhat renewed the avoidant behavior, but in time the animal could learn that even this was harmless. Spontaneous working-through represents what might be called the normal method of getting over a fright—at least the unassisted method—but it can easily go astray if anxiety is too strong, in which case the situation remains permanently frightening.

A Human Example

With respect to relearning after fright, cats and young children are not as far apart as might be supposed. This can be illustrated by the example of a 2½-year-old girl who developed a powerful fear of using the toilet. The fear proved to be specific to the act of defecation; the little girl could urinate freely on the toilet, but in order to avoid having to defecate there she would steal away to some private spot and move her bowels in her pants. It is evident that this fear had not been created by an experimental blast of air, nor could the parents recall any incident in the course of their attempts at training that seemed capable of producing such a result. One of the findings that emerged from the work of Freud and his followers, however, was that young children have fantasies surrounding their excretory processes, and that these fantasies, primitive but powerful, may sometimes be alarming. The toilet is a place where things are washed down and disappear. Very young children have been known to be afraid that they would be flushed down if they sat on the toilet, or to believe that the feces that disappear are a valuable part of themselves. Thus it is possible to believe that this little girl's phobia came into existence not because of an externally initiated fright but because of an imagined danger.

If a fear of this kind appeared in a slightly older child, the first helpful step would be to try to dispel it by information: the toilet is not wide enough to flush down a child, the feces are not precious and we are always making more of them. Many a fear has been abated simply by setting the actualities straight. But it can easily happen that the parent's reassuring explanation has no effect on the avoidant behavior, as if it did not communicate with the child's own conception, which indeed may well be the case when the child's cognitive development is not far advanced. If the parents cannot reorganize the child's cognition so radically that defecating in the toilet becomes a different and safe stimulus, their options in dealing with the phobia become similar to those of Masserman in dealing with the cats. The first or *forced* solution would consist of placing the child forcibly on the toilet and awaiting the desired result. This tended to produce panic in the cats and would predictably make the problem worse. The third solution, *spontaneous working-through*, would call for doing nothing, in the hope that the child would eventually prefer to use the toilet in normal fashion, like her parents and siblings, and overcome her anxiety at her own pace. This entails the risk that nothing will happen, leaving the fear more fixed than ever, and in any event it might take an extremely long time. The second alternative, *retraining*, was therefore the one actually chosen by the parents in this case.

The retraining followed the principle of operant conditioning whereby new behavior is shaped by a program of rewards. To assist the desired result, fruit and liquids were made prominent in the child's dinner menu. Immediately after dinner, before she could go elsewhere, her father instituted daily 20-minute training sessions: while she sat on the toilet he sat next to her, entertaining her and telling her stories. Periodically she was urged to push hard and make gas in the toilet, and whenever she succeeded in making gas she received a small M & M candy and a lot of praise. This first step proved easy, so that after a few sessions she was regularly winning several M & M's each evening. However, she soon reached a critical point when the urge to defecate was so strong that she could no longer make gas without also having a movement. This frightened her and she held it in, often with great effort, despite all her father's exhortations and other tactics. Finally, he spanked her once, crisply

167

but not very painfully, which resulted in an immediate bowel movement. This triumph earned her four large M & M's, abundant praise and affection, and the summoning of the rest of the family to share in the celebration. The procedure was repeated the next two times the urge was obviously strong, with the surprise of the spank serving to relax the taut sphincter. Thereafter no spanking was necessary, resistance to pushing diminished, and she began to look forward to the evening sessions.

Soon she decided to name her feces as they arrived. Depending on size, they were first called Papa Bear, Mama Bear, and Baby Bear, but the idea of naming suggested wider possibilities. Before long, usually in an expansive mood, she began announcing in advance the characters to be produced, so that in the end all the local pet animals, all her relatives, and most of the neighbors had the honor of being on her guest list.

Overcoming the phobia took a long time. Treating anxiety is not a place to look for quick victories. Nearly a month of regular sessions occurred before the child went directly to the bathroom without hesitation. Only after eight weeks had her movements become so regular as to avoid accidents. At this point candy rewards could be discontinued; social recognition was sufficient to maintain the new behavior. Even so, there was a brief setback at ten weeks, with an unexplained accident in her pants and obvious renewed fear of the toilet. This time, however, three evening sessions with candy and guest lists were enough to subdue the anxiety, and thereafter the little girl had no further trouble.

Defensive Obstacles to Relearning

The difficulty of relearning after fright, as we have seen, comes from the circumstance that avoiding a dangerous situation is incompatible with finding out that it may not really have been dangerous. The cats in Masserman's experiment were capable of tolerating a blast of air while feeding, but their response to the first few experiences of the bizarre event prevented their finding this out. As long as they cowered at the far end of the cage there were no more blasts and no fresh appraisal of consequences. These cats, of course, were captive. Denied to them were the usual feline options of running away, climbing a tree, and permanently looking elsewhere for their food. The little girl was also in a sense captive. She was not allowed to use her chosen avoidant response, which was to move her bowels in her pants and thus make the toilet unnecessary. When fright is experienced and an avoidant response works, it is a sound principle of survival—as well as a sound principle of learning—to keep on using that response on future occasions of danger. Pressure is required—the cats boxed in and made hungry, the child pushed toward socialized behavior—to counteract the seemingly sensible plan of keeping away from what scares you.

The plan is not as sensible as it seems. Our evolutionary heritage has equipped us to frighten too easily. Fear is an extremely unpleasant tension,

168

and behavior that reduces it is likely to be powerfully reinforced. This is all very well in a dangerous world, but for a child in a family it often happens that events are not as dangerous as they seem. Toilets will not swallow you up, parental anger will not lead to injury and death, scolding does not imply abandonment, belittlement does not signify being forever cast out. Avoidant responses can be learned to any of these things, but it is evident that development will be seriously crippled if the child tries for total avoidance of parental anger, scoldings, and belittlements. Along with cognitive growth, these human stimuli require discrimination, an increasing knowlege of the extent of their effects under different circumstances, so that responses can be modulated and made more appropriate. But this implies continual reappraisal, and it is just this step that cannot be taken if avoidance has the right of way. Mowrer's expression, the *neurotic paradox*, refers to just such an outcome. Patients do not do what is good for them; for instance, they fail to stand up for their rights and allow themselves to be pushed into a disadvantageous position. This can happen when self-assertion has remained indiscriminately associated with anxiety, so that the need for anxiety-reduction overcomes the desire for one's rights.

The adaptive process is thus capable of being crippled and made inflexible when the avoidance of anxiety demands too much of it. The result can be visible in the behavior of animals and young children, but in the human cognitive field there are counterparts of avoidance that manifest themselves less obviously in overt behavior—what might be called mental maneuvers for controlling anxiety. The yield from Freud's painstaking investigations of the recollections and free associations of his patients included much information about this form of defensiveness, conceptualized as defense mechanisms.

DEFENSE MECHANISMS

The concept of defense was introduced by Freud in some of his earliest writings. Before long he substituted repression, which became for a while one of the keystones of his thinking. Later he reversed his position to the extent of reinstating defense as the general concept, with repression standing as one of the defense mechanisms along with projection, reaction formation, regression, turning against the self, and four or five others. Anna Freud (1937), in her book on defense mechanisms, takes the same general position, but recognizes that repression is entitled to a somewhat special status. She points out, for instance, that other defenses are very often combined with repression, and she entertains the possibility that "other methods have only to complete what repression has left undone." Repression, in her view, is entitled to a unique position because of the amount it seems capable of accomplishing and because of its damaging consequences.

169

Repression

Freud arrived at the concept of repression, as we have seen, in his early work
with hysterical patients, when stubborn resistances to free association gave way
and events of great emotional importance were restored to awareness. It
seemed evident that the resistance was not simply to talking about the events;
the patient was truly unable to recall them until a deeper resistance had been
overcome. This suggested that the original forgetting of the incidents was of
an unusual character. Instead of fading out because they were unimportant,
the memories had been pushed out because they were especially important but
also acutely painful. In one of his definitions Freud (1915) said that "the essence of repression lies simply in turning something away, and keeping it at a
distance, from the conscious" (p. 147). In a later work, when he had given
anxiety a central position in his theory of neurosis, he described repression in
more clearly defensive language: memories, images, and impulses were excluded from consciousness when they tended to arouse unmanageable anxiety
(Freud, 1926). It was not Freud's idea that this sort of thing occurred all the
time. He did not imply a general law that we tend to forget the unpleasant. A
whole series of laboratory experiments designed to test the concept of repression, but using relatively innocuous situations, did not at all come to grips
with the problem (MacKinnon & Dukes, 1962). Repression occurred only in
situations that involved grave anxiety; moreover, it occurred most frequently
and importantly in early childhood, when cognitive development was still at a
primitive level. In addition, Freud showed by his usage that the most likely
candidates for repression were wishes arising from instinctual urges that if expressed would lead to disastrous consequences. Not just specific situations, but
all images connected with sexual or aggressive urges might have to be kept at a
distance from consciousness if linked to anxiety.

Repression can thus be described as a primitive mental maneuver for avoiding anxiety. Danger-inviting impulses are excluded from awareness and thus
also from overt behavior. This form of avoidance shares the shortcoming of
overt avoidant behavior: it makes no provision for renewed encounters with
danger and thus blocks the process of extinction. The dangers of early childhood are not simply isolated happenings, like witnessing an accident or nearly
being run down by a locomotive. Whether we emphasize parental behavior or,
like Freud, the impulses in the child that evoke parental behavior, the typical
dangers are recurrent. The parents will again be punishing or rejective, the
child will again have impulses toward naughtiness and self-assertion. It is vital
for development that the alleged dangers in these interactions be reappraised
and discovered to be manageable to some extent. Repression prevents this
from happening. This makes it, in Anna Freud's words, "the most dangerous
mechanism. . . . The withdrawal of consciousness from whole tracts of instinctual and affective life may destroy the integrity of the personality for good and
all" (A. Freud, 1937, p. 54).

Repression of erotic impulses in childhood was judged by Freud to have especially long-lasting consequences. In his treatment of anxiety disorders in the late nineteenth century, he repeatedly discovered great resistance to recalling any episodes, past or present, in which the patients had experienced sexual inclinations and fantasies. Childhood erotic tendencies, which in those days were often visited by violent disapproval, had been repressed only too well, so that in adult life even the most legitimate sexual feelings evoked anxiety sufficient to keep them out of awareness. But the sexual urge, of course, was not thereby eliminated, and the result was a state of tension in which its energies sought indirect outlets in dreams, disguised fantasies, and other symbolic manifestations. Later in the history of psychoanalysis, childhood aggression received similar emphasis: patients resisted the recall of anything that meant they had been angry, but their associations were filled with symbolic evidences of destructiveness. Repression was historically an essential aspect of the concept of unconscious motivation that has had such a large influence on contemporary thought.

Projection

Close inspection of other defense mechanisms shows that they regularly presuppose an element of repression. In other words, they consist of a defensive inhibition followed by secondary adjustments that serve to make the inhibition more secure. These secondary adjustments are part of the repertory of normal behavior. They become defense mechanisms only through their linkage with repression, which causes them to have the characteristics of excess and rigidity.

Projection is usually defined as the attribution of one's own thoughts, feelings, and impulses to other persons or objects in the outside world. Its basis lies in the fact that our own feelings tend to influence our perception of the world. Murray (1933) performed an experiment in which children were given two opportunities to judge the emotions being expressed in a series of photographs. Between the first and second judging, the children played a scary game of "murder," with the result that they found the faces markedly more malicious when seen the second time. Sears (1936) used a method in which subjects rated themselves and each other on various personality traits. When subjects lacked insight into their own traits, they tended to give unduly high ratings on these traits to their acquaintances. It is out of such raw materials—such motivationally colored perceptions—that the projective process is constructed. It becomes a defense when the recognition of one's own feeling entails anxiety and evokes protective inhibition. Projection then has so much work to do in maintaining the defense that it may reach the pathological proportions of a loss of reality testing.

Most people can recollect occasions in everyday life where they attributed a humiliating error to something outside themselves. The baseball batter who

171

This is how Casey's moment of truth might have appeared to him. To externalize blame eases the guilt for personal failure.

swings and misses, then glowers at the bat as if it had opened a hole for the ball to slip through, can stand as the symbol of this very human tendency to externalize blame. If this were serious projection, however, the player would go on to have the bat examined for holes and would believe that the pitcher was in league with magical enemies. Projection occurs in its strongest form in paranoia and paranoid schizophrenia, in which patients are deeply convinced that they are objects of hostility, plots, and sexual aggressions by others. Therapists who try to argue them out of these convictions may soon find themselves classified as part of the enemy forces.

Reaction Formation

This mechanism means the development of tendencies or traits that are the very opposite of tendencies we do not like in ourselves. To take a simple example, suppose a man comes to realize that he is very dependent and, feeling a bit ashamed of this discovery, resolves to be scrupulously self-sufficient in all

172

respects. He may carry his independence somewhat to a fault, but it does not reach the proportions of desperate defense. Normal development often proceeds in just this way. Suppose, however, that his reaction formation had occurred in childhood, and had resulted from acute shock, say a sudden belittling rejection by the people on whom he depended, so that he repressed his own dependent impulses. Now the reaction formation serves the purpose of a daily denial of a threat still felt to be intolerable. He has to be self-sufficient to avoid fear, and his reaction formation will probably be extremely rigid. He will be one of those people who cannot even ask for a match.

Now that Freud's ways of thinking have become so much a part of the culture, we are all perhaps a little too ready to interpret behavior as reaction formations. People who have developed a derogatory style feel more shrewd and sophisticated if they assert that another person's behavior is not what it seems to be, but covers up for the opposite. If a man boasts about sexual prowess and is strongly assertive with women, we wonder whether he is reacting to fears of impotence and passivity. If a woman is strong in the cause of women's rights, we think of the possibility that she is denying her domestic inclinations and maternal feelings. In some cases these guesses might be correct, but knowledge that reaction formation has occurred depends on unusual familiarity with the person's history. Not everything we do is a cover-up for its opposite. To interpret behavior correctly as a reaction formation, we must establish that the opposite characteristics were at one time, and perhaps still are, subject to intense anxiety that is controlled by excluding them from awareness and enacting their opposites.

Displacement

This variety of defense is twice illustrated in the case of a young woman described by Anna Freud (1937). The central problem was a jealous hatred of her mother, which, however, she dared not express lest she lose her mother's precious love. The first protective maneuver was a *displacement* of the negative feelings onto another woman. "Her mother continued to be a love-object, but from that time on there was always in the girl's life a second important person whom she hated violently." This hatred entailed less anxiety than hating her mother, but it still caused her suffering. Next she *turned inward* the aggression that was felt toward others. "The child tortured herself with self-accusations and feelings of inferiority, and did everything she could to put herself at a disadvantage and injure her interests, always surrendering her own wishes to the demands made on her by others" (pp. 47, 50). That this could be a solution shows the force of her anxiety lest her mother desert her, but after a while it too became unbearable. To relieve herself of such a burden of guilt, she resorted to projection and began to imagine herself the innocent victim of hate and persecution by others.

Intellectualization

Under this heading belongs a group of defensive processes that are of central importance in compulsive anxiety disorders. These processes have the characteristic tendency of taking emotional conflicts into the sphere of intellect, divesting them of affective and personal meanings, and working on them as problems in metaphysics, religion, political theory, and so on. The word *rationalization* has been applied to this type of defense, though usually not in its original meaning of "making rational" but in the debased sense of "making excuses." Special forms of intellectualization have been called *isolation* and *undoing*. The details of these processes can best be left to the later chapter in which we study compulsive disorders. At this point it is sufficient to notice again that we are dealing with a normal adjustive process that becomes a rigid mechanism only by association with a primary defensive inhibition. The whole normal attempt to understand the world means capturing it in the realm of intellect and making allowance for possible distortions that spring from emotions and personal meanings. Only when intellectualization is preceded by

The defense mechanism of intellectualization denial. Laurel to Hardy: "I just let them fall. They broke all by themselves."

the repression of threatening personal tendencies and is prostituted in the service of concealing such tendencies can we call it a pathological mechanism.

In this account of defense mechanisms we have adhered to the idea that they are based on normal patterns of adaptive behavior that have been captured and rigidified in order to control anxiety. Each defense mechanism has its normal counterpart that contributes to adaptation. Thus intellectualization can be seen as a defensively distorted form of logical thinking, projection as a misuse of the empathic understanding of others, repression itself as an indiscriminate version of our powers of holding back impulses until circumstances are appropriate. This conception is more fully discussed in an essay by Kroeber (1963) and is implicit in a recent systematic book, *Coping and Defending*, by Norma Haan (1977).

PROTECTIVELY BURDENED PERSONALITIES

What happens to the development of personality when strong conditioned avoidance responses are not extinguished? What happens when "whole tracts of instinctual and affective life" are repressed and their alleged dangers not properly reappraised? Obviously these unchanged residues of childhood anxiety will be handicaps, but not enough to prevent growth from going forward. Their effect can best be described as imposing a pattern of restrictions on development: nothing must be done, no situations must be entered, that tend to arouse the original anxiety. Growth can take place so long as it meets this limiting condition.

The effect can be clarified by taking the simpler example of a physical handicap. Suppose that a boy is afflicted with infantile paralysis and recovers with substantial loss of locomotion. His whole development must now take place in such a way as to allow for his limitation. In building up competence and seeking the esteem of others, he will be unable to use athletic achievement. Social adjustment must be accomplished without his being able to dance or to drive a car. Some interests will be closed to him because they demand prolonged standing. This particular defect does not preclude a well-rounded and even distinguished career, but it nevertheless illustrates with simple clarity the effect of a limitation on the process of development.

When there are important unextinguished childhood anxieties, development must similarly proceed to take account of a limitation. The defense of warding off all memories of childhood danger situations, and all impulses that might recreate those dangers, may serve well enough at the time, but it leaves the person in a vulnerable position. New situations may be forcible reminders of the danger. Aggressive, sexual, or other tendencies are bound to be aroused, and the person has to build up a life in such a way as to forestall the arousal of what is repressed. Taking as an example children who sense real danger of losing parental affection, we can say that they have got to develop so

175

that they will never, so far as possible, offend their parents. The surest means of doing this is to subordinate their own wishes to those of their parents. As the world expands outside the family circle, fear of rejection may be so generalized that they become vulnerable to additional threats. Rejection by teachers, by playmates and friends, later by spouse and employers and business associates, has the power to call up severe anxiety. All of them must be pleased. Any coolness, inconsideration, or belittlement must be avoided at all costs. The whole pattern of traits and tendencies is colored by this necessity. It sounds like a bad pun, but we might truly say that an infantile paralysis grips any tendencies that might create a situation strongly reminiscent of the danger experiences of childhood. One can see the far-reaching limitation that affects human relationships. Others must never be offended, and they must always treat one well. The many traits and tendencies developed in order to bring about this result constitute in the end a sort of protective organization.

Every person grows up amid limitations that tend to restrict the full flowering of personality. Many of these limiting conditions are actual and contemporary; we are today more sharply aware than ever before of the crippling effects of poverty and cultural deprivation. Our concern here, however, is with the special kind of limitation imposed by unextinguished anxieties dating from early life that no longer correspond to actual dangers but that nevertheless impose themselves on adaptive behavior. Development can be seriously handicapped by obsolete conceptions of what is dangerous. We refer to the result as a *protectively burdened personality*—a pattern of personality that is burdened by having to maintain excessive protection against obsolete dangers.

It is convenient to distinguish two kinds of constituents that make up a burdensome protective organization. In the first place there is usually evidence of *overdriven strivings:* certain goals in life and certain types of relationship with other people are pursued with a relentless intensity that betrays underlying anxiety. In the second place there are evidences of *protective traits* that serve to prevent the person from being stimulated in ways that would arouse particular anxieties. If we conceive that both these constituents have the purpose of making the person feel safe, the overdriven strivings accomplish this goal by an active seeking of symbols of security, whereas the protective traits achieve it by resistive exclusion of symbols of threat. The distinction does not imply, of course, that the two methods are mutually exclusive. We would expect to find them both at work in any well-developed protective organization.

Overdriven Striving

An overdriven striving should not be conceived of as wholly different in character from a normal or healthy striving. It is rather an exaggeration and rigidifying of an ordinary way of behaving. Nowhere is it more important than here to bear in mind the continuity between healthy and disordered behavior. Overdriven strivings are exaggerations of certain tendencies that are almost universal in human behavior. They become exaggerated in the service of defense against anxiety.

These points can be made clearer by examining Karen Horney's broad classification of overdriven strivings, which she called "neurotic trends" (1945). Believing that the more important anxieties have to do with relationships with people, she proposed that overdriven strivings should be grouped under the three headings: moving toward people, moving against people, and moving away from people. Moving toward people, also called a compliant trend, implies that the person feels a certain helplessness and tries to win the affection and esteem of others in order to lean on them for support. Moving against people, also called an aggressive trend, means that the individual strives to surpass and defeat others, becoming strong enough to disregard their possible hostility. Moving away from people, detaching oneself from others and building up a more or less independent existence, has the effect of avoiding whatever threats may be contained in human relationships. Clearly these purposes are not in themselves abnormal. There are times when each one of the three is fully appropriate and highly desirable. Overdriven strivings are thus not brand new ways of behaving toward other people. They are exaggerated and rigidified versions of strivings that appear in everyone.

Normal people differ a great deal in the balance they establish among moving toward, moving against, and moving away from others. We would expect different patterns to result from different kinds of parental encouragement and from the social opportunities afforded by the neighborhood and the available groups. We would expect differences of temperament and ability to be influential. A considerable overemphasis on one or another trend is not inconsistent with good adjustment. We cannot call one of these strivings overdriven unless in addition to having been favored by temperamental and environmental influences it is being seriously overworked in the interests of defense.

Criteria for Judging a Striving To Be Overdriven

There are three criteria by which defensive overworking can be recognized. (1) The first is indiscriminateness: a given attitude is assumed not only when appropriate but even in the most unsuitable circumstances. A person who craves affection and approval, for instance, must have it from everyone, even from bus drivers and store clerks who are of no real importance in his or her life. It may even be required from children and pet animals. The trend has a compulsive intensity that does not permit it to be adapted to circumstances. (2) Another attribute of overdriven strivings is their insatiable character. The person seems never satisfied, does not reach repose, but always needs a little more of the same kind of satisfaction. The person who moves toward people wishes that even a very congenial evening had been a little more congenial. The person who seeks triumphs wishes that even a signal success had been a little more glorious. The person who manages to separate from all close ties

177

wishes to be also free from minor personal contacts. (3) The blocking of over-driven strivings creates disproportionate frustration, probably with signs of anxiety. If aggressive competitiveness, for instance, is serving a protective purpose, to be beaten in some competitive enterprise will throw the person into a state of desperation. The defeat means vital threat.

Need for Affection

That a striving to obtain affection could be overdriven was early recognized by Freud and his followers. The overdriven need for affection has been best described by Horney (1937). To have affection is certainly a good thing in itself. Such a striving, therefore, qualifies as overdriven only when it meets the three criteria just described: it is indiscriminately compulsive, it is insatiable, and when frustrated it gives rise to disproportionate despair if not outright anxiety. This intensity comes from the fact that the striving for affection is also serving as a striving for security. The person must have affection not only because it is good in itself but also in order to feel safe.

Horney pointed out that the individual who seeks security in this particular trend keeps unwittingly creating situations of conflict. A woman, for instance, thus overdriven is in great need of love from others, but she is more or less incapable of giving anything in return. The original difficulty contained a repression of hostility in the interest of retaining parental affection. Lurking within her, but kept very firmly out of her awareness, is a resentful distrust of other people. Emergence of this hostility into consciousness would constitute a basic threat, calling up the original danger situations in which anger had to be repressed lest it offend the parents. But in every relationship from which she seeks to gain affection, this dangerous hostility is stimulated. She needs too much affection; she cannot tolerate the other person's being interested in some third person, and she cannot bear to be the object of any demands or criticisms. In other words, she expects a degree of blind devotion that she is highly unlikely to obtain from anyone, and she is therefore continually frustrated. She continues, however, to think of herself as loving the other person. Unable to become aware of the mixture of hostility in her feelings, she can never allow for them, outgrow them, perceive her deficiencies as a giver of love, and achieve in her relationships a reasonable balance of give and take. "In short," says Horney, "for a person who is driven by basic anxiety and consequently, as a means of protection, reaches out for affection, the chances of getting this so-much-desired affection are anything but favorable. The very situation that creates the need interferes with its gratification" (p. 114).

Because rejection was originally a danger signal, this protectively burdened woman is highly sensitized to it. As a result she overreacts in indiscriminate fashion to anything that may be considered a rebuff. If an appointment has to be changed, or if she is kept waiting a few minutes, her equilibrium will be badly upset. It will be hard to take the initiative in seeking affection because she is so acutely sensitive to the possibility of being rejected. This is typical of the self-defeating conflicts that arise out of overdriven strivings. She must have affection, but at the same time she hardly dares seek it. If she is lucky enough to find an affectionate relationship, she will almost inevitably wreck it by sensitiveness, demandingness, and failure to give anything in return. Under these circumstances it is obvious that the whole development of personality will be badly impoverished. The vital problems of friendship and love can never be made to come out right.*

Needs for Superiority and Power

Both Adler and Horney were shrewd observers of overdriven strivings for power. In a culture that places a high value on competitive success the goals of power and prestige are attractive to many people. Striving for these goals might be described as already culturally overdriven in many sectors of American society. This makes it easy for power and prestige to become symbols of security and to be chosen as the objects of overdriven strivings on the part of people whose basic anxieties have to do with inferiority and humiliation. When the need for power is overdriven by childhood anxieties it soon exhibits the familiar qualities of indiscriminateness and insatiability. There is a constant search for new worlds to conquer. A man, for instance, thus overdriven is an autocrat in his office, takes a commanding part in business conferences, tells his wife and children how things are to be done at home, tries to raise the biggest dahlias of anyone in town, dominates the discussions at the parent-teacher association, and can be heard as the loudest and most frequent speaker even in casual gatherings. At the same time he is tremendously vulnerable to any obstruction of his need for power and prestige. It is then that anxiety creeps up on him, perhaps even to the extent that he looks for psychiatric rescue.

Implicit in the overdriven striving for power is the belief that everyone is hostile. Life is a competitive struggle, and the only way to avoid going under is to be on top. Along with the desire to have control over others there is usually an interest in recognition, in having one's power affirmed and acclaimed by others as an additional guarantee that they will not dare to be openly hostile. The intense concentration on the relationship of power, and the distrust of others that it both implies and engenders, crowds out other relationships and thus impoverishes the person's life in other dimensions. It will be hard for a husband, for instance, to think of his wife in any other way than as a person to be dominated to satisfy his own needs or as a person who will enhance his social position and economic prospects.

*The subtle ramifications of a burdensome overdriven striving can be fully appreciated only by reading a detailed individual case. In her classic book, *Self-Analysis*, Horney (1942) gives such a case, centering around a young woman's "morbid dependency" on a man. See pp. 47–52, 75–88, 190–246.

Competitive striving for success pervades our society as well as many others. We all cheered this hero in the film *Breaking Away*.

Protective Traits

In the course of growth a person builds up an array of traits that facilitate adaptation to the surrounding world. Characteristic and relatively fixed ways of doing things are developed. Gestures, for example, may be typically bold and sweeping in one person, small and hesitant in another; speech may be loud or soft, fast or slow; desks may be kept tidy or messy; work habits may be regular and persistent or spasmodic but intense. Such traits, like strivings, can be lured into the service of defense against anxiety. In addition to their convenience in general adjustment they can participate in a protective action against possible arousals of unextinguished childhood threats. A well-developed series of protective traits can serve as a police patrol against the outbreak of anxiety.

This possibility is unusually well illustrated in the speech and surface traits of a psychoanalytic patient described by Reich (1949), who introduced the striking expression *character armor* to describe protective behavior of this kind. When first seen, the patient created an immediate impression of refined arrogance. His facial expression was haughty, his speech quiet and measured, his gait slow and restrained. He lay down on the couch in a composed fashion, his legs neatly crossed. Even when discussing painful recollections he maintained his evenness and dignity; in fact, these traits became more conspicuous when he approached topics presumably of high emotional importance. "One day tears came and his voice began to choke; nevertheless, the manner in which he put the handkerchief to his eyes was composed and dignified" (p. 181). This patient was suffering from a severe anxiety disorder, and he knew that his cure depended on a free expression of his feelings during his hours with the psychoanalyst; yet he was so strongly armored with habitual protective traits that for many weeks it was impossible for him to do anything but resist his own cure.

The services performed by protective traits became clearer when, as in the course of psychoanalytic treatment, they can be slowly broken down. When this occurred in Reich's patient, a second layer of character armor came to light. Beneath the courtly surface his attitude toward other people, including the physician, was highly critical, hostile, and derisive. He took delight in the misfortunes of others and was constantly on the alert for their shortcomings. Yet this, too, was in the nature of a defense, for it concealed very sharp and painful feelings of inferiority. A person who carries a burden of inferiority feelings can ease the load somewhat by discovering equal or greater weaknesses in others, but to express such disparagement openly would invite dangerous reprisals and counter-criticisms. By his dignified protective traits the patient managed to look politely contemptuous while at the same time preventing any real arousal of his own disturbing feelings of hostility and inferiority.

Protecting the Self-Picture

Traits do not usually stand as separate items in a person's repertory of behavior. They form an organized pattern, and to some extent they participate in each person's image or picture of self. Most people are inclined to cherish and defend a favorable self-picture. To do so is by no means an abnormal phenomenon. Gardner Murphy (1947) described, as follows, the human tendency to paint the self-picture in the best possible colors.

> Both perception and valuation of the self are complicated processes that take a long time to crystallize. But the result of all these developments is that like the childhood rag doll, the self, scarred and tattered as it is, becomes a deeply treasured possession; for most of humanity, at least in competitive cultures, it is probably the central value of existence. However poor, confused, and inconsistent it is, it is central, and it must be defended not only against outer attacks but against a clear perception of its unloveliness (pp. 529–30).

When there is a heavy burden of anxiety, the self-picture becomes involved in the protective organization. Its defense becomes an acute issue. The patient cannot tolerate any blemish on this outermost layer of armor, even in matters that seem remote from central anxieties. Like other processes captured for defensive ends, the self-picture becomes rigid and cannot be modified in the light of new experiences. It also becomes, as Horney (1945) has shown, much

181

more a creation of fantasy designed to put overdriven strivings and protective traits in a noble and glorious light. Reich's patient provides a perfect illustration. One day the analyst, commenting on his aristocratic surface, called his behavior "lordly," and this led to the discovery that he cherished a very real image of himself as an English lord. This fantasy was based on a mere rumor that his grandmother had had an affair with an English lord and that his mother was half English; it included the notion that he was not the true son of his father, a small Jewish merchant in the German town where they lived. These fantasies had been elaborated consciously during the patient's childhood, and at puberty he had been able to translate them into actual protective behavior by imitating a very lordly and immaculate school teacher. The necessity of defense against obsolete dangers caused the patient to preserve and act on this juvenile self-picture well into adult life.

The Costs of Protective Organization

The protectively burdened personality operates at a cost. To keep the unextinguished anxieties of childhood from being aroused with disruptive force, it may be necessary to maintain an unusually exacting self-picture, to restrict one's behavior by means of rigid protective traits, and to overdrive certain natural strivings that have become entangled in the web of defense. These ways of behaving have all been unduly strengthened because they have reduced anxiety and increased a feeling of security. But they tend to impair the flexibility of the adaptive process. They restrict the freedom available to the person in dealing with problems both of change and of persistence. Finding the right vocation, for instance, may be hampered by a pretentious self-picture that demands nothing less than top status, by protective traits that make for coldness and lacking involvement, or by an overdriven striving that necessitates pleasing everyone by one's choice. When protective burdens are heavy, a disproportionate part of a person's choices is dictated by defense and a disproportionate share of energies is devoted to security. When the problem is seen in this way it becomes legitimate to speak of certain consequences or costs of the protective organization. Most common among these are disturbing tensions and chronic dissatisfaction.

Disturbing Tensions

Even a generally successful protective organization is not likely to be uniformly effective. The situations that arouse anxiety cannot always be avoided, and the urges that are felt to be dangerous cannot be held entirely in check. The result may be restless tension or spells of irritation and frustration that do not seem sensibly related to existing circumstances. Furthermore, overt anxieties of a diffuse kind may from time to time disturb the protectively burdened person. Without really reaching panic, the person may be bothered by fears of accident, fears of death, fears of going insane. The fear of going insane bears no relation to any real likelihood of doing so; it expresses in a symbolic way the person's dread of the confusion and anxiety that would ensue if the protective organization were to break down. Tensions of this kind are likely to disturb sleep and may produce dreams that are full of trouble and foreboding. Sound sleep requires true relaxation, and protective organization cannot always work so effectively as to produce this boon.

Another source of unease is the tendency of overdriven strivings to create conflict. Because of their compulsive intensity they block and exclude other tendencies and even conflict with one another. As Horney (1945) pointed out in her discussion of moving toward, against, and away from people, if any one of these attitudes is lifted to compulsive intensity it more or less wrecks the chances of using the other two. Yet because the other two represent more or less universal human needs, it is not really possible to subordinate them completely. A person whose anxiety in human relationships can be held in check only by an overdriven striving for seclusive withdrawal does not thereby obliterate wishes for affection, esteem, and glory. These wishes become needling from time to time and prevent feeling satisfied with the limitations imposed by the chief defense. If a second trend is also reinforced in the interests of defense, the situation is still more difficult. There is anxiety if seclusion is impossible and anxiety if competitive success proves elusive. The very intensity and indiscriminateness of overdriven strivings make it almost impossible to harmonize them with each other and with the rest of a person's tendencies.

Chronic Dissatisfaction

Protective burdens tend to wax and wane, depending on the extent to which the obsolete anxieties are stimulated by external circumstances. But running through these ups and downs there is apt to be a thread of chronic dissatisfaction and hopelessness. Overdriven strivings tend to be insatiable, so that even when circumstances permit them a large amount of gratification they do not lead to enjoyment and repose. Because they are serving in the cause of defense as well as enjoyment, and because the childhood dangers remain unextinguished, the goal of satisfaction can never quite be reached. Furthermore, it is possible that natural desires, perhaps even imperious bodily cravings, become blocked by overdriven strivings. The original fear might have nothing to do with sex, for example, but adequate sexual satisfaction would be blocked if an overdriven tendency toward seclusive withdrawal became dominant in the person's life.

The eternally unsatisfied need for security and the other needs that may become blocked in protective organization are capable of creating a feeling that life is not rewarding or fully satisfactory. If the situation does not improve in the course of time, the person may become increasingly depressed. A change of job may be tried, or a move to another place, or getting married or divorced, but these alterations may well fail to relieve the costs of protective or-

183

ganization. Even if the conclusion is reached that the obstacles to happiness lie within, no way may be seen to change or remove these obstacles. Thus it can happen that a person seeks psychological treatment not because of symptoms, not because of a disease, but because of wanting to find a way out of the discouragement and futility that result from the protectively burdened pattern of life.

Comparison with Normal Organization

Before leaving this topic, it is well to remind ourselves of the continuity between normal and abnormal behavior. Tension and dissatisfaction are part of the human lot; no one can go through life without considerable visitations by these unpleasant states. Obviously one cannot always be contented, buoyant, and optimistic, especially in a time like the present when we are beset by formidable real problems. It is hard to draw any line between disturbing tensions or chronic dissatisfactions that are suitable responses to a real situation and those that result from the exactions of a protective organization. Such a judgment has to rest on some criterion of appropriateness. Responses that are being made to the obsolete dangers of childhood would be expected to show less appropriateness to the current reality, more rigidity, more compulsiveness, more occurrence both in season and out of season. Ideally, we should be able to respond in an appropriate way to each situation as it arises, perceiving both what is old and what is new about it and adapting our behavior accordingly. No one ever reaches such a standard—probably no one ever gets through childhood without residues of defense against its anxieties—hence the concept of the protectively burdened personality is a relative instead of an absolute one. It is most applicable when the pattern of living is clearly restricted by overdriven strivings and protective traits and when there are clear costs in the form of disturbing tension and chronic dissatisfaction—which are not appropriate to the actual circumstances and therefore presumably referable to childhood anxieties and defenses.

SUGGESTIONS FOR FURTHER READING

The problem of anxiety is not at all the exclusive concern of abnormal psychology. It has been placed in its proper perspective as a general problem of the twentieth century by Rollo May in *The Meaning of Anxiety* (1977), who examines the contributions of psychologists, philosophers, social historians, and other students of humanity, and who attempts to formulate their ideas so as to find common ground for further inquiry. The first six chapters of this book provide an illuminating excursion through modern thought on this significant problem. Of similarly broad intent, surveying historical and contemporary views of anxiety, is a small book by W. E. Fischer, *Theories of Anxiety* (1970).

Recently there has been heightened interest in studying how we cope with anxiety and other types of stress. This interest is represented in the wide-ranging papers collected by G. Coehlo, D. Hamburg, & J. Adams in the book entitled *Coping and Adaptation* (1976).

The best book on defense mechanisms is Anna Freud's little classic, *The Ego and the Mechanisms of Defence* (1937). T. C. Kroeber's paper, "The Coping Functions of the Ego Mechanisms," which is Chapter 8 in R. W. White, ed., *The Study of Lives* (1963) develops in detail the relation between defense mechanisms and general, adaptive processes.

More than any other worker, Karen Horney tried to trace the ramifications of defense throughout the personality. Her most relevant books are *The Neurotic Personality of Our Time* (1937) and *Our Inner Conflicts* (1945), books that are still illuminating for a later time. Of similarly lasting significance is Gardner Murphy's early explicit relating of human defensive tactics to the protection and enhancement of the self-picture; see his *Personality: A Biosocial Approach to Organization and Structure* (1947).

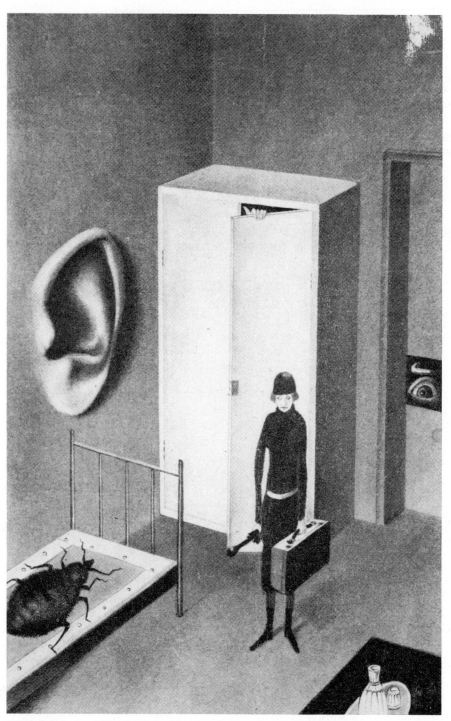

The Hotel Room (ca. 1930) by Anton Macher. The New York Public
Library.

6
Anxiety Disorders

The two most common symptoms of psychological disorder are anxiety and depression. In a study of hospitalized psychiatric patients they were the two most frequently reported complaints in *every* diagnostic group, with both appearing in more than three-fourths of all patients (Lewine et al., 1978). They are probably equally prevalent in less serious disorders that do not require residential hospital treatment. For this reason it is appropriate to devote this chapter to psychological disturbances that feature anxiety in its myriad forms, and a later chapter to affective disorders in which depressed mood is prominent.

For most of this century, anxiety disorders have been labeled *neuroses*, which means literally "abnormal or diseased conditions of the nerves." That

187

unfortunate term has a history that should long ago have been led to its abandonment. Early on, these "nervous diseases" were shown to be precisely the ones that defied explanation in neurological terms. Charcot exposed the neurological nonsense of such hysterical symptoms as glove anaesthesia or paralysis that could be removed by hypnotic suggestion. Freud elucidated the anxieties, defenses, and symbolic meanings that made it possible to think of these disorders as an outcome of misdirected adaptive effort. By the 1920s neurosis signified a disorder in which—however widely the learning process had gone astray—there was *nothing* wrong with the neurons! Unfortunately this semantic contradiction did not earn the term a decent burial. Instead, the adjective "neurotic" was picked up in both professional and popular speech and applied to almost any behavior suggestive of anxiety, inhibition, or indeed any quality that one did not happen to like. Gone thus riotously out of bounds, "neurotic" became a handy epithet for putting down rivals in arguments, and it was even applied to whole societies by their critics. With simple but compelling logic Costello (1976) argued: "Perhaps we should abandon the term neurotic for the time being and concentrate on attempting to unravel the function of anxiety, mild or severe, in our lives" (p. 45).

Bravely, the third edition of the *Diagnostic and Statistical Manual of Mental Disorders* or DSM-III (American Psychiatric Association, 1980) has relegated the term neurosis to secondary preference in the most recent classification system, and we reinforce that noble decision by expunging the word from our technical vocabulary. However, we do not follow the DSM-III in replacing that rubric with four new categories (anxiety, factitious, somatoform, and dissociative disorders) because we prefer to encourage students and clinicians alike to think of people in descriptive terms of process and behavior, instead of proliferating categorical labels that often confine or distort our understanding of the people involved. It seems preferable to use classificatory terms *as adjectives* to signify processes, behaviors, and often intensely personal experiences instead of as substantives that typify people. To illustrate, we prefer to talk about anxious persons with physical complaints related to their anxiety, instead of about "neurotics" with "conversion hysteria."

Historically, anxiety disorders have been recognized by fairly specific complaints or troublesome symptoms. The most common of these are panic attacks, phobias, obsessions and compulsions, amnesias and dissociated states, and a whole gamut of physical symptoms. It is perhaps not necessary to limit the concept literally to just these patterns, but care must be taken not to extend it as a blanket term to cover difficulties of living that do not come to a head in some relatively specific disabling symptom. The importance of this point will become clear in later chapters on psychological treatment. Treating a phobia is quite a different matter from trying to be of assistance in a struggle to achieve warm personal relations or in a puzzled search for identity.

This chapter is occupied mainly by descriptions of several varieties of anxiety disorders. These descriptions, however, will point toward a final section where, with images of the disorders freshly in mind, we can take up important and controversial theoretical questions. These include the nature of the presenting symptoms, the part to be attributed to anxiety and defense, the relative weight of past history and present problems, and the relation of the form of disorder to acquired strategic style and to constitutional vulnerability. Despite our strong condemnation of the misleading labels for these disorders early in this century, we intend to keep an open mind about physiological and anatomical factors that may play a role in causing them.

ANXIETY STATES AND PANIC ATTACKS

On first thought, it might seem that panic attacks refute the whole theory of anxiety disorders. If the disorder, with all its cost to the person, arises in the first place to prevent anxiety, how can one of its symptoms be the very anxiety it is supposed to prevent? This apparent dilemma vanishes when we recall that anxiety can break through in a variety of ways under a particular set of circumstances. If a phobic person suddenly encounters the object that was being avoided, anxiety can occur in panic proportions. If a patient with a hand-washing compulsion is prevented from washing, acute discomfort and dread will be experienced. Furthermore, people who complain only of anxiety states do not have them all the time; only on occasion do they find themselves bordering on panic. It is therefore still possible to think of panic attacks as representing the momentary failure of protections that usually keep the person reasonably serene.

The diffuseness and indefiniteness of the danger are the most trying features of panic attacks. Nothing in the actual situation seems to warrant the eruption, hence no sensible steps can be imagined to avoid it. The cartoon by Steig captures this frustration in telling fashion: because the little gesticulating demon is at the end of a stick attached to the back of a person's head, the demon always remains out of sight behind him, no matter which way the victim turns. Anxious people may feel that they are going insane, that they are trapped

This cartoon by Steig, called simply "Anxiety," tells its own story.

amid dangerous forces, or merely that something indefinably dreadful is going to happen. Many devices may be tried to keep control, like physical activity or intense mental work, but often these are of no avail. The sense of losing one's grip may add to the panic.

The psychotherapist who receives such a person for treatment necessarily subscribes to the view that the seemingly causeless anxiety must have causes. Not much can be done before discovering what the person fears—what the stimulating conditions are that set off the anxiety attacks. This can be achieved only by a careful scrutiny of precipitating situations, as well as the person is able to report them. Understanding current situations can sometimes be amplified by examining those that the person recalls from earlier life. Certain common features may be apparent in the series of fright-provoking situations, thus establishing a pattern of immediate causes of which the person had never been fully aware.

The onset of anxiety disorders ranges from 16 to 40 years of age, with the average in the mid-twenties, and their prevalence has been estimated at 2 to 5 percent of the normal population in the United States and Britain (Marks & Lader, 1973). Half the patients with anxiety disorders have secondary diagnoses of affective disorder and the majority also report symptoms of heart disturbance, such as chest pain, palpitations, and breathlessness (Woodruff, Guze, & Clayton, 1972), so it is not surprising that an estimated 10 percent of patients in cardiology practices suffer from anxiety disorders (American Psychiatric Association, 1978).

An Illustrative Case

Leon (1977) reported the case of Richard Benson, age 38, who applied for therapy because he suffered from severe and overwhelming anxiety that sometimes escalated to a panic attack. During periods of intense anxiety it often seemed as if he were having a heart seizure, with chest pains and heart palpitations, numbness, shortness of breath, difficulty swallowing, and a tightness over his eyes that restricted his vision to objects directly in front of him (tunnel vision). The patient had been anxious most of his life, but it was only since his promotion at work six months previously that the feelings of anxiety became a severe problem. The intensity of his symptoms was very frightening to him; on two occasions his wife had rushed him to a local hospital because he was in a state of panic, sure that his heart was going to stop beating and he would die. The symptoms were relieved with an injection of tranquilizing medication.

Benson had had a chronic problem of bladder and kidney infections as a child, but none occurred after the age of 11. Nevertheless, he continued his childhood practice of always learning the location of a bathroom whenever he was in an unfamiliar place. He was afraid of wetting his pants if he could not find a bathroom immediately, should he have an urge to urinate. This problem had become more intense in recent months and had generalized to many other circumstances.

Family History. The patient was the only child of white native Americans living in an urban, working class environment. His parents had an unhappy marriage, arguing continually. They finally separated when the boy was eight years old and he never saw his father after that. His mother obtained a job working as a waitress in a restaurant. The boy played with other children in the neighborhood when he was growing up, but he was a fearful youngster and rarely fought back if one of the children started picking on him. He was extremely afraid of going to elementary school because there were no bathrooms near his classroom, so his mother had to force him to attend every day. During a bladder or kidney infection it was difficult to control his bladder, and urination was extremely painful. Several times in school he partially wet his pants when the teacher did not allow him to go immediately to the bathroom. He was intensely concerned that other children would notice his wet trousers and make fun of him. Subsequent to these episodes, he developed an overwhelming need to urinate whenever he was in a place where no bathroom was available. This pressure would not abate until he actually did urinate. Benson described his mother as extremely nervous, not very demonstrative of affection, but a devoted mother who was concerned about his physical health and of whom he was fond. She rarely administered physical punishment, and usually reprimanded him verbally when he misbehaved. She closely supervised his play activities and left him in the care of a relative when she went to work. As a teenager he learned to live with his anxiety about urinating involuntarily. With a note from the family physician he was permitted to go to the bathroom whenever he felt the need, which greatly lessened his fear of being confined in a classroom. He had several friends and sometimes associated with girls as part of a large group, but he seldom participated in social activities at school and usually stayed home or visited relatives with his mother on weekends.

Young Adulthood. After graduating from high school Benson obtained an office job in a large investment corporation. Here he became acquainted with the woman, employed as a secretary, who later became his wife. She was the only woman he had dated for any length of time, although she had gone out with several men before they met. After three years of courtship, carefully saving their money, they were married. Their marital relations were harmonious despite their sexual inexperience at first. His wife was very understanding about his "interest" in bathrooms and usually helped him to locate them in any new places they went. Before the recent onset of severe anxiety symptoms he had been an easygoing person, able to converse well with others, which he considered an important occupational asset that probably was a factor in his recent promotion to a more responsible position. On the other hand, he usual-

191

ly gave in to the wishes of others in order to avoid being pushy, overbearing, or argumentative. Rather than engage in a dispute over politics, for example, he would change the subject and avoid discussing the issue any further. Admittedly, his interpersonal style often left him feeling angry and helpless, but the thought of freely expressing his opinions made him quite anxious.

Present Problem. The anxiety symptoms intensified markedly soon after he was promoted. His new responsibilities required immediate decisions and frequent conferences that lasted an hour or more in unfamiliar buildings. If he did not locate a rest room before beginning to confer, the familiar urinary urgency would build until he finally broke off the meeting to find a place to relieve himself. Conversations came to make him feel trapped, on the edge of panic, even if he knew the location of a bathroom. Such fears would also arise in his car in heavy traffic, or in a tunnel, or on a bridge. Periodic tests by his family physician ruled out urinary infections or other physical problems, and he was referred for psychiatric treatment when the symptoms reached catastrophic proportions. By the time he was hospitalized the anxiety symptoms were incapacitating him. He had begun to worry about when another acute attack would occur and this apprehension made him more anxious still. He expressed concern about his health and became sensitive about any fluctuations in his breathing or difficulties in swallowing. He began to note the location of doctors' offices and hospitals wherever he went and became extremely anxious if medical help were not close by. Though he had previously enjoyed bicycle riding with his children on the weekend, he resisted it now because of the lack of bathroom or medical facilities on the trails. Eventually he gave up cycling even on familiar trails with hospitals near by, for fear that the rest rooms would be occupied when he needed to use them. The anxiety states now spiralled frequently to panic attacks of heavy perspiration and rapid heart beat, which could only be brought under control with a tranquilizer injection by a physician. Ultimately he was unable to eat or go to work. He was staying home most of the time to avoid contact with people, and his wife was losing patience with his hypochondriacal idiosyncrasies. Finally, he took sick leave from his job and admitted himself to a psychiatric hospital for intensive treatment. We will review the treatment and the outcome in Chapter 7.

Analysis. Richard Benson's problems can be understood in social learning terms if one evaluates the interpersonal as well as the situational and physiological factors influencing the development of his symptoms. Because of the childhood occurrence of severely discomforting physical symptoms, he was classically conditioned to respond with anxiety to cues of bladder distention. The painful bladder and kidney infections and the associated pain during urination made this natural event highly aversive. With his fear of urinating involuntarily, the anxiety response generalized and included all situations where a bathroom was not immediately available. Many social situations consequently became occasions for anxiety because he anticipated embarrassment over a possible "accident." The conditioned anxiety response might eventually have extinguished in childhood if the response pattern had not been so generalized and so strongly reinforced by anxiety reduction. The anxiety response persisted, however, even after the infections terminated because it had been conditioned to so many physiological and environmental stimuli. Seeking closer proximity to a bathroom and urinating became instrumental responses that reduced anxiety in a variety of stressful interpersonal situations. Anxiety reduction followed each repetition of the behavioral sequence, further strengthening the avoidance conditioning process. Eventually, interpersonal situations alone elicited the instrumental response of seeking a bathroom. He was able to get along with his handicap as long as he could restrict his social environment, but when the expanded job responsibilities precluded these restrictions he was forced to face the anxiety more directly. The following escalation of physiological responses interacted with his increasingly maladaptive coping strategies because, as the level of anxiety intensified, the amount of relief achieved by social avoidance, medical contact, and tranquilizers increased commensurately, continually reinforcing his dependence on them. The progressive sense of helplessness further heightened his anxiety until he was virtually in perpetual panic. The irony of his tragic situation prompts one to give simple-minded advice: "So wet your pants already! That can't be as bad as what happens from trying to avoid it." Sadly, even that would not help because the chain of maladaptive responses was by now so elaborate, so pervasive in his life, and so much overlearned.

Obviously, not every child with a painful bladder disorder later falls victim to such a psychological disorder. It is likely that the physical symptoms came to have some personalized, symbolic meaning for Benson, which lent a special significance to their interpretation (cf. Chapter 3, "The Adaptive Process"). A more complete understanding of what those personal symbolic issues might be would require more intensive psychological evaluation than is presently available.

PHOBIAS

A phobia can be defined as an irrational dread of an object, act, or situation. The word "irrational" differentiates it from a normal fear, and is inserted to indicate that we speak of a phobia only when the thing that is greatly feared offers small actual danger. When a person shows intense fear of something that is in fact harmless, we have to assume that some distortion has occurred in the person's learning history to account for the unrealistic behavior.

Phobias cannot readily be classified. They have sometimes been named according to the object or situation that is feared. At one time medical writers favored attaching Greek prefixes to indicate every possible object of morbid dread. A few of these fancy names, such as claustrophobia (morbid dread of closed or constricted spaces), have become harmlessly lodged in the scientific vocabulary. In older medical literature there were literally hundreds of them: for instance, melissophobia (morbid dread of bees), gephryophobia (morbid dread of crossing water), parthenophobia (morbid dread of virgins), homilophobia (morbid dread of sermons). This list becomes endless because there is really nothing that cannot be an object of morbid dread. Lest the reader fall victim to onomatophobia (morbid dread of names), let us reassure you that this pretentious vocabulary is now largely obsolete.

Most people are familiar with fears they know to be out of proportion to real danger. Many adults are more afraid of snakes or rats or mice than is warranted by the harm likely to come from these creatures. Others experience irrational uneasiness on high places, in small enclosures, or in crowds. In an age when airplane travel has become common, several travelers have recognized a discrepancy between published statistics of risk and their own discomfort while

 Acrophobia is the fear of high places, which may be quite exaggerated in some cases.

Claustrophobia is the fear of closed spaces.

in the air, and some have found it impossible to use this method of transportation. The prevalence of such fears in an average community has been studied by interviewing a representative sample of the population. Fear of snakes was reported by 39 percent—this in a region with few poisonous snakes—while fear of heights was mentioned by 30 percent. These fears may be considered mild phobias, but they usually have less serious effects. In the same community the prevalence of mildly disabling phobias was 7.5 percent and of severely disabling ones much less than 1 percent (Agras, Sylvester,& Oliveau, 1969). To fear snakes and high places may be annoying, perhaps also a small insult to pride, but one's life is not really disrupted by avoiding them. With a full-blown phobic disorder the disruption becomes grave. Perhaps the person cannot leave the house unaccompanied, cannot go to work, cannot go shopping or cross streets or ride in cars, cannot take part in any social life. Avoidance of anxiety reaches proportions that interfere in critical ways with normal living, as we saw with Richard Benson. Phobic symptoms are relatively common. They were observed in 20 percent of the psychiatric patients in one study, somewhat more often among women, which may relate to biological sex differences (that are not understood at present) or to greater socialization pressures on boys to act fearlessly (Marks, 1973).

Taken together with anxiety states, phobia can be considered the simplest form of anxiety disorder, though the distinction between the two may be important because phobias generally respond better to psychological treatments

195

such as desensitization (Marks & Lader, 1973). In our historical introduction we noticed a large convergence of opinion on the idea that the central problem in these disorders is anxiety and its management. On this fundamental proposition there is agreement between psychodynamic theorists, whose ideas can be traced back to Freud, and learning theorists, whose original inspiration was Pavlov. Whatever else may be involved, the conditioning paradigm offers a helpful way to think about phobias.

Phobias as Conditioned Anxiety Responses

The excessive and inappropriate anxiety that characterizes a phobia suggests a conditioned anxiety response laid down in one or more situations of unusually acute fright. This conception is developed by Eysenck and Rachman (1965), who postulate that neutral stimuli that are relevant to the fear-producing situation or that make an impact on the person are likely to be included as conditioned stimuli for the anxiety response. Especially in childhood, when perception is still relatively global and undifferentiated, a large cluster of stimuli may thus become dangerous, and the range may be further extended by generalization to stimuli of a similar nature. The process is illustrated, as we saw in Chapter 3, by the child Albert, who was experimentally conditioned to fear a pet white rat and who became afraid also of rabbits, a dog, light-colored furs, and cotton wool (Watson & Rayner, 1920). Through these learning processes a basis is laid for later phobic fear of objects slightly similar or associatively linked to the original cause of fright.

This conception, based on Pavlov's model of the conditioned response, can be supplemented by explicit use of the concept of operant conditioning. Ullmann and Krasner (1975) contend that operant conditioning plays a major role in both the development and maintenance of phobic behaviors. The behavior associated with phobic stimuli is avoidance, and this response is reinforced by anxiety reduction, as we saw in Richard Benson. Phobic avoidance was maintained and strengthened over time until he was unable to go cycling with his children or to work. The avoidance response prevents new learning. Extinction cannot occur if the feared stimulus is so sedulously avoided that no new appraisal can be made of its danger.

Phobias in childhood can often be understood in these simple terms. The historic case of Peter (Jones, 1924), who feared rabbits but recovered from this fear by gradual deconditioning, appears to require no additional methodological or treatment concepts (although different theoretical explanations might be offered for Peter's recovery). Equally straightforward is an adult case of phobia, described in detail by Wolpe (1969), which seemed to be entirely the consequence of a recent motor accident. The car in which the person was riding was hit violently at a crossing by another car moving against a red light. Physical injuries kept the person at home for only a short time, but when she tried to go out again in the car she suffered unbearable anxiety. She also suffered, of course, almost unbearable boredom and frustration if she could never leave home. The treatment was difficult, requiring in the end 60 therapeutic hours, but it was all concentrated on deconditioning the various stimuli to fright—cars approaching from the side, cars crossing in front, and so forth. The plan of treatment used in this case made it possible for the woman to ride again in cars without discomfort.

Clinical studies suggest, however, that considerable complications may be involved in a fully developed phobia. These can be interpreted as complications of the basic principles of learning and motivation, but they have often been described in somewhat different language. Conceivably, the woman's symbolic interpretations of the accident contributed to the difficulties in treatment.

Phobias as Protective Displacements

Frequently it seems that the object of which a person is afraid is only a fragment of any likely situation of fright. The phobia is of sirens, or of streets, or of sporting goods shops, or even of anything that involves the number 13. Such objects of dread may have had some part in the original constellation of fear stimuli, but they seem like peripheral items instead of central dangers. It is as if the boy Albert were thrown into panic only by cotton wool while no longer being upset by the pet white rat. To explain this characteristic, the proposal has been made that anxiety aroused by the central stimuli has been blocked and then displaced to peripheral stimuli that have the property of being more avoidable. Especially when anxiety is linked to recurrent impulses of one's own that are being contained by repression, a gain in security may result from concentrating fear on an avoidable outside object. For a woman to have a phobia of being alone on the street may be a more comfortable solution than recognizing impulses to seek sexual contacts there. For a man to have a phobia of shops where guns are displayed may give him less distress than becoming aware of his own urges toward violence. Repression of dangerous impulses is kept secure by this maneuver of externalization.

Displacement presumably occurs along associative channels, depending initially on stimulus generalization. We examined such a process in Chapter 3 when studying Diven's research (Diven, 1937). In that experiment associative connections served as effective guides for generalization, even when the subject was unaware of the original stimulus, so that anxiety responses became linked to all rural words in a list as well as to the word "barn," which had been followed by electric shock. Using such channels, the phobic person may be said to fasten on associations that neatly substitute for the real source of threat. But there is more to it than is implied by stimulus generalization. Unlike Diven's normal subjects, who became uneasy about "barn" and everything rural, the phobic person is terrified only by some rural item such as "plough," and does not manifest anxiety about barns. This is the peculiarity that is ac-

197

commodated by the concept of repression plus protective displacement. The central danger is more successfully avoided by pushing the threat some distance away.

We have seen how much energy Richard Benson devoted to finding bathrooms, locating hospitals and doctors, and urinating—far more than was realistically justified by the objective circumstances. But all that expenditure of effort deflected his attention from other deeply threatening issues: making decisions, being assertive, confronting disputes openly, and dealing with people socially. From this perspective we can see that his phobic behavior preemptively shielded him from dealing directly with his deep-seated interpersonal insecurities. This illustrates precisely the concept of protective displacement.

Phobic Vulnerability and Current Stress

Not uncommonly a phobia assumes extreme proportions at some point in adult life after having been quiescent since early childhood. This requires the assumption that something has happened recently to increase the strength of the anxiety response so that it reaches a newly disruptive level. Such strengthening would seem improbable if the revived dangers were merely historical and had nothing to do with the person's current problems. The model of events that appears most applicable is the same one we used in studying anxiety states. Childhood panic occurs, and this creates a liability to experience panic again if the person encounters forcible enough reminders of the original dangers. But as the child grows up, perceives with more discrimination, and becomes capable of more competent action, situations of great helplessness are largely avoided and violent anxiety is not touched off. Then come problems in adult life that cause diffuse anxiety in their own right. This lowers the threshold for all responses to danger and thus calls up fairly soon those that were conditioned in the early situation of panic. The phobic symptom is a product of current anxiety utilizing responses that were first laid down under past stress.

This abstract statement can be made clearer by an example. No phobia has ever been so carefully studied as that of William Ellery Leonard, a poet, writer, and teacher who made his disability the central theme of a highly detailed autobiography (1927). At the age of 36, he had the extraordinary experience we used in Chapter 5 to illustrate the subjective state of panic, an experience of overwhelming dread as he stood on a bluff overlooking a lake, along the other shore of which a freight train was moving. From that day on, he suffered from a crippling phobia that kept him from going any distance away from home. By taking quarters across the street from the university he became able to resume his work as a teacher, but trips away from home, even not very long walks, would quickly be stopped by rising panic. Leonard received some professional advice, but he was largely his own physician, using relaxation and so-called "auto-hypnosis" to increase recall of earlier frights and thus, he hoped, blunt their force. He eventually remembered what was probably the initial panic, when at age 2 he stood too near the track on a station platform and was almost run down by a thundering locomotive—the "locomotive-god" of his title. Another major fright occurred at age 9 when he was chased out of the schoolyard by a group of jeering children after disgracing himself by making a puddle on the floor under his desk. From then until 36 he had occasional mild attacks of seemingly senseless uneasiness, but he was not unusually fearful and his freedom of movement was unrestricted, even when traveling by train. He married the daughter of a family much respected in the community, a woman known to be highly sensitive and subject to depressions. A few weeks before his attack on the bluff she committed suicide. The community, which had come to regard Leonard as demanding and self-centered almost unanimously blamed him for her death. His level of anxiety mounted uncomfortably until the intensified feelings of disgrace and rejection touched off the long quiescent panic responses of early childhood. On the bluff he had apocalyptic visions with details drawn from both early scenes. Then amnesia descended on this horrible experience, but now he dared not ever venture any distance from home.*

In the clinical literature it is sometimes reported that phobias tend to spread. The person is at first afraid only of riding in elevators, but then small rooms become taboo, the subway must be given up, perhaps all public enclosed places must be avoided. When avoiding elevators provides insufficient relief, stimulus generalization begins to operate and more things are imbued with properties of danger. The process is understandable but misguided, so to speak, in that it controls current anxiety only by imposing increasing restrictions on everyday living.

Secondary Gain from Phobias

When a person suffers from anxiety, this fact has certain effects on the environment. One of the most common results is that the individual enters the status of a sick person instead of a foolish or irritating or selfish one. This may produce gains in the form of sympathy, excuse from work, and providing of services by other members of the household. Adler was particularly fond of pointing out these gains from illness. Perhaps a need to dominate is served by the symptom: fear of going on the street forces some member of the family to accompany the afflicted person at the latter's pleasure. Perhaps it is escape from hopeless competition that is served: nobody expects a sick person to be out winning victories and setting records. Leonard's phobia appears to have had certain punitive consequences related to guilt over his wife's death yet anger at being held to blame for it. It was painful to narrowly restrict his life space but painful as well when he tried to extend it. But perhaps there was also

*Excerpts from this case will be found in Kaplan (1964), pp. 311–22.

an attempted punishing of the community, saying in effect, "Look what you have done to me by blaming me for my wife's death." The ultimate consequences of a phobia can be far-reaching.

Effects of this kind are often given the name of *secondary gain*. This usage follows a distinction originally made by Freud. *Primary gain*, he argued, lies in the control or better management of anxiety. This form of gain may be disadvantageous in every other respect, imposing crippling restrictions on the individual's life. *Secondary gain* consists of whatever advantages are found to accrue from the fact of having symptoms: gains from illness and other effects on the person's environment. Sometimes a symptom seems to have been guided from the start by anticipation, however unwitting, of the effect it would have on the environment. This is less characteristic of phobias, where secondary gains are really secondary and often not especially large. But when they occur they are certain to add to the difficulty of bringing about a favorable change in the person.

The extent to which a phobia is complicated by protective displacement, involvement in current life problems, and secondary gain probably varies a great deal from one person to another. The techniques of behavior modification, aimed straight at removing the symptom without searching for anything that might lie behind it in the past or present, have had their greatest success with phobias. The implications of this finding will be considered in detail in the chapters on psychological treatment. In general, however, during the last twenty-five years prospects have improved for successfully treating phobia within a reasonably short length of time.

COMPULSIONS

Anxiety disorders frequently are manifest in compulsive thoughts or actions. It is common to refer to these as *obsessions* and *compulsions*, but they are usually closely linked: for instance, the obsessive thought that there may be dangerous germs on one's hands leads to the compulsive act of handwashing. Therefore we will follow Carr's (1974) suggestion to use compulsion as the generic term, modifying it sometimes to indicate whether the compulsive behavior is cognitive or motoric. Carr also emphasizes the importance of distinguishing between compulsive *symptoms* and *traits*, so to avoid confusion, let us distinguish between compulsive *anxiety disorders* and compulsive *personality types*. A compulsive personality is characterized by traits of thoroughness, consistency, punctuality, and carefulness, but the behaviors associated with these traits do not necessarily occur against the will of the individual, nor to the detriment of everyday existence; they are integral parts of the person's character. Neither is there a clear relation between this cluster of traits and the occurrence of compulsive symptoms. In this chapter we consider only compulsive anxiety disorders, which arise from acute anxiety and in which overt symptoms (whether active or passive) *serve to reduce anxiety*. Carr (1971) monitored autonomic activity during the performance and interruption of compulsive behaviors and concluded that they occur at high levels of anxiety and reduce the anxiety to tolerable levels.

Characteristics of the Symptoms

A compulsion is a "recurrent or persistent thought, image, impulse, or action that is accompanied by a sense of subjective compulsion and a desire to resist it" (Carr, 1974, p. 311). Minor compulsions are familiar in everyone's experience. We keep wondering whether we turned off the gas burner, or we knock on wood after mentioning our good fortune. These everyday phenomena resemble clinical compulsions to the extent that they are sensed as irrational. We know they are foolish, but they seem to have a little push of their own and it is easier to let them have their way. In clinical compulsions this quality is greatly magnified. The ideas and actions are like foreign bodies, forcing themselves on the person yet not experienced as part of the self. Moreover, they often betray their defensive nature. If the person tries to stop the ruminations or rituals, he or she plunges into an attack of anxiety.

Compulsive symptoms occur in great variety. The person's mind may be full of thoughts about infection and disease, making it necessary to wash the hands a hundred times a day and to take precautions that would put a modern hospital to shame. There may be rituals in regard to dressing or going to bed that make these actions laborious and time-consuming. Blasphemous thoughts may intrude during nightly prayers. Orderliness may become the demon of one's existence, requiring an endless task of straightening, arranging, recording, and filing. Particularly trying are obsessions concerning harmful and violent acts: the person is invaded by ideas of burning the house down, cutting someone's throat, strangling the children, diving in front of a truck. The danger that such acts will be carried out is small to the vanishing point, but the person has no feeling of control over them and constantly fears that they will turn into realities. The lives of compulsive individuals are easily reduced to ineffectiveness and misery. Their energies are tied up in symptoms, and they are filled with doubt, vacillation, uneasiness, and helplessness. Occasionally an attack of anxiety breaks through.

Close scrutiny of the contents of compulsive symptoms show that they can be classified under two headings: (1) Part of the symptoms give expression to aggressive and sexual impulses. Murderous hostility, destructiveness, dirtiness, and sexual urges in a crude and violent form reveal themselves in the content of compulsive thoughts. It is as if the suppressed *antisocial impulses* returned in this guise to plague the person. (2) The rest of the symptoms give expression to *self-corrective tendencies*. Orderliness, rituals, cleanliness, propitiatory acts, self-imposed duties, and punishments all testify to the person's need to counteract and set right antisocial tendencies. Guilt feelings are almost con-

201

Judith Anderson tries in vain to remove the abhorrent blood from Lady Macbeth's hands in Shakespeare's poignant description of a compulsive ritual. Lady Macbeth: "Out, damned spot! Out, I say! . . . What, will these hands ne'er be clean? . . . Here's the smell of the blood still. All the perfumes of Arabia will not sweeten this little hand."

stant companions. Reading in the paper about a murder that was committed many miles away may evoke guilt as intense as if the person had actually *committed* the murder and deserved terrible punishment. The division of the symptoms into these two classes, *antisocial impulses* and *self-corrective tendencies,* gives an immediate insight into the nature of the conflict. A childish conception of evil joins battle with a childish conception of righteousness and punishment.

Compulsive symptoms sometimes have a sudden onset, but very often they make their appearance gradually. When the symptoms develop gradually, it is almost always the self-corrective ones that make the first appearance. The symptom picture is first occupied by derivatives of the defensive process. Only later do signs of the anxiety-linked impulses creep into the scene.

Distinctive Features of Compulsive Disorders

Although compulsive disorders frequently overlap with others, especially with phobias, a number of characteristics roughly differentiate them from other patterns.

1. Elements of conflict are more fully represented in consciousness than in any other anxiety disorder. Antisocial and self-punitive tendencies can be read in compulsive thoughts and actions, although they are often disguised and symbolic and not experienced by the person as a part of the self. These impulses "feel" like foreign bodies that intrude themselves from unknown parts of the mind, leaving them semi-detached from the self.

2. The struggle between anxiety-linked impulses and defensive processes is carried on in the realm of intellect, making extensive use of displacement. The person may ruminate on the philosophical antagonism between love and hate instead of recognizing hateful impulses toward some loved one. This tendency may interfere with treatment, giving rise to theoretical disputes with the therapist over basic assumptions about clinical practice, for example.

3. Aggressive impulses occupy an unusually large place among basic conflicts in compulsive disorders. Sexuality is by no means excluded, but hostility is usually the predominant issue.

4. Certain character traits are common in compulsive disorders, showing a distinctive pattern of protections. Compulsive people often show great interest in orderliness and cleanliness, which they carry to extremes. They are inclined to be conscientious and idealistic, wanting always to be kind and considerate of others, never angry. Two other traits often appear in the pattern: stubbornness and stinginess. These features of personality imply strong compensation against aggressive, destructive, and messy tendencies, as well as strong needs for self-direction.

These distinctive features of compulsive disorders imply a pattern of adaptation—a strategic style—that is different from what is seen in other anxiety disorders. This style has been characterized in various ways. Salzman (1968) emphasized the interest in absolute control, along with the feeling that any loss of control would constitute an unbearable public display of inadequacy and imperfection. This requires the guidance of one's life by conscious rules, principles, and conventions, and careful preparation in advance to meet all possible emergencies. Salzman mentions the example of a lawyer in court who had an anxiety attack when opposing counsel introduced an argument he had not anticipated. Actually the argument was of no importance, but the mere fact of being surprised and caught unprepared was a sufficient stimulus to violent anxiety. A different aspect of the adaptive style was emphasized by Angyal (1965), who spoke of a *pattern of noncommitment* that he thought might arise from a childhood atmosphere conducive to abiding confusion as to whether the world is basically friendly or inimical. This pattern is especially clear when decisions have to be made; long delay, and a careful balancing of factors that always seem equal, show the person's reluctance to undertake a final course of action. Shapiro (1965) described the compulsive style as one of tense deliberateness and effortfulness. More or less continuous pressure is exerted against oneself, while at the same time suffering under the strain of that pressure. But the demands are not experienced as one's own; they seem instead to arise from a job to be done, an expectation to be met, a duty to be

203

performed—some intrinsic requirement outside the self. Shapiro likens the compulsive person to *a dutiful soldier in search of an order*. There is little room for zest and enthusiasm in a life thus structured, and there tends also to be some loss of the experience of conviction. The acute symptoms of compulsive disorders exhibit many of these characteristics in exaggerated form. Finally, in a risk-taking study of psychiatric patients Steiner (1972) found that compulsive patients were much more cautious than any of the other groups, which Carr (1974) attributes to their chronic overestimation of the probability of undesired outcome, with an accompanying high level of perceived threat and felt anxiety. Such pessimism would naturally engender both conservatism and apprehension.

Example of the Mechanisms of Isolation and Undoing

It is hard to convey the degree to which the compulsive person's actions and thought processes become clogged unless we can use actual illustration. A boy of seventeen had severe conflict over masturbation. His pastor gave a talk denouncing the practice, and advised that one should never associate with a boy who masturbated. The boy had an acquaintance who masturbated, and he now found it difficult to keep away from him. But when he passed him on the street he felt distinctly uneasy. The first symptom was a little ritual of turning around and spitting whenever he passed the wicked boy. This is a perfect example of *undoing*: the boy cleansed himself and expressed rejection immediately after permitting the danger of contact. The symptom was insufficient, however, to deal with the anxiety generated by these threatened contacts, and the next defensive strategy was a phobia. He developed a morbid dread of meeting the bad boy, avoiding the possibility as much as possible. The phobic system began to expand until it included the whole section of the city in which the other boy lived. Further, he made a compulsive stipulation that no member of his own family should enter that section.

From this point the symptoms invaded his thinking more and more fully. A severe compulsive disorder took the place of the phobias. The boy found himself thinking about the forbidden section of the city. Even this contact in thought had to be prevented. He developed an elaborate technique of *isolation*: he would stand still and fix on an image of the forbidden region until the image was bereft of all meaningful connections and stood all alone in his mind. To effect one of these isolations took quite a while, often as much as an hour. Before long he was dividing the whole world into good and bad, which increased the scope of his isolations. Even language fell into the two categories, so that he had to choose carefully lest a good and bad word make contact by being in the same sentence. The whole thing became so laborious that he deliberately thought about the forbidden things in order to strengthen the images and make their isolation easier. Thus the anxiety-linked impulses crept stealthily back into the symptoms.

204

This excerpt from a case history has been given only to illustrate the mechanisms of undoing and isolation and the general blocking of normal thought processes that occur in compulsive disorders. The reason for his extreme anxiety on the subject of masturbation must be assumed to lie somewhere in the boy's childhood history. We now examine a longer excerpt from another history to show the process of disturbance in relation to the whole development of personality and to specific crises occurring in the course of life.

An Illustrative Case: Peter Oberman

Peter Oberman had the misfortune to lose his faith in both of his parents at about the same time. While small he enjoyed his mother's affectionate and watchful care and the weekend visits of his father, who was a traveling salesman. Growing independence soon taught him to regard his mother as an object of contempt. She was an extremely timid woman who felt the world to be a dangerous place in which one must be constantly on guard against sickness, injury, accidents, and kidnappers. She constantly restrained him with images of danger, and as he became an active boy of eleven he resented the resulting overprotection. With a boy across the street he began to study electricity and radio. His mother, who greatly feared electricity, expressed her apprehension, and this was the last straw for Peter. He saw the full absurdity of her timid ways and began to treat her as a fool.

At this juncture his father changed jobs and was at home a great deal. He interested himself in his son's affairs and seriously interfered. Very close with his money, he would occasionally buy expensive presents for which he would expect the deepest gratitude, but they were never the right presents. When Peter wanted a photography set, his father got him a pool table; when he wanted a bicycle, he was given a moving-picture outfit. His father deplored his taste in radio programs and forbade the boy to listen. If Peter came home a minute later than the expected time, he had to brace himself for a veritable tirade. He was terrified, and he could see that his mother also was terrified by his father's insistence and anger. Furious at the domestic dictatorship, he never quite dared to resist it. At length things came to a more severe crisis. He frequently saw his mother in tears, comforted by his grandfather. The father had fallen in love with another woman and was spending nights away from home. Peter's emotions were deeply involved in the tangle; he swore at his father and used obscene language about the other woman. The father, now harboring some guilt feelings of his own, would stalk away in silence.

Both of Peter's identification figures thus crumbled into the dust of his contempt. From neither could he expect esteem or really considerate love. He turned to his grandfather, lately a widower, who occupied the apartment upstairs. The lonely old man responded warmly, and soon there was an active sharing of interests. The grandfather, a scholarly man, was an ardent admirer of Marx and the doctrine of economic determinism. He and Peter followed

205

political events with intense interest. The grandfather bestowed much affection, and at the same time inspired the eleven-year-old boy with ideas about science and the social order that must have been somewhat beyond his understanding.

Since he had rejected his mother and his father, since the atmosphere at home was completely intolerable, it became for Peter Oberman an overwhelmingly important matter not to lose his grandfather. The old man had suddenly become his only source of reliable affection. The idea of losing him aroused a desperate anxiety. But he was old; like the grandmother, he might die. Peter began to be visited by anxious thoughts that seemed to force themselves into his mind. He had images of the house catching fire; he was afraid it would be struck by lightning or shattered in a high wind. He thought of various ways in which harm might come to his grandfather, and then he began to develop symptoms that had the character of magical acts designed to prevent this catastrophe. If the thought crossed his mind that the house might burn, he felt compelled to touch something in order to avert the danger. If he had such a thought while stepping on a crack, he had to step on the crack again to cancel the thought. Soon he needed to perform extra touchings for good measure, and sometimes he would spend nearly an hour going through one of these operations. When people began to notice his peculiar behavior, he developed a technique for discharging all the unlucky thoughts of the day in the privacy of his bedroom at night. If he pointed four times (a lucky number) to the southwest (a lucky direction), he could counteract the danger. But he never felt satisfied. He had to point $4 \times 4 \times 4 \times 4$ times, 256 times, and this took half an hour. He invented short cuts like stamping his foot to stand for groups of numbers, but in the end no time was saved. If the ritual could not be completed, he felt absolutely miserable. He was at the mercy of *compulsive thoughts* and *actions*, all of which had the significance of *undoing* the harm contained in a destructive thought.

It may seem paradoxical that Peter should entertain destructive thoughts that included his grandfather, the very source of his remaining security. It becomes less strange when we consider the circumstances from the point of view of an eleven-year-old boy whose faith in his father and mother has lately been shattered. He well knew that his father could show loving affection, yet quickly withdraw it and let him down. He well knew that his grandfather represented in a sense a false security, because he was old and would presently die. The trouble was that he needed love so badly that he could not resist the grandfather's affectionate interest, yet it was a restraint, an unwelcome restraint, for an eleven-year-old boy to spend so much time with an old man and hear him talk endlessly about barely comprehensible subjects. Although for the most part he could not stand the thought of his grandfather's dying, there were times when part of him secretly desired this event.

When Peter was twelve his grandfather did die. The fatal ailment was attributed by relatives to distress over the father's love affair — a further proof of the father's power to destroy Peter's happiness. Peter's grief was uncontrollable. His tearfulness lasted for several months, and his digestion was badly upset. He wanted to preserve his grandfather's apartment just as it was, and when this proved impossible he photographed every room from every angle, not even omitting the toilet, keeping the negatives locked up where no harm could befall them. He began a diary in which was recorded every incident that in any way reminded him of his lost protector. But his feeling of weakness and helplessness was now so great that he required more far-reaching reassurance. His maturing intellectual powers seized on ideas received from his grandfather and developed the notion of a universal determinism, the understanding of which would give him complete control over everything. He dedicated his life to the laws of the electron and the atom, which he conceived as universal laws applicable to society as well as nature; his grandfather had already schooled him in economic determinism. Then he began to draw up life plans for himself, listing his liabilities and assets, taking hours to get every detail in perfect order. At fourteen he read Einstein, believing that if he could understand this great man he could understand anything.

This turn of events represents the launching of an overdriven striving. To restore some measure of confidence in himself, he developed a compensatory striving for superiority in the special form of omniscience. Through understanding, through familiarity with the basic laws of nature, he was going to control everything, including his father and his own tempestuous emotions. That a boy with superior intellectual gifts should become interested in philosophy between twelve and fourteen and should be attracted by sweeping generalizations is not in itself extraordinary. In Peter's case, however, curiosity was a secondary motive; he was using philosophy to compensate himself for a feeling of weakness, to make himself feel masterful and omnipotent. His preoccupation with ideas and future plans was more than a natural unfolding of real powers; it was a desperate measure designed to avert anxiety. As a result he overdid it, set his goals too high, and spent fruitless hours struggling to work out an unchallengeable system of truth. It is this excess, this rigidity, that distinguished his overdriven striving from a straightforward expression of healthy impulses.

When Oberman reached college, his condition had considerably improved. At high school he had done well, achieved some social participation, and contrived to overcome his compulsive rituals. His overdriven striving gave sufficient security without wrecking his social adjustment. The new environment, however, revived several of his problems, and the threat of compulsory military service touched off many of his early childhood fears. His first course in philosophy challenged the naturalistic system he had worked out for himself. He spent so much time trying to revise his thinking and free it from contradictions that he neglected his regular studies, lost his appetite, and, as he himself put it, "walked around in a daze all summer." When in the company of his classmates he found himself showing off, giving a "big line," trying to impress with his superior knowledge, even telling lies in his struggle to put himself foremost. Any little failure brought on protracted daydreams of omnipotence. One day he bungled a recitation in elementary German: for hours he daydreamed about a future invitation from the university to give a series of lectures in German. The overdriven striving was speeded up and stiffened to a point where it was again indistinguishable from obsessive symptoms.

Impending military service awakened a host of fears. He was afraid of being kicked around at training camp, and especially of physical injury. His relations with his father had not prepared him to react well to authority. Anxiety mounted steadily, so that after two months in training he arrived at complete psychological breakdown. Separated from the service, he sought professional help for thorough treatment. This took a long time, as is often the case with compulsive disorders, but the results were good. He presently entered an exacting course of professional training and has maintained a successful career in medicine for thirty years.

DISSOCIATIVE PROCESSES

Dissociative phenomena are distinctive features of some anxiety disorders that have been associated historically with "hysteria," a diagnostic category of questionable utility (Slater, 1965; Reed, 1975) that we award the same neglect as "neurosis." The metaphor of dissociation was used originally by Janet (1907) to describe a process whereby idea-complexes were split off or *dissociated* from normal consciousness. The term refers most often to peculiarities in the realm of memory, the central feature of which is forgetting personal identity. These may include a brief *amnesia*, a more extended *fugue*, or a fully developed *double* or *multiple personality*. The disorder may include forgetting one's own name or place of residence. Symbols of one's identity may be lost, as well as memories of previous life events that normally support a continuing sense of selfhood. Sometimes the person is so confused by the loss of memory that he or she approaches a police officer to ask for help. In other cases—the ones technically called *fugues*—the individual may go on for quite a while functioning adequately as a new person, perhaps with a new name. There are reports of these conditions lasting for months and even years. Conceivably, such a change might be permanent, but we would have no access to these cases. Literally, *amnesia* means any kind of abnormal forgetting, whether caused by drugs, brain injuries, old age, or psychological factors. The cases we are considering here represent a particular type of amnesia, the forgetting of personal identity, which is motivated by anxious conflict and represents an attempt to do something about that conflict. Genuine amnesia for serious crimes is a relatively common occurrence. Episodes of "ego-alien behavior" accompanied by varying degrees of amnesia accounted for 1.3 percent of military psychiatric admissions in 1968–70, but figures ranged from 5 to 14 percent during World

War II, undoubtedly reflecting acute combat reactions (Kirshner, 1973). Kirshner argues that dissociative phenomena may "lie on a continuum, perhaps overlapping with everyday absent-mindedness, concentration, and impulsivity, and serve a variety of psychological needs. These phenomena might better be redefined as reluctance to recall or acknowledge bits of experience, following a culturally determined pattern of evasion (amnesia). Seen in this way, situational variables, 'actual conflicts,' are central if not all-determining. Evidence suggests that amnesia is a fairly common means of dealing with conflict and may be entirely within the sphere of the ego as an adaptive device" (p. 707).

Amnesia for Personal Identity

The following example reported by McDougall (1926) is remarkable for its transparency. A British color-sergeant in World War I was carrying a message, riding his motorcycle through a dangerous section of the front. All at once it was several hours later, and he was pushing his motorcycle along the streets of a coastal town nearly a hundred miles away. In utter bewilderment he gave himself up to the military police, but he could tell absolutely nothing of his long trip. The amnesia was ultimately broken by the use of hypnosis. The man then remembered that he was thrown down by a shell explosion, that he picked up himself and his machine, that he started straight for the coastal town, that he studied signs and asked for directions in order to reach this destination.

It is clear, in this case, that the amnesia entailed no loss of competence. The soldier's actions were purposive, rational, and intelligent. The amnesia rested only on his sense of personal identity. The conflict was between fear, suddenly intensified by his narrow escape, and his duty to complete the dangerous mission. The forgetting of personal identity made it possible to give way to his impulse toward flight, now irresistible, without exposing himself to the almost equally unbearable anxiety associated with being a coward, failing his mission, and undergoing arrest as a deserter. When he achieved physical safety the two sides of the conflict resumed their normal proportions and his sense of personal identity suddenly returned.

Many cases of amnesia and fugue occur in civilian life under less violent circumstances, but generally in connection with what amounts to an emotional crisis in the person's life. Often these involve some social or financial or family conflict, which supports the idea that forgetting one's identity is a defense against intolerable anxiety when some powerful need or wish becomes uncontrollable. Ordinarily such a need is suppressed out of concern for one's reputation or social position. When the need is strengthened, usually by some external crisis, so that it can no longer be suppressed, personal identity is blotted out, as if the person were saying, "It can't be I who does such a thing."

Valuable information can be obtained by studying what people recall about the situation in which a symptom came into being. By analyzing tape-record-

209

ings of therapeutic interviews, it has been possible to do this the moment they occur (Luborsky & Averbach, 1969; Luborsky, 1970). The key is to examine the conversational context just preceding the mention of any symptom: pain, headache, fast heartbeat, or anxiety. Among the symptoms studied in this way is momentary forgetting, as when the client starts to say something and then cannot remember what it was. These are, of course, minor instances of amnesia with fairly prompt recovery of the lost thought, but there is almost always a clear connection between the memory failure and a sensitive or embarrassing issue. The forgettings of these clients, not unknown also to the rest of us, may be small models of what happens on a large scale in amnesia for personal identity.

Multiple Personalities

A clinician may live out a long and active professional career without encountering a single case of multiple personality because they are so rare. After combing the literature Horton and Miller (1972) found less than a hundred reported cases, and fewer than a dozen of those were published in the last fifty years. Nevertheless, multiple personalities are worthy of mention because of the important problems they raise.

Multiple personalities can be considered as more extreme forms of amnesias and fugues. In well-developed cases there is a loss of personal identity, but instead of the amnesic period being dominated by one imperious wish, it becomes an arena in which a whole new personality develops. Nemiah (1978) illustrates this with the case of Margaret B., a woman of 38 brought to the hospital with a paralysis of her legs following a minor car accident that had occurred six months before. Until three years before her admission to the hospital she had enjoyed smoking, drinking, visiting night clubs, and other social activities. At that point, however, she and her alcoholic husband were converted to a small, evangelical religious sect. Her husband achieved control of his drinking, she gave up her prior social indulgences, and the two of them became completely immersed in church activities, which included extensive practical nursing among the sick of the congregation. It was soon determined that the paralysis was not organically based, and further history revealed that she often heard a terrible voice telling her to say and do things, and threatening to "take over completely." Finally, it was suggested that she let the voice "take over." She closed her eyes, clenched her fists, and grimaced for a few moments during which she was out of contact with those around her. Suddenly she opened her eyes and one was in the presence of another person! Her name, she said, was "Harriet." Whereas Margaret had been paralyzed, and complained of fatigue, headache, and backache, Harriet felt well, and she proceeded at once to walk around the interviewing room. She spoke scornfully of Margaret's religiosity, her invalidism, and her puritanical life, professing that she herself liked to drink and "go partying" but that Margaret was always going to church and reading the Bible. "But," she said impishly and proudly,

210

"I make her miserable. I make her say and do things she doesn't want to." At length, at the interviewer's suggestion, Harriet reluctantly agreed to "bring Margaret back," and after more grimacing and fist clenching, Margaret reappeared, paralyzed, complaining of her headache and backache, and completely amnesic for the brief period of Harriet's release from her prison.

It can be seen that the dissociative process provided a defense for Margaret against undesirable feelings over which she was in conflict, driving from conscious awareness her inclinations to indulge in pleasures that, from her religious perspective, were sinfully improper. Identification also played an important role in fashioning her secondary personality. As a child, Margaret had been devoted to a playmate named Harriet. When both were six, Harriet was taken ill suddenly with an acute infectious disease and died in three days. Margaret was deeply upset at the time and wished to die in her friend's place. At some undetermined time after that event, Harriet had gone "inside Margaret," as Harriet reported when she held sway in consciousness, and she had lived there quite happily until the point when Margaret "got religious" and their tastes for entertainment and pleasure diverged. Internalizing the image of her dead friend appeared to have protected Margaret from despair and sorrow at her loss. These emotions emerged unspent when, under hypnosis, the adult patient was directed to revive the memories of an event then thirty years past.

It is well to be skeptical about multiple personalities, especially when the opportunity exists to dramatize them in hypnotic states. Undoubtedly a case of multiple personality can be played up or down according to the clinician's predilection. Still there probably are quite genuine instances that occur without any help from the doctor. This appears to be true of the case reported by Horton and Miller (1972), who had no prior expectation that multiple selves would appear and who took pains to offer no encouragement. Their client nevertheless disclosed three different selves, amnesic for one another, that had been in existence at various times during the four years since her father's death. In addition, a fourth personality included the memories of all the others but had great difficulty living with their highly conflicting tendencies. These authors also attach great significance to identification processes. If during development the situation favors many unstable identifications instead of a few stable ones, the chances are increased that the resulting "selves" will be difficult to integrate. In addition, it seems likely that multiple personality reflects a pervasive self-dramatizing adaptive style. This trait has often been mentioned in connection with the more physical forms of anxiety disorder.

PHYSICAL ABNORMALITIES

From our historical introduction (Chapter 1) we already know that unusual, sometimes quite bizarre, physical symptoms first drew the attention of such physicians as Charcot, Janet, Freud, and Breuer to anxiety disorders. They diagnosed these physical anomalies (paralyses, sensory deficits, anaesthesias, spells, and the like) as symptoms of "hysteria," a syndrome that also featured histrionic personality traits: dependency, hypochondriasis, attention-seeking emotional lability, self-concern, suggestibility, vanity, egocentrism, and provocative but frigid sexuality. The juxtaposition of these obviously pejorative descriptions of personality with "phantom" neurological symptoms betrays a profound sexist prejudice in the minds of those great men. The term "hysteria" stems from the ancient Greek word for *womb* and was coined to imply disturbances of the womb, on the assumption that the disorder was confined to women. We must disclaim as obsolete these theoretical preconceptions and draw a sharp distinction between conversion *symptoms* and the *traits* of hysterical personality type, a conception still widely used.

Varieties of Conversion Symptoms

Conversion symptoms take a wide variety of bodily forms. On the motor side are the *paralyses* that may include an arm, a leg, both legs, or one whole side of the body. These symptoms can be distinguished from true organic injuries by the fact that normal reflexes are retained in the paralyzed area, and that little or no muscular degeneration occurs. Sometimes the diagnosis is made still easier by the anatomical nonsense that characterizes the symptom: both hands, for instance, may be paralyzed, while the arms retain their motility, a state that could be produced organically only by a highly peculiar nerve injury in both wrists. Other motor symptoms are *mutism* (inability to speak), *aphonia* (inability to speak above a whisper to "voice" the speech), *tremor*, and *tics* (spasmodic jerking in a small coordinated group of muscles). On the sensory side there are the many varieties of *anaesthesia*. These may accompany the paralyses, but they sometimes occur alone. Within any one sense department the anaesthesia may take a number of forms. In vision, for instance, the possibilities include total blindness, blindness in one eye, contraction of the visual field to a small focal point, blindness in the left half or right half of both eyes, and many other curious fragmentations of the visual process. "Spells" may occur, which in some respects resemble epileptic seizures but can generally be distinguished from them. Finally, there are sometimes *twilight states* in which the person is confused and distressed, experience having an unreal and dreamlike quality. The loss of contact with reality is less complete than in psychosis.

Symptoms of this sort have for some time been known as *conversion reactions*. The term is derived from an idea of Freud's that the energy of a repressed instinctual urge becomes diverted into sensory-motor channels in such a way as to block the functioning of some organ. Regarded even by its inventor as difficult to understand or to verify, this notion of converted energy is of no value today, but the name persists, and with it the fact that the bodily symptoms are not plausible consequences of physical impairment. Discarding the language of hypothetical energetics, we still have to explain what Charcot originally discerned as the oddly mental character of the bodily disabilities.

Psychological Basis of Conversion Symptoms

Like other forms of anxiety disorder, the physical symptoms can profitably be considered a defense against anxiety. "Its essential and distinctive feature," according to Fairbairn (1954), "is the substitution of a bodily state for a personal problem; and this substitution enables the personal problem as such to be ignored." Enlarging on this statement, Ziegler and Imboden (1962) proposed that not just anxiety but any strong negative feeling—shame, disgust, loss of self-esteem—may be the reason for defense. They further emphasize the communicative aspect of the symptom. The patient with a conversion symptom enacts the role of a person with "organic" illness, symbolically communicating distress by means of somatic symptoms. The symptom diverts attention from the personal problem, whatever its nature, and may be used as an instrument to negotiate interpersonal transactions. In everyday life it is sometimes observed that a person with weighty emotional problems becomes relaxed and serene when afflicted with a primary organic illness, which provides a blameless excuse for shelving the problems and accepting the invalid's role. Conversion symptoms achieve much the same result.

Since Freud it has been widely believed that anxiety is *not* found in conversion disorders, because the symptoms were thought to protect or defend the sufferer from anxiety, but recent evidence (Marks, 1973) shows that patients with chronic conversion symptoms rate themselves as more anxious than anxious phobic patients and have correspondingly higher autonomic activity, which indicates fearful arousal. Related to this is the problem of emotional escalation that we considered in anxiety states and panic attacks. Mechanic (1972) emphasizes the importance of anxiety aroused by unusual body sensations, especially in people with inadequate means or information to explain the sensations or express their concern about them. Simple reassurance may not be helpful unless it incorporates an explanation that is plausible enough to allay the anxiety *about the symptoms*. In short, the person must be helped to construe the bodily symptoms in a plausible and predictably reassuring way.

Other Features

Templer and Lester (1974) found that 24 percent of psychiatric patients show at least one conversion symptom, but they estimate that only 9 to 18 percent of these display hysterical personality traits. It is interesting that 88 percent of them were women, which may reflect the true state of things now or indicate continuation of the sexist prejudice in modern mental health scientists. Conversion symptoms were most prominently associated with passivity and dependency, but several studies have found them associated with antisocial personality traits.

213

Slater and Glithero (1965) followed up patients diagnosed for "hysteria" seven to 11 years later and found that more than half of them had explicit or latent (but previously undetected) organic diseases. Various kinds of visual disturbance (blindness, blurring, visual field constriction) have been attributed to "hysteria," meaning that the disturbances were believed to have no organic basis, though this presumption is now being questioned. For example, Rada, Meyer, and Kellner (1978) have detected tubular visual fields as the source of the disturbance in some cases. So there is some danger in misdiagnosis if (potentially treatable) organic causes are disregarded. Guze (1970) reviewed five follow-up studies that showed 20 percent of conversion reaction patients several years later had either neurological diseases or psychoses. In general, conversion symptoms or a diagnosis of hysteria based on them did not predict a uniform course of illness or outcome, which is consistent with the observation that conversion symptoms occur in a wide variety of psychiatric, neurological, and general medical conditions. On the basis of his review Guze offered the plausible proposal to use the conversion reaction diagnosis primarily in a descriptive way, to refer to unexplained symptoms suggesting neurological disease, of which amnesia, unconsciousness, paralysis, "spells," aphonia, urinary retention, difficulty in walking, anaesthesia, and blindness are the most common examples.

Stefánsson, Messina, and Meyerowitz (1976) estimated the incidence of conversion disorders at 11 to 22 per 100,000 per year in general populations and 4.5 percent of patients seen in psychiatric consultation. They are found predominantly in women, nonwhites, and people from low social classes, with the onset of symptoms usually in the middle adult years between 25 and 45. These results suggest that people low on the social power hierarchy develop conversion symptoms as a form of body language or symbols that express meaning, allowing the powerless to gain some measure of influence.

An Illustrative Case

Two elements require explanation in anxiety disorders with conversion symptoms: the personal problems from which escape is sought, and the mechanism whereby symptoms are produced. Both elements are illustrated in the following example (Malamud, 1944).

A married man of twenty-eight was in a motor accident. He sustained minor scratches and was otherwise apparently unhurt, but he emerged from the accident completely blind. The absence of any injury that could be responsible for loss of vision led to a diagnosis of hysteria. It was discovered that the accident occurred while he was driving to the maternity hospital to see his wife and first-born child. His first remark to the psychiatrists was that he could not tie his wife down to a blind man and would now divorce her.

This strange sequence of events becomes intelligible if we work out the patient's history and discover the personal meaning of the situation that so star-

tlingly made him blind. First we discover a clearly *overdriven striving* in the
patient's previous behavior, an exaggerated trend toward independent self-sufficiency. He early separated from his parents and established an independent life for himself, resolving at the same time that he would never marry. He was attracted to women, but kept all relationships at a purely sexual level and discontinued them at the first hint of deeper feeling and especially at the faintest threat of marriage. His history showed that the purpose of this overdriven striving was to hold in check all feelings of dependence on women. The mother had been extremely domineering and the father weakly submissive. While we cannot precisely recover the earliest anxiety in this case, it evidently had something to do with the parental relationship. Dependent longings entailed unwilling submission to the mother's iron rule, a thing to be hated and feared because it made him resemble the weak and helpless father. Therefore dependent longings constituted a danger, and the trend toward self-sufficiency served to hold them in check.

The patient's overdriven striving was not allowed to prevent the satisfaction of his sexual needs; it functioned merely to prevent his relationships from satisfying anything besides sex. His safety lay in his freedom to walk out of any relationship. An equilibrium was established that worked well enough for several years. *Disturbance of the equilibrium* began when his sexual adventures brought him in contact with a woman who in certain respects reminded him of his mother and stimulated his dependent longings. This was so satisfactory that he permitted the relation to develop. He sought her advice and allowed her to make decisions. He grew increasingly uncomfortable—anxiety was evidently stirring—but he finally consented to marriage on the condition that they would never have children.

One can say at this point that he had suspended his overdriven striving in order to gratify dependent longings, but he kept the guarantee that he could escape at any time if this new equilibirum proved unbearable. His tension and discomfort show that it was only just bearable. Then suddenly his avenue of escape was blocked: his wife became pregnant. He demanded an abortion, but she refused. Throughout the pregnancy he was increasingly uneasy. He did not know why he felt this way, but in the course of later analytic treatment he recovered memories that showed how earnestly he had hoped the pregnancy would not mature and how tenaciously he clung to the notion that escape from the marriage would still be possible. When his wife went to the hospital his anxiety came into the open, taking the twisted form of terror lest something happen to the mother or child. Finally he learned that both were well, and that he could see them. He jumped into the car and drove toward the hospital. Then the accident happened, and he was unable to see them.

Knowing about the patient's past and his chief overdriven striving, we can understand that the successful birth of the child pushed him to the point of panic. But this does not account for the highly specific symptom of blindness. By what process was it possible for this symptom to come to his rescue? We

215

know only that the patient apparently considered blindness an adequate
ground for divorce, now that his wife had a child to support. If this idea was in
his mind before the motor accident, it might have influenced the direction
taken by defensive inhibition. One can easily speculate that the patient had
hoped he would never live to see the proof of his permanent bondage, thus focalizing the danger on seeing, so that going blind became a way of preventing
contact with the threat. But there is no direct evidence for such associative
connections, and even if they were operative in the patient they would not fully
explain the conversion symptom. There are many things in our lives that are
painful to see, but we see them none the less.

Placement of the Symptoms

The problem of the location and form of physical symptoms in anxiety disorders is still so poorly understood that we can only suggest some possibilities.
Sometimes symptom formation begins with a primary organic injury. There
are various reflex responses that tend to immobilize an injured limb so that,
for example, a wounded leg will stiffen to prevent further motion and pain. If
these immobilizing reflexes should be prolonged and reinforced for psychological reasons, a temporary injury may be turned into a permanent disability. In
a study made at a Veterans' Hospital in Appalachia, conversion symptoms
were found in something like a quarter of the patients, a far larger proportion
than would be expected in a civilian population (Weinstein, Eck, & Lyerly,
1969). The symptom was commonly placed in some organ that was the site of
previous injury or disability. The investigators suggested that histrionic physical symptoms are more readily expressed in people much given to overt displays of aggression and to blaming their frustrations on external circumstances, including physical health.

Direct connection between some organ system and a serious life conflict
may serve to determine the location. This is particularly true in *occupational*
disorders, such as mutism or aphonia in a salesperson, paralysis of the fingers
in a pianist, writer's cramp in an author, or—taking some liberty with the
meaning of "occupation"—sexual impotence in a Don Juan. In such cases
there are conflict and anxiety over carrying out the occupation successfully,
and the symptom definitely prevents further performance. A further example
of occupational disability also illustrates the role of *secondary gain* in maintaining these disorders. A veteran—from Appalachia, as it happened—who
worked as a railroad brakeman developed a mysterious weakness in his right
hand that prevented him from exerting a sufficient grip on levers to continue
working. A minor war injury to his right hand (frostbite) some years before
suggested the site of the symptom, and since the original injury was a *service-
connected condition*, the veteran received financial compensation that almost
equaled his wages as a brakeman. In such cases it is difficult to draw the line
between anxiety disorders and *malingering*, but often the secondary gain from

the symptom cannot be consciously anticipated nor the symptom voluntarily devised.

In many cases, the symptom is in part a product of imitation. This is shown, for instance, in a study of student naval aviators who developed conversion symptoms that put them out of action during training (Mucha & Reinhardt, 1970). In 70 percent of the cases the site of the symptom was an organ system in which one of the parents had suffered serious illness. The assumption might be made that when a symptom is needed to avoid acute anxiety, so to speak, patterns of illness are unwittingly adopted that have been seen in the person's past experience to provide legitimate exemption from struggle. The role of illness is more easily copied than invented, though it should also be pointed out that purely constitutional vulnerabilities may also be inherited genetically.

The study also showed that naval aviators are recruited from highly achievement-oriented backgrounds, have typically done well in competitive sports, tend to accept no excuses for anxiety or failure, and thus see physical illness as the only legitimate ground for escaping unbearable strain. Presumably the more tolerant a society becomes about accepting anxiety, nervousness, depressed feelings, and other subjective complaints as grounds for exemption from full participation, the less urgent is the need for a symptom that emulates a physical disease. In this connection it appears that medical knowledge has a real effect on symptom formation. The dramatic old-fashioned symptoms like glove anaesthesia are no longer available to educated people, especially those trained as physicians, nurses, or medical secretaries. More often among relatively sophisticated people the physical symptoms take the form of pain (Stefánsson, Messina, & Meyerowitz, 1978).

THE RELATION OF SYMPTOMS TO PERSONALITY STYLE

Recall that compulsive symptoms are often reported in persons that otherwise do not conform to the compulsive personality style, and dissociative and conversion symptoms are frequently observed in people without other prominent histrionic features of personality. Nevertheless it is plausible to hypothesize that people with distinctively compulsive personality types (Shapiro, 1965) would be more prone to compulsive thoughts and rituals under anxiety and stress than to other constellations of anxiety symptoms. We all have acquaintances who might be described as habitually "cerebral" in the sense of thinking about their experience, turning things over in their minds, and rarely acting with impulsive abandon or dramatic flair. Compulsive symptoms appear to be consistent extensions of these qualities. We know other people who are more inclined to leap before they look, who immerse themselves in each experience, who seek excitement and a touch of drama in everything they do. It would surprise us if such a person, even under great stress, displayed the repetitive rituals and philosophical entanglements that ensnared the "cerebral" Peter Ober-

217

man. Amnesias and mysterious physical symptoms seem to be more consistent extensions of a dramatic, communicative style of living. In short, we may hypothesize that the personality type shapes to a certain extent the form that anxiety symptoms may take, even though the symptoms themselves are not necessarily dependable reflections of personality type. Stated in other words, inferences about the form of symptom expression can be made from personality style, whereas inferences about style based on symptoms are less reliable.

Current Research

There is now considerable research that bears in one way or another on individual differences of the kind just described. Commenting on this research, Korner (1971) postulates two regulatory principles for dealing with stimulation. One of these "will serve to sift, to diminish or to make manageable incoming stimuli" by means of analysis and reflection. The person will tend to avoid strong and novel excitations, and when dealing with anxiety will most easily employ defense mechanisms of intellectualization and isolation. The other principle favors "the management of strong stimulation through motor or affective discharge, through hypermotility, impulsivity, action rather than reflection," and it is characteristic that novelty and excitement are welcomed instead of avoided. Korner's own research, done with infants 2 to 4 days old, indicates that differences in the management of stimulation already exist at birth, and other workers have found similar stable preferences during the first few years of life (Thomas et al., 1963; Escalona, 1968). Especially relevant is the finding by Kagan and co-workers (1965) that as early as the age of two, and more clearly during the school years, children differ stably regarding speed of processing information. This was shown, for instance, in a test of problem solving involving selection of the best among several responses. School children having a "fast conceptual tempo" answered quickly with the first thing that struck them as appropriate, and made many errors. Other children, the "reflective" ones, delayed their response as if considering the alternatives, and made few errors (Reppucci, 1970). The cognitive differences disclosed in this research may ultimately distinguish histrionic from compulsive personality types.

The most thorough and persistent research on basic dimensions of personality has been done by Eysenck (1970). Using a large number of tests and relatively precise experimental measurements, and treating the results with sophisticated mathematical analysis, Eysenck has built up evidence for two stable independent dimensions along which people vary, one called *neuroticism*, the other called *extraversion-introversion*. The neuroticism dimension covers qualities with respect to which all varieties of anxious people tend to differ from the normal. "At the one end we have people whose emotions are labile, strong, and easily aroused; they are moody, touchy, anxious, restless, and so forth. At the other extreme we have people whose emotions are stable, less easily aroused, people who are calm, even-tempered, carefree, and reliable" (Eysenck & Rachman, 1965, p. 20). The second dimension, extraversion-introversion, owes something to Jung's historic speculations about the outward or inward turning of interest, though some change of meaning inevitably results from translating Jung's shrewd impressions into practical measurements. This is the dimension that bears on the form of anxiety disorder. Conversion symptoms and dissociated states are related to extraversion, while phobias and compulsive disorders go with introversion. By giving the tests to criterion groups consisting of patients independently diagnosed, Eysenck claimed that these relationships were satisfactorily confirmed.

In studying dimensions it is easiest to describe the ends, the extreme cases, but necessary to remember that the majority of people fall somewhere in the middle. Eysenck uses the following expressions, among others, to describe the extreme extravert: "sociable, needs to have people to talk to, craves excitement, acts on the spur of the moment, likes change, prefers to keep moving and doing things; altogether his feelings are not kept under tight control." The extreme introvert, in contrast, is described as "quiet, retiring, introspective, reserved; he tends to plan ahead, does not like excitement, likes a well-ordered mode of life, and keeps his feelings under close control" (Eysenck & Rachman, 1965, p. 19).

Even restaurants understand what extraversion is all about.

219

Anxiety Disorders and Difficulties of Living

As we saw in the historical introduction, study of the anxiety disorders began in connection with medical practice, and they were interpreted to be forms of disease. When the nervous disorders proved to have no sensible relation to disordered nerves, they were considered psychological in origin but still cast in the medical model. When it became clear that psychological disorders resulted from learning processes and responses to difficulties in living, and when in consequence their correction had to be defined in terms of relearning, the educative process was still described as one in which a doctor treated a patient for a disease. This bit of history offers a wry commentary on inertia in human thinking, but the medical model escaped challenge while most of the work remained in the hands of physicians. The appropriateness of this model becomes a sharp issue today because professional workers trained in other ways than medicine, especially psychologists, have been able to deal successfully with anxiety disorders, and want to establish the right to use their skills in this way. It is the scientific problem, however, not the professional one, that concerns us at this point. With evidence now at hand, how can we best understand anxiety disorders?

Understanding seems to require that we keep in mind at least four considerations: (1) constitutional vulnerability, (2) vulnerability created by early anxieties, (3) adaptive style, and (4) current stress.

Let us assume that a child is born with an inherited disposition toward neuroticism, which might mean mainly a low threshold for anxiety. That child may very well get into trouble with anxiety somewhere along the way, under the right conditions of stress. On the other hand, if the child starts with a relatively extreme endowment for extraversion, it might be more likely for later stress to evoke dissociative and physical symptoms. If strongly introverted by nature, the child may be more vulnerable to phobic or compulsive patterns when severe difficulties of living are encountered. Such outcomes obviously do not follow inevitably, but their likelihood may be influenced by inherited temperamental characteristics.

Differing life circumstances expose children to varying amounts of severe anxiety. If a single fright is very severe, or if, probably more typically, there are repeated situations of danger such as incurring parental anger or loss of love, patterns of anxiety response may be learned by the child that will surface again later in extreme circumstances as an adult. Being blamed for a wife's suicide would be stressful for anyone, but it precipitates a stubborn phobia only when childhood experience has established special vulnerability.

Extraversion and introversion are associated not only with different symptom patterns but also with different adaptive styles. Adaptation requires flexibility, and this will be restricted if one style is overdeveloped. People whose style is "cerebral," like Peter Oberman, may do well in occupations requiring reflective thought or detailed workmanship but experience difficulty when de-

220

cisions have to be made or when strong feeling is appropriate. The success of a strongly preferred adaptive style thus depends on the circumstances of one's life. Preferred style may work well for a time, only to fail when circumstances change. Adaptive styles, of course, are not confined to the two that we have examined in this chapter. In an account based on clinical studies, Shapiro (1965) described in addition to the hysterical and compulsive, a paranoid style and an impulsive style, with the impulsive style associated with behavior tending toward delinquency. A person's adaptive style determines the types of situation *least* likely to be manageable and hence *most* stressful. If the stress is sufficiently acute, anxiety symptoms develop that are congruent extensions of the preferred adaptive style.

Whatever the importance of past conditionings and vulnerabilities, current stress is an essential ingredient of anxiety disorders. Peter Oberman's case is especially instructive: he was ridden with symptoms after his grandfather's death, when he first went to college, and when he was drafted for military service, but between these occasions he had periods of successful functioning. Current difficulties of living are most likely to precipitate an anxiety reaction when they have one or more of the following features: first, they duplicate important psychological aspects of earlier conflict situations; second, they upset the preferred adaptive style, defensive traits, and overdriven strivings; third, they call out increased defensive processes that become crippling. To illustrate, let us suppose that a man whose personality has developed along coolly intellectual lines becomes attracted to a warm, expressive woman. The situation is enough like his childhood relation to his mother to arouse anxieties connected with his early childhood experience. It threatens his "cerebral" adaptive style and blocks his overdriven striving toward impersonal aloofness. It thus accelerates these protective operations so that he becomes phobic about feminine companionship and obsessively entangled with inner debates about love, hate, dependence, and freedom. Being attracted, falling in love, and contemplating marriage can be regarded as intrinsically stressful but not, for most people, to such an extent that it elicits an anxiety disorder. To have such drastic effect, current stress must touch certain vulnerabilities, innate or acquired, and must threaten preferred security operations.

Viewed in this way, anxiety disorder is a phenomenon of learning and a way of coping with difficulties of living. These disorders differ from other outcomes of this universal struggle because they come to a focus on one or another of those crippling states of mind and/or body that historically have been described as symptoms. When we look closely at these symptoms, they become intelligible as products of conditioning and learning in circumstances where avoidance of anxiety looms large. It may be counted an historical accident that anxiety disorders were originally conceptualized as diseases, for in many respects they do not fit the classical model of medical disease. It is important to emphasize this point as we turn to the subject of psychological treatment. The literature on this topic is still pervaded by the imagery of a doctor treating

221

a patient for physical illness, whereas modern methods of treatment often benefit from more flexible procedures and roles based on psychological models that emphasize relearning more than healing.

SUGGESTIONS FOR FURTHER READING

The older literature on the "neuroses" contains a wealth of description that is still valuable today. P. Janet's book, *Major Symptoms of Hysteria* (1920), is unsurpassed for its clinical descriptions of dissociated states and "hysterical" symptoms. M. Prince's classical study of Miss Beauchamp, *The Dissociation of a Personality* (1913), is fascinating reading, though a little on the dramatic side. It should be followed by his more circumspect paper, "Miss Beauchamp: The Psychogenesis of Multiple Personality," which is reprinted in Prince's *Clinical and Experimental Studies in Personality* (1939). An excellent discussion of the problems raised by multiple personalities, both for abnormal and general psychology, is available in Chapter 18 of G. Murphy's *Personality: A Biosocial Approach to Origins and Structure* (1947). The psychoanalytic gospel according to Otto (Fenichel, *The Psychoanalytical Theory of Neurosis*, 1945) is still interesting, though dated and exceedingly detailed reading. A. Krohn offers a competent, but doctrinaire, recent psychoanalytic account of "hysteria" in *Hysteria: The Elusive Neurosis* (1978). A somewhat more balanced psychoanalytic account of the dynamic bases of psychopathology and the anxiety disorders is provided by J. C. Nemiah in Chapters 9 and 10 of *The Harvard Guide to Modern Psychiatry* (1978).

An independent psychodynamic view is taken by A. Angyal in *Neurosis and Treatment: A Holistic Theory* (1965), a posthumous work edited by E. R. M. Hanfmann & Jones; "hysteria" is described as based on a pattern of vicarious living, compulsive disorders on a pattern of noncommitment. F. R. Hine presents a concise, modern psychodynamic model of human conflicts that draws on both psychoanalytic and learning theory in *Introduction to Psychodynamics: A Conflict-Adaptational Approach* (1971). C. G. Costello's *Anxiety and Depression* (1976) is a short, thoughtful essay on the two most common symptoms of psychological disorder. D. Shapiro's *Neurotic Styles* (1965) contains surely the most instructive and balanced description of four salient abnormal styles of personality (compulsive, paranoid, hysterical, and impulsive); it is thoroughly psychodynamic in orientation. In *The Causes and Cures of Neurosis* (1965) H. J. Eysenck & S. Rachman give a strictly behavioristic interpretation of anxiety disorders, making the subject sound as simple as Fenichel makes it sound complex.

Of relevance to the topics covered in this chapter are three (of 20) extensive case histories presented by G. R. Leon in *Case Histories of Deviant Behavior* (1977), including the case of Richard Benson. Undoubtedly the most authoritative scholarly account on the subject of anxiety is the pithy volume by M. Lader & I. Marks, *Clinical Anxiety* (1971), which manages to cover the entire subject in merely 183 pages, 25 of which are devoted to *listing* 542 references! This book is unique because it manages to avoid taking sides in theoretical disputes. The more theoretically oriented reader may find useful an extended essay by D. E. Berlyne on the relation between behavioristic theory and personality in *Handbook of Personality Theory and Research* (1968).

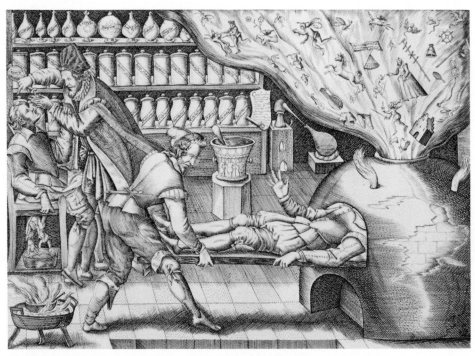

The Physician Curing Fantasy (ca. 17th century) by Matthaus Greuter.
Philadelphia Museum of Art. SmithKline Corporation Collection.

7
Psychological Treatment:
Individual Methods

This is the appropriate point in our study to take up psychological treatment. As we saw in the historical introduction, the psychological way of thinking about disorders—the psychological model as contrasted with the medical model—came out of attempts to treat what were then known as the neuroses. There is a presumption that the people so dramatically cured by Mesmer, and later by hypnotism, belonged mainly in this category, as did the patients studied by Charcot, Janet, and Freud. At this point in the book we have studied the anxiety disorders, in which psychological factors play a central part. We have also examined a large variety of maladaptive patterns arising from development and leading to difficulties of living. Psychotherapists everywhere, including those on college campuses, are quite as likely to find themselves dealing with troublesome dependence, inferiority feelings, social ineptitude, sexual problems, and identity crises as with disorders that manifest themselves as phobias, compulsions, and seemingly physical symptoms. Furthermore, psychological treatment has specific uses in connection with many of the disorders described in the rest of this book. Understanding these applications will be easier if we take up at once the nature and varieties of psychological treatment and the kinds of results that can be expected.

NATURE OF PSYCHOLOGICAL TREATMENT

In this book we use *psychological treatment* as an inclusive term to designate all forms of intervention into maladaptive and abnormal behavior that work fundamentally through the learning process.

Reading the literature of the last twenty years, one might conclude that there were two distinct and exclusive schools of thought: *psychotherapy* and *behavior therapy.* The latecomer, behavior therapy, which became popular only twenty years ago, has sometimes been defended with a partisan zeal that magnified its differences. To minimize the differences is a mistake, but we must beware of any implication that these two varieties of treatment have little in common. They share three highly important points: (1) they both fit the psychological model better than the medical model; (2) they both assign an important place to anxiety; and (3) they both operate by influencing the learning process. Where they differ is in ancestry and in resulting preferences about technical method. Today's psychotherapy owes much to Freud's lengthy explorations of personal life, and although many current concepts and methods are quite different from Freud's, it is still usual to view the patient's complaint as part of a larger pattern of personality. Behavior therapy sprang from experimental psychology; it undertakes to change behavior according to relatively simple laws of conditioning and learning, laws that were first established in laboratory experiments with animals.

A visitor from another culture, told of these differences, might remark that psychotherapy keeps things too complicated, while behavior therapy makes them too simple. If psychotherapists addressed themselves more intensively to the actual mechanisms of change, and if behavior therapists made more allowance for human cognitive complications, the two streams might be found flowing together. This is exactly what is happening. Although we will take up the two traditions in succession, we do not have the slightest doubt that they belong together in the same chapter.

To complete our survey, we will also describe a group of methods now commonly put under the heading *humanistic-existential psychotherapy.*

Promotion of Relearning

Calling a disorder psychological means thinking of it as a pattern of learning that is faulty in the sense of yielding unworkable results in current circumstances. One's conception of learning, as we saw especially in Chapter 3, may emphasize in different degrees such aspects as conditioning, insight, cognitive fields, emotion, and motivation, but there is no doubt that a phobia, for instance, is learned and that unlearning is the best cure. Seen in this light, all forms of psychological treatment involve attempts to create a situation that is favorable for relearning. In one-to-one treatment, which we concentrate on in this chapter, the favorable situation has to be started by means of conversation taking place in the therapist's office.

There are more than ordinary obstacles to the kind of relearning that is necessary to ameliorate difficulties of living or to lift anxiety symptoms. We regard it as normal, though not necessarily easy, for our patterns of behavior to change if in new circumstances they turn out badly. When people turn to psychotherapy it is because their behavior fails to change. They continue to repeat the same patterns even when the consequences are uncomfortable and self-defeating. The therapist must try to bring about change in behavior and in feelings that have already shown themselves to be stubbornly resistant to change. Typical of this rigidity are forms of behavior that have been strongly overlearned during childhood, that serve as defenses against anxiety, or that satisfy some unwitting resentful or protective purpose in current life. The therapist is called on to change what neither circumstances nor the client's own efforts have thus far been able to change.

Corrective Emotional Experience

It is, of course, a mistake to think of this relearning as a wholly intellectual process. Although Freud described the goal of psychoanalysis as replacing what is unconscious by what is conscious, and although much has been written about increasing the patient's insight, it became a tenet of psychoanalytic theory that the curative forces do not lie in the realm of intellect. This is recognized in a formulation by Alexander (1946), who wrote that the basic principle is "to re-expose the patient, under more favorable circumstances, to emotional situations which he could not handle in the past." The patient must "undergo a corrective emotional experience," and "intellectual understanding of the genetics has only an accessory significance" (pp. 66–67). Other theorists have been equally explicit in locating the essential change in the realm of feeling, and there is widespread agreement, which includes behavior therapists, that the reduction of anxiety is one of the most central problems. It is useless to tell the phobic child that the rabbit is not dangerous. The child must learn through controlled exposures that actually arouse some degree of anxiety but produce no painful consequences, that a rabbit is not a reason for pan-

227

ic. Similarly the adult anxiety patient must progressively feel the anxiety derived from earlier history, and thus learn to respond to obsolete dangers at
their true current value. Conditions must be created in which the patient will
dare to reappraise anxieties and relax defenses.

Initial Steps

The therapeutic situation is initially established by what the therapist does in
the first few meetings. Some of the things that happen are common to all
schools of thought. Information must be exchanged: the therapist must learn
about the client's life situation and about the complaints that prompt seeking
treatment; in return, the therapist must give some idea of what is involved in
treatment. Whatever else is done, there must be a certain minimum of interviewing, history-taking, and explanation. The manner in which these initial
steps are carried out goes far toward defining the therapeutic relation.

In the nature of the case the therapist is cast in the role of an expert from
whom help is sought. On the whole, however, psychotherapists have been inclined to play down the superior–inferior aspect of the relation so as to maximize those aspects that resemble friendship and represent sympathetic understanding. Much has been written about the importance of a display of warmth
by the therapist, but this pleasant word, suggesting an emanation of heat from
a radiator, does not carry us far toward understanding actual transactions.
More definite is the therapist's attentive interest and grasp of the import of
what is said. In a clinical report on work with combat troops who had undergone schizophrenic breakdown, Eissler (1952) noticed that the patients responded favorably to indications of interest on his part, even when what they
were saying was relatively trivial. He remarks on the "special joy" that is experienced when an attentive listener gives himself fully to what you have to say.
There is threefold value to a client in feeling understood. The client experiences a sense of competence at having communicated successfully, gains reassurance that the therapist's guidance will be appropriate, and feels pleasure at
being taken as a person of value. What is often described as routine history-
taking can thus be much more than a routine. It can serve to vivify the therapist's understanding, respect, and wish to be of help.

In one of his earliest works Carl Rogers (1942) advanced an idea that has
proved illuminating. He distinguished between responding to the content and
responding to the feeling in what another person says. This is not as easy as it
sounds. All our habits of conversation are built on responding to content. If
someone tells us of going to a disco dance we are likely to ask where it was, how
was the music, how large was the crowd, and perhaps make no comment on
the shining eyes that say how our informant felt about the evening. In one of
Rogers' examples a student says that his study habits are wrong and that he is
not really so stupid as his grades indicate. Asking about the study habits and

the grades is a response to content; recognizing the student's disappointment with his grades and concern that they not be taken as the true measure of his ability is a response to feeling. A good example of responding to feeling was given in our clinical introduction at the beginning of the case of Walter Lilly.

People come to psychological treatment often in desperation but usually with hope. Their motivation seems strong, but it is not yet channeled into what will actually be required of them. As treatment proceeds, the therapist "constantly faces the task of urging the patient to examine old fears and to experiment with new patterns of behavior" (Stieper & Wiener, 1965, p. 124). This can be hard, often painful, and the motive of getting well may falter badly if not aided by a sense of alliance with the therapist. Businesslike initial steps accomplish less than those that are directed toward building this alliance.

Specific Techniques

What has been discussed thus far is common to all methods of psychotherapy. What more can the therapist do? After the initial steps one moves on to the specific techniques that one considers most likely to produce the unlearning of old and the learning of new adaptive patterns. In an older tradition the therapist might rely entirely on suggestion, hypnosis, persuasion, or plain physical relaxation. In the psychoanalytic tradition one would instruct the client in the none too easy art of free association. If direct methods of behavior modification are to be employed, one will teach the client the part to be played in whatever procedure is chosen. It is from this point on that we enter the realm of controversy. Agreement on the basic principle that psychological treatment means relearning does not in the least guarantee agreement on how the relearning can best be accomplished. Psychological treatment is a burgeoning field, with a large crop of new publications and new claims—a difficult literature to evaluate unless one keeps fundamental principles in mind.

We will examine individual psychological treatment under three main headings: psychodynamic therapy, behavioral treatment, and humanistic-existential psychotherapy.

PSYCHODYNAMIC THERAPY

In the historical introduction we noticed that Freud's discoveries led to an interpretation of personality that is often called *psychodynamic*. This means that importance is attached to the striving aspect of behavior, the motivation that lies behind what we do. Psychodynamic therapy, which is often called just plain psychotherapy, is treatment that gives similar prominence to motives. It is based on the idea that abnormal behavior, feeling, and thinking stem in large part from distorted internal motivations that can be rectified through insight and relearning in a supportive human relationship. Clients seeking treatment do not always report their complaints in motivational terms. They may even describe a symptom as an isolated intrusion into an otherwise normal existence. Those who practice psychodynamic therapy believe that disorders are more likely to be caught up in the organization of personality and to represent at least a little more than shows on the surface. An important part of treatment therefore consists of discovering the motivations—the dynamics—that sustain the maladaptive behavior.

Historically, psychodynamic therapy is derived from Freud, but by now the derivation is often fairly remote. Departures from Freud began early with Jung and Adler and continued with Sullivan, Fromm, Horney, and other so-called "Neo-Freudians." Some psychodynamic therapists today who admire Freud's ways of thinking refer to their work as "psychoanalytically oriented." Others follow different patterns of thought and may adopt new names for their special way of working. Despite the diversity, we think it possible, following the lead of Korchin (1976), to describe the main features of psychodynamic therapy. These features form the core of what is nowadays involved in treatment, the core also of what is taught to students preparing to enter this specialty.

The Therapeutic Alliance

The most time-taking activity in psychodynamic therapy is conversation. If the relevant motivations are to come to light, there has to be detailed familiarity with the client's present and past experience. Present feelings, of course, are the crucial point, but it is often easier for a client to understand them by remembering their relation to the adaptive efforts of the past. The story could be told more briefly if the client knew it all at the start. More likely, however, the relevant part is a thicket of contradictory feelings and actions. Much time and repetition may be needed to cut a path to the habits and distorted motivations that are causing the client's discomfort. The therapist must inform the client that treatment will take time, the extent of which cannot easily be guessed at the start. Most treatment of this kind, with meetings perhaps twice a week, goes on for at least several months.

Those who practice psychodynamic therapy attach great importance to the therapeutic relation. They see it as a vital part of the process of treatment. The relation is almost certain to be unique in the client's experience. The listening therapist is a person with scientific training who is committed to the goal of health. This person is presumed to be wise in human suffering and experienced in setting it right. The client is not blamed for fears, shames, and inhibitions, which are taken seriously as the seat of the trouble and of its possible change. One looks in vain among the other relationships of life for just this combination of qualities. The pastor may be too strongly identified with standards of right and wrong. The friend may not listen long without giving nervous reassurance or talking about his or her own troubles. The loved one may listen, but cannot be counted on to give authoritative advice. No one hits the happy combination of interest, detachment, and knowledge that characterizes a skillful psychotherapist. It is this unique atmosphere that supports the client's growth.

In a recent systematic study of the various meanings attached to psychotherapy, Reisman (1971) takes this unusual combination into account. Arguing that psychotherapy should be defined by what the therapist does rather than the effects produced, he concludes that psychotherapy is "the communication of person-related understanding, respect, and a wish to be of help." Person-related understanding represents the sphere of the therapist's expertness, respect stands for the attitude of valuing and not blaming the client, and the wish to be of help signifies motivation to persist in promoting relearning as long as there are beneficial results.

Essential Processes

Flow of Communication. Given a good therapeutic relation, clients are generally able to provide a flow of informative conversation. They talk about their complaints, their experiences and feelings, their wishes and fantasies, their memories of the past, their problems and plans for the future. The therapist's respectful interest encourages the flow, which may be further aided by judicious steering of the conversation and asking for additional information. When the client shows signs of pain and anxiety, progress is helped if the therapist explicitly recognizes these feelings while encouraging the client to go on. But often it is wiser, especially in the early stages, to let the client veer off or circle around what appears to be painful. The topic will probably reappear in good time when the client's confidence has increased; if it does not, the therapist can choose a time to ask for it. The flow of communication goes in more personal directions to the extent that the therapist is able to respond to the feeling instead of the content of what is said. The client becomes progressively convinced that feelings are what count.

Examining the Client's Experience. The flow of conversation enables both client and therapist to study the client's experience. Even in single incidents we tend to reveal characteristic ways of perceiving, thinking, defending, and striving. This is shown in the following example and commentary taken from Korchin (1976).

THERAPIST: You look sort of downcast today.
PATIENT: Yes, I feel miserable. Yesterday was my first day on the new job. Everything was wrong. I couldn't even sleep last night. I may not even go back tomorrow.
THERAPIST: What happened?

231

PATIENT: Everybody ignored me. Nobody seemed to care that I was there; they barely said "hello." I suppose I can do the work OK, and I certainly need the money, but who wants to work in such a place? The vibes were all bad. I don't think there's one person there I could relate to.

THERAPIST: Can you be sure? You were only there one day.

PATIENT: Well, I suppose I could give it another try. I didn't really get to meet everyone. But they all looked the same, as if they didn't like me and didn't give a damn about me.

THERAPIST: You said you didn't sleep last night?

PATIENT: Yeah, I got to thinking about it, and got to wondering if I had done something wrong. Maybe I gave them the impression that I thought they were a bunch of clods. Anyway, I kept thinking about it, feeling miserable, thinking that maybe I had acted pretty snotty. Aw, the hell with it, I'm not going back.

Even in this brief exchange we can develop a number of reasonable hypotheses about the person's needs, cognitive style, emotional responsivity, and defenses. The patient greatly wants to feel warmly accepted, even in a work situation which might serve other needs and even before there is a reasonable basis for relationships to be formed. He is quick to sense rejection, though also realizing that he may provoke it. Intellectually, he is quick to overgeneralize and, emotionally, to overreact. As defense, he retreats from a potentially threatening situation, but not before he has dwelt on it and allowed it to make him miserable. In the course of therapy each of these themes would be explored, not once but likely several times, the therapist encouraging the patient to examine and view himself from different perspectives by offering interpretative hypotheses. In the present episode, attention was called, and quietly at that, only to the tendency to overgeneralize (pp. 310–311).

Exploring the Client's Past. Another result of continued conversation is learning about the client's past life. Since it is present feelings that really count, no pressure is exerted on clients to recover the past for its own sake, but the antecedents of present feelings flow naturally in the talk and often assist in dealing with them. If the patient just described recalls episodes of rejection by schoolmates, then perhaps disappointments in a family circle that favored another child, these prior instances may help him to comprehend the push behind his current tactics of defense and counter-rejection. They may help him in the end to change these tactics in a way that encourages a more friendly response. In psychodynamic treatment, understanding the past is useful to the extent that it assists in changing the present and future.

Exploring the Therapist-Client Relation. Of no small value in treatment is the examination of the therapist-client relation. When they are together so much, the client exhibits in direct interaction with the therapist a characteristic array of personal attitudes and social tactics. These may reflect the client's ordinary repertory, but they soon include specific attitudes toward the therapist. Among these are likely to be some that are borrowed from the client's past and transferred to the therapist without much realistic justification. Thus a client who was long jealous of a favored sibling may become angrily resentful that the therapist sees other patients. *Transference* reactions show that attitudes toward important people in the client's past are still operating with inappropriate force in the present. When the inappropriateness becomes clear, the client is likely to modulate the response to take better account of the therapist's actual characteristics.

Material for change is available to the client in another way: through *identification* and *modeling*. This may be a conscious process; more likely it is an unwitting copying of the therapist's ways of thinking and acting. The imitation may show in trivial ways, but the gain will be substantial if the client "has learned to plan actions instead of acting impulsively, to remain calm under stress, and to face his own inadequacies rather than denying them, inspired in part at least by observing these qualities in his therapist" (Korchin, 1976, p. 314).

Interpreting the Client's Feelings and Meanings.

The part played by the therapist in these processes might be described as quietly active. The therapist can facilitate the conversation by recognizing the client's feelings, clarifying what the client has said, and asking for additional information. Of special importance is interpretation. The use of this tool requires great skill and sensitivity. Most of us, perhaps in a moment of annoyance, have interpreted another person's remarks—"You say that because you are fixated on your mother"—and have noticed that our wisdom has been received with something less than gratitude. In psychodynamic therapy interpretation rarely consists of such omniscient reconstructions. More likely the therapist will simply call attention to ignored or inconsistent elements in what the client has said, or point out relations among experiences discussed on different occasions. Perhaps the therapist makes a generalization: "It seems that when you get into a frustrating situation you feel like giving up." Perhaps the therapist calls attention to an unacknowledged feeling: "You seem to be very angry when you talk about him." Perhaps an inconsistency is pointed out: "You say you respect him, but I keep hearing you make disparaging remarks about him." Interpretations of a more inclusive kind are generally held back for later stages of treatment, when the strengthened therapeutic alliance will make them less threatening.

The timing of an interpretation is of critical importance. Because the therapist adds something to what was said, clients in early stages may feel as if they were being corrected. They may not be ready to admit that they sound angry or give up too easily. An interpretation made too soon simply sets up resistance and delays progress. There is a critical point at which a client benefits, often

233

with a pleased sense of insight, and can put the knowledge to work. "I've been thinking about what you said last week and I decided to try it out by acting differently with my wife." Korchin (1976), from whom these examples have been drawn, cautions us not to expect blinding flashes of insight in which clients see all their problems solved. Insights are slowly cumulative, must be repeated often to extinguish the associated anxiety, and must be rightly timed—the ultimate test of therapeutic skill.

Translating Insights into Actions and New Life Patterns.　As time goes by, the content of the conversations shifts from inner feelings to outside realities, from maladaptive handicaps to adaptive potentials, from past problems to future prospects. When the client brings up a possible plan for the future the therapist can now, without setting off anxiety, ask about the details and talk more as an equal about the realities involved. This stage is obviously necessary for the treatment to be considered successful, but psychodynamic therapists agree that in most cases it cannot be hurried. Pushing too directly for the desired goals of treatment, before the client's feelings are unscrambled and anxieties reduced, only mobilizes resistance and delays progress. It is one of the easiest ways to make treatment a failure.

An Illustrative Case

Several essential processes are illustrated in the following fairly brief but successful treatment of an anxiety disorder (Alexander & French, 1946).

A business executive of forty-two years had suffered for a long time from an uncontrollable jerking of his arms. On three occasions he had had brief periods of unconsciousness. Neurological examination failed to disclose any sign of brain injury that might account for these attacks or for the jerking. The patient had a long history of irritability and a domineering attitude that injured his human relationships. At one point his wife divorced him because of these intolerable traits, but later they were remarried. The immediate occasion for seeking help was the fact that his wife was again considering separation. In addition, for a number of weeks he had suffered a complete loss of sexual potency.

This information was given during the first few interviews. The flow of conversation then moved to the patient's father, where it continued for some time. This suggested that the patient's father had a lot to do with the trouble. The father had been a self-made man with huge self-confidence and a violent temper. He was a tyrant both at home and in his business. He never tired of making the son feel inferior, and though at times there was sharp conflict between them, the son always gave in. Among other things the father had intimidated the patient in the matter of sexual expression. To meet all this pressure and somehow preserve self-respect, the patient had built up his own assertive and domineering attitude. He was ruled by a vast compensatory need to appear important and strong. When the father died, the patient took over the family glassware works and with great energy expanded it well beyond what his father had been able to accomplish. He felt impelled to surpass his father, yet along with all his competition and rebellion there was a great deal of admiring devotion.

From the very start the patient reproduced in the therapeutic situation his combined attitudes toward his father. The phenomenon of transference came unusually early and with great force in this case. The patient wanted rules to be made for him, and scrupulously obeyed one or two that had to be suggested. But his conversation was otherwise designed to impress the therapist with his importance, and whenever the therapist explained anything he quickly began to explain something about which he himself was expert: business or sports. He literally tried to force the therapist to become tyrannical so that he could rebel and compete with him. This attitude was so clear that the therapist undertook to create a corrective emotional experience by behaving in just the opposite fashion. He let the patient take the lead, avoided statements that could be thought arbitrary, admitted the limitations of psychotherapy, expressed admiration for the patient's good qualities, took an interest in his business and social activities. Under this treatment the patient became distinctly confused. He plainly thrived in the permissive, encouraging atmosphere, but he was unable to check his competitive feelings and still tried to fight battles with the therapist. This offered the perfect opportunity for interpretation. The patient could not help seeing that his aggression was completely out of relation to the therapist's behavior. His chief overdriven striving was exposed and he became able to enter a more genuine relationship with the therapist.

The change in his attitude toward the therapist was soon reflected at home. He became less domineering and was able to assume a more appropriately benevolent and helpful role toward his son. But his need to make a tyrant out of the therapist finally yielded only after a particularly vivid dream and its aftermath. The patient dreamed that he had manufactured some glassware and that the therapist angrily broke it all to pieces. The dream reminded him of an occasion when his father smashed a set of glassware because he did not like the design. During the subsequent hour the therapist asked the patient to tell more about his work. The patient eagerly embarked on a condescending lecture that soon became calmer and more confident. The contrast between the angry, destructive therapist of the dream and the appreciative listening therapist of reality was a decisive experience for the patient. At last he could have a friendly relation of give and take with an authoritative person without intrusion by father. With this decline of father's power the patient discovered to his pleasure that his sexual potency had returned.

The remaining hours of treatment were devoted to fuller discussion of the transference relationship. In childhood the patient had often been obliged to accept help from his father, but the father had always made him feel inferior on such occasions. This led him to react with a compensatory striving to prove

235

that he was really the better man. Accepting help from the therapist had thus reanimated from the start the very core of the problem. The therapist's radical assumption of exactly the opposite role, giving help along with interest, permissiveness, and a complete lack of the father's dogmatic self-confidence, led to an unusually rapid corrective emotional experience. At the end of treatment the patient's arms no longer jerked, which may be taken as presumptive evidence that the jerking originated from the tension of suppressed rage. His emotional and sexual relations with his wife were better than ever before, talk of separation had ended, and his irritable and domineering tendencies had greatly diminished.

In obvious ways the case illustrates the exploring of present and past experience through a flow of conversation. It shows the patient readily translating insights into changed actions at home and at work. What it exemplifies most dramatically is the transference reactions, and their interpretation, that enabled the patient to come face to face with his chief overdriven striving, which was at the heart of his difficulty. Aided by the fortunate circumstance that the therapeutic situation so easily brought out the overdriven striving, the treatment required only three months for its successful conclusion.

Variant Forms

There are a number of variant forms of psychodynamic treatment, some of which have been given names of their own. We classify here as psychodynamic those variants that largely make use of the essential processes described above, while putting special emphasis on some aspect of the treatment considered of special importance.

Individual Psychology. The earliest variant was that of Alfred Adler, who separated from Freud early in both their careers. Adler gave to his ideas and methods the title of Individual Psychology. He attached great importance to a person's style of life, an adaptive style developed in early childhood and often not successfully outgrown. In patients with anxiety disorders the style was faulty, being heavily grounded in feelings of inferiority and compensatory struggles to dominate and be superior to others, at the expense of friendly and loving human relations. Adler cautioned against taking a moralistic attitude, and repeatedly said that the patient's neglected social feeling could grow only in an atmosphere of warmth and support. In practice, however, he worked for early understanding, and relatively early interpretation, of the maladaptive life style, believing that no progress could be made until this obstacle to growth had been softened. Adler seems also to have relied on his persuasive power to help the growth of social interest (Ansbacher & Ansbacher, 1956).

There are today only small numbers of therapists who call themselves Adlerians or practitioners of Individual Psychology. This gives a false impression of Adler's influence. Many of his ideas have gone into the stream of contemporary thought and have become the accepted clinical common sense of our time.

Rational-Emotive Therapy. An influential contemporary variant has been developed by Albert Ellis and christened Rational-Emotive Therapy (Ellis, 1962). Like Adler, Ellis believes that there are initial obstacles to progress that have to be removed, but he sees them as beliefs rather than styles of life. Clients' suffering results from the irrational ways in which they construe the world and the unrealistic expectations that follow. Recalling the client mentioned earlier who reacted so badly to his first day on a new job, Ellis would say that he held the following belief: "I must be loved and accepted by everyone in my life, and if I am not, it is terrible." Holding such a belief, no doubt unwittingly, the client has often felt frustrated, angry, and anxious but has failed to learn from experience that one can live contentedly without everybody's love. Another client might believe that it was necessary to do everything exceptionally well and make no errors; anything less would mean rejection and disgrace. Ellis deals early and vigorously with these obstructive beliefs, using a combination of encouragement, challenging, interpreting, and assigning homework of systematic self-observation. It is this cognitive orientation, this early appeal to reason, that most distinguishes Ellis's methods. A similar cognitive variant has been developed by Beck (1976) especially for use with depressed patients.

Briefer and Crisis-Oriented Therapy. The expansion of public psychological services during the last fifteen or twenty years has brought many clients to treatment who have neither time nor inclination for extended work. Sometimes they complain of a highly specific problem, sometimes they have been thrown by an unexpected crisis. Treatment must be brief, perhaps six to ten interviews—sometimes only one—but it can be of significant value to the client especially in crises (Caplan, 1961; Lindemann, 1965). Obviously there will be no time for extended conversation and exploration. The nature of the difficulty must be rapidly assessed, and limited, practicable goals must be set. This may mean simply restoring an upset client to the pre-crisis level of functioning. It may mean ameliorating an especially crippling symptom. There is always a chance that coping ability will be increased by better understanding of the present disturbance (Butcher & Koss, 1978). In a few cases brief treatment can lead to larger insights and larger improvements, setting the client in a more constructive direction. These goals can be better attained if the therapist is somewhat active and directive, keeping the conversation on course and the goals in mind. Brief psycho-dynamic treatment needs highly experienced therapists who can make quick and accurate judgments and interact skillfully with clients. Under favorable circumstances these foreshortened treatments can yield encouragement, advice, and perhaps somewhat more.

237

Freud's Psychoanalysis

As we saw in the historical introduction, Freud developed a form of treatment based on free association, interpretation, and a search for earliest childhood origins. Conducted in this way, psychoanalysis took a long time, even up to several years with five appointments a week. This feature, with the associated expense, made it unavailable to all but a few fortunate people. As an instrument of research it played an historically unique part, but it could not meet the rising demand for psychological services. Today it is used mainly for training future therapists, who can profit from unusually thorough self-understanding, and for a small number of patients with stubborn anxiety disorders that have not yielded to other treatments.

Why does Freud's form of treatment, usually known as full-length or standard psychoanalysis, take such a long time? There are at least three outstanding reasons.

1. Free association takes a great deal more time than conversation. Alexander (1937) summarized as follows how the patient is instructed:

> The patient is requested to report everything that occurs to him in the analytic session. He is asked to verbalize everything that occurs to him in the original sequence and form without any modification or omission. He is asked to assume a passive attitude toward his own trains of thought; in other words, to eliminate all conscious control over his mental processes to which he gives free rein and merely report them (pp. 40–41).

The method, of course, is intended to encourage the emergence of feelings, including feelings that are usually repressed. It leads to resistance, interpretation, and a specific lowering of anxiety. But it allows the patient to swim aim-

238

lessly in the stream of consciousness, arriving only slowly at significant recollections. The analyst interprets obvious evasions but in so doing must be
careful not to get in the way of emerging feelings. Attempting to speed up free
association could easily destroy its value.

2. Freud believed that the critical conditionings of anxiety took place in early childhood, and that their current consequences could not be changed without full recall of the original situations. Effective reduction of anxiety, in his
view, required vivid recall and reliving of the original events. Present evidences of anxiety, including character armor and overdriven strivings, only
pointed the way back, often through a long series of events, to the original
childhood panic. It took time to cover so much ground.

3. Furthermore, Freud believed that in patients with anxiety disorders there
was typically more than a single root. He would probably have been unsatisfied with the treatment of the man with the jerking arms, partly because the
earliest interactions between patient and father were not recovered, partly because the patient's relation with his mother and with other family and household members were not thoroughly probed. Full cure, in Freud's view, meant
working through all the anxiety-generating relationships of early childhood,
besides the defenses, armor, and protective traits to which they had given rise.
This really meant a major reshaping of the personality. Only thus could the
patient deal confidently and realistically with whatever might happen.

Few people today accept such a sweeping goal of permanent cure. Few
workers have found that intense reliving of the infant's conflicts in the family
circle is requisite for a satisfactory solution of more immediate problems. But
there is reason to believe that such conflicts occur and may well exert a detrimental influence on later development. Those who have practiced full-length
psychoanalysis report the regular occurrence, after some time, of a phenomenon called "transference neurosis" in which the patient repeats with the therapist all that once went on with parents. Hendrick (1939) described this as
follows:

> Because this occurs with such consistency in every analysis, we can understand that
> the transference has developed to a point where the transference emotions are more
> important to the patient that the permanent health he is seeking. This is the point
> where the major unresolved, unconscious problems of childhood begin to dominate.
> They are now reproduced in the transference with all their pent-up emotion. The
> patient is unconsciously striving for what he failed to gain or to do without in actual
> childhood. Only those who have observed it will appreciate how fully much of the
> reaction to the analyst at this period is like a child's. Petulance, irritability, defi-
> ance, even a childishness in tone of voice are frequent, even in people who are
> otherwise quite mature.

Such behavior, so far at odds with the actual situation, lends itself especially
well to interpretation. The interpretations must be repeated a good many

times before the stormy emotions and the anxiety subside. Working out the "transference neurosis" is thus an example of the gradual extinction of conditioned anxiety.

BEHAVIORAL TREATMENT

In the preceding chapters we have touched several times on matters related to behavioral treatment. When examining the adaptive process (Chapter 3) we mentioned Pavlov's historic work on conditioned responses, including the processes of acquisition, generalization, and extinction. We also took note of Skinner's ideas about operant conditioning and reinforcement, illustrating with an experiment in which the content of mental patients' conversation was changed by the staff's paying attention to certain themes and paying no attention to others. When describing the anxiety disorders (Chapter 6) we noticed the applicability of conditioning principles especially in understanding anxiety states and phobias. It is evident that certain long-recognized principles of learning have a direct bearing on disordered behavior.

What distinguishes behavior therapy from other forms of psychotherapy is the attempt to base all procedures on principles of learning already demonstrated by experimental work. In practice this usually implies principles of conditioning and deconditioning as originally demonstrated in experiments with animals, although some use can be made of the more complex learning processes studied in human beings. The goal is to make treatment an application of experimental psychology, and in the behavioristic tradition to conceive of it as a modification of behavior instead of as a change in subjective states like feeling, confidence, or self-respect.

An Early Example: The Treatment of Enuresis

Success along these lines was obtained some years ago by the Mowrers (1938), who invented a technique to overcome bedwetting in children. An apparatus was devised whereby the first moisture on a pad placed in the bed set off a bell loud enough to wake up the child. In due course the stimuli preliminary to urination became connected with the response of waking, enabling the child to exert control long enough to reach the bathroom. The method has had considerable use ever since. In a review covering twenty-five years, Lovibond reports that an initial arrest of bedwetting is obtained on the average in 90 percent of the cases treated. This good news is somewhat marred, however, by figures showing a rather high rate of subsequent relapse. Weighing several relevant studies, Lovibond sets 34 percent as a probable figure for relapse as shown by follow-ups one to three years later; "the main problem still appears to be the reduction of the relapse rate." Some workers think the results can be better (DeLeon & Sacks, 1972), but even if only two out of three cases are

240

promptly cured, conferring on the children a gratifying sense of mastery and on the parents a welcome relief from anxiety and the washing of sheets, the achievement is by no means negligible.

Systematic Desensitization

The deconditioning technique known as systematic desensitization was devised by Joseph Wolpe (1958), who more than anyone else was responsible for bringing behavior therapy to life after thirty years of only sporadic interest. Reasoning from experiments with animals and children, Wolpe searched for a way to produce gradual deconditioning of anxiety responses in adults. This proved to be possible if the patients vividly imagined the objects of their dread, provided they were at the same time thoroughly relaxed and calm in the therapist's reassuring presence. Pains had to be taken to keep them from imagining so vividly as to precipitate an acute attack of anxiety. To this end, therapist and patient worked out beforehand a list or hierarchy of situations the patient feared, arranged from least to most provocative of anxiety. A hierarchy on fear of high places might start with looking up at one from below and proceed through graded steps to a climactic scene in which the patient stands on a precipice looking down. Treatment began with imagining the most innocuous scene several times over until it no longer aroused uneasiness; then the next scene would be imagined and deconditioned; and so on up the list until the patient in fancy could stand on the dreaded spot looking serenely down into the depths below. Such a result could not, of course, be obtained quickly. Many repetitions and occasional setbacks usually stretched the work on a single list over 15 or 20 sessions, and if the patient had more than one focus of fear, so that several hierarchies had to be constructed, even more time might be required. On the average, however, systematic desensitization called for less time than did other methods of psychotherapy applied to similar disorders.

The reader may be surprised that just imagining the things of which you are afraid should have so much power to reduce fear. And what happens when the patient gets up on the real precipice? It is therefore important to recognize the power of imagination, under just the right circumstances, to elicit strong affective responses. When therapist and patient are at work constructing the hierarchy, the patient can admit being most terrified by high places without actually going straight into a panic; one can report what one knows without experiencing its full affect. In a dream of high places, however, the patient would indeed be panic-stricken, and a scene vividly imagined in a relaxed or drowsy state can have the affective properties of a dream. Wolpe's procedure involves training the patient to relax deeply; in some cases hypnotism is used to promote both physical relaxation and vivid imagery. Then the therapist proposes each scene and the patient imagines it, with the safeguard that a signal can be given to call the scene off and encourage renewed relaxation if the

241

patient gets too scared. Real anxiety is unquestionably involved, and the de-conditioning can be almost as effective as if the therapist accompanied the pa-tient through a hierarchy of real events. Case reports show that, although it may be something of a jolt to pass from the imagined to the real precipice, the majority of patients can do it. This is, of course, more than they could have done prior to treatment.

Systematic desensitization can be interpreted as a simple process of extinc-tion. Conditioned anxiety stimuli are given, no painful consequences follow, and the conditioned response thus becomes weakened to the vanishing point. Wolpe believes that a second principle is involved, which he calls *reciprocal inhibition*. Extinction of the anxiety aroused during the treatment is assisted by activation of an antagonistic bodily response, in this case calm relaxation. The theory depends on the known antagonism between the sympathetic and parasympathetic divisions of the autonomic nervous system, which govern re-spectively preparation for emergencies and maintaining peaceful vegetative processes, and by the common sense thought that one cannot be anxious and calm at the same time. Wolpe attributes the manageability of the anxiety aroused during systematic desensitization to the damping effects of the in-duced relaxation. Not all behavior therapists agree that reciprocal inhibition is an important principle. Reverting to our discussion of the therapeutic situa-tion, it is worth pointing out that the reassuring presence of the therapist may have a good deal to do with the patient's tolerance of anxiety. Desiring the therapist's esteem, reassured by the implicit promise to stop scenes that be-come unpleasant and to restore calm, the patient may well be emboldened to find out how much anxiety can be tolerated.

An Example of Systematic Desensitization

To make the therapeutic process clearer we will take an example originally re-ported by Rachman (1959). The patient, Miss A. G., a 24-year-old teacher, suffered from a phobia of injections, dating back at least to the age of six or seven. When an injection could not be avoided she was panic-stricken and al-ways fainted. She sought treatment when an impending trip that was impor-tant to her entailed a series of inoculations. This phobia was her central com-plaint, but she also had an intense fear of inserting internal sanitary pads, and she mentioned a sexual problem consisting of pain and anxiety during inter-course; in addition, her answers on a standard test gave evidence of general feelings of insecurity. The therapist chose systematic desensitization for the two focalized complaints and undertook "to relieve the feelings of insecurity by discussion and reassurance."

Two hierarchies were constructed, one dealing with injections and one with sanitary pads. The first started with picturing a hospital in the distance and led up to receiving an injection in a doctor's office. The second began with an image of an unopened box of pads in a drugstore and proceeded to imagining the act of insertion, which in reality the patient was unable to perform. In the

242

course of 22 sessions spread over several months, the desensitization procedure was carried out successfully through both hierarchies. At the end of this, A.G. had no difficulty with sanitary pads, and she received her requisite injections somewhat nervously but without fainting or lasting upset. She was elated at this success and reported that she felt in general a lot better. Follow-up after five years showed that she had held her gains and that her symptoms had not recurred.

The elimination of the two phobic responses seems clearly related to the desensitization procedures, but Rachman's report suggests that reassuring discussion made more than a negligible contribution to the total result. At the fifth session A. G. talked about her protracted love affair and her doubts about it; "after some discussion, her feelings and motives became more lucid and she experienced some relief." To the twelfth session she came so depressed because of a setback in her love affair that desensitization was postponed in favor of "nondirective, cathartic discussion." At the fifteenth session she told of having to give up an attempt at sexual intercourse because of intense pain and anxiety; this made her wonder whether or not she had a physical defect. Questioning showed that there had been inadequate foreplay, so she was "given information and advice about love-play and was told to relax fully before love-making." At the eighteenth interview she told of having intercourse without "even the slightest pain," which greatly reassured her on the subject of sexual adequacy. Without detracting from the accomplishments of systematic desensitization, we have to allow that another problem area, sex and her love affair, was being simultaneously treated by techniques of advice, information, and sympathetic listening, evidently with satisfactory results. A literal-minded scientist might see in this an experiment spoiled: there is no way to determine the relative contribution of the different techniques to the total result, or to decide what interaction there might have been between the diminishing phobias and the improving sexual situation. But if we were to consult Miss A. G., she would almost certainly say that she had received good therapy.

The Phobic Element in Anxiety Disorders

Systematic desensitization is at its best when the patient complains of phobia — a circumscribed irrational fear of a specific object or clearly defined situation. Extinguishing an anxiety response can be straightforwardly accomplished if there is a known, restricted conditioned stimulus to which the patient can be systematically exposed. It has been remarked that behavior therapists seem to encounter more phobic patients than the adherents of other schools of psychotherapeutic thought do. This apparent difference may well be due to the method of diagnosis: behavior therapists take special pains to look for phobic elements in their patients' complaints, trying to pin down specific stimulus patterns that are most conducive to anxiety. When we studied phobias in the last chapter, however, we encountered evidence that an irra-

243

tional fear might not be just itself, so to speak, but part of a more complex adaptive operation. Lazarus (1971), a behavior therapist who espouses a "broad-gauge" approach, cites the case of a man who developed a sudden crippling phobia of crossing bridges. No earlier history involving bridges could be elicited, but it came out that the patient crossed a long bridge every day to get to work, that he had been offered a promotion, and that he had experienced heavy reluctance to accept so much new responsibility. The bridge phobia is here part of a larger pattern of threat to self-esteem; it could be considered a face-saving device. Its removal would be unfortunate if the therapist were not prepared to deal also with the conflict between the patient's self-esteem and his dread of responsibility. This further step might also be accomplished by principles of behavior therapy, but the more "broad-gauged" the techniques become, the less different they seem from those practiced by other schools of thought.

Operant Conditioning Methods

Wolpe's work is founded on the model of Pavlov's conditioning experiments. He describes a large number of techniques based on this model and adapted to purposes other than desensitizing a phobia. Some of these methods, however, involve principles of operant conditioning, and it is often hard to draw the line within a given technique between these two modes of influence. "Behavior therapies that apply the principles and technology of the operant learning paradigm," say Kanfer and Phillips (1970), "are more widely used for a greater diversity of target symptoms, and within more varied social contexts, than are any of the other behavior therapy models." What distinguishes operant conditioning, as we saw in Chapter 3, is its emphasis on the consequences of behavior instead of the stimulating conditions. Reinforcement is the key concept, and the goal is to control the reinforcement contingencies in such a way as to diminish the frequency of undesirable responses and increase the frequency of desired ones. Operant conditioning thus provides a means of promoting and shaping new behavior as well as suppressing pathological modes of responding. The principle was illustrated in Chapter 2 in the case of Walter Lilly, when parents, teachers, and therapist alike agreed to pay no attention to the boy's crying, screaming, and fears of dying—especially to excuse him from nothing and let no benefits accrue on account of this behavior—but to show interest and engage in conversation when he talked in a more mature way. This principle is effective, of course, only to the extent that the therapist is in control of the reinforcement contingencies. Not by accident, the most striking instances of behavior modification through operant conditioning have occurred in institutions, where the staff had extensive control over the environment.

244 Operant conditioning can be carried out in a great many different ways. Among its virtues is flexibility: procedures can be devised that meet the pecu-

liar conditions present in each case, and workers with the method have shown great ingenuity in this respect. In one-to-one treatment with adults, the therapist's approval or disapproval is probably a critical reinforcing agency. The motive of wanting one's troubles alleviated gains significant support to the extent that one comes to care about the therapist's interest and esteem. With children the rewards can be more primitive—child therapists are large purchasers of fruit and candy—but generally with the intention later to replace food reinforcements with social ones. When a client's behavior is marked by deficiencies, as is usually the case—poor social initiative, lack of assertiveness, sexual timidity, feeble power of concentration—programs of reinforcement, often coupled with those intended to reduce anxiety, can bring about beneficial change within a reasonably short time.

If positive reinforcement can shape desirable new behavior, can negative reinforcement be used to suppress undesirable responses? This raises the much discussed question of punishment as a method of control. The therapeutic version of this larger problem is known as *aversion therapy*. It consists of connecting pathological behavior with an immediate aversive stimulus powerful enough to suppress it. If a client's problem is alcohol, a drink can be given along with a drug that quickly induces nausea and vomiting. If homosexual interest is the trouble, an experimental situation can be created where looking at same-sex nude pictures brings on painful electric shock that is relieved by looking at opposite-sex pictures. Aversion therapy is certainly capable of suppressing an undesirable response rather quickly, but it is, as Lazarus (1971) remarks, "usually a harrowing experience" that tends to "hurt people or rob them of their human dignity." This can be somewhat mitigated by combining aversive therapy with positive training, and perhaps altogether avoided in a method advocated by Cautela (1967) in which aversive imagery takes the place of overt punishing events. In a thorough review, Kanfer and Phillips (1970) note that "misgivings about possible undesirable side effects" have held back both research and application, but they conclude that these are unnecessary "when the procedures are properly constructed and applied to suit the individual circumstances."

Operant conditioning has been used with a variety of problems not hitherto considered to be within the scope of psychotherapy. A collection of fifty case studies edited by Ullmann and Krasner (1965) shows the wide range of these endeavors. As mentioned earlier, Ayllon and others have modified the behavior of severely disturbed mental patients by combinations of food and social rewards so that the patients became more comfortable, manageable, and socially responsive. Mute schizophrenics have been induced to speak, patients with bizarre and inconvenient habits have given them up, and occasionally there has been sufficient progress to justify discharge from the hospital (Lanyon & Lanyon, 1978). Mentally retarded children have also benefited from operant methods, becoming trained in ways that make institutional or home care much easier and that facilitate maximum use of capacity (Baker &

245

Ward, 1971; Thompson & Grabowski, 1977). The human value of such work should not escape our notice even if it seems more natural to call it training than psychotherapy.

Token Economies. Useful in institutions is a form of operant conditioning known as token economy. The object is to give the staff a regular and simple means of reinforcing desired behavior and reducing the troublesome variety. This is accomplished by establishing a medium of exchange—tokens of some kind—that can be used to secure privileges like candy, TV time, movies, special foods, or weekend passes. Patients earn tokens by various kinds of behavior, from making beds to taking on larger job responsibilities, that make life easier on the ward. They can spend them as they please, accumulating them until they have the price of the privilege they most want. Token economies have been tried in mental hospitals, schools for the retarded, centers for juvenile delinquents, institutions for prisoner rehabilitation, and even in school classrooms. There is now a large data base supporting the conclusion that token economies are effective in changing behavior (Kazdin, 1977). This means in effect that where tried they have produced a better level of behavior than prevailed before. Critics who say that the method is merely a way of buying good behavior are perhaps a little too harsh. Inmates and staff alike profit from a reduction of disturbing and inconsiderate behavior, and the atmosphere that results is surely more conducive to growth. Krasner (1971) points out that in a token economy one learns to behave so as to better elicit positive reinforcement from others, and this experience may carry over outside the institution. Token economies are not intended to have large effects on severely disordered and maladaptive behavior. They are not a substitute for psychological treatment, and should be judged instead as a form of human management.

Biofeedback. Another application of learning theory, useful especially in psychophysiological disorders, goes by the name of biofeedback. There have been plentiful hypotheses about physical changes in disorders like chronic high blood pressure or migraine headaches, but only recently have sophisticated methods been developed for the continuous monitoring of such changes (Schwartz, 1973). It now turns out that a person can sometimes achieve a measure of control over a bodily system previously considered involuntary by watching a continuous recording of bodily functions and learning the actions or thoughts that change them. Thus a person hoping to lower blood pressure can produce changes in the readings and find out what reactions preceded the changes. There are presumably intrinsic rewards in seeing the blood pressure decrease, and this can be further reinforced in several ways by an attending therapist.

246 The technological magic in biofeedback appeals perhaps too much to some workers, but Kazdin (1978) points out that research evidence for the usefulness

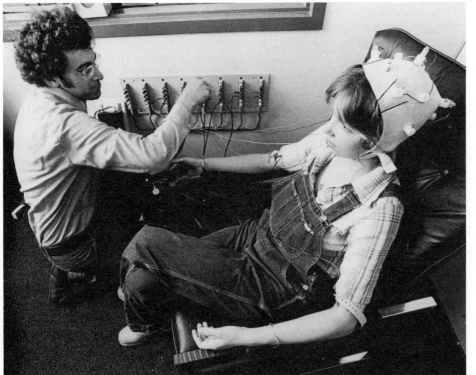

Biofeedback conditioning involves some rather complicated paraphernalia, but the experience of the subject is quite comfortable and safe. Electrodes attached to the arms may measure blood pressure or perspiration; electrodes in the helmet measure electrical impulses from the brain.

of this method is still rather slim. What systems can be influenced, and how much they can be influenced, are still largely to be determined.

Reinforcement in Operant Conditioning. In order to make the principles plain we have undoubtedly made behavior modification, especially operant conditioning, sound easy. Reinforcement is a seductive term. Vanity may prompt us to believe that simply by conferring our smiling approval, communicating our frowning displeasure, or withholding our interest, we can omnipotently shape the behavior of everyone around us. What undercuts this happy conceit is the recollection that others are simultaneously engaged in shaping us. But in any event disordered behavior is the kind least likely to change in response to superficial reinforcement; otherwise it would have changed long ago. To be an effective therapeutic reinforcer requires training, skill, and sensitivity. It requires a therapeutic relation in which the client trusts and respects the therapist and comes to care a great deal about meeting

247

the therapist's expectations. It requires also a detailed knowledge on the therapist's part of such technical problems as what schedules of reinforcement are more appropriate in different circumstances and how to manage transitions from one type of reward to another. Before concluding that behavior therapy is easy, one should read the solid 600-page book by Kanfer and Phillips, (1970), who describe in detail the abundant research and clinical observations that constitute the necessary learning foundations for practical work in this field.

Assertiveness Training

The method of behavior modification known as assertiveness training was included by Wolpe (1958) in his first book and has become part of the technical equipment of most behavior therapists.

> Assertive training, generally speaking, is required for patients who in interpersonal contexts have unadaptive anxiety responses that prevent them from saying or doing what is reasonable and right. . . . The patient may be constantly placating other people because he fears to offend them, or because he feels a moral obligation to place the interests of others before his own. He may allow people to maneuver him into situations he does not desire. He may be unable to express his legitimate wishes (Wolpe, 1969, p. 63).

Assertiveness training represents a head-on attack on social inhibition, on what in Chapter 4 we called social enslavement. This is different from dealing with a phobia. Social anxiety is diffuse and can be aroused by a large variety of stimulating conditions. True to his theories, however, Wolpe tries to focalize the problem. He seizes on the particular relation in which the patient's lack of assertion has its most damaging consequences—perhaps the relation with spouse or employer—and works for a modification of behavior at just this one point. To one patient Wolpe reports using these words: "What I expect of you is to stand up for your legitimate human rights, to express your views as clearly and as forcefully as possible no matter how critical of you other people appear to be. Stop being on the defensive, and stop apologizing for yourself" (1958, p. 123).

Social anxiety is very common. A certain amount of it can be considered the average result of human socialization. Countless people have become aware of this in themselves, have been angry at themselves for such submissiveness, and have resolved to be more assertive next time. Undoubtedly this self-treatment sometimes works, but it is a common experience to realize after the next time that one has been as submissive as ever, held back by a powerful reluctance. What is there about assertiveness training that makes it any better than self-help? Remembering the therapeutic situation and the therapist's expectations so clearly communicated, we can presume that the patient faces a conflict of anxieties. There is dread of being assertive, but there is also dread of reporting

248

failure and unworthiness back to the therapist. Assertiveness treatment is essentially an application of the time-honored method of persuasion. Success depends on the client's having developed a strong respect for the therapist and a powerful need to live up to expectations.

Experience has shown that Wolpe's rough method leaves much to be desired. Assertiveness training is nowadays conducted more gently and gradually. As described by Lanyon and Lanyon (1978), it begins with a considerable amount of conversation. An important function of this talk is to bring the client to discriminate between assertiveness and aggression. Submissive clients typically confuse the two; the most legitimate request or statement of rights feels like an expression of hostility, and is subject to the anxiety connected with hostility. When asked what would happen if they asserted themselves, clients may picture counter-hostility and destructive attack. As the client becomes better able to think of assertive behavior that is not hostile, opportunities are created to rehearse such behavior and imagine its consequences. Only then is the client considered ready to attempt assertion in the real world. The therapist's encouragement must continue for some time while these trials go on. Reinforcement from outside may come slowly; acquaintances who have always dominated the client will not simply subside and take it when the worm begins to turn. When proper account is taken of these complications, however, assertiveness training has proved one of the most successful ventures in behavioral treatment.

Illustrative Case.   In the last chapter we described the case of Richard Benson (Leon, 1977) to illustrate severe anxiety disorder. He was given behavioral treatment that in the end—after two years—gave him almost complete relief. The therapist first undertook systematic desensitization, hoping to extinguish the anxiety connected with situations where a bathroom was unavailable. This was unsuccessful, perhaps because the anxiety was elicited by more stimuli than could be captured in the imagined scenes. The therapist then tried a different plan for extinction: he assigned a graded series of tasks centered around Benson's bicycle riding. The easiest was to ride where there were frequent known rest-rooms, stopping at each to comb his hair but not urinating if he could help it. When this could be done without anxiety or urination he moved up to more difficult tasks, until finally he could ride alone through unfamiliar routes and also ride in the company of others. This time the procedure was successful, but the therapist felt that Benson's more general fear of social embarrassment needed modification, and for this he employed a vigorous extinction strategy called "implosive therapy" (Stampfl & Levis, 1967). The therapist generated vivid images of the most embarrassing situations possible and urged Benson to maintain them in painful detail until his anxiety subsided. This method, obviously dangerous for patients who cannot tolerate strong anxiety, proved well-timed in Benson's case and did in fact reduce his fear of embarrassment. Finally, assertiveness training was undertaken, with modeling, role playing, and practice, in order to raise his level of social competence. Benson's therapy, like that of Walter Lilly (Chapter 2), illustrates the value of flexibility in behavioral treatment. Different techniques have to be chosen to meet different aspects of the patient's trouble.

Cognitive Behavior Therapy

Behavioral treatment grew rapidly during the 1960s. Based on the psychological model of maladaptive behavior, it attracted many psychologists well-trained in learning theory. Clinical experience, with its expectable complexity, presently led to a significant enlargement of concepts. Behavior was seen to be determined not just by external stimuli but by the individual's perception and interpretation of them. It was necessary to consider cognition, a topic once rejected by strict behaviorists because it involved subjective happenings.

In a history of behavior modification Kazdin (1978) describes the changes as follows:

> The inclusion of cognition-based treatments represents a new direction in behavior modification that evolved out of dissatisfaction with stimulus-response explanations of behavior and in response to research that has demonstrated the role of thought processes in controlling behavior. Another reason for recognizing the importance of cognitive processes in behavior change is that many problems requiring therapeutic interventions are themselves based upon cognitions (e.g., obsessions, self-critical statements). Overt behaviors are not always the problem that serves as a basis for seeking treatments. Hence, focusing on thoughts, feelings, self-verbalizations, and other private events is required (pp. 307-308).

For a movement that started as a direct offshoot of behaviorism this is a radical change of view. The early behaviorists, like John B. Watson, believed that the private worlds of thought and feeling had no place in science because they could not be directly observed and verified by other scientists. As Kazdin shows, clinical work with individual human beings drove therapists out of this ideal of pure objectivity. But when thoughts and feelings and beliefs are taken seriously in treatment—when cognition is admitted as a legitimate concern— the distance between behavioral treatment and psychodynamic therapy is very much reduced (Wachtel, 1977). We would expect cognitive behavior therapists to put more stress on learning and reinforcement contingencies, while psychodynamic therapists would be more concerned with motivation and insight. But the conversations with clients in which each would engage might not sound very different. Cognitive therapists claim Albert Ellis (1962) as one of themselves, whereas we described his rational-emotive therapy as a variant of psychodynamic treatment. His way of discussing clients' irrational beliefs at the outset as a means of removing obstacles to further progress is similar to Adler and similar also, as we will see, to some cognitive treatment practices.

As an example of changing initial beliefs, Goldfried and Davison (1976), who call the process "cognitive relabeling," cite the case of a student who suffered from examination anxiety. Systematic desensitization had been used but did not produce a lasting result. Conversation revealed that the student had a fantastically high standard of preparation and adequate knowledge. He would sit surrounded by books, although the textbook alone would prepare him sufficiently; before long he would become confused by too much information and anxious because he was not retaining it. The examination as such was not the cause of anxiety as much as the way the client interpreted it and the consequent self-defeating manner in which he prepared. When he could accept this relabeling of his study habits as excessive and inefficient, the client's treatment advanced successfully.

Value is claimed for self-instruction as a means of producing change. Children commonly use this process as a means of controlling their own behavior. At first aloud, but later silently, they give themselves orders to do this and not do that, orders that may first be borrowed from parents but presently become their own. This general phenomenon is turned to account by Meichenbaum (1977), who seeks to bring about favorable change by altering clients' habitual self-instructions. He believes that children isolated by shyness, for example, constantly give themselves instructions to avoid the dangers of contact even when they might like to join. Alteration of these self-instructions proceeds through a training program that uses films, modeling, discussion, and rehearsal, at the end of which the children are equipped with a more up-beat set of self-instructions for use when entering a social situation.

It is a short step from this technique to a variety of methods designed to bring about stronger and more appropriate self-control. Lanyon and Lanyon (1978) use this development to refute the charge often made that behavioral treatment coerces and controls clients from the outside. Self-control procedures, they say, "increase the patient's ability to determine his own destiny and fulfill his potential" (p. 128). Once it is allowed that subjective processes influence and guide behavior, training in self-control can be described as helping a person to become more fully aware of present behavior, and going on to teach the principles of learning that might lead to change. Self-observation is encouraged by asking detailed questions, sometimes requiring that a detailed diary be kept. Clients are then told how to administer self-rewards and self-punishments to produce substantial change. Further instruction includes practical wisdom about stimulus control and training to use alternative responses—for instance, learning to relax when anxiety threatens. Self-control methods have many uses. They have been applied, for instance, to giving up smoking, coping with obesity, and improving study habits.

Evaluative Comments

Looked at historically, behavioral treatment came as a fresh breeze at a time when psychoanalysis was passing the peak of its popularity and when Freud's theoretical scheme was beginning to look like an obstacle to further progress. There is an appealing directness about the analysis of disordered behavior into the specific situations that most upset the client and the circumstances that keep reinforcing maladaptive responses so that they are not unlearned. There is a refreshing air of common sense about going straight to the task of reducing anxiety and encouraging new behavior, and applying for these purposes the most elementary principles of learning. Readers of the literature are likely to feel that behavior modification is a no-nonsense approach, working for definite goals by definite means, dispelling a lot of theoretical clouds, and using concepts that lend themselves to being tested.

Yet it was this very simplicity that from the beginning received the most strenuous criticism. Sloane (1969), Wilkins (1971), and Locke (1971) took behavioral treatment to task for trying to explain change in mechanical terms— extinction, reinforcement, reciprocal inhibition—without giving proper credit to the therapeutic relation, although this relation lends itself to a naturalistic explanation in terms of learning and motivation. Breger and McGaugh (1965) considered the learning principles invoked too simple and asked that a larger place be made for the more complex meanings characteristic of human experience, as contrasted with animals. But behavior therapists themselves soon discovered the limitations of their first formulations. Actually working with patients, running up against those more complex meanings, they evolved cognitive therapy that, as we have seen, brought them closer to the older traditions of psychotherapy. In the course of time it may happen that the polemics of a few years ago will fade and that psychological treatment will become a reunited discipline.

HUMANISTIC-EXISTENTIAL PSYCHOTHERAPY

Both classes of treatment thus far described stand in the tradition of natural science. However broadly and humanly they are interpreted, psychodynamic therapy and behavioral treatment both assume that behavior is mainly determined by unwitting motives, environmental contingencies, or other processes described as external to the self. This has been criticized as making people sound less than human. By contrast, a humanistic outlook gives main attention to purposes, values, options, and self-determination, and it sees as the highest human motive an urge toward self-actualization (Maslow, 1970). Humanistic therapy proceeds by encouraging the growth of self-understanding, especially of self and world as the client experiences them, and by raising the client's awareness of freedom, responsibility, and choice. These changes are held to open the way toward fuller self-actualization.

Existential Psychotherapy

Existential psychotherapy originated in Europe out of an attempt to modify Freud's scientific outlook with the view of man arising from existential philosophy. Giving philosophical debts to Kierkegaard, Husserl, and Heidegger, it has been especially developed by two Swiss psychiatrists, Ludwig Binswanger (1956) and Medard Boss (1963). Existentialism raises questions about the scientific understanding of human behavior; as Binswanger put it, "man is no longer understood in terms of some theory—be it a mechanistic, a biologic or a psychological one." The emphasis is shifted to *being,* to personal experiencing in the present. Psychotherapists, according to Rollo May (1958), must ask themselves: "Can we be sure that we are seeing the patient as he really is, knowing him in his own reality; or are we seeing merely a projection of our own theories *about* him?" They must further ask themselves: "How can we know whether we are seeing the patient in his real world, the world in which he 'lives and moves and has his being,' and which is for him unique, concrete, and different from our general theories of culture? In all probability we have never participated in his world and do not know it directly; yet we must know it and to some extent must be able to exist in it if we are to have any chance of knowing him." Existential therapy differs from other forms in calling not for new techniques but for an uncommonly high standard of knowing another person as that person really is. Even more than that, according to Laing (1967), psychotherapy must be "an obstinate attempt of two people to recover the wholeness of being human through the relationship between them" (p. 53).

Existential therapy has had wide popularity in Europe and is a significant movement in the United States. Many have felt that it addressed itself more directly than other methods to the deeper contemporary concerns of humanity. Ford and Urban (1965) give existential therapists good marks on a number of points.

> They share with others, such as Adler and Rogers, an emphasis on the importance of subjectively observable responses; attention and awareness are fundamental, not only as they affect a person's present behavior but also as they determine what he will learn and how he will change in the future. These writers share with Adler the notion that how a person represents future events to himself (goals and objectives) has much to do with the way he can behave in the present. They have not missed the critical purpose of psychotherapy, and they stress the importance of the patient actually performing new and constructive responses in the everyday world; these concrete patterns of interaction become the ultimate test of the success of psychotherapy. . . . They point to a pattern of difficulties frequent in present-day patients, isolation and loneliness, which they interpret to result from the person's learned avoidance of significant interactions with people. They emphasize a person's identity, or awareness of himself, as a basic antecedent to human behavior.

Client-Centered Therapy

As an example of humanistic-existential psychotherapy we will take a method introduced by Carl Rogers (1942). It is one of the simplest versions of this form of treatment, and is widely used; it will also repay careful examination.

Rogers first gave his method the title of nondirective counseling. This reflected his belief that the client should always take the lead in the therapeutic process. As described by Rogers, the counselor does not intervene by asking questions, by giving information or advice, or even by directing the course of the conversation. The goal is to help the client grow in the client's own directions, and the role is confined to encouraging and ratifying this growth. To this end, the counselor employs a single therapeutic tool called the acceptance, recognition, and clarification of feeling—a tool we described earlier in the chapter. The special quality that makes a conversation therapeutic, as Rogers first stated it, is responding to feeling instead of content.

In a later publication Rogers (1957) changed the title of his method to *client-centered therapy*. He now amended his account to avoid the elusiveness of the word "feeling." The counselor must learn to perceive things as the client perceives them, to enter as fully as possible into the client's "internal frame of reference," and to "indicate to the client the extent to which he is seeing through the client's eyes." This more existential description does greater justice to the cognitive aspect of what is to be recognized: not just loose feelings, so to speak, but matters of deep concern to the client. Still later, Gendlin (1970) arrived at a further refinement. "Feelings are really 'felt meanings,'" he wrote; "implicitly complex experiencing of situations. . . . Not to distract or digress from the experiential process of the client's concretely felt meanings, but to point to them, help him wrestle with them, carry them forward by our personal and exact response to them or inquiry concerning them—that is the principle."

Difficulty in finding the right words to convey just what the client-centered therapist accepts, recognizes, and clarifies should not be taken to mean that it is unimportant. We will not go far wrong if we think of it as the client's deepest personal concerns, whatever they may be at a particular time. When the therapist's recognitions are successful, the client is in a unique situation. Feelings, the way things look, the things that really matter are constantly appreciated and are clearly the things in which the counselor, too, is interested. Successful recognition of the internal frame of reference thus leads to the expression of more and more feelings. The client has probably never before had a listener who showed such awareness of personal concerns. As a result, it often happens that within a single hour more is communicated than has ever been said to anyone else.

The consistent use of this single therapeutic tool distinguishes client-centered therapy from other forms of treatment in which advice, information, interpretation, conditioning procedures, and practical assistance may be intermingled. The Rogers technique deserves its original title of "nondirective." At times almost amusingly evasive, the therapist replies to anxious queries by acknowledging that the client feels anxious, or parries a request for advice by recognizing that the client would like someone to settle the question. But the therapist sticks to the principle of responding to the experiential process as it is disclosed, and the client soon learns to take the initiative.

Changes Occurring Through Client-Centered Therapy.   Success is of course not univeral, but this method is clearly capable of producing significant changes. A substantial number of research studies based on many series of recorded interviews tends to confirm a fairly regular course of events (Rogers & Dymond, 1954). Time is spent at first in defining or *structuring* the situation. More than likely clients will want direction and will accept with difficulty the idea that the hour belongs to them. As they get used to this, clients at first use the opportunity to pour out *negative feelings:* doubts, guilts, inferiorities, anxieties, and hostilities. This is followed by "one of the most certain and predictable aspects of the whole process," the faint and tentative expression of *positive impulses.* Social feelings, love, self-respect, the desire to be mature make their appearance in client conversation. When these are duly clarified there begin to be distinct signs of the *achievement of insight.* Having expressed so many feelings on both sides of the ledger, clients begin to see themselves in a new light. They begin to talk about possible decisions and courses of action. Before long one witnesses the *initiation of positive actions,* possibly minute but generally significant. The timid high school boy takes the step of going to a dance; the formerly frantic and resentful mother devises a way of showing affection and respect for her child; the prim and prudish young girl comes to the decision of styling her hair as the other girls have done. The first positive actions may be hardly more than symbolic. They may be initiated only after a series of attempts to persuade the counselor to sanction or advise them. But in any event they are important because they represent just the kind of step clients have been unable to take before. They constitute the first short but crucial steps in the journey toward greater self-confidence and greater self-insight that characterize clients successfully treated.

In spite of the gentle character of the influence brought to bear in client-centered therapy, it is capable of producing a corrective emotional experience. We must put the question, therefore, whether the change is profound, whether it is enduring, whether the accompanying insights have a lasting effect on future development.

To look first on the bright side, we take one of Rogers' most successful examples, the case of sixteen-year-old Barbara (Rogers, 1942). During her junior year in high school this girl had what was described as a "nervous breakdown," characterized by "fears and sensations of an overwhelming sort which were very troubling." Her case appears to qualify as at least a mild anxiety disorder. The root of her difficulty was discerned to be in an overstrict religious background and in a too strong identification with her scholarly father. Sixteen sessions of client-centered therapy brought about the following changes in her insight, accompanied by appropriate positive actions. (1) She passed from rather fantastic intellectual ambitions and an intense desire for perfection to a more realistic acknowledgment of what any one person, and herself in particular, would be able to achieve. This progress did not end in a sad sense of limitation but rather in a cheerful acceptance of things as they are. (2) She changed from an "ultra-saintly person, afraid of any social instincts, to a person who wanted to get along with and enjoy other young people." Her social interests were very greatly expanded. (3) She had always "hated sweetheart stuff," but as the interviews progressed she was first able to acknowledge a distinctly affectionate interest in a certain man friend, then later to appreciate the "puppy-love" character of this infatuation, recognizing its shallowness compared to what she really wanted. (4) Starting from the position that she wanted to be a man and greatly disliked children, she gradually came to feel that the role of woman and wife would not be objectionable. Her dislike of children began to evaporate.

If these changes sound bland and conformist, we must remember that her earlier positions had not worked; they led to breakdown. Considering her youth and her apparent capacity for change, there is little reason to doubt that the benefit would be permanent. Unfortunately the amount of change does not always seem to be so large as it is in this example. When one studies the case of Herbert Bryan, for instance, an anxiety patient in his late twenties, whose eight interviews are printed verbatim in Rogers' book, there is room for considerable doubt as to whether the improvement was more than transient. Many problems clearly touched on in the client's conversation were as unsolved at the end as at the beginning, and it is hard to feel confident that the brief spurt of self-assurance shown in the last two interviews would carry him through future difficulties. In contrast to Barbara, the course of whose life appears to have been set right by client-centered therapy, Herbert Bryan, older and with a more stubborn disorder, sounds as if he left treatment very much as he came to it.

Evaluation of Client-Centered Therapy. The method developed by Rogers has been widely adopted, especially by nonmedical counselors. It is appreciated for its clarity, its consistency, and the fact that it is unlikely to do the client any harm. It is all too easy during a therapeutic interview to mix up the principles one is employing and thus to destroy the efficacy of any of them. Thus an inexperienced or careless therapist may proceed for a while nondirectively, thus affirming respect for the client's self, then be tempted into an interpretation that says in effect that the client's self cannot be trusted, then hope to go back to the nondirective atmosphere as if the client's self had not just been wounded. Rogers has shown how to proceed consistently on the basis of respecting the client's self. His work has been importantly clarifying in the training of therapists.

The main criticism directed against client-centered therapy was the inflexibility resulting from the use of only one technique. The method seemed most suitable for intelligent, reflective, puzzled young people struggling with diffi-culties of living but having no more than mild anxiety complications. Critics were quick to point out shortcomings in such a method for severe anxiety dis-orders that other kinds of psychological treatment appeared to benefit. Not enough information was obtained or guidance given, according to Thorne (1944), to keep a client from "browsing along the edges of his problem, com-ing to grips with it only in terms of a few partial insights." But Rogers' ideas and methods should not be dismissed as necessarily superficial. Modified somewhat to meet different needs and serve a wider variety of clients, they have been successfully used even with hospitalized schizophrenics (Gendlin, 1966; Hatcher & Brooks, 1977). Like Adler's contributions, they have become part of today's clinical common sense. In his later work Rogers (1957) contrib-uted importantly to defining and measuring those qualities in a therapist that make for a superior therapeutic relation.

Humanistic Therapy and Meaning

The humanistic-existential outlook, with its emphasis on meaning, seems highly suitable to meet certain contemporary problems that appear to be on the increase. In an exposition of the work of Rollo May, Reeves (1977) points out that although problems of repression and inhibition have become less common, treatment is more than ever in demand. Clients are now likely to complain of "a puzzling loss of feeling and an apprehension of insecurity de-spite the new 'freedom' of 'self-expression.' "

> From the patients themselves came spontaneous expressions of dismay at their own diminished ability to feel moved or enthusiastic about anything, at the continuing

Mass industrial production often involves personal regimentation that may stifle indi-vidual initiative and foster conformity in people.

257

Production lines increase efficiency and cost economy in manufacturing, but at the
cost of time stress and monotony for the workers.

disappointment of loneliness, boredom, and isolation. . . . Social living, which
ought to have been free and vital, had become instead a flat, dull, meaningless
round of routine. . . . Far from solving the problem of man's psychological difficulties, the new 'freedoms' of affluence, sexual permissiveness, and educational and
moral experimentation, seem to have generated a whole new range of problems,
from anxiety and disorientation to apathy and complete loss of interest. Patients
were bringing to psychotherapy, therefore, not psychosomatic illness, not ultimately
a precisely psychological problem, but rather a philosophical question, the question
of meaning. For them it was and is a question of attempting to discover a constructive answer to the meaninglessness that they experience so intensely (pp. 23-24).

It can hardly be asked of psychotherapy to supply meaning to those who have not found it in their personal lives today. But humanistic-existential treatment can aid in the searching process. In particular, this treatment can help clients become more familiar with the inner aspect of themselves: their authentic feelings and their powers of initiative and choice. "It is somewhat amazing," Ruitenbeek (1970) writes, "to find out in talking to these patients that the idea of confrontation and decision-making in their personal lives is something alien to them" (pp. 28–29). It seems as if they had been lived by their lives rather than living them. What they have done has all been externally defined, the result of job requirements, expectations, conformity; it has not been experienced as coming from within and subject to control. Bugental (1976) describes in great detail his treatment of six cases all of whom suffered, though in quite different ways, from this oversocialized helplessness. His therapeutic task was to bring forward and show the clients their own preferences, their authentic wishes, and their power to be active agents. Therapists are not the people to confer meanings on a client, but they can help clients significantly in learning to look for their own meanings.

PSYCHOLOGICAL TREATMENT WITH CHILDREN

Psychological treatment with children is not fundamentally different from treatment with adults. The same principles operate, but their emphasis and application have to be adjusted to the fact that the client is immature and dependent. Children do not come for treatment of their own accord. As a rule they do not perceive themselves as in need of treatment. The therapist therefore has to proceed differently in several respects.

Differences from Adult Treatment

In the first place, the therapist has a somewhat different task in creating a therapeutic situation. This task is to prove to be a helpful, kindly companion who can become an interesting part of the child's world. Sometimes this can be accomplished in the first meeting, but often it takes a longer time for the young client to accept the therapist. Anna Freud (1959) describes an example in which a ten-year-old boy, whose problems included phobias, deceptions, and thefts, was convinced only after many meetings that it was worthwhile to bother with the therapist. "I had to inveigle myself," she says, "into a confidence which would not be won directly, and to force myself upon a person who was of the opinion that he could get along very well without me." She accomplished this by adapting herself to the child's whims, making herself an interesting participant in his play, proving herself useful when he was in trouble, and allying herself with him by returning things he had stolen and protecting him from punishment. When a person comes for treatment with any other

Play therapy allows children alternatives to verbal speech for expressing their feelings, using toys and puppets to help. This child obviously found much to talk about.

motive than a felt need for help, the therapist has to work hard to create a therapeutic situation.

The expression of feelings must also be accomplished in a different fashion. For younger children, at any rate, conversation is a poor medium for this purpose, and the principle of free association cannot be grasped. Fortunately a good substitute is available. If left to themselves, children will play, and the therapist can do no better than encourage this play. Play is a spontaneous and unguarded activity, the child's natural mode of expressing feelings, developing interests, and working on problems. When play was first suggested as a substitute for conversation, it was considered largely a means of diagnosis. Soon it became apparent, however, that play was itself to a certain extent therapeutic. Children use it not only to express anxieties but also to reduce them by putting themselves in the position of actively mastering the danger. By introducing the young client into a small world of toys—dolls and animals, houses and furniture, cars and trucks, water, sand, and building blocks—two things are accomplished at one stroke. The therapist opens an easy path for creating the initial friendship, and also becomes linked to the child's own preferred means of expressing feelings and achieving corrective emotional experience.

A third process that is altered in work with children is transference. The child develops various feelings, sometimes quite violent ones, toward the therapist, but these may constitute a new relationship rather than a transferred repetition of attitudes toward parents. As Anna Freud (1959) neatly expresses it, "The child is not ready to undertake a new edition of its love relationships because the old edition is not yet out of print. Its original objects, the parents, are actually in existence as love objects, not in fantasy." Often it happens that a child who is well-loved at home mistrusts the therapist, whereas a rejected child strikes up a warmly affectionate relationship. At other times a child repeats in relation to the therapist the emotions felt toward one of the parents, but little would be gained by trying to point this out.

Finally, there has to be a different handling of the positive actions that may be initiated by the child as treatment proceeds. New behavior can serve as corrective experience only when it is met with a favorable reception. Children are in a poor position to make their environments treat them differently, even when their own behavior has greatly changed. Dependent and relatively helpless, they still occupy their accustomed places in the family and among their playmates. Sometimes progress is possible only by putting the child in a new environment: a new school, a camp, or even a foster family. The other alternative is to try to change the existing environment so that it will treat the child differently. Most workers feel it is futile to treat children under fourteen unless the parents can be influenced at the same time.

Simultaneous Treatment of Mother and Child

Because the mother is usually the one who brings the child for treatment, the first step in implementing this policy was to draw her into a simultaneous ther-

261

apeutic relation. While the child was in one therapist's office, the mother gave her version of the difficulty to another therapist, receiving client-centered counseling, advice, encouragement, and support as might be needed. In an early account of work based on this plan, Allen (1942) pointed out that since mother and child are likely to have a deeply entagled relation, their separation at the clinic provides a good setting for the work of untangling. The child experiences the novelty of being able to behave without maternal supervision and criticism. Children often try to make the doctor assume responsibility; they want him to treat them the way their mothers do. The significant step of doing things because they want to, rather than to please or resist the doctor, comes later and with difficulty. The mothers meanwhile change in much the same direction. Frequently the mother has been as much enslaved to the child as the child has been to the mother. Both parties need to be disentangled so that they can become individuals in their own right.

The procedure is illustrated in the case of Solomon, a ten-year-old boy suffering from tics and general nervousness (Allen, 1942). Whatever their origin, the symptoms served the purpose of enslaving an already devoted mother who fussed anxiously over Solomon's difficulties. The child soon discovered that the therapist was not going to fuss anxiously over his complaints, and these were rarely manifested at the office. At the third interview Solomon stated that his mother thought he was better. At almost the same moment the mother was telling the social worker that the symptoms were very much worse; then she suddenly blurted out, "What will I have left when the children are grown?" Her own difficulty in letting Solomon, her youngest child, grow up was clearly a contributing cause of his illness. Solomon, meanwhile, began to learn the satisfactions of growing up, though he resisted them stoutly for a time. There were several scenes in which he debated whether he should bravely go to bed alone instead of having his mother take him upstairs at night. He tried to cajole the therapist into ordering this new behavior, and his feelings were hurt when the therapist said that the act should not be done simply to please him. Finally, however, Solomon began to do things on his own initiative. He expressed an interest in growing up and being like his older brothers. The change in both child and mother was neatly symbolized at the close of the last interview. For the first time Solomon struggled uncomplainingly to put on his heavy coat with its awkward collar, working until he succeeded, and for the first time his mother did not offer to help him.

It seems likely in this case that work with Solomon alone would have gone to waste. He readily gave up his symptoms at the office, but would he ever have been able to discontinue them at home if his mother solicitously fussed over him and thus rewarded the symptoms? Treatment of the mother alone would also have gone rather slowly. Would insights gained at the office survive the primitive appeal of her child's tearful trembling at the prospect of going to bed alone? Each party could make rapid and substantial progress only when the other party also changed.

Simultaneous treatment of mother and child is for practical reasons still much used, but treatment of the whole family, which we discuss in the next chapter, comes closer to the ideal of influencing the young client's main social environment.

Current Trends

Allowing for all these differences between children and adults, most methods of treatment described in this chapter can be used with children. In different ways, psychodynamic therapy, behavioral treatment, and client-centered counseling have proved suitable. It is encouraging to report that a present trend in this field, according to Schaefer and Millman (1977), calls for therapists to be able to use most of them. Theoretical differences seem to have melted faster in work with children than in the treatment of adults. Schaefer and Millman notice that "professionals are showing more and more interest in developing clinical skills that cut across disciplines, theories, and specialty fields. Consequently, there seem to be fewer distinctions and more cooperative interplay between the various professional and therapeutic camps." The goal is coming nearer of fitting type of treatment to the needs of the individual case. Aiming for this goal, therapists have paid closer attention to specific processes, and have become creative in devising special procedures for special needs. This bodes well for future practice.

That an alert and eclectic attitude is needed becomes apparent when we glance at the variety of complaints found in clinical work with children. A listing of these includes the following common problems:

Anxiety Disorders
   Nightmares, compulsive behavior, hysterical behavior, depression, school phobia, fears, and reactions to trauma.
Habit Disorders
   Tics, eating difficulty, enuresis, sleep disturbance, self-injurious behavior, thumbsucking.
Antisocial Behaviors
   Temper tantrums, destructiveness, aggressiveness, stealing, firesetting, running away.
Hyperkinetic Behavior
   Restless, hyperactive behavior, short attention span, impulsiveness and low frustration tolerance.
Disturbed Relationship with Children
   Social isolation, overt hostility toward peers, sibling rivalry.
Disturbed Relationship with Parents
   Overt hostility toward parents, overdependent relationship with parents.

Obviously a therapist who tried to deal with such different problems with a single favorite technique would be in for trouble. Indeed for many workers

263

one of the attractions of this field is the challenges it offers to the therapist's intelligence and inventiveness.

Growing recognition that the individual child's well-being is closely dependent on the human environment prompts a second current trend, preventive in spirit. Therapists are beginning to spend more time in the community teaching ways to head off psychological difficulties. In Schaefer and Millman's (1977) words, "Thus therapists are actively teaching courses on parent effectiveness training, building marital relationships, coping with developmental crises, sex and drug education, assertiveness training, and effective study habits. Psychological growth and inoculation against predictable crises and problems of living are the goals of these efforts" (p. 6). In the past, not all mental health education has been well done. Sometimes it has created anxiety instead of confidence. Furthermore, training to be a therapist is no guarantee of being a good teacher; the role is very different. But this trend toward making the adult community more aware and competent in psychological matters also bodes well for children's future.

RESULTS OF PSYCHOLOGICAL TREATMENT

One might suppose that the results of psychological treatment would long ago have been measured and put on an objective basis. If the whole enterprise were new we might think it legitimate to proceed experimentally without being sure of the results, but the assessment of outcomes should certainly be given high priority; otherwise there is a risk of continuing to offer treatment that does no good and may even be harmful. By now, surely, outcome research should have spoken in clear tones, giving therapists a fairly precise idea of what they are likely to accomplish. By now, therapists should know what kinds of treatment produce what kinds of results with what kinds of clients, so that intelligent treatment decisions can be made and guesswork and waste of time eliminated. By now, when care is being extended to greater numbers of people and health costs have become a national problem, it should be possible to state the cost-effectiveness of different kinds of treatment, in terms of both time required and results obtained.

These seem to be sensible expectations, but they dissolve the moment one starts to think about the problems of measurement.

What do we mean by a successful or unsuccessful outcome? Do we mean greater flexibility and insight in certain broad areas of living, do we mean elimination of a troublesome symptom, do we mean a profound reshaping of the whole personality, do we mean the discovery of one's true nature and powers of initiative? Can we properly compare results when what various therapists have tried to accomplish is so different? And if we decide to make such comparisons anyway, how are we going to measure the different changes that are implied? If research has not come up with clear and satisfactory answers on the results of psychological treatment, it is not because of failure to recognize the importance of the problem. It is because of the almost insurmountable difficulty of making the necessary measurements.

Reported Overall Results

In an early attempt to assess the overall value of psychological treatment Eysenck (1960) was able to assemble more than 50 reports covering 15,000 patients. Results were generally expressed in terms of several degrees of improvement; but if we gather into one group such headings as "cured," "much improved," and "improved," calling these successful outcomes, and interpret "slightly improved" and "not improved" as unsuccessful outcomes, the findings showed a reassuring consistency. With adult patients the proportion of successes hovered around two-thirds. With children, results at termination of treatment showed almost exactly this same proportion of successes, while results estimated from later follow-up studies carried the figure above 70 percent. Taking these figures at face value, being able to help two-thirds of one's patients would be ground for considerable satisfaction.

This was not, however, Eysenck's message. Quite correctly he pointed out that quantitative statements of results could not be taken at face value. What was needed was a comparison with similarly troubled people who received no treatment. One could not assume that their rate of change would be zero; everyone knew that spontaneous remissions sometimes happened. The real test of the effectiveness of psychological treatment would be how much better it could do than would happen anyway without therapy. What was the base rate for spontaneous recovery? Here Eysenck threw a bombshell. He dug up two pieces of research on neurotic individuals who received no treatment; over a period of time two-thirds of the cases had recovered. It followed that psychological treatment had not been shown to do any good at all.

Naturally this caused a stir in psychological circles. In the ensuing controversy many workers seemed hypnotized by the idea that the base rate for spontaneous recovery from anxiety disorders was two-thirds and that psychological treatment must do better than that, or must do it in less time, to prove its value. In fact it was not difficult to show that Eysenck's supposed control groups were "quite useless as a basis for comparison with results of psychotherapy" (Subotnik, 1972). The patients in the two studies were not comparable to those who typically receive psychological treatment, and the criteria of recovery could not be accepted as valid indicators. But Eysenck's claim had one good side effect. It stimulated an active search by those who wanted to study the effects of treatment to find real control groups for comparison with their treated cases. Bergin and Lambert (1978), examining 18 reports that bear on recovery without treatment, find "a median spontaneous remission rate of 43 percent, with a range of 18 percent to 67 percent" (p. 146). Only the top study in the range equaled the original estimate of two thirds suggested by Eysenck.

Studies of therapeutic results continue to report a success rate of around 65 percent, which against a base rate of 43 percent justifies the conclusion that "psychotherapy is better than no therapy" (p. 152). The results of psychological treatment are not spectacular, but treatment is distinctly better than doing nothing. Compared to spontaneous remission, it can be expected to produce better results in a shorter time.

Investigating Specific Processes

What variety of psychological treatment works best? As far as overall results go, comparisons among psychodynamic therapy, behavioral treatment, and client-centered therapy show that all forms have about the same rate of success. But one has to ask whether the question is legitimate, whether overall figures can provide useful information. Can the results of behavioral treatment be compared with those of humanistic-existential therapy when the goals of the two methods are so different? Is it not even misleading to compare behavioral methods as different as systematic desensitization and cognitive behavior therapy? Psychological treatment is not a unitary phenomenon. It includes a lot of different methods, different events, and different outcomes.

Realizing this, investigators have been turning their efforts to more specific processes, asking what kind of transactions, initiated by what kind of therapists with what kind of clients, produce what kind of changes. Formidable as this sounds, it means getting down to brass tacks and learning about the measurable specifics of behavior change. Therapists of the future should be better equipped to judge what to do when with a given client to produce a needed change. Such knowledge can be expected to improve the proportion of good results.

Only a few findings from this active and expanding field of research will be mentioned here. There is evidence that the therapeutic relationship deserves the importance assigned to it by earlier workers. Orlinsky and Howard (1978), examining a considerable literature, cite research evidence that effective psychotherapy "is distinguished most consistently by the positive quality of the bond that develops between the participants" (p. 317). In successful outcomes, therapist and client have both invested time and energy in their relation, they have developed good personal contact with mutual comfort, trust, and lack of defensiveness, and they agree in affirmation of the goals to be sought. The interpretation given to these research findings sounds familiar: "This safe, stimulating, but supportive atmosphere balances and makes tolerable the direct expression of deeply painful, frightening, and abrasive sentiments—sentiments that might be (and probably have been) overwhelming in other, less resiliently cohesive relationships" (p. 317).

Another line of research indicates that successful outcomes are associated with an increased sense of mastery. In Chapter 4 we saw that a sense of competence contributes importantly to personal confidence and self-esteem. A person's security and satisfaction depend, says Frank (1976), "on a sense of being able to exert some control over the reactions of others toward him as well as his own inner states" (p. 47). An experiment is reported by Liberman (1978) in which patients were given, along with their treatment, certain tasks to perform for a research worker. Half the patients were told that their improvement in these tasks was due to their own efforts; the other half were told that it was due to a pill (actually a placebo) they had been given. The two groups were equally improved at the end of treatment, but at follow-up three months later the patients from the "mastery" half had continued to improve, while the "placebo" subjects had on the average slipped a little backward. Both groups, it seems likely, profited from the therapeutic relation, but those whose sense of mastery had been strengthened had something more to go on when the relation ended.

The measurement of results has proved under scrutiny of research to be anything but a simple problem. Information can be obtained from therapists, patients, independent trained observers, and a variety of questionnaires and tests. Inconsistency often exists among these sources, and when different judges are used to evaluate the available material they may be far from agreement. There is not, according to Strupp and associates (1977), even a consensus as to what constitutes recovery and good mental health.

> Three major interested parties are concerned with definitions of mental health: (1) *society* (including significant persons in the patient's life); (2) the *individual patient*; and (3) the *mental health professional.*
>
> 1. *Society* is primarily concerned with the maintenance of social relations, institutions, and prevailing standards of sanctioned conduct. Society and its agents thus tend to define mental health in terms of behavioral stability, predictability, and conformity to the social code. . .
>
> 2. The *individual client* evaluating his own mental health uses a criterion distinctly different from that used by society. The individual wishes first and foremost to be happy, to feel content. He defines mental health in terms of highly subjective feelings of well-being—feelings with a validity all their own. . .
>
> 3. Most *mental health professionals* tend to view an individual's functioning within the framework of some theory of personality structure which transcends social adaptation and subjective well-being. . .

These three viewpoints on mental health are not always in disagreement, but they may be so. Clearly research workers should be quite explicit in giving their criteria of improvement.

When carefully done, studies of outcome usually reveal that a certain number of clients get worse. Bergin and Lambert (1978), who call this the "deterioration effect," make the reasonable point that "treatments which are capable of producing beneficial effects are capable also of producing harmful effects" (p. 152). Though nobody doubts that failures occur, their number, as Bergin

267

and Lambert's review shows, is fortunately not very great. Being made worse means emerging from treatment with impaired energy, decreased competence, increased symptoms, a sustained dependence on the therapist, expectations that are beyond the client's capabilities so that they generate feelings of failure—some or all of these. The available research links failure with initial level of disturbance: schizophrenic tendencies, weak social adjustment, poor coping capacity, general disorganization. It is often hard to tell beforehand, but some patients must be considered too sick for psychological treatment, and some cannot endure the stress it entails. Unfavorable characteristics of the therapist have been investigated less. Research in this area should lead to greater care in selecting patients and in choosing candidates for training in psychological treatment.

Spontaneous Remission

If spontaneous remission occurs in 43 percent of untreated people otherwise similar to those who receive treatment, the process certainly deserves attention. In studying anxiety disorders (Chapter 6) we saw that current stress generally makes a contribution to onset, even when earlier experience and learning also play a part. Present situations may heighten reminders of earlier dangers and upset habitual adaptive strategies. But circumstances can also move in the opposite direction. A person who experienced childhood panic about rejection, for instance, may come into a congenial group that gives constant evidences of acceptance, or a person who has all but crippled his endeavors by excessive caution and meticulous attention to detail enters an occupation where these qualities are of great importance and are hailed as rare excellencies. Furthermore, an untreated anxiety disorder may eventually build up so much desperation that the person, feeling that he or she cannot go on like this any longer, will at last take active steps to lead a more rewarding life and will tolerate the increased anxiety that this at first entails. Other agencies besides psychological treatment are designed to contribute to growth. Religious organizations try to build confidence and acceptance in a setting of meaningful ideals. Secular institutions give counsel and advice that may turn a person in a new and valuable direction. There are courses that teach social competence and books that describe self-help. One or more of these influences may speak to an anxiety-burdened person in a way that proves helpful. Naturally there are influences on the other side that may deepen a disorder. But it is impressive that 43 percent of the people studied found ways to move upward.

The Client's View

Research results do not convey a vivid impression of how it feels to be cured. A study by Strupp and associates (1969) puts emphasis on what clients think of their treatment, and clients are certainly entitled to a hearing.

The Strupp research was conducted by sending an extensive questionnaire to former patients of a group of therapists who agreed to this procedure. The therapists in the sample were mostly psychoanalytically oriented, and the patients had been seen for a minimum of 25 interviews, with the average number being 70. The success rate of these relatively long-term treatments fell close to the usual 67 percent. The majority of patients considered their therapy "exceedingly beneficial," enabling them to "deal more effectively with the vicissitudes of a decidedly imperfect society." The answers tended to confirm the importance of the therapeutic relation, apart from the specific techniques employed.

> Irrespective of variations in the form of therapy and other considerations, the emergence of a "warmth" factor was particularly noteworthy. It permeated all ratings and assessments — those of patients as well as therapists. We concluded that a sense of mutual trust was unquestionably a *sine qua non* for successful psychotherapy; in its absence, little of positive value was accomplished. There was additional evidence that overshadowing this attitudinal-emotional factor was the patient's conviction that he had the therapist's respect. This faith in the integrity of the therapist as a person may be called the capstone of a successful therapeutic relationship under which all other characteristics are subsumed. When it existed, both patient and therapist were articulate about its presence (pp. 17–18).

To the clients it was an asset to feel that the therapist was keenly attentive, natural, unstudied, reassuring, and careful not to injure self-respect. More common when the outcome was unsuccessful were comments that the therapists made the client feel like "just another patient," that they appeared neutral and passive, that they missed some of the client's real feelings, that they talked in abstract language, and that they caused or allowed the client to be angry with them. Perhaps the clients wanted more attention and friendship than was compatible with a professional relation. Some of them mentioned as a sign of progress their acceptance of being in fact "just another patient" instead of the therapist's sole concern.

The chief changes in themselves described by the clients are listed under these headings: better interpersonal relations; increase in self-esteem; greater interest, energy, and satisfaction in living; and a greater sense of mastery. Following are some of the actual words used:

> I like being around people, which I did not before. . . . Many times I put myself in the position of a "therapist" and listen — and try to understand other people's problems as they relate to them rather than to myself.
>
> Another big change was one of really listening or involving myself; now I find I see people in a different light.
>
> I think the greatest change has been getting my confidence back.
>
> I'm sure I'm a different person in attitude. I feel so much more relaxed — more confident, sure of myself, more attractive, and above all, my husband and my daughter enjoy me more.

I now feel capable of accomplishing certain goals which I formerly regarded as desirable but unattainable. I rarely need tranquilizers (or beer) to cope with tension.

I'm able to find satisfaction and happiness in small ways that I had overlooked before, probably because I was too busy worrying about myself.

Most importantly, I am able to feel joy and pain, which even with the latter is good, because *I'm* living, and not just something parasitic. I can trust another person enough to care, and to risk the consequences of the caring.

Much better able to lead my life as I please and better able to cope with life as it comes day to day. Feel freer to tell others what I think and where to get off! Better able to live with fussy and "disturbed" parents (pp. 67–71).

Excerpts of this kind make it clear that psychotherapy can be experienced as producing important and desirable changes. These changes, furthermore, are consistent with the general idea that the task of psychotherapy is to create conditions favorable for corrective relearning that involves strong feelings. The lowering of anxiety and guilt, the relaxing of defensive inhibitions, and the learning of more rewarding patterns of behavior are all represented in the descriptions. The fundamental principles of psychotherapy need not be regarded as hopelessly complex. They all have to do with removing blocks in the learning process and promoting new growth. The processes are partly understood and wholly understandable.

SUGGESTIONS FOR FURTHER READING

The literature on psychotherapy has become voluminous in the last few years. A fine initial orientation, with historical sweep, can be obtained from Jerome D. Frank's *Persuasion and Healing: A Comparative Study of Psychotherapy* (1961). A collection of case studies representing a large variety of therapeutic methods has been assembled and edited by A. Burton, *Case Studies in Counseling and Psychotherapy* (1959). For an excellent brief survey, lucid and nonpartisan, see R. W. Heine, *Psychotherapy* (1971).

The best survey of psychodynamic therapy is given by S. Korchin, *Modern Clinical Psychology* (1976), Chapter 13. The same author's description and evaluation of psychoanalysis today is in the next chapter, pp. 324–334.

A brief, clear, and lively introduction to behavioral treatment will be found in R. I. Lanyon & B. P. Lanyon, *Behavior Therapy: A Clinical Introduction* (1978). For greater depth and detail see A. S. Bellck & M. Hersen, *Behavior Modification: An Introductory Textbook* (1977), which is especially strong on research foundations.

The most instructive work in English on existential psychotherapy is R. May, E. Angel, & H. F. Ellenberger, eds., *Existence: A New Dimension in Psychiatry and Psychology* (1958), which includes translated case histories by Binswanger. A more recent work by W. V. Ofman, *Affirmation and Reality: Fundamentals of Humanistic-Existential Therapy and Counseling* (1976), treats with commendable clarity such topics as ways of looking at people, the therapeutic relation, and restoring freedom of choice. For client-centered psychotherapy the sources are two books by C. R. Rogers, *Counseling and Psycho-therapy* (1942) and *Client-Centered Therapy* (1951). These should now be supplemented by a book edited by C. Hatcher & B. S. Brooks, *Innovations in Counseling Psychology* (1977).

Michael Rutter, in *Helping Troubled Children* (1975), has written a clear and informative survey of child psychiatry, intended for nonprofessionals involved with or interested in children. More detailed and technical is the survey, *Therapies for Children* (1978) by C. E. Schaefer & H. L. Millman.

Those who hunger for definite results of psychotherapy can now search the pages of S. L. Garfield & A. E. Bergin's encyclopedic *Handbook of Psychotherapy and Behavior Change,* 2nd edition (1978), a notable reference book. Korchin discusses results in Chapter 16 of *Modern Clinical Psychology* (1976).

Various attempts have been made to analyze the central processes in psychotherapy, those that might be supposed common to all methods. In a book describing ten different "systems," D. H. Ford & H. B. Urban, *Systems of Psychotherapy: A Comparative Study* (1965), attempt this synthesis in their final chapter. It is also the subject of an essay by J. M. Reisman, *Toward the Integration of Psychotherapy* (1971), and more recently has been treated at length and with great care by P. L. Wachtel in *Psychoanalysis and Behavior Therapy: Toward an Integration* (1977).

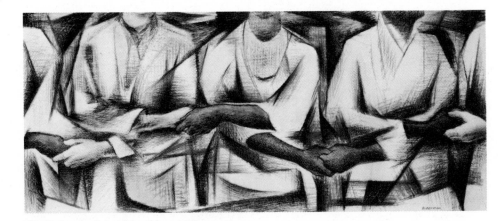

The Chain, mural detail by Edward Biberman.

8
Psychological Treatment:
Group Methods

Compared to individual psychotherapy, the treatment of people in groups has a short history. Group psychotherapy began over sixty years ago as a time-saving device in dealing with patients in mental hospitals, and its larger potentialities were only gradually perceived. It came into its own after World War II and is now widely used, either as an adjunct or alone, for many varieties of disordered behavior. Reflecting on all that was said in the preceding chapter, we can easily understand the misgivings aroused by the proposal to treat people in groups. Individual psychotherapy is a difficult, delicate, and highly personal proceeding; would not the presence of other people simply create interference and nullify the possible good effects? Group methods, however, parallel with important trends in the understanding of human behavior, trends away from an individualistic toward a social or interactive conception. Clients who are seen alone in the therapist's office are in fact members of families and of other social groups. Their complaints often center on interactions with these other people, whose behavior may have a good deal to do with what is wrong. Treating people in groups is thus in a sense more realistic than the "one-to-one" relation; getting along better with other people is facilitated by having some of them there. But we should not conclude from this that group methods are necessarily superior. Our task is to discover what they accomplish under what conditions, and what they presumably cannot be expected to accomplish.

As practiced by Freud, psychoanalysis involved a minimum of contact with people in the patient's social orbit. Change was expected to occur through reduction of resistance and anxiety, especially through the analysis of transference. The patient was responsible for carrying over the gains to the outside world. When psychoanalysis was extended to children, however, the plan of isolating the treatment was clearly impractical. Change in a child's behavior could not long survive if there were no answering change on the part of the parents. As we saw, simultaneous treatment of child and mother by two therapists soon became standard clinical practice. A similar shortcoming of individual psychotherapy became evident in marriage counseling. It takes two to make a marital crisis, and if peace can be restored this must be through a change of feeling in both contending parties.

FAMILY THERAPY

The bold step of trying to influence the whole family is in accord with present thinking about the nature of social systems. It is not enough to treat a child and mother unless they are indeed an isolated pair in the world. Under average circumstances child and mother are part of a social system consisting of father, siblings, and any other persons living in the home. According to systems theory it is not just the sick child—the "designated patient"—who needs to change, but instead the whole system of which the child is a part. In practice it is no small feat to secure the participation of all family members. Unfamiliar with systems theory, the other members suppose that treatment is for the designated patient alone and do not imagine that their own problems have anything to do with it. If they are willing to come at all, it is simply to provide information.

Treating the Family as a System

Ackerman (1958), a pioneer and strong advocate of family therapy, favors interviewing the whole family at the very beginning, and points out that the first

interview can provide useful clues. Much can be deduced from the way the members enter the room, offer greetings, and distribute themselves among the available chairs. Conflict, confusion, the dominance hierarchy, and preferred modes of acting as a family may reveal themselves sharply in the problem of seating. Significant family alignments, alliances, exclusions, and scapegoating may come to light early in the proceedings. The therapist meanwhile tries to create an atmosphere of rapport that will favor a reduction of concealments and defenses. To achieve a therapeutic result "he must permit himself to be drawn into the center of the family disturbance," but must also preserve objectivity and freedom to serve as umpire and even as controlling authority if things threaten to get out of hand (Ackerman, 1961). Family psychotherapy is obviously no job for a novice. To improvise appropriate action in what can easily become a whirlpool of passions requires rare gifts of alertness and a seasoned skill in grasping the meaning of behavior.

It is not easy to shift one's focus from individual to family therapy. Haley (1970) brings out the difficulties in a paper in which he contrasts the outlook of the beginning family therapists with that of the experienced worker. Trouble begins with the word "patient." The beginning therapist, out of habit, may fall in with the family's designation of the patient and perceive the task as curing this patient with the help of the rest of the family. As Haley puts it, "the experienced family therapist . . . struggles to find a better term than 'patient' for the family member chosen to be it." The trouble is not inside one person; it lies in the entire family system, in the whole set of relations prevailing among all the members, and it will not be resolved without changes in the system. The beginning therapist, again, true to previous experience, may start by taking a lengthy history and trying to establish a diagnosis of the problem. But any family arriving for help is likely to be in a state of crisis. The experienced therapist tries to intervene almost at once to reduce acute tension and otherwise to show that something useful can happen. The beginning therapist may be tempted to make interpretations and point out to the family members how much, for instance, they hate one another. This can go to the point of "torturing a family by forcing them to concede their unsavory feelings about each other." The experienced therapist avoids this useless exercise and tries in a more positive way to resolve the difficulties that are creating the hostility.

A damaging mistake, according to Beall (1972), is for the therapist to become too quickly allied with certain family members and to accept their myths. By the simple act of accepting one member as "the patient," for example, the therapist may implicitly make a "corrupt contract" with the others that exempts them from any share in the trouble. Readers will recognize this taking sides as a blunder, but in all fairness they should think of families they have recently met and notice how hard it is to keep from taking sides when controversies exist.

In a paper reflecting on more than fifteen years of experience with family treatment, Ackerman (1966) describes the method as "therapeutic intervention on the emotional processes of a natural living unit, the family entity, viewed as an integrated behavior system." The interview unit consists ideally of the whole family, although at certain points some members may be excused in order to concentrate on a particular pair, possibly the husband and wife or a child and a parent. The goal can be described as producing a more healthful, satisfying family life. This implies easing the anxieties, competitions, and resentments that spoil the positive aspects of interaction. The therapist's task is to provide a timely challenge to the rationalizations and defensive disguises whereby the members conceal from themselves the destructive aspects of their relationship. This is mainly accomplished by a device Ackerman calls "tickling the defenses."

> This is essentially a technique of confrontation which points especially to contradictions between conscious attitudes and patterns of action, to discrepancies between verbal utterances and nonverbal communication, as reflected in facial expression, movement, mood, posture, and gesture. Especially important here is the exposure of unreal and impossible demands, the challenge of fruitless blaming and vindictive encroachment on other family members, and the undermining and challenging of hypocritical self-justifications.

Obviously the therapist must be expert in tickling the right defenses at the right time, as well as expert in maintaining a sense of justice and impartiality, distributing the challenges fairly among the members. The therapist's whole usefulness depends on being trusted as a person who has the sympathy to understand but the wisdom to stand apart from the family conflicts.

Family therapy can be of great value. It is capable not only of relieving the suffering of the person designated as patient but of improving the conditions of family life for everyone involved. But it is not a panacea and cannot be expected to work in all circumstances. It cannot be used at all, of course, unless all family members are willing. Best results appear to be obtained when the "designated patient" is an older child or adolescent, and the method seems especially suited to problems of adolescent separation (Korschin, 1976). It is important that the family desire and hope for an improved life together. Sometimes the therapist enters the scene too late to check forces that are making the family fall apart. Sometimes a member other than the "designated patient" proves unable to stand any "tickling of defenses," and reacts destructively to any improvement in others. Ferreira (1971) points out that a family self-image or "myth" may be so ingrained that no member can tolerate its being challenged. He describes, as an instance, a family in which the father was a happy man, always smiling, bothered by nothing, setting a tone for all the other members. Everyone had symptoms of some kind, and disturbed family life was easy to infer, but the family sat with fixed grins, "as if saying in a sort of nonverbal chorus, 'See how happy we are.'" The therapist finally challenged the father's happiness, saying that he appeared profoundly unhappy behind his cheerful mask. The shot struck home: the father's smile disappeared and he looked serious and sad. But first one, then another member came to the rescue, pronouncing the therapist wrong and the father unfailingly happy, until the father's smile returned in full force. Challenge to the myth of happiness was more than this family could bear.

In recent writing about family psychotherapy there is a strong tendency to speak of the critical events in terms of communication theory. Many family therapists think of their function chiefly as improving communication among the members. This is valuable provided one keeps in mind that strong feelings and motives are present; family disorders do not consist just of defects in communication. But poor communication tends to increase misunderstanding, especially when words of appreciation remain unspoken and annoyances are allowed to mount into chronic resentments. Thus when a family is basically motivated to stay together but disturbed by conflicts, much of the therapeutic work takes the form of opening channels of communication so that the forces of solidarity can prevail over those of disruption.

What Happens in Family Therapy

These general statements may leave the reader mystified as to what actually goes on in family psychotherapy. Recorded transcripts are especially helpful in making the proceedings vivid; two useful books are Minuchin (1974) and the collection of cases by Papp (1977). For illustration here we choose a sam-

An important advance in conjoint family therapy is achieved when the family members, especially the children, talk to one another instead of to the therapist.

277

ple of conversations from Virginia Satir (1967), *Conjoint Family Therapy.* These involve a family consisting of Joe and Mary and their children, Johnny (10) and Patty (7); Johnny's poor work and unmanageable behavior at school is the avowed reason for undertaking family therapy. In an early conversation the therapist asks the children what ideas they had about coming.

PATTY:	Mother said we were going to talk about family problems.
THERAPIST:	What about Dad? Did he tell you the same thing?
P:	No.
TH:	What did Dad say?
P:	He said we were going for a ride.
TH:	I see. So you got some information from Mother and some from Dad. What about you, Johnny? Where did you get your information?
JOHNNY:	I don't remember.
TH:	You don't remember who told you?
MOTHER:	I don't think I said anything to him, come to think of it. He wasn't around at the time, I guess.
TH:	How about you, Dad? Did you say anything to Johnny?
FATHER:	No, I thought Mary had told him.
TH:	(To Johnny) Well, then, how *could* you remember if nothing was said?
J:	Patty said we were going to see a lady about the family.
TH:	I see. So you got your information from your sister, whereas Patty got a clear message from both Mother and Dad. . . . (To Mother) Were you and Dad able to work this out together— what you would tell the children?
M:	Well, you know, I think this is one of our problems. He does one thing with them and I do another.
F:	I think this is a pretty unimportant thing to worry about.
TH:	Of course it is, in one sense. But then we can use it, you know, to see how messages get across in the family.

This incident illustrates the practice of bringing each member of the family into the conversation, letting each person speak for him- or herself. When members try to speak for each other, the therapist may stop them and insist that even the children must speak for themselves. Parents may thus for the first time hear themselves described by their children. The excerpt also brings to light the parents' unwitting preconception that Johnny, as "the patient," need not be given the courtesy of an explanation, whereas Patty, the well child, was told where they were going. The failure of communication with Johnny is further shown in the following excerpts:

M:	(About Johnny) His pleasure is in doing things he knows will get me up in the air. Every minute he's in the house, constantly.

TH: There's no pleasure to that, my dear.

M: Well, there is to him.

TH: No. You can't see his thoughts. You can't get inside his skin. All you can talk about is what you see and hear. You can say it *looks* as though it's for pleasure.

M: All right. Well, it looks as though, and that's just what it looks like constantly.

TH: He could be trying to keep your attention, you know. It is very important to Johnny what Mother thinks.

Here the therapist tries to introduce an alternative explanation of the child's behavior that is less negative. In the following conversation with the father, this enlightenment is produced by hearing directly from the child.

F: I mean, he never wanted me to stay and watch him play baseball.

TH: Tell me, how did you explain this to yourself? Why do you think he didn't want you to watch?

F: Well, that's the trouble, I never have been able to figure it out.

TH: Well, one way to find out is to *ask*. Let's ask Johnny. He can tell you. Maybe he is uneasy when Dad is around.

J: I'd just get embarrassed, sometimes.

TH: You'd get embarrassed.

J: Uh huh. Cause he had Patty with him and Patty is always making a fuss. The other guys would laugh.

Even these few exchanges suggest a situation in which Johnny has become a focus of parental anger and Patty is preferred to him. Johnny's "symptoms"—his school difficulties—are part of a problem in family interaction and are not likely to abate until the whole system of interactions has changed. The therapist thus becomes concerned with all the relationships, including the marital one, which is approached in the following conversation beginning with the children.

F: Somehow, I don't know, somehow she has this way of making me feel that it's me—that I am the one who . . . .

TH: Mary's tears make you feel you have been the one who is wrong, is that it? You feel at fault?

F: Exactly. She won't listen when I try to explain.

TH: What about you, Mary? How do you know when Joe is displeased?

M: He turns on the TV so loud you can hear it in the laundry room.

TH: So then he shows his anger by shutting you out, is that it? And she shows her anger by shutting you out with her tears. And either way you can't find a way to get close enough to work things out.

(The therapist then asks how the disagreement is finally solved.)

F: I give in. That's what I do.

M: That's what you think. You're as stubborn as they come.

F: How? How am I more stubborn than you?

TH: I think that . . . .

J: Daddy, when are we going to the beach? You promised we could go, and we never do.

F: As soon as it's warmer we'll go. It's too cold to go to the beach.

M: Of course we did promise them . . . .

TH: I think we should . . . .

P: You said we could go a couple of weeks ago.

TH: I think both children get upset when their mother and father disagree. Maybe they think someone will get hurt. But I don't see any dead bodies around, do you? Mother looks in one piece. Dad looks in one piece.

M: They do get upset. We try not to argue in front of the kids.

TH: But of course they know when their parents have pain. The important thing is that ways can be found to work on this. That's why we are here, to find ways to work on this.

The insights that occur through conversations of this sort do not produce immediate miraculous changes in behavior. Joe and Mary may soon quarrel again in front of the children. Johnny may continue to be exasperating, and favor may again be shown to Patty. But the automatic character of these interactions may well have been broken, so that the members of the family can begin to imagine avoiding an impasse, behaving in alternative ways, getting around the customary blocks in communication. The next occasion of conflict may catch them unawares, but afterwards they will see more clearly what could have been done to avoid useless battles. Over time considerable change can take place, so that all members experience family life as more harmonious and rewarding.

MARITAL COUNSELING

After this introduction to family psychotherapy the value of joint treatment for marital problems seems obvious. Time was required, however, to unseat the preference even here for individual psychotherapy. Kohl (1962) describes numerous cases in which the more troubled member of a discordant pair sought individual treatment and began to improve, whereupon the other member became increasingly troubled and was obliged to seek help. Nothing could demonstrate more clearly the interactive nature of marital disorders. Discordant partners were sometimes assigned to two individual therapists who every so often consulted together. Occasionally a person passing the door when one of these consultations was in progress would be amused to hear the voices of the two therapists raised in an angry quarrel as each defined his or her own client's point of view. Marital counseling is best performed by bringing the contending parties together in the presence of one counselor, sometimes two, who can point out the failures of communication at the very moment when they occur.

This conclusion is espoused by Haley (1978) who describes the discrepancy between what the members of a marital pair report and what actually happens between them.

> When a couple presents a marital problem, the therapist's views can depend on who is interviewed. If the therapist sees the wife alone, he or she may sympathize with her for having such a problem husband. When such an interview is followed by an interview with the husband alone, the therapist usually discovers that there were a number of things the wife neglected to mention and that the husband has a justified point of view too. When seeing them together the therapist discovers patterns of action between them that show the marriage to be quite different from what either spouse described. With experiences of this kind, the therapist learns not to naively take sides with one spouse against the other and learns the value of seeing how people actually deal with each other rather than listening to reports about how they do (p. 157).

Describing marital tensions as seen in a psychological clinic, Dicks (1953) calls attention to the important part played by role expectations. Frequently, he points out, we project on the person we love and marry a set of expectations derived from previous experience with parents, or even from fantasy. The role of spouse is thus overlaid with personal meanings, and disappointment may be felt if the actual spouse enacts the role in some different fashion. The son of a mother who waits on her husband and the daughter of a father who waits on his wife might find in marriage that each was expecting what the other least expected to give. Discrepancies of expectation with regard to dominance, submission, and initiative can also create frustration and resentment. The case of Benton Child, described in Chapter 2, illustrates an initial harmony between a passive-dependent husband and a dominant wife, followed by discord after the birth of children, when the husband proved unequal to paternal responsibilities and the wife needed help in caring for the family. Benton's expectations were derived from his mother's indulgent spoiling, which applied both to his father and to himself.

A somewhat similar example of marital discord is described by Main (1966), who notes the complicating presence of a mutual projection on the partner of unacceptable tendencies in the self. The husband, who greatly feared his own assertiveness and hostility, magnified these qualities in his wife and was himself docile and sexually impotent. The wife, who was anxious about her lack of education and social training, magnified these faults in her husband and badgered him to the point that he seemed more stupid than he actually was. Each party thus behaved in a way that exaggerated the faults of the other, but in the end it proved possible to abate these trends and put the marriage on a workable basis.

Results of Family and Marital Therapy

Because of the relative newness of the methods thus far described in this chapter, there has not been much time for investigation of results. In a searching review, however, Gurman and Kniskern (1978) point out a sharp increase of research during the last few years and find at least two hundred studies bearing on the problem. Most reports of effectiveness thus far are based on judgments by therapists and by clients. As yet there is little work that includes independent judges and little tackling of the difficult problem of measuring improved family climates. To date the research is not perfect, but neither are the reported results negligible.

The outcomes for family therapy are curiously reminiscent of those reported in the last chapter for individual psychological treatment: 71 percent of children and adolescents are improved and 65 percent of adults. In the light of studies comparing family with individual treatment, the authors conclude that family therapy is the method of choice not only for obvious family conflicts but for problems usually seen as individual that prove to involve other family members.

Results for marital counseling show an average improvement rate of 65 percent. Here it is possible to draw a contrast with individual marital therapy, where only 48 percent are reported improved. Gurman and Kniskern have examined those reports that admit to making certain clients worse. For conjoint marital therapy the average rate is about 5 percent, for individual marital therapy about 11 percent. The authors conclude that "individual therapy for marital problems is a very ineffective treatment strategy. . . . Couples benefit most when both partners are involved in therapy, especially when they are seen conjointly."

Conjoint Sexual Therapy

Sometimes a couple seeking help defines the difficulty simply as a sexual problem. This may in fact be the main trouble: a couple otherwise happy and wanting to continue their life together has difficulty with sex and wants to make this aspect of experience more satisfactory. Perhaps sexual behavior has been reduced to a routine, perhaps timing and technique are poor, perhaps the pair has difficulty discussing the subject; at all events there is a sense of losing something that might make life much happier. Conjoint sexual therapy was originally designed for people with this problem. Obviously, marital discord in other spheres can invade sexual relations, which then have to be seen as part of a larger problem. In such cases conjoint sexual therapy becomes an adjunct to marital counseling.

A fairly brief form of sexual therapy has been developed by Masters and Johnson (1970). The client couple is asked to spend two weeks or so at a center removed from the distractions and responsibilities of home. This is to promote relaxation and allow plentiful time for learning and practice. The procedure begins with individual interviews, the man with a male and the woman with a female therapist; sexual histories are investigated in detail. Then follow joint sessions in which histories are compared and problems discussed. Instruction plays a large part in the therapist's contribution. The clients are usually ill-informed about the possibilities of sex, but what they learn they are told to practice in the privacy of their bedroom. Often they need to learn to enjoy sensual pleasure for itself, not just as a short preliminary to intercourse. Specific methods are also taught for dealing with such problems as impotence, premature ejaculation, and frigidity (Kaplan, 1974).

There is no reason why the straightforward procedure developed by Masters and Johnson should not be called as it has been, "the new sex therapy." Care must be taken, however, not to assume that there is anything else new about it. When a problem first presented as sexual turns out to have other important aspects, these must be dealt with by whatever regular modes of treatment seem most appropriate. As Sollod (1975) points out, the so-called "new sex therapy" is a "therapeutic amalgam" combining a variety of already familiar techniques with the essentially educational program of Masters and Johnson. This may work well. Improved sexual functioning may convince a couple that change is possible and thus encourage them to seek help for other problems. Or, in reverse, a couple that has profited by marital counseling may still need specific sex therapy.

In a case history reported by Hogan (1978), the husband illustrated the first sequence and the wife the second. The wife had been in regular treatment for some time, but came to sex therapy because of a continuing inability to relax that made intercourse impossible. The husband agreed to sex therapy, and in fact the couple's sexual performance became much more satisfactory to both. But there were many quarrels occasioned by the wife's anxiety and the husband's resentment at having his wife and the woman therapist directing his behavior. These problems were so disturbing that the wife continued her regular therapy and the husband decided that he, too, would enter psychological treatment.

PSYCHODRAMA

Another form of psychotherapy using people in groups is the *psychodrama* originated by J. L. Moreno (1946). The essential principle of psychodrama is to stimulate the expression of feelings through unrehearsed, spontaneous play-acting. Other patients take part in the action, and still other patients and observers make up the audience. Moreno himself surrounded the procedure with

283

an array of grandiose concepts, but the central ideas seem to be quite simple. Drama stands as a midway point between fantasy and reality. It is real in the sense that there is a stage with lights, a group of spectators, and other actors toward whom one is behaving. It is unreal in the sense that the whole thing is only a play. Unrehearsed drama has a certain similarity to free association. Giving free associations is real in the sense that a therapist is listening and that relief from a disorder is being sought. It is unreal in the sense that what one says is illogical and fantastic, quite unsuitable for communication in everyday life. Proponents of psychodrama maintain that it is better than free association as a means of securing expression. Although at first it may be hard for patients to act with freedom, they can be slowly induced into an atmosphere in which they learn to express themselves with great spontaneity and often with great enjoyment.

The following case report by Sarbin (1943) will make the procedure clearer. A seventeen-year-old high school boy seemed quite incapable of social relationships. Listless and shy, he stayed by himself most of the time, but from interviews and tests it was clear that he fantasied himself as a popular high school boy. He was first asked to participate as a spectator while other patients acted their psychodramas. Then he was asked to prepare a short scene of his own for a subsequent session. He chose the role of a radio commentator and gave a simple scene that required no supporting characters—altogether a safe and undemanding performance. At the next meeting he was requested to serve as a minor character in a drama being enacted by other patients. He was the buddy of a soldier who received abusive treatment from a tough sergeant. He was able to imitate freely the actions of his buddy and even develop them

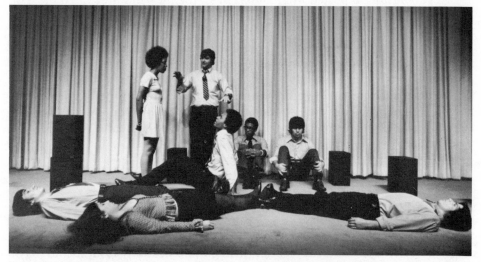

A psychodramatist here sets the scene for enactment of a psychodrama with participants at Daytop Village, a center for treatment of drug dependency.

in his own way. For his next assignment he prepared an original scene calling for several supporting characters. For the first time he was able to act without self-consciousness, genuinely absorbed in the drama. Next he took the part of father in another young patient's drama. This role proved highly congenial; he "stole the show" as he acted out what were unmistakably his own father's attitudes toward him. Only after this success was he requested to enact what corresponded to his own most cherished fantasy. He was asked to depict a day in the life of a high school boy. Choosing various characters to represent his parents and his fellow students, he put on a spontaneous drama remarkable for its animation and conversational freedom as well as its revelation of his emotional difficulties at home.

There were various other sessions, but what concerns us more is the patient's off-stage progress. Instead of sitting alone he began to come into the center of the group. Instead of retiring between scenes he began to use the intervals for conversation with others. Listless shyness gave place to more alert participation. The parents were surprised at the rapid increase of interest in people and events and at his spontaneous seeking for companionship. The patient even gained weight while these improvements were going on. In the realm of psychodrama he had become able to behave in a way that corresponded to his ego-ideal and that gave him self-esteem. The change carried over into new behavior in everyday life.

Psychodrama would seem to be an excellent technique for people with a certain degree of generalized inhibition and difficulty in expressing themselves. It supplies just the right lift and social support for overcoming inhibitions that are not too deeply rooted. New behavior can be rehearsed under fictional conditions before being attempted in real life. Moreno has used psychodrama for marriage problems and even for matrimonial triangles. Here it is sometimes successful in liberating the deeper feelings that discolor and clog the relationships. A scene can be started from whatever clues the parties offer in their preliminary interviews. Although these clues may have to do with superficial or side issues, "it is a reliable psychodramatic experience," according to Moreno, "that, once the subjects are working on the therapeutic stage, they are carried by the momentum of psychodramatic dynamics from the surface to the deeper level of their relationship" (p. 329).

Psychodrama has had a less spectacular rise than family psychotherapy. According to Polansky and Harkins (1969) it "has not had the widespread application its potentialities warrant." They regret this because, in their view, "it is a mode of treatment which can be helpful to a substantial portion of patients a large proportion of the time—which is about all one can say about any of the psychotherapies." They recognize that not all therapists find it congenial to participate so actively, exhibiting the "interpersonal energy, moment-to-moment inventiveness, and occasional controlled flamboyance" that make the method effective. They recognize also that there are risks in a situation that sometimes mobilizes so much feeling in several patients at once. But they re-

285

port favorably on a program of psychodrama in a private psychiatric hospital, where as an adjunct to individual treatment it has sometimes "brought to life" a listless or withdrawn patient who otherwise was not making progress.

During the 1970s psychodrama continued to be used. Gonen (1971) showed that its effectiveness with hospital patients was increased by videotape playback. Books have appeared by Greenberg (1974) and by Starr (1977). Starr considers the method especially applicable to alcohol and drug problems, to depressions and certain forms of schizophrenia, and for use on psychiatric wards, where among other things it provides patients with interesting occupation.

GROUP PSYCHOTHERAPY

If we were to be fussy about language we would say that this section needed a more exact title. Family therapy, marital counseling, and psychodrama certainly qualify as group psychotherapy, but in practice this more general term has come to imply groups of a particular kind. Typical of group psychotherapy as currently practiced is a meeting of a therapist and perhaps eight adult or adolescent patients who at the outset are unacquainted. In the course of a series of sessions the members of the group will become well acquainted, and sometimes lasting friendships are formed. In essence, however, group psychotherapy involves work with a group of strangers, and one of its strengths may well lie in the circumstance that the members are bound by no formal ties after the work is completed. Social learning in the group can thus be a trial run or dress rehearsal, so to speak, with people toward whom one has no future commitments. In this respect it differs sharply from family treatment and marital counseling.

Within this definition there is room for great variety. Early workers with group therapy, experienced in individual treatment, enacted their new roles with as little change as possible from their old ones. Before long there was much the same range of opinions about group therapy as existed regarding individual treatment. Some workers advocated a strictly "group-centered" procedure that copied the permissiveness and nondirectiveness of Rogers' client-centered psychotherapy (Hobbs, 1951). Some adhered as closely as possible to Freudian psychoanalysis and concentrated on interpreting the transference reactions that occur during meetings (Ezriel, 1950; Sutherland, 1952). Others favored a principle of flexibility, using different degrees and kinds of activity according to circumstances (Slavson, 1955). Still others, chiefly those working with more seriously disturbed people, found it advisable to use tactics of a more directive character (Klapman, 1946). Similarly, there was a range of opinion about the length of time required to secure good results. Twenty to forty weekly sessions represent an average duration in many clinics and outpatient services, but one worker, George Bach (1954), who argued strongly that

group therapy should be intensive, considered a group still new when it had
met only fifty times and stated that "intensive group psychotherapy certainly
does not represent a short-cut in terms of therapy hours, although it is economically easier for most patients." Already in 1955 group psychotherapy was
being offered in a variety of shapes and sizes.

The Course of Group Therapy

It will be clear from the variations just described that we cannot give a standard account of the course of group therapy. Yet in order to convey some idea
of what happens we must select certain features, even if they are not universal.
In work with anxiety patients the group is likely to number about eight. Meetings are held once or twice a week, with leader and group members sitting in-
formally around a table. At first the members direct all their remarks toward
the leader, and it is evident that they expect the leader to answer questions,
give advice, and generally function in an authoritative manner. The leader
meets this by a method originally described by Foulkes (1951) as "leadership
by default"; simply saying, "Let me hear what *you* think about this question."
As in individual therapy, patients at first find this nondirectiveness quite frustrating, but the leader's "defaulting" eventually forces them out of their initial
attitude of dependence. It can now be observed that patients begin to talk to
each other rather than to the therapist; they may even begin to favor each
other with therapeutic suggestions. From this point on, the leader serves chiefly as an alert interpreter, though occasionally more active steering is necessary
to protect a member from being overwhelmed by advice or diagnosis on the
part of other members. Presently the leader begins to raise questions about the
motives behind what is being said. What prompted A to give the advice he just
gave to B? This examining of motives is gradually taken up by the group
members, who start to become aware of their own motives and the consistent
kind of impact they have on others. C discovers, for example, that her remarks
are always directed toward the less assertive patients, and she thus learns that
she tends to be fearful of reprisal. D discovers that he always intervenes when
there is tension between two other patients, and he thus realizes the force of his
own fear of hostility. Much of this discovery is made spontaneously or with the
help of other group members. The leader is no longer the only source of interpretations.

What is talked about in these meetings? The patients discuss their symptoms
and other things that are troubling them. They air the exasperations of their
current life. They talk about the process of therapy and speculate on what is
involved in getting well. A good deal of time may be spent in narrating important episodes in their past lives. As time goes on, the conversation turns more
and more to what is happening in the group: how the patients feel about the
leader, how they themselves seem to affect others. This bringing to expression
of feelings and counter-feelings, so different from what happens in ordinary
social life, constitutes a unique experience in human relations and may well

287

prove to be the central advantage of group psychotherapy over individual treatment.

An Illustrative Example

The following episode, taken from a book by Berne (1966), illustrates several aspects of group psychotherapy, including the fairly uncommon one of humor used to increase insight.

> Sophia was always ready to complain about how things were at the office, and each week she said she could not make up her mind whether to continue in the group or go to Europe. When the other members of the group said that she was really trying to make her mind up whether to get better or to look for a magical solution to her troubles in Europe, she evaded the issue for a long time. On this particular day, she asked them again if she should stay in the group or travel. They replied rather effectively, wondering again how they were supposed to deal with a question like that, and politely asked her to explain its purpose. But Dr. Q thought from the way she broached the question on this occasion that she was perhaps ready for a showdown, so he decided it was best to interrupt them and go to the heart of the matter. She had previously been asked several times why she did not want to get better, and had pretended not to understand the question. On the hypothesis that she was now ready to answer, Dr. Q therefore asked:
>
> "Why don't you want to get better?"
>
> She replied, laughing nervously, "Because getting better would mean doing the things my parents always wanted me to do, and I have to spite them."
>
> "That reminds me of a story," said Dr. Q. "One night in the middle of winter a policeman found a drunk sitting on a doorstep, shivering and shaking and freezing, and he asked him what he was doing there. The drunk said, 'I live here,' so the policeman said, 'Then why don't you go in?' The drunk said, 'Because the door's locked,' so the policeman said, 'Why don't you ring the bell?' The drunk said, 'I did, they didn't answer,' so the policeman said, 'Then why don't you ring again? You'll freeze to death out here.' And the drunk said, 'Oh let them wait.' "
>
> Almost everybody in the group laughed. Two nodded, and Jim said, "That's me, all right." Sophia also laughed. Then Dr. Q added:
>
> "Unfortunately, parents sometimes say things that are right. Are you planning to spend the rest of your life getting back at your parents, or do you think some day you'll get better?"
>
> "Well," replied Sophia, "maybe some day I'll get better."
>
> "Well, if you're going to die eventually, why not do it now, and save all that time and grief?"
>
> "I'll think about it," answered Sophia, whereupon Dr. Q immediately turned his attention to someone else (pp. 254–56).

288 Even in so short an episode it is possible to observe the alertness, skill, and sensitivity that is needed for the conduct of group psychotherapy. The therapist picks up through some clue—manner, tone of voice, choice of words—that the patient may now be ready to consider more seriously her repetitive question. It would have been easy to think, "There she goes again," and pass on to more promising topics. When the answer comes, representing a significant gain in the patient's insight, the therapist at once tells a story that illustrates humorously the patient's plight—the self-destructive character of spite. This procedure is hazardous: had the story not been perfectly appropriate, or had the mood of the group been slightly different, the patient might have felt that she was being ridiculed. Happily, another member says, "That's me," and everyone is able to laugh together. The therapist then clinches the interpretation in a challenging statement and attempts to persuade the patient to act soon. Why does he so quickly give this up and turn away? It would have been easy to insist a little triumphantly upon the correctness of the insight and the changed behavior that might well follow. But the patient's reply—"I'll think about it"—is not negative or resistant. She accepts her insight and the therapist's enlargement of it, but she asks for time to get used to its difficult implications. The therapist recognizes that she should have this time, and by changing the subject protects her from possible further comments by other members of the group. It would have been easy indeed to bungle some step in this brief transaction and thus throw away the chance to help the patient.

The Group as Environment for Change

Appreciation of the value of group psychotherapy has increased steadily over the past thirty years. At first considered superficial, recommended chiefly for clients who could afford nothing better, it is now accepted as a method having properties of its own that make it for many purposes superior to individual treatment. One of its best services is a quick decrease in the sense of isolation. The clients become vividly aware that other people have problems like theirs and that these problems need not be cause for shame. At first a patient may feel strange and inhibited in the group, but there is a good chance that feelings of group solidarity will presently prove helpful in bringing about a beneficial change.

Another valuable property of group treatment is that social behavior comes under direct observation. In individual treatment the therapist learns about the client's social interactions only through the client's biased report. A therapist whose client had sketched himself as unusually charming and interesting was once surprised to hear at a social gathering that this same person was highly unpopular because everything he said was in a condescending tone of voice. The group method allows both therapist and group members to see what really happens in the client's relations with others. They can observe what tactics are employed, what defenses prevail, and what distortions there may be in social perception. At appropriate times the therapist can point these out, and the group members are likely to assist by telling the client how they feel about the behavior.

For all of us there are gaps between our self-pictures and how we actually sound. Group therapy is a perfect setting for perceiving the discrepancy. Clients may be unpleasantly surprised to learn that their tone of voice is condescending, that their apologies are irritating, that their wisecracks are a bore, or that their superficial chatter keeps everyone at arm's length; pleasantly surprised if their stumbling attempts to express appreciation and understanding meet with a warmly encouraging response. The therapeutic group provides an unusually favorable opportunity to learn changes in interactive behavior.

In a thoughtful paper Gutmacher and Birk (1971) point out additional advantages of group psychotherapy. The group therapist, they believe, offers a more realistic identification figure. Unlike the individual therapist who serves as permissive audience for one patient, the group therapist is seen in action, so to speak, participating in a social group. Furthermore, the client must from the start share the therapist with other group members; the role of favorite child is closed and intimations of sibling rivalry are constantly present. On this account, the authors believe, group treatment is especially appropriate when passive and manipulative dependence are important problems. They cite the instance of a client who was stuck in the gratification provided by an individual therapeutic relation and who made progress only after being transferred to a group that dealt forthrightly with her exorbitant demands. They advocate group treatment also for clients, variously categorized as "acting-out," delinquent, or "character-disordered," who locate the source of their trouble exclusively in the outside world. At the start these clients are serenely unaware of their own part in their destructive and self-destructive behavior. "In individual therapy," the authors say, "such problems may be extremely difficult to confront because the patient does not come with anxiety about his behavior and a wish to change it. However, in the group setting his behavior can be faced more squarely. The patient cannot be so evasive because his actions are directly observed and his distorted view of them can be challenged." They cite the case of a young woman who was fearful of men because, as she told it, starting with her father they had always treated her so badly. Presently she began to form a relation with a young man in the group, and soon everyone could see the force of her resentment and the active way she provoked hostile responses from her would-be friend. For the first time she realized her own part in her persecutions and was motivated to change her behavior. Becoming aware of unsuspected aggression in oneself is probably the most common therapeutic happening. When patients are asked to recall a critical incident in their treatment they are most likely to report a sudden upsurge of anger toward another group member (Yalom, 1975). Benefit lies in the fact that a therapeutic group accepts such an outburst and no permanent harm results.

Group psychotherapy is currently in wide use with many kinds of clients. It has an accepted place in mental hospitals with psychotic patients. It is frequently used either alone or as an adjunct in treating anxiety disorders. With suitable adaptations it is appropriate for other disorders and for a great variety of problems in living. But individual treatment has advantages of its own;

This is a group therapy session taking place at a hospital day center. As often happens in an active meeting, the group here has taken the lead away from the leader, and is discussing things among themselves. The process facilitates the formation of relationships among the participants, and they may learn as much from that as from the leader.

it is unlikely to be displaced by group methods. Encouraging as the group may be, it cannot provide quite the security of the individual session, nor can it permit the long-continued probing and struggle that may be necessary to change defensive habits dating from early childhood. Not all kinds of desirable change require a group environment; not all kinds would be facilitated by the presence of other patients. In clinical practice the recommendation is often made, when staffing is available, that a patient receive both individual and group psychotherapy. This reflects the belief that each has its virtues and that both together will maximize the possibility of change.

Applications to Children

Some adolescents respond well to a method that consists outwardly of sitting around and talking, but children require fewer words and more action. Early in the history of group psychotherapy Slavson (1943) began to meet these needs by organizing activity groups. Children in the age range from eight to thirteen were provided with the opportunity to meet, play, practice handicrafts, and occasionally take trips, all under the guidance of a carefully trained leader. There was no discussion of problems, nothing that overtly resembled treatment, but social learning occurred through the calm, steady, appreciative, fair-minded influence of the leader. Taking as little notice as possible of disruptive outburts, the leader set a pattern of organized behavior and supportive appreciation; the children presently discovered that imitating this pattern made the meetings more interesting. Both disruptive children and shy children, if their tendencies in these directions were not too severe, were reported to benefit from participation in the Slavson activity groups.

Group treatment of children has subsequently branched out in many directions, but the idea of relearning through activity continues to be an important theme. In residential treatment for boys with severe emotional disturbances, for instance, the staff tries to replace emotional outbursts with more competent ways of dealing with frustration (Trieschman, Whittaker, & Brendtro, 1969). Through good management one can sometimes show a child that screaming and indiscriminate blaming over a lost toy is ultimately less rewarding than making a careful search or planning for a replacement; similarly, that trying to break up other children's games produces a poorer result than asking quietly to join. Bardill (1972) reports a successful application of a token economy, which he calls "behavior contracting," with a similar group of difficult young clients. Conduct points, ultimately convertible into money, could be earned by listerning to others, making helpful comments, and refraining from various forms of disturbance. While this procedure greatly improved the group sessions, we do not yet know whether experiencing the good results of competent behavior—the intrinsic reinforcement—is helped or hindered by introducing the money reward. Another application, this one especially adapted to shy, withdrawn adolescents, combines social training in the group with videotape feedback (Savin, 1976). Social skills are explained, modeled, rehearsed and coached by the leaders, after which the subjects witness on the screen their own performances. This awakens anxiety at first, but in time the subjects become able to concentrate on their own social behavior and find ways to improve it.

Behavior therapy was originally devised for individual treatment, and those who practiced it were not at first much interested in group methods. The last two examples are part of a change in this respect. Lately there has been a quickening interest in applying behavioral methods to both children's and adults' groups. Expositions of this trend have been published by Rose (1977) and Harris (1977).

Gestalt Therapy

We place Gestalt therapy at this point because it is commonly practiced in groups and because it seems to stand midway between formal group therapy and the encounter groups we examine next. Gestalt therapy is, however, sometimes practiced individually, and it is often classified as a form of humanistic-existential treatment. Originated by Frederick Perls, a Viennese refugee from the Nazis, it justifies the claim to be existential by constant emphasis on the here-and-now, with professed disinterest in both past and future. Perls derived many of his ideas from the earlier school of Gestalt Psychology, which had effectively criticized the analysis of behavior and perception into elements without regard to overall properties—Gestalten, or forms. Applied to personality, this meant attention to the person as a total functioning being, and to symptoms and complaints as failures in natural wholeness. Gestalt therapy aims to recover wholeness so that organismic self-regulation can be restored. If this statement sounds bafflingly indefinite, this would not have bothered Perls, who was fond of saying, "lose your mind and come to your senses" (Perls, 1970). He meant by this that through precocious use of "mind" we build up a protective facade of strategies, defenses, roles, and self-conceptions that prevents us from "sensing" or feeling some of our most real and important needs. Instead of being harmoniously self-regulated by our true natures, we are guided discordantly by a collection of ideas.

The task of Gestalt therapy is to keep steering people away from their ideas about themselves by making them aware of how they actually feel—right now. The therapist may call attention to unwitting gestures that speak louder than words, to tones of voice, perhaps to slips of speech, and usually requires acceptance of responsibility for the indicated feelings. "The curative factor," says Korchin (1976), "is awareness—a realization of one's needs, as well as realization that they need fulfillment." Published verbatim reports (Perls, 1969) show that Perls operated with considerable dramatic flair and originality, but Gestalt therapy is more than a personal style. Since his death it has continued as a recognizable form of psychological treatment.

ENCOUNTER GROUPS

In recent years there has been a fast proliferation of experiments with meetings designed to promote better human relations. Perhaps the widely used word *encounter* will serve as a heading for the many variations that have developed. These meetings have a good deal in common with group psychotherapy, but their intent is different. The purpose is training instead of treatment. The earliest training groups (T-groups) were developed shortly after World War II, when worldwide destructiveness had again emphasized the dire need for a better understanding of human relations. In 1946 the first Human Relations Conference was held at Bethel, Maine. Here a group of generally successful people discovered how much they could learn about social interaction simply by interacting and focusing their attention on how they did it. In a research done much later with problem-solving groups, Moment and Zalesznik (1963) called attention to two dimensions of competence, the technical and the interpersonal. The "technical specialists" contributed good ideas about the objective features of the problem to be solved, but they were obtuse to the feelings of others and engaged in constant put-downs. The "social specialists," less fertile with solutions to the problem, listened to others, expressed appreciation and respect, suggested compromises, and thus maintained a har-

293

monious atmosphere for work. Some, of course, could do both, and some neither, but the two kinds of "specialists" dramatize the dual nature of cooperative work. The original purpose of T-groups was to increase sensitivity to the human relations aspect of joint endeavors. T-groups were designed, according to Argyris (1962), "to provide maximum possible opportunity for the individuals to expose their behavior, give and receive feedback, experiment with new behaviors, and develop awareness and acceptance of self and others." Usually present was the additional goal of understanding the conditions that make group work productive and efficient.

The reported success of training groups presently suggested purposes of a more general kind. Could not the group method be used to increase human contact, to melt defenses and promote direct, warm, spontaneous interactions? Would it not be possible in a group of similarly disposed strangers to drop the conventional images, role enactments, and protective human encounters? There followed a rapid spread of sensitivity training groups, encounter groups, marathon groups, and other groups designed to stimulate powerful emotional experience. Although some of these groups have a regular schedule of meetings, there is a strong trend toward making them short and intense. Marathon groups, for instance, meet continuously for two days, with

A special objective of many encounter groups is to break down inhibitions against intimate relationships by encouraging physical contact with strangers and members of the opposite sex.

294

time out only for a night's sleep. Institutes such as Esalen at Big Sur in California, dedicated to the enrichment of experience and release of potential, offer weekend programs as well as more lasting group meetings. Along with this trend goes a multiplying of what might be called "shock" methods: free use of the sense of touch, nude bathing, emotional catharsis, and the development of dramatic scenes that elicit direct expressions of support and love. Such experiences are seen, for instance by Schutz (1967), as opening the way for "the fulfillment of one's potential." An institute called Orizon provides participants with "the opportunity to take a sufficient leave from your daily self" in order to open "the potentialities for deeper experiencing of life" that are "within each of us" (Goldberg, 1970). Not just those whose personal behavior is disordered, but "each of us" is seen as a suitable client.

Compared to the purposes of group psychotherapy these goals seem extravagant. Compared to the methods of traditional group treatment, which entail a gradual learning process extended over time, the one-shot weekend seems an improbable shortcut. On the face of it there is little reason to suppose that marathon weekends are likely to displace either group or individual psychotherapy in the treatment of people with well-rooted disorders of behavior. But the argument is made by Ruitenbeek (1970) that brief intense encounters have appeal and possible value to people, increasingly numerous in our time, who are seriously alienated from their own feelings. This complaint can be a side effect of inhibition or of psychotic withdrawal, but there is reason to regard it as often a problem in its own right. Many contemporary clients, according to Ruitenbeek, are vague in their complaints but discontented with life. "Their childhood memories are not necessarily traumatic or even very bad, but there is not too much they feel good about." They function well but somewhat mechanically in everyday life, but "they lack the touch of intimacy and warmth, which are the ingredients for plain happiness and satisfaction." For this particular malady an important gain may come from a concentrated attempt to mobilize strong unaccustomed feelings.

Reported results of the encounter group experience range from the ecstatic to the direful. Some participants report that they feel reborn and go home with a much improved feeling about family and friends. They become eloquent advocates of sensitivity training and may even be drawn into the encounter movement as a life work. Others have a wonderful time but are presently found to have gone elsewhere for more sessions, as if the encounter were an exhilarating intoxication that did not carry over to sober everyday life. Reports appear in medical journals about serious anxiety disorders or psychotic breakdown following an encounter experience. These results are not necessarily inconsistent. Strong emotional arousal can easily be healthfully stimulating to some, pleasant but transient to others, and severely disturbing to still others.

This way of putting it is in harmony with the results of controlled studies. Lieberman, Yalom, and Miles (1973) studied a large number of groups including more than 200 individuals, with 69 subjects serving as controls. According to judgments that included independent observers and tests, a third of the subjects in encounter groups made substantial gains especially in social values and self-concepts. Followed up at later times, these subjects proved to have held their gains. Encounter groups, on this showing, are capable of having strong, lasting beneficial effects on one out of three participants. The same research shows a regrettably high rate of bad effects. Eight percent of the subjects became "psychiatric casualties" who required professional assistance, and eleven percent more were rated lower than they had been at the beginning. Beneficial effects looked somewhat larger in a survey by Knapp and Shostrom (1976), whose tests showed large average gains in "self-actualizing" maintained for at least a year. Specifically, the encounter subjects scored more inner-directed, more spontaneous, more capable of intimate contact, and more accepting of aggression. But this again must be balanced by a survey of nine studies (Hartley, Roback, & Abramowitz, 1976) that, while showing great variation in reported deterioration effects, does not challenge the eight percent average previously reported.

In thinking about these findings we should first bear in mind that encounter groups are designed to promote growth rather than treat disorders. That many of the participants are already "well" in the technical sense gives all the more credit to encounter groups for helping substantial numbers to become

An outgrowth of the feminist movement has been the proliferation of women's support groups, which may operate with or without a leader.

more well, but it puts the rate of failure in a poor light. Here there is a second point to bear in mind: the selection of clients and the training of leaders is below the standards that prevail in psychological treatment. With groups that are at least partially open to the public it is impossible to do more than a superficial screening of candidates. Furthermore, the skill required for screening, especially for recognizing candidates likely to be more disturbed than helped, implies extensive experience with mental patients, but group leaders are not necessarily drawn from professional mental health workers, whose training has certainly not encouraged the use of methods so informal, so improvised, and at times so theatrical. Many leaders of encounter groups have fallen into the work because it felt congenial and they found themselves good at it. One of the most important functions of professional organization is to set and maintain standards governing the selection of trainees, their training, and the guidelines of practice, including the selection of clients. The encounter movement has thus far moved only partway toward this degree of organizational maturity. In the meantime it is unfortunately necessary to say that anyone thinking of trying such a group should look carefully into its antecedents, claims, and leadership in order to be protected from cranks and commercial exploiters who have crept into the field.

THE THERAPEUTIC MILIEU

Turning back to more institutionalized forms of therapeutic activity, we close this chapter with brief notice of a changed approach in mental hospitals and correctional institutions. The older concept of an asylum, where the mentally sick could be removed from society, and kept out of harm's way—symbolized by building mental hospitals on remote hillsides far from the crossroads of life—has gradually given way to the idea of the hospital as a therapeutic environment (milieu) in which everything is arranged to be conducive to recovery. An early step in this direction was the introduction of occupational therapy, through which in an unthreatening setting of work with inanimate objects the patients might find interests and a revived sense of competence. Another step was the self-service cafeteria, offering patients the opportunity, whether they took it or not, to make mealtime social contacts of their own choosing. Exercises, games, birthday parties, dances, and other recreations followed in all hospitals aspiring to leadership. During the 1950s there was a rapid expansion of experiments in mental hospitals, correctional institutions, and homes for the retarded. The aim was to organize these institutions, considered as social systems, in such a way that all inmates would have a chance to benefit from being there (Jones, 1953; Stanton & Schwartz, 1954; Greenblatt, Levinson & Williams, 1957).

In practice this proved to be slow work. Quite apart from possible administrative and financial difficulties, the shift from custodial to therapeutic practices involved a profound change in the attitudes of the hospital staff. This

297

meant a change in the outlook not only of doctors but also of nurses, attendants, and other workers who are in contact with the patients most of the time. One is reminded of the old joke about librarians who consider it their duty to keep books clean and intact rather than to have them read; if the job is perceived and valued in this way, it is quite a wrench to change to a less orderly but more educational conception. In like fashion, the nurse—as in Kesey's *One Flew Over the Cuckoo's Nest* (1962)—who prided herself on keeping the patients in her ward clean and tidy or the attendant who measured his success in terms of keeping the ward quiet and controlling aggressive outbursts could not easily sacrifice their established virtues as custodians for the unknown possibilities of a therapeutic role. Nor should we suppose that the new view was always easy for doctors, who had to manage the hospital community and who were aware that there is, after all, a custodial element in the whole operation, failure in which will bring down the wrath of relatives and civic authorities.

The transformation of custodial wards into therapeutic ones was well described by von Mering and King (1957). They pointed out the great force of what they called the "legend of chronicity," the assumption that the patients were there to stay and could not be expected to get better. The unfortunate thing about this legend was that it guaranteed exactly what it predicted: the attitudes of those who believed it created an atmosphere in which the patients did indeed not get better. The staff acted to get the day's work done with the least fuss, and the patients were allowed to sink ever more deeply into their own preoccupations. Quite different is the situation when someone becomes convinced that the ward can be run on a therapeutic basis. When the patients are given generous attention with the implication that things can be better, even severely regressed schizophrenics, who no longer keep clothes on and are incontinent, can recover their lost habits, respond a little to the staff, show an interest in the activities of the ward, and even make a few awkward steps toward helping one another. Less disorganized patients can accomplish much more: they may take over many of the routine jobs, working in groups as dormitory or linen closet helpers; they may arrange birthday parties and other festivities; and they may work out a program of improving and redecorating the ward. Such projects generate pride in the living quarters and reawaken pleasure in social interaction.

> While sitting around the tables making things to improve the appearance of their ward, the women began to talk to each other as they had never done before. It was as if a group of apartment dwellers, who formerly had only nodded to each other in passing, were suddenly thrown together in close association, and for the first time began to find out what their neighbors were like (p. 123).

Yet all of this was accomplished with a minimum of prodding by the staff. It represents the salutary influence of a warm interest that also implies confidence and respect.

Administrative resistance to experiments of this kind is often overcome by the discovery that the financial cost of a "remotivated" ward is less than it was before. The human profit is decidedly encouraging. Some patients advance to making home visits and perhaps to ultimate discharge, while those who remain as permanent residents have the benefit of more alert and rewarding lives. When the "legend of chronicity" is replaced by a "legend of recovery" the results are, to be sure, less than miraculous; but there is a distinct change, and it is almost always in the direction of better lives for everyone concerned.

When we say it is better for everyone concerned, we include the staff along with the patients. As Greenblatt (1957) pointed out, there are in American mental hospitals about twenty attendants or aides to every nurse and every doctor, a large corps of people in constant contact with patients but untrained to be more than watchdogs. Often these workers have no feeling of participation in the therapeutic process. One of the most promising moves away from the custodial concept is the training of attendants to realize their importance to the patients, to treat them with friendly respect, and thus to exert a true therapeutic influence. Increasingly attendants and nurses are being used as therapeutic agents in behavior modification programs aimed at fostering independence and self-care, shaping positive social behavior, and reinforcing self-assertion.

Another plan that has proved successful in some places is to establish a form of patient government. This allows the patients to take major responsibility for recreational and social life, raise money to purchase supplies and equipment, supervise housekeeping and the serving of food, and help to orient new patients to hospital life. Participation with management in running the hospital makes it distinctly their concern, and serves as a useful vehicle for effective reality testing.

Tranquilizing drugs, which we consider later in the book, have played an important part in these developments. Without the calming effects of these drugs the humanizing of mental hospitals would certainly have proceeded more slowly.

It is curious that these improvements have gone on at the very time when hospitals are being assigned a more restricted place in mental health practice. There is pride today in the shrinking of hospital populations and in the closing of buildings. Mental health is now seen as a community problem: with proper local facilities many patients, it is believed, do better in their own communities than in isolated institutions. As yet, local facilities—community mental health centers—are not abundant enough to take over the full load. In any event it seems likely that some patients some of the time will continue to need the protection provided by a mental hospital. But going to a hospital no longer means entering a state of permanent custody. It may well mean going into a therapeutic milieu in which a great deal will be done to send a more healthy person back to the community.

299

SUGGESTIONS FOR FURTHER READING

On the subject of family psychotherapy a good starting point is Virginia Satir's *Conjoint Family Therapy* (rev. ed., 1967), a straightforward presentation with numerous excerpts. Recommended also is N. W. Ackerman's *Treating the Troubled Family* (1966). Help in grasping the complicated happenings of family therapy can be obtained by reading some or all of the 13 cases, each written by a prominent family therapist, given in P. Papp (Ed.), *Family Therapy: Full Length Case Studies* (1977).

On marriage counseling Bernard Greene's *A Clinical Approach to Marital Problems: Evaluation and Management* (1971) will be found both comprehensive and practical. Conjoint sexual therapy is described by W. H. Masters & V. E. Johnson in *Human Sexual Inadequacy* (1970) and by H. S. Kaplan in *The New Sex Therapy* (1974).

The inescapable classic on psychodrama is J. L. Moreno's *Psychodrama* (1946), which most readers will find exceedingly difficult. An easier acquaintance with this method can be made through an essay by L. Yablonsky & J. M. Enneis, "Psychodrama Theory and Practice," in *Progress in Psychotherapy*, Vol. 1, edited by F. Fromm-Reichmann & J. L. Moreno (1956).

Especially recommended as an authoritative work on group psychotherapy is I. D. Yalom's *The Theory and Practice of Group Psychotherapy* (2nd ed., 1975). Growing interest on the part of behavior therapists is shown in two books: S. D. Rose, *Group Psychotherapy: A Behavioral Approach* (1977), where stress is laid on setting definite goals, orderly planning of sessions, and careful assessment and monitoring of progress; and G. G. Harris (Ed.), *The Group Treatment of Human Problems: A Social Learning Approach* (1977), which contains ingenious applications and innovations.

For a readable and thought-provoking survey of encounter methods, sympathetic yet critical, there is H. M. Ruitenbeek's little book, *The New Group Therapies* (1970). The encounter movement receives judicious evaluation in S. J. Korchin's *Modern Clinical Psychology* (1976), pp. 406–422. Marathon groups are described and weighed by Elizabeth E. Mintz in *Marathon Groups: Reality and Symbol* (1971). For detailed studies of recent progress in sensitivity training (T-groups) see the book edited by R. T. Golumbiewski & A. Blumberg, *Sensitivity Training and the Laboratory Approach: Readings about Concepts and Applications* (1977).

The therapeutic milieu as developed in mental hospitals is discussed by G. L. Paul, *Psychosocial Treatment of Chronic Mental Patients* (1978). A lively paper by B. B. Zeithin, "The Therapeutic Community—Fact or Fantasy?" together with three rejoinders appeared in *International Journal of Psychiatry*, Vol. 7, April, 1969, raising a number of critical issues.

The Headache (1819) by George Cruikshank. The Philadelphia Museum of Art. SmithKline Corporation Collection.

9

Psychophysio-
logical
Disorders

Up to this point we have been concerned primarily with the psychological side of human behavior. Human development, the organization of personality, the adaptive process, and various maladjustments, including anxiety disorders, were construed mainly as psychological problems: motivation, learning, anxiety, and defense. We have touched briefly on physiological aspects of anxiety disorders, but our study thus far has not attached much signifcance to the body and the nervous system. This is not because of an inclination to regard people as disembodied spirits. It is because, until recently, much less has been known about the neural and visceral processes that accompany learning.

Our attention must now turn to a group of disorders in which the physiological complications are *at least* as important as the psychological. Disorders of adjustment are linked up with bodily processes in such a way as to produce genuine organic illness. The person complains of stomach pains or heart trouble; perhaps it is asthmatic attacks or skin diseases or frequent headaches that require a physician's attention. The ailments are not in the least imaginary. Examination discloses serious malfunctioning in the organs complained about, sometimes even such tissue changes as ulcers in the stomach or eruptions on the skin. The physical symptoms require treatment in their own right. Ulcers must be dealt with by rest, diet and medication, or by surgical means; high blood pressure must be controlled by anti-hypertensive medication, exercise, and diet. But a growing body of evidence indicates that disorders of this kind do not result solely from organic weakness nor from purely local tissue changes. Emotional stress also plays a role in causing these bodily disorders. Medications may relieve them, but recurrence is likely unless the emotional problem can be set right.

Disturbances in which emotional stress leads to chronic dysfunction in some organ system have historically been referred to as *psychosomatic disorders*, but the more precise term already recommended in DSM-II (1968) is *psychophysiological disorders*. Psychophysiological disorders are limited here to cases where the physical dysfunction is in organs controlled by the autonomic nervous system. This excludes certain anxiety disorders, which otherwise qualify perfectly as psychophysiological, because the bodily symptoms — for example, the sensory and motor symptoms such as paralysis and anaesthesia — occur in organs innervated by the cerebrospinal portion of the nervous system. Psychophysiological disorders occur in such regions as the gastrointestinal tract or the circulatory or respiratory systems, which are under the control of the autonomic division.

Prevalence of Disorders

During this century the frequency of psychophysiological disorders has increased greatly. Figures on neuropsychiatric breakdowns during military service show a relatively smaller incidence of anxiety disorders in World War II than in World War I, but a much greater frequency of psychophysiological disturbances. Before World War II the incidence of peptic ulcers in the U.S. Army was 1.6 per 1000 soldiers. In 1941 it rose to 3.2 and in 1942, after the war began, it was 5.8 per 1000 (Treisman, 1968). Thus there is evidence of sharp increases as a result of acute stress as well as a more gradual increment over time. Similar trends are clear in statistics based on civilian populations (Schwab et al., 1970) but recent surveys indicate that chronic digestive disorders showed about the same prevalence (9 percent) in 1975 as in 1968, with even a slight decline in ulcer disorders in 1975 (Drury & Howie, 1979). The trend here may be leveling off.

To some extent, changes in the prevalence of disorders result from fashion in diagnosis. Some disorders are now called psychophysiological that might have been classed as hysteria three generations ago. To a certain extent, moreover, increase in the frequency of a given disorder may reflect the advances of medicine. For instance, in the United States death rates for cardiovascular disorders increased from 287 (per 100,000 population) in 1910 to 520 in 1966. Meanwhile, the rates for influenza and pneumonia dropped from 196 to 33 and deaths from miscellaneous other causes dropped from 776 to 146 (U.S. Department of Health, Education and Welfare, 1968). The greater frequency of cardiac disorders may partly reflect the increasingly stressful pace of modern life, but it also arises because a larger proportion of the population now survives acute respiratory infections, for example, that would have been fatal seventy years ago. Consequently, more people live to the middle and later decades when cardiac disorders are in any event more common.

These reasons, however, do not wholly explain the general increase of psychophysiological disorders, and the social implications of the trend are disturbing (Schwab et al., 1970). Many disorders have been occurring with increasing frequency among younger age groups. Sex ratios have changed: peptic ulcer used to be four times as prevalent in men as in women, but the ratio has been reduced to little more than two-to-one. On the contemporary social scene, as women participate more actively in the occupational and social arena, they are exposed to added stresses, with greater conflict and ambiguity in their roles. As a result we can expect an acceleration in stress disorders among career women and working mothers. The prevalence of psychophysiological disorders is two to four times as great in lower social classes as in other classes. Death from hypertension is seven times more common in nonwhites than in whites. This may reflect genetic disposition in part, but discrimination and segregation also induce psychological stress and frustrations than can contribute to this outcome. There is increasing susceptibility to psychophysiological disorders in urban centers and among mobile people, which has been attributed partly to the recurrent emotional arousal evoked by noise, crowding, appetizing media advertisements, and driving in heavy traffic (Pilowsky et al., 1973). Even public speaking has been shown to cause rapid heart beat and increases of adrenaline and fatty acids in the blood, which contribute to heart disorders (Taggart, Carruthers, & Somerville, 1973). Experiments have indicated that overcrowding and disruption of social organization can induce hypertension in mice (Henry, 1975); apparently there is similarity in this respect between mice and men: both require space and social order to be content.

The cost of health care in this country is estimated at $115 billion a year—8 percent of the Gross National Product (Thomas, 1975). A large part of that pays for treating the symptoms of psychological distress, because repeated studies show that at least one-third of all patients receiving medical care suffer primarily from emotional and nervous disorders (Spaulding, 1975). In a large survey of a county in northern Florida 14 percent of the respondents reported

305

In certain respects mice are like humans: both experience stress from crowding and disorganization. Crowding has brought about population decline, as shown in the top photo. Many of those below wish it had done the same there.

suffering from hypertension, 5 percent from asthma, and 4 percent from ulcers or colitis (Schwab, Fennell, & Warheit, 1974). More than half regularly experienced psychophysiological symptoms (headaches, indigestion, constipation, nervous stomach, stomach aches, diarrhea, high blood pressure, asthma, peptic ulcers, colitis, or weight problems). And these were significantly more common among blacks, females, the old, and the poor, which has important social implications. Indeed, life stress has become such a prominent focus of recent research in all kinds of psychophysiological disorders that we consider it as a general issue before turning to the specific disorders themselves.

Life Stress

Harold G. Wolff, one of the greatest pioneers in psychophysiological research, started studying the onset of illness in the late 1930s. He and his colleagues, notably Thomas H. Holmes, found that unusual life events help to cause many diseases, including colds, tuberculosis, and skin disease. More than 5000 patients were asked to tell about the life events that preceded their illnesses, and they reported a wide range of events: death of a spouse, a change of job, divorce, birth of a child, outstanding personal achievement. So many patients mentioned mothers-in-law so often that the researchers came to consider them a common cause of disease in the United States (Holmes & Masuda, 1972)! Life events clustered in a two-year period before the onset of illness. (Women, married or not, tended to become pregnant at times of great life change.) Not all the events were so negative or traumatic that they would obviously cause stress. Most were such ordinary experiences as children leaving home, taking a mortgage, changing residence or schools, things that happen to everyone sometimes, though not often. What was important about them was that (especially when they happened in bunches) *they required adaptation or coping behavior*.

Holmes and his associates (Holmes & Masuda, 1974) developed a Social Readjustment Rating Scale comprising 43 of the most common life events reported. Hundreds of people were asked to rate the amount of social readjustment required for each of the events on the list, assigning an arbitrary value of 50 to *marriage* and comparing the other events to that standard. The scale is reproduced in Table 9-1, showing the resulting average weights assigned for each item. The extraordinarily high value assigned to *death of spouse* is borne out by a study from the National Health Service in England (Parkes, Benjamin, & Fitzgerald, 1969). In a sample of 4000 widowers during the first six months of bereavement, death occurred at a rate 40 percent higher than expected, based on national figures for married men of the same age; coronary artery disease was the principal cause of death. The magnitude of life changes has been associated with the incidence of major illness, likelihood of hospitalization, sudden cardiac death, onset of heart attacks, occurrence of bone fractures, teacher absenteeism for illness or injury, risk of football injuries, and minor psychophysiological symptoms (Holmes & Masuda, 1974). A chart of

307

Table 9-1   Social Readjustment Rating Scale

Rank	Life Event	Mean Value
1	Death of spouse	100
2	Divorce	73
3	Marital separation	65
4	Jail term	63
5	Death of close family member	63
6	Personal injury or illness	53
7	Marriage	50
8	Fired at work	47
9	Marital reconciliation	45
10	Retirement	45
11	Change in health of family member	44
12	Pregnancy	40
13	Sex difficulties	39
14	Gain of new family member	39
15	Business readjustment	39
16	Change in financial state	38
17	Death of close friend	37
18	Change to different line of work	36
19	Change in number of arguments with spouse	35
20	Mortgage over $10,000	31
21	Foreclosure of mortgage or loan	30
22	Change in responsibilities at work	29
23	Son or daughter leaving home	29
24	Trouble with in-laws	29
25	Outstanding personal achievement	28
26	Wife begin or stop work	26
27	Begin or end school	26
28	Change in living conditions	25
29	Revision of personal habits	24
30	Trouble with boss	23
31	Change in work hours or conditions	20
32	Change in residence	20
33	Change in schools	20
34	Change in recreation	19
35	Change in church activities	19
36	Change in social activities	18
37	Mortgage or loan less than $10,000	17
38	Change in sleeping habits	16
39	Change in number of family get-togethers	15
40	Change in eating habits	15
41	Vacation	13
42	Christmas	12
43	Minor violations of the law	11

Source: Holmes and Rahe (1967), Table 3, p. 216.

one patient's history of illness is depicted in Figure 9-1. Thus life change stress plays a role in the causation, time of onset, and severity of diseases of all kinds.

Sarason et al. (1978) developed a more refined measure of life change, the Life Experience Survey, that separates positive change from negative change. They found that negative change has greater psychological impact, that is, it correlated significantly with anxiety and personal maladjustment. No particular event seems to be linked to a particular disorder (Goldberg & Comstock, 1976; Holmes & Masuda, 1972), so the study of these general precipitating events reveals little about specific etiology. For that we must look more closely at human physiology and the role of emotion.

EMOTION AND BODILY PROCESSES

Emotion is obviously related to certain bodily states, and many common phrases recognize this. The heart is said to ache or to be broken; in its more turbulent moments it can be in one's mouth or go down to one's boots. The color of the face can change over a wide range from white as a sheet to purple

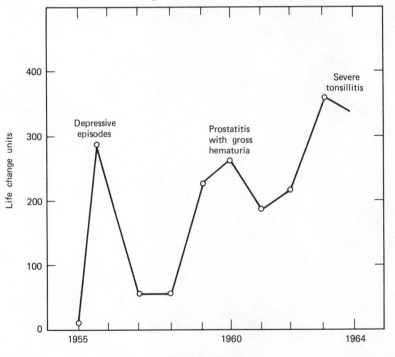

Figure 9-1

Temporal relationship of life crisis and disease occurrence. (From Rahe & Holmes, unpublished, 2a.)

with rage. We say that we have no stomach for a job or that we· haven't the guts to do it. In China it is appropriate for a man to say to his lady love that his intestines tie themselves in knots while she is away. Language would hardly have become so replete with such phrases unless there were some kind of factual basis.

Everyday Observations

Turning from metaphor to empirical observation, we still need not set up an experimental situation to find examples of psychophysiological relationships. Everyday observation teaches us quite a few lessons on this subject. As a first example we can take the nervousness that many people feel when they have to make a speech or appear in some other capacity before an audience. Stage fright carries with it a number of well-known bodily reactions. For the last

 Such life changes as moving to a new home create stress which can take its toll on psychological equilibrium.

meal preceding the public appearance there is poor appetite, possibly even a complete inability to eat. As the great moment approaches, the heart beats rapidly, the mouth becomes dry, the hands tremble and grow cold, and there is a strong desire to urinate and move the bowels. The upset state of mind is reflected in an upset state of body. A contrasting example is offered by the emotion of joy. This will show itself not only in erect posture, springy step, bright eyes, and smiling face, but also in systems under autonomic control. The joyous person usually shows a good color, has a strong deep pulse, breathes deeply, has a good appetite, enjoys food, and digests and eliminates well. The viscera share in the mental well-being. For a third example we can take grief, which is usually accompanied by marked somatic distress (Lindemann, 1942). There is apt to be an aching tightness in the throat, sometimes a choking sensation, shortness of breath, and a frequent need for sighing, all of these related to a feeling of wanting to cry. Another element is a feeling of weakness and easy exhaustion, so that the bereaved person can scarcely summon energy to climb the stairs or walk for any distance. Disturbances of eating are highly characteristic: appetite is extremely poor and the person complains that all food tastes like sand. Grief ramifies throughout the body, affecting a large number of functions controlled by the autonomic nervous system. We have no reason to doubt that other feelings and emotions besides nervousness, joy, and grief have a widespread influence on the whole bodily economy.

Early Research Using Hypnosis

Lipowski (1977) delineates the years 1925 to 1955 roughly as the first phase of psychophysiological research in this country. The early work was heavily dominated by the psychoanalytic theory of Franz Alexander (1950), which postulated a decisive role for unconscious conflicts and related emotions in the development of asthma, colitis, thyroid disorders, essential hypertension, rheumatoid arthritis, skin disorders, and peptic ulcer. It was hypothesized that distinctive attitudes and traits of personality predispose a person to particular types of psychophysiological disorder. Perhaps because of the emphasis on unconscious motivation much research employed hypnosis. For example, on the basis of intensive clinical interviews Graham and his associates (Grace & Graham, 1952; Graham, Stern, & Winokur, 1958) discerned specific attitudes associated with different psychosomatic disorders, such as hives and Raynaud's disease. They hypothesized that the emotional correlates of these attitudes might contribute, via physiological processes, to the somatic pathologies observed. Hives sufferers felt mistreated and were preoccupied with what was happening to them, but had no wish to retaliate. Patients with Raynaud's syndrome, on the other hand, felt a strong wish to take some direct, usually hostile, action. The clinical symptoms of these two disorders are as different as the specific attitudes linked with them. In hives the skin becomes hot and swells up in wheals or patches that itch intensely. In Raynaud's disease the skin of the extremities, especially the hands and fingers, becomes cold and

311

moist and numb. You have probably experienced this in very mild form while watching your favorite athletic team playing in overtime in a championship game. Physiologically, Raynaud's syndrome is produced by constriction of blood vessels in the skin, hives by dilation of these vessels.

To test their hypothesis, Graham et al. hypnotized a group of normal young men and suggested to them the attitudes specific to hives and Raynaud's disease while monitoring continuously their skin temperature. For the hives attitude the subject was told that Dr. X was going to burn his hand with a match and he would feel very much mistreated, but would be unable to do anything about it or even think of anything to do. He would think only of what was happening *to* him. To stimulate Raynaud's disease, the subject was given the same suggestion but told in addition that he would feel so mistreated that he would want to hit Dr. X as hard as he could, to choke him and strangle him. He could think *only* about how much he wanted to hit Dr. X. The "hives-specific attitude" produced a sustained rise in skin temperature, while the "Raynaud's specific-attitude" produced a steady decline. The conclusion drawn was that, if suggested attitudes can produce such distinct physiological effects, real ones, especially when long sustained, might well contribute to psychophysiological illness. In a replication of that study (Peters & Stern, 1971) subjects showed decreases in skin temperature when hypnotized and increases when not hypnotized, *regardless of which "disease attitude" was suggested*, which casts some doubt on the earlier findings.

Hypnotic suggestion has also been used to suppress allergic skin reactions (Black, 1963). Allergens such as pollen extract were injected into the skin of the forearm of allergic subjects in the normal waking condition, and then again under hypnosis with the following suggestion: "You will have the same injection again, but this time there will be no response; there will be no heat, no redness, no swelling, no itching, no reaction. Your arm will no longer respond to the fluid as it did before. It will be just as if water had been pricked in." The allergic response, as measured by the swelling of the skin and increase in skin temperature, could be reduced by this hypnotic suggestion.

As we saw in the historical introduction, Charcot and Janet, and afterwards Freud, came to believe that the mysterious symptoms of "hysterical neurosis" could be both caused and cured by *ideas* alone. We see here an interesting parallel: that ideas, and feelings, can contribute to and can remedy psychophysiological symptoms. Experiments of this kind are often classed with the wonders of hypnotism. It is more accurate to class them with the wonders of psychophysiological processes. The contribution of hypnotism is not uniquely important—it consists merely in heightening the imaginative processes and giving direct suggestions. It evokes stronger physiological reactions, perhaps because the trains of thought suggested under hypnosis are not opposed by competing mental activities that normally occur in the waking state. Similar effects can be obtained by imagination without hypnosis. Digestive secretions can be provoked merely by talking about thick juicy steaks or other relished foods. For our present purposes the important thing is the close relation be-

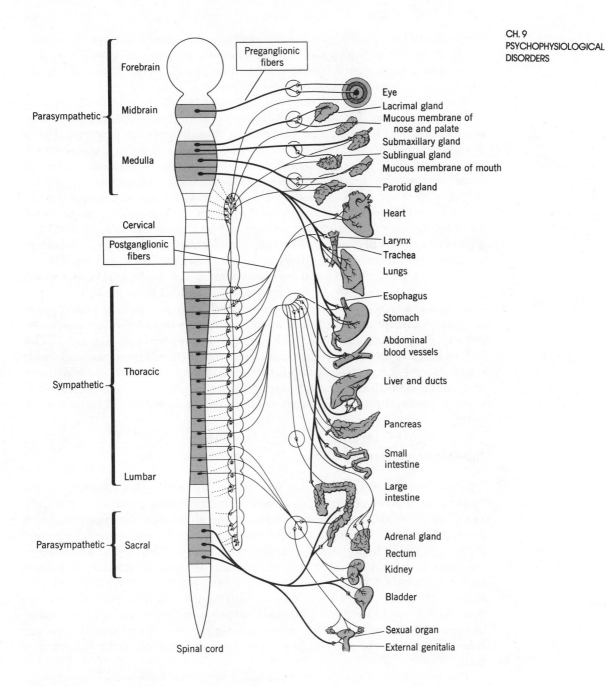

Figure 9-2
Autonomic nerves and the organs that they innervate. As shown, most organs receive fibers from both the sympathetic and parasympathetic portions of this system.

313

tween psychological and physiological processes. States of conflict, feelings of
relish or disgust, thoughts and fantasies about eating are all closely linked to
bodily processes governed by the autonomic nervous system. This is the basic
fact that lies behind psychophysiological disorders.

We consider later some theoretical shortcomings of the "specificity hypothesis" that accounted for its waning influence during the second phase of research in this field, dating roughly from 1955 to the present (Lipowski, 1977).
Wolff initiated a second major research tradition, marked by careful scientific
and experimental design, quantification of the variables studied, a focus on
conscious (and thus more readily elicited) psychological factors, and *a concern
with the mechanisms that mediate between symbolic and physiological processes*. This tradition has exerted greater influence in recent years—the well-
known program of investigation on life stress by Holmes and Masuda (1974) is
a good example—because it was compatible with the precepts and methods of
modern social science. The present phase of research is marked by relatively less emphasis on individual psychodynamics and more emphasis on psychophysiological responses to environmental stimuli. Theoretical perspectives
have broadened to include the effects of social factors on health: family interaction and disruption, conditions and relationships on the job, urbanization,
poverty, migration, and rapidly changing value systems and life-styles. This
has added a social and ecological dimension that has enriched—and vastly
complicated—the previously two-dimensional (psychodynamic and physiological) conceptions that prevailed during the earlier phase. To understand these
modern conceptions we must first review some basic aspects of human physiology.

The Autonomic Nervous System

The autonomic nervous system, sometimes called the "involuntary" or the
"vegetative" nervous system, is a system of motor nerves governing what Cannon (1929) called "the domestic affairs of the interior of the organism." It is
intimately connected with the cerebrospinal system, having centers in the medulla, midbrain, hypothalamus, and cerebral cortex, yet it is to some extent
set apart both anatomically and functionally. In general, the axons of autonomic neurons do not proceed from the central nervous system directly to
muscles or glands; instead they pass to outlying ganglia that serve as relay stations on the way to the final goal. In contrast to the cerebrospinal system that
innervates the striated muscles responsible for movement and posture, the autonomic system acts on the glands and smooth muscles of the viscera and
blood vessels.

The autonomic is divided into two subsystems that have somewhat antagonistic effects. The *sympathetic* system is mainly concerned with mobilizing the
resources of the body for use in work or in emergencies. Anatomically it is well

designed to act more or less as a whole: the sympathetic ganglia lie in an interconnected chain so that excitation at any one level is likely to spread upward and downward to reach all the organs affected by the system. The *parasympathetic* division is mainly concerned with conserving and storing the body resources. Its action is less unified (the ganglia are not interconnected), but some of its nerves branch in such a way as to reach several organs. The vagus nerve, for example, reaches the heart, the bronchi, the stomach, and the intestine. Thus both divisions of the autonomic act with less precision and more diffuseness than the cerebrospinal system.

It is easy to exaggerate the antagonism between the two divisions. Cannon originally conceived that all strong emotions such as anger and fear activated the sympathetic, suppressed the effects of the parasympathetic, and thus put the organism on an emergency footing. The studies of Gellhorn (1964) and others have shown that this conception of an emergency reaction is somewhat too simple. If the organism is to react effectively in a crisis, a rise in parasympathetic activity must closely follow the initial burst of sympathetic discharge. The interaction between the two divisions proves to be quite complex; reciprocal action is necessary to maintain an effective bodily state either in emergencies or in quieter times. For our present purposes it is probably better to emphasize not the two parts but the action of the autonomic system as a whole in managing the domestic economy of viscera, blood vessels, and glands.

The autonomic response to a danger signal brings about a marvelously complete preparation for fight or flight. Consider, for example, a deer grazing contentedly in a clearing when a leopard emerges from the forest some distance away. Upon perceiving movement along the edge of the forest, alarm registers immediately in the deer's brain. Involuntarily the deer freezes into immobility, its ears are pricked, its head is turned straight in the direction of the danger, and it sniffs the wind. Meanwhile its body goes through the emergency preparations to flee. Its muscles tense because then they can contract faster and with more power than if they are relaxed. Its liver releases into the bloodstream a large supply of sugar that will be needed as fuel for the muscular effort during flight. Its heart beats faster and its blood pressure rises so that the blood can deliver sugar and oxygen to the muscles faster. The hunger that led it out into the clearing disappears in a flash, because a species as poorly armed to fight as the deer would not survive long if they continued eating in such circumstances.* In a sudden attack of diarrhea the deer empties its bowel so that it can run faster, much as airline personnel jettison the cargo of a plane that is in danger of losing altitude. Now the deer is prepared for the tumultu-

---

*Dogs and large cats, on the other hand, growl or roar when threatened during feeding and they eat faster if danger increases. Fear does not destroy their appetite because they are armed well enough to survive by fighting. In this respect we resemble the deer: fear wipes out hunger because we are better equipped to flee than to fight. These observations and the illustration of the deer and leopard are drawn from Simeons (1962).

315

These birds are differently equipped to deal with intruders at mealtime. If a human
approached the rose-breasted grosbeak (top) it would flee rather than finish its meal.
However, the hawk (below) would continue eating as long as possible and would be as
likely to attack the intruder as to flee.

ous exertion that will be required to save its life if that movement off in the distance turns out to be a leopard.

It is easy to see that psychophysiological disorders in humans involve the same physiological functions as these emergency mechanisms. Peptic ulcers and colitis are disturbances in the timing and intensity of digestive functions. Essential hypertension and cardiovascular disease result from dysfunctions in blood pressure and heart rate. Diabetes is a disorder in the regulation of blood sugar. Asthma is a respiratory disorder. Hives and Raynaud's syndrome are disturbances in skin function and the regulation of body heat. As a general statement we can say that psychophysiological symptoms result when emergency reactions of the autonomic nervous system are chronically invoked in circumstances in which physical survival no longer depends on them, though we will see later that this is not the whole story.

Normally the autonomic nervous system maintains an effective equilibrium. Strong emotion is accompanied by overactivity in some part of the system, but strong emotion is usually transient. Anger subsides, and heart rate and blood pressure go back to normal levels. Acute grief passes, and appetite returns to its customary state. The healthy digestive tract, heart, circulation, and respiratory system are equal to quite a large amount of overactivity if occasion demands. Naturally there are limits, beyond which prolonged activity tends to create serious dysfunction and even permanent injury. In order to explain psychophysiological disorders it is necessary to show why certain patterns of autonomic discharge remain persistently active in the absence of what appear to be suitable circumstances.

Chronic Autonomic Stimulation

Curiously enough, it is upon our capacious brains that we must lay the responsibility for psychophysiological disorders. The human cerebral cortex, vastly developed in comparison with the deer's, must be reckoned a great evolutionary success, but some of its side effects are troublesome. As Simeons (1962) points out, the cerebral hemispheres developed initially to discriminate incoming sensory stimulation, so that mammals need not respond instinctively to all of them. This function was better performed if the brain could maintain a large storehouse of memories readily available to guide behavior in new situations. But this requirement eventually led to the possibility of reflecting about the past and imagining the future. This placed additional burdens on autonomic mechanisms, which were now often called into action by imagined and symbolic threats. In Selye's (1956, 1975) formulation the adaptive reaction to stress occurs in three stages: an *alarm reaction* that quickly mobilizes the body's defensive forces, a *stage of resistance* to sustain the response to continued stress, and, if the stress continues too long, a *stage of exhaustion* in which protective reactions fail and the animal succumbs. A tough and healthy creature can sustain a long hard fight or flight, but there is a time limit to the

317

internal protective reactions, and if pressed close to this limit they begin to produce destructive tissue change in the organs that are involved.

Animals respond mainly to situations immediately present and do not, as far as we know, worry very much about the future. They may have hot wars but they do not have cold wars. Emergencies in the lives of humans are quite commonly of longer duration. They use the autonomic reaction patterns designed for hot wars in those more extended emergencies that are analogous to cold wars. Future events may be the subject of worry long before they happen; past deeds may be regretted long afterwards; resentments may simmer for a long time. Despite the adages, we *do* cross bridges before we come to them and cry over spilled milk. Since people must use what they have, they adapt "for long-term purposes devices designed for short-term needs" (Cobb, 1950, p. 138). And if the term lasts too long, destructive tissue changes may happen in the organs that participate in the physiological protective reaction.

The protective reactions may be used not only for too long a time but in a way that is not appropriate to the actual situation. Thus the body may be mobilized to fight—to engage in strenuous muscular activity—when the real provocation to anger has been of a social or symbolic kind. Perhaps the source of annoyance is a child's misbehavior that must be dealt with by verbal punishment; perhaps it is a slur cast by an acquaintance that must be countered by repartee or an intelligent argument; or perhaps it is an insult by the boss that you dare not repay for fear of losing your job. In the ensuing behavior if the mobilized bodily resources are not used for muscular exertion, as they were originally intended, there may be a long delay in restoring the internal physiological balance. When such symbolic provocations occur repeatedly, even continuously, then the body remains in a continual state of emergency and those are the conditions that may lead to psychophysiological breakdown.

GASTROINTESTINAL DISTURBANCES

Formation of Peptic Ulcers

The prevalence of duodenal ulcer at autopsy has been reported at 9 percent in Germany and Scotland (Weiner, 1977). If one considers ulcers in the stomach as well, then probably more than one in ten people develops a peptic ulcer at some time. The formation of ulcers usually comes after a prolonged period of chronic gastric distress. Discomfort is felt about two hours after eating and can be alleviated by taking food. During the day the person can keep fairly comfortable by frequent snacks, but at night the distress is likely to increase. Ulcer formation results from chronic overactivity and oversecretion by the stomach. Under normal circumstances the stomach becomes active when a meal is to be digested. With the accomplishment of this task and the passing of the meal into the intestines, the stomach comes to rest and its acid secretion stops. Severe stress or protracted emotional conflict can work in several ways to upset the normal digestive cycle (Simeons, 1962). First, the alarm system may shut down the blood supply to the stomach, just as if a predator were approaching. If this is mild, it strangles the thin-walled veins and blocks the drainage of blood from the stomach, which produces congestion (gastritis or stomach irritation). But if the constriction is strong, it shuts down even the strong-walled arteries. This, in turn, causes the uppermost cells of the stomach lining to lose their oxygen supply and die, exposing the lower layers to erosion by the gastric acid. These lower cells are endowed with less resistance than the upper cells, so they succumb easily to the powerful acid and leave small incipient ulcer craters in the lining. Under normal circumstances such sores would heal very quickly, even in a few hours. However, psychological stress can thwart this natural therapy by activating the parasympathetic system and increasing the secretion of stress hormones, both of which make the stomach secrete more acid, even after the food has left the stomach. Since there is no food to absorb the acid secretions, they only irritate and inflame the mucous lining of the stomach and the upper part of the small intestine (duodenum). This makes the small ulcers even larger, and the continuing hyperacidity makes it difficult for them to heal.

Various experiments with animals have shown that prolonged acid secretion in the stomach elicited by stress eventually produces ulceration (Ader, 1971). These results are sufficiently conclusive, but hardly as dramatic as those obtained with a human patient by Wolf and Wolff (1947). The patient at the age of nine had drunk some scalding soup that seriously burned his esophagus so that it became closed with scar tissue. In order to feed him, a surgical opening (gastric fistula) was made directly into the stomach through the abdominal wall. At the age of fifty-six the man was in excellent health and rarely suffered digestive difficulties. The fistula was in regular use; it was sufficiently large to permit observation of the stomach walls, and, to make matters perfect for science, a collar of gastric mucosa had grown out to surround the fistula, thus exposing to direct view a small amount of tissue essentially similar to that which lines the stomach. We will have more to say about this man in a moment. What is important here is the experimental demonstration that gastric juice produces ulceration. A small erosion occurring on the exposed gastric mucosa, where the supply of mucus was poor, was artificially kept moist with gastric juice for four days. The erosion increased in size, resembled in every way a chronic ulcer, and was painful when touched. When a dressing was placed so as to protect the ulcer from gastric juice, the area healed completely in three days, leaving no trace of a scar.

We know then that ulcers result from loss of blood supply and excessive acid secretion in the digestive tract, which are stimulated by the parasympathetic division of the autonomic nervous system, acting through the vagus nerve.

319

Various studies have shown that gastric ulceration is produced by chronic vagal stimulation resulting from injuries in the midbrain, drugs, or the shock caused by severe burns. Enlargement of the size of the stomach may be a factor in peptic ulcers, perhaps because the larger number of cells increases the volume of acids and enzymes secreted (Weiner, 1977). For these reasons, surgery to cut the vagus nerve or remove part of the stomach or both is reported to be 93 to 99 percent effective at curing intractable ulcer disease (Eisenberg, 1978). Now we can consider what constellations of factors in everyday life conspire to create the conditions for peptic ulcers to develop. We will examine them in terms of three principal determinants: prolonged stress, predisposing biological or constitutional factors, and certain types of personality patterns.

Prolonged Stress

The level of gastric acid is readily affected by the emotions, especially unpleasant ones like tension, anxiety, or anger. Brady has demonstrated that such stress can cause peptic ulcers in animals if sufficiently prolonged. Pairs of monkeys were placed in restraining chairs and subjected to brief electric shocks every twenty seconds for six hours of every twelve. One of them (the executive) was provided a lever that, when pressed, prevented the shock to either animal. If he failed to press it in time, both monkeys received the shock. The control monkey also had a lever but it was useless, so the executive monkey was responsible for the welfare of both partners. They shared the same amount and frequency of punishment and the same degree of restraint, but the executive had the additional burden of repeatedly making decisions and taking action to prevent unpleasant events. Naturally it learned very well how to avoid shocks by pressing the lever, so both monkeys received relatively few shocks. However, within a few weeks the executive monkeys died of perforating ulcers, while the control monkeys remained healthy. Davis and Berry (1963) generalized Brady's results to humans, using college students, but not carrying the experiment to the same drastic lengths (which made it easier to recruit subjects). Only the subject who could prevent an electric shock showed an increase in gastric motility during the experiment or after it was over. There has been some dispute about the implications of Brady's experiment (Weiss, 1972) but there is general agreement that it shows the damaging effects of prolonged stress.

A natural human experiment concerned Dr. Hoelzel, a Chicago scientific specialist in the physiology of the stomach who regularly monitored his own gastric juices (Wright, 1945). In January 1928 his landlady was shot dead during an attempted robbery. Hoelzel was responsible for the arrest of the culprits, and for ten days following their apprehension he was acutely anxious that he would be killed in revenge. On the morning of the shooting, his gastric acid was 100 percent higher than the highest level it reached normally, and it remained more than 30 percent about the normal level until he moved to a safer place.

Finally, we illustrate the close connection between gastric hyperacidity and psychological stress with the following dream of a man with a history of chronic, mild irritation of the digestive tract (gastritis, colitis):

He was in his childhood home with his family when they were accosted by a strange gang of hoodlums. In the ensuing fight he and several others in his family were wounded by pistol fire. The hoodlums fled through the back alley in the family's car. After lying low for a few minutes, the family left the house to seek help from the neighbors. But just as they emerged from the front door they spied the hoodlums returning through the back way. Thinking they must have returned "to finish the job" so no witnesses would be left to testify against them, the family hurried back into the house to lock the doors and call the police. The man himself realized that this was not a very safe defense because the hoodlums could quickly cut the telephone line, force their way into the house and have the family at their mercy. Therefore, as soon as the rest were locked inside the house he made a break for the neighbor's house next door. He realized this was risky because he was the most seriously wounded, bleeding profusely from gunshot wounds in the lungs and elsewhere. If no one were home next door, he might not have the strength for a longer chase to other houses further down the street. But it appeared that he had no other choice. The others in his family were too horrified to think clearly and it was certain death for all of them to be trapped in the house. The hoodlums saw him as they came out of the garage and they began to give chase. Now he realized that his neighbor would be in the same jeopardy as his own family. Therefore, his only chance was to alert as many neighbors as possible before he was caught so that at least one of them could get a phone call through to the police before their lines were cut. But the hoodlums were not far behind and he was already beginning to get dizzy. . . .

At this point the man awoke, understandably in a state of intense anxiety. He was sweating, breathing heavily, passing gas, and feeling extreme pressure to urinate. He felt a painful tingling and soreness about the walls of his whole abdomen that was similar to what he felt after a severe bout of indigestion. He had to drink several glasses of water before the discomfort was relieved. Upon inquiry about the dream, he immediately associated it with a meeting of top level staff in his company that was held the previous day. He had only recently joined the firm and was already beginning to feel "very much at home with his new family," thinking he might want to stay there permanently. At the meeting a policy issue was discussed that he felt had far-reaching implications for the future direction of the company and his role in it, which would influence greatly how happy he could be with his work if he stayed there. Consequently, he took a strong stand on the issue in order to persuade his colleagues to his way of thinking. However, he was opposed by a small, but very vocal, group of junior employees, whom he easily identified as the hoodlums in his nightmare. The decision of his colleagues went against him, leaving him angry about their poor judgment and depressed about the long-term viability of the firm. Apparently no one else shared his sentiments.

321

This case illustrates our pernicious capacity to symbolize potential threats and to magnify their future significance, often without full awareness. Unfortunately, the human body does not come equipped with a thermostat that adjusts the physiological responses for degrees of psychological abstraction.

Predisposing Physiological Factors

We introduced physical symptoms when studying the development of anxiety disorders. Constitutional factors are even more important in psychophysiological disorders. From our discussion of the mechanics of ulcer formation we can hypothesize that people with 1) low cell resistance in the stomach or 2) high levels of acid secretion are more prone to peptic ulcers. No definitive evidence exists on the first hypothesis but it is known that the resistance of body tissues in general depends on hormone levels and there are wide individual differences in these. The second hypothesis has been confirmed by Mirsky and co-workers (1957). They measured levels of gastric secretion in 2073 army inductees at the beginning of basic training. They selected for follow-up 8 to 16 weeks later 63 with pepsinogen levels in the top 15 percent of the total distribution and 57 from the bottom 9 percent. Four draftees had duodenal ulcers to start with and five more developed an ulcer by the second examination. All nine were in the group with the highest rates of gastric secretion. Psychological testing indicated that the draftees with ulcers had strong underlying needs to be fed and supported. They were anxious about expressing hostility for fear of losing desired support. But when support was withheld, they were unable to express the anger they felt. From this we can see that stress, level of gastric secretion, and personality all contribute to the etiology of peptic ulcers.

Baron (1962) tested 100 medical students for gastric secretion and followed them for 27 years. Nine of them eventually developed duodenal ulcers, and those nine had secreted—as medical students many years before the disease onset—more gastric juice, with greater acidity, than the rest of the subjects. These studies show that increased acid and pepsin secretion are sufficient to cause ulcers, but about half of all ulcer patients are *not* hypersecretors. To explain their illness it is necessary to consider blood supply and the protective role of mucus in the stomach lining.

The hypothalamus is extremely important in controlling the autonomic nervous system. It regulates the rage and flight responses and can influence the motility of the gut and the supply of blood to the muscles. For this reason regular stimulation by electrodes implanted in the hypothalamus can produce ulcers in animals (Treisman, 1968). The hunger center is also located there and these drive systems interact. We tend to be irritable when hungry, perhaps because our ancestors had to be prepared to hunt and fight for their food when they were hungry. Ask any parents about the mood of their children just before suppertime and you will understand why so many are grateful that engaging television programs are scheduled at that time. On the other hand, we are more contented and agreeable when well fed. Not much is known about

322

individual differences in hypothalamic function, but almost certainly this is the source of many of the keys to the causes of ulcers.

Ectomorphic body build, blood type O, and low levels of blood group antigens ABH are replicated genetic markers of ulcer susceptibility, but their role in the etiology of the disorder is probably weak (Weiner, 1977). The blood antigens may help to build up the cells of the gastric lining to resist erosion.

Personality Patterns in Cases of Peptic Ulcer

Brady chose to call his ulcer-prone monkeys "executives" because ulcers occur frequently in ambitious, hard-driving business executives and others in responsible positions (though actually they are more common among blue-collar workers). Peptic ulcers once had the nickname of "Wall Street stomach." Consequently, much early research centered on personality traits of ambition, efficiency, achievement striving, and active living. Subsequent studies showed, however, that these qualities were also common in other types of disorder (e.g., coronary artery disease) and in healthy individuals. Alexander (1950) attempted to salvage the theory by emphasizing *unconscious* conflicts. Although they presented themselves as productive, responsible, aggressive, and self-sufficient leaders, unconsciously these individuals craved love, rest, and nurturance. In a more recent study (Alexander, French, & Pollack, 1968) "blind" diagnoses of peptic ulcer disease based solely on psychodynamic formulations were somewhat better than chance in men, but not in women. The authors concluded that their results confirmed the etiological theory of unconscious orally passive and dependent wishes for men. The problem with that interpretation is that oral dependent imagery may represent symbolic *effects* of the disease that appear only *after* the onset of symptoms. There may be some truth to the hypothesis that the hard-driving executive personality type or unconscious dependency conflicts dispose a person to ulcer formation, but it is doubtful that such a disposition is specific *only* to that particular form of psychophysiological disorder.

Other negative emotions have also been implicated in the genesis of peptic ulcer. Anxiety, hostility, and resentment are known to increase motility and acidity in the stomachs of ulcer patients and some normal individuals, and these can be reduced by inducing feelings of commitment and well-being. The man with the gastric fistula reported by Wolf and Wolff (1947) behaved in a similar fashion. Pathogenic changes came at moments in his life when he was dominated by feelings of anger and resentment. They were particularly acute when he was discharged from a small outside job on grounds of inefficiency, and when a man who lent him money tried to meddle in his affairs. When he experienced fear or sadness, on the contrary, the gastric mucosa became pale and both motility and acidity dropped.

Case histories of ulcer patients show that gastric pain and ulceration are sometimes precipitated by conflict with a mother figure, personal rejection or withdrawal of interest by a loved one around the time of childbirth, or as a result of guilt over sexual relations. Sometimes the precipitating cause is an event that creates a sense of failure, or arouses anger and aggression. These descriptions argue against a specific emotional constellation as to the cause of the gastric conditions that lead to ulceration. All the emotions discussed here bear a plausible relation to gastric dysfunction because of what we have learned about their connection with the hypothalamus and its mediation of the digestive processes. The evidence is less clear about any *learned associations* between specific emotional states and gastric function, especially if it involves infantile or unconscious learning. That is not surprising since one is then moving into the sphere of *personal meanings*, a realm always marked by great diversity. Philip and Cay (1972) found that two-thirds of peptic ulcer patients showed the ubiquitous psychiatric symptoms, anxiety and depression, and those *without* them had generally better prognosis for recovery from the ulcer disease. However, psychological testing of personality traits did not show differences from other medical patients or normal populations at large, so they concluded that there is no distinctive "peptic ulcer personality."

Anorexia Nervosa

We turn next to a disorder characterized by a highly negative attitude toward food. Appetite and eating is suppressed to such an extent that much weight is lost, in some cases until death by starvation occurs. The disorder is far more common in women than in men and usually occurs during adolescence, in connection with the onset of puberty, sexual relationships, and marriage. Typically, a teen-age girl stops eating and begins to lose weight. The menstrual periods cease and people close to her become quite concerned, urging her to eat. But she deviously evades the matter or dismisses it cavalierly as unimportant, while maintaining a level of vigorous physical activity that is quite astonishing for someone so emaciated. The disorder may be medically confused with severe pituitary disease because of the regression in sexual function and lowered basal metabolism, but it is unclear whether anorexia nervosa is a disorder of primarily psychological (Meyer, 1971) or endocrinological (Mawson, 1974) origin. Endocrine investigation reveals a reduced output of pituitary gonadotrophin, associated with low sex hormone levels, that can lead in turn to cessation of menstruation in women or sexual impotency in men. What is not clear is whether the sexual malfunction is a sequel of malnutrition or a primary feature of the illness. If treatment is successful, return of sexual functions usually follows improvement in nutrition.

Distortion in body image, anxiety, and obsessional symptoms occur in many cases, and severe anorexia has been observed in a few cases to precede florid psychotic symptoms (Meyer, 1971). Usually the core of the problem is a severe crisis in psychological maturation. Sometimes the motivation seems to turn on the desire to remain thin, flat-breasted, and sexually unattractive; there is anxiety connected with becoming sexually mature. Bruch (1973) studied a hypothesis put forward by Sigmund Freud that anxiety in anorexics arises from unconscious fear of oral impregnation. She found little evidence of such fantasies and misconceptions among her anorexic patients, but noted that they are exhibited rather commonly among normal adolescent girls, in a childish misunderstanding about how babies are conceived. In still other cases anorexia has the significance of an aggressive resistance to parental demands or a refusal to become like the same-sexed parent. The attitude most commonly observed in anorexia is disgust (etymologically, the opposite of taste). Often the disgust is focused on food, but that is usually symbolic of distaste for other aspects of one's life. One patient reported that the disgust "can spread out from eating to the whole world, to the whole of life" (Meyer, 1971, p. 541). Many patients talk freely about the central problem: not wanting to grow up, not wanting to become like their mother. It is easy to see that eating is closely associated with developmental advances throughout childhood, from nursing to drinking from a cup, from being fed to feeding oneself, and "you must eat well in order to grow up to be big and strong like your parents." The natural concern of parents about their children's eating makes it an obvious symbol for expressing resistance to any frightening or mysterious aspect of growing up. The diversity of personal meanings associated with the refusal to eat makes it necessary to study each case individually in order to understand the etiology of the disorder in that instance.

Following the theme of family relations, Minuchin (1974) suggests that the child's anorexic symptoms emerge from a dysfunctional family pattern, serving the function of a stabilizing force; the family must concentrate on the anorexic, thereby diverting attention away from underlying family conflicts. Successful treatment therefore consists of restructuring the enmeshed dysfunctional family system.

Mawson (1974) sees the disorder as a phobic avoidance response to food, resulting from sexual and social tensions generated by the physical changes of puberty. The same areas of the hypothalamus regulate feeding, sexual behavior, and menstrual activity, all of which are disturbed in anorexia, suggesting hypothalamic dysfunction may be a central problem. This is by now a familiar theme in psychophysiological disorders.

In a follow-up study Morgan and Russell (1975) found that 39 percent of anorexic patients made good recoveries within four years, though an alarming 10 to 23 percent die from the disorder (Van Buskirk, 1977). Premorbid personality disturbances, disturbed relationships with family, and previous psychiatric treatment are common. A 5 to 20 year follow-up study (Goetz et al., 1977) found the best recovery in patients with histrionic, manipulative personality styles and the poorest outcomes in those with schizoid adjustment, which suggests a close relation between prognosis and the quality of personal adjustment.

Disorders of Elimination

Let us recall the deer that was literally "scared shitless" by its perception of the leopard. The physiological mechanism that evacuated the bowel was an instinctively triggered contraction of the muscles that surround the colon. In hu-

325

mans the same mechanism can be invoked by perpetual emotional arousal. Chronic overaction of the parasympathetic pathways causes excessive secretion of mucus in the colon and spasm in the muscles, which impedes the circulation of blood and leads to congestion. In mild cases, this results in chronic constipation that later passes over into diarrhea, generally of a painful character because the colon is irritated. Experimental stimulation of parasympathetic fibers does not produce *colitis*, but there is strong evidence for their overactivity. Tension is usually created by strong emotions, such as anxiety, resentment, and guilt. Colitis sufferers are often overconscientious, dependent on the opinion of others, rigid, and inclined to obsessive thinking, which gives rise to long periods of brooding preoccupation. Acts of injustice to themselves or others fill them with resentment, which brings guilt in its train. Constant preoccupation with these matters is believed to be responsible for the prolonged muscle tension and for the action of the parasympathetic system on the colon.

Liss, Alpers, and Woodruff (1973) studied patients with irritable colon and found most of them met research diagnostic criteria for psychiatric disorder, usually an anxiety or depressive disorder. The psychiatric symptoms normally appeared prior to the onset of gastrointestinal symptoms. Symptoms in the upper gastrointestinal tract occurred frequently in association with those of the colon, suggesting that the syndrome is diffuse rather than being confined to the colon.

In more extreme cases the muscle spasms strangle the arteries that feed the inner surface of the colon, causing the death of the cells lining the gut. This condition is called *ulcerative colitis*. Movements are very frequent, as many as twenty times a day, but they consist mostly of blood, mucus, dead bits of tissue, and very little fecal matter (Simeon, 1962). Like peptic ulcers, ulcerative colitis is peculiarly resistant to medicinal treatment. Drugs, folk remedies, and surgery may be tried, but the condition will persist unless the underlying emotional tension is relieved, usually by psychological means. Engel and Schmale (1967) hypothesized that depression, caused by real or fantasied relationship loss, leads to impaired blood supply in the colon, which makes that organ vulnerable to ulceration.

CARDIOVASCULAR DISORDERS

In the United States 55 percent of all deaths are due to cardiovascular disorders, and probably half of these deaths result from essential hypertension (Lipowski, 1975). That is, one in four people dies from the effects of hypertension in one or another of the vital organs, usually the heart, brain, or kidney. We see that cardiovascular disorders are not unlike gastrointestinal disturbances in their etiology, but they present the gravest threat to life, more so than cancer. Moreover, heart conditions and hypertension account for 22 percent of the chronic disorders that cause restriction of activity, for example, work, housekeeping, or going to school (United States Department on Health Education and Welfare, 1968, p. S = 23). Our primary purpose here is to describe some distinctive features of cardiovascular disorders that bring up important new points.

To understand cardiovascular disorders let us begin, as before, with a brief synopsis of the system's normal function (Simeons, 1962, pp. 145-146). In a sudden emergency an immediate increase in arterial blood supply is required by the heart and body muscles, the brain, kidneys, and many other organs, but not the intestinal tract. To bring this about quickly the sympathetic division of the autonomic nervous system constricts the peripheral arteries through little muscles in the arterial walls. This increases blood pressure through the body just as squeezing on a hose increases the force of water from a lawn sprinkler. Meanwhile, the hormonal systems gradually increase the pace of the heart until the volume of blood pumped is adequate to the increased needs of the body's musculature. When that is accomplished, the peripheral arteries relax, lowering the pressure, because the volume of blood fed into the organs is sufficient for the exertions of fight or flight. This secondary relaxation of the arteries and the normalization of blood pressure causes the phenomenon called colloquially "second wind," the feeling of renewed strength and vigor after the initial exertion has apparently used up one's physical resources. But second wind can occur only if the additional blood supply is actually used in muscular effort. If not, blood pressure remains high; the autonomic system continues to react as if further preparation were still needed for fight or flight, prolonging the emergency constriction of arteries.

Essential Hypertension

The term "hypertension" does not refer to general tenseness but to the specific symptom of high blood pressure. Chronic elevation of blood pressure can result from various organic conditions. Hypertension is called "essential" only in those cases that prove to be free from organic disease initially. Hypertension can create unpleasant symptoms such as headache and dizziness; if prolonged, it may lead to fatal vascular accidents or cardiac failure. It can be effectively controlled medically with tranquilizing drugs or in severe cases by radical surgery that cuts the sympathetic fibers to the heart. This operation allows patients to lead a fairly normal life, but they have to observe certain restrictions in regard to effort; heart rate may not be much increased to meet extra demands.

Organic factors are often not the primary cause for essential hypertension. Constant vasoconstriction and acceleration of the heart result instead from an enduring state of emotional tension. The emotion of anger is obviously implicated, inasmuch as rage produces precisely this effect on the circulatory system. Therefore it is not surprising that many studies have found difficulties in the management of hostility and aggression among chronically hypertensive patients (Graham et al., 1962). Hypertensive people may be gentle in their outward manner but boiling inside with rage. This intense and chronic anger is usually strongly inhibited but not repressed. They may be well aware of their rebellious hostility, recognizing it clearly even though they control it. This can create a unique psychological impasse where they cannot express the hostility more openly or suppress it entirely. This curious midway position of hostile impulses, neither expressed nor repressed, seems to be a recurrent feature of essential hypertension. In itself there is nothing unique about a conflict between dependent submission and hostility. The conflict can be solved in various ways, such as avoiding situations that evoke submissive behavior, expressing the rebellion more openly, or submerging the hostility more deeply so that it manifests itself, if at all, in anxiety symptoms instead of a psychophysiological disorder. This particular constellation is especially distinctive in essential hypertension: a double blocking where the person submits but is never reconciled to submitting, feels furious but never discharges the fury.

Experimental evidence confirms the validity of this rationale (Hokanson & Shetler, 1961; Hokanson & Burgess, 1962). Normal subjects were angered deliberately by the experimenter while their blood pressures were being recorded. A control group was treated courteously. Later, half of each group was given an opportunity to administer electric shock to the experimenter. In the angry group, venting the anger in this way brought the blood pressure back to normal, but pressure remained high in that half of the angry subjects who had no chance to shock the experimenter.

Some occupations dispose people to hypertension more than others. Cobb and Rose (1973) found a higher incidence of hypertension in air traffic controllers—by a factor of four!—than among second class airmen who are exposed to much less stress. Those controllers working with high traffic densities showed more cases of hypertension, and at an earlier age, than those working with low traffic densities. Even such a seemingly innocent pastime as driving an automobile, which many of us do uneventfully every day, may contribute to high blood pressure. Little, Honour, and Sleight (1973) found short periods of raised arterial pressure while driving, related to such episodes as overtaking other cars. It is plausible to assume that stresses, work pressures, and interpersonal aggravations of these kinds cumulatively contribute to the chronic disorder of essential hypertension.

Constitutional Factors in Essential Hypertension

We have emphasized the role of emotional tension in causing essential hypertension, but there is strong evidence that an inherited predisposition for vascular and endocrine hyperreactivity can also contribute to the disorder (Miall & Oldham, 1963; Pickering, 1965). With marked vulnerability, little emotional stress is required to cause hypertension. In fact, Friedman and Iwai (1976) conducted an animal experiment that suggests psychic stress may produce hypertensive effects *only* in genetically predisposed individuals. When chronically exposed to an approach-avoidance conflict (food accompanied by

328

electric shock), rats genetically inbred for susceptibility to hypertension developed persistent high blood pressure, whereas rats inbred for genetic resistance to hypertension did not.

Hypertension usually develops in two stages. Keeping angers and conflicts from open expression may repeatedly provoke rises in blood pressure, but in the earlier phase this is brought back to normal by homeostatic mechanism. However, high blood pressure throws a strain on blood vessels, kidneys, and other organs, which may gradually produce changes in them that cause the pressure to be maintained at a high level for physiological reasons, even if the original emotional causes no longer operate. In this later phase of *chronic hypertension*, psychological intervention alone may not be sufficient to prevent the malignant effects of the disorder.

Lest we think that constitution tells all the story, we should keep in mind a study by Winklestein, who found elevated blood pressure in nonrelated persons living in the households of hypertensive patients (Schwab et al., 1970). This suggests an element of social contagion that underlines the significance of interpersonal factors in the etiology.

A Case of Essential Hypertension

Weiss and English (1957, pp. 246-249) report a case that illustrates dramatically many of the points discussed here. A 29-year-old truckdriver was treated for rather severe hypertension. His father suffered from valvular heart disease and his paternal grandfather died of a stroke after the age of 60. Both of these cardiovascular conditions point to the hereditary vulnerability of the young patient. His father had worked for the same firm and was killed in an accident, but the family was denied compensation. The patient was "burned up" about that. He wanted to get involved in union activities where he would have an opportunity to avenge his father. He had previously been denied this opportunity because it meant too much work and excitement. Given permission now, he became an organizer and worked hard for the union, six hours a day, in addition to his regular eight hours on the job. Still he actually improved during the two years he was engaged in union activities. His symptoms got better and his blood pressure was normal. Then the union broke up. Again he was "choked with rage" and his blood pressure went up. This continued until his death at 38 of malignant hypertension. His body was relieved of internal tension as long as the union provided an effective outlet for channeling his frustrated aggressive impulses. When he was deprived of that outlet, it is as if his body resumed the burden and quite prematurely succumbed.

Coronary Heart Disease

The most common malignant effect of chronic hypertension is coronary heart disease (CHD). In an extraordinary program of studies Rosenman, Friedman, and their associates in the Western Collaborative Group not only investigated the causes of CHD but predicted its occurrence with impressive success (Friedman, 1969; Friedman & Rosenman, 1974; Rosenman et al., 1975). In their initial studies they found that the people most prone to CHD have top levels of occupational responsibility, a family history of parental CHD, and a personal history of high blood pressure, but they were less likely than average to have had peptic ulcers. The two most distinctive features of CHD victims were a characteristic personality constellation that the investigators labeled *behavior pattern A* and high levels of lipids (fat) in the blood. The characteristics of behavior pattern A were: (1) intense, sustained drive for achievement, recognition, and advancement, (2) extraordinary mental and physical alertness, (3) busy involvement with diverse responsibilities and an acute sense of urgency about deadlines for completion, (4) competitive, aggressive, and hostile feelings toward others and toward the clock. Behavior pattern B showed the opposite characteristics. Far more people of the A type than the B type suffered from CHD, though fewer than one in five knew of their heart condition. Starting in 1960 the authors measured the overt behavior pattern, blood lipids, and other aspects of 3524 men, 39 to 59 years old, employed in ten California industries. About half were classified "blindly" as Type A individuals, and they had significantly more cholesterol, fatty acids, and neurochemical by-products of stress in the blood, especially during working hours, than those classified as Type B. They also found the Type A pattern in 62 percent of the sons of the prospective study subjects exhibiting that pattern (Bortner et al., 1970), which may be attributable to genetic transmission or modeling or both.

They were able to follow 3154 of the subjects who were well at initial examination in 1960 for a period of 8 to 9 years, in order to test how well various risk factors could predict the occurrence of heart disease (Rosenman et al., 1975). During the follow-up period 8 percent of them developed heart disease, twice as many from the 50 to 59 age range as from the 39 to 49 age range. They found eight factors significantly associated with CHD: parental history of CHD; reported diabetes in the subject; lack of education; smoking habits; Type A behavior pattern; blood pressure; blood levels of cholesterol, triglyceride, and lipids; and lack of exercise in the older group. Type A behavior was strongly related to the incidence of heart disease, even when its correlation with other risk factors was statistically discounted. For example, more than twice as many A types (2.1%) as B types (1.0%) died from heart disease. Of particular importance is the finding that nearly all the differences and relationships observed were substantially stronger among the older (50–59) men than among the younger (39–49) men. Insofar as this relates to personality type, this suggests that the Type A life-style of long standing has a more decisive effect on the risk of heart disease. There is also some evidence that Type A individuals have significantly higher life stress scores (Sheehan & Hackett, 1978).

330 Some controversy has permeated the literature on personality types in cardiovascular disorders. Mordkoff and Parsons (1968) reviewed the entire literature on coronary personality and found no consistent support for any particular personality configuration, nor for focal conflicts, conscious or unconscious, in CHD patients. Friedman et al. (1974) failed to confirm the Type A prediction of heart attacks, using a questionnaire procedure of limited relevance to Type A assessment. This is one of those rare instances, however, when we can say the critics are probably wrong. In addition to the compelling predictive results described above, Jenkins et al. (1977) demonstrated a strong association between the psychological typology and actual tissue changes in the blood vessels. Using angiographs, they measured the amount of atherosclerotic pathology (narrowing of the four principal coronary blood vessels) in the prospective study subjects. Arterial pathology was significantly correlated with two clusters of psychological variables: (1) Type A behavior pattern, and (2) sustained, intense, painful emotions such as anxiety, depression, and internal conflict. The men with the most severe atherosclerotic changes scored high on both clusters. They concluded that men who are most vulnerable to atherosclerosis are hard-driving, hard-working Type A individuals who put pressure on themselves to solve problems, meet deadlines, and move up the social ladder. At the same time these men are uncomfortable in interpersonal relationships and feel awkward and insecure when in groups. In an admittedly *post hoc* analysis, they speculate that such men obtain their rewards in life from seeking achievement instead of socializing with people. They also seem to have a low theshold for becoming tense or depressed. These conjectures are consistent with results from a follow-up study of heart attack victims (Hackett & Cassem, 1973), which found that mortality and morbidity were lower in groups who denied worry and were optimistic about their heart conditions. Sheehan and Hackett (1978) claim that antihypertensive medication remains the mainstay of treatment for heart disease; we have no reason to dispute that opinion, but the studies just reviewed indicate that there is also plenty of room for psychological interventions.

Migraine Headaches

Attacks of migraine headache occur periodically in some individuals, usually on one side of the head. Constriction of blood vessels in the brain produces symptoms that forewarn of an impending attack: dark spots in the visual field, tingling sensations on the skin, speech difficulty. The body then overcompensates with extreme dilation of the blood vessels, which causes intense pain, light sensitivity, and vomiting. Attacks may be followed by euphoric mood swings. A wide variety of personality profiles has been associated with the disorder, but no consistent typology has emerged. It is generally agreed that emotional stress may lead to an attack in vulnerable individuals. Medication to prevent the vascular dilation can often be effective in controlling the headaches if taken as soon as the preliminary symptoms appear. Biofeedback techniques have been used to abort the headaches by conditioning people to warm

331

their hands as a general means to achieve relaxation, though clinical relief may come about in such procedures directly from redistribution of blood flow from other parts of the body to the hands (Taub, 1977).

BRONCHIAL ASTHMA

The suggestion that asthma may in some cases be a psychophysiological disorder is often met with immediate opposition. Asthma is a chronic respiratory disorder in which psychological conflicts and emotional stresses play a prominent role in precipitating the symptom attacks. It is a mistake, however, to emphasize the psychological aspects of the disorder to the exclusion of the physiological aspects, because allergies and infections often lead to the first attack. Gold (1976) classifies 30 to 50 percent of all cases as *extrinsic* or *allergic asthma*, which usually begin before the age of 40 and are associated with sinus congestion or eczema and a strong family history of allergy. Food allergies are common and attacks are often seasonal. Antigens combine with antibodies in the blood, which leads to constriction of the bronchial passages and symptom attacks. *Intrinsic asthma* occurs primarily in middle-aged people, frequently following viral infection of the lung. It is less often associated with food or skin allergies. Attacks tend to be perennial, instead of seasonal, and may not respond to drugs. Death is more common in the intrinsic form. After the first signs of the disorder, either infectious, allergic, or psychological factors may predominate in initiating an attack in either form of the disorder.

When attacks are regularly associated with a certain emotion or a particular type of stressful situation, it is reasonable to assume a psychophysiological basis for the disorder, and it is clear that emotional factors can contribute to, or intensify, asthmatic attacks of primary allergic origin. McNichol and Williams (1973) found that 43 percent of a group of children aged 14, who had not more than five wheezing attacks overall (and thus would not be classified as asthmatic), reacted positively to at least one of six allergens on scratch testing, which suggests there is a very wide potential for the disorder. On the other hand, several studies show more emotional disturbance in asthmatic children and in their parents if allergic predisposition in the children is low (Kagan & Weiss, 1976).

Physiological Basis of Bronchial Asthma

The parasympathetic nervous system controls weeping and the respiratory defenses against airborne allergens. These responses include the secretion of tears by the eyes, the dilation of small blood vessels in the nose that causes nasal congestion, and the constriction of the bronchial passages in the lungs. The last response serves to restrict the amount of allergens inhaled but it also hinders breathing, especially exhaling, and in severe asthmatic attacks this hindrance approaches suffocation. These parasympathetic responses may be

332

activated reflexively by local irritation of bronchial tissue or by direct innerva-
tion from the hypothalamus. The latter is the mechanism by which emotional
states probably bring about asthma attacks. Various pollens, certain food proteins, and animal hairs cause the same result by the reflex mechanism in people who are allergic to them. In either case the asthmatic attack is characterized
by extreme breathing difficulty, choking, and wheezing. Many believe that
bronchial constriction is a conditioned physiological response that, once initiated by infection or natural allergic reaction, may subsequently be elicited
by psychosocial factors, as well as allergens and infectious agents.

Asthma tends to run in families in the extrinsic form although the majority,
with the intrinsic form, have essentially negative family histories (Purcell &
Weiss, 1970).

Prevalence and Course of the Disorder

Approximately one in twenty-five persons in the United States suffers from
bronchial asthma. A third of these are children and about half of the asthmatic adults developed the disorder as children (U.S. Department of Health, Education and Welfare, 1979). Twice as many boys are afflicted as girls, although
the sex ratio evens out during the adult years (Purcell & Weiss, 1970). Improvement is the rule: most asthmatic children improve considerably, usually
during or soon after adolescence. However, asthma can be a very serious condition. In this country it causes 4000 deaths annually, and it accounts for
twice as many of the chronic conditions that restrict necessary everyday activities as peptic ulcer. Asthma is estimated to be responsible for nearly a fourth
of the school days missed because of chronic illness in children (U.S. Department of Health, Education, and Welfare, 1968 and 1979).

Emotional Precipitation of Asthma Attacks

Early attention was focused on the extreme dependent attachment of psychoanalyzed asthmatics to their mothers (French & Alexander, 1941). Outwardly
they presented a wide variety of personality patterns, but the common feature
was a deep unconscious fear of being separated from the mother. In these
cases an asthmatic attack was interpreted as the equivalent of a repressed cry
for the lost mother. The physiological basis for such a connection is plausible
enough and other investigators have been struck with the dependent attachments of asthmatic individuals, but subsequent evidence has not confirmed
the hypothesis of a specific personality constellation or nuclear conflict, and
Purcell and Weiss (1970) have pointed out that either conscious or unconscious attempts to suppress weeping may be avoidance responses because crying in itself can provoke an attack.

Rather than speak of specific types of personality or interpersonal needs, it
is more accurate to say that asthmatic attacks can be precipitated or intensified
by emotional states, like anger, excitement with pleasurable feeling, anxiety

333

or worry, and depression. Various kinds of stress may give rise to these emotional states. The manner in which this happens will depend on the needs and personal experience of each individual; wide diversity must be expected. In one case, separation anxiety may be the common precipitant. In another, it may be fear of having an attack when the medicine has been left at home. In still another, it may be resentment against parental restrictions.

An experiment reported by Stein (1962) illustrates how the personal meanings an individual applies to a situation can provoke an asthmatic attack, even in the absence of allergenic irritants. A 32-year-old man with a history of asthma and severe eczema was locked in a small allergen-free chamber with a door about as thick as the usual bank vault. His initial remark was, "I'll be locked in a box and what will happen if you two suddenly collapsed and died?" The situation made him extremely apprehensive and led shortly to severe asthmatic symptoms. At the height of the attack he complained, "This is the worst I have felt in weeks." At this point an attempt was made to relieve the attack using suggestions and a nebulizer filled with saline.* When this placebo had no effect, the attack was promptly terminated by substituting the appropriate medicine for the saline.

A case reported by Metcalfe (1956) illustrates how a particular kind of social situation repeatedly provoked asthma attacks. A young single woman kept a detailed diary of her activities for 85 days, during which time she was a patient in a hospital but free to come and go as she pleased. She suffered asthma attacks on 15 days, about one each week. Metcalfe plotted the time relations between those attacks and the patient's contacts with her mother. None of the 15 attacks (60%) occurred within 24 hours of being with her mother, whereas only 14 of 70 (20%) asthma-free days were preceded by a visit with her mother. Looked at another way, asthma attacks followed about two contacts of every five (39%) with her mother although they occurred only once every ten days (10%) otherwise. The degree of association between the attacks and the visits was statistically highly significant. Moreover, further analysis showed that the attacks were substantially more likely to occur if the meeting took place at home rather than outside the home. Clearly the combination of meeting with her mother and being at home was the principal psychosocial impetus for the attacks. A study of the patient in depth would be required to ferret out precisely which psychodynamic aspects in that situation were stressful for her.

It has been observed that many asthmatic people have dreams and fantasies about water and drowning, and psychodynamic theorizing has been devoted to it. However, the simplest explanation is that such fantasies symbolize subjective impressions during the attacks, when they may feel as if they were drowning in their own bronchial secretions.

In response to experimental stress, asthmatics showed greater decrease in air passage conduction and slowed breathing; they also reported feeling less

334 *A nebulizer is a small oral inhalator that usually emits an epinephrine mist or other stimulant that relieves the bronchial constriction by way of the sympathetic nervous system.

anger in response to the provoking stress (Mathe & Knapp, 1971), which might suggest some suppression of emotional expression. In another study (Luparello et al., 1970) asthmatics showed less increase in airway resistance if led to believe that the chemical inhaled was a "dilator" than if it was called a "constrictor," showing that respiratory functioning can be altered by suggestion.

The Role of the Family

Minuchin et al. (1975) offer a conceptual model for the role of the family in bronchial asthma. Certain types of family organization are closely related to the development and maintenance of psychophysiological symptoms in children, and the symptoms play a role in maintaining family homeostasis. For example, some family conflict may induce emotional arousal in the child, triggering physiological response. Normally, arousal and symptoms would subside as the child's physiological functioning returned to normal levels, but this natural recovery may be handicapped by the nature of family members' involvement with each other around the conflict. In other words, family interaction patterns may trigger the onset or hamper the subsidence of psychophysiological processes, or both. Families in which this occurs are typically deeply enmeshed in one another's lives, overprotective of children, rigid, and resistant to conflict resolution. In such circumstances, the child's illness may be used as a mode of communication within the family, and as a tool for conflict avoidance.

Example. A mother was unable to express her rage that her husband refused to protect her from his mother's attacks. The asthmatic son was highly involved as the mother's protector, and he could state her complaints. He urged his father to protect her from her mother-in-law. The father tried to persuade his son to reject the mother's "childish" demands, but the wheezing boy maintained his adult stance. This is cited as an example of *parent–child coalition*. If emotional arousal contributes to the boy's asthmatic condition, symptom relief would depend at least partly on resolving the conflict between the parents.

Separation of severely ill asthmatic children from their families results in marked improvement of the condition for about half the children, which underlines the significance of the role that the family can play in initiating or maintaining the disorder. For this reason it has been facetiously observed that "parentectomy" may be a beneficial operation for asthmatic children.

Lest we be too harsh in our depiction of the parents of asthmatic children, let us keep in mind that they must bear an enormous realistic burden throughout the child's development, and this can take its toll. David (1977) found a high frequency of clinical depression in the mothers of severely asthmatic children, which the author attributes primarily to the mother's concern over the health of the child. Clearly there is mutual interaction between the illness and family relations.

335

Treatment of Bronchial Asthma

In treating asthma one must keep in mind that allergens and emotional factors can *both* contribute to an attack, regardless of which is the primary causative agent. For this reason an investigation of the causes in Metcalfe's case should not overlook the possibility that the mother may keep a favorite flower in her home to which the patient is sensitive. Obviously, where allergens are involved prevention may be possible through insight and avoidance of the irritants or through injections to increase the body's tolerance. Symptomatic relief may be obtained with antihistamines in mild attacks, regardless of the cause. More severe attacks may require epinephrine or another medication by oral inhalation or injection. A few extreme cases can only be treated by intensive hospital care.

Both medical and psychological methods have been used with some effectiveness to treat the psychological causes of the disorder (Purcell & Weiss, 1970). Biofeedback and tranquilizers can facilitate relaxation and inhibit extreme emotional reactions to stress. Counseling, psychoanalysis, and family therapy usually seek some insight into the complex interpersonal transactions that habitually trigger the attacks and attempt to remedy them with appropriate role changes. Behavior therapy has attempted to desensitize patients to the psychological and social stimuli that cause anxiety or excitement, on the assumption that diminished responsivity will alleviate the severity of the attacks. Although no single type of personality disturbance is characteristic of all asthmatic patients, disturbance of some kind is the rule (Knapp & Nemetz, 1960). Appropriate psychological treatments aimed at correcting those disturbances can reasonably be expected to alleviate the respiratory symptoms as well.

CONCEPTIONS ABOUT ETIOLOGY

Having examined several varieties of psychophysiological disorder, we are in a position to consider various conceptions about the causes of disorder and the placement of the symptoms. The issues here are similar to those we considered in anxiety disorders, with the chain of events extending into the domain of the autonomic nervous system and of bodily physiology. Probably nowhere in the field of mental health is holistic theory more necessary than here, for in the human organism mind and body interact continuously, oblivious of the possibility that they might be separated through the intellectual machinations of scientists and therapists. It is just as reductionistic to consider this field the study of "the psychological causation of physical illness" as it is to attribute these disorders solely to germs or allergens (Lipowski, 1977). The earlier work in this field centered, as we saw, around two relatively simple hypotheses. The first invoked constitutional differences: a disorder would appear in the weakest or most vulnerable organ system. On the other hand, the specificity hypothesis held that each variety of psychophysiological disorder was associated with a specific emotional constellation that affected the autonomic system in a particular way. Both hypotheses tended to polarize thinking about the causes of disorder. More recent research has clarified a great deal, especially about the physiological mechanisms that mediate between psychological processes and physiological disruptions. Now we know that neither model can stand alone in sovereign form. Human lives just aren't that simple.

The Specificity Hypothesis

Take first the specificity hypothesis. Certain connections of a quite general nature have been confirmed by several different researchers, but the attempt to correlate highly specific emotional constellations with particular disorders has had only mixed success. There is some support for the view that suppressed anger or hostility is a common emotional problem in essential hypertension, dependency in peptic ulcer and bronchial asthma, guilt in ulcerative colitis, and Type A behavior in heart disease. These general associations, however, do not go far toward explaining the location of symptoms. As we include more kinds of disorder we run out of broad emotional constellations to distinguish them. Anxiety, dependence, passivity, guilt, anger, and aggression recur with monotonous frequency. The explanatory power of these general associations is further weakened by such contrary evidence as that hostile feelings as well as dependent ones can activate the digestive processes that lead to ulcers. The ambiguous status of the specificity hypothesis is not surprising, because that approach "causally linked variables of very different levels of abstraction, e.g., conflict and peptic ulcer, without due regard to the intervening psycho-physiological mechanisms. Validation . . . proved predictably difficult" (Lipowski, 1977, p. 235).

While the early formulations of the specificity hypothesis have not been confirmed, a reduced version of it has been somewhat widely accepted. For each individual the kinds of stress, emotion, and autonomic response are reasonably regular, and the pattern of association among them can usually be understood by careful study of the personal meanings attached to them. These personal meanings and their autonomic associations seem to originate quite early in life and are extremely diverse across individuals. Thus, unless there is some built-in connection, as between anger and elevated blood pressure, no universal association can be assumed between emotional constellation and physiological disorder. The connection is an individual matter determined by experience and personal meaning.

Constitutional Vulnerability

The constitutional hypothesis has fared much better; indeed it has been strengthened in recent years. The relation between physique and type of disorder is ambiguous, at best; however, a limited but reliable hereditary predisposition has been found in studies of twins and family pedigrees for peptic ulcer (Weiner, 1977), essential hypertension (Hermann et al., 1976; Shapiro,

337

1973), bronchial asthma (Knapp, 1975; Weiner, 1977), and ulcerative colitis (Kirsner, 1971). Various experimental studies bear on the question of individual differences in the patterns of autonomic response. Of particular relevance is a report by Lacey and Van Lehn (1952), who studied a group of normal children at the Fels Institute. Each child was given the cold pressor test, in which a lively autonomic response is evoked by immersing the hand for one minute in painfully cold water. Autonomic activity was measured in several ways, including blood pressure, heart rate, and perspiration. It was found that the children exhibited characteristic individual profiles of autonomic reaction, and that these profiles could be reproduced through a later administration of the test. There seems to be, in other words, a hierarchy of autonomic responses that is stably characteristic of each individual so that it can be referred to as an "autonomic constitution." With one child the response to stress may be most conspicuous in heart rate, with another in peripheral blood pressure, with another in perspiration, and so on (Lipton, Steinschneider, & Richmond, 1960; Thomas et al., 1960). Research with adult psychological patients does not supply such telling evidence of early individual differences, but it yields results of the same kind. Cardiovascular patients, for example, respond to laboratory stress situations with predominant cardiovascular changes and little change in muscular tension, whereas patients complaining of head and neck pains react to the very same stress with marked muscular tension and little change in the cardiovascular system (Malmo, Shagass, & Davis, 1950; Schachter, 1957).

There is no reason to doubt the existence of individual differences in the pattern of autonomic responses under stress, and there is no reason why we should hesitate to believe that some of them are innately determined. Constitution, however, does not operate in a vacuum. Almost at once it manifests itself in the child's behavior and affects the responses of others to the child. A greedy or fussy or passive infant obviously will elicit distinctive patterns of response from the mother. Constitution, in short, exerts substantial effect on the transactions that take place between the child and the early human environment.

A Synthesis

Both lines of our inquiry have arrived at the same point. On the one hand, we have been forced back from adult emotional constellations to the childhood conditioning of autonomic patterns; on the other, we have been forced forward from innate differences to the effect these differences may have on conditioning autonomic patterns in the child's early environment. In either case the conclusion is the same: stress responses and visceral response patterns are shaped and individualized in early life experience (Reiser, 1975a). Initially, the human infant is a mass of undifferentiated responses under stress. Differentiation of autonomic patterns soon starts, however, and may have advanced a long way before the child emerges from a preverbal life of feeling into more organized psychological patterns. Sometimes early infections or enzyme deficiencies begin the process of accentuating some and suppressing other parts of the autonomic repertory. This process is in any event strongly influenced by the atmosphere of the nursery, the circumstances of feeding, the manner in which training is carried out, the use of diets, laxatives, enemas, and special medications, in fact by anything that tends to subdue some functions and overload others. The result of all this early conditioning can be observed in many ways, but the adult anxiety response furnishes a particularly good example. Each individual has a particular way of feeling anxious, no matter what the nature of the threat. With some people there are sinking abdominal sensations, with others shortness of breath, with others diarrhea, with others vomiting, with others palpitations, and so on through hundreds of variations. The general protective reaction has become individualized through conditioning in childhood.

Assume that every individual inherits certain constitutional vulnerabilities and develops a characteristic physiological response style early in life. What else needs to be considered to account for psychophysiological disorder? The most recent advances in the field instruct us about the importance of *precipitating stresses*, which may be as general as "being under pressure at the office" or as specific as inhaling an allergenic pollen, and of *coping strategies*, which encompass the entire psychological history of the individual.

The telephone, the cigarette, and the clutter in his office tell the story of this executive's tense work.

339

Symbolic activity influences organismic processes at all other levels of organization down to the cellular level. It has been found that stress and the suppression of emotion may even increase the susceptibility to cancer in animals exposed to carcinogenic viruses (Riley, 1975) and in humans (Abse et al., 1974; Greer & Morriss, 1975). Social situations and events obviously are the most significant source of symbolic information, which the individual appraises and endows with subjective meaning. Such thinking is a condition for arousing emotions that in turn activate physiological, cognitive, and behavioral responses (Lipowski, 1977). Conflicts and frustrated strivings may disturb one's psychological equilibrium and impose adaptive demands on the person. Such *psychosocial stress* does not necessarily cause illness: its effect on health depends on the person's coping capacity, social support, and other factors. Bereavement, loss of job, disturbed family interaction, specific work conditions, and sensory overloads are examples of psychosocial stressors. If the precipitating stress implies threat, loss, or personal insignificance for the individual, negative emotions (fear, anxiety, grief, depression, guilt, or shame) are liable to be evoked. These emotions play a crucial role in activating one of three defensive reactions: fight, flight, or immobility (Engel & Schmale, 1972). If the stress persists and overwhelms the person's coping capacity, then psychophysiological disorder may result.

Obviously, a stimulus or life situation can evoke a stress reaction by psychological means only if it is *interpreted* by the person as harmful or threatening (Lazarus, 1977). Potential harm can be minimized through coping processes, which include all the psychological defenses and adaptive strategies we considered in the earlier chapters. There is a growing conviction among experts in the field today that good ego strength and the ability to express basic drives adaptively are characteristics that increase "host" resistance to a wide variety of illness (Katz et al., 1970).

Psychophysiological disorders do not end with the initial onset of symptoms. Many important psychological changes follow. The perception of the disorder and its meaning become increasingly elaborated in the person's self-image and incorporated into ongoing mental life, especially if conflict is involved (Reiser, 1975a). Symbolically powerful ideas become associated with distressing symptoms and enmeshed in the person's social relations and intrapsychic life as well. This lends heavy meaning to the disorder, its signs and symptoms, sometimes creating the impression that the disorder originated as a symbolic conversion reaction. One is liable to fall into this conceptual trap by interpreting the specificity hypothesis too literally. Today's asthmatic attack does not mean that the person is in conflict precisely over the issue of acting on an impulse or confessing it to mother. That may once have been a vital issue, to which bronchial constriction became a conditioned part of the stress reaction, so that now any prolonged reaction to stress is likely to culminate in asthmatic symptoms. Specific emotional constellations may have existed in childhood at the time when autonomic patterns were being differentiated and conditioned. Present problems *may be* very similar to the original ones, but they *do not have to be* to produce the symptoms. All that is needed is prolonged stress. The historically conditioned autonomic patterns will do the rest.

Implications For Treatment

It is not surprising, in view of this, that rather modest therapeutic results have been reported for most psychodynamically oriented treatment methods (Kellner, 1975). The alteration of childhood autonomic patterns cannot really be expected. They are something with which the person must learn to live. Marked benefit can result from freeing blocked impulses like the hypertensive's simmering anger; furthermore, the person can learn to perceive threats in a more circumspect, discriminating way that makes them less threatening. It is probably through such peripheral changes that the reported successes in psychotherapy actually come about. On the other hand, promising initial results have been reported for limited physiological improvements in illnesses as diverse as cardiovascular disorders, anorexia nervosa, and bronchial asthma by means of relaxation training (Stone & DeLeo, 1976; Alexander, Miklich, & Hershkoff, 1972), operant conditioning (Van Buskirk, 1977) and biofeedback conditioning (Goldman, Kleinman, & Snow, 1975; Vachon & Rich, 1976).

IMPLICATIONS FOR GENERAL MEDICINE

Psychophysiological research raises far-reaching problems and carries radical implications regarding the general practice of medicine. The fact that at least a third of the medical cases seen in general practice are based on emotional maladjustment gives new meaning to the old ideal of a sound mind in a sound body. Originally the implication of this phrase was that you could not have a sound mind unless you had a sound body. Now we may wonder whether it is possible to have a sound body without a sound mind — or, as we would be more likely to say — without first attaining sound adaptation.

It is foolish to exaggerate the psychological aspects of any disorder. A diagnosis of essential hypertension should not be made without first making thorough tests for kidney, vascular, and other possible organic disorders. Neither should psychotherapy be recommended for asthma willy-nilly without making skin tests or other diagnostic tests for allergies. When we speak of psychophysiological disorders, we should not lose sight of the fact that the human spirit resides in a human body.

The general practitioner of medicine is at present neither well trained nor well situated to practice psychological treatment. Patients do not usually expect their physician to advise in other than strictly bodily matters and might well resent anything that resembled meddling in their "private affairs." These expectations may change slowly, especially as public awareness of psychophys-

341

iological disorders increases, and the doctor must always respect those expectations. Furthermore, the training of physicians does not generally include sufficient background in psychology to warrant their treating problems of emotional adjustment. More harm than good may be done by the physician who, having excelled in chemistry and learned to regard a patient as a complex piece of machinery, leans back in a swivel chair and tells the piece of machinery how to lead its life. Psychological treatment is a difficult profession that calls for practiced skill. Some educators believe, however, that it is both possible and necessary to train the general physician along this line, and some new programs are doing that. It is important to recognize emotional complications and show the patient that bodily processes can be closely related to emotions. Active efforts should be mounted to prevent the patient from sinking into a routine of invalidism and medication—especially in this era of self-medication and drugs on demand—if there is a chance the emotional adjustment can improve. The physician must be trained in psychophysiological diagnosis, and know when and how to refer a patient for psychological treatment, just as for any other kind of specialized treatment. In order to fully understand a patient's bodily economy, some acquaintance with spiritual economy is also necessary. The physician of the future will be forced more and more to take account of our emotional nature.

SUGGESTIONS FOR FURTHER READING

Part Two in the fourth volume of the *American Handbook of Psychiatry* (Reiser, 1975b) contains 16 authoritative chapters on psychosomatic medicine, which are full of medical jargon but decipherable and extremely comprehensive. A stimulating, brief summary of knowledge in this field from a psychological perspective is the chapter by M. Treisman in P. London & D. Rosenhan's *Foundations of Abnormal Psychology* (1968). A more contemporary review from a medical viewpoint is available in the readable chapter by D. V. Sheehan and T. P. Hackett in A. M. Nicholi's *The Harvard Guide to Modern Psychiatry* (1978). The book by A. T. W. Simeons, *Man's Presumptuous Brain* (1962) is a fascinating little essay written for lay readers. It is beautifully and audaciously written, full of sound medical insights (and a few unsound ones) that are palatably interpreted. If you must choose only one book to read and you can do it without scientific documentation—this has none—pick this one and enjoy yourself.

More serious readers will appreciate H. Weiner's *Psychobiology and Human Disease* (1977), an exhaustive, rather opinionated, technical review of the principal psychophysiological disorders. Almost all the relevant research is included, though it is not entirely current in all areas covered. Useful compendia are J. H. Nodine and J. H. Moyer's *Psychosomatic Medicine* (1962) and C. G. Costello's *Symptoms of Psychopathology* (1970). O. Hill's book, *Modern Trends in Psychosomatic Medicine* (1976), is the third in a series of collections by authoritative experts on a wide variety of topics, essentially representing British and European viewpoints.

E. Gellhorn and G. N. Loufbourrow's *Emotions and Emotional Disorders* (1963) gives thorough treatment of the physiological basis of emotional disorders. L. V. DiCara's *Limbic and Autonomic Nervous Systems Research* (1974) offers a collection of contributed chapters for advanced students and investigative specialists about recent research in an area that has seen spectacular growth in the last decade. The edited volume by A. Monat and R. S. Lazarus, *Stress and Coping: An Anthology* (1977), surveys research on stress, with a unique emphasis on cognitive aspects of coping with it. A more specialized collection that focuses specifically on life change research is E. K. E. Gunderson and R. H. Rahe, *Life Stress and Illness* (1974). A similar volume with a wider focus and more general appeal is B. S. Dohrenwend & B. P. Dohrenwend, *Stressful Life Events: Their Nature and Effects* (1974). F. Alexander, T. M. French, & G. H. Pollack provide a spirited defense—with empirical data at last!—of the specificity theory of psychophysiological disorders in *Psychosomatic Specificity: Experimental Study and Results* (1968). D. T. Graham's chapter in N. S. Greenfield & R. A. Sternbach's *Handbook of Psychophysiology* (1972) also takes a modern position that supports specificity theory.

The book by M. M. Eisenberg, *Ulcers* (1978), is a popular essay by a practicing clinician (with too little time to give scientific references) that tells everything you ever wanted to know about ulcers. An important monograph on heart disorders is M. Friedman's first report of the Western Collaborative Study, *Pathogenesis of Coronary Heart Disease* (1969), and a more recent summary is available in M. Friedman & H. Rosenman, *Type A Behavior and Your Heart* (1974). An interesting array of cases is brought together by H. H. W. Miles, S. Cobb & H. C. Shands in *Case Histories in Psychosomatic Medicine* (1952). An excellent, concise review of the field from a historical perspective is contained in the article by Z. J. Lipowski in the *American Journal of Psychiatry* (1977).

343

Playground by Paul Cadmus. Courtesy of the Midtown Galleries.
Photo by Geoffrey Clements.

10
Crime, Delinquency, and Conduct Disorders

The psychological origins of disordered personal behavior were discovered in the course of treating anxious and depressed patients. Disturbing emotions and their psychological treatment, to which we have devoted the last four chapters, can thus be regarded as the classical themes in modern dynamic psychology. From them we have learned to look for causes of disordered behavior in such realms as attitudes learned in the family circle, critical problems in childhood emotional development, the personal meaning of events, objective stressful circumstances, and above all the effects of anxiety and the defensive operations used to hold it in check. The illumination provided by this way of thinking is not confined to anxiety disorders and psychophysiological disturbances. In this chapter, and the next two we extend our survey to several more varieties of disordered behavior in which psychological factors play a significant part.

Anxious or depressed people typically conform in outward ways to social expectations, taking out their inner conflicts and frustrations upon themselves in the form of symptoms, suffering, fatigue, and chronic dissatisfaction. In contrast, the people to be studied here can be described as *acting out* some part of their problems at the expense of others, violating codes and conventions for personal gain, and sometimes doing harm to their victims. Conscience in people with anxiety disorders or psychophysiological disorders is usually strong and quite effective in suppressing unsocialized impulses. For this reason psychological treatment puts such emphasis on the expression of imprisoned feelings. In this chapter we deal with people in whom conscience either is feeble or can be circumvented to permit leakage of antisocial conduct at certain points.

Delinquency and criminal behavior are defined by society and the law instead of by psychology and medicine. A young person is designated delinquent, an older person criminal, when his or her behavior violates the rules and standards of society. The child who runs away from home, the truant from school, the gang member who breaks windows and steals from fruit stands, the professional thief, the racketeer, the embezzler, and the first-degree murderer all qualify for membership in the social outgroup we consider in this chapter. It is obvious that we are not dealing here with a single type of disorder. We can assume in advance that among the people classed as delinquent or criminal there will be many varieties of personality and many kinds of contributing cause. Our problem is to consider the numerous ways in which a person comes into opposition to the standards of society. Delinquent and criminal behavior bear a significant relation to surrounding social and economic conditions. The whole problem forms a chapter in social pathology as well as a chapter in abnormal psychology.

CRIME IN THE STREETS

"If New York has 31 times as many armed robberies as London, if Philadelphia has 44 times as many criminal homicides as Vienna, if Chicago has more burglaries than all of Japan, if Los Angeles has more drug addiction than the whole of Western Europe, then we must concentrate on the social and economic ills of New York, Philadelphia, Chicago, Los Angeles, and America" (National Advisory Commission on Criminal Justice Standards and Goals, 1973, p. 352). In a single breath that stark statement both diagnoses a significant social problem in our society and recommends some solutions. Few social issues concern Americans more than the threat of physical violence or loss of personal property in the streets or in their homes. In the last 20 years it has been an important issue in political campaigns. The matter touches the deepest feelings of safety and security in all of us, so we all have a stake in understanding it.

Especially in large cities, where crime rates are high, many citizens deal with their fears of physical violence or loss of personal property by barricading their doors. To some of us the extra precautions may seem extreme, but the threat is very real.

Street crimes are usually classified according to the *Uniform Crime Reports* published each year by the U.S. Department of Justice, which include among *violent crimes against persons* murder, forcible rape, robbery (armed or unarmed), and aggravated assault, and among *property crimes* burglary, larceny-theft, and motor vehicle theft. Property crimes are much more common, accounting for 90 percent of the 10,935,800 Crime Index offenses reported for 1977 (U.S. Department of Justice, 1978). That publication includes a clock obviously intended to cause alarm by depicting that, on the average, a property crime occurs once every three seconds in this country and a violent crime against a person occurs once every 31 seconds. Using police arrests as an indicator, men committed 78 percent of the property crimes and 90 percent of the violent crimes in 1977. Except for forcible rape, by far most of those crimes were directed against men, though some cross-cultural studies imply that the proportion of crimes against women may increase as they become more involved in professional, business, and other activities outside the home. The perpetrators of street crimes come predominantly from lower social class backgrounds; two-thirds of major violent crimes are committed by blacks against blacks or hispanics against hispanics (Curtis, 1974) and many of the assailants

347

and the victims live in lower-class conditions. These statistics reflect the despair within lower-class and minority communities in this country where social institutions that should be supportive are in a state of great disrepair. Alcohol is found to be associated with the majority of crimes of violence, in both the assailant and the victim (Goldstein, 1975). This is a distinctive and dangerous feature of alcohol, as relatively few drugs are known to foster violent behavior directly.

It is not very reassuring to know that only 21 percent of the Index crimes reported in 1977 were *cleared*, that is, solved by arrest. A higher proportion of crimes against persons are cleared than crimes against property—for example, 75 percent of murders—because crimes against persons usually involve acquaintances and there are often witnesses available who can identify the perpetrators. This underscores the importance of citizen responsibility for crime detection. On the other hand, an arrest, once made, usually leads to conviction: 80 percent of the adults arrested in 1977 were prosecuted and 76 percent of those prosecuted were convicted as charged or for a lesser crime (U.S. Department of Justice, 1978).

The Difference Between an Assault and a Homicide Is a Gun

Perhaps nowhere is the complicity of the affluent classes in abetting crime more apparent than in the case of gun-control legislation. More than half of all murders are committed with handguns—not rifles or shotguns or other sporting weapons—so repeated attempts have been made to require through legislation the licensing of handguns. These attempts have consistently been effectively thwarted by the National Rifle Association, which represents about a million members and $2 billion a year in commercial trade. The effectiveness of their political efforts is indicated by the familiarity of their key lobbying slogans: (1) "Gun control is unconstitutional"; (2) "Guns don't kill people—people do"; and (3) "When guns are outlawed only outlaws will have guns." Despite public polls showing that 71 percent of our citizens feel no one should own a gun without a police permit (McCaghy, 1976), our national congress has repeatedly failed to enact such legislation.

Forcible Rape

In recent years feminists have drawn great public attention to the problem of rape for obvious reasons. It is degrading for a man to force himself sexually on an unwilling person, of either sex. Women are the victims in 99 percent of the cases reported (U.S. Department of Justice, 1978). Physical violence is sometimes involved, and victims are occasionaly coerced to engage in demeaning and revolting sexual practices. Tragically, many victims have been subjected to further insult and debasement by unsympathetic police officers when reporting the crime. Feminist leaders have been successful in bringing about legislative and judicial reforms, as well as raising public consciousness, to protect women from potential rapists and rape victims from further humiliation after the crime.

A study of 646 forcible rapes in Philadelphia (Amir, 1971) belied some popular myths about rape, and contributed unfortunately to at least one of them. The following lists the popular myths, followed by the factual results of the study:

1. Black men commonly rape white women; in fact, 77 percent of the rapes studied involved black men and black women.
2. Rape is a hot-season crime (the "thermal law of delinquency"); in fact, the Philadelphia rapes were spread evenly over all seasons and months of the year. Nationally, rapes do peak during the summer months, so there is some truth to the myth.
3. Rape usually occurs among total strangers; in fact, more than a third involved close neighbors and acquaintances, and others had had previous encounters.
4. Rape is associated with drinking; in fact, alcohol was absent from the rape situation in two-thirds of the cases.
5. Rape victims are innocent persons; in fact, 20 percent had police records, especially for sexual misconduct, and another 20 percent had "shady" reputations. This knowledge and experience has probably led to some prejudice against rape victims among police personnel.
6. Rape is predominantly an explosive act; in fact, three out of four rapes were planned events, especially when it took place in the residence of the victim or offender, or when the rape was a group event.
7. Rape takes place in dead-end streets or dark alleys; in fact, there was a significant association between the place of initial acquaintance and the place of the rape.
8. Rape is always a violent crime involving physical brutality; in fact, 87 percent required only temptation and verbal coercion initially to subdue the victim.
9. Women usually resist rape; in fact, over half did not resist their attackers in any way.
10. Rape is a one-to-one forced sexual relationship; in fact, 43 percent involved two or more assailants. Indeed, 26 percent were group rapes, usually involving teenagers.

PROFESSIONAL CRIME

Crime in the Suites

Exhaustive classification of criminals is not possible because half to three-quarters of all crimes are never reported, but if it *were* possible, almost everyone would be included. A national survey found that 91 percent of the sample interviewed had committed violations for which they might have received jail or prison sentences (*The Challenge of Crime in a Free Society*, 1968). It is almost equally impractical to document precisely the extent of the most common form of crime in our society: white collar crime. This includes embezzlement, fee-splitting, illegal financial manipulations, tax evasion, price-rigging, bribery, patent infringements, false and misleading advertising, unfair labor practices, bankruptcy fraud, corrupt business practices, consumer fraud, illegal competition, and the most intricate form of modern crime: computer embezzlement from banks. McCaghy (1976) describes a panorama of corporate swindles that boggle the imagination: stealing dress designs, selling faulty burglar alarms, price-fixing, monopolistic price-warring, fraudulent warranty sales, falsified product testing, air, water, and food pollution, misleading advertising, evasion of employee safety regulations, fraudulent manipulation of pension benefits, and collateral frauds for corporate financing. Most of these crimes are never exposed; they get lost or covered up in the complications and convolutions of business procedures. Few of those convicted for these crimes ever go to jail.

Politicians and government employees directly misappropriate public funds, pad payrolls, illegally employ relatives, take kickbacks, grant favors to business (e.g., through commissions on public contracts), issue fraudulent licenses, and underestimate tax evaluations. These practices increase with economic and industrial advancement among nations (Clinard & Abbott, 1977). At the present time, *several* members currently serving in the United States Congress stand convicted of such crimes. Though crimes in the streets are committed primarily by people from the lower social classes in our society, crimes in the suites belong mainly to the higher echelons. Opportunity seems to be greater among people in advantaged positions.

Too little heed is paid to white collar crimes because most of them do not present a direct, recognizable threat to personal safety, and the victims are usually collective society instead of specifiable individuals or groups. Consider the following example, showing the collusion of both big business and big government (Sampson, 1973). The International Telephone and Telegraph Corporation (ITT) is a huge multinational conglomerate that grew by business acquisitions from the 52nd largest American corporation in 1959 to the ninth largest in 1976. It has over 300 subsidiaries and more than 700 subsidiaries of subsidiaries. ITT attempted to acquire the Hartford Fire Insurance Company in 1969, with the intention of drawing on its cash reserves to support other operations. A suit was filed by an assistant attorney general on antitrust grounds: it would give ITT too much monopolistic power. The Watergate exposé revealed that, while litigation over this matter proceeded in the courts, top ITT officials met repeatedly with top administration officials, including the Vice President and the Attorney General, seeking a way to sidetrack the government action. During the course of these negotiations the company pledged $400,000 to the Republican national convention. Nine days later, it was ruled in court that ITT could keep the Hartford Company.

"You have a pretty good case, Mr. Pitkin. How much justice can you afford?"

Drawing by Handelsman; © 1973
The New Yorker Magazine, Inc.

Sutherland (1961) has shown that corporate crime is pervasive. He investigated 70 of our largest corporations and found that *every one of them* had been found guilty by a court or regulatory commission for violation of anti-trust, false advertising, patent, copyright, or labor laws. The average number of violations was 14. Probably the most celebrated example of corporate crime is the conspiracy of 29 electrical equipment companies to fix prices illegally, which resulted in prison sentences for seven high ranking executives in such corporations as General Electric and Westinghouse (Herling, 1962). The offenders in this case were quite aware that their activities violated the law, and they took elaborate precautions to prevent detection. All of these men were affluent and otherwise law-abiding and scrupulous; their criminal behavior cannot be explained by poverty, defective socialization, or personal pathology. Basing his analysis on the study of embezzlers, Cressey (1970) argues that white collar criminals must rationalize their behavior in such a way that a violation of trust or law does not appear *wrong*. It may even be construed as appropriate, under the circumstances. In the testimony of the electric company executives a typical justification was that price fixing is commonly accepted practice.

The Cost of White Collar Crime. It is likely that the cost of white collar crime is substantially greater than the economic cost of "ordinary" crime (Winslow, 1968). For example, the yearly cost of embezzlement and pilferage exceeds by several billion dollars the losses sustained throughout the nation from burglary and robbery. Fraud is a major cause for closing about five banks each year. More than 30 percent of all business failures each year result from employee dishonesty. The annual bill for all purchases in one state dropped 40 percent following exposure and prosecution of business executives and government officials for bribery and kickbacks. As shown in Table 10-1, *excluding* the cost of price-fixing illegalities, industrial espionage, and soci-

Table 10-1   The Annual Cost of Some White Collar Crimes (Millions of Dollars)

$ 80		Bankruptcy fraud
3,000		Bribery, kickbacks, and payoffs
100		Computer-related crime
21,000		Consumer fraud, illegal competition, and deceptive practices
	5,500	Consumer victims
	3,500	Business victims
	12,000	Government revenue loss
1,100		Credit card and check fraud
	100	Credit card
	1,000	Check
7,000		Embezzlement and pilferage
	3,000	Embezzlement (cash, goods, services)
	4,000	Pilferage
2,000		Insurance fraud
	1,500	Insurer victims
	500	Policyholder victims
3,500		Receiving stolen property
4,000		Securities thefts and frauds
$41,780		TOTAL (millions)

Source: Adapted from *A Handbook on White Collar Crime* Washington: U.S. Chamber of Commerce, 1974).

ety's efforts to combat such crime, the total annual cost of white collar crime is no less than $40 billion, or almost 3 percent of our Gross National Product (U.S. Chamber of Commerce, 1974).

And Then There Was Watergate. The scandal first broke in June 1972 with the discovery of illegal electronic eavesdropping and a break-in of the Democratic National Committee headquarters in the Watergate Hotel in Washington, D.C. Those arrested in the break-in were discovered to be hired by a fund-raising organization for President Nixon, the Committee for the Re-election of the President. During the next two years the scandal grew as evidence emerged of illegal actions by presidential aides and Cabinet officers. The investigations revealed that high-level individuals in the administration had obstructed justice by such means as paying hush money to the Watergate burglars, wiretapping many telephones on absurd national security pretexts, pressuring the Internal Revenue Service to harass political "enemies" with income tax audits, instigating other burglaries to obtain evidence against American radicals, and using "dirty tricks" to disrupt and discredit Democratic candidates. Still other charges emerged from the Watergate investigations: Presidential misuse of public funds, the President's support of a lobby's political interest in exchange for a $2 million campaign contribution, and fraudulent preparation of the President's income tax returns. Finally, it was disclosed that the President was personally involved in the cover-up of the Watergate case. The full dimensions of the corruption in the Nixon administration may never be known, but the extent of it is at least signified by the kinds of persons who either admitted illegal activity or were convicted of such activity: the Acting Director of the FBI, the Secretary of the Treasury, two Attorney Generals, the Secretary of Commerce, the White House Chief of Staff, the chief domestic advisor to the President, plus numerous special counsels and aides to the President. In little more than half of a single presidential term of office all those officers resigned or were imprisoned, Vice President Spiro Agnew resigned in disgrace following disclosures that he took bribes and evaded taxes, and ultimately President Richard Nixon resigned in order to avoid impeachment. In a final irony, the new President, Gerald Ford, pardoned the ex-President to spare the nation further turmoil, so that Nixon was never prosecuted for his crimes. Never in the history of the United States have so many of the most politically powerful been implicated in such a wide web of corruption and abuse of power (McCaghy, 1976).

A good many people who almost as a matter of course commit crimes in the business world behave entirely differently in private life. They may adhere to firm standards of kindness and consideration at home and private life; they may be exemplary members of the community, giving time and money to valuable enterprises. They seem to be governed by two inconsistent value systems, one for home and one for business. So sharp is the separation that a father will see nothing incongruous in scolding his son for a self-serving lie and conferring

353

next day with his advertising manager on how best to fool the public about the company's product. This paradox finds its explanation in the nature of our economic system. In theory, the provision of economic wants operates under a larger historic moral code that includes consideration of the interests of others. But in fact the so-called free enterprise system makes a virtue of competition. It offers egoistic prizes of profits and power to those who compete ruthlessly and learn to work the system to their own advantage. Business is business, we often hear: if you do not bribe foreign potentates their order for weapons goes to your rival, and you are a failure. Being of service is the basic justification for business activity, but being successful, rich, and powerful can too easily be achieved by manipulating the system without much regard for service.

Obviously, white collar crime is extremely difficult to detect or prevent, and some might argue that it is not worth the effort and cost to do so. However, in one sense it is the most threatening of all forms of crime because of its corrosive effect on the moral standards of our society. Fraudulent business practices, blatant income tax evasion, and political corruption promote cynicism toward society and disrespect for the law. Effective control of white collar crime would necessitate substantial restriction of what is now felt to be personal liberty, a price we are reluctant to pay.

Organized Crime

Organized crime refers mainly to a vast business empire called the Mafia, the Syndicate, or La Cosa Nostra, which controls illegal gambling, loan sharking, and narcotics. Most of its income derives from gambling, which grosses between $9 billion and $20 billion a year, all of course tax-free (*The Challenge of Crime in a Free Society*, 1968). The Mafia is, in fact, a federation of coordinated racketeer "families" whose criminal activities are governed by a council of about a dozen overseers. Some of their "business dealings" utilize strong-arm tactics and blatantly illegitimate methods: extortion, terrorism, monopolization, bribery, fraud, and the like. For example, between 1919 and 1967 there were more than a thousand gang murders in Chicago alone (Mulvihill & Tumin, 1969). However, the core of their activity consists of covertly supplying illegal goods and services, which is enormously profitable because there is a huge market for them despite the laws against them. Much of their profits are in turn invested in legitimate business enterprises with which the Mafiosi identify themselves publicly. The leaders own grocery stores, bars, restaurants, automobile agencies, race tracks, and are highly placed in the garment industry, the coin-operated machine industry, the olive oil and cheese business, construction, trucking, and many others.

The motivation for organized crime bears some similarity to that for white collar crime. Racketeers consider themselves as businessmen who take advantage of lucrative opportunities for profit, and they probably feel justified in their criminal activities much as do corporate executives who conspire to rig retail prices. However, the Mafia is in most respects a deviant subculture like the street gangs we discuss next, with a distinctive organizational structure and an explicit code of conduct and values at odds with those of society at large. The principal elements of that code, originally formulated in 1892, are familiar to most of us who have been tutored by Mario Puzo and Marlon Brando:

1. Reciprocal aid in case of any need whatever
2. Absolute obedience to the chief
3. An offense received by one of the members to be considered an offense against all and avenged at any cost
4. No appeal to the state's authorities for justice
5. No revelation of the names of members or any secrets of the organization (Ianni, 1972).

The code has been so successful and the "business" so profitable that it is easy to see how people in some segments of society are recruited and assimilated in that subculture. Thus we are dealing here with a group that is socialized to an alien system of moral standards. The economic advantages and social solidarity of the subculture are powerful inducements to adhere to its moral code, so "treatment" consists mostly of enforcing the law, and rehabilitation is, understandably, extremely difficult.

In case you think the Mafia is defunct, consider the execution of Carmine Galante in July 1979 (*Time*, 1979). Galante spent almost half his life behind bars, starting at ten when he was sent to reform school as an incorrigible delinquent. He worked his way up through the ranks of the organization, specializing primarily in drug trafficking, pornography, loan sharking, and labor rackets. He was considered a ruthless gangster who would "shoot you in church during High Mass." After the death of Carlo Gambino in 1976, Galante was considered the top candidate to succeed him as *boss of bosses*, but he failed to unite the other leaders behind his candidacy because he pushed for greater involvement in the drug rackets, especially heroin and cocaine, despite the heavy legal penalties associated with them. Early in 1979, at the age of 69, Galante asked the Mafia's governing commission for permission to retire after putting his affairs in order, which was approved. But within a short time the commission discovered that he had secretly built up a force of 30 "greenies," hardened young recruits from Sicily. Suspecting that Galante was about to double-cross them, the commission met again in early July and decided that he should be retired more permanently. A few days later, as Galante was eating lunch in a Brooklyn restaurant, a car drew up outside and five men wearing ski masks rushed into the restaurant. Six feet from the table, they opened fire with shotguns and semi-automatic rifles, killing Galante with shots in the left eye and chest, killing his bodyguard and another associate who owned the restaurant, and wounding the owner's 17-year-old son. No, the Mafia is not defunct.

JUVENILE DELINQUENCY

If you ask average citizens what forms of crime they are most concerned about, they would list first the violent crimes against persons. Next would come crimes against property, which are by far the most common, the popular image in the communications media notwithstanding (Ohlin, 1971). Of least concern are the so-called "victimless" crimes like drunkenness, disorderly conduct, gambling, prostitution, and vagrancy, which are by far the most common crimes committed, but present little threat to personal safety or the social order. Our interest here focuses primarily on the first two kinds of criminal behavior, which share the psychological distinction of bringing direct, and usually deliberate, harm to the welfare of others. Most of these crimes are committed by juveniles or young adults.

"Studies made of the careers of adult offenders regularly show the importance of juvenile delinquency as a forerunner of adult crime" (*The Challenge of Crime in a Free Society*, 1968, p. 152). The earlier a juvenile is arrested or brought to court for an offense, the more likely he or she is to carry on criminal activity in adult life. And the more serious the first offense is, the greater likelihood of committing serious crimes later. Therefore an understanding of criminal behavior must begin with the study of juvenile delinquency. Three personality types found by Jenkins (1966) in delinquent children and guidance clinic referrals are prominent. *Socialized* or *subcultural* delinquents are typically characterized by association with bad companions, gang activities, cooperative stealing, habitual truancy from school and home, and staying out late at night. *Overanxious* youngsters are mostly shy, apathetic, sensitive, and submissive, but lack the impulsive and aggressive tendencies of other delinquents. *Unsocialized aggressive* delinquents start fights, are assaultive, cruel, defiant of authority, maliciously mischievous, and have inadequate guilt feelings. Probably many of the last group would be diagnosed in adulthood as *sociopaths*.

Cultural Deviance

Behavior that is called delinquent sometimes results from an entirely normal process of psychological development. If a boy is brought up in a clan of pirates, he will develop a superego that tells him never to work for something when it is possible to steal it. Identifying with his father, he will build an ego-ideal of bigger and better piracy. In such a case the process of socialization is accepted. The person is called a criminal by the major society, but within the minor society of pirates he is simply growing up to be a solid and respected citizen. Before concluding that a given case of delinquency represents a failure to accept prescribed standards of conduct, it is necessary to ascertain what standards of conduct prevail in the family and in the immediate neighborhood. Merrill (1947) reported the case of the three Maguire brothers who during late childhood and early adolescence ran up a collective total of twenty-four court appearances. The mother was always in court to defend them, and the father saw no objection to their eking out the slender family income derived from his business as a peddler. The Maguires were a well-knit, affectionate family, free from conflicts and emotional disorders, handicapped only by somewhat limited intelligence that made it difficult to earn a living. Every social agency knows cases of this kind in which the whole family pattern is one of delinquency.

In such cases the boy is not delinquent from that segment of society which is closest to him. He is better described as a *cultural deviant*: a product of a particular subculture that sanctions activities considered antisocial or inadequate by the larger society. He may be a loyal and conforming member of his subculture, identified with others, capable of feeling guilt if he violates their standards, free from guilt when he acts in sanctioned opposition to the alien larger society. The situation can be dramatized by an item from a case history: a mother expected her children to provide food for the family by stealing it from neighboring vegetable gardens and roadside stands, and the children were punished if they returned from their missions empty-handed. There may be nothing capricious about the discipline or vague about the standards in a deviant subculture. It is only to the larger society that the cultural deviant presents a problem.

Deprivation and Social Disorganization

Most street crime is committed in the slums of large cities, where predominantly minority groups reside, schools are inferior, and social disorganization is extreme. People move constantly. The neighbors of today are gone tomorrow, and their place is very likely taken by a family of different national origin and different language. Diverse cultural standards flourish side by side with little interaction and little community solidarity. Under these circumstances it is difficult for parents to maintain control over their children, even though the majority try to do so. The parents have to work single-handedly without reinforcement from the neighbors. In a stable community each family is known and each child is known in the neighborhood. Reputations have to be maintained, and behavior is governed by neighbors and acquaintances as well as by members of the family. This extended reinforcement of standards is lacking in a disorganized area. In its place are the street corner gangs and the opportunity to become an apprentice in an adult criminal group.

Prison populations reflect the same factors. The majority are young, single men who are poor, undereducated, and come from disorganized families. They typically have had limited access to educational and occupational opportunities (*The Challenge of Crime in a Free Society*, 1968). Often the first step in the rehabilitation of criminals is to teach them how to read and write. Naturally, being reared in circumstances of extreme relative deprivation breeds envy and hostility toward the privileged people who enjoy easy access to the desirable rewards of affluent life. For an uneducated slum hoodlum, mugging a rich banker in Central Park represents not only a unique economic gain but

357

also a small retribution for being frustrated and deprived of those same rewards for no understandable reason.

Immaturity

Many criminal actions are simply immature solutions to difficulties in life. As can be seen in Table 10-2, police arrests indicate that the majority of all crimes covered by the FBI Crime Index are committed under 30 years of age, and the frequency of arrests declines steadily with age. This is consistent with the interpretation that with increasing maturity criminals abandon the life of crime and, presumably, find alternative ways to achieve their goals legitimately. As a counter-argument one might reason that criminals improve their techniques so they elude capture more effectively as they get older, or that fewer crimes are committed by older criminals because most of them are incarcerated, but neither of these arguments is borne out by the study of criminal careers.

Further evidence for the hypothesis of immaturity is the fact that more than half of all homicides, aggravated assaults, and forcible rapes are committed against family members and personal acquaintances (U.S. Department of Justice, 1978). Domestic disputes account for as much as half of a patrol officer's calls in a high crime area, many involving violence (Remington, 1971). Crimes that occur in these circumstances are seldom deliberately planned, but erupt impulsively in the heat of anger or sudden temptation. To illustrate, during a lovers' quarrel a man hit his mistress and threw a can of kerosene at her. She retaliated by throwing the liquid on him, and then tossed a lighted match in his direction, causing his death (Mulvihill & Tumin, 1969). A significant proportion of murder victims contribute substantially to their own deaths in similar ways, and often the precipitating issue in the dispute is a trivial matter. Such crimes occur less frequently as domestic life becomes more stabilized, or alternatively as resignation and acquiescence increase. Auto theft and forcible rape occur less frequently as the adventurousness and passions of youth dwindle and legitimate access to cars and sexual partners improves. Crimes against property probably diminish with age because perpetrating them is both strenuous and hazardous. And we may even hope that some criminals give up the life of crime because they get caught or "see the light" and find better ways to achieve their goals in life.

Table 10-2   Frequency of Arrests for Street Crimes by Age

	Total Arrests by Age					
	10–19	20–29	30–39	40–49	50–59	Over 59
Percentage of distribution	35.3%	33.9%	14.1%	8.9%	5.5%	2.3%

Source: Uniform Crime Report for the United States—1977 (U.S. Department of Justice, 1978).

A formal diagnostic system has been developed that classifies juvenile offenders according to interpersonal maturity, with seven levels from lowest to highest (Sullivan, Grant, & Grant, 1957; Miller, 1972). Youths at the lowest levels are considered the least psychologically mature, by which is meant that they have no feeling of control over their destiny, are cognitively simple and concrete, have no internalized values or standards, are impulsive and cannot delay gratification, and are "time-bound" to the present, with little appreciation for future or past events. Youths at higher levels have achieved varying degrees of progress toward maturity in these respects. Treatment at youth correctional institutions is calibrated to each youth's particular level of maturity, with specific procedures designed to help every one acquire the psychological skills that are needed and can be learned.

Failure to Internalize Parental Standards

Socialization can be regarded as the outcome of a bargain that is struck between parents and child. The child's part of the bargain is to give up the privileges and unrestraint of a small child in favor of the responsibilities of a larger one. The parents' part of the bargain is to set models of considerate and socialized behavior and to make it worth the child's while, in the coin of affection and praise, to undertake the required sacrifices. The parents, who are in the position to manage the bargain, must steer a middle course and maintain a workable balance. The demands they make must be neither too small nor too great in proportion to the rewards they give. Conversely, the rewards they give must be neither too small nor too great in proportion to the demands they make.

One pattern is for the parents to make no demands and set no standards. The child is simply "spoiled," allowed to do everything it pleases with no loss of rewards. This provides no motive to take the uphill road toward socialization. The child expects everything to come easily, as its just due, and it is easy to slip over into the attitude that anything is there for the taking. This kind of training produces indifference, perhaps mild contempt, toward the restraints and ideals of society. Often enough, however, the result is merely a passive, dependent, irresponsible attitude instead of a career of crime. Indulgent overprotection may, but probably does not regularly, predispose to enduring delinquency.

A contrasting pattern is that where demands are made but rewards of love are more or less completely withheld. The parents are severe and unloving; they require that socialization take place, but they give the child no praise or affection for success, only punishments for failure. The child's sacrifices are thus made unpleasant, and nothing is offered to cancel the resentment that is felt in submitting to such a bargain. As a result the child submits to it less and less and eventually becomes an avowed rebel against the constraints of society. The outcome is not only indifference to social standards; it is active hostility toward them.

359

In the 1930s, the Cambridge-Somerville Youth Study was launched to determine some of the causes of juvenile delinquency and what could be done to prevent it. Extensive material, including the family background, was gathered on more than 500 boys who were believed to have a high risk for delinquency. Years later, when it was known which boys had actually become delinquent, the family backgrounds of the delinquent and nondelinquent groups were compared (McCord, McCord, & Zola, 1959). One of the most important influences proved to be the cohesiveness of the family and the consistency of discipline. Much higher rates of subsequent delinquency were associated with families described as quarrelsome, neglectful, and lax in discipline. Particularly conducive to a criminal career was a regime of punitive but erratic discipline; whereas consistent discipline, even when severe, led to better socialization. With respect to parental behavior the investigators found that love on the part of the mothers, even when they were anxiously overprotective, and warmth and a relative passivity on the part of the fathers were associated with fewer delinquent outcomes. When fathers were cruel, neglectful, or absent, and when mothers were cruel, neglectful, or passively helpless, the rates of ultimate delinquency were high.

In a study of aggressive adolescent boys by Bandura and Walters (1959), the findings are related more closely to theory. Serious delinquency turns not only on failure to absorb parental standards but on an active, hostile opposition to them. This opposition depends on the possibility of hating the parents, at least the one most closely associated with standards. If the child clings to a hope of getting love from the parents, his hostility will be repressed and emotional disturbance may result. Bandura and Walters therefore attach importance to the vicissitudes of dependence and to the hostility growing out of shortages and deprivations of love. Once the scales are tipped toward hostility, the boy embarks on a course characterized by active aggression and self-sufficiency. When established, this course tends to be self-perpetuating: dependence is feared, signs of love and esteem are mistrusted, and friendly relations are thwarted by a quick display of aggression. One of the findings of Bandura and Walters was that aggressive adolescents fared less well with everyone, even with their contemporaries, than did the control group. The investigation also showed the importance of relations between fathers and sons. "The fathers of aggressive boys were typically hostile to, and rejecting of, their sons, expressed little warmth for them, and had spent little time in affectionate interaction with them during the boys' childhood" (p. 354). Antisocial aggression was especially likely to be the outcome when the mothers, instead of mitigating this state of affairs, added to it by discouraging dependence and perhaps subtly rewarding the steps toward self-sufficiency.

It is clear that the causes of delinquency are numerous and that their influence is often reciprocal. A secure relation with the mother can counterbalance a hostile one with the father, but if the security is insufficient the two relations may become a joint influence toward delinquency. Erratic punitive discipline and a disorganized neighborhood may combine to produce a result that neither would often produce by itself.

Membership in Delinquent Groups

In an earlier chapter we studied the importance of group memberships in the development of personality. We saw that in early adolescence group membership rose to a peak of importance in the individual's life, taking over to a considerable extent the functions of emotional support previously concentrated in the family. Many delinquents are unhappy at home. Long before puberty they welcome and need whatever support and recognition can be obtained from group memberships. The group may early become the boy's or girl's only home in an emotional sense. Groups outside the home generally mean more in the lives of delinquents than they do in the lives of other children (Cohen, 1955).

Of itself, however, this fact does not explain the superior attraction of *delinquent* groups over those that stay out of conflict with law and order. Even in an area that suffers from maximum social disorganization there is a choice of groups. The peculiar attraction of the delinquent group arises from the exciting and lawless character of its activities. Delinquent groups are often in a state of crisis. The excitement is highly advantageous to one who wants to drown the memory of a distressing home life. Even more important is the lawlessness. The individual who needs support in rebelling against parental standards finds this support in good measure in a group that rebels against all of society's standards.

Walter Miller has studied street gangs intensively for many years and he considers them a stable part of urban lower-class life that complements the family in socializing the adolescent, albeit sometimes in unfortunate directions (1970, 1977). Most street gangs engage in some form of illegal activity, but this activity does not comprise more than a minor portion of the gang's total range of customary activities, which include: playing, talking, flirting, gambling, spectator sports, fighting, dancing, listening to music, love-making, drinking, drug use, property destruction, and various forms of theft and vandalism. The ages of adolescent street gangs usually range from 10 to 23 for boys and from 10 to 18 for girls. Through participation in a gang a youngster acquires vital knowledge of lower-class culture, training in individual competence, the uses and abuses of authority, the reasonable limits of law-violating behavior, and the skills of interpersonal relations. In contrast to the extreme disorganization of the neighborhood and family, the gang may be the most reliable and rewarding form of human association. Since gangs are oriented primarily around recreation and crime, their leaders are usually selected for their athletic prowess, crime skills, and fighting ability. One leader, for example,

361

Many of the socializing functions of the family are taken over by street gangs in urban lower-classes. Some of their activities are criminal, but most are oriented toward recreation and socializing with peers.

had especially wide authority because he was a hard drinker, an able street fighter, a skilled football strategist and team leader, an accomplished dancer and smooth ladies' man, and one of the most criminal of the older gang members, being among the relatively few who had "done time." Since criminal activity is a prime source of prestige, aspiring leaders step up their criminal involvement in order to assume or solidify their leadership positions. This is dangerous, of course, because it increases the risk of apprehension. The social structure of the gang is quite flexible, however, and when a leader gets caught, other standy-by leaders are ready to take his place.

There is an obvious hierarchy within the gang. Younger and less capable members have inferior status, while older, more experienced members serve as surrogate parents for their protégées, with the responsibility for showing them the ropes. Identification processes normally found within the family are transferred to the gang, so that the reputation of the gang and the gang leaders take on tremendous psychological significance. Most of the fabled gang fights result from some form of threat, real or imagined, to someone's reputation as a man (Short & Strodtbeck, 1965). And, of course, within the delinquent subculture successful crime is one of the principal symbols that adulthood has been achieved.

Emotional Disturbance

The subcultural delinquents discussed to this point may become *socially* deviant without necessarily being *psychologically* deviant. Some delinquents also have psychological conflicts that cause tension, guilt, remorse, depression, and discouragement (Peterson, Quay, & Tiffany, 1961). All these elements are illustrated in the case of Bert Whipley. He consciously chose delinquent companions when others were available, and he went joyriding in stolen cars because it was great fun. He found welcome esteem from older boys when he successfully stole some number plates for them. He greatly enjoyed the thrill of riding at high speed while a rain of police bullets spattered around the tires. Particularly important was the chance to defy, insult, and outwit the police. Joyriding in stolen cars is easier than might appear. Bert completed something like fifty such missions without being caught or hurt. It was a perfect means of demonstrating the powerlessness of all that his father espoused. However, combined with this audacious behavior was the paradoxical motive to seek punishment in order to alleviate an unconscious sense of guilt. Strictly speaking, it is a sign of emotional disturbance, showing that part of the parental standards had been fully internalized. Thus we can see that both the doing and undoing of Bert's antisocial behavior served distorted emotional needs.

Treatment of Juvenile Delinquency

As we have seen, juvenile delinquency is not a single syndrome. It is a way of behaving that is adopted by many different kinds of children for many different reasons. The prevention of juvenile deliquency is thus an operation on many fronts. The obstacles presented by deviant subcultures and delinquency areas do not belong strictly in the psychologist's province, yet it may be that little can be done to change the family atmospheres that contribute to delinquency until these central economic and social problems are brought nearer to solution. In the meantime, the attempt to bring favorable influences to bear on young people through social service and recreational agencies may show little outward result. This was the conclusion of the ten-year Cambridge–Somerville Youth Study, which found little difference in the incidence of delinquency between a group of boys given abundant services of this kind and a group given no special services (Powers & Witmer, 1951). The forces disposing toward delinquency seem to outweigh those that can be mustered in later childhood by social agencies.

The alternative to prevention is treatment, and our interest here is in the possibility of psychological treatment methods. In any attempt at treatment the therapist starts at a serious disadvantage. To the delinquent any mental health professional appears as an enemy, representing law and order and presumed to be trying to convert the client to the hated cause. Few delinquents come willingly for psychological treatment. The therapist has to convince them that it is worth their while. Recognizing the difficulty of engaging the individual in therapy, some programs of *guided group interaction* have been set up, which attempt to shape the attitudes and norms maintained by a group of delinquents, instead of the behavior and attitudes of any one of its members (Wheeler, Cottrell, & Romasco, 1967). It is reasoned that, since the normative support for delinquency comes from the peer group, it is necessary to change the values of the whole system by working directly with the group as a unit. In such programs group members have a stake in the fate of all other members because they participate with the staff in solving any problems that come up.

In an ingenious departure from the conventions of psychotherapy, Slack (1960) has shown that chronic delinquent boys who are unreachable because of their contempt for professional help can be brought into a kind of treatment by the expedient of hiring them for pay. They are engaged to assist the experimenter by telling their life stories to him and his tape recorder, and by taking a number of psychological tests. The subject need not perceive for some time that any personal benefit is intended. During this time he has a chance to contemplate his own life, to establish confidence in the therapist, and to find out what psychotherapy would be like. Confidence will be felt more readily if the boy finds in the therapist someone who can see things from his point of view and convey a sense of alliance, yet not be taken in by the bluff and big talk that is part of his usual stock in trade.

In a residential setting a behavior therapy program has been used with some success, by systematically rewarding cooperative and prosocial behaviors, while punishing (by withholding positive reinforcers) lying, stealing, and cheating (Burchard, 1967). In a similar effort Schwitzgebel (1967) found that positive rewards brought about desired changes in the behavior of his delinquents, whereas punishments did not.

SOCIOPATHIC PERSONALITY DISORDER

We turn now from the broader consideration of delinquency and criminal behavior to a problem more strictly psychological. It is evident that delinquents and criminals cannot be characterized in any simple way and that their difficulties with society have important roots in disordered social and economic conditions. The possibility remains, however, that *some* criminals suffer *primarily* from true psychological disorder which interferes with the process of socialization. While disturbed delinquents like Bert Whipley have secondary psychological conflicts, the psychopathology in these cases must be quite fundamental to explain their persistent and callous antisocial behavior.

A Problem in Psychiatric Classification

Psychopathic personality originated as a diagnostic concept with an English psychiatrist, Pritchard, who in 1835 described a "form of mental derangement" in which intellect seemed unimpaired but moral principles were "perverted or depraved," the "power of self-government" was lost or diminished, and the individual was incapable of "conducting himself with decency and propriety in the business of life" (p. 15). It was generally believed that they suffered from some hereditary weakness of the nervous system; hence the term *constitutional psychopathic inferiority* was commonly used. These two ideas—a defect in the realm of socialized behavior and an innate weakness lying behind it—have continued to dominate most thinking about sociopathic personality. It has proved impossible, however, to reach general agreement as to what should be included under this heading. Kraepelin distinguished seven subtypes: the Excitable, the Unstable, the Impulsive, the Eccentric, Liars and Swindlers, the Antisocial, and the Quarrelsome. Some current textbooks add sexual deviations to the list, and others include addiction to alcohol and drugs. Such liberality tends to defeat the purposes of psychological understanding.

More recent diagnostic formulations, offering various labels (*character disorder, sociopathic personality, psychopathic personality*), have consistently attempted to narrow the category and define it in more positive terms (Cleckley, 1964). Gunn and Robertson (1976) examined "psychopathic" prisoners, but could find no objective evidence of a cluster of traits that fit the classical diagnosis of *psychopath* or *sociopath*. We will use simple descriptive terminology, *sociopath*, while recognizing that this is also not very satisfactory. The people so diagnosed have developed in such a way that parental and social standards have never been internalized; they have failed to respond adequately to the process of socialization. Cleckley rules out those cases in which social standards are rejected only in respect to some one particular kind of behavior, such as alcoholism or deviant sexual behavior in a person otherwise adapted to social demands. He also rules out cases in which crime is adopted as a positive way of life—the subcultural criminals who are enemies of society but loyal and stable members of culturally deviant groups. Besides the disturbed delinquents, who have sometimes been referred to as *secondary psychopaths*, a group of criminals with primary personality disturbance remains. Let us emphasize that it is unclear whether there is a truly homogeneous group of such people, as Cleckley claimed, or merely a diverse group who share certain traits in common.

Some Descriptions of Personality Traits

Some sociopaths make an unusually pleasing impression in interviews: superficially charming, alert, well-informed, able to talk well. Intelligence in these individuals is good and does not deteriorate. Others may be rather taciturn and dull-witted. Nervousness, signs of anxiety, delusions, and irrational thinking are usually absent. One soon finds out that they are very unreliable, inclined to lie and deceive. They do not accept blame for their misconduct nor feel shame about it, but readily give a plausible excuse for everything that has oc-

365

curred. While able to reason satisfactorily, in some cases even brilliantly, they show very poor judgment about their behavior. They get into the same trouble over and over again, never learning from their experience. No life plan is followed consistently unless it is a plan to make life a failure. In their personal relations they are egocentric and incapable of real love or attachment. Strong, deep, and lasting feelings do not seem to exist. Although they may talk a great deal about feelings, they give the impression of merely using words without insight into the nature of real emotion. Cleckley has termed this tendency toward verbalizations devoid of emotional meaning *semantic dementia*. They know the words but not the music, so they are incapable of empathy or genuine concern for others (Johns & Quay, 1962). Understandably, their sex life is usually impersonal, superficial, and poorly integrated, presumably because they treat their partners as sexual objects instead of as genuine lovers. They manipulate and use other people for their own ends, yet often manage to persuade them through glib explanations of their sincerity and good intentions. Sociopaths are impulsive and unable to delay gratifying their needs, regardless of future consequences; although they may understand the advantages of postponing gratification in an intellectual way, future events—whether good or bad—have no emotional significance for them. Although they may *simulate* emotional reactions, they actually experience little anxiety or fear. Vanity is another common characteristic: an exaggerated concern with appearance, status, and reputation.

It is clear that we are dealing with a fairly serious disorder, with grave disturbances emotionally, in foresight, and in the control and organization of behavior. Cleckley considers the condition serious enough to be classed as a psychosis. Sociopaths may outwardly present a "convincing mask of sanity" and a mimicry of human life, but they have lost contact with the deeper emotional accompaniments of experience and with its purposiveness. To this extent they may be said to have an incomplete contact with reality, and it is certainly very hard to approach them and influence them therapeutically (Cleckley, 1964).

A Sample Case

A particularly good example is Dick Hickock, one of two men who slaughtered a family of four in a vain robbery attempt in their home (Capote, 1965). He was raised in a good home on a farm in Kansas. His parents were strict, religious, hard-working, and loving. The children were hardly ever allowed to leave the yard and visit with playmates. They were always "semi-poor," not well off but with the necessities and a few luxuries provided for, like most Kansas farm families during the Depression and war years. Dick was not a bad pupil in school, and could have done better than average if he had applied to his studies only a fraction of the effort he gave to sports. He was a star athlete in basketball, baseball, track, and football. Two colleges offered him football scholarships, and he wanted to go to college to become an engineer, but his family had no money to afford the other college expenses, so after graduating from high school he took a job as a railway trackman. Subsequently he worked periodically as an ambulance driver, car painter, and garage mechanic.

Through most of his childhood Dick was no trouble to anybody, a cheerful boy who got along well in school, was popular with his classmates and obedient to his parents. The first inkling of criminal tendencies came at 17, when he was arrested for breaking into a drugstore. The next year he suffered head injuries in an auto accident that left his handsome face slightly askew and, according to his father, changed his personality so he "just wasn't the same boy." Now he became sulky and restless, ran around with older men, drank and gambled. Not everyone agreed with his father's testimony, which after all was given at his son's murder trial, where evidence for brain damage might have swayed the jury to recommend a milder sentence. A neighbor claimed that Dick would "steal the weights off a dead man's eyes"; he would have gone to jail "more times than you can count, except nobody around here ever wanted to prosecute. Out of respect for his folks."

He was married and divorced twice, having three sons by his first wife, all in the short space of about six years. Both his wives were only 16 years old. Dick was a *pedophile* who delighted in seducing pubescent girls, which was at least a sign of immaturity on his part if not a bizarre feature of psychological disturbance. He got deeply into debt from gambling and imprudent living shortly after his first marriage at 19. Though he was working, he began stealing things and writing fraudulent checks. Eventually he served seventeen months in prison for stealing a neighbor's hunting rifle, and the experience soured him, making him feel the whole world was against him. When he returned home he was contrite, promising his father he would never do anything more to hurt him because he had been a "pretty good old dad" to Dick, and he seemed to mean it sincerely. But this mood did not last.

Even as a hardened criminal Dick was personable, clean-cut, and affable, "a fellow any man might trust to shave him." He was a likable extravert with a wonderful smile that really worked, "sane but not too bright" (though his I.Q. was tested at 130). He was fastidiously attentive to personal hygiene and the condition of his fingernails. His athletic body was covered with sexy, aggressive, and sentimental tattoos: bosomy nudes, dragons devouring human skulls, and bouquets dedicated to Mother and Dad. There was also a hard side of his personality. To Perry Smith, his partner in crime, Dick was authentically tough, pragmatic, invulnerable, "totally masculine." Less appealing were his lack of aesthetic appreciation and his callous insensitivity to the feeling of others. He felt no guilt about making empty promises of marriage to ensure the seduction of a teen-age Mexican girl, and it thrilled him to run over mongrel dogs on the highway. He was an expansive, dominant type who spent his money freely for vodka and women after a windfall from passing bad checks. Dick had a way with women and boasted conceitedly of his amorous conquests.

While in prison Dick learned from another inmate, Floyd Wells, of a prosperous farmer named Clutter who usually had about $10,000 in a wall safe,

367

Dick Hickock (right) was a smooth talking con artist who swore they would leave no witnesses. Notice the skew in his facial appearance, a residual effect of a boyhood accident. Perry Smith (left) was the softer person of the two, but also seriously disturbed. He actually executed the murder of the four helpless members of the Clutter family.

and an attractive 16-year-old daughter. Dick began to devise a "flawless" plan to steal that money and leave no witnesses, even if there should be a dozen people in the home that night. To this end he chose as his partner Perry Smith, a "cold blooded killer" who claimed to have beaten a "nigger" to death with a bicycle chain, just for the hell of it. (In fact, he had never killed anyone.) Incredible as it sounds, Dick seems to have reckoned that he would be less vulnerable to prosecution in the event of capture if Perry did the killing, but there would be no capture if, as he insisted over and over again, they left no witnesses. At the scene of the crime Dick was brutal and sadistic to the victims; he obviously gloried in having them tied up at his mercy. It was Perry who put pillows under their heads to make them comfortable and reassured them that everything would be all right, and it was Perry who prohibited Dick from raping the girl. Dick was angry that there proved to be no safe and no $10,000;

they found less than $50 altogether. Yet despite all his bluster and threats, Dick only held the flashlight while Perry slit Mr. Clutter's throat and finished off all four helpless victims with shotgun blasts to the head. (Perry had a seriously disordered personality diagnosed as "very nearly that of a paranoid schizophrenic.")

Much of Capote's book concerns the escapades of the pair after the killing: repeated sprees of check forgery in Kansas City and Florida; a brief sojourn living it up in Mexico; looking vainly for a motorist to rob, kill, and discard in the desert. It is hard to believe that a man as shrewd as Dick Hickock would think they could travel with impunity throughout the Southwest, even returning to his home territory to pass bad checks in Kansas City. He was planning to impersonate an Air Force officer, so he could pass "a bundle of confetti" (worthless checks) on the Strip at Las Vegas, when they were apprehended. Dick had concocted a fantastically convincing alibi for the night of the murder, which he delivered with disarming facility, but the two men were tried and convicted of first degree murder. They had taken precautions, but not enough, and they ultimately confessed to the crime. After more than five years of appeals, both men were hanged in 1965. In character to the end, Dick's last statement before the execution was: "I just want to say I hold no hard feelings. You people are sending me to a better world than this ever was." Then, as if to emphasize the point, he greeted with a handshake and a charming smile the four men who were mainly responsible for his capture and conviction.

Psychological Aspects of the Disorder

The most important clue about psychological factors in such cases appears to lie in the shallowness of feeling toward other people. The emotional blunting, the lack of affectional ties, the mimicry of love without evidence of real feeling all point to a possible disturbance in the child's early human relations. Parental rejection immediately comes to mind; but, as we have seen, this can also produce other kinds of emotional disturbance and delinquent outcomes. Anxiously disturbed people often crave human relations, the delinquent fights them, but sociopaths seem to be merely indifferent. We can hypothesize a very early injury to affectionate relations, a serious deficit of gratifying love and care, perhaps even in the earliest years. Lacking strong initial attachments, in growing up the child may learn to adapt shrewdly enough to the surrounding realities and may become socialized to the extent of presenting a pleasant front; but the real meaning in life is still the direct gratification of impulse, and this childlike value is not importantly tempered by close affectional ties or by a feeling of involvement in the human community.

The concept of parental rejection does not seem to fit the childhood situation in the case just described, although some emotional distance between the boy and his parents was implied. However, several investigators consider parental rejection a primary etiological factor (Jenkins, 1966; McCord & Mc-

Cord, 1964). It has been found repeatedly that sociopaths have more than their share of parental loss through death or separation (Oltman & Friedman, 1967; Robins, 1966). However, this is also common for drug addicts, alcoholics, schizophrenics, and many other forms of psychological disorder (Watt & Nicholi, 1979), so by itself it could not explain the sociopathic outcomes distinctively. Robins argues that broken homes do not *cause* sociopathic disorders, but instead reflect pathology in the parents, especially the father, which simultaneously contributes to sociopathic outcome in the child and marital discord between the parents.

How might the childrearing practices of the parents shape the traits characteristic of sociopaths? Clearly moral behavior is learned through experience with rewards and punishments administered, usually, by the parents. Typically, bad behavior is penalized immediately and directly because parents, like research psychologists, have learned that delayed or indirect punishments do not effectively produce resistance to subsequent temptation (Solomon, Turner, & Lessac, 1968). However, Maher points out that "sometimes the punishment may be forestalled or at least reduced in severity by suitable expressions of repentance and promises not to repeat the behavior" (1966, p. 216). In learning theory terms, the child who can consistently avoid punishment in this way learns verbal repentance behavior while losing any fear of punishment for forbidden acts. Consider our sample case in the light of this hypothesis. We were told that the Hickock parents were hard-working, conscientious and strict, yet loving. Capote's account makes clear that the father, the main disciplinarian, was also extremely loyal to his son and denied repeatedly any criminal intent in Dick's actions. If it were characteristic of Mr. Hickock to set stringent restrictions on Dick as a child but continually postpone punishments for violations when the boy gave evidence of repentance, he might well have molded a manipulative moral attitude and extinguished fear of punishment. It may seem a large leap from smooth-talking your father out of a spanking to getting away with murder, but with a lifetime of reinforcement behind it such developmental experience might be a significant determinant.

Vaillant (1975) argues that sociopaths are, in fact, anxious people with long histories of parental deprivation. Their immature defenses against human intimacy give the *appearance* that they are unfeeling, unmotivated to change, guiltless, and unable to learn from experience. He therefore recommends treatment oriented around close relationships, especially with groups, dealing firmly and objectively with their acting out, manipulative behavior and repulsive maneuvers.

Another possible source of antisocial behavior is modeling. As we saw in Chapter 5, modeling plays a major role in the acquisition of conscience. How often it has been demonstrated that children do as their parents *do* rather than as they *say* (Aronfreed, 1968; Bandura & Walters, 1959)! Antisocial tendencies may be acquired, in part, by imitating one's parents. Consistent with this is Robins' finding that many fathers of sociopathic offspring are themselves antisocial or impulsive. In the Hickock case, the evidence is insufficient, but it does not seem to point in this direction. On the other hand, Sutherland and Cressey (1977) emphasize that criminal behavior is often learned from other people, typically in groups, through communication, modeling, and the shaping of moral attitudes. After his automobile accident and departure from school, Dick Hickock apparently was exposed to such negative influences by consorting with older men with whom he drank and gambled. And of course he learned many of life's wrong lessons from well-qualified tutors during his terms in prison.

Still another possibility has to do with delay of gratification. Arieti (1967) hypothesizes that a child learns to postpone gratification through consistent training to expect substitute rewards at progressively longer intervals of time. In place of an immediate reward a mother may offer love and praise and a promise of a future bonus if the child can inhibit the impulse or postpone the pay-off. Thus promises and hopes of future gratification retain a flavor or echo of mother's approval and tenderness, secondarily reinforcing the postponement. Now if we assume that a child is reared in a broken home or has rejecting parents, forbearance may hold no such emotional compensations, which may give rise to a permanently childlike attitude toward impulse gratification. In the Hickock case we do not have the necessary information about the mother, though difficulty in delaying gratification was certainly prominent in the son's behavior.

Biological Aspects of the Disorder

During the second half of the nineteenth century there were repeated attempts to show that criminals were constitutionally inferior. This conception of the problem was a natural consequence of the "somatogenic hypothesis" that for a time completely dominated psychiatric thinking. Criminals behaved differently from other people, therefore something must be different about their constitutions or nervous systems. The results of these investigations are not particularly impressive. Although voices are still raised for constitutional inferiority, there is no compelling evidence for biological causes of sweeping magnitude.

Less easy to dismiss is the much more specific hypothesis that the particular disorder we are discussing here—sociopathic personality—is related to brain injury or brain inadequacy. Sometimes following a severe head injury, as happened with Dick Hickock, and sometimes following an attack of encephalitis (which is known to damage brain tissue), the behavior of a previously well-adjusted child will change in what might be called a delinquent direction. The child may become overactive and aggressive, have outbursts of emotion and irritation, and be unable to concentrate or to accept the restraints of the classroom. There seems to be some loss of regulatory control that previously characterized the child's behavior. Under such circumstances it is harder to tolerate the restraints of socialization. The control of impulse and temper, the

371

postponement of immediate satisfactions, the mere requirement to sit still at table or at school become suddenly more difficult than they were before. In view of these facts it is at least a legitimate hypothesis that some subtle inadequacy of cerebral function might contribute to the inability of sociopaths to be governed by the standards and restraints of society.

There is impressive consistency in a multitude of studies showing abnormal electrical activity in the brain, as measured by electroencephalogram (EEG), among 31 to 58 percent of all sociopaths (Arthurs & Cahoon, 1964). The abnormalities are mainly of two kinds. Most commonly reported is an exceptionally high frequency of very slow waves, which are characteristic of normal infants and young children but diminish with increasing age (Bay-Rakal, 1965). Within the sociopathic groups the slow-wave pattern has been found to be associated with aggressiveness, impulsiveness, poor motor coordination, developmental retardation, and inadequate socialization. The second type of abnormality is a positive spike in the EEG recordings, found in as many as 40 percent of highly impulsive and aggressive individuals (Hughes, 1965). This pattern appears mostly in cases with a history of overwhelming aggressive and destructive urges, often triggered by trivial provocations and resulting in severe damage to property and injury to others. These "attacks" are so violent and unrestrained as to suggest an epilepsy-like seizure, yet they often include actions requiring considerable skill and precision, and afterwards the person can discuss them with full awareness and no apparent feeling of guilt or anxiety.

An obvious hypothesis is that sociopathic behavior reflects cortical immaturity, especially in cases where slow waves are frequent. Many sociopathic traits are childlike: egocentricity, impulsiveness, inability to delay gratification. If the hypothesis of maturational retardation is correct, one might expect sociopathic behavior to decrease with age. Consistent with this is Robins' (1966) finding that a third of her sociopaths became less grossly antisocial with age, usually between the ages of 30 and 40, and the finding by Gibbens et al. (1968) that sociopaths with EEG abnormalities have a better prognosis than those with normal EEGs, presumably because of outgrowing their cortical immaturity. There are limitations, however, to the hypothesis. It does not explain how the EEG abnormalities come about. They might be acquired during childhood through infection or head injury; they might result from birth damage or injury during the fetal period; or they might be the product of hereditary influences. Furthermore, one should not exaggerate the parallels between childlike and sociopathic behavior, which may represent quite different processes. Finally, the hypothesis is a little shaken by the fact that 15 percent of the general population exhibit EEG abnormalities and do not become sociopathic. On the other hand, it is certainly plausible that cortical immaturity *contributes* in some way to sociopathic behavior; for example, it may explain the sociopath's alleged inferior capacity for conditioning, especially of fear responses, and the consequent undersocialization (Eysenck, 1964).

Another speculative formulation is summarized by Hare (1970). Many of the slow waves and positive spikes found in sociopaths' EEG records apparently emanate from the temporal lobes and the associated limbic system. Though poorly understood, the limbic system is believed to play a central role in sensory and memory processes and the central regulation of emotions. Specifically it has been implicated in the regulation of fear-motivated behavior, including learning to inhibit a response in order to avoid punishment (McCleary, 1966). Hare hypothesizes that the clinical observations of impulsivity and social insensitivity may be attributable to malfunction of inhibitory mechanisms in the limbic system.

Genetic Abnormalities. About one male in every 1000 births has an extra masculine sex chromosome, or XYY genotype. By contrast, a pooled estimate of 2 percent of the men in mental-penal institutions such as hospitals for the criminally insane have an extra Y chromosome (Hook, 1973). Nielsen and Christensen (1974) found that men with the double Y chromosome were taller than normal, had lower than average intelligence, were more often imprisoned for criminal behavior, and more often impaired in their reproductive capacity. Psychologically, they were *not* aggressive but had many difficulties at school, were mentally immature, more impulsive than their siblings, and had difficulty in making relationships with others. On the basis of the accumulated evidence, Hook (1973) concluded that the association between XYY genotype and incarceration is proven, but the extra sex chromosome hardly predicts antisocial behavior with confidence. Men with XXY chromosomal abnormality, born at a similar rate of one in 1000 births, are also over-represented among institutional populations, but they are more likely to be mentally retarded. The XXY condition is referred to as Klinefelter's syndrome. It is also not known to be associated with aggression.

Treatment

The treatment of sociopaths is anything but an inviting task. They seldom are motivated for psychotherapy because they see nothing wrong with their behavior. Most dynamic forms of therapy are ineffective because they presuppose a future orientation and substantial capacity for emotional relationship with the therapist, both of which are usually lacking. Under present laws governing commitment to mental hospitals, sociopathic patients cannot be kept long at an institution because they are not mentally deranged in the sense of intellectual confusion or disorientation. For the most part they move in and out of the portals of institutions as readily as they move in an out of jobs, spending a good part of their time at liberty where they are costly to society. Nevertheless there is promise in some therapeutic ventures such as that reported by the McCords (1964) for 15 sociopathic children at the Wiltwyck School in New York.

373

They attributed the effectiveness of the program to four factors: the rapport between children and counselors; the absence of punitive frustration; the subtle but powerful social control exerted not only by the adults but also by the boy leaders; and individual and group psychotherapy. There was, unfortunately, no control group against which to compare their improvement. Similar programs in Denmark and Holland have also had some success (Hare, 1970).

Authoritarian programs may be useful for institutional treatment. A British study compared the effectiveness of two treatment regimes, one essentially self-governing, with tolerant staff members and intensive group therapy, the other more authoritarian, with a sympathetic but firm type of discipline and only superficial individual counseling (Crafts, Stephenson, & Granger, 1964). After six to nine months of treatment, patients were permitted to take day jobs in the community, returning to the hospital each night. Neither group showed changes in personality or adjustment during the treatment, but the group treated under the authoritarian regime were convicted of significantly fewer offenses during the year after discharge. Thus work training in a friendly but disciplined residential setting may be more effective for treating sociopaths than the permissiveness that is usually recommended in the treatment of other psychological disorders.

Many criminals give up their antisocial behavior in middle adulthood, attributing the change to fear of further punishment or loyalty to their spouses (Robins, 1966). Instead of concentrating our efforts on extended hospitalization or psychotherapy, which have not proved very effective, Robins therefore recommends supporting the pressures toward conformity in the social environment and trying to prevent isolation from family, friends, or neighbors. They may be able to do what highly trained professionals can not: limit further antisocial activities.

Behavior therapy is normally used to reduce anxiety or remove symptoms, and therefore has seldom been employed for treating sociopaths. Hare (1970) offers the intriguing suggestion of using behavioral techniques for the opposite aim, namely, to increase fear and anxiety in order to augment their motivating influence. It is problematic what the response to such conditioning would be but it is an experiment worth trying.

SOCIETY'S RESPONSE TO CRIME

A basic dilemma has evolved in modern law over what response society should make to criminal behavior. In a cogent analysis of this dilemma Maher (1966) points out that selecting the right response has proven difficult because criminal punishment is intended by society to serve more than one purpose. On the one hand, punishment is considered a morally justified retribution for violating society's laws. This *revenge* motive is based on the premise that everyone is responsible for one's own behavior, so anyone who commits an offense against society *deserves* to suffer for it. This is a remnant of the old principle: "an eye for an eye, and a tooth for a tooth. . . ." On the other hand, punishment is intended by society to prevent the recurrence of crime either by directly detaining the criminal (incarceration) or by rehabilitation or by deterring future violations with the threat of stiff penalties. Holding to both of these objectives has caused society to work at cross purposes with itself. The revenge motive calls for penalties against previous actions, with the severity of the penalties graduated, understandably, according to the seriousness of the crime. The prevention motive, however, calls for penalties gauged to probable future actions, which obviously requires assessment of the psychological motivation for the crime and may be quite unrelated to its magnitude.

Judges, lawyers, legislators, and clinicians have striven conscientiously to reconcile this melange of purposes so as to serve best the interests of society and still protect the rights of the offender. The effort has had only modest success. The McNaghten Rules provided the guidelines for many years to judge whether an offender was morally responsible for alleged criminal actions, and hence subject to full retribution for the crime. When a plea of insanity is entered, the question whether the defendant committed the crime is not contested; only whether punishment is deserved for it. Traditionally, insanity has been ground for exoneration, when based either on the McNaghten Rules or on the ground that the crime was motivated by a pathological irresistible impulse. In practice, of course, the legal decision about responsibility has become simply a decision about treatment, with different dispositions reserved for those who are responsible and those who are not. A psychiatrist or psychologist asked to testify about a defendant's responsibility is really being asked: "What should we do with this person?" Much confusion and probably some injustice has arisen at this point in the judicial process because the courts have tried to satisfy simultaneously the public demand for retribution and the often contrary dictates of rehabilitation.

The dilemma is probably best illustrated in the case of murder. By far the most murders are committed by usually law-abiding citizens in the heat of ex-

---

THE McNAGHTEN RULES

In 1843 Daniel McNaghten murdered a government clerk whom he mistook to be Sir Robert Peel, the Home Secretary for the British government. McNaghten said he was instructed to commit the murder "by the voice of God," and was acquitted by reason of insanity. A committee of judges was convened to recommend general criteria for "legal insanity." They concluded that a defendant is legally insane who labored under such defect of reason from disease of the mind as not to know the nature and quality of the act allegedly committed, or if the person *did* know it, that he or she did not know it was wrong to do it.

treme provocation against friends or relatives. At almost any other time they would not desire or be inclined to carry out the act, and once it has been done they typically feel great guilt and remorse over it. Follow-up of such murderers, once released after serving their sentences, shows that they seldom repeat the crime. Current laws call for severe penalties for murder because of the magnitude of the crime: death or imprisonment for life or a very long term. This serves mainly the purposes of retribution and deterrence. If the law were designed, however, to serve *only* the purposes of rehabilitation and the prevention of recurrence in this individual, many murderers of this type might receive light sentences or none at all. Obviously laws must seek some compromise between general deterrence and individual rehabilitation, but we may hope that the gradual abandonment of capital punishment and other recent flexibilities in applying the law indicate that modern society is outgrowing the archaic need for revenge.

Defendants considered to be insane are said to be "incompetent to stand trial" and are usually sent to a mental hospital for observation or treatment until they are ready or competent to stand trial. Steadman and Braff (1974) indicate that such "incompetency diversions" of arrested criminals have been used as alternatives to prison which circumvent the due process of law and, in effect, deprive the defendants of their legal rights. One patient in a state mental hospital admitted candidly in an informal interview that he had stolen 17 automobiles and was hospitalized rather than prosecuted for the last offense. He would have preferred conviction for car theft, for which the prison sentence would have been about six months, whereas his present stay in the hospital had already lasted more than two years!

The other side of that coin presents clear dangers for society. If the plea "not guilty by reason of insanity" is accepted in court, the defendant is usually sent for psychological treatment in a hospital. When treatment is judged to be completed, the person may be returned to the community, sometimes years before the minimum sentence for a "guilty" verdict would have elapsed. Many people feel that this is an unreasonable risk for society to bear; as a result some legislative initiatives are being taken to replace the plea "not guilty by reason of insanity" with the plea "guilty by reason of insanity," with appropriate sentencing options that ensure periods of surveillance commensurate with the seriousness of the crime committed.

Psychological Differentiation of Criminal Types

As society moves toward a judicial system more oriented to prevention and rehabilitation, the mental health professions can expect to be called on more and more to provide the knowledge to assess the criminal's prognosis and to enlighten society's response to criminal behavior. Of particular service in this regard is Brown's (1965) formulation of how moral behavior is acquired. The critical aspects of moral behavior are knowledge, feelings, and conduct. Moral knowledge, or awareness of the rules of society, is acquired through concept formation and cognitive learning. Moral feelings, such as guilt, shame, and remorse, are learned by classical conditioning. Moral behavior is dependent on knowledge and feelings, and is governed by the principles of instrumental and imitative learning. From this perspective it is obvious why the sociopath has the poorest prognosis of the four types of delinquents considered in this chapter. Sociopaths know, on a cognitive level, what society considers right and wrong, but they behave immorally because they are unable to experience moral feelings with sufficient intensity for awareness of the rules of society to have any impact on their behavior (Hare, 1970). This aspect of the sociopathic personality has played havoc on the legal definition of insanity. It may be argued that sociopathic criminals are no less insane because their knowledge of right and wrong is *emotionally* blocked from bearing on their conduct than are schizophrenics whose knowledge of right and wrong is *intellectually* inaccessible. In the Hickock trial the prosecution realized that a full psychiatric diagnosis of "severe character disorder" could be used by the defense to mitigate the penalty for the murder, and therefore objected to the court-appointed psychiatrist giving any further testimony than to answer "yes" or "no" to the question whether the defendant knew right from wrong at the time he committed the crime. The objection was upheld. Thus limited by the McNaghten Rule and prohibited from elaborating, the psychiatrist was forced to declare that the defendant did indeed know right from wrong, foreclosing any further consideration of insanity.

Treatment of sociopaths should concentrate on kindling some spark of moral feeling, as indicated in the last section, unless this proves impossible because of some constitutional inability to be conditioned. In either case, neither judicial leniency nor conventional psychotherapy seems indicated, though Vaillant's (1975) recommendations for group treatment are worth pursuing.

Disturbed *delinquents* know the rules and have some capacity for moral feeling, but misbehave presumably because of some distortion in the process of socialization, which allows antisocial behavior to serve disturbed emotional needs. Psychotherapy and other conventional treatments for psychological disorder would seem to have the best prospect of helping in this case, though firmness and some attention to supporting moral feelings would probably not be amiss. Delinquents are delinquents, after all, because they break the rules.

Socialized or *subcultural delinquents* have good knowledge of the rules of their subculture, strong moral feelings, and good conduct by the standards of that subculture, but they follow the wrong rules. Society's response in this instance should be to expose continually the discrepancies between the two moral codes, and to reassert constantly that the deviant code cannot win. This may be accomplished to some extent by public education, but inevitably society must also set limits against individual violations by enforcing the law. Psychotherapy hardly has much to offer here, except as an adjunct to rehabilitation when the criminal is willing to "go straight."

The *white collar criminal* knows the right rules, has strong moral feelings and generally good conduct, but in circumscribed areas distorts intellectually

377

the interpretation or application of the rules in such a way as to evade moral culpability for criminal conduct. In most cases of this sort the prognosis should be good, even with moderate penalties because the social censure of criminal conviction is a powerful instrument in the lives of affluent, otherwise respectable, citizens. There are, of course, some white collar criminals who violate the law with *conviction*, and these may be regarded and treated like subcultural criminals who adhere to a deviant code of ethics.

Balancing Effectiveness Against Fairness in Law Enforcement

Modern labeling theory (McCaghy, 1976) underlines an important problem in law enforcement: deviance is not a property *inherent* in certain forms of behavior; it is a property *conferred on* these forms by the audiences that directly or indirectly witness them. A critical variable, then, is the social audience that defines deviance. There are elements of discretion in how society creates and enforces its laws that make society an integral cause of deviance. Much deviant behavior emerges from conflicts between parties or classes struggling over scarce resources. Rules are necessary to control the conflict if a society is to survive, but rules favoring the powerful magnify the differences between the powerful and the powerless. In the process the powerful place the blame for deviance on those without similar influence over the administration of law, which creates serious problems of morale and respect for the law. As we have seen, criminal deviance is present at all levels of society.

An infuriating illustration of the problem is described by Seymour (1973). Two cases were called for sentencing before a United States District Judge in Manhattan's Federal Court on January 15, 1973. The first case concerned a 22-year-old Puerto Rican woman with two children, five and four years old, who pleaded guilty to aiding in the theft of part of a group of welfare checks amounting to a total of $2,086. The woman had come to New York only a few years before, could not speak English, and was on welfare herself. She was living with her husband in a poverty-stricken section of Brooklyn. Her husband was a diabetic and she provided insulin for him. She had no prior criminal record. The judgment of the court was imprisonment for 18 months. The second case concerned an educated white-collar defendant who pleaded guilty to commercial bribery and extortion in the amount of $23,000, as well as perjury and inducing another to commit perjury. The judge went out of his way to point out, along with other considerations, that the defendant had two young children and no prior criminal record. The judgment of the court was a suspended sentence!

Prescriptive Penology

Making the state's reaction fit the offender's potential for reform is called *prescriptive penology*. To make it work, Glaser (1972) accurately observes, will require much more than the one percent of correctional expenditures that is currently spent on *research* to measure the effectiveness of alternative correctional practices. Prescriptive penology has been a major theme during the 1970s, along with three specific trends: (1) crime has been redefined to limit offenses for which penalties are imposed to those that produce a definite victim; (2) punishment policies have been based increasingly on controlled experiments to test the effectiveness of penalties as general deterrents, instead of on a passion for revenge; and (3) correctional measures for persistent offenders have become more diverse and flexible, calibrated to the life history of the criminal more than to the seriousness of a particular crime. Here the primary focus is on facilitating success in legitimate alternatives to crime rather than merely on restraining offenders for some duration of confinement. This means more emphasis on training for legitimate employment and more liberal use of probation and work release programs that allow prisoners to work during the day in the community, returning to confinement at night. Prescriptive penology made eminently good sense early in the 1970s. Though it did not promise to resolve every problem of law enforcement, it seemed to be a step in the right direction.

The pendulum may swing back the other way, however, during the 1980s. Scott and Vandiver (1974) conducted an empirical study of the practice of "indeterminate sentencing" or individualized disposition of criminal cases based on the character of the offender, instead of identical disposition of all persons convicted of the same offense. The rigidity and subsequent harshness of uniform sentencing without consideration of mitigating factors led to the development of the indeterminate sentence and the utilization of parole boards to determine when offenders had undergone sufficient punishment (or rehabilitation). The danger in this practice is that parole boards might abuse their discretion by requiring different periods of incarceration for the same offense without justification. The original idea was for the parole board to review periodically each inmate's case and order release at the optimum time to readjust and function adequately in society. The judge, schooled in law and not human behavior, would not be as well qualified to determine how much rehabilitation (punishment) specific inmates needed, or how they would respond to the various treatment programs offered. The solution was to create parole boards, staffed by citizens trained to understand human behavior, to decide when the inmate was ready to return to society. The data from the study showed that, in fact, parole boards based their decisions primarily on legal criteria, such as the seriousness of the crime committed, which were precisely the ones the judge used to decide on sending the offender to prison. This lends itself to low morale among prisoners if they perceive the parole board decisions as either capricious or rigid. Institutional adjustment and personal development of the offender were not being used effectively by the parole boards and were *not* correlated with recidivism (repeated offenses after release from prison).

On July 1, 1979, the state of Colorado put into effect a new determinate-sentencing law, establishing more exact sentences from which to choose as judges make sentencing decisions (*The Denver Post*, 1979). Under the previous law, indeterminate sentences were available to judges. For instance, a forger might receive an indeterminate-to-five-year sentence and a murderer a 15-to-30-year sentence. The decisions about release time were made by a parole board, which may eventually be eliminated under the new system. The new law clearly will restrict the discretion of law enforcement officers in deciding how long convicted criminals must remain in prison. Let us hope that, in seeking fairness in law enforcement, the changes of the 1980s do not abolish the important advantages of prescriptive penology.

SUGGESTIONS FOR FURTHER READING

A good place to begin the study of criminal behavior, as obviously many others have done, is with the authoritative textbook by E. H. Sutherland and D. Cressey, *Criminology, 9th ed.* (1974). A systematic study of the influence of child-training practices and family relations in delinquency is made by A. Bandura and R. H. Walters in *Adolescent aggression* (1959). For a vivid account of the lives and thoughts of youth gang members, read L. Yablonsky's *The violent gang* (1969).

 The Report of the President's Commission on Law Enforcement and Administration of Justice (1968) is an extremely informative and authoritative source of general information about crime and delinquency, and was written by the nation's leading experts in criminology. The Federal Bureau of Investigation publishes each year a compendium of valuable statistics on crime and law enforcement, *Crime in the United States: Unified crime reports* (1978). The volume edited by L. Radzinowicz and M. E. Wolfgang, *Crime and Justice, 2nd ed.* (1977), is a useful collection of papers by leading authorities. J. F. Short's *Modern criminals* (1970) presents a selection of papers with a sociological slant on various types of criminals; the papers were previously published in *Trans*-action magazine. D. Glaser's essay, *Adult crime and social policy* (1972), provides an extremely erudite and provocative analysis of crime as a social problem.

 H. Cleckley's *The mask of sanity, 5th ed.* (1976), is a thorough study of sociopathic personality disorders, liberally illustrated with interesting histories. The whole subject is well reviewed, with a study on treatment, by W. McCord and J. McCord in *The psychopath: An Essay on the criminal mind* (1964). R. D. Hare's *Psychopathology: Theory and research* (1970) is a brief, well-written volume on the same subject, with emphasis on the somatic basis of the disorder. *In Cold Blood* (T. Capote, 1965), though written by a literary figure, is an extremely compelling psychological study of two extraordinary criminals that is well worth reading.

 C. H. McCaghy's sociology textbook, *Deviant behavior: Crime, conflict and interest groups* (1976), available in paperback, covers the whole range of deviant behavior, but is especially informative about white collar crime. J. H. Goldstein's paperback, *Aggression and crimes of violence* (1975), provides an intensive psychological study of aggression and crimes of violence.

380

Illumined Pleasures (1929) by Salvador Dali. Collection of Sidney Janis. Photo by Geoffrey Clements.

II
Drug
Dependence

Those who write darkly about the problems of contemporary society are almost certain to mention drugs. In recent years the availability and use of drugs has increased rapidly, and problems connected with their misuse appear often in the news. The American Psychiatric Association's system of classification (DSM-III), described at the beginning of Chapter 2, includes a category somewhat oddly named *substance use disorders*, which we can read to mean disorders resulting from excessive use of drugs. In addition to their part in these disorders, drugs contribute to traffic accidents and crime in the streets, and they are implicated in a variety of physical ailments.

Some readers, sitting down to this chapter with a cigarette in hand and a cup of coffee beside them, may be incensed to find that caffeine and tobacco are included among the substances that can produce disorders. Others will protest against giving a bad name to drugs they have heard about or experienced as producing agreeable effects. In moderate amounts different drugs can stimulate and "turn on," soothe and relax, create a friendly mood, bolster self-confidence, facilitate sexual performance, yield insights and expanded awareness, and help us to forget. Some readers may say that without cigarettes they could not sit still long enough to read this chapter. Some may point out that without coffee they would become too drowsy to understand what they were reading. Others might argue more broadly that the stresses of modern life, which are partly responsible for psychological disorders, can be better endured with the help of drugs that soften our natural responses of anxiety and depression. A good many drugs, used with intelligent restraint, can be claimed as allies of comfort and well-being.

But when we turn to excessive use there is no question that we have entered the realm of disorders. All the substances discussed here, including coffee and tobacco, contain chemicals that affect the central nervous system. In small quantities the effects are pleasant, but larger amounts become distinctly hazardous to health and happiness. More important, from a clinical viewpoint, the effects may acquire an attraction so strong that it defies rational control. We can then speak of drug dependence—an enslavement that can be very difficult to break. The line between moderate and excessive use of drugs is hard to establish, but everyone should have the available information about it. Too often, people have crossed that shadowy line without realizing it and then found it difficult to get back. We will start with caffeine, the drug least likely to get out of hand in this way, but that still has limits of safe use.

CAFFEINISM

It is a common observation that coffee and tea promote rapid thinking, intellectual effort, and mental acuity, and reduce drowsiness, fatigue, and reaction time—all especially valued commodities in an achievement-oriented society. The caffeine in these and many other commonly consumed preparations (see Table 11-1) dilates blood vessels near the heart and lungs, increases heart rate and gastric secretion, stimulates the bowels, relaxes muscles in the chest, strengthens the contraction of skeletal muscles, and increases basic metabolic rate. It also seems to counteract the sedative/hypnotic effect of many medications. Plainly, caffeine is a powerful stimulant (Greden, 1974)! Unfortunately, heavy use of caffeine also produces dependence and tolerance, and if its use is stopped there are such withdrawal symptoms as nervousness, irritability, lethargy, inability to work effectively, restlessness, palpitations, disturbed sleep, gastrointestinal irritation and diarrhea, and headache. Caffeine withdrawal headaches have even been produced experimentally; they usually respond to

384

Table 11-1   Some Common Sources of Caffeine

Source	Approximate Amounts of Caffeine per Unit
Beverages	
Brewed coffee	100–150 mg per cup
Instant coffee	86– 99 mg per cup
Tea	60– 75 mg per cup
Decaffeinated coffee	2– 4 mg per cup
Cola drinks	40– 60 mg per glass
Prescription medications	
APCs (aspirin, phenacetin, caffeine)	32 mg per tablet
Cafergot	100 mg per tablet
Darvon compound	32 mg per tablet
Fiorinal	40 mg per tablet
Migral	50 mg per tablet
Over-the-counter analgesics	
Anacin, aspirin compound, Bromo Seltzer	32 mg per tablet
Cope, Easy-Mens, Empirin compound, Midol	30 mg per tablet
Vanquish	32 mg per tablet
Excedrin	60 mg per tablet
Pre-Mens	66 mg per tablet
Many over-the-counter cold preparations	30 mg per tablet
Many over-the-counter stimulants	100 mg per tablet

Source: Greden (1974, p. 1090).

caffeine but tend to recur the next day. The clinical symptoms of caffeinism are virtually indistinguishable from those of anxiety disorder. There is no question that psychiatric patients use caffeine like a drug: in one study patients with pain-killers available on demand used significantly fewer of these medicines if they were high caffeine consumers (Winstead, 1976). About 20 to 30 percent of Americans consume more than 500 to 600 mg of caffeine per day, the equivalent of five cups of coffee (Greden et al., 1978). The symptoms of caffeinism are likely to occur above that level of consumption.

Greden et al. (1978) studied the clinical correlates of caffeinism in 83 psychiatric patients. They classified the patients into three levels of daily caffeine consumption: low (0–249 mg), moderate (250–749 mg), and high (750 mg or more). The majority of the consumption was from coffee, but as much as one-quarter of the daily quantities derived from other sources. Among the low consumers 70 percent reported they were in good physical health, as compared with only 46 percent and 44 percent of the moderate and high consumers. High and moderate consumers were significantly more anxious and

385

depressed, feeling tired, blue, like crying, in a state of tension over recent concerns; difficulties seemed to be piling up. High consumers reported also significantly greater use of minor tranquilizers, sedative-hypnotics, alcohol, and cigarettes than the other groups. High consumers were less likely to have their sleep impaired by drinking coffee before bedtime, which may indicate either greater tolerance for caffeine or innate differences in caffeine metabolism. Withdrawal headaches were commonly reported when daily coffee was omitted. In correlational studies of this kind it is ambiguous whether dependence on caffeine is a cause or an effect (or both) of the clinical symptoms. At the least, the authors reason that caffeinism accentuates the symptoms.

A Case Illustration

A twenty-seven-year-old nurse who was married to an Army physician applied for evaluation at a military outpatient medical clinic because of lightheadedness, tremulousness, breathlessness, headache, and "irregular heartbeat" occurring sporadically about two or three times a day. The symptoms had developed gradually over a three-week period. She denied precipitating stresses. When the evaluating physician commented on her apparent anxiety, she admitted being apprehensive but correlated it with the presence of palpitations, chest discomfort, and irregular heartbeat, Physical examination and a multitude of laboratory tests were all within normal limits. An electrocardiogram revealed characteristic premature ventricular contractions. She was given medication for the heart symptoms, should they recur, and she was referred to the psychiatric outpatient clinic with a diagnosis of "anxiety reaction, probably secondary to the fear that her husband would be transferred to Viet Nam." However, the patient refused to accept this assessment despite continuation of her symptoms. She diligently searched for a dietary cause (perhaps *hypoglycemia* or low blood sugar?) and after about 10 days she convincingly correlated her symptoms with coffee consumption. In retrospect, she was able to trace symptom onset to the purchase of a fresh-drip coffee pot. Because this coffee was "so much better," she had begun consuming an average of 10 to 12 cups of strong, black coffee a day—more than 1000 mg of caffeine. She withdrew completely from her coffee regimen and within 36 hours virtually all symptoms disappeared, including her cardiac arrhythmias. She complained of fatigue for one week but then began noting that she was "truly awake in the morning for the first time in years." She was later "challenged" twice with caffeine after periods of abstinence. Subjective anxiety recurred, along with heart symptoms. Proud of her diagnostic skills, the nurse vowed to refrain from excessive use of coffee or tea in the future, and a two-year follow-up revealed that the symptoms have never recurred.

There may be a moral to the story we've just recounted: don't trust a diagnosis of anxiety reaction if you're drinking 10 to 12 cups of strong coffee every day! A simpler and more fundamental lesson is that caffeine is a powerful drug that should not be overused. Some people find that even small quantities make them feel tense and jittery; they are better off without it. Others experience only good effects from four or five cups a day and view caffeinism without alarm. But it might be a good plan, in view of coffee breaks, coffee machines in workplaces, and coffee served everywhere, to make an occasional count of one's daily consumption. Many people drink a lot more coffee than they realize. In most lives there is enough to worry about without adding the tension produced by too much caffeine.

SMOKING

The facts about tobacco are rather simple, not nearly so ambiguous to the impartial observer as the great controversy surrounding it would lead one to believe. Annual per-capita cigarette consumption in the United States increased from less than 50 at the turn of the century to about 4200 in recent years (Mausner & Platt, 1971). At the same time consumption of other forms of tobacco—pipe and chewing tobacco and cigars—has declined substantially. The rapid increase in cigarette smoking reached a plateau in the early 1960s, probably because of the growing suspicion that it might endanger physical health (Skinner, 1970). From 1957 on there were various public statements by Surgeon Generals of the United States reporting with increasing confidence the causal connection between smoking and various lung and heart diseases, most notably cancer of the lung. In 1964 the Advisory Committee on Smoking and Health published its report documenting the hazards (U.S. Public Health Service, 1964). They assembled evidence from animal experiments, clinical and autopsy studies, and population studies, all of which were consistent with the conclusion that cigarette smoking causes cancer and other diseases of the respiratory system and contributes to a variety of other diseases of the heart, circulatory system, and abdomen. The most compelling evidence came from prospective studies that kept track of 1,123,000 men starting in 1951 and included 37,400 who died before 1964. The investigators compared the death rates of smokers and nonsmokers from various diseases. Among smokers there were almost eleven times as many deaths from lung cancer. The mortality ratios were less, but still overwhelmingly impressive, for bronchitis and emphysema (6.1), cancer of the larynx (5.4), oral cancer (4.1), cancer of the esophagus (3.4), peptic ulcer (2.8), and other circulatory diseases (2.6). Overall, 68 percent more smokers than nonsmokers died from all causes. Moreover, the death rates were highly correlated with the number of cigarettes smoked each day and the duration of the smoking habit.

It was predictable that cigarette consumption would decline, and it did in 1964 by 2 percent (Skinner, 1970). But anyone familiar with habitual smoking could have predicted that it would rise in 1965 to about the same level as in 1963. What this and a multitude of experimental studies showed is that new information about health hazards may change attitudes about the danger and

387

temporarily reduce smoking, but over the long term it has little effect on smoking behavior (Swinehart, 1966). In 1966 a law was passed that required every cigarette package sold in this country to display prominently the following warning: "CAUTION: Cigarette Smoking May Be Hazardous to Your Health." Much more stringent measures were proposed in Congress, but they failed. Tobacco is a $10 billion industry that spends over $250 million annually on advertising, and 21 of the 50 states derive a substantial portion of their income from tobacco production (Meserve, 1968).

Subsequent reports from the Public Health Service confirmed and strengthened the conclusions of the first report. They showed that some of the initial conclusions were too conservative; for example, it was found that the death rates of people who smoke more than a pack a day are 30 times as high as the rates among nonsmokers (Horn, 1968). As the evidence mounted, pressure on government agencies increased until all cigarette advertising was finally banned from radio and television in 1971. A Gallup poll showed that 40 percent of a national sample of adults smoked cigarettes five years after the Surgeon General's report, contrasted with 45 percent of those polled six years before it was published. A third of the nonsmokers had previously smoked but

"THE HEALTH WARNING ISN'T ALL BAD — THINK OF ALL THE MASOCHISTS WE'RE PICKING UP."

given it up, and 41 percent of the smokers reported that they had cut down on
cigarettes. What is most striking about these figures is that so many people continued to smoke in spite of the known dangers. Some reasoned, no doubt, that bad consequences did not happen to everyone and would not happen to them, at least for a long time. Others tried to stop smoking but failed. Evidently, smoking yields gratifications that are not easy to give up.

The Tobacco Habit

Most people begin smoking before they are twenty because it is symbolically associated with adult status, independence, adventure, and attractiveness. The smoking habit is both acquired and maintained in part for social reasons. Initially, the group pressures for social conformity are great and smoking, once initiated, becomes a powerful cue symbolizing affiliation, group cohesion, and the sharing of pleasure. It is easy to observe that when one person lights up after a meal or at a party, other smokers in the group find it difficult not to follow suit.

The rewards most often cited for smoking are that it relaxes and reduces tension. Nicotine is a mild stimulant that is not especially toxic. Tars are the principal cancer-causing component of cigarette smoke, but the stimulating properties of nicotine may play a significant etiological role in cardiovascular diseases.

It is unclear whether smoking should be characterized as an *habituation* or as an *addiction*. The World Health Organization (1957) offers four distinctions between drug addiction and drug habituation. In contrast to an addict, an habituated person desires to continue taking the drug but does not have an overwhelming compulsion to get it at all costs; shows little or no tendency to increase the dose; manifests some degree of psychic dependence on the effect of the drug but no physical dependence and hence no abstinence syndrome (withdrawal symptoms); and does not carry behavior to a point that is detrimental to society. Habituation is not presumed to reflect serious personality defects from underlying psychological disorders that might become manifest in other ways if the drug is removed.

By these criteria it might seem possible to classify smoking as an habituation, not an addiction. Treatment aimed at counteracting the chemical needs established by smoking has been generally less successful than methods designed to reduce the psychological urges (U.S. Public Health Service, 1964; Mausner & Platt, 1971). But it is not always true that nicotine creates no dependence and no abstinence symptoms. Some tolerance for the drug does develop, and fairly consistent symptoms of withdrawal exist, especially for heavy smokers: nervousness, drowsiness, and headache. Schachter (1977) has shown that smokers adjust their habit to maintain a relatively constant level of nicotine in their systems. One of the effects of stress is to increase acidity in the urine, and nicotine is then excreted at a faster rate than when urine is alka-

389

line. For this reason Schachter believes that more cigarettes are smoked under stress in order to maintain constant nicotine levels in the body. In a study consistent with this theory, subjects under stress did not increase their smoking after drinking sodium bicarbonate, which makes urine more alkaline (Schachter, Silverstein, & Perlik, 1977). These results support the argument that physiological dependence on nicotine accounts at least partly for the stubborn persistence of smoking habits.

In summary, the habitual use of tobacco is related primarily to psychological and social drives, and at least secondarily to the chemical actions of nicotine on the central nervous system and on body chemistry. Smoking improves the self-image, fosters feelings of social affiliation, and relaxes tension. The habit is reinforced and perpetuated by nicotine dependency, which explains why nicotine-free tobacco and other substitutes do not yield satisfaction. There is some evidence that smokers are more extraverted and have more emotional problems than average, but extraversion might be an *effect* of greater exposure to social stimuli and social influence instead of a cause for smoking. Smoking increases under temporary stress, so it evidently serves a tranquilizing function.

The Will To Break the Habit

The first step in breaking the smoking habit is a firm decision to stop. Mark Twain was a devoted pipe and cigar smoker often quoted as saying he could quit with the greatest of ease and had in fact done so "hundreds of times." He would point out that life is nothing more than one calculated risk after another and "nobody ever comes out of it alive." Obviously treatment stands little chance of success in a happy recidivist like Mark Twain. However, even firm resolve is often not sufficient to ensure success. It is remarkable that two renowned psychologists as committed to rationality as Gordon Allport and Sigmund Freud should die of cancer because they could not stop smoking. Allport smoked cigarettes until he learned that he had terminal lung cancer, less than a year before his death in 1967 at the age of seventy. Freud's lifelong war with tobacco is an epic with such poignancy that it merits recounting in some detail (Rodale, 1970).

Freud suffered an attack of influenza in 1894, at the age of thirty-eight, which left him with an irregular heartbeat. His best friend and closest associate at the time, Dr. Wilhelm Fliess, informed Freud that this was the result of smoking cigars, and ordered him to stop. He tried to stop or cut down his ration, but failed. Later he did stop but his subsequent depression and psychophysiological symptoms proved unbearable and within seven weeks he was smoking heavily again. Fliess persisted in ordering Freud to stop and once more he did—for 14 very long months. He suffered throughout this period and then resumed because the torture was "beyond human power to bear." On another occasion he decided to stop again, since his pulse was very bad and he couldn't keep to a ration of four cigars a day; this time he was smoking

The story of Freud's ambivalent struggle with his cigar had all the elements of a tragic epic.

again within a month. Freud continued smoking 20 cigars a day, and struggling against the habit, until he developed cancerous lesions of the right palate and jaw in 1923, when he was sixty-seven. A successful operation was performed, the first of 33 he would have to bear before he died. He was free of cancer for eight years although other places in his mouth began to go through the familiar series of precancerous stages. He was repeatedly warned by eminent specialists whose judgment he trusted that smoking was the cause. Occasionally he tried very hard to stop and thought he had succeeded, but each time he resumed because, so he insisted, it helped him to think. By now Freud was having recognizable attacks of "tobacco angina" whenever he smoked; even partially denicotinized cigars produced cardiac discomfort. In 1930, at seventy-three, Freud was hospitalized for his heart condition. He recovered almost overnight simply by giving up cigars. But after 23 days he started smoking a cigar a day. Then two. Then three or four, and soon twenty again. In 1936, at the age of seventy-nine, and in the midst of his endless series of mouth and jaw operations for cancer, there was more heart trouble, which was again relieved as soon as he stopped smoking. Freud was, of course, a peculiarly interested analyst of compulsive habits and he was thoroughly disgusted by his own inability to break the smoking habit. By now his jaw had been entirely removed and an artificial jaw substituted; he was almost constantly in pain; often he could not speak or eat or swallow. Still he smoked an endless series of cigars until he died of cancer in 1939, at the age of eighty-three, after many years of intense suffering.

Many might feel that Freud's case was so extreme that he was in fact *physiologically* dependent on cigars, but it is clear that he was not. The crucial test was during abstinence: at no time that he quit, cold turkey, did he have withdrawal symptoms (e.g., fever, chills, nausea, delirium) such as are found in alcoholics or heroin addicts. Quite the contrary, his physical health improved because of relief from nicotine stimulation. That he suffered so abominably demonstrates that *psychological* dependence is not to be dismissed lightly. Freud's sensory and emotional needs had become so structured around smoking that the courageous will to stop, which he amply demonstrated, was outweighed by the attendant costs to his whole emotional economy. Let us therefore not underestimate the power or tenacity of psychological habituation.

Influencing Smoking Behavior

Three kinds of measures have been used to limit smoking: educational and public information campaigns; restrictions on the sale, advertising, and use of tobacco; and various forms of treatment for the smoking habit. Early reports have shown little success in any of them. Public information has quite effectively persuaded most people of the health hazards in smoking, but regular smokers lag behind ex-smokers and nonsmokers in accepting this conclusion (Wakefield, 1969). To prevent the development of habitual smoking, several educational experiments have been attempted in public schools. These also have succeeded in making children's attitudes toward smoking more negative without influencing their action very much (Leventhal, 1968). The legislative actions to raise taxes on tobacco, require the warning on every cigarette package, and restrict advertising in the media have not been decisive. While tobacco consumption shows signs of slight decline, the impact has by no means been substantial. Ironically, concerns about ecology and the resultant peer or social pressure may prove to affect smoking habits more than concerns about health have done.

Various treatments for the smoking habit have been tried, including nicotine substitutes like *lobelin*, placebo therapy, psychotherapy, group therapy, aversive conditioning, and tranquilizing drugs. One ingenious procedure was derived from an operant conditioning rationale. The premise was that smoking behavior is usually maintained by a regular pattern of social cues in the daily rituals: mealtimes, social gatherings, coffee breaks, stress periods, and so on. Therefore, smokers were equipped with an electric timing mechanism programmed to ring a bell at random times throughout the day as a signal to smoke. Then and only then were they to light up. In this way the smoking habit would be dissociated from the powerful social cues and attached instead to various *irregular* places and times of the day, so it would later be easier to give up smoking altogether. Most treatments for the smoking habit have had results like those reported at the Norwegian "weaning clinics": dramatic success immediately followed by many relapses, especially in the first few months after treatment (Wakefield, 1969). Follow-up studies showed that 85 percent stopped smoking by the end of treatment, irrespective of method, but the number of "cures" dropped to 30 percent after six months and to 16 percent after eighteen months. The last figure is possibly no larger than the number who would have given up smoking without treatment.

William Thackeray, the nineteenth-century novelist, wrote: "I vow and believe that it [smoking] has been one of the greatest creature-comforts of my life—a kind companion, a gentle stimulant, an amiable anodyne [pain killer], a cementer of friendship" (Skinner, 1970). Apparently a lot of people agree, both before and after treatment. If it just didn't do such unfortunate things to the lungs and heart. . . .

PSYCHOACTIVE DRUG DEPENDENCE

Because the "drug problem" has forced itself rather dramatically into public awareness in recent times, it comes as a surprise to many people that dependence on psychoactive drugs has a history reaching back thousands of years. In some cultures drug addiction is as common and as widely condoned as alcohol abuse is in the United States today. There is good reason, however, to argue that the magnitude of the drug problem has changed. Partly this is because the number of drug abusers has increased substantially. More important is the sudden upswing in detrimental effects on society at large. Drug overdose and drug-related crimes of violence are now the leading cause of death between ages fifteen and thirty-five in New York and other metropolitan cities (Whitten & Robertson, 1972). That same report estimated that $3 billion in thefts each year and more than half of all crimes against property in New York City were committed to maintain heroin habits. That proportion dropped to 48 percent in 1973 and even more sharply to 23 percent in 1976, though Manning (1977) disputes the claim that this was due to harsher criminal penalties and procedures. Probably the greatest cause of concern is the growing proportion of addicts among younger age groups and minority races, where it can be expected that the users take to drugs because of immaturity or their disadvantaged status in society (Fraser, 1972). Previously drug dependence was concentrated among whites and distributed throughout the adult age range; now most users are minority group members in their twenties or teens.

The reasons for taking psychoactive drugs may be initially similar to those for drinking coffee and smoking tobacco: pleasure, stimulation, relaxation. But the effects can be much more distinctive and emphatic—the drugs are called "psychoactive" because they produce marked changes in consciousness—and this probably explains in part how easily they can induce dependency. There are, of course, wide differences in the effects of various psychoactive drugs. Popularly these substances are classified as "uppers" (stimulants) and "downers" (depressants). However, we will consider them in five groupings according to the distinctive ways they are used, in each case focusing on one particular drug for illustration. These groupings are *cannabis*, especially marihuana; *hallucinogens* like LSD ("acid"); *stimulants* like cocaine and the amphetamines ("speed"); *sedatives* like nembutal and seconal ("barbs," "goof balls"); and *narcotics* like heroin.

Cannabis

Marihuana is obtained from the dried or crushed leaves and flowering tops of cannabis, an Indian hemp plant that grows wild in many parts of the world, including the United States. Typically, the small crushed fragments are rolled into thin homemade cigarettes, called joints, that are smoked for their special pleasurable effect. Although illegal in many countries, marihuana continues to be used by millions, especially in Asia and Africa, just as it has been for several thousand years. The use of "pot" has shown the sharpest increase of all the psychoactive drugs in this country, especially on college campuses. Health authorities believe that 35 to 40 million Americans have tried the drug at least once in their lives, with almost 15 million of them regular users (Bryant, 1977). Perhaps four million of these are "potheads" who make chronic marihuana intoxication a way of life. Cannabis does not cause strong physical dependence, as do heroin, barbiturates, and some tranquilizers, but evidence shows that the body *can* develop profound tolerance to the drug at sufficiently high dose levels, making increasingly larger doses necessary to get the same effects (Domino, 1972). Abstinence from chronic cannabis use produces relatively mild withdrawal symptoms: irritability, insomnia, and loss of appetite, but many scientists believe that it can produce extreme psychological dependence if taken regularly.

Hashish is the potent dark brown resin from the tops of high quality cannabis. Because of the high concentration of resin, it is often five or six times stronger than marihuana, although the principal psychoactive ingredient, *tetrahydrocannibol* (THC), is the same. Therefore, the physical and psychological effects are quite similar, differing only in intensity. The main effects of cannabis are stimulative, although in very large doses this shifts toward de-

THE FACTS ABOUT CANNABIS TOLERANCE

Some readers may have experimented with pot occasionally and found that it took less to get "high" each successive time they smoked. It may startle them to learn that cannabis produces tolerance, and leave them doubting the claim. The facts are these. In two recent double-blind studies, experienced marihuana smokers were unable to distinguish between the intoxicating effects of active marihuana cigarettes and placebo "joints" with the active drug (THC) removed. In animal studies, rats and pigeons have developed *profound* tolerance to THC; pigeons have gradually been built up to daily doses *nine* times the amount that is normally lethal! Chronic hashish users in Greece have been observed to smoke *ten* times as much as would cause a novice to collapse (Russell, 1978). Therefore there is little doubt that tolerance can develop to the active ingredients of cannabis if the amounts taken are large enough. The opposite effect of "reverse tolerance" or sensitization experienced by occasional pot smokers is attributable more to psychological factors than to the physiological action of the drug. It probably depends on expectation and on giving oneself more fully to the new experience (Domino, 1972).

pressant effects. The subjective experience depends greatly on the user's expectations, the circumstances, and the strength and quantity of the drug used. Typically the earliest change is toward a more dreamlike consciousness in which the sharp edges of unpleasant reality and logic are smoothed away and sensory experience becomes agreeably vivid. Although thinking and judgment are actually impaired, they may be experienced as better than usual, yielding pleasing new insights. Sounds and colors are intensified, space may seem enlarged or otherwise changed, time can be much extended so that five minutes seem like an hour. Sensory illusions are common, but hallucinations or delusions are rare, except with heavy doses. Frequently the user withdraws passively and just savors the "high." Occasionally uncontrollable laughter or crying may occur. Sometimes the effects are quite frightening or very unpleasant, giving rise to unfounded suspiciousness or marked anxiety. In a few cases, especially among emotionally vulnerable youths, such reactions may border on panic or lead to a paranoid state or a temporary break with reality.

Before 1970 most of the marihuana consumed in this country was grown domestically; it was low in THC content: 0.2 percent or less. This may help to explain why many observers in the early years came to the conclusion that marihuana was a harmless drug. By 1970 Mexican marihuana with an average potency of 1.5 to 2.0 percent THC had replaced the domestic variety and held a virtual monopoly in the American market over the next few years. By the end of 1973 Jamaican, Mexican, and Colombian marihuana with an estimated potency of 3 to 4 percent THC entered this country in increasing quan-

395

tities. It is disquieting that young people are now starting in on this form of the drug without realizing that it is stronger. In the years 1975-77, the proportion of daily users among high school seniors increased from 6 percent to 9 percent. Unfortunately, many young people, well aware of the risk of regular use of psychoactive drugs, still cling to the older idea that marihuana is an exception and need not be considered harmful (Russell, 1978).

What sort of people prefer to use cannabis? Kay et al. (1978) obtained self-descriptions of the personality traits of users, continuous nonusers and switched nonusers (those who had given it up) among male college students. One important difference was in *conformity*. Nonusers described themselves as deferent, self-controlled, highly socialized, mature, responsible, and highly concerned with order, social standards, and intrapersonal structuring of values. By contrast, the users saw themselves as relatively irresponsible, rebellious, emotionally labile, and hostile to rules and conventions; they claimed strong needs for autonomy, change, and exhibition. Another difference was in their *orientations toward achievement*. Nonusers emphasized their personal traits that lend themselves to social and vocational achievement within conventional channels: efficiency, organization, industry, achievement, persistence, and personal adjustment; their replies obviously demonstrated a more positive attitude toward their place in society. On the other hand, the users prized most their independence, spontaneity, adventuresomeness, and novelty-seeking. One might infer that impulsive extraverts are more inclined to use marihuana. The authors point out that the findings support popular beliefs about college-age drug users and may reflect, in part, social expectations as perceived by the subjects. However, a different study of high school drug users found similar results: users valued feelings and experience—a kind of interpersonal responsiveness—over planning and logic, which are certainly more conducive to social conformity and achievement (Graham & Cross, 1975). The *switched nonusers* reported that they had never used marihuana in their first year at college, but did become users in subsequent years; their scores on the personality questionnaires fell midway between those of the users and the continuous nonusers during all four years at school (Kay et al., 1978). Their self-descriptions changed significantly over time on only one scale (flexibility), which supports the contention that certain personality types may be susceptible to marihuana use rather than that its use results in personality changes.

A great deal of controversy has surrounded the use of marihuana. From a clinical viewpoint, it has been known for a long time that smoking it interferes immediately with thinking, speech, and recent memory. It can impair judgment and logical thinking and simultaneously cause the subjective impression that mental functioning is as good as ever or even enhanced by the drug. Performing any complex task that requires good reflexes and clear thinking may be impaired, so that driving, for instance, becomes more hazardous—a danger that earlier had been discounted. The difficult question is whether chronic use has any long-term insidious effects that are damaging or irreversible. De-

396

fenders of the "recreational use" of marihuana often cite a study of 30 chronic
users and 30 nonusers among Jamaican natives by Beaubrun and Knight
(1973). They found no significant differences between the groups in the incidence of mental illness or abnormalities of mood, thought, behavior, despite
the fact that the users had smoked pot daily for no less than seven years. Sharp
criticisms have been raised about the research methods used in that study
(Russell, 1978). Many experienced clinicians in this country have observed severe insidious effects of chronic cannabis use: deterioration of memory, inability to think clearly or concentrate, loss of will power, impairment of judgment, unstable and shallow emotion, impairment in orientation, massive and
chronic passivity, and lack of motivation—the so-called "amotivational syndrome." The resulting controversy has generated an awesome amount of empirical research, the results of which leave little question about the health hazards of using cannabis.

Empirical Research on Health Hazards.   THC accumulates in the fatty tissues of the body, especially in the liver, lungs, reproductive organs, and brain.
THC is very slowly metabolized, unlike alcohol for example, so that residues
remain for one or two weeks, and they accumulate from chronic use, possibly
irreversibly. Such accumulations definitely can cause impotence and various
respiratory pathologies, and possibly also brain atrophy when used chronically
for many years. In rhesus monkeys, who readily learn to smoke, as little as two
joints a week for three months (a total of 20 cigarettes) causes abnormality in
electrically recorded brain activity that may be permanent. The primary focus
of THC action appears to be a particular region of the brain, the limbic system, which contains the so-called "pleasure center" and controls visceral and
sexual functions, perceptual sensations, drives, and the expression of emotion.
These changes in electrical activity do *not* register in scalp recordings, which
are commonly used and were the *only* ones used in the Jamaican study; the recordings must be made with electrodes implanted deep in the brain (Russell,
1978). Using an electron microscope, Heath et al. (1979) found structural
changes at the cellular level in the brain of pot-smoking monkeys: a widening
of the juncture between adjacent nerve cells, abnormal deposits, and early
signs of nerve cell degeneration—all localized in the septal region of the limbic
area where abnormal brain wave patterns were recorded. Cannabis has also
been shown to precipitate seizures in epileptics.
  Perhaps the most serious criticism of research on these health hazards has
been that unrepresentatively large doses of the drug were required to produce
the physical pathologies observed. For this reason, the most compelling evidence yet available concerns reproductive impairment. Sassenrath and her associates (1979) gave the equivalent of 1 to 3 "good" marihuana reefers daily to
female rhesus monkeys, who metabolize the drug very similarly to the way humans do. Of those that became pregnant while taking the drug, 44 percent
lost their babies during pregnancy or soon after birth. The control group of **397**

nondrugged mothers had only a 12 percent birth loss. The experimental babies that survived had lower birth weights than controls and were hyperactive: playing harder, sleeping less, and being more aggressive than their peers. Further studies with rats, mice, rabbits, and monkeys at other research centers replicated the high infant mortality rate and specified at least part of the physiological mechanisms involved: shrinkage in the uterus and ovaries of the mothers and sharp alterations in the hormones that control reproduction. Damage was also found in the sperm cells of human male pot smokers, suggesting that reproduction is impaired in both sexes. Those who doubt these results should examine the photographs on page 397.

In summary, it is clear that marihuana is toxic or poisonous to the body and especially to the brain. There can be no doubt that it is physically harmful when used regularly in large amounts, and it can also be psychologically disastrous. Occasional pot smokers are entitled to protest that none of these consequences have been shown to happen if the drug is used with sensible moderation. Whether light and occasional use has detectable adverse effects still needs to be investigated. In the meantime, everyone should be aware that marihuana cannot be given special status as a totally innocuous drug. If it is used, care must be taken not to slip over the line into regrettable drug abuse.

Legal Sanctions. The federal laws against possessing, selling, or giving away marihuana were moderated in 1970, classifying such offenses as misdemeanors rather than felonies, but the potential penalties still remain large: up to one year's imprisonment and/or a $5000 maximum fine. The penalties are even more severe for second and subsequent offenses, especially for providing the drug to minors under eighteen years of age. The laws are severe because for many years marihuana was considered addictive. There has been strong resistance to relaxing the legal restrictions because it has been found that about 80 percent of narcotic addicts have used marihuana previously. Does this mean that smoking pot leads to (causes) the abuse of other, more dangerous drugs like heroin? In fact, very few of the millions who use marihuana go on to use narcotics, so no causal connection has been established. Probably some persons who are disposed to abuse the drug may be more likely to abuse other, stronger drugs. We do not yet know how much easy access to marihuana may influence these people to try narcotics.

The opinion of experts on drug abuse seems now to be shifting clearly toward reducing the legal penalties against marihuana use (Grinspoon, 1971; Brenner, 1972). When discussing this issue, people frequently refer to Prohibition, the "noble experiment" that failed to shut off the flow of alcohol, which is a more costly menace to society than marihuana. If 35 to 40 million Americans have used pot and 15 million of them still do it regularly, then enforcement of laws against using it would be difficult, at the least. The problem is complicated all the more because smuggling across our southern border is now a very profitable business. Recent trends in law and public opinion seem to be

Electron microscope pictures of sperm cells. Photo A shows normal sperm from a control subject. Photos B and C show the changes in the sperm of chronic hashish users in Athens, Greece.

coming around to the view that marihuana use and abuse should be treated as a social and medical problem, not a legal one.

Hallucinogens

The best known and most fully researched hallucinogenic or psychotomimetic drug is lysergic acid diethylamide. Since most people can't pronounce the last word, under the influence of the drug or otherwise, it is usually referred to as LSD or acid. Other less known but powerful hallucinogens include peyote, mescaline, psilocybin, CMT, and STP. LSD is an artificial chemical obtained from a fungus that grows as a rust on rye grain. It is so powerful than one ounce of LSD provides 300,000 average doses. An average dose amounts to a tiny speck of colorless, tasteless, odorless material that is usually taken in pill or capsule form, although the amount of active material is so small it can be placed in a cube of sugar or almost any other food. Its effects usually last from eight to twelve hours (U. S. Public Health Service, 1970).

The physical effects are like those of most stimulants: enlarged pupils, flushed face, chilliness, perhaps a rise in temperature and heartbeat, and a slight increase in blood pressure. The psychological effects can be quite dramatic. Marked changes in sensation, especially vision, are typical. Unusual patterns are seen and the meaning of what is seen is transformed. *Synesthesias* occur in which one experience is translated or merged into another so that, for example, smells may be felt or sounds may be seen. Illusions and hallucinations can occur and delusional thoughts are sometimes expressed. The sense of time and of self are strangely altered. Emotional variations are marked, ranging from bliss to horror, sometimes within a single experience. One of the most confusing, yet common, experiences is to feel two strong but opposing feelings at the same time: happy and sad, or depressed and elated, or relaxed and tense. Arms and legs may feel simultaneously heavy and light. The normal feeling of boundaries between one's body and space may be lost. Memory and logical thinking remain intact, up to a point, but they become impaired with larger doses, giving way to feelings of great understanding, new insights, a sense of rebirth. Nearly always these "enlightenments" turn out to be fleeting or spurious. Many experts believe that chronic or continued use of LSD distorts judgment and impairs the ability to concentrate and think rationally. Christopher Mayhew, a member of the British House of Commons, captured the sublime ambiguity of the "psychedelic experience" in a letter to the London *Times* describing his own experiment with an LSD-type hallucinogenic drug. "I experienced the beatific vision, eternal life, heaven. It was all there as the saints had described it—ecstasy, timelessness, illumination and unity, or if you prefer it, depersonalization, time disturbances, light hallucinations and the disintegration of the ego." Some users believe that LSD fosters creativity because it heightens sense impressions, but objective studies show conclusively that paintings, writings, and other works created under the influence of the drug are noticeably poorer than otherwise. The enhancements claimed are entirely subjective and not consensually valid.

The overwhelming majority of people take LSD for the "high"—to feel better. This may be because they are unable to deal with life's frustrations, or feel alienated. Other reasons given are: curiosity, because friends do it, "kicks," self-understanding, or a search for religious or philosophical insights. Unhappily, not all "trips" produce euphoria, pleasant sensations, and gratifying im-

400

agery. Sometimes the trip is a bad one or "bummer" in which the images are terrifying and the emotional state is full of dread and horror. Because of the distorted time sense—a few minutes may drag on like hours—this may seem like a terrible nightmare that will never end. In extreme cases panic may ensue as the user grows more and more frightened by not being able to "turn off" the drug's action. It is common to forget that a drug has changed one's thinking and feeling, and thus one becomes more vulnerable to the fear of losing one's mind. *Flashbacks*, or recurrences of some of the features of the LSD trip days or months after the last dose, may occur without apparent cause, leading to the subjective fear that the user is becoming psychotic. In some individuals this concern has caused anxiety and depression leading to suicide. Even good trips have led to accidental death. Cases have been reported, for example, where LSD users felt they were invulnerable or could fly and consequently walked in front of moving cars or attempted to fly from high windows, with disastrous results.

An LSD Trip with Extra Mileage

There is some question whether LSD in itself can cause mental illness in an emotionally stable individual, but there is little doubt that the drug can precipitate acute and sometimes long-lasting disorders in susceptible persons. Often those who are most vulnerable emotionally are the most attracted to LSD, in the hope that it will solve their problems or provide "instant insight." A professional psychologist found out about this danger the hard way. He was a clinical researcher and very much interested in the mind-altering potential of the hallucinogens. Early in the 1960s he was corresponding with Professor Timothy Leary, who was experimenting with all sorts of drugs. At one point Leary wrote that he had acquired incredible insights from taking LSD. Among other things he had come to understand that there is but *one mind*. In the fall of 1960 his correspondent also began some experiments with the drug, using volunteers and himself as subjects. Usually he administered small doses, but one time he himself took 2000 micrograms, a very large dose. A few days after that he delivered an enthusiastic lecture about LSD at a Veterans' hospital. Several clinicians in the audience were struck by a subtle but unmistakable looseness in his thinking. His lecture was slightly grandiose, rather disjointed, and contained several large leaps of inference. No one mentioned a clinical diagnosis of manic psychosis, but there was general consensus among those who attended that this was a very eccentric psychologist. He became increasingly agitated in succeeding weeks, reportedly without taking any more drugs, until he was hospitalized about two months later in such bad shape that he had to be transported to the hospital in a straitjacket. There followed a deep psychotic depression that lasted several months, despite the very best treatment available in an exclusive private hospital. Within weeks after his release and about seven months after the first talk, he delivered another lecture

401

to a professional audience. This time he carefully analyzed the subjective enthusiasm that LSD had created in him initially and then gave a sober account of his long psychotic episode. From this presentation one got the impression that the awesome power of LSD has both enhancing and destructive aspects.

It is not yet known how LSD works in the body, but it seems to affect the levels of certain brain chemicals like serotonin and norepinephrine (see Chapter 15) and to produce changes in the brain's electrical activity. Animal experiments suggest that the brain's normal filtering and screening processes become blocked, causing it to be flooded with unselected sights and sounds. Chronic LSD users continue to be overloaded with sensory stimulation, which may explain their inability to think clearly and to concentrate on a task or goal. Considering the potent impact of LSD it is not surprising that many studies indicate that it may cause chromosomal damage in the user and offspring (Nichols, 1972). Two cases of acute leukemia have also been attributed to LSD (Cohen, 1970). However, other studies have found contrary results and it is still too soon to conclude that there is a direct link between LSD and chromosomal damage or birth defects. The evidence is sufficiently strong so that women of childbearing age are particularly urged not to use the drug. The federal penalties for possessing, producing, selling, or giving away LSD illegally are quite severe, and there is not much public sentiment to change them because of the general consensus that it is a dangerous drug.

Stimulants

Cocaine is probably the oldest and most widely used stimulant in the world. For centuries it has been the practice of natives in the Andes Mountains of South America to chew coca leaves, and it is estimated that six million still do so regularly in Bolivia and Peru (Cameron, 1972). The most commonly used stimulants in this country are amphetamine (Benzedrine), dextroamphetamine (Dexedrine), and methamphetamine (Methedrine). Slang terms for these drugs are "uppers," "bennies," and "speed." They stimulate the central nervous system and are best known for their ability to counteract fatigue and sleepiness. Drivers take them to stay awake on long trips; students take them while cramming for exams; and athletes take them to get "hyped up" for competition, although sporting associations have banned their use. In one instance, a gold medal for first place in a swimming contest at the 1972 Olympics was revoked when tests after the race showed traces of a stimulant in the winner's urine. For many years the athlete had been taking the drug for an asthmatic condition (see Chapter 7), but he had failed to obtain the necessary clearance to take the drug while competing.

The Japanese used stimulants to reduce aviator and industrial-worker fatigue during World War II, unaware of their abuse potential (Seevers, 1970). Civilian use in Japan began in 1945 and it was estimated in 1954 that two million Japanese used amphetamines intravenously, with 600,000 believed to be

These Peruvian Indians routinely suck on cocoa leaves, but it seldom creates a social problem for them.

chronic users. Placing the drug on prescription was inadequate to halt the epidemic, so the government passed very stringent laws against its use and initiated a massive educational campaign that finally brought the problem under control by 1958.

Amphetamines stimulate the release of norepinephrine (a substance stored in nerve endings) and concentrate it in the higher centers of the brain. This speeds up the action of the heart and the metabolic processes for converting

403

food into the chemicals the body needs. Besides increasing the heart rate, they are capable of raising the blood pressure, cause heart throbbing and rapid breathing, dilate the pupils, and cause dry mouth, sweating, headache, diarrhea, and pallor.

Psychologically, amphetamines (in moderate doses) produce feelings of alertness, self-confidence, and well-being. These last for some hours, but eventually they give place to a letdown with mildly depressed feelings. At one time physicians sometimes recommended to patients inclined to fatigue and drowsiness during part of the working day that they take a daily small dose of amphetamine. This dose, like coffee, produced no immediately noticeable effect but kept the patients pleasantly alert throughout the day. Ill effects have not been demonstrated for this very moderate use except that people might push themselves beyond their true physical endurance and reach periods of real exhaustion. Stimulants do not produce physical dependence as do the narcotics, but the body does develop a tolerance so that larger doses are required to feel the effects. But increasing the dose was risky: the effects of the drug on heart rate and blood pressure could be unpleasant, even occasionally fatal to people with vulnerable circulatory systems. On this account, if for no other reasons, federal law now prohibits physicians from prescribing amphetamines except for certain narrowly specified conditions.

The psychological situation is different, however, when heavy doses of a stimulant are taken. The experience goes far beyond general well-being and it is felt immediately. This is more true when instead of pills the drug is taken in liquid form by injection into a vein—often a critical step in becoming addicted. Injection of a stimulant is known as "speeding" or "shooting up." The first intravenous injection produces almost at once an ecstatic experience called a "rush" or "flash" that has been likened to a full body orgasm (Smith, 1972). Indeed some individuals claim to have reached sexual climax shortly after injection. Before long the drug is likely to be taken in a spree over a day or two, and gradually the sprees become longer, the doses larger, and the injections more frequent, in order to get the same level of "flash" and perpetuate the high. After a period of several months the user is a "speed freak" who injects the drug many times a day in large doses, and remains awake continuously for three to six days, becoming increasingly tense, shaky, and paranoid as the "run" progresses. The runs are interrupted by bouts of profound sleep, called crashing, which last a day or two before another run begins. The severity of the crash is related to the length of the run, the amount and quality of the drug taken, and the physical and psychological condition of the user. For the novice after a short run it is mildly unpleasant, with fatigue, mild depression, and ravenous hunger. As the length of the run is extended and the condition of the user deteriorates, the crash includes deep depression, hallucinations, and extreme fatigue, which are so unbearable that experienced speed freaks try to blot it out by taking a depressant drug such as a barbiturate or heroin to induce sleep immediately (Kramer, 1972). Alternating the drugs or taking speed and heroin simultaneously often leads to narcotic addiction. It is not surprising that most of the young white heroin addicts in the Haight-Asbury district had previously used speed compulsively.

The pattern of serious drug abuse is fairly regular (Cohen, 1972). Stronger forms of a drug tend to displace weaker ones. More rapid techniques of acquisition become preferred to slower forms of absorption. Speed may be taken first as a pill, then "snorted" for more immediate effect and ultimately injected. This should come as no surprise to psychologists because immediate reinforcements are the most powerful ones, and a needle in a vein provides the quickest delivery of a drug to the brain. Experimentally arranged intravenous self-injection of amphetamines in rats is just as strongly reinforcing, and is characterized by periods of intake and abstinence entirely analogous to the patterns seen in human speed freaks (Pickens, Weisch, & McGuire, 1967; Pickens & Harris, 1968). Finally, more dangerous (and expensive) drugs displace less dangerous ones. *Once a person is assimilated in the drug culture*, the steps of progression are predictable: from pot to LSD, from LSD to speed, and from intravenous anything to intravenous heroin.

The use of stimulants, and cocaine in particular, increased dramatically in the 1970s, especially among college students and affluent, educated adults. Most of them seriously underestimate the dangers of these drugs. They take too lightly the life-threatening potential in the "recreational use" of stimulants, for instance the real danger of cardiac arrest. They also fail to respect the power of "mere" psychological dependence. In the case of stimulants, the startingly pleasant results of the "rush" or "flash" are extremely strong reinforcers, making a repetition hard to resist. "Drug dependence results basically from the reproducible interaction between an individual and a pleasure-inducing biologically active molecule. The common denominator of all drug dependence is the psychological reinforcement resulting from reward associated with past (use of the drug) and the subsequent increasing desire for repeated reinforcement" (Nahas, 1975, pp. 187–188).

The Violence Associated with the Speed Culture

The life style of speed freaks is so frantic that most people not on speed can't stand to be around them, so they congregate together, talk and fantasize, bicker endlessly, and share their plans and dreams for the future. A lot of attention is naturally given to maintaining their supply of drugs. Occasionally there are sudden outbursts of violence, especially if the group has been "running" for a long time on large doses of speed. On long runs their activity becomes very frantic and irrational. Roger Smith (1972) cites as an example the torture-rape of a teenage girl who was a heavy user of speed and barbiturates. She was accused by another girl in a large group of stealing a barbiturate pill. The girl denied the theft, but the accuser began to assault her. This focused the attention of the entire group on the victim, and they proceeded to "train"

405

The photograph above shows the elaborate paraphernalia used to prepare for snorting cocaine, which the woman below is doing through a rolled up twenty dollar bill. The scene behind shows that cocaine is often used for recreational purposes at parties.

or gang-rape her. When a member of the group was later asked why he didn't try to stop it, he explained that this would put him on her side, in the minority, which is a very dangerous place. "You have to imagine how heavy those people were into that; if you go against them you best come out shooting."

Because the law prohibits (albeit ineffectively) the nonmedical use of stimulants, the speed scene is a criminal subculture in which most users lead a marginal existence. To maintain that existence and provide a steady supply of drugs, it is common to resort to prostitution, robbery, or one of several "hustles" involving the distribution of drugs to other users. The primary cause of violence is related to the practice of "burning," or selling highly adulterated drugs. Street hustlers usually deal in small quantities, hoping to realize enough profit to pay for the cost of their own drugs. But in the euphoria and expansiveness created by an injection they may shoot all the speed purchased for resale and then have no money to buy additional drugs. Then they may package any substance that looks like speed and attempt to sell it on the streets. They may be lucky for a while, but veterans in the speed culture consider "burning" an offense than cannot go unpunished. After all, there is no police force to ensure the quality of the drugs they buy. Punishment may take the form of a large monetary fine or a beating. Some "burn artists" are knifed or shot. Many of the overdose deaths in the drug culture are not accidental, but are deliberately executed sentences. In one instance, a burn artist was given the choice of being shot or taking a massive dose of LSD (ten 500-mcg capsules). He chose the overdose and was discovered by the police days later, wandering the streets naked and totally incoherent.

The medical complications of chronic stimulant abuse or an overdose are severe hypertension, cerebral hemorrhage, hepatitis (from poor hygienic techniques during injection), convulsions, coma, and sudden death (Louria, 1972). Angrist and Gershon (1972) reported the case of a twenty-four-year-old man who had taken amphetamine heavily for two years, shooting a "spoon" of street speed because he began to feel influenced by electric waves and forces possibly emanating from a machine operated by "people in the background," and became convinced that a police raid was imminent. To avoid prosecution, he had swallowed the remaining three "spoons" in his possession and then jumped from a second-story fire escape to elude his persecutors. In the hospital he showed auditory hallucinations that cleared after two days, and ideas of influence that diminished gradually over two weeks. The diagnostic impression after clearing was chronic paranoid schizophrenia with superimposed intoxication. About a year later he was caught in an actual police raid and swallowed what is estimated at 10 to 15 grams of amphetamine to destroy the evidence. (Even one gram is a very large dose.) Three hours later he was totally disorganized, throwing his arms up in the air and rolling his head around, so far gone that he didn't realize what was going on. He was taken to a hospital in shock and assisted by a respirator, but he died less than fifteen hours after taking the overdose.

The graffito sometimes written on the wall of a drug clinic reads: "Just give me Librium or give me Meth" (D. E. Smith, 1972). It reflects an attitude of many young drug users who come to the clinic because they just took the "wrong drug" or too much of the "right" one, but do not question the life style of drug involvement. In the case just reviewed, one could claim that the young man's premature death was due to an overdose caused by the criminalization of drug dependence. That is partly true but an additional cause of death was a whole life style gone wrong. Speed kills.

Sedatives

These are a large group of drugs made for medical purposes to relax the central nervous system. The best known are the barbiturates, made from barbituric acid, which was first manufactured in 1846. There are long-acting, slow-starting forms like phenobarbital (Luminal) and amobarbital (Amytal). The most commonly abused forms are short-acting, but with immediate effect, like phenobarbital sodium (Nembutal) and secobarbital sodium (Seconal). Slang terms for these are "downers," "barbs," and "goof balls."

In normal doses barbiturates mildly depress the action of the nerves, skeletal muscles, and heart. They slow down the heart rate and breathing, and lower the blood pressure. For these effects they are beneficial for diagnosing and treating mental illness, relaxing patients before and during surgery, and treating tension disorders like ulcers, high blood pressure, epilepsy, and insomnia. In higher doses the effects resemble drunkenness, with confusion, slurred speech, and staggering. There is impairment of the ability to think, to concentrate, or to work, and emotional control is weakened. Users may become irritable, angry, and combative, and then finally fall into deep sleep (U.S. Public Health Service, 1969).

Barbiturates distort sense perception and slow down motor reactions, so they are an important cause of automobile accidents, especially when combined with alcohol abuse. Barbiturates tend to heighten the effects of alcohol, which explains in part why one study found more than half of the psychiatric patients who abused sedatives had also abused alcohol at some time (Bakewell & Wikler, 1966). Reactions to the drug are stronger at some times than others and users become confused about how many pills they have taken, which leads to accidental overdose and sometimes death. Barbiturates are a leading cause of accidental poison deaths in the United States and one of the most common means for committing suicide.

Almost all sedatives produce physical as well as psychological dependence. Barbiturate addiction is considered by some experts more difficult to cure than narcotic addiction. The body requires increasingly larger doses to feel their effects. Abrupt withdrawal of the drug produces an abstinence syndrome with cramps, nausea, delirium, convulsions, and in some cases sudden death. Therefore withdrawal should take place under medical supervision in a hospi-

408

tal with gradually reduced dosages over a period of several weeks. Several months are required for the body to return to normal.

The sale of sedatives, like that of stimulants, is closely regulated by federal agencies. All sales to the public must be obtained by prescription. The penalties for illicit dealing in the drugs include heavy fines and imprisonment. However, one in four of all the prescriptions doctors write for mood-affecting drugs is for a barbiturate, and probably an equally large supply is obtained illegally, without prescription. A large number of the people who abuse sedatives are mature adults, business executives, homemakers, and professionals, who lead productive lives and use the drugs to relax tension, blow off steam, and forget their worries. Because of their respectability, barbiturate addiction was not regarded as a very serious social problem until it found its way recently into the urban youth culture, where in combination with speed and heroin it contributed to crime and the corruption of younger and younger lives. Then the magnitude of the problem and the dangers of these drugs became clear. This evolution of social consciousness may seem self-serving and unfair to young dissidents who believe in their right to use the drugs as they choose, but behind it lies a sound, if vaguely articulated, principle. There is tolerance for individuals to abuse drugs to the extent of damaging or even destroying their own lives, but society sets limits when such abuse reaches epidemic proportions and especially when the individual's abuse impinges substantially on the lives of others. Following the Japanese example, we can only hope that individuals will set their own limits when the dangers of the drugs are publicized widely enough.

Narcotics

The principal narcotics are opium and pain-killing drugs derived from opium, which is obtained from the juice of the poppy fruit. The derivatives include heroin, the most widely used by far, morphine, paregoric, and codeine. The opiates can be taken orally or inhaled, but they are most often injected intravenously by addicts. Heroin depresses the central nervous system and reduces hunger, thirst, and the sex drive. For this reason many heroin addicts lose tremendous amounts of weight and suffer from malnutrition. Emotionally, heroin reduces tension, relieves fears and worries, and creates a glowing sense of euphoria. Its effectiveness in killing pain accounts for its principal medical use. The "high" makes a person feel very self-confident, and this is followed by a period of inactivity bordering on stupor. It is well known that heroin leads to addiction, both physically and psychologically. Once the habit is started, the body develops a tolerance for the drug. Because it is outlawed for nonmedical use, heroin is expensive on the street. As the habit gets bigger and more expensive—some habits cost hundreds of dollars a day—the addict is usually forced into a life of crime to pay for the drugs. Like the speed freaks described earlier, most narcotic addicts pay their way through drug dealing,

409

prostitution, and a variety of street "hustles." Even more of the serous crimes of burglary, armed robbery, and forgery are associated with narcotics. Once crime and degradation have become a way of life, the emotional dependence on heroin is locked in as a way to escape facing life. The abstinence syndrome on withdrawal can be quite severe, as with barbiturates, but the symptoms may be alleviated under medical treatment. Fear of the withdrawal keeps many addicts "hooked" (U.S. Public Health Service, 1969).

The health of addicts is often bad. They may be sick one day from the effects of withdrawal and sick the next from an overdose. They can never be sure of the purity of the heroin they buy on the street and this leads to accidental overdoses. Their life span is drastically shortened. The medical complications of chronic narcotic abuse are heart infection, tetanus and hepatitis (both from unhygienic use of needles), and various respiratory and circulatory difficulties (Louria, 1972). At least one percent of heroin addicts die every year, a mortality rate 2.5 to 3.0 times the average; 1400 died in New York City alone during 1974, more than half from adverse drug reactions, 40 percent from violence (usually homicide) and 5 percent from infection (Platt & Labate, 1976). In 1972 one of 27 infants born in New York City was to a heroin-addicted mother; most of these babies showed signs of withdrawal within 48 hours after birth (Zelson, 1973).

Cimino et al. (1973) estimated the prevalence of heroin addiction nationally at 700,000 to 800,000, although there is some indication that the number is declining. Among black addicts, who are in the majority, drug use often starts around sixteen or seventeen years of age; they typically grow up in poor familial environments during the formative periods of their lives, with serious parental problems of emotional and physical health, parental absence, socioeconomic and general deprivation (Platt & Labate, 1976). By the time they become drug users they are likely to be socially deviant already: school dropouts, marital failures, and chronically unemployed (Ball & Chambers, 1970). They are usually in trouble with their families and almost always in trouble with the law. Immaturity and alienation permeate the descriptions of most addicts. Perhaps the most uncharitable characterization is made by Chuck Dederich, a reformed alcoholic and the founder of Synanon, which will be discussed shortly: "Dope fiends shoot dope. As long as they are dope fiends, they are not much good; they are slobs and thieves, with the temperaments of nasty little children. When they stop using dope, they're something else again. They need self-respect and then general respect more than they do sympathy" (Yablonsky, 1965, p. 379).

A Case History

The life of Charlie Hamer demonstrates that narcotic addiction signifies much more than habitual dependence on a chemical (Yablonsky, 1965, pp. 16–25). He was born in 1903 in Henryetta, Oklahoma, the youngest of five

410

children. He was fatherless at the age of one. His mother reared the children with little supervision, for which she had neither the time nor the ability. He was arrested at ten for stealing coal and chickens and at seventeen for drunkenness, disturbing the peace, and fighting. At nineteen a local Chinese family introduced him to opium, which he smoked for three years. His first hypodermic injection took place at twenty-two with the residue from an opium pipe. One year later he began using morphine intravenously. This drug was obtained in the pure form from unethical doctors, pharmaceutical houses, and peddlers. He built up a larger tolerance and used 15 to 25 grains per day, obtaining money for the drugs by theft, robbery, confidence games, and the like. Then he began alternating with cocaine and was introduced to heroin at thirty. When he was thirty-four he migrated to California and was free of drugs for six years but used alcohol to excess. Then he began to use opium again, both orally and by injection, shipped out with the Merchant Marine and for two years used many drugs throughout the world: heroin, cocaine, hashish, morphine, the works. When he returned he used heroin constantly until joining Synanon when he was fifty-six years old. He was married and divorced three times between the ages of twenty-two and forty-four. He was arrested dozens of times for forgery, theft, robbery, vagrancy, suspicion of robbery, possession of narcotics, addiction, and forgery of narcotic prescriptions. Almost half of his adult life was spent in county jails, state penitentiaries, and federal hospitals for addicts. That he was alive and able to function after all that abuse indicates how strong his constitution was.

Psychological Aspects of Drug Abuse

Bearing in mind the different effects of the drugs we have been describing, one might suppose that each user would have a favorite drug and would become addicted only to the one that best fitted his or her needs. This should apply especially to "downers" and "uppers"; it seems paradoxical to crave both unless they have been worked into a complementary temporal pattern. We would guess from everyday experience that there are people who, perhaps as a matter of innate constitution, feel slightly "down" a good deal of the time: quiet types who tire easily, often feel a little sleepy, and never refuse a cup of coffee. Before amphetamine was placed under legal restriction, a small daily dose was sometimes prescribed for people of this type, who reported themselves to be more alert and lively as a result. But for these same people a daily dose of a tranquilizer would be harmful, lowering their energy still further, whereas maintenance doses of a tranquilizing drug are often felt to be indispensable by people who otherwise would suffer all day from tension and jumpy nerves. Eysenck (1970) has shown experimentally that extraverts and introverts, as defined by his measuring instruments, respond to different drugs in ways that are reliably different. Are we not therefore entitled to suppose that "speed" abuse will take hold in people who have difficulty getting up speed, that narcotics will get their grip on those who crave a dreamy escape from trouble and pain, and that LSD will seduce people whose habitual boredom is drowned in the excitement of novel, unearthly experiences?

It is not improbable that preferences of this kind exist and influence the course of drug abuse. But there is the case of Charlie Hamer who tried them all, and his story is not unusual. Widespread today is a pattern of drug abuse that includes everything; the use of drugs is accepted as a way of life. The implicit expectation seems to be that one's whole feeling experience, up or down alike, is to be produced and guided by chemical means. The underlying rationale is a caricature of push-button technology. There is a switch, a pill, a drug for every need, including how one feels. The appeal of drugs is that they can switch on all kinds of feelings, soothing, exciting, mystical, even blasting, and one wants to be sure to experience them all. We can infer that the main psychological need satisfied by drugs as a way of life is the need to overcome what might be called an affective anaesthesia. There is a marked parallel here to what we noticed in Chapter 8 when studying encounter groups; there, too, much importance is attached to securing a strong, even violent, expression of feeling. Probably those who crave emotional encounters and those who crave drugs come from overlapping groups, sharing an emptiness of feeling that seems to be common in our time. Another feature of contemporary alienation that adds to the attraction of drugs as a way of life is a deep-seated passivity. As we saw, Ruitenbeek (1970) described this quality, often encountered in contemporary young patients, as a seeming unfamiliarity with expending personal effort and making personal decisions. If one does not have command over one's actions and associated feelings, the temptation may soon become overwhelming to let drugs do it all.

To the extent that alienation of this sort lies behind drug abuse it is difficult to mobilize the motivation necessary for successful treatment. Many who lead the drug way of life come from grievously depressed backgrounds; one cannot honestly picture for them a glowing future if they kick their habit. Others come from affluent homes, but have rejected the "establishment" in such wholesale terms that no glow is possible in their own picture of the future. The situation illustrates once more the close relation between personal pathology and social conditions. Sometimes anxiety becomes enlisted on the side of treatment: the drug abuser becomes panic-stricken about medical consequences. A more valuable ally, however, is the need for self-respect, and sometimes this need can be rekindled from the ruins that would be considered, objectively, a human wreck.

Treatment for Drug Dependence

Synanon was founded in 1958 and staffed with drug addicts. It was originally housed on the beach in Santa Monica, California, but now has several chapters scattered through the country. What success this organization has had in curing addiction comes from recognizing at the start that treatment only works if the addict genuinely wants it to work. Often the crucial test is the initial willingness to undergo the agony of withdrawal by kicking the habit "cold turkey." The two cardinal rules of living at Synanon House are: no drugs and no physical violence. One of the most controversial aspects of the treatment is the verbal-attack therapy employed in the "synanon sessions." This is a form of encounter group experience in which each member takes a turn being challenged, grilled, and criticized for faults, emotional weaknesses, suspect motives, and behavior at Synanon (Yablonsky, 1965). The rationale behind this vicious cross-examination is that the fundamental causes for becoming and remaining a drug addict are emotional faults for which a variety of subterfuges and defenses are devised to cover up. Once the secondary symptom of chemical addiction has been cured, the brutal exposure of the synanon sessions is used to uncover the primary emotional pathology. Catharsis is obviously an important mechanism in the treatment. Social support is even more significant.

Consider, for example, Charlie Hamer's "treatment." He was among the first to come to Synanon in 1959, weighing 118 pounds rather than his natural 170, and carrying a life-long heavy habit. On entering he met three junkies, all old friends, who were "clean" (free of drugs) and very enthusiastic about Synanon. Charlie couldn't believe it. He spent the first several days on a divan, sick as a dog, trying vainly to persuade some of the other junkies to get him some dope. Two women nursed him day and night, giving him bed baths and wiping up his vomit. Every day Dederick stopped by to shake his hand and taunt him that he could not stick it out. But he did, because he was afraid of his habit and sick of the demoralization it caused him. Within a week he kicked the habit and took his first job, as breakfast cook, but reluctantly. He hadn't bought Synanon; he just figured to stay thirty days so when he got back to the streets the habit would cost only about half as much as before. But before long Dederich astonished him by entrusting him with $3 or $4 of the organization's precious little money to buy groceries and get a meal together. It was a terrific challenge and an important milestone when Charlie managed to get past the drugstore on that first errand. Within a few months he was chosen as a director of Synanon. He didn't know what to do about that. He was flattered and pleased, of course, but also frightened about the responsibility it would entail, and he still was bent on leaving soon. After considering the matter for a few days, a seemingly trivial incident convinced him of his course of action. He was walking down the hallway on the second floor, on his way to the toilet, when he saw a cigarette butt on the floor. He reached down to pick it up and put it in the butt can, and that started him thinking. If he had acquired such a sense of proprietorship that he was now picking up butts off the floor, then he must have decided already to stay at Synanon. The next morning he went downstairs with a clear look in his eye and started acting like a director, poking his nose into things he didn't know anything about, like other people's responsibilities. Charlie Hamer remained "clean" at Synanon ever since. He has

413

been in charge of the young-adult group and for a time directed the Synanon House in Reno, Nevada. Understandably, he has been an outstanding role model for younger members, who could derive hope for themselves from the example of his personal success.

The leaders of Synanon have kept the evaluation of their success rate in treatment and rehabilitation a closely guarded secret, because they consider the organization rather like a cult or a religion whose success depends on its mystery and charisma. Some facts, however, have recently emerged. Of 844 entering the program over a five-year period (1959–1964) 54 percent left prematurely (Scott & Goldberg, 1973) and 75 percent of those who completed the program and left the sheltered community relapsed to drug use within two years (Switzer, 1974). On the other hand, 43 percent of the 844 remained in residence and free of drug use.

A tragic footnote should be added to the Synanon story. Over the years the organization became quite large and fabulously wealthy. Stories were told that Dederich ruled over the empire in the manner of a tyrant. Finally, in 1979 criminal charges were brought against him for threatening violence against his enemies and for ordering members of his staff to implement the threats. Incriminating recordings of his staff meetings were presented as evidence in court. When papers were served for his arrest at a luxurious residence in Arizona, he was found in a drunken stupor at the age of 66, psychiatrically unfit to stand trial for the alleged crimes. Apparently the temptations of power were too much for the reformed alcoholic; he violated his own first cardinal rule and eventually succumbed again. He was institutionalized for psychiatric rehabilitation before being brought to trial on the criminal charges.

The Synanon treatment, which is best characterized as rehabilitation, has been emulated elsewhere, for example, at Daytop Village in New York City. There are limitations to such programs. Obviously, not every drug addict can find a good job like Charlie Hamer's. And unfortunately many cannot be persuaded that they want to be rehabilitated or to give up drugs. Either voluntarily or by court commitment, many are treated at federal hospitals in Lexington, Kentucky, and Fort Worth, Texas, but success has been limited for involuntary patients.

Decriminalizing Drug Dependence

In an unusual sense, laws are one of society's forms of treatment for drug dependence. In the opinion of some experts, our present stringent laws have failed to control drug abuse but have caused several undesirable side effects (Stachnik, 1972). Criminal penalties make addicts reluctant to seek help and also add to the grief of their families. Confiscation and ultimate shortage of drugs keep their price high, by the laws of supply and demand, and thus encourages crime to support the habit and fosters aggressive recuitment of new

414

Synanon pioneered in the use of a form of intense encounter group treatment for drug addicts. A lot of powerful emotion is also being expressed in this encounter session at a youth center in New York.

users as the safest way to raise money. Legal prohibition makes illegal traffic more profitable, raises the chances of police corruption, and diverts law enforcement from other crucial crime protection. Felony conviction subjects users to the dehumanizing effects of imprisonment and hampers job rehabilitation, which is critical. And the penalties fall mostly on poor minority groups, who use drugs for escape from the unpleasant realities of their lives, for which the affluent white "establishment" is partly at fault.

Stachnik offers a radical counterproposal that merits careful attention: that we remove the present criminal penalties and treat psychoactive drugs like any other potentially harmful substance (medicine, cigarettes, alcohol). He would treat drug dependence as a medical problem by offering users a choice of heroin or methadone or any other drug in maintenance dosages at community clinics for minimal cost or nothing. Several advantages of this procedure are cited. It would reduce the amount of urban crime, more than half of which is presently committed to support heroin habits. Clean equipment would reduce hepatitis and other illnesses caused by nonsterile injection. Overdose deaths and murders associated with criminal traffic in drugs would be reduced.

415

METHADONE TREATMENT

Methadone is a highly addictive drug that is antagonistic to heroin. It prevents heroin-induced euphoria as well as the excruciating symptoms of heroin withdrawal. The main advantages of methadone are that it does not induce a tolerance necessitating steadily increased dosages, as heroin does, and it produces only mild abstinence symptoms, even with rapid withdrawal. Methadone is the most widely used of several "alternatives" to heroin currently offered on an experimental basis to addicts who want to kick the habit. Goldstein (1977) reports that approximately a third of those who begin methadone maintenance programs emerge several years later substantially improved; Freedman (1977) offers 35 to 40 percent as a conservative estimate of success.

Moreover, this would provide the first benign contact between the "establishment" and the heroin subculture, which could be followed with careful attempts to shift heroin habits to methadone, initiate rehabilitation, and so on.

Radical as it sounds, such a program has already been tried in Britain, with encouraging initial results. It used to be that every physician in the United Kingdom could use discretion about prescribing narcotics for addicts, with the result that known heroin and cocaine users tripled in number from 1964 to 1967 (Jaffe, 1972). Thereafter authorization to prescribe for narcotic addicts was restricted to specialized clinics attached to major teaching hospitals. As long as the addict remains registered with a Drug Dependency Center, he or she may receive prescriptions for any drug at a standard cost of 52¢ (or free if the person cannot afford to pay). A special effort is made to switch heroin addicts to methadone and, if possible, to give up drugs altogether. A number of rehabilitation programs are available if the addict wishes to participate. Most of Britain's registered heroin addicts are now being supplied with methadone. In the first three years of the program the number of British addicts has declined slightly, while during a comparable period the number has more than doubled in the United States (Whitten & Robertson, 1972).

Though the matter is extremely controversial in this country, a consensus is growing among drug treatment experts that some kind of maintenance programs must be tried out, at least experimentally. We must keep in perspective that maintenance programs only treat the peripheral symptoms of a profound disorder, both in individuals and in society at large. Without simultaneous efforts at prevention and rehabilitation, maintenance programs could at best only mark time. The least that can be said is that experimental maintenance programs are no less reasonable than the American agreement to pay a $35 million subsidy to Turkish poppy growers to stop raising their crops by the end of 1972, a scheme that defied the laws of both economics and reason (Whitten & Robertson, 1972).

Prevention

It is ironic that in handling pressing social problems, efforts at prevention often come last, after programs for relief of symptoms and the rehabilitation of past victims, whereas logic would seem to dictate the reverse priority. Prevention may also come last because to be effective it requires the most knowledge about causes. Although we know little about the precise patterns of etiology for drug dependence, it appears that primary prevention must begin in the family home. A questionnaire study of 8865 high school students in Toronto suggests that the drug-use patterns of parents may influence their children's (Smart & Fejer, 1972). Fewer students reported using tobacco, marihuana, barbiturates, heroin, speed, LSD, and other psychoactive drugs if the parents used neither tobacco nor alcohol. Mothers who frequently smoked and drank were most likely to have their children turn to illicit and stronger drugs. These findings might be discounted as showing only that ascetic parents produce ascetic offspring while indulgent parents produce indulgent offspring, a plausible result without very profound implications. However, students whose parents were regular users of tranquilizers were twice as likely to smoke marihuana, three times as likely to use hallucinogens, and eight times as likely to follow the example of drug use set in their households. On the one hand, this might implicate some kind of genetic vulnerability to drug dependence. It also may mean that children learn their attitudes and behavior regarding drugs from parental role modeling.

Prevention has been attempted mainly through a variety of public education campaigns sponsored by the U.S. Public Health Service and various professional associations. These feature popular sports stars in brief videotape clips during intermissions of televised sports programs exhorting the viewing audience not to mess around with drugs, and advising them to write to the National Institute of Drug Abuse for free booklets with the facts about drugs. It is hoped that identification with sports heroes and a knowledge of the dangers of drugs from the booklets will dissuade youngsters from turning to drugs in the first place.

CHRONIC ALCOHOLISM

We consider last the drug that is abused more and costs society more than all other drugs combined: alcohol. This is partly because the use of alcohol is legalized almost everywhere and two-thirds of American adults drink at least occasionally (U.S. Public Health Service, 1971). This observation may seem to compromise the proposal to decriminalize drug use, which was favorably presented earlier. It is indeed powerful evidence against *legalizing* the use of psychoactive drugs. Stachnik's (1972) proposal was to remove criminal penalties

417

for drug use and to authorize the provision of addicting drugs under government control, but *not* to legalize them or allow their open distribution and use according to individual discretion. We see below that the proposal to remove criminal penalties has equal merit for alcohol use, except of course for serious crimes such as drunken driving.

It is estimated that nine million people in the United States, or 7 percent of the adult population, abuse alcohol. Excessive use of alcohol is a contributing cause of 28,000 traffic fatalities, half of the total each year, a third of the suicides, more than half of the criminal homicides, 40 to 50 percent of all police arrests, and 60 percent of all commitments to mental hospitals (U.S. Public Health Service, 1971). Alcohol costs our economy $15 billion a year for health and welfare services for alcoholics and their families, time lost from work, property damage, and medical expenses (Richard, 1969). Like the other forms of drug dependence, alcohol can be woven into the texture of almost any kind of disorder. Therefore it is impossible to specify a particular developmental history or physiological predisposition for the disorder. Still, some broad regularities have been established.

The Effects of Alcohol

Alcohol is a natural substance formed by the reaction of fermenting sugar with yeast spores. The colorless, inflammable liquid is a major ingredient in beers, wines, and liquors, with varying degrees of distillation or concentration. Although we often speak of its stimulating effects, alcohol is actually a central nervous system depressant. This is clear enough when a person is quite drunk, with failing locomotion and incoherent speech. The initial stimulating effect results from its selective action on neural mechanisms. Its depressant effect touches first the most recently evolved areas of the cerebral cortex, which have a predominantly inhibitory function. Disinhibition produces a sense of well-being and relaxation, freedom of thought, and pleasant affect. It is conducive to conversation, hence the wide use of alcohol as a social lubricant. Both animal and human studies show that moderate amounts of alcohol reduce fear, anxiety, and emotional tension (Lowe, 1977).

As intoxication increases, events take a fairly regular course. There is some difference of opinion about this course, depending on whether or not the observers participate. To a slightly intoxicated judgment it will be apparent that everyone is talking with great zest, wit, and wisdom. The world is full of glowing possibilities; the heart is full of warm, friendly, and expansive feelings. But sober observers will be apt to see the picture a little differently. They will agree on the zest and expansive feelings, but they may have some reservations about matters of judgment and intellectual keenness. It will occur to them to question whether the person who is informing the company on how to construct outdoor fireplaces is really an authority on that subject, and they will doubt whether the great plans for world reform being loudly developed in an-

418

other part of the room will prove practicable in the cold light of morning reality. If they stay around long enough, they will observe further signs of deterioration as sedation progresses to other parts of the nervous system. Speech, hand coordination, and locomotion become increasingly impaired until finally a state of stupor is reached (Eysenck, 1961, pp. 664–670).

It is commonly observed that people behave more amorously after drinking, so alcohol is often thought to be an aphrodisiac. The truth is that alcohol influences sexuality in the same indirect ways that many psychoactive drugs do. Moderate amounts release inhibitions and can help to overcome lack of confidence or feelings of guilt about sex, which may facilitate sexual activity. But concerning larger amounts, Shakespeare was right: drink "provokes the desire, but it takes away the performance" (*Macbeth*, Act II, Scene 3).

Normal and Abnormal Drinking

There are many people who use alcohol frequently but never to excess. In some circles moderate drinking is part of the routine life, though immoderate drinking is regarded as reprehensible. These facts make it possible to speak of *normal drinking* and to look for some kind of a line beyond which drinking can be called *abnormal*. Such a line might be drawn according to external signs: drinking in the morning, being unable to face any important situation unless "fortified," being unable to drink socially without getting drunk, and so on. All these external criteria, however, get their meaning from the strength of motivation toward alcohol. The crucial question is how urgently and for what the alcohol is needed. The mild disinhibition that is obtained from one or two drinks, with its relaxation, sense of well-being, freedom from restraint, and easy flow of conversation, is a temporary benefit that most people can appreciate. People who need alcohol for this benefit and for nothing more are normal drinkers and likely to remain so. They are under no serious temptation to drink beyond the point where this benefit is obtained, and it is not worth it to them to wake up next morning with a hangover. Furthermore, they are not so dependent on this benefit that they cannot forego it when circumstances so require. Normal drinkers, in short, have no strong further motive for using alcohol beyond the enjoyment of its mild disinhibitory effects. A similar "exoneration" could be claimed for the great majority of "recreational" users of marihuana or cocaine, who smoke or snort only occasionally under the same circumstances and for the same reasons. The legal implications differ, of course, and the health hazards may be substantially greater, but those considerations have little to do with the psychological motivation for drug use.

Alcohol has further potentialities, and these constitute its appeal for the person who becomes an abnormal drinker. As intoxication increases, as restraint and judgment dissolve, impulses may come to expression that are in no way satisfied in everyday life. Take the case of a college student whose outward personality was marked by a tendency toward derogatory verbal criticism and

419

a certain aloofness from all but his closest friends. Under the influence of sufficient alcohol he became extremely belligerent, picking quarrels and coming to blows with men in bars. His friends often had to rescue him because, although he fought like a demon, his slight physique was really unequal to these encounters. At mixed parties he regularly passed through the belligerent stage to expressions of a different character. He would lay his head on a girl's lap and weep piteously for her loving care, describing himself as a lonely outcast. The following day he would dimly remember his aggressive adventures but his extreme show of dependence would be safely wrapped in amnesia.

This is the sort of case that is likely to progress fron normal to abnormal drinking. There is a *repressed* but still active craving for loving maternal care. There is also a very strong aggressive need, *suppressed* by circumstances to the extent that it comes to expression only in verbal form. Alcohol does a lot for these two needs. It permits the young man to act as aggressively as he really feels, without forcing him to assume full responsibility for his actions. It permits him to gratify his dependent cravings without forcing his sober consciousness to become aware of them. Alcohol thus allows him to satisfy strong needs without disturbing the protective organization that ordinarily keeps them in check. One can easily see the fatal attraction of alcohol for a personality organized on these lines.

On the basis of experimental studies, McClelland et al. (1972) argue that *men* drink primarily to feel stronger, to increase the feeling of personal power, with less feelings of social responsibility, reality orientation, time concern, or social influence. In this way the male drinker savors the subjective feelings of potency and invincibility without the necessity to render full social account for their expression.

Abnormal drinking sets in when alcohol fits into personal motivations in some such way as those described. When it temporarily alleviates conflict by allowing expression to otherwise blocked needs, especially when its amnesic properties are utilized to prevent realization of the needs that have been expressed, alcohol is likely to become irresistibly attractive. In this case the charm of mild disinhibition is only a minor part of the motive for drinking. The major goal is relief from conflict and the expression of cravings that cannot be satisfied in real life.

Alcohol Addiction

With habitual drinking the body develops some tolerance for alcohol, and definitely becomes physically dependent on it. The withdrawal symptoms can be quite severe. Recurrent in the literature is the suspicion that some people have an unusual physical vulnerability. Studies of adoptees in Denmark show that the *sons* of alcoholics are four times more likely to become alcoholic than are the sons of nonalcoholics, whether they are raised by their alcoholic parents or by foster parents (Goodwin et al., 1977). No such difference was found for the *daughters* of alcoholics; it is important to recall that the Danish culture condones heavy drinking by men but not by women. At least 25 percent of the male relatives of alcoholics are alcoholic. The prevalence of alcoholism in Denmark is 5 percent in men and 1 percent in women (Goodwin et al., 1977). Whitney et al. (1970) demonstrated that a preference for alcohol, perhaps related to enzyme activity, can be experimentally accentuated through inbreeding in mice and rats. The evidence of a constitutional basis for alcoholism remains tentative, however, and much more attention has focused on psychological and cultural causes (U.S. Public Health Service, 1971). The disorder is most closely associated with alienation, anxiety, and impulsivity—traits we are familiar with from our study of psychoactive drug abuse. Alcoholism is found most commonly in men of minority races who have experienced exceptional hardships: limited job opportunities, unequal housing and schooling, inadequate medical care, childhood stress, and parental drinking problems. We already know that most serious psychological disorders fall on the disadvantaged, but the last point underscores again that young people learn methods for coping with stress, including maladaptive ones, from imitation and identification with adults. Alcoholism occurs most frequently among those aged thirty-five to fifty-five, when the stresses of work (or lack of it) and family responsibilities are most acute, and usually evolves slowly from problem drinking over many years (Plaut, 1967).

The prevalence of alcoholism is lowest in cultures where drinking customs and sanctions are unambiguous, widely known, and congruent with other cultural values. In these cultures people drink in a definite pattern. "The beverage is sipped slowly, consumed with food, taken in the company of others—all in relaxing, comfortable circumstances. Drinking is taken for granted. No emotional rewards are reaped by the man who shows prowess of consumption. Intoxication is abhorred" (U.S. Public Health Service, 1971, p. 3). (Incidentally, the same casual attitude is taken by South American natives toward chewing coca leaves, which explains in part why that form of drug dependence is seldom pathological there.) On the other hand, maladaptive drinking, drinking without food, and intoxication are most common in those populations where attitudes toward alcohol are ambivalent. The United States is unfortunately one of these. We assign special significance to the use of alcohol, consume increasing quantities of it, but feel guilty about it, perhaps because of our strong Puritan heritage. The result is that we have a high prevalence of alcoholism.

The medical complications of alcohol addiction are extremely serious. It shortens the life span by ten to twelve years and is a primary or related cause of brain damage, cirrhosis of the liver and other digestive organs, heart and nutritional disease, and endocrine disorders.

Treatment of Alcoholism

The treatment of alcoholism offers at least one peculiar difficulty. The main symptom is so available and so attractive that the person often cannot resist it.

At any point where treatment proves emotionally costly, there is a terrific temptation to escape into drunkenness. Alcohol constantly offers an easy solution to the problems both of life and of treatment. Most patients stubbornly cling to the idea that after being cured they will become normal drinkers. Most therapists, on the other hand, believe that only total abstinence will work in a person who has been alcoholic. An exception among experts in this field is Pattison (1976), who challenges the claim that alcoholics must achieve total abstinence from drinking to be rehabilitated. Pointing out that abstinence is not highly correlated with improvement in other areas of adjustment (emotional, interpersonal, vocational, and physical health), he argues that stabilized or controlled drinking may be a reasonable goal of treatment, if improvement in other areas of adjustment can be maintained. The argument is frankly not very convincing regarding most alcoholics; records of treatment are full of relapses that begin when the clients decide that their improved condition has made them capable of normal drinking.

A systematic review of 265 studies of alcoholism treatment showed that psychotherapy resulted in at least some improvement for two-thirds of the clients; a third were unimproved, and only 6 percent were actually worse after treatment (Emrick, 1974). A third of the clients treated were totally abstinent. A further survey of the literature showed that differences in treatment methods did not significantly affect long-term outcome (Emrick, 1975). *Abstinence rates did not differ between treated and untreated alcoholics, partly because 13 percent of the untreated ones became abstinent without professional help,* but more treated than untreated alcoholics improved, suggesting that formal treatment at least increases an alcoholic's chances of reducing the drinking problem.

Special methods have been employed to block a relapse into drinking. Many drugs have been tried, with limited success, to reduce the craving for alcohol. Clearly the best results have been obtained with *disulfiram* (Antabuse), which causes violent vomiting when combined with alcohol (Hoff, 1970). Antabuse must be taken daily and voluntarily by the alcoholic in order to prevent a return to drinking. The client is carefully instructed about the extremely adverse physical reaction caused by alcohol when taking Antabuse, or may be exposed to a mild demonstration reaction personally. The chief value of the drug is that it relieves the person from the worry of drinking impulsively, because its effects last several days, providing a "temporal cushion" during which any craving for alcohol is checked by knowledge of the unpleasant consequences. The decision to take Antabuse, and the practice of taking it, are closely related to the alcoholic's motivation to abstain. It is usually chosen by younger and less deteriorated clients who are the most highly motivated. Some older clients cannot be given the drug because of physical deterioration, but otherwise it is considered relatively harmless. Because motivation is so critical, Hoff recommends that the clients take the medication unsupervised, without reporting to members of their family or their employers. They are advised to take the drug in the quiet of their rooms and specifically reexpress their own

acceptance of the fact that they cannot drink, and that they have chosen to accept another day of abstinence. In this way, taking the medication serves to reinforce and sustain their own motivation for abstinence, and their own recognition that they are unable to drink safely. Used in this way, Hoff reports
improvement for 76 percent of Antabuse-treated alcoholics.

Some success has also been claimed for aversive conditioning. As mentioned
earlier, the client is given alcohol together with a strong emetic that causes
prolonged nausea and vomiting. The desired result is that the client acquire a
conditioned avoidance response to alcohol. Since the influence of Pavlov has
been strong there, the Russians have developed these techniques assiduously.
The story—perhaps apocryphal—is told that a World Health Organization
representative on a tour of hospitals in the Soviet Union was shown an experimental ward for the treatment of alcoholics. A group of patients who had
completed the cure were lined up to meet the distinguished visitor. Without
warning, the physician-in-charge pulled out of his pocket the paper label from
a vodka bottle and displayed it to the patients, whereupon they began vomiting
right on cue. Less dramatic results than this are usually reported elsewhere.

Aversive conditioning has achieved some limited success in helping alcoholics to overcome their craving to drink. Here a man in treatment watches with peculiar fascination as a drink is poured for him. Consumption of the alcohol will be accompanied by
an unpleasant electric shock applied to electrodes attached to the little finger and
thumb, so that eventually alcohol will acquire the noxious connotations in the man's
mind of the painful stimulation.

423

These methods, like hospitalization itself, should be regarded as technical aids to treatment. The real work has to be done on the problems of maladjustment that have made the person an abnormal drinker in the first place.

Alcohol abuse rates as one of our most serious public health problems, surpassed only by cancer and heart disease. Major efforts are now being made, especially as a result of the passage of the "Comprehensive Alcohol Abuse and Alcoholism Prevention, Treatment and Rehabilitation Act of 1970," to treat alcohol abuse as a health problem instead of using traditional, punitive, legal methods that don't work. One of the provisions of the Act was to set up the National Institute on Alcohol Abuse and Alcoholism, which among other duties is charged with public education about the dangers of alcohol abuse. Brief videotape clips are presented on television designed to dissuade people from driving after drinking and from coaxing reluctant guests to drink more than they want.

One of the most successful methods of dealing with alcoholism is by the movement known as Alcoholics Anonymous. This movement was originated by a group of cured alcoholics (*Alcoholics Anonymous*, 1955). It is now represented in a great many American cities. The nucleus is a local voluntary association. The meetings are given over to discussions of the common problem, sometimes with testimonials from members who have been cured, and to a sort of leaderless group therapy. When new members are added, very likely still deeply alcoholic but genuinely desirous of changing, they are given at once some responsible task in the society so that they will more readily become identified with the group. In short, every attempt is made to provide an immediate sense of fellowship and group support as a counterpoint to the old haunts and drinking companions. The new life must be more attractive than the old. Another feature of the program consists of providing strong individual support when a member is in the grip of the old temptation. Other members will spend considerable time, perhaps even staying for days on end, to keep the comrade from relapsing into drink. The success of such maneuvers naturally depends on the fact that all members have had their own troubles with alcohol. When people are really struggling to overcome addiction, they welcome the help of others who have been through it all themselves. In certain respects a fellow-sufferer can be a better therapist than a trained person who has never been alcoholic. The success of Alcoholics Anonymous gives testimony to the healing power of both group membership and sympathetic insight. Now that organization also extends its support to the families of alcoholics, who bear much of the burden of suffering.

SUGGESTIONS FOR FURTHER READING

"Must" reading, even for the lay person, is the excellent report of the Advisory Committee to the Surgeon General on smoking and health (U.S. Public Health Service,

1964). A more recent report of a similar nature was published by the Royal College of Physicians of London (1971). Collections of papers presented at national research conferences have been published by E. F. Borgatta and R. R. Evans in *Smoking, health and behavior* (1968) and by S. V. Zagona in *Studies and issues in smoking behavior* (1967). Former U.S. Senator Maurine B. Neuberger (1963) discusses the political and economic aspects of the tobacco problem in *Smoke screen: Tobacco and the public welfare*. W. I. Skinner's *Tobacco and health: The other side of the coin* (1970) speaks for the defense; his being in the tobacco industry does not discredit his case for tobacco, but the logic of his argument does.

In an area of psychopathology with the epidemic possibilities and rapid changes in scientific knowledge of the psychoactive drugs, it is difficult and important to keep up with the latest research advances. Useful for this purpose are a number of brief publications available from the National Clearinghouse for Drug Abuse Information, Washington, D.C. 20013, and from the Bureau of Narcotics and Dangerous Drugs, U.S. Department of Justice, Washington, D.C. 20537. Among these, a booklet prepared by the Justice Department, *Fact Sheets* (1970) contains useful information about drugs and a contemporary bibliography on each of the drug groups discussed in the present chapter. *Students and Drug Abuse* (U.S. Public Health Service, 1969) is a similar booklet oriented to educating college students. Broad representation of viewpoints is included in the second Rutgers Symposium on Drug Abuse (J. R. Wittenborn et al., 1970). An *excellent* source with a medical perspective is *Drug Abuse: Proceedings of the International Conference* (C. J. D. Zarafonetis, 1972). J. C. Ball and C. D. Chambers' *The epidemiology of opiate addiction in the United States* (1970) contains a collection of their papers on the epidemiology of opiate addiction in the United States. For a history of Synanon and an account of the more human side of drug dependence and rehabilitation the reader should not miss L. Yablonsky's *The tunnel back: Synanon* (1965). J. J. Platt and C. Labate (1976) offer an extremely comprehensive account on heroin addiction in *Heroin addiction: Theory, research and treatment*. G. J. Russell (1978) provides a succinct and readable summary of the latest medical findings on the effects of marihuana smoking, written especially for the lay person, *Marihuana today: A compilation of medical findings for the layman*.

A comprehensive summary of all aspects of alcohol abuse is contained in the First Special Report to the U.S. Congress from the Secretary of Health, Education and Welfare (U.S. Public Health Service, 1971). Also very useful is *Alcohol problems* (T. F. A. Plaut, 1967). *World Dialogue on alcohol and drug dependence* (E. D. Whitney, 1970) is a collection of papers by experts in the field of alcoholism from throughout the world. R. V. Phillipson's *Modern trends in drug dependence and alcoholism* (1970) is a similar collection with mainly British and American viewpoints. *Alcoholics Anonymous* (1955) tells the story of a most interesting experiment in treatment. A study of social and family backgrounds is given in W. McCord and J. McCord, *Origins of alcoholism* (1960). C. D. Emrick's articles for the *Quarterly Journal of Studies of Alcohol* (1974, 1975) include an exhaustive compilation of research studies of psychological treatment for alcoholism.

425

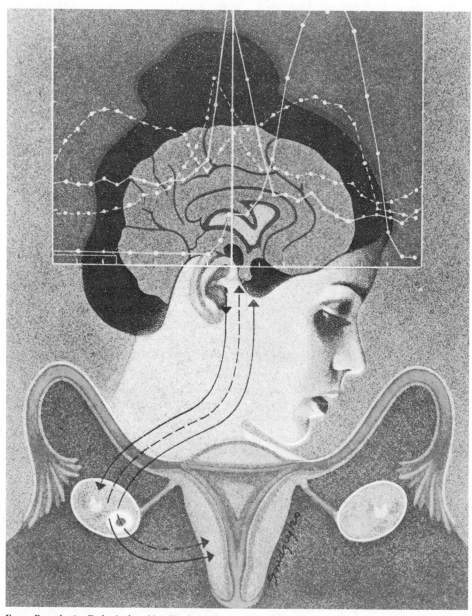

From *Reproductive Endocrinology*, New York, Medcom, Inc. 1973 (Alex Gnidziejko, artist.) By permission of the publisher.

12
Sexual Disorders

In this chapter we analyze a group of disorders specifically in the realm of sexual behavior. Considering the frequency with which sexual problems are involved in other kinds of disorder, it may seem arbitrary to single them out for separate consideration. This procedure is justified, however, by the fact that sexual abnormality sometimes occurs in people who in most other respects lead relatively unburdened and productive lives. It is thus possible to think of sexual deviance as a separable form of disorder even though it is more commonly caught up in larger patterns of troubled living.

Since the start of the century, when Freud shocked respectable Western society by disclosing the far-reaching subterranean activity of sexual urge and fantasy, there has been a change amounting to a

revolution in cultural attitudes toward sex. The patients from whom Freud
derived most of his information had been brought up in an atmosphere conducive to a suppression of sexuality so powerful that whole tracts of experience
were sometimes banished from consciousness. Sexual impulses, too insistent to
be fully contained, were thus forced into devious channels and might sometimes break through in overt aberrant behavior. Psychoanalytic findings made
it possible to believe that sexual disorders had their roots in excessive repression. Evidence was brought in by anthropologists that such disorders were
more frequent in societies where sex was culturally suppressed (Malinowski,
1927; Seward, 1946). These ideas contributed to a widespread loosening of
sexual constraints both in expressed values and in actual behavior, and it was
hoped that the new freedom would eventually put an end to deviance in the
sexual sphere. Possibly the revolution is still too young, not yet widely enough
diffused, to have this effect. But there is also the possibility that there are intrinsic problems in human sexual development and functioning that cannot
be made to vanish simply by unrestrained expression.

The topic of sexuality has a remarkable capacity to arouse human sensitivities, which gives rise to myths, rumors, and prejudices that somehow resist extinction in the face of reality. Consequently, an important part of our task
here, besides surveying the results of research, is to debunk the myths that are
demonstrably false and to question those of uncertain validity.

In Chapter 4 we considered, from a psychological viewpoint, the normal
course of sexual development and the various points at which adaptive difficulties might occur. We begin this chapter with a brief synopsis of some important features of sexual development and functioning, mainly from an organic and physiological perspective.

BIOLOGICAL FOUNDATIONS OF HUMAN SEXUALITY

From an evolutionary perspective human sexuality is first and foremost a
mechanism for reproducing the species. There can be no human reproduction
without a union between individuals of opposite or complementary gender.
Therefore an understanding of human sexuality must begin with an account
of the difference between males and females. This difference begins at conception with the pairing of the sex chromosomes from the egg and the sperm.
If the X chromosome from the mother is paired with an X chromosome from
the father, the offspring will be female, but if the father donates a Y chromosome, the offspring will be male. In normal embryonic development, the primordial gonad begins its differentiation as a testis, if that is to be its fate, after
the sixth week of gestation, or about six weeks ahead of the timing of ovarian
differentiation (Money, 1977). If both embryonic gonads are removed prior to
the critical period when the other sexual anatomy is formed, then the embryo
will proceed to differentiate structurally as a female, regardless of genetic sex.

Nature's rule apparently is that something must be added for masculinization to occur. Later in gestation further structural differentiation occurs, largely in response to production by the testes of the male sex hormone, *testosterone*. Excess testosterone, whether introduced naturally or artificially, can cause masculinized genitalia in the female, and too little can result in feminized genitalia in the male, so here again there is evidence that masculine development is superimposed, so to speak, on feminine potential.

If all goes according to the ontogenetic plan, the baby is born with distinctively differentiated genital structures and internal reproductive organs, including the gonads. At birth, the baby has already passed through two of the three critical phases of gender differentiation: (1) the *genetic/reproductive phase* transpires at conception with the assignment of the sex chromosomes and initial cell development; (2) the *phase of morphological development* takes place largely *in utero* during gestation, primarily under the control of sex hormones generated by the mother and by the gonads of the embryo itself. The third phase, *psychosocial differentiation*, begins at birth and is brought about through patterns of childrearing, modeling, and social interaction with parents and significant others, primarily during early childhood. Gender differentiation can best be understood as a serial program (Money, 1977). Phyletically written parts of the program exert their determining influence particularly before birth, and leave a permanent imprint. Even at these early stages of life, however, the phyletic program may be altered by idiosyncracies of personal history, such as toxins or excess hormones. After birth the programming becomes—by phyletic decree—a function of biographical history, especially social biography. The social biography program leaves its imprint as surely as does the phyletic. The long-term effects of the two are equally fixed and enduring, and their different origins are not easily recognized. Aspects of human psychosexual differentiation attributable to the social biography program are often mistakenly attributed to the phyletic program. For example, there is abundant evidence from animal research to show that sexual object choice is heavily influenced by social and environmental factors in early childhood (Beach, 1977a). Congenital sex differences in behavior potential can be extended and exaggerated, obliterated, or even reversed by social conditioning, and different societies have managed to achieve all of these modifications to greater or lesser degree. The only behavioral differences that are never contravened by any society are those essential to its own survival—namely, those necessary for reproduction.

Sexually differentiated behavior patterns known to depend on hormones in other species involve responses essential to reproduction. In humans sexual behavior includes many patterns with no reproductive significance. Both reproductive and nonreproductive sexual behavior develops in the individual under the directive influence of personal experience and social learning. Consummatory responses like orgasm are essentially reflexive and require no experiential preparation, but various forms of preparatory or appetitive behavior

Both of these rhesus monkeys were reared in isolation from birth at the University of Wisconsin Primate Laboratory, and this has disturbed their sexual behavior as adults. The male is attempting an abnormal sexual mount, and the female is making an abnormal positional response. Sexual disturbances of all kinds have been found likewise in human societies.

(e.g., courting or sexual foreplay) are acquired through learning and elaborated by experience. Hence sexual object choices and preferred methods of sexual arousal depend heavily on learning through social experience (Beach, 1977a).

Gender Identity and Sex Role Development

Gender identity may be defined as the sameness, unity, and persistence of one's individuality as male or female, especially as it is experienced in self-awareness and behavior (Money, 1977). *Gender role* or *sex role* comprises everything that a person says and does to indicate to others or to self the degree that one is male or female; it includes, but is not restricted to, sexual arousal and response. Gender identity is the private or subjective experience of one's sex role; sex role is the public expression of gender identity. Gender identity and sex role are obviously central components of human personality. Many factors contribute to the establishment of both: assigned sex and sex of rearing, external genital structures, internal reproductive organs, fetal and pubertal sex hormones, brain function (principally in the hypothalamus), and psychosocial experience (Money, 1971). Money espouses a kind of imprinting theory: that one's sexual role is determined primarily by experiences during the first few years of life. It is "abundantly clear that nature has ordained a major part of human gender-identity differentiation to be accomplished in the postnatal period" (Money, 1977, p. 77).

The period in which this development can be most easily observed begins with toilet training and the onset of language acquisition, at about 18 months, and continues until the age of three or four. Primary responsibility for ambiguity in psychosexual differentiation during this period, if it occurs, resides with the parents. Money especially emphasizes the importance of *complementation* in shaping the child's sex role behavior; children learn their gender identity and their sex role behavior by accommodating themselves to the behavior of members of the opposite sex, as well as by identifying with members of the same sex. Although we have heard most about the processes of identification and modeling, Maccoby and Jacklin (1974) conclude from their review of the literature that modeling plays only a minor role in the development of sex-typed behavior. They emphasize that the learning of sex-typed behavior is a process built on biological foundations that are sex-differentiated to some degree.

Most sexual and reproductive behavior in animals and humans is influenced to a high degree by hormones; for example, hormones initiate the preparations for sexual activity, make possible sexual consummation, and require nurturant behaviors (such as nest building) that follow reproduction. The most important way in which hormones affect sexual behavior is to induce temporary changes in brain function (Beach, 1977a). Experience affects the organization of these mechanisms. The basic mechanisms for feminine and masculine behavior are present in all normal individuals of each sex — organically, both sexes are fundamentally bisexual with one important qualification: in genetic males the masculine system is more completely organized and more easily activated (especially by androgen, a male sex hormone) than the female system, and vice versa for genetic females, who respond primarily to estrogen (a female sex hormone).

Finally, we should note that it has been demonstrated that sexual activity can be either stimulated or blocked through experimental manipulations in the brain, largely focused on the hypothalamus, though there is no specialized "sex center" in the brain (Whalen, 1977).

It is common to regard children between birth and puberty as sexually neuter or latent, but this is obviously misleading because *most* of the important psychological differentiation of the sexes and consolidation of gender identity takes place during that period. It is true that puberty marks the period of dramatic physical growth that initiates *organic* sexual maturity, but most of the significant *psychological* choice points have been reached and resolved long

431

Sex role differentiation begins early in our society, and is heavily reinforced by socializing experiences. Is there any question what kind of roles the boy above and the girl below have chosen for themselves?

The budding body builder on the left and the aspiring electronics technician on the right are doing their part to stem the tide of sex role stereotyping in our society.

433

before that time. The unanimity of opinion among experts in the field concerning this issue is impressive (Beach, 1977b). For example, in retrospect many homosexuals and transexuals report feelings of conflict in gender identity occurring as early as six to ten years of age (Diamond, 1977) and the pivotal events may have occurred even earlier. "All things considered, it seems feasible, as a working hypothesis, to say that the Anlagen (organic rudiments) of behavioral normalcy, anomaly, ambiguity, or incongruity of gender identity are laid down long before hormonal puberty" (Money, 1977, p. 81). Hormonal changes at puberty may influence the *degree of arousal* to an image already predetermined to have some arousal power, but not the *stimulus* to which the person will respond with sexual arousal. That is established long before puberty.

Let us summarize what has been said thus far. All humans begin embryonic life with the same structural foundation, which is fundamentally feminine, but normally become structurally differentiated as to gender before birth. Psychological differentiation of gender and of sex role is a lifelong process influenced strongly by both organic developments and social experience, especially in the first few years of childhood. Organic sexual maturity takes place at puberty, largely in response to hormonal changes, but gender identity is principally established some years before that.

Human Sexual Response during Intercourse

Most college students can write their own scenario of life events leading from puberty to a full sexual life in young adulthood, if not from personal experience then drawing on their cultural indoctrination, which—for better or worse—probably includes trashy novels, *Playboy*, and such instructive documentaries as "Animal House." We will add here only some elements of information that may have been slighted in that indoctrination: a summary of the normal patterns of human sexual response during intercourse. This will provide a perspective from which to consider various aspects of human sexual disorder.

Human sexual response is initiated in the social context of selecting a mate. Traditionally, in this process two people of the opposite sex meet and fall in love, which means that they enjoy one another's company and find their personal relationship mutually self-confirming. If marriage and reproduction are potential objectives of the pair, other considerations may be important, such as age, physical health, religion, parental approval, financial means, career aspirations, and moral values, because such matters may have a significant bearing on prospective family life. Obviously, physical attraction plays an important role, either in "one-night stands" or in more enduring relationships, but its significance depends on the life situation of the partners. As cultural values have become liberalized and dependable means of birth control have become available, there has been increasing use of sexual encounters as a form

434

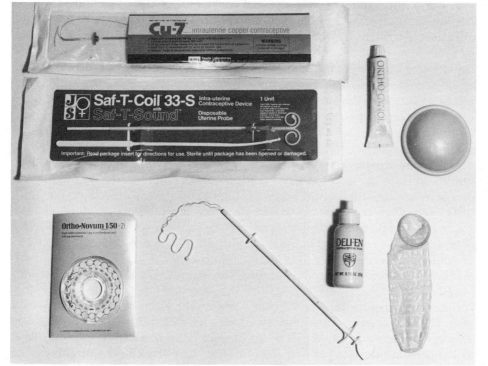

Birth control is a fact of modern life. Pictured here are a variety of the most commonly used birth control devices. In the lower left corner is a package of oral contraceptive pills, one for each day of the month; when taken regularly they prevent ovulation. In the lower right corner is a condom, which is placed over the man's penis during sexual intercourse to capture the semen that is ejaculated. To the left of it is a bottle of contraceptive foam that can be applied in the woman's vagina, preferably before sexual intercourse, to neutralize sperm cells. In the upper right corner is a diaphragm, which is inserted in the vagina prior to intercourse to block the union of sperm with egg. The tube to the left of it contains a contraceptive cream that is applied simultaneously with the diaphragm. The remaining three items are different intrauterine devices (IUDs) that prevent implantation of fertilized egg in the uterus. No birth control method is perfectly reliable, so it is wise to obtain expert medical advise before using any of them.

of recreation that is sometimes quite casual. There is also increasing public awareness of "alternative" sexual life styles, such as communal living and gay life, which diverge sharply from the traditional patterns for mate selection and mating. In considering all forms of mating we should not lose sight of the age-old widom that successful sexual intercourse is a profound interpersonal experience as well as a gratifying physical one. Trite as that statement may sound, we will see that there are few biological sexual abnormalities that are not preceded or accompanied by difficulties in the interpersonal sphere.

435

It is a natural part of the process of courtship for the prospective lovers to caress one another and exchange both physical and psychological gestures of affection. As their relationship becomes more intimate and their emotional commitment to one another deepens, initially tentative kissing and embracing usually gives way to more passionate necking and petting until the partners agree at some point, either explicitly or implicitly, to engage in sexual intercourse. When that happens the partners will usually think about, and often talk quite frankly about, birth control procedures. For people of all ethical and religious persuasions there are precautions that can be taken to influence the likelihood of conceiving a child, and it is a very naive person indeed—usually an inexperienced teenager—who does not carefully *plan* a pregnancy. Once a mutual decision has been made to make love, passionate petting will merge into sexual foreplay. There are at least two ways to describe what transpires from that point on. A relatively predictable sequence of physiological responses takes place in both partners, and at the same time they share a complementary emotional experience with distinctive subjective feelings. The physiological account may sound distastefully clinical, but it provides an important foundation for understanding the more pleasing subjective experiences.

Sexual intercourse takes some time. Despite the French films you may have seen, it is not usually done between lunch and coffee during the noon hour. The age-old phyletic ritual *can* be accomplished in five minutes, or even less, as happens in massage parlors, sleazy hotels, and penthouses every day. The reason most people take their time in making love is because it can be a profoundly pleasurable emotional experience, one they want to savor. And that is probably the way nature intended it. As we saw in the account of autonomic functioning in Chapter 9, the body has an impressive innate capacity to anticipate physiological needs. Obviously, people do not go through life in a constant state of sexual excitement. They build up to that condition gradually, primarily by means of affectionate mutual pleasuring during foreplay. A number of generalized body reactions occur (Steen & Price, 1977). Muscles in the arms, legs, abdomen, and buttocks contract. Heart rate and blood pressure increase. Blood vessels in the pelvic region become engorged. The rate of breathing increases and perspiration forms over much of the body. The breasts swell and the nipples become erect. The skin over much of the body reddens (the so-called sex flush).

Masters and Johnson (1970) have observed four phases of sexual response in the genital organs: excitement, plateau, orgasm, and resolution. The first two phases transpire during foreplay; orgasm usually occurs at the climax of intercourse; and resolution brings the body back to its normal quiescent state. During excitement or arousal erection of the male's penis results from increased blood flow, making it larger in length and diameter. The testes are partially elevated and increase in size. Meanwhile the inner surface of the female's vagina becomes moist with internal secretions, the clitoris grows larger, and the

436

uterus is elevated. In the plateau phase there is an increase in circumference of the *glans* at the tip of the penis and full elevation of the testes in the male. Mucous secretion from internal glands forms at the tip of the penis. In the female there is substantial engorgement and swelling of the vagina and the flesh around the genital area, with ballooning of the innermost parts of the vagina and further elevation of the uterus and cervix. The uterus becomes enlarged and the clitoris elevated. Mucous secretions from internal glands appear. At the point of orgasm, ejaculation of semen results from involuntary contractions in the male, accompanied by contraction of the anal and urethral sphincters. The female experiences contraction of the uterus, vagina, and the anal and urethral sphincters, but nothing in the nature of an ejaculation occurs. During resolution or detumescence there is a reduction of blood flow and loss of penile erection in the male. A refractory period lasting a few minutes or hours sets in, during which he may be unable to have another orgasm. There is a reduction of blood flow in the female sex organs as well, with decreasing size and elevation, but she can readily return to orgasm without any refractory period.

All the organic changes recounted above are designed through evolution to optimize the chances for successful intercourse and reproductive conception. The added lure of the experience, which assures that humans won't forget how to do it, is the emotional accompaniment of intercourse. Wagner (1974) elicited subjective descriptions of the experience from college students in introductory psychology, which we can divide into three clusters regarding foreplay, orgasm, and afterglow. During foreplay there is an extraordinarily pleasant building of tension, accompanied by a warm feeling of affection and love for the partner. Breathing becomes more rapid as exhilaration and excitement increase with waves of pleasurable sensations and mounting anticipation. There is a feeling of tightening inside, with palpitating rhythm and a tremendous buildup of pleasure. The body tingles, beginning in the thighs, lower back, and genital area, then spreading everywhere with pressure building in the genitals as if something under the skin were pushing out. As orgasm approaches there may be buzzing sensations, rectal contractions that start a series of chills up the spine, and a feeling of loss of muscular control. Orgasm is described as a momentary experience lasting perhaps 3 to 5 seconds: a rush or flash of pleasure, a sudden explosion in the genital area with intense muscle spasms, pulsating sensations, shuddery contractions, and hot-cold feelings that make the tremendous work of releasing the pleasure worthwhile. The physical movements at climax are spontaneous and involuntary, and they are accompanied by lightheaded or fluttering sensations, dizziness, and weakening — almost a total loss of conscious sensation for the surroundings, except for the other person. The culmination is a fantastic sensation of tension release, as if all nerve endings burst and quiver, sending the whole body and mind into a state of beautiful oblivion. This state of elation and euphoria gives way to an intense feeling of relief that blossoms over the whole body, which one student

437

likened to jumping in a cool swimming pool after hours of sweating turmoil. What follows in the afterglow is a feeling of floating, a sense of joyful tiredness and warmth. There is a deep sense of peace, relaxation, and satisfaction, pervaded by an emotional feeling of love for the partner and a great desire for sleep.

The vivid descriptions of sexual experience by these college students show a remarkable resemblance to the "highs" reported from intravenous injections of stimulants and narcotics. Understanding the powerful reinforcing aspects of sexual response helps to explain why sexuality implicitly pervades our private fantasies, social relationships, commercial enterprises, advertising, indeed the whole of consciousness in modern society. With this understanding it is also easier to comprehend the great attraction and the possible frustrations attached to variations and distortions in the use of these simple but powerful reproductive mechanisms. We turn our attention to these variations now.

VARIETIES OF SEXUAL DISORDER

Sexual excitability and sexual interests exist in childhood. They take the form of masturbation, curiosity about the genitals, self-display, mutual investigation with other children, and crushes and affectionate relationships sometimes accompanied by possessiveness and jealousy. For the most part the sexual tendencies of children would be called perverted if they persisted into adult life. An extensive process of relearning goes on at puberty, colored by the new level of genital excitability and aided by surrounding social expectations. The usual result is that childish object choices and childish modes of satisfaction are put aside in favor, sooner or later, of sexual relations with someone of opposite sex.

This was the picture drawn by Freud (1953) in an influential paper published originally in 1905. Here he advanced the idea that the various forms of deviant sexual behavior should be regarded as developmental disorders instead of expressions of constitutional abnormality; further, that they represented continuations of childhood sexual tendencies. Normally the diffuse "partial impulses" that constitute the child's sexuality are gathered into a new pattern at puberty, submerged by the excitability of the genitals and contributing to the central goal of copulation. If for some reason this integration cannot be achieved—if "genital primacy" remains incomplete—one or more of the earlier patterns may persist and become the preferred mode of sexual expression. On this basis Freud classified sexual aberrations under two headings: deviations of sexual *object* and deviations of sexual *aim*. To cover the clinical varieties of sexual disorder it is necessary to add a third category, wherein object and aim are normal but there is trouble with sexual *performance*.

The chief disorders of sexual performance are *impotence* and *premature ejaculation* in the male and *frigidity* in the female. The most common variation of object choice is *homosexuality*, the choice of an object of the same sex. In this category belong also the peculiarities known as *fetishism*, in which some small part of the object, such as a hand, a shoe, or a lock of hair, captures special power of sexual arousal. Disorders of sexual aim include such phenomena as *exhibitionism* and *voyeurism*. In exhibitionism, displaying the genitals or the naked body becomes the essential element in obtaining a satisfactory sexual experience. In voyeurism, observing the bodies and sexual acts of others plays the same indispensable part. These can be regarded as exaggerated perpetuations of childish display and curiosity. *Sadism* and *masochism* have similar counterparts in childhood when the relation between sexual and aggressive feelings is often misunderstood and confused. The sadistic deviation makes violence and giving of pain an indispensable condition for sexual satisfaction. The masochistic deviation similarly associates sex and the receiving of pain.

Newspaper readers are acquainted with another category, that of "sex fiend." This is a journalistic classification, not a scientific one. The expression is likely to be used about males whose behavior exhibits a confusion of sex and aggression, as in combined rape and murder; in other words, for acute examples of sadism. It is also employed for adults who direct sexual behavior toward children, a deviation in object choice. Another everyday expression, "sex offenders," designates a legal category rather than a psychological one. In an institution for sex offenders there are likely to be inmates with sexual disorders, but there are others who are not deviant regarding performance, object, and aim. They are there because their sexual behavior has been so immoderate as to arouse complaint. We have already dealt with forcible rape in the chapter on crime, delinquency, and conduct disorders because the immoral and aggressive aspects of rape are more salient indications of psychological disturbance than the sexual aspects.

DISORDERS OF SEXUAL PERFORMANCE

If a man seeks advice on troubles with sexual intercourse, his complaints are likely to be either that he cannot secure an erection, or that he cannot sustain it long enough for successful insertion, or that he reaches ejaculation so quickly that his partner remains unsatisfied. If a woman seeks advice, her complaint is likely to be that she cannot relax physically or mentally, that she does not feel pleasurably aroused, that intromission is uncomfortable if not painful, and that she does not reach the point of orgasm, all of which means that neither she nor her partner is satisfied. From these common complaints it is easy to deduce that mutually satisfactory sexual intercourse requires wholehearted abandonment to the bodily sensations and feelings that carry it to completion. This abandonment can be blocked by conflicting feelings such as anxiety, disgust, or guilt.

439

Sexual intercourse improves with experience, and novices can hardly be expected to perform like seasoned veterans. Episodes of impotence and frigidity are common while the sexual act is still novel, unfamiliar, perhaps a little awesome. Anxiety about one's adequacy as a sexual partner is entirely natural, but anxiety is precisely one of the feelings that can interfere with sexual arousal. Even a tense concentration on technique, on how best to bring about mutual arousal and appropriate timing, can interfere with the involuntary aspects of the experience, although novices can hardly be expected to avoid it. Shortcomings of performance that are due to inexperience cannot be considered disorders, but this designation becomes appropriate if poor performance persists too long or appears at some later point as a falling off from a level previously achieved.

Contributing Causes

Improvement in sexual performance is a learning process that requires reinforcement, and conceivably a person's initial ineptitude may be perpetuated by an unfortunate pattern of reinforcement contingencies. If a young man on his first attempt is impotent because of anxiety, he may be more anxious on the second attempt. Desires for success and enjoyment will be on the side of persisting, but if his partner gives no help, expresses disappointment, and adds to his humiliation, he may well develop a settled conviction of inadequacy. If a young woman in her first experiences is more tense than aroused and thus has more discomfort than satisfaction, and if her partner unhelpfully proceeds to his own consummation, she may well develop a settled conviction that she is naturally frigid. The partner's response is an important part of the reinforcement contingencies, and if the partners encountered in early experience tend to strengthen a sense of inadequacy it becomes hard to build up the confidence requisite for satisfactory intercourse.

Perhaps nothing creates more insecurity about sexual competence in our society than the belief that the size of the sexual organs determines the adequacy of sexual performance in oneself or one's partner. Of course such cosmetic considerations may influence the degree of sexual attraction between partners, but the truth is that the sexual satisfaction of either partner is *not* related to the size of the male penis or the female vagina (Price & Steen, 1977). The female orgasm depends more on stimulation of the clitoris and other accessory structures than on the vagina, so any penis capable of penetrating the vagina is usually adequate to induce the desired response. By the same token, the engorgement of the female sex organs that takes place during intercourse permits gratification of the male in a vagina of virtually any normal size. Similarly, the size of a woman's breasts has no relation to her capacity for sexual response nor for sustaining a baby through breastfeeding. Despite the popular image of glamorous Hollywood sex symbols like Loni Anderson and Arnold Schwartzenegger or the ineffectual image of Woody Allen and Gilda Radner,

440

This walking billboard added significantly to his masculine image by becoming a successful racing driver after achieving stardom as a movie actor, but appearance bears little relation to the quality of one's social and sexual life.

there is no factual basis for making any presumptions about the sex life of any of them.

Residues of past experience make a significant contribution to sexual performance. Sexual experience is approached with preconceptions and attitudes built up throughout the personal past. One set of preconceptions has to do with the sense of competence. The vigorous boy athlete, successful in a number of different sports, may anticipate sexual experience as another of those physical accomplishments at which he is bound to be great. The awkward, clumsy boy may approach the same situation with a firm expectation that here too he will be awkward and clumsy. Similarly a popular girl, accustomed to feeling that she pleases boys, will enter this new branch of experience more confidently than a girl who has come to doubt her charm. A second set of preconceptions is derived from cultural and family attitudes toward sex. Less

441

often than in the past, but still often, children gather from their parents' attitudes and warnings that sex is dangerous, degrading, dirty, and disgusting. These briefings may occasionally be so effective that sex with a partner is never attempted. The more common consequence is to surround intercourse with negative affects that interfere with arousal and good performance; whatever pleasure is obtained tends to be spoiled by subsequent feelings of guilt or shame. Such attitudes may be outgrown, but sometimes they persist throughout life. Contemporary parents occasionally swing to the opposite extreme and constitute themselves as a cheering section for their adolescent children's sexual initiatives. This may build up such high expectations that at first the reality seems tame by comparison. As one newly experienced adolescent put it, "Is that all that has to happen to make me mentally healthy?"

An important part in disorders of sexual performance is sometimes played by hostility. This is most clearly seen in marriages that have begun to go wrong. Poor sexual performance has the effect of disappointing the partner. It reduces physical satisfaction and at the same time communicates a message that the partner is no longer an attractive, arousing object. In such cases, of course, the sexual disorder does not stand alone; it is part of a deteriorating human relation, and it may be confined to that relation. When hostility is an habituated part of a person's attitude toward others, its spoiling effect can be general. Competitive feelings, jealousy, chronic resentment, self-preoccupation all interfere with the generous spirit that is implicit in a mutually satisfying act. In some cases of impotence, furthermore, the sexual act is interpreted as destructively aggressive, and the anxiety aroused by one's own hostility has an inhibitory effect on performance.

Treatment

Recent developments in treating disorders of sexual performance have produced decidedly encouraging results. Reporting on work that has had widespread publicity, Masters and Johnson (1970) find that 80 percent of their 790 cases of sexual dysfunction were essentially cured and remained so throughout a five-year follow-up period. Admittedly their patients had a better than average prognosis. For the most part they were married couples who valued their marriage, hoped to improve it, and especially wanted to eliminate the sexual difficulties that seemed to be its only flaw. Few of these subjects showed signs of other forms of disorder (Maurice & Guze, 1970) and presumably most of the couples enjoyed good rapport. Masters and Johnson acted on the assumption that the sexual disorder could be treated directly without reference to other possible factors. In their view, the marital relationship is the "patient," and the cure consists of each partner's learning how to achieve, and how to help the other partner achieve, sexual satisfaction. Part of the program involves getting the partners to feel comfortable together in sexual situations: relaxed, frank, able to communicate freely. This is best accomplished if they

Drs. Masters and Johnson use dolls to illustrate a point about technique in love-making for a couple in sex therapy. Relaxed and explicit discussion of potentially embarrassing matters of technique is an integral part of such treatment, but the personal relationship between partners is often a significant issue also.

can spend some time away from home near the treatment center, free from domestic distractions, having a sort of second honeymoon. It is further favored by not having complete sexual relations for the first several days, to avoid the anxiety over performance that has been plaguing the partners. The other part of the program consists of detailed instruction in the art of love-making with practice by the couple in private. This starts with what might be called "sensuous exercises," an extended sexual foreplay without going any further, designed to allow the partners to rediscover and enjoy the pure pleasure of sexual arousal. From this beginning the couple advances by slow degrees to complete intercourse, no new step being taken until there is full confidence about the preceding steps. In effect the married pair, caught in an habitually tension-ridden sexual performance, is told to back off and learn the whole thing over again.

This direct approach to treatment can properly be called behavior modification, and it is similar to the principles described by Wolpe (1969). In treating impotence and premature ejaculation, assumed to occur because anxiety is strong enough to inhibit full arousal, Wolpe recommends rearranging the situation so that sexual excitement can gain the upper hand over anxiety. The technique for doing so is much like the one employed by Masters and Johnson, consisting of foreplay alone until anxiety disappears, then gradual approxi-

443

mations to complete intercourse, each step being taken only when it no longer raises anxiety. When patients do not seek treatment in pairs, for men there is always the practical problem of finding a female collaborator with the kindness, patience, and frustration-tolerance to help through the many sessions, maybe as many as 15 or 20, during which he cannot yet give her any real satisfaction. Wolpe reports that of a series of 31 patients treated under relatively favorable circumstances, 21 became wholly satisfactory performers, 6 were improved, and only 4 received no benefit. For the treatment of frigidity a different method is used. Assuming that frigidity is a conditional inhibition resulting from frightening events and frightening parental attitudes in early life, Wolpe treats it like a phobia by means of systematic desensitization, as described above in Chapter 7. If the frigidity is specifically with the husband, his collaboration greatly increases the probability of a successful result.

Commercial exploitation is a predictable problem in this area. Steen and Price (1977) estimate that there are from 4000 to 5000 "clinics" or "treatment centers" for the treatment of sexual problems, although only 50 to 100 of them have staff who are adequately trained to provide sex therapy. Such "clinics" are suspect if they immediately offer sexual engagement with the clinician or readily provide surrogate sexual partners for the clients. Those services are more appropriately associated with prostitution than with authentic treatment by professionally qualified sex therapists. Experienced sexual partners *have* been employed in legitimate clinics to gradually induce sexual arousal in a member of the opposite sex, with the objective of conditioning the client to associate pleasurable sensations and sexual arousal with heterosexual stimuli (Masters & Johnson, 1970). These individual treatments may have important implications for teaching inexperienced or anxious persons sexual skills, but their use is still exceptional because treatment of couples is considered more efficacious.

In using these direct methods it is assumed that the sexual disturbance is either the whole trouble or at least sufficiently separable to be treated by itself. Considering what we have learned about the growth of personality, the assumption may be too simple in many cases. Intensive clinical evaluations often disclose both a complex history and a complex interaction with other aspects of personality. A spread of this kind is found in a case described by Lazarus, in which the patient, a man of thirty-three, announced on his first visit: "I have come to you in order to prove to myself that our social values are depraved" (1965, pp. 243-245). It was a long journey from this pronouncement through a tangle of social judgments derogatory to women before the patient disclosed that he was sexually impotent. Being a behavior therapist, Lazarus organized the treatment around systematic desensitization, but anxiety had to be reduced for four different situations: sexual initiative, assertiveness toward women, physical violence, and social rejection. In this case, impotence did not stand alone; it was part of a whole system of anxiety-laden attitudes toward other

444

people. Lazarus reports that treatment required 57 desensitization sessions over eight months, but the final result was wholly satisfactory.

From such considerations it might seem that treatment concentrated too heavily on sexual performance might send patients away with improvement in one sector but unchanged regarding other important personal problems. This may happen, but it does not necessarily constitute an argument against using direct methods. Insight-oriented treatment, usually requiring a long time, is apparently less successful than behavior modification, very likely because it does not concentrate enough on teachable skills and practical devices for controlling anxiety. Psychological treatment, as we have seen, must often be directed not at everything that conceivably might be done but at some one point where adaptive change is feasible. When a person complains chiefly of a disorder of sexual performance this is surely the place to start, and improvement in this sphere may have a favorable effect on confidence in other spheres.

HOMOSEXUALITY

Before the advent of psychoanalysis, a sexual preference for members of one's own sex was widely believed to be a biological abnormality. Following Freud, emphasis shifted to the psychological side of the problem, and homosexuality was interpreted as a developmental disorder. Recently the study of sex roles and of gender identity has added substantially to the developmental picture, though many empirical findings are contradictory and at least one expert suggests that research on homosexuality has reached the stage where it should go back to the drawing board (Bell, 1975). We do not yet have a definite explanation of what brings about homosexual object choice, nor for that matter can we explain heterosexual object choice either. To assume that either one occurs "naturally," without assistance or training, is probably too simple. Let us review what we do know.

Biological Aspects

The part played by biological abnormality has been reviewed by Money (1970). A prominent hypothesis is that homosexuality might be related to an abnormal balance in the secretion of androgen and estrogen, the male and female sex hormones. In one study, exclusive and near-exclusive male homosexuals had lower levels of male sex hormones in the blood, markedly lower sperm counts, and more misshapen sperm cells than controls did (Kolodny et al., 1971). Replication studies by other investigators have yielded contradictory findings, so the hormonal hypothesis may apply only in a minority of cases. An inferential problem here is that, even if hormonal abnormalities should be confirmed, these might be the *result*, rather than the *cause*, of the

445

WHY STUDY HOMOSEXUALITY?

A certain number of clients seek medical or psychological treatment because of homosexuality. They view this condition as a handicap, a source of distress, and an obstacle to a desired normal family life. In their minds it rates as a disorder of which they would like to be cured. Homosexuality is a deviation from the sexual object choice that is usual and that must be reckoned natural in the evolutionary sense that without it the species would not have survived. These reasons have always seemed to justify the inclusion of the topic in books on abnormal psychology.

In recent years, however, homosexuality has become the subject of strenuous political controversy. Some of the people so oriented have rebelled against their repressive treatment by society, have brought their preference into the open as something to be respected, have fought against discriminatory legal restrictions, and have found allies among civil rights groups and liberals, though also incurring much hatred and counterattack. Gay organizations maintain that it is grossly unfair for the heterosexual majority to impose restrictions on the homosexual minority, who should have an equal right to express their erotic urges without prejudice or legal handicaps. In the tense atmosphere of this crusade it has been vehemently argued that homosexual object choice not be considered a disease or a disorder. Influenced by this argument, formal votes have been taken by the American Psychiatric Association and the American Psychological Association, and homosexuality has been removed from DSM-III (1980) as a diagnostic category of mental illness.

There is a good deal to be said for this decision. It has long been known that many homosexuals lead productive and relatively happy lives and are sometimes gifted with great talents. Many have no desire to change their orientation and are quite prepared to cope with the disadvantages their preference may entail. These positive possibilities in gay life are easily obscured by a classification of disorder or disease. Certainly there can be no justification for the powerful prejudices built up in the past against gay people or for the harassments that have often deprived them of their civil rights. The inclusion of the topic in this book does not signify a stand on classification. It means that homosexuality is worth studying, that people should know whatever is known about it, and that those who have studied it in clinical settings deserve to have their contributions heard.

different patterns of sexual behavior. In the few systematic twin studies, concordance for overt homosexual object choice in monozygotic twins has been significantly greater than in dizygotic twins. This suggests that genetic factors may play some role in determining homosexual behavior. The newly developed techniques of chromosome counting have not disclosed any significant average differences between homosexual and heterosexual individuals. Only

Contary to popular stereotypes, many homosexual couples lead rather conventional domestic lives apart from their atypical sexual practices.

447

in certain rare cases has a genetic abnormality been demonstrated. Males with Klinefelter's syndrome, a eunuchoid body build with late and weak virilization (masculine development) at puberty, prove to be endowed with an extra female sex chromosome; this leads often, but not inevitably, to homosexual object choice.

In a series of detailed case studies, Stoller (1968) has made a cautious argument for a basic biological influence on object choice. He cites instances, including Klinefelter's syndrome, in which the sex assigned by the obstetrician to the child at birth, based on the appearance of the external sex organs, has been wrong, with the internal structures and genetic constitution proving later to be those of the opposite sex. Some persons thus miscast and brought up in the wrong role report always having felt like members of the other sex. In spite of their training, they have never experienced sexual impulses appropriate to what they were supposed to be. Such cases are essentially homosexual, and from their ranks come those individuals called *transsexuals* who request surgery to change their sex. A follow-up study of boys referred to a clinic because of markedly effeminate behavior showed that many more than average were bachelors, homosexuals, or transsexuals (Lebovitz, 1972).

The weight of evidence, however, is heavily in favor of learning instead of biologically determined preference. This is nowhere more dramatically revealed than in studies of hermaphrodites (people with reproductive organs of both genders) by Money and the Hampsons (1955). One form of female hermaphroditism, the adrenogenital syndrome, which if untreated produces a somewhat virilized woman, leads sometimes to assignment at birth as a male, sometimes as female. If the assignment passes unquestioned during childhood in the minds of the parents, the child grows up without apparent conflict to be boy or girl, as expected. Surgical and biochemical treament can then be used to make the genital organs more masculine or feminine and sexual life can in many respects approximate the normal (Money, 1968). Genetic sex is the same in all such cases, but environmental expectations and training can take the child's gender identity in either direction and plant it firmly.

Homosexual object choice does not, of course, necessarily imply the full range of feelings considered appropriate for the opposite sex. Some male homosexuals are active and assertive toward their partners, preferring them younger and perhaps aspiring to be their heroes. The attitude is traditionally masculine, there is no tendency toward feminine interests, and the problem is wholly confined to object choice. The female counterpart is a traditionally feminine woman who stipulates only that her partner be of the same sex. These instances differ from the common stereotypes of effeminate "fairies" and masculine "lesbians," and it would be less appropriate to invoke a biological factor behind a preference so largely confined to the visual appearance of the partner. Nor do biological causes seem convincing for those individuals, usually called "bisexual," who have agreeable relations with either sex.

448

Developmental Aspects

If sexual object is the result of experience, one hypothesis might be that homosexual seduction during late childhood or early adolescence was responsible for the unusual conditioning. Two reasons make this simple logic unimpressive. The first of these came to light in the Kinsey reports, which revealed an unexpectedly high incidence of homosexual experience in the population at large (Kinsey, Pomeroy & Martin, 1948). Of the total male sample in the Kinsey studies, 37 percent, nearly 2 out of every 5, had some form of overt homosexual experience during the course of life; the figure was 50 percent for males who remained single until the age of thirty-five. The figures do not disprove the seduction hypothesis, but they show that homosexual experience is more common than had been supposed, and they suggest that it does not necessarily have a strong emotional impact and can coexist with heterosexual interest. Exclusive and permanent homosexuality was reported in only 4 percent of the total male sample. Gebhard (1972) estimates that four million (2%) of the people in the United States (including women) are predominantly homosexual.

The second and more telling reason for doubting the importance of seduction at or after puberty is the undeniably strong evidence that the preference starts much earlier in life. This is widely noticed in clinical cases, where the patient is likely to report homosexual preference as far back as he or she can remember, fortifying the statement with recollections from childhood long before the onset of puberty. An early origin is also reported by homosexuals of both sexes who have accepted their preference and made it a way of life, never seeking psychological help. Whatever happens later, homosexual object choice does not typically begin at puberty and may go back to early childhood.

There are several possible ways of understanding this early choice. Some homosexuals recollect from ages as early as five or six an unexplained fascination with an acquaintance of the same sex. The experience is remembered as analogous to being in love. It is easily distinguished from other friendships at that age. Children around this time are often described as exhibiting strong sexual interests in forms like masturbation and curiosity. Conceivably they might sometimes be capable of *premature object choice* and of being in a sense really in love. Such choice would be as easily homosexual as heterosexual at a time when secondary sex characteristics have not developed. If it were heterosexual it would presumably not create future problems. While this speculation does justice to what seem like valid early memories, it cannot easily be further tested. We do not know how strong and how lasting the influence of premature choice on later development might be.

According to another hypothesis, homosexual choice is encouraged by *difficulty in feeling oneself into the heterosexual role*. In a study of the natural

449

history of homosexuality, Saghir and Robins (1971) selected for intensive interviews 89 male and 57 female homosexuals, secured through homophile organizations, who met the criteria of being productive members of the community, never having been in prison, and never having sought psychiatric
help. In contrast to heterosexual control groups, a majority of the homosexual
subjects showed during their childhood a crossover of role preferences and
identification. The boys typically lacked contact with other boys, shunned
rough games, and preferred girl playmates and feminine interests. The girls
had mainly boy playmates, were actively involved in sports, and expressed a
dislike for dolls and domestic activity. The unusual role preferences appeared
to be stably fixed well before puberty, and they became transformed into overt
sexual interest in a way that was analogous to the normal heterosexual awakening described by the control subjects. Evans (1969) obtained corroborating
self-descriptions: as children, male homosexuals were frail, clumsy, not athletic, and often loners, avoiding fights and preferring to play with girls. Stephan
(1973) likewise found them socially isolated as children, feminine, rejected by
male peers but friendly with female playmates.

This theory becomes more convincing if we assume a constitutional element: it is the temperamentally "gentle" boys and "tomboy" girls who experience the most difficulty feeling at home in sex roles. A different possibility,
less dependent on constitution, attributes homosexual choice to the *characteristics of available role models.* If the father's role seems vastly superior, the little girl may like it better; likewise, the boy may be attracted to superior qualities of the mother in contrast to a worthless masculine model. This formula is
doubtless too simple, but there is research bearing on the subject of role
models and emotional patterns in the family.

Bieber and associates (1962) studied male homosexual patients in long-term
psychoanalytic treatment. They called on a large number of their colleagues
to fill out a detailed questionnaire about male homosexual patients they had
recently treated, with the items designed to bring out whatever had been revealed about early memories and family experience. The investigators were
impressed by a frequent, though not universal, pattern of relations among
father, mother, and boy child. The relation between father and mother was
not satisfactory; the mother became maternally overprotective of the son but
also transferred to him her thwarted marital love; the father, like a defeated
rival, treated the son with some combination of criticism, rejection, and sulky
withdrawal. In half or more of the homosexual patients the mothers were
"dominant wives who minimized their husbands," had "a closebinding intimate relationship" with the sons, preferred the sons and allied with them
against the husbands, and were either "explicitly seductive" or had a closeness
with the sons that "appeared to be in itself sexually provocative." These influences were already at work when the sons were 3 to 5 years old, the time when
sexual arousability undergoes an increase and also when male and female social roles are being learned. One might suppose that the chief consequence

would be premature heterosexual interest; but the mothers, though seductive up to a point, frustrated and thus surrounded with guilt the more open signs of erotic feeling, while frequently making clear their contempt for the male role as exemplified by the husbands. Thus the boys remained attached, dependent, gratified yet frustrated, and nudged toward the feminine role.

There is evidence from other sources that this family constellation occurs with marked frequency in the histories of male homosexuals. To check on its generality, Evans (1969) made a questionnaire study using a sample of men who had not sought psychiatric treatment; the men themselves, rather than their doctors, provided the information on family life. In spite of the difference in method and in the sample the replies confirmed the Bieber studies; the same pattern was found in a large number of the cases.

Female homosexuality provides additional evidence on the developmental background. Exclusive homosexual object choice occurs, according to the Kinsey report, only a third to a half as often in females as in males (Kinsey et al., 1953). In a study of female homosexuals using reports from the same psychoanalysts who provided the Bieber group with 106 male cases, there were only 24 female cases (Kaye et al., 1967). This study disclosed a partial converse of the constellation described for males. A good many of the fathers answered the description of having been overintimate and close binding, and the mothers tended to be puritanical and hostile, but they also emerged as dominant, which was not at all a quality shown by the fathers of male patients in the Bieber study but is quite consistent with the results of other research.

Kremer and Rifkin (1969) directed their attention to 25 high school girls, twelve to seventeen years old, in a low status neighborhood, whose inclinations were at least in some degree homosexual. Many subjects came from disorganized and broken homes. The fathers were hostile, exploitative, and detached; the mothers were neither rejecting nor dominant but were mainly overburdened and hardly adequate for their responsibilities. One point came out sharply: "The caretaking women, mother or surrogate, held or expressed strong negative attitudes toward their own mates and much skepticism about men generally. Warnings to the girls about men were frequent. The girls in turn expressed many negative attitudes toward their fathers and about men." Clearly, their childhood indoctrination had discouraged a central attitudinal aspect of feminine sex role development.

More recent research suggests that the most general feature of the relations between homosexuals and their parents may be *alienation*. Lester (1975) points out that mothers of homosexuals have been described as either close-binding, intimate, and controlling, or as hostile and rejecting, but all studies agree that fathers are detached, hostile, and rejecting. For example, Stephan (1973) reported more father absences because of both death and divorce; fathers were more distant, hostile, and less encouraging of masculine behavior in their sons. Mothers were more dominant but less liked and respected by their sons, and they encouraged feminine attitudes and behavior. Parents of

451

both sexes regarded sex as shameful more often than control parents. The resulting effects on the offspring are predictable: heterosexuals see themselves as more similar to their same-sexed parent than to their opposite-sexed parent, whereas in homosexuals the difference between those perceptions is not significant (Thompson et al., 1973). Taken as a whole, the results of these studies show a greater indication of alienation from parents, especially of the same sex, than of positive identification with the parent of the opposite sex.

There is evidently some relation between homosexual object choice and patterns of family interaction. But it has not been shown that the connection is a tight one. Hooker (1969) warns that patterns such as those discovered by Bieber never occur in all cases, sometimes appear in controls, and are similar to patterns often detected in the childhood histories of schizophrenic patients. Alienation from parents and unusual characteristics of available sex role models can work mischief for development, but they do not regularly produce the specific result of homosexual object choice. We have still much to learn.

The most consistent theme in the research we have examined is an *attitude inculcated by the mother that sex is dangerous, disgusting, and contemptible*, something to be avoided at all costs. Boy and girl alike grow up in an atmosphere in which pleasing mother means steering wide of wicked sexual feelings, and this can be construed as steering wide of the whole sex role. Some homosexuals have reported that for a considerable time after puberty it did not occur to them that their agreeable friendships, even when they evolved into physical relations, were really sexual—that they could possibly be the degrading, disgusting thing they had been trained to avoid. The barrier of anxious negative feeling built up by their briefing encouraged persistence in the homosexual pattern longer—with more reinforcement—than might otherwise have been the case.

Confronted by several possible explanations of a given result, we should not necessarily assume that one is right and the rest wrong. Premature object choice, difficulty in feeling oneself into the usual sex role, peculiarities of available role models, alienation from parents, strong negative briefings by mothers—several of these in combination may be necessary to produce and confirm homosexual preference. Here as elsewhere in the study of personality, combinations of influences can be considered more typical than single causes.

Changing Homosexual Orientation

Through most of the history of abnormal psychology homosexuality has been regarded as hard to treat. When deviant object choice was attributed to a biological defect, treatment was not even attempted. Freud and his followers made much of the developmental aspects, but rates of improvement following psychoanalytic treatment were reported to be not as good as those obtained with anxiety disorders. A somewhat more optimistic view is taken by current workers who use variants of psychoanalysis or who favor the techniques of be-

havior modification. If homosexuality depends hardly at all on biological peculiarities, if it is almost entirely a consequence of learning, then relearning,
the essence of psychological treatment, ought to be effective. But the relearning of sexual orientation turns out to be not as simple as it sounds.

The first problem has to do with motivation. There are many homosexuals,
of course, who do not want treatment, who build their sexual preference into a
way of life they consider to be worth the practical difficulties. As our society
grows increasingly tolerant on the subject of sex, the legal and social handicaps of homosexuality become appreciably less severe, though still heavy.
Sometimes a person who has more or less accepted the unusual orientation
while young begins in the course of time to have second thoughts. With youth
vanishing, a stable life with marriage and a family looks increasingly attractive. Progress in one's vocation and a growing place in the community may
make a person feel more vulnerable to possible scandal and adverse social
judgments. Thus a person may come for psychological treatment with curiously mixed motives. The desire to change sexual orientation may be wholly
sincere, but there is lingering reluctance to surrender an important source of
satisfaction. Giving up the sexual objects to which one feels spontaneously
drawn is a profound sacrifice; resentment is understandable that such a price
must be paid to obtain what comes naturally to other people. Motivation is
more favorable if the person does not accept the deviant preference, has perhaps just discovered it, regards it as a weakness or a vice, and wants to be
rescued from its grip. Self-respect, an important ally, is then on the side of a
successful outcome, but sexual inclination is still on the other side.

Considered as a problem in learning, treatment can be broken down into a
number of processes to which the several techniques of behavior therapy appear to be applicable. To reduce the strength of homosexual behavior it is
possible to use aversive methods. Lowering the anxiety connected with heterosexual behavior seems a proper place to apply systematic desensitization. Encouraging the client to attempt heterosexual activity might call for assertiveness training, and if difficulties of performance are encountered there are the
methods already described for dealing with impotence and frigidity. Schemat-
ically, everything can be covered by those straightforward techniques for behavior modification, but it must be remembered that the therapist's resources
—the available rewards, punishments, and response contingencies—are not
unlimited, and the conditionings to be changed are likely to be deeply en-
trenched.

Of these several methods, aversive treatment has proved to be the most controversial. The best known method is a pictorial technique worked out by
Feldman and MacCullock (1971). As used with male clients, pictures of males,
some clothed and some nude, are shown on a screen and associated with a
painful electric shock. The client controls the disappearance of both slide and
shock by means of a switch, but he is supposed to leave the slide on the screen
as long as he finds it sexually attractive. In a later stage female slides appear

453

when male ones are switched off, receiving positive reinforcement through the cessation of pain. Contrived as this sounds, the authors claim considerable success, and report that of 25 patients successfully treated 52 percent were still normally heterosexual a year later, while 48 percent had to a greater or less extent relapsed. Wolpe (1969), referring to this as a "gratifying finding," nevertheless concludes that "it does not justify the use of aversion as the primary treatment of homosexuality." He considers it more important to deal first with the anxiety surrounding heterosexual behavior, and cites a case in which the lowering of social anxiety produced a spontaneous change from homosexual to heterosexual interests. It would seem in any event an obvious therapeutic blunder to try to block homosexual behavior before the patient had made progress toward the heterosexual alternative.

Systematic desensitization is considerably less hazardous and is especially appropriate when strong anxiety is focalized on the anatomy of the other sex and on the act of intercourse. In the male homosexuals studied by Bieber's group the female genitals were objects of fear or disgust in a majority of the cases. When this feature is prominent, the condition resembles a phobia, the type of disorder with which desensitization has its best results (Lamberd,

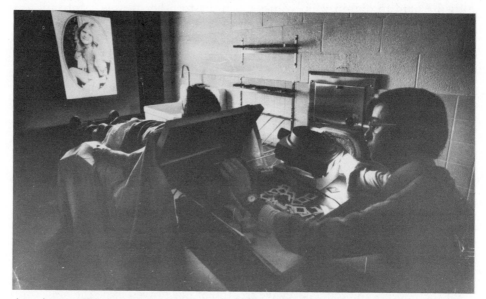

Aversive conditioning is one of the most controversial treatments for sexual disorders. The man being treated here has been imprisoned repeatedly for molesting children. The treatment consists of a mild electric shock on the inner thigh whenever a slide of a naked child, copied from pornographic magazines, is flashed on the screen, but there is no shock received when a slide of an adult is shown. By counterconditioning, the objective of the treatment is to reduce the man's attraction to children, but to increase attraction to adults.

1969). However, a good outcome is not likely to be obtained by concentrating the treatment too narrowly. Homosexuality involves more than an attitude toward genitals and intercourse. Gender role preferences, interests, interpersonal relations, even the whole self-concept may form part of the pattern, and the spread of anxieties may be fairly wide. Some workers who started with highly focused techniques of behavior modification have moved toward a broader conception of treatment, drawing on some of the older traditions of psychotherapy (Fox & Di Scipio, 1968).

Psychoanalytically oriented methods take more time, but they afford more insight both into what lies behind the object choice and what happens during the process of change. This can be illustrated by a case described by Ovesey (1969), who emphasizes the interpersonal attitudes entangled with homosexual inclinations, especially those having to do with dependence and power.

An Illustrative Case

The client was a thirty-year-old unmarried businessman who complained of severe and increasing anxiety in his work. He reported being strongly competitive and hostile toward male colleagues, whose counterhostility made him acutely anxious, and he felt that his position was in peril. In the course of history-taking he disclosed that he led an active homosexual life and had only once had heterosexual intercourse, more or less under duress. He had not thought of deviance as curable, and was surprised, pleased, yet somewhat anxious at the therapist's assurance that it might be treated. That night he dreamed that the lobby of the building in which he lived had been reconstructed overnight, transformed into new strength and elegance; he saw the dream as a symbol of his own awakened hopes.

The client's family background partly fitted the pattern described by Bieber. The father, a moderately successful professional man, was "weak, inadequate, and totally intimidated by the mother, who was the dominant member of the household." The mother was "sharp-tongued, aggressive, self-willed, and obviously brighter than the father," but the client was fond of her and felt only contempt for his father. Throughout childhood the client felt that he was not manly. He was the youngest of three brothers and was physically small; moreover, his mother, disappointed at not having a daughter, kept him too long in girls' clothes and long hair and made him do chores of sewing, cleaning, and cooking. Although he dated girls during high school, he began to be plagued by homosexual thoughts. At nineteen he was drafted into the Army, where most of his companions were bigger, tougher, and not above taunting him because of his small stature and gentleness. It was at this time, "when he felt particularly unmanly," that he had the first of what became a long series of homosexual relationships. He preferred an assertive role in these encounters, practicing anal intercourse; "in this way, he not only satisfied himself sexually, but also enhanced his deflated masculinity by making a woman out of his partner."

455

During the second month of treatment the client began to date women. Even though he made no sexual advances, these meetings caused him constant anxiety. Talking about it to the therapist, he kept harping on his father's weakness in the face of his mother's strength. When asked what this could possibly have to do with his current difficulties, he gradually recognized his own "fears of standing up to the mother" and "anger with the father for failing to protect him." His conception of the heterosexual relation was so heavily dominated by his early experience in the family circle that he could not yet construe it afresh and was still victimized by the old emotions. But he persisted in his direct attempts to overcome anxiety. He undertook sex play with his dates, even though he felt more anxious than excited, and presently he began to attempt intercourse. Several times he was impotent, but eventually, encouraged by the therapist not to give up, he was successful and began a gratifying sexual life with his partner of that occasion. Six months from the start of treatment he believed himself cured, ready to marry the woman, no longer bothered by homosexual feelings, free of the troubles that had bothered him in his job.

Had the client been dismissed at this point, his case would doubtless have been recorded as a complete success obtained in a relatively short time, In fact the therapist did not consider him out of the woods and construed his rapid improvement as a "transference cure." This expression refers to a "cure" in which pleasing the therapist, borrowing strength from his encouragement, and earning his respect produces a degree of initiative that temporarily suppresses anxiety, but that cannot survive the ending of the therapist's support. The reader will perceive here a moot point that is actually more factual than theoretical, but the facts are hard to ascertain. The therapist might have judged that although the client's anxiety of women was not fully deconditioned he could safely terminate treatment, trusting that sexual gratification and feelings of self-respecting manliness—important positive rewards—would progressively limit the power of the old alarms. He might reason that he should let well enough alone and have time for another client. He might question the wisdom of further exploration as tending to stir up problems that could safely be let lie. In fact, the therapist decided to continue, and what happened next undoubtedly assured him that he was still needed.

After a favorable start, the client's relations with his girlfriend rapidly deteriorated. As bickering increased, the woman emerged as an aggressive person not unlike the client's mother, and in the heat of quarrels she presently began to taunt him and question his manhood. Once more he found himself thinking about sex as if it were dirty, aggressive, and certain to lead to emasculation by the angry woman. The client disengaged himself from his girlfriend, gave up the company of women, and thought longingly of resuming his homosexual life. He complained once more about competition with other men at the office. For the moment, he was right back where he started, and he might have stayed there without the therapist's continuing encouragement to keep trying.

456

Resuming the struggle, the client entered a period during which he compulsively tried to seduce every attractive woman he met, but he felt no lasting interest in these partners. His assertiveness at the office continued, and he exhibited competitive and hostile feelings toward the therapist. While thus attempting to be the dominant male on all fronts, he became aware of the dependent tendencies against which he was fighting. As a small boy he had been fond of his father and dependent on him as well as on the mother; this presently led into an Oedipal situation from which he emerged fearing the anger of both parents. That the lure of dependence was still strong is shown in an incredible piece of folly: he tried to resume the relation with his first girlfriend, only to discover almost at once the same frictions and anxieties as before. Once out of this trap, the client gradually learned "that he need not look upon all women as his mother," and that "his ultimate answers lay neither in compensatory aggression with men, nor in passive dependence, nor in homosexuality." In the course of time his behavior lost its compulsive extremes, his life became happier, and he found and married a woman with whom his relation could be congenial.

This course of treatment took a long time. Therapist and client met on 347 occasions in the course of three years. Such length, as we have seen, is the frequent by-product of a technique that gives wide scope to free association and the uncovering of early childhood cognitions. The case shows, however, that an improvement promptly achieved may not be final; anxieties surrounding intimate personal relations, early ingrained and stimulated in a variety of subtle ways, are all too easily reawakened after apparently successful inhibition. When seen in follow-up the client believed that his ability to discriminate among his own reactions, to perceive the occasions when current stimuli tended to touch off anachronous responses, had helped him to remain steady through situations of potential stress.

Fetishism

In its extreme form, fetishism involves being attracted and sexually aroused by some small stimulus that most people would regard as an insignificant part of the whole. The fetishist is not fascinated by another person but by locks of hair, shapely hands, beautiful shoes, fur garments, articles of adornment. There are intermediate degrees, in which one feature is of major interest but sexual intercourse may follow. In the fully developed case, however, the fetish gains exclusive possession of the field, and collection of the desired objects may take the place of physical satisfaction. Vernon Grant (1949) in a theoretical paper gives two examples to illustrate these possibilities. The first, drawn from an early paper by Alfred Binet, is the case of a man who preferred a beautiful hand above everything else in the opposite sex (1887). Contemplation of such a hand gave him great pleasure and an erection, and he remem-

457

bered in minute detail every hand that he had thus enjoyed. "He pretended to a knowledge of palm reading as an excuse for the minute examination of women's hands." Much as he was fixated on hands, however, he was still responsive to the woman as a whole, and the fetish "offered no obstacle to normal sexual relations." The second case comes from Wilhelm Stekel (1930). It is summarized as follows by Grant (1949).

> The stimulus consists of aprons, of certain well defined colors and patterns; the susceptibility dates from a very early age. The fetishist has an extensive collection of those aprons that meet the requirements of his taste. He is never sexually excited by the aprons, nor does he use them in masturbation. He is strongly attracted at sight of an apron of the proper design and feels an urge to possess it. At night he takes the apron which is "dearest" to him to bed; at other times he may stroke and kiss the aprons. He has never had sexual intercourse, even during several years of marriage; his attachment to the aprons, he states, makes such a relationship impossible, and has itself functioned as an erotic outlet (pp. 25-26).

If the study of abnormal psychology were intended for entertainment, like a trip to the zoo, fetishists would provide some of the most amusing exhibits. But Grant (1951) brings us back to sober reality by pointing out that there are fetishistic elements in even the most normal sexual attractions. Men who cast an appreciative eye at women's legs or the shape of their breasts should recognize a certain cousinship with the patient who pretended he was a palmist; mild focusing of sexual interest on certain anatomical features, far from being an abnormality, is not in the least uncommon. Furthermore, it is characteristic of sexual object choice to be highly selective in accordance with individual preference and taste. We do not call it a disorder if men prefer blondes, or if they prefer brunettes, or if they reserve their real interest for redheads; we do not even chide them if they choose women in smart clothes or, vice versa, in ragged T shirts and worn dungarees. Sexual attraction is guided to a surprising extent by properties that we experience as aesthetic qualities inherent in the object, and there are great individual differences in what thus allures us. In fetishism this selectivity is carried to an extreme. The fetish can become the exclusive condition for erotic arousal, or its possession can substitute for genital erotic satisfaction.

The theoretical problem posed by fetishism is how to explain the extraordinary narrowing and focalizing of the erotic stimulus. That such a result could be produced wholly by uncomplicated conditioning seems hardly plausible, especially in cases like the apron fetish. One can reason that the choice represents evasion, displacing erotic feeling from sexual ideas that arouse anxiety to peripheral images that are safer, but this again lacks credibility, especially in cases like the fetish of shapely hands. Psychoanalytic thinking emphasizes the potential symbolism of repressed wishes; for example, a wish that the sexual partner be a mother could lie behind the fascination with aprons. As yet there is no convincing explanation for fetishism. The chain of events that leads to homosexual object choice is difficult enough to understand; the one (or more) that leads to fetishism is a good deal more obscure. The one thing that most experts agree on is that fetishism represents a development failure (Steen & Price, 1977).

DISORDERS OF SEXUAL AIM

In a historically important book on juvenile delinquency, William Healy (1917) showed that certain cases of stealing result from an association between this act and sexual excitation. Such association occurs most readily before puberty, when sexual excitation is still diffuse and none too clearly understood. Healy's cases include many like the following. A girl of eight went around with older girls who taught her to steal in shops and who also aroused her interest by free talk about sex. Presently this girl began compulsive stealing accompanied by unmistakable sexual excitement. A boy of eleven often went to the beach with other boys who would steal from shops along the way and later, when undressed, practice mutual masturbation. Before long the boy felt an irresistible impulse to steal whenever he heard talk about sex. These examples are not too serious cases, but they shed a certain light on those which become more serious. There is a plastic quality to the sexual urge, especially in childhood. Under a peculiar combination of circumstances, presumably involving serious anxiety, stealing might become the only stimulus to sexual excitement; it might even crowd out any normal form of consummation.

The clearest cases of disorder in sexual aim are those in which some other aim has totally displaced the normal one. More commonly, however, the aim of heterosexual intercourse is still present, but associated with some condition without which it is mechanical and unexciting. The typical *sadistic* pattern, for instance, calls for inflicting pain during sexual foreplay, and it is this that produces thrilling excitement and fully gratifying coitus. The reverse is true of *masochism*, which in its restricted meaning as a sexual disorder requires the experience of pain as a prelude to fulfillment. In the disorders that involve looking and being seen, *voyeurism* and *exhibitionism*, the substitute aim more easily attains a kind of autonomy, so that, for example, a chronic Peeping Tom may obtain excitement and orgasm on his perch on the fire escape if a suitable scene lies in his field of vision. In the disorder called *transvestism* there may be a similar autonomous thrill to dressing oneself and appearing in public in clothes appropriate to the other sex. All of the behaviors designated by these technical terms occur in casual and playful forms in everyday life, and some of them more openly during sexual foreplay. They become disorders only through excess, and through serious interference with heterosexual behavior. Experienced as irresistible impulses, they can put the person in serious conflict with the police and the courts.

The literature shows quite clearly that transvestites and transsexuals have normal sex chromosomes (Lester, 1975). Those with Klinefelter's syndrome (XXY) appear to be genetically predisposed to defective psychosexual differentiation, which may be related to the high frequency of mental retardation and passive-dependent personality found in such men. Among 16 men with Klinefelter's syndrome, Money and Pollitt (1964) found two transvestites, two homosexuals, and one arsonist. (Arson is believed in many cases to provide perverse sexual gratification.) There is also little evidence for hormonal abnormalities in transvestites (Lester, 1975). Attention has therefore centered on psychological determinants of dual gender identity, especially as found in genetic male transvestites.

> It is characteristic of this condition that, in the dissociative manner of Dr. Jekyll and Mr. Hyde, the two gender identities may be expressed alternately. Each of the transvestite's two personalities has its own name and its own wardrobe, male or female. The degree to which each personality will appear publicly convincing will depend, for the most part, on the extent of its experience in eliciting gender-appropriate reactions from other people, until its own responses, in turn, become habitual and artless. Of course, this usually means that the male transvestite first becomes publicly convincing as a male since this usually is the way he is required to dress. He may, nevertheless, practice cross-dressing from early boyhood, and in consequence become able, by the time of adolescence, to present himself very convincingly in the female role. It is possible for impersonation to be so effective that one is hard pressed to believe that the person to whom men feel erotically attracted in the role of 'Brenda,' is the same person whom women fall for as 'Bob' (Money, 1977, p. 79).

Some *exhibitionists* are immature, use dark locations, and expose themselves openly to children for sensual pleasure. Often this is done to stimulate an impotent penis or as a means to solicit further sexual involvement with the children; these types usually try to avoid arrest. Others have organic brain disorders and exhibit out of carelessness, loss of their sense of social propriety, or inability to distinguish right from wrong. Still others are tense, anxious and conscious of the impropriety, but act under compulsion, unable to resist the impulse. The first two types are obviously severely impaired psychologically. The third type is usually embarrassed about the behavior and depressed after the act, which clashes with his personal moral code. Exhibitionism in such cases may be likened to a compulsive disorder that is focused on sexual and social inhibition (Lester, 1975).

There is an obvious kinship between many of these forms of sexual perversion and anxiety disorders, with prominent features of dissociation, compulsion, and anxiety.

Treatment of a Case of Exhibitionism

An actual case will be more useful at this point than general statements to make vivid what is involved in such disorders and their treatment (Bond & Hutchinson, 1965). The patient was a married man of twenty-five who had already run up a police record that included 24 charges of indecent exposure, 11 convictions, and 9 prison sentences mostly of only a few months' duration. The first remembered occurrence of his symptom was at age thirteen when he engaged in sex play with a girl of ten, became angry at her indifference, and exposed his erect penis to her. In general he suffered from feelings of inferiority that included the size of his penis, and the gesture of exposing himself sounds like a reassurance, a moment of desperate courage. During adolescence the tendency developed out of all bounds. When he saw an attractive girl in the park, on the streets, even in a department store, he would experience an irresistible sexual excitement along with dread, leading to what he called "a grim determination to expose, come what might." Becoming erect and extremely tense, he would expose himself, but "the spell would be broken" by the shocked response and, trembling with anxiety, he would attempt flight. Several efforts at treatment had been of no avail, so it was decided to undertake a program of systematic desensitization, the patient being brought to the sessions by his wife lest he err on the way.

The patient proved capable of deep relaxation and strong visualization of scenes. Out of the initial interviews a hierarchy of scenes was constructed that involved, with various degrees of closeness, women of the type who appealed to him in locations like streets and stores where he was likely to become excited. The patient imagined each scene in turn until it no longer excited him, with the theoretical assumption that the relaxed state would inhibit the tense condition that always preceded his exposures. In the course of 46 sessions, interrupted twice by lapses that caused his arrest, he reached a point of complete control over his symptom. If momentarily attracted by a woman he told himself to relax, and the sequence of rising tension was stopped at its source. For the next 13 months the patient was free of trouble, and his life, including his relations with his wife, became much happier.

Like the homosexual client previously described, however, this patient suffered a relapse. This happened after he lost his job and was for some months unemployed and short of money. This situation was a blow to his sense of adequacy and self-respect; it revived the inferiority feelings of his previous life. Three episodes now occurred in which he followed a woman into a public toilet and exposed himself there. It is interesting that toilets had not been included in the deconditioning hierarchy, so that the patient, still immune on streets and in stores but now again beset by feelings of inferiority, found women in toilets an irresistible stimulus. Further treatment had to be undertaken to close this avenue of stimulation. It seems plain, however, that an improvement in the patient's precarious sense of adequacy would provide more lasting insurance against future relapses.

An Example of Multiple Perversions

While it is convenient to describe sexual disorders one by one, several may occur together in a single patient. The strange complications in such cases can

461

be illustrated by an example that in its time had wide publicity. A seventeen-year-old student was found guilty of three brutal murders and a large number of burglaries (Freeman, 1955). On the wall of one apartment, in which he killed a young woman, was found written with lipstick, "For heaven's sake catch me before I kill more; I cannot control myself." Sexually deviant behavior began in his case at the age of nine and took the form of fetishism and transvestism. He repeatedly stole women's underclothing, took it to his room, and dressed himself in it with great sexual excitement. At thirteen he began securing the desired objects by going into houses through windows. Sexual excitement gradually became concentrated on this act. He often struggled to prevent himself from leaving home at night, but sometimes desire would break down his resolutions. At the sight of an open window at a place that might be burglarized, he experienced sexual excitement with erection. Usually as he passed through the window he experienced orgasm. If so, he generally left without taking anything. The impulse to kill came only if he was startled in the act of burglary. On one occasion, however, he experienced orgasm when he hit a woman who interrupted him, and he left at once without hitting her again.

Reports on this case do not disclose the sequence of events and fantasies that led the sexual need into such peculiar channels. They do show, however, that there were severe blocks on normal channels. At first he indignantly denied that he had ever practiced masturbation, but he later admitted having tried it twice without being able to secure any sexual excitement. With equal reluctance he admitted occasional petting with girls, but reported the experience to be so upsetting and repulsive that he usually burst into tears. The pattern of guilt feeling could hardly be stranger. He was much less upset in speaking of his brutal murders than he was when questioned about normal sexual behavior.

CONCLUSION

It is clear from this survey that sexual disorders are for the most part the result of unusual patterns of learning. Biological factors play a part that is decisive only in cases of fairly gross bodily abnormality, and even then they are sometimes overruled by learned gender identity. The conclusion follows that what is learned can also be unlearned, but in practice many sexual disorders do not yield easily to therapeutic endeavors. This is least true with disorders of *sexual performance* such as impotence and frigidity. Here the more open attitude toward sex that prevails today has made it possible to devise direct methods of treatment that appear to have a good rate of success. When the unusual feature is in *sexual preference*, as in homosexuality, or when the trouble lies in *sexual aim*, as in voyeurism and exhibitionism, change occurs with greater difficulty. Methods of intervention that are traditionally long often take longer; methods that seek economy of time do not save as much time; and unsuccessful results must be expected a little more frequently than in the treatment of anxiety disorders.

It is a common finding, when exploration of the past is thoroughly carried out, that the learning relevant to later difficulties began in early life, even before five or six. By that age sexual feelings become of some importance and sexual identity and role are first being learned, but cognitive development is limited and unusual learnings can occur. These learnings are influenced by the child's relation to the parents and the parents' relation to one another, and they are steered by briefings about sex that may be strongly repressive. When problematical early learning becomes entwined with anxieties, defenses, identifications, sex role acquisition, and sense of personal adequacy, we need not be surprised that what has been learned may be difficult to unlearn.

One reason for the difficulty is the powerful attraction of behavior that has been reinforced by sexual satisfaction. Whatever the consequences, the unusual aim or object choice is experienced as the spontaneous form of sexual fulfillment, loss of which seems a grievous sacrifice. This introduces conflict with regard to change. Even when the form of expression leads to social rejection, hostility, entanglement with the law, and serious curtailment of rights and opportunities, there may be reluctance to give up one's preferred mode of sexuality. In recent years homosexuals have argued that their preference is not a disorder and should be respected. The gay rights movement has had at least some success in softening prejudice and protecting the often violated civil rights of homosexuals. Therapeutic experience shows, however, that when change is actively sought, and when motivation, patience, and persistence are adequate, unusual sexual preferences and aims can be treated with a fair prospect of satisfactory results (Adams & Sturgis, 1977).

SUGGESTIONS FOR FURTHER READING

S. Freud's monograph, *Three contributions to the theory of sex*, originally published in 1905, is to be found in his collected works (Freud, 1953) and in paperback. It represents the first attempt to understand deviant sexual behavior as a developmental disorder. Two books on homosexuality, based on psychoanalytic treatment but with a theory somewhat more adaptational than Freud's, are I. Bieber et al., *Homosexuality: A psychoanalytical study* (1962) and L. Ovesey, *Homosexuality and pseudohomosexuality* (1969). The methods of treatment described by Ovesey form an interesting contrast with those of behavior modification advocated by H. J. Eysenck and S. Rachman in *The causes and cures of neurosis* (1965). A strictly behavioristic method of treating inadequate sexual response was first described by J. Wolpe in *Psychotherapy by reciprocal inhibition* (1958). Recent work along somewhat similar lines has been pursued and developed extensively by W. H. Masters and V. E. Johnson in *Human sexual inadequacy* (1970).

Disorders having a biological basis, and the complex relation between these and

463

gender identity, are discussed by J. Money in *Sex errors of the body* (1968) and by R. P. Stoller in *Sex and gender* (1968), which pays special attention to transsexualism and transvestism. D. Lester's *Unusual sexual behavior: The standard deviations* (1975) contains a digest of most of the forms of sexual deviation.

F. A. Beach (1977b) provides an authoritative compendium written by 10 experts from a wide variety of disciplines in *Human sexuality in four perspectives*; it approaches human sexuality from four different perspectives, and is especially instructive about the biological foundations of sexual function. E. B. Steen and J. H. Price's *Human sex and sexuality* (1977) is a very readable elementary textbook, in paperback, on human sexuality. *Sex and the college student* now in paperback, prepared by the Group for the Advancement of Psychiatry (1968), deals with sexual development and with campus sexual issues, including college policies and the regulation of sexual conduct. Z. Luria and M. D. Rose's *Psychology of human sexuality* (1979) is an excellent textbook.

Timons of Athens (1936) by Rockwell Kent. Courtesy of the Rockwell
Kent Legacies.

13
Schizophrenic Disorders

Schizophrenia is the most extreme form of psychosis, usually requiring psychiatric hospitalization at some time. Starting early in life, often during adolescence and still more often in the decade of the twenties, it can wreck the person's whole adult career and seriously limit the possibilities for making any useful contribution to society. If spontaneous recovery does not occur, or if treatment is not successful, a schizophrenic person may become a public charge for most of adult life, whether in hospitals, halfway houses, or other public facilities. Because the disorder may last so long, schizophrenic patients constitute something like half the inmates in psychiatric hospitals at any given time. The annual cost of schizophrenia is estimated at between $12 and $20 billion, or 1 to 2 percent of the Gross

467

National Product (Gunderson & Mosher, 1975). Less than a fifth of that cost is for direct services of all kinds; the vast majority of the cost is attributable to loss of work productivity. Only 15 to 40 percent of all discharged schizophrenics work, as compared with 40 to 75 percent for other psychiatric disorders. The early onset of schizophrenia (18 to 35 years) deprives its victims of both vocational training and early employment experience, thus jeopardizing their future job prospects as well. The disorder must be considered highly costly, whether we reckon the cost in dollars spent or in the more important coin of human lives gone wrong.

The prevalence rate usually cited for schizophrenic disorders is one percent (Slater & Cowie, 1971), although 1.5 percent is probably more accurate. This means that there are about two or three million schizophrenics in the United States today. The question that may be of more direct interest than these rather abstract statistics is: What are the chances that I or someone I know will become schizophrenic? The answer is that about three people out of a hundred that reach age fifteen develop schizophrenia during their subsequent lifetime (Yolles & Kramer, 1969).

There is a common misconception that most schizophrenics reside in psychiatric institutions, but some simple calculations can show that this is not so. The 1970 census reported that there were 457,000 patients hospitalized in state, county, private, and VA hospitals (U.S. Bureau of the Census, 1970). Half of them, or 228,500 can be assumed to be diagnosed schizophrenic. If there are two million schizophrenics altogether, then there are eight times as many who live in the community as in institutions. This might seem frightening to some because schizophrenic people are known to do unpredictable and dangerous things. Contrary to impressions created by newspapers, Lehmann (1975) reports one homicide committed per year among 10,000 patients in one community over 30 years, which is very close to the rate for our general population (U.S. Department of Justice, 1978), and these homicides are usually connected, like suicide, with hypersensitive reaction to perceived rejection by an important support figure. We will see that there are good reasons—economic, humanitarian, and psychiatric—why schizophrenic people should not be "locked away" any longer than is absolutely necessary for the welfare of all concerned. Surely the best reason was given by Harry Stack Sullivan (1962): everyone, even such a disorganized person as a schizophrenic, is much more simply human than otherwise. Humanity required several centuries to grasp the full implications of that idea.

The term *schizophrenia* was introduced by Bleuler in 1911. It now supersedes the name *dementia praecox* originally coined by Morel in the middle of the nineteenth century and made popular by Kraepelin around the turn of the century. The older title reflected the belief that dementia, running a slow progressive course, was characteristic of all cases. We know now that the disorder does not always start early, true dementia seldom follows, and many people recover (most, if the diagnostic formulation is broad), so the term is no longer appropriate. Bleuler's term means a splitting of the mind but is not meant to suggest such gross "splits" as occur in dissociative reactions and multiple selves. Bleuler had in mind a general loosening of associative connections and disorganizations of mental life and behavior. He considered this fragmentation of integrated behavior to be the truly central disorder of schizophrenia.

The different forms of schizophrenia exhibit a tremendous diversity of symptoms, leading some to question Kraepelin's historic step of classifying these divergent pictures under a single heading. The majority of experts, however, agree with Kraepelin that the different varieties have enough in common to warrant giving them a common name, but the basic nature of the disorder is not thereby established. Most cases have obvious psychodynamic features, with the psychosis coming as the culmination of a history of unsuccessful adjustments. On the other hand, certain phenomena are so bizarre and so extravagant that it has seemed impossible to explain them without resort to biochemical and neurophysiological hypotheses as well. We begin our account of this mysterious group of disorders with clinical descriptions of the behavior and subjective experiences that characterize them.

A HINDOO FABLE

Over half a century ago Kraepelin wrote: "The causes of dementia praecox are at the present time still wrapped in impenetrable darkness" (1919, p. 224). Despite massive research efforts in the intervening years, we still don't know precisely what goes wrong in schizophrenic disorders or what causes them, although we know quite a bit more than in Kraepelin's time. An analogous investigative dilemma and the solutions to it were poetically preserved for posterity by Saxe in 1873. It concerned the "six men of Indostan to learning much inclined, who went to see the Elephant (though all of them were blind)." Each found a different part of the animal: the side, tusk, trunk, knee, ear, and tail. And each reached a different conclusion about what it was like: a wall, spear, snake, tree, fan, and rope. "And so these men of Indostan disputed loud and long, each in his own opinion exceeding stiff and strong, though each was partly in the right, and all were in the wrong!" The moral is worth quoting for students of schizophrenia: "So oft in theologic wars, the disputants, I ween, rail on in utter ignorance of what each other mean, *and prate about an Elephant not one of them has seen!*" (pp. 135–136).

Like the six blind men, investigators have studied schizophrenia with exhaustive thoroughness from virtually every perspective—genetic endowment, physiology, biochemistry, the nervous system, intellectual functions, emotions, adjustment and defense, early experience, social environment—and not arrived at a compelling portrait of "the nature of the beast." Since the darkness has not been dispelled, our account here must reflect the same inquisitive bewilderment.

469

CLINICAL MANIFESTATIONS

There is a greater degree of disturbance in intrapsychic function, character structure, and interpersonal relationships in schizophrenia than in any other form of psychological disorder. Intrapsychic problems are reflected in thought, speech, mood, and sensory perception. Because particular intrapsychic modes of responding to early interpersonal relationships determine to a great extent the ultimate character structure, an individual's past history is reflected in current functioning. In both past and present, schizophrenics show extreme disturbance in every sphere of functioning (Day & Semrad, 1978).

Bleuler (1911) emphasized that the *fundamental* disturbances that distinguish schizophrenia are found in associations, affect, autism, and ambivalence ("the four A's"). "When associative links between thoughts are loosened or destroyed, looseness of associations occurs and bizarre, illogical and chaotic thinking results. When affect is split, it becomes inappropriate and mood exaggerated, indifferent, shallow, or flattened. Autism is the absorption in private, subjective ideas, including daydreams, delusions and hallucinations; as these increase, the patient loses contact with reality. Ambivalence is expressed in uncertain, hesitant affect. The combined result of these four disturbances is that the patient is unable to organize meaningful, logical, consistent thoughts, behavior or interactions" (Day & Semrad, 1978, p. 210). Symbolism in schizophrenic thinking is private and peculiar, in part self-expressive and in part defensive. Schizophrenics may express their feelings less frequently and less intensely than most people, so they often appear indifferent or apathetic, emotionally shallow, and devoid of empathy with others. They may be unable to experience pleasure, especially in relations with other people. Ambivalence, negativism, and fear of the destructiveness in their negative wishes may impair or paralyze their will. All of us experience ambivalence, but it is much more intense in schizophrenics, and it serves to help them avoid dealing directly with conflicts. It is common to find extreme disturbance in interpersonal functioning, such as excessive dependency on others, impairment in social competence, and vulnerable self-image (Grinker & Holzman, 1973). An alarming proportion of schizophrenic people, 19 percent, attempt to commit suicide (Day & Semrad, 1978).

Historically, the hallmarks of schizophrenic disorders have been the dramatic symptoms: hallucinations, delusions, negativism, stupor, and the like. However, Bleuler considered these *accessory* symptoms that are less crucial for the diagnosis of schizophrenia than the four fundamental disturbances. We may think of the accessory symptoms as particular mechanisms of defense employed to deal with the inner tensions created by the primary disturbances of thinking and emotion. This is an important distinction because we will see that neither the particular clinical symptoms nor the pattern of defenses relate dependably to the severity of the disorder or to the long-term outcome of the

Schizophrenic disturbances in thinking, mood, and perception are often revealed in artistic productions. Disorganization is often the first step in making artistic creations, so some schizophrenic people show appreciable talent in this form of human expression, as reflected here. The melange of diverse elements in this picture is typical of schizophrenic art work. The startling figure at the lower right obviously captures our attention, but the prominent eye near the top reminds us that we are being watched, a vigilant preoccupation of schizophrenic people with paranoid inclinations.

illness. That should be kept in mind as we review several varieties of schizophrenia.

VARIETIES OF SCHIZOPHRENIA

Kraepelin originally divided schizophrenic disorders into three subgroups (paranoid, hebephrenic, and catatonic) and Bleuler added a fourth (simple)

471

that was accepted by Kraepelin but is no longer used in this country. These subtypes or syndromes have been employed diagnostically throughout the world for most of this century, even though subsequent research has shown that these groupings are not mutually exclusive; they overlap, with the predominant symptoms changing markedly in the course of the illness, requiring a shift in diagnosis. Because the subtypes are not stable over time and have no *functional* coherence, treatment and prognostic decisions based on them are not very dependable. Nevertheless, the categories offer a convenient format for *describing* the disorders concisely. Many other subtypes have been suggested, for example, borderline, pseudoneurotic, and schizo-affective, but we consider only the last of these. It may be useful to think of the subtypes primarily as patterns of tactics for coping with the fundamental aspects of pathology: disorganization, loosening of associations, sensory overload, and the like. In this scheme of things the accessory symptoms can be thought of as specific mechanisms for coping with these extremely upsetting changes, whereas the subtypes are *clusters* or *patterns* of these mechanisms that feature, for example, efforts at motor and emotional control in the case of catatonia, or cognitive control and intellectual explanation in paranoid solutions (Shakow, 1977).

The Disorganized Form (Formerly Hebephrenia)

This form of schizophrenia is not seen very often nowadays, in part because the principal defining symptoms are various forms of regression that can now be prevented by drugs and improved hospital management. The chief symptoms are silliness, inappropriate smiling and laughter, bizarre disorganized ideas, and an incoherent stream of talk studded with words made up for the occasion (neologisms). There are scattered delusions and hallucinations that have little continuity and no organization. Some of these patients are infectiously good natured. One man frequently laughed ostentatiously during ward meetings and when asked why he disturbed the meetings with his outburst (which was no accident) he would eagerly relate the story of how he bought that laugh for $50 from a fellow in Chicago back in 1945. A young psychiatrist chose to live as a patient in this man's ward for two weeks for the announced purpose of "seeing what it was like"; at the end of the second day the patient came over to the doctor, put his hand protectively on his shoulder and confided with mock earnestness, "You know, Doc, I think you're much better already."

Language and Communication. Loosening of associations is apparent when ideas slip off one track onto another that is completely unrelated or clearly but obliquely related. Sometimes the frame of reference may shift idiosyncratically. Ideas expressed may be vague, too abstract or too concrete, repetitive, or stereotyped; patients may speak at great length but convey very little information. Thinking may be illogical or incoherent; facts are obscured,

472

distorted, or excluded, and conclusions reached on the basis of inadequate or faulty evidence. Less common language disturbances are perseveration and blocking, in which a particular idea either dominates the patient's communication or can't be expressed at all.

Affect. One of the most ominous symptoms of schizophrenia is emotional *blunting*, a severe reduction in the intensity of affect, or *flattening*, in which there are virtually no signs of affective expression (monotonous voice, immobile face), or the person may report having no feelings at all. Inappropriate affect is observed when feeling tone is discordant with the content of speech or ideas, for example, smiling while describing one's torture with electric shocks. There may also be sudden, unpredictable changes in emotion, such as inexplicable outbursts of anger.

Volition. Disturbance in self-initiated, goal-directed activity can grossly impair work or other role functioning. There is commonly a loss of interest or drive, an inability to complete a course of action, marked by ambivalence or vacillation.

Regression in Behavior. If deterioration occurs the patient may be found eating with the fingers, neglecting dress and toilet habits, smearing feces, and otherwise dropping the restraints of socialized living. The disorganized form of schizophrenia is usually associated with poor premorbid (childhood) adjustment, early and insidious onset of symptoms, and a chronic course of illness without signficant remissions. Social impairment is often quite extreme. For these reasons, many of these patients may be classified as *process* schizophrenics (to be described in the next section).

An Example. The disorganization and fleeting strange ideas are well illustrated in the following piece of ward conversation (White, 1932, p. 228). The doctor addresses the patient, a black, with a standard question to which he receives a surprising answer.

"How old are you?"
"Why, I am centuries old, sir."
"How long have you been here?"
"I have been now on this property on and off for a long time. I cannot say the exact time because we are absorbed by the air at night, and they bring back people. They kill up everything; they can make you lie; they can talk through your throat."
"Who is this?"
"Why, the air."
"What is the name of this place?"

473

"This place is called a star."

"Who is the doctor in charge of your ward?"

"A body just like yours, sir. They can make you black and white. I say good morning, but he just comes through there. At first it was a colony. They said it was heaven. These buildings were not solid at the time, and I am positive this is the same place. They have others just like it. People die, and all the microbes talk over there, and prestigitis you know is sending you from here to another world . . . I was sent by the government to the United States to Washington to some star, and they had a pretty nice country there. Now you have a body like a young man who says he is of the prestigitis."

"Who was this prestigitis?"

"Why, you are yourself. You can be a prestigitis. They make you say bad things; they can read you; they bring back Negroes from the dead."

In this conversation the hebephrenic jumps from image to image and merely returns now and then to a theme. Everything is jumbled. Even the feelings seem jumbled and pulled out of coherent relation to events. The patient may weep when explaining how well she feels or laugh foolishly when describing an attack on her mother, as Kathi Hermann did. She was diagnosed hebephrenic, although she was quite young and obviously not at an advanced stage of the disorder. Still one can see in her case inappropriate emotions, presumptuous behavior toward ward personnel, and incipient elements of social restraints dropped or neglected.

A combination of paranoid and disorganized characteristics appears in the following excerpt from an essay written by a patient. The attempt at system is typical of the paranoid form. The use of language, however, is a nice example of what a French writer has called "word salad," a phenomenon that is particularly well developed in the disorganized form. The essay is entitled "Mother of Man" and begins with this paragraph.

This creation in which we live began with the Dominant Nature as an Identification Body of a completed evolutionary Strong Material creation in a Major Body Resistance Force. And is fulfilling the Nature Identification in a like Weaker Material Identification creation in which Two Major Bodies have already fulfilled radio body balances, and embodying a Third Material Identification Embodiment of both; which is now in the evolutionary process of fulfillment but fulfills without the Two Parents' Identification Resistances, therefore shall draw the resistances and perpetuate the motion interchanging of the whole interrelationship; thus completing this Creation in an interchanging Four in Three Bodies in One functioning self-contained, self-controlled and self-restrained comprising the Dominant Moral Nature and consummating a ratio balanced Major Body of maximum resistance, in a separated second like Weaker Material Major Body Functioning Counter Resistance Force to the Strong Material Major Body Resistance Force, the beginning of this creation; and the Dual Force Resistances then as a major Body and Major Body

Functioning completes a University in material balance functioning the preservation of all things.

The reader may experience difficulty in grasping the patient's thought, but to the patient herself it was full of significance. She had gone over her typescript with great care, correcting the punctuation and inserting words or phrases to clarify any possible obscurity in her meaning. Her paragraph is not without a theme. One can infer that she is writing about the creation of new life by the union of two bodies, though she is careful to keep her subject at a metaphysical plane. But the language gets completely out of hand. Words are strung together in incongruous chains, happily liberated from their usual task of conveying precise ideas. Whatever the patient had in mind, one cannot say that she achieved successful communication. To communicate with others, either through speech or writing, is a social act, and it is in the sphere of social acts that the schizophrenic disorder is most apparent.

The Catatonic Form

In the catatonic variety of schizophrenia the focus of the disorder is on movement. There are peculiar postures and gestures, curious grimaces, and stereotyped actions that are repeated endlessly. More dramatic are the phases, sometimes alternating, of catatonic stupor and catatonic excitement. The excited episodes are usually of short duration, but while they last they are often extremely violent with real danger of both homicide and suicide. Sometimes the frenzy is accompanied by delusions, hallucinations, and feelings of great power; at other times it looks more like a wild, disorganized outbreak of energy. Much of the activity, however, has symbolic significance that can be related to the patient's personal problems and fantasies. The stupors are of longer duration, going on sometimes for weeks and months. The patient sits in one position and does not speak. Immobility may extend to the point that urine and feces are not passed until they move involuntarily and that saliva is not swallowed so that it accumulates and falls from the mouth. The patient has to be dressed and undressed, moved in bed, and fed through a tube. This state of exaggerated immobility may start suddenly, last for months or years, and disappear in an instant. Older theories that posited degenerative changes in the nervous system were discredited by these abrupt onsets and remissions.

Careful study of catatonic stuporous states has shown that they are less passive than they appear. It is usually more accurate to say that the patient is in a state of active immobility. Any attempts to force a change of position will be met with strong muscular resistance. The patient is not in a limp state, nor in a state of mental stupor necessarily. Despite the refusal to react, the mind is often alertly observant of what is going on. Afterward the patient may report in great detail the things that happened and were said by others during the period of apparent stupor. It is more accurately described as a state of acute negativism, so acute that it invades the whole motor system, but vigilance is not

It would be extremely uncomfortable for most people to sit in this position for more than a few minutes, but this catatonic man may remain like this, immobile, for hours and hours.

suspended. It can be inferred that rumination and fantasy are prominent during these periods of mutism. Sometimes they end in response to an hallucinated command, evidently the climax of some silent inner drama.

Abrams and Taylor (1976) found that only 7 percent in a sample of hospitalized catatonics met the research criteria for a diagnosis of schizophrenia, but 69 percent met the criteria for affective disorder, mostly of the manic type. At follow-up after one year, two-thirds of them had shown marked improvement or full remission. Morrison (1974) also found that many catatonics of the excited type met research criteria for affective disorder. On follow-up 40 percent had recovered completely, and the motor symptoms (posturing, mutism, rigidity, grimacing, and negativism) were not related to outcome. The salience of affective disturbance and high rate of recovery might be taken to indicate that catatonia should be classified with the affective psychoses instead of the schizophrenic disorders. As an alternative, Lewine, Watt, and

476

Fryer (1978) combined catatonics with other affectively colored schizophrenic disorders in a single *schizo-affective* subgroup of schizophrenics expected to have good premorbid adjustment and good prognosis for recovery.

Day and Semrad (1978, p. 214) offer the following brief synopsis of a catatonic case:

A 27-year-old coal heaver lost his father and, within six months, became withdrawn, gestured inappropriately, and frequently fell to his knees to pray and crossed himself at home, in the street, and at work. He also, uncharacteristically, took lessons in ballroom dancing. He was admitted to the hospital in a state of excitement, complaining that voices called him a queer and that cars came by the house, flashing their lights on and off as signals. He became negativistic, then blocked in speech and thought to the point of muteness. His bouts of demonstrative silent prayer often ended in an attack on one of the staff or other patients. After he had been subdued by several attendants and sedated, he would be silent and withdrawn for an indeterminate period, which would be followed by renewed prayers and violence. Finally, after he had attacked and hurt several people, he was lobotomized. (Lobotomy is a brain operation; these events occurred before modern drug treatments were available.)

The Paranoid Form

This is by far the most common form of schizophrenic disorder. Mild elements of paranoid symptoms are frequently found in other disorders, as we saw in Benton Child's unfounded (premature) belief that his wife was unfaithful to him and in Kathi Hermann's feelings of persecution by her clique of acquaintances. In paranoid schizophrenia the delusions are usually more richly developed. The delusions are typically changeable, numerous, fantastic, and accompanied by hallucinations. Delusions are nothing more than distorted or unrealistic personal beliefs, but they may be exaggerated to preposterous dimensions. Paranoid people do not rest content with thinking that they are being persecuted; they hear others murmuring against them, see figures lurking at the windows, feel the electric ticklings directed at their skin, taste the poison that has been slipped into their food. They do not stop with the mere belief in being Christ or Napoleon or Hitler or Joan of Arc; they hear voices announcing their fame and bringing important message of state. In the early stages of the illness it is generally possible to see the connection between these misinterpretations of reality and the patient's personal wishes, needs, and fears. As time goes on, however, the delusions may spread out in a disorganized fashion. Magical forces and mystical powers come into the picture, and strange influencing machines are presumed to exist that the person may draw in great detail. The whole universe created in the person's mind becomes increasingly bizarre.

477

Frequently, paranoid schizophrenics are jealous, angry, or argumentative, even to the point of bringing legal suits against their enemies. (Not surprisingly, mental health practitioners often give such litigious patients a wide berth!) Some paranoid people are fearful and express concerns about autonomy, gender identity, and sexual preference. Gross disorganization of behavior is rare in paranoid disorders and intelligence is quite high in some cases. Emotional responsiveness usually remains intact, though interpersonal relations often have a formal, stilted quality or an extreme intenseness. Onset of the paranoid subtype commonly occurs later in life than in other subtypes and the symptom pattern is more stable.

To illustrate, let us consider two cases that would both be diagnosed paranoid schizophrenic, though the outlook for the two would obviously be very different. The first, a man of thirty-eight, was admitted to a Veterans' hospital in an acutely anxious and depressed state. He was an extremely conscientious and hard-working family man, with three children, who until recently had considered himself happily married. He had been working under a lot of pressure, putting in long hours on the job. At home he had several run-ins with his neighbors, particularly the man next door. To complicate matters he and his wife had not been getting along well, especially in their sexual relations. (Experienced clinicians would wonder here which problem came first.) Over the last several months he had begun to wonder what the neighbors had against him. This was coupled with his observation that his wife increasingly displayed herself naked with casual abandon in the bedroom, in full view of the neighbors. To his accusations, his wife replied impatiently that the curtains were drawn and the lights were out, so no one could see in. But he insisted on pulling the blinds as well, and now he began to keep an eye on the neighbors. His suspicious behavior eventually drew some complaints to the police, and this convinced him that they too were involved in the plot. One day he came home from work exhausted and frustrated, to find the *front door open* and *his wife's underpants lying on the bedroom floor. That* convinced him that his wife was having an affair with the man next door! His work was suffering noticeably because he heard voices at work talking about his domestic problems, so he lost his job. Shortly thereafter he was admitted to the hospital.

His recovery was amazingly rapid. With rest, intensive drug treatment, and individual and group psychotherapy he gradually began to distance himself from the delusional system. He was helped to understand that the pressure he felt on the job was primarily attributable to his own intense desire to provide well for his family, and not intrinsic to the job itself, as his employer made clear. He was persuaded that his neighbors were not more covetous of his possessions or his wife than most people are, but that any attentions they showed were magnified out of all proportion by his own insecurity, for which he compensated in part by extreme industriousness at work. He began to see, though reluctantly at first, that his wife's provocative sexual behavior was really directed at him, and stemmed from their increasing alienation from one another over the past several months. He was released from the hospital in much improved condition after six weeks and was welcomed back at home and by his previous employer. On follow-up a year later he was free of symptoms and doing well.

The second case is a pleasant spinster in her fifties who was encountered at a convention of the American Psychological Association in San Francisco. Without introduction she struck up a conversation in a coffee shop at one of the convention hotels, explaining that she attended all the conventions although she herself was not *formally* trained in psychology. She had always been fascinated with the mysteries of the mind, extrasensory perception, mysticism, and occult matters. Through her reading and travels she had learned a great deal of psychology. She sponsored popular seminars at her home in New York City. Timothy Leary, the professor-turned-psychedelic-specialist, had given a presentation along with several Indian mystics of world renown. Her psychiatrist encouraged her to do this because it was good for her. She obviously could easily afford these seminars and it gave her something to do. On learning that her listener was from Harvard, she immediately dropped the names of Henry Murray, Gordon Allport, and others of her close friends there. Harvard, of course, is where a cyclotron is located, the one that exploded a few years ago. According to her, that was the machine used to burn out the pineal gland in her brain. It was done by remote control many years ago. That started all the trouble that led to her being hospitalized so many times, prevented her from achieving the level of recognition for which her talents entitled her, and caused her to lead an eccentric and lonely existence.

The delusions of persecution in the first case were much more comprehensible in the context of the patient's recent history. This was his first major psychological disturbance and his distorted belief system had fortunately not become stabilized. In the second case the delusional system was much more extensive and implausible. We can guess that this patient had quite a long history of serious psychological disturbance, which had now stabilized at a tolerable level of eccentricity.

There is a form of psychosis, paranoia, in which the symptoms are confined to the development of a delusional system. This psychosis is generally assigned independent status outside of schizophrenia. The clearest distinguishing feature is the absence of hallucinations. Falsification of reality is restricted to misinterpreting events; what happens is correctly perceived, but peculiar inferences are drawn from it. Except for the delusional system, these people are perfectly oriented and quite normal in their conduct. The personality does not become disorganized, and interest in the environment is substantially preserved. One might say that paranoia is a restricted psychosis, sufficiently circumscribed so that it does not invade and disintegrate the personality as a whole. We will consider presently the nature and origins of paranoic thinking. The disorder is mentioned here because of its similarity to the paranoid form

479

of schizophrenia. Both show an extensive use of the mechanism of *projection*. In paranoid schizophrenia, however, there is a more far-reaching loss of interest, loss of contact with reality, and general disintegration of personality.

By means of projection people may spare themselves intolerable anxiety by attributing some of their own tendencies to other persons. Wishes and fears may thus be transformed into external facts for which personal responsibility can be disclaimed. When a woman claims that od has chosen her to lead humankind to its salvation, she is expressing an extremely grandiose wish but not assuming responsibility for it. When she claims that pursuers and unseen forces are preventing her from achieving great things, as the pleasant spinster did, she is expressing both a grandiose wish and a fear of incompetence to fulfill it, but avoiding responsibility for this conflict. One man voluntarily entered a hospital because he thought he was being followed by five FBI agents, and he pointed to the five trees in front of the hospital behind which they were now hiding. When asked why they were following him, he explained that somehow the rumor had gotten around that he was a homosexual. He vehemently disclaimed any truth to the rumor, but he was sure that was the reason because he had recently been the victim of homosexual advances in several bars that, admittedly, were known as homosexual haunts, but he had as much right to drink there as anyone else. It was clear that he was getting vicarious sexual gratification from these encounters, while neatly disclaiming any homosexual inclinations in himself because that was anathema to a man of his conventional background. Unfortunately, the guilt this created in him was too overwhelming. The delusional and hallucinatory aspects of paranoid schizophrenia are thus intelligible in terms of desire, anxiety, and defense. Further principles of explanation, however, are needed to understand the more strictly schizophrenic aspects of the disorder: the loss of interests, the growing confusion, and the gradual deterioration of thought and conduct.

The Schizo-Affective Form

We add this fourth clinical subtype not because of its wide use in the past but because it is likely to be used increasingly in the future. Since Kraepelin first created his diagnostic system it has been a troublesome dilemma to distinguish between the affective and schizophrenic psychoses. It has always been recognized that the outcomes of the two groups of disorders differ sharply, but the importance of the distinction has increased because of two developments in recent decades. First, with the discovery and refinement in the application of psychotropic drugs since the early 1950s, we have learned that affective psychoses respond to very different medications than schizophrenic disorders do. Second, research has shown that not all schizophrenic disorders lead inexorably to deterioration; indeed, a substantial proportion of them can lead to at least partial recovery, *especially* if elements of affective disorder are prominent in the clinical picture (McCabe et al., 1971).

When a depressive or manic syndrome of at least one week's duration precedes or develops along with psychotic thought disorder symptoms, schizoaffective schizophrenia may be diagnosed. The symptoms of thought disorder may run the gamut: delusions of control; auditory hallucinations with no apparent relation to depression or elation; preoccupation with delusional ideas or hallucinations; loosening of associations. Emotional blunting or flattened affect are usually not prominent features. There is typically an acute onset and resolution of the illness, with recovery to previous levels of functioning likely. There is high prevalence of affective disorders but low prevalence of schizophrenic disorders among family members.

Is Schizophrenia a Unity?

What common features are to be found that justify placing these syndromes under a common heading? One thing that can be said about all of them is that they show a disturbance of relationship with people. Sometimes the attempt to communicate is abandoned altogether. Such extreme withdrawal is usually accompanied by preoccupation with ideas and fantasies that are egocentric and illogical, where objective facts tend to be obscured, distorted, or excluded. It seems clear, however, that this process of withdrawal does not explain all the strangeness of schizophrenic behavior. Just as we cannot explain depression as the uncomplicated result of discouragement or loss, so we cannot understand the bizarre character of schizophrenia as a direct outcome of social withdrawal. There is a degree of disorganization that goes beyond anything we might reasonably ascribe to lack of human contact. Contact with inanimate surroundings also becomes seriously impaired. While interpersonal withdrawal is a typical precursor of schizophrenia and a cardinal feature of the clinical picture, it is not the essential psychotic process. Many people withdraw who never show schizophrenic disorganization. What turns withdrawal into a disorder is progressive personality disorganization, a breakdown of integrated thinking and integrated adaptive behavior. It is perhaps here that one can make the strongest case for the unity of the several forms of schizophrenia.

Disorganization was the central point of Bleuler's theory of schizophrenia, advanced in 1911 and now regarded as a historical milestone. We have pointed out that the more dramatic symptoms—the delusional systems, frightening hallucinations, the catatonic excitements—were to be regarded as secondary developments. Bleuler believed that the central disorder could exist in various degrees of severity and that it could run a variety of courses. With some patients there would be steady deterioration, with others, intermittent attacks; the disease might take a chronic downward course, but it might be subject to arrests and remissions. Because of these variations in onset, course, and prospects, he often referred to the "group of schizophrenias." On the basis of 515 cases admitted o the Swiss hospital where he worked, he reported that 22 percent advanced to severe deterioration and that 60 percent recovered suf-

481

ficiently to be capable of earning a living. He did not regard the recovered patients as completely well, and some of them eventually relapsed, but others apparently remained free from incapacitating illness.

How far have we been able to advance beyond Bleuler's view of schizophrenia? We can specify much more precisely the prognosis of a case in advance, as we see in the next section. And the length of hospitalization for schizophrenic disorders has been greatly reduced. A study in West Germany (Meyer, 1967) found that the average hospital stay was 1033 days during the period 1929–1931 (before electroshock therapy was introduced), but was down to 353 days in 1949–1951 (before antipsychotic drugs were discovered), and 113 days in 1959–1961 (when drugs were the primary mode of treatment). Nowadays the average length of hospitalization has been reduced to only a few weeks. Indeed, many schizophrenics are treated solely as outpatients. Nevertheless, the chances of complete recovery were 2 to 4 percent 50 years ago and they are not much better today; after five years of illness 60 percent recover socially, 30 percent remain socially handicapped but still live in the community, and 10 percent require continuous hospitalization (Day & Semrad, 1978). This seems to indicate a disorder of a fundamental magnitude that is still beyond the reach of current knowledge and clinical practice. And so it is.

THE PROCESS-REACTIVE DIMENSION

Bleuler's observation of the variations in onset and course of illness has given rise to a much more fruitful classification that offers some promising connections with etiology and with prognosis, which Kraepelin's categories did not. Some cases of schizophrenia develop slowly over many years with gradually increasing withdrawal and signs of disorganization, until the person's maladjustment can no longer pass unrecognized and professional help is required. Other cases develop much more rapidly, as in the case of the thirty-eight year-old paranoid schizophrenic man described earlier. Usually such rapid onset occurs at a time when the person is under serious psychological stress, such as a major vocational setback, a domestic crisis, or the loss of a loved one. Adolph Meyer (1906), a contemporary of Bleuler, construed schizophrenia in such cases as a reaction to severe social circumstances and hence considered it more susceptible to recovery. This implied a direct connection between present psychotic behavior and previous social experience and opened the way to a whole new approach to schizophrenia, from the viewpoint of social and psychological development. Sullivan extended this viewpoint, concentrating his own attention on the early adolescent years of development. There followed a vast amount of research designed to isolate the cardinal characteristics that distinguish *reactive schizophrenias* with good prognosis from *process schizophrenias* with poor prognosis. The results have been remarkably consistent (Vaillant, 1962; Robins and Guze, 1970; Garmezy, 1970). Good prognosis is associated with acute onset, obvious precipitating stresses, good premorbid adjustment, confusion, prominent depressive symptoms, and a family history of affective disorders. Poor prognosis is associated with gradual onset, schizoid premorbid adjustment, emotional blunting ("flat affect"), lack of confusion in thinking, and a family history of schizophrenia. In short, the chances for recovery are less if there is clear evidence of a familial predisposition for schizophrenia instead of depression, if schizoid withdrawal seems to be an established way of life and if the psychotic experience seems neither very disturbing nor different from the person's customary behavior.

A convincing demonstration of the validity of the process-reactive concept was made by Stephens and Astrup (1963), although a number of other investigations have achieved similar results (Nameche, Waring & Ricks, 1964; Vaillant, 1964). They classified 143 schizophrenics as either process or nonprocess types while in the hospital, and compared the two groups on independent ratings of improvement at discharge and on follow-up 5 to 13 years later. The results were as follows:

Follow-up of Process and Nonprocess Schizophrenics*

Clinical Rating	At Discharge		At 5–13-Year Follow-Up	
	Process	Nonprocess	Process	Nonprocess
Recovered	7%	17%	10%	38%
Improved	38	51	41	59
Unimproved	55	32	49	3

*Adapted from Stephens & Astrup (1963).

The risk of deterioration, which was the principal defining characteristic of the disorder in Kraepelin's work, was very slight in the nonprocess schizophrenics but about 50 percent in the process cases. This opens the encouraging prospect that schizophrenic disorders may be reliably classified for probable outcome, not so much on the basis of salient clinical symptoms as on pertinent social and life historical criteria. It may be noted that these authors found a substantially higher rate of recovery among the nonprocess group than Day & Semrad found for schizophrenic patients in general.

Organic versus Psychodynamic Etiology

Bleuler (1924) described reactive schizophrenia as a morbid reaction to an affective experience, whereas process schizophrenia is conditioned by a morbid process in the brain, although the two forms cannot be distinguished clinically because the symptoms intermingle. There is some empirical support for this hypothesis. In a variety of studies process schizophrenics have shown more impairment of abstract thinking, greater deficit in physiological responsiveness, more "organic" signs on the Rorschach, and so on, but it is impossible to de-

483

termine from these studies whether the defects reflect *causes* or *consequences* of the disorder. More compelling evidence is based on data gathered prior to the onset of psychotic symptoms. Ricks and Nameche (1966) found that "soft signs" of neurological impairment (rigidity, speech abnormalities, abnormal gait, poor coordination, impaired attention span, enuresis, hyper- and hypo-activity) were the best predictors for chronicity in the guidance clinic records of adolescents later hospitalized for schizophrenia.

Another source of convergent evidence is the recent study in Denmark that traced the biological family histories of adopted children who were hospitalized for schizophrenia as adults (Kety, 1978). Schizophrenic disorders were found among the biological relatives of the adoptees who developed chronic schizo-phrenia and borderline schizophrenia, but none were found among the rela-tives of the acute (reactive) schizophrenics. This suggests that genetic pre-disposition is significant for chronic and borderline schizophrenias, both of which can be considered process types because they constitute general life styles, but not for the more episodic reactive schizophrenias. Winokur and his associates (McCabe et al., 1971; Fowler et al., 1972) take the argument a step further. They found more schizophrenia in the relatives of poor prognosis schizophrenics and more affective disorders in the relatives of good prognosis schizophrenics; they concluded that the latter (reactive) form of the disorder is genetically related to affective psychosis instead of schizophrenia. This of course ties reactive schizophrenia to a biological cause although a different one than for process schizophrenia. However, we will see later that there are limits to the power of genetic evidence for explaining any form of psychosis.

An alternative view is offered by Phillips (1968), who considers the process-reactive dimension as a continuum of psychological development. Reactive schizophrenics achieve demonstrably higher levels of social competence prior to breakdown and have for this reason greater adaptive potential after the acute phase has passed. Differences in genetic predisposition or other organic factors are not incompatible with this view, but they would be significant etio-logically only insofar as they affect the whole course of the person's social and psychological development. There is an important departure here from most conceptions that emphasize the regressive aspects of schizophrenic disorder. Phillips argues that the disorder represents a continuous process in which the premorbid, intermediate, and ultimate stages are meaningfully related. Knowing the level and modes of adaptation prior to onset makes seemingly anomalous aspects of the psychosis comprehensible, and, most importantly, explains the variations in outcome.

It is still too soon to place these hypotheses and empirical facts definitely in a theory of etiology. Clearly Kraepelin's system of classification is being super-seded by other systems based more on personal history than on clinical symp-toms. Strauss and Carpenter (1974) found that even the most ominous constel-lations of schizophrenic symptoms at hospital admission do not reliably predict outcome two years later. Referring to the studies in Copenhagen (Kety,

1978), those authors point out that inadequate or poor premorbid personality appears to have stronger genetic links to schizophrenic family history than does the clinical symptom picture at breakdown. Hawk et al. (1975) extended the follow-up of Strauss and Carpenter's sample to five years with the same results.

From many viewpoints reactive forms of schizophrenia are coming to be distinguished from process forms, despite their similar symptoms. This may lead ultimately to a formal revision of diagnosis for the functional psychoses, perhaps along the lines suggested by Astrup and Noreik (1966). These workers would classify as *schizophrenia* only the process psychoses that have a high risk of schizophrenic deterioration. The cases with a significant mixture of "true" schizophrenic indications and depressive signs would be called *schizoaffective psychoses*; they would carry a medium risk for long-term defects. Reactive psychoses would be grouped along with mania and depression as *affective psychoses*, and would carry low risk of deterioration.

Acute Schizophrenic Episodes with Recovery

The outbreak of unmistakable schizophrenic behavior sometimes occurs under circumstances that illuminate the nature of the patient's inner turmoil. A girl of eighteen returned from a year in Europe in an acute schizophrenic condition, withdrawn, guilt-ridden, frightened, preoccupied with delusions of persecution. The year abroad was her first time away from home and she had always been sheltered and restricted by her overprotective father. While in Europe she became acquainted with boys for the first time, and became infatuated with one in particular. They had lain together in bed and kissed, so now she was certain that she was pregnant! She knew that her father would have disapproved of her behavior, and this made her feel doubly guilty. She was certain that everyone knew about her sinfulness, even the garbage collectors, so she was afraid to go outside alone. This young woman was helped by some fundamental sexual information. Her parents and older sister were advised to reassure her about the presumed "transgressions" and to encourage her to more active social participation. In this case the natural sexual experiences were interpreted as great personal shortcomings and abnormalities because of misinformation and misguided moral attitudes. The immediate cause of breakdown was a sharp blow to self-esteem that may well have been already precarious. This was mirrored in her belief that everyone "knew about her" and led to her withdrawal and rather serious disorganization of behavior.

Transient schizophrenic episodes can be described as retreats from reality. When viewed in the light of their later outcome, however, they can better be characterized as tactical retreats having the function of a delaying action until the person gets organized for a fresh attack on the problem of new adjustment. A prominent aspect of the clinical symptoms in the case just cited was guilt, which Phillips (1968) considers a good prognostic sign because "turning against the self" in times of stress, in contrast to "turning against others" or "avoiding others," reflects a high level of psychological development. This case, like most of those with acute onset, would be classified as a reactive type of schizophrenia.

Gradual Onset with Progressive Disorganization

In cases of gradual onset, warning signs may be detected that something more than withdrawal is taking place. A child may give evidence of "clinging to the mother's apron string" and avoiding rough, competitive play. Often there is early success with schoolwork and a continuing interest in studies. Thus far, the pattern of adjustment might be called unassertive, but not morbid. It would be more serious, if, before long, a general retraction of interest were observed, with less intense and less numerous participations in things of previous interest. The individual may experience subjectively a growing sense of passivity and alienation, that outside events are losing their meaning. The youngster ceases to make new friends, even older or younger friends, and interest in schoolwork declines into dreamy inattentiveness. This change for the worse is likely to occur at puberty. So long as interest is maintained in some form of constructive activity—art or writing, for example—there may be a chance to find the way back, along the lines of some specialty, to social acceptance and participation. But if interests are retracted to the point of listlessness and apathy, so that fantasy reigns without further correction by real experience, then the condition must be regarded as ominous.

Ideas of reference (attributing personal significance to events that are unrelated to oneself in fact) may tend to creep gradually into the picture without at first assuming the status of delusions. Incipient schizophrenics are keenly aware of outside stimulation, even without overtly responding to it. For a long time they may recognize that the source of difficulties resides inside the self. Nevertheless they cannot help feeling that the world is a little hostile, or at least inconsiderate. Being highly aware of their own fantasies, they wonder what other people would think if they knew what was going on in their heads. It is a short step to occasional fleeting delusions. They half believe that people are actually saying derogatory things and behaving in a hostile fashion. They may remain for some time in this borderland of half belief, only gradually slipping over to the point where insight and perspective are lost. People in this psychological borderland are overly sensitive to perceived or imagined failures on their part or to criticism from others, so we may suppose that any important slippage or jolt in self-esteem may precipitate overt psychosis.

The general retraction of interests can be considered a first sign of impending disorganization. It is not a logical consequence or natural extension of defensive withdrawal from people. This is an indication of giving up the attempt to move forward even along asocial lines. Sometimes the retraction of interest finds expression in ideas that the world has changed and that everything is dying. The internal affective change is perceived as a physical change in the world.

The following case illustrates both the gradual appearance of disorganization and the way in which events can progressively deepen a schizophrenic reaction. A boy in high school was considered by his friends to be sensitive, solitary, and a little eccentric. They knew that he was an orphan and lived with an elderly, somewhat peculiar foster mother. The boy was good in his studies, especially in history and literature. His English teacher, who constantly read his literary productions, noted distinct talent but many eccentricities of content. Themes of death and decay, images of dilapidated castles and gardens gone to seed, scenes of an ancient glory now crumbling to dust—these and similar gloomy ideas dominated his beautifully written verses. Although the boy spent a good deal of time alone, he had several friends among the students who were preparing for college. At graduation he was separated from his chums, since he himself was unable to go to college. Occasionally he visited them, but it was clear that he resented his inferior position and the interruption of his own education. His friends now began to suspect that he was building up fictions about himself. He showed them an application blank that he had received from an art school. They believed that he had prepared it on his own typewriter. He also discoursed at length on his distinguished French ancestry, a theme he was able to fill out convincingly from his knowledge of history. He repeatedly mentioned that his real mother, a countess, was now living in the city, and that he was in frequent communication with her. The friends began to feel that he was a liar, and they laid plans to expose him. One day they confronted him with numerous fatal inconsistencies in his stories and accused him of fabrication. He thereupon admitted that his stories were not true, but explained that he had been forced to disguise himself in this way in order to elude a hostile power known as the Third Element. He now claimed that he and his mother, the countess, had collaborated in preparing a set of disguising fictions to keep the Third Element off their trail. He told his accusers that the situation was growing increasingly serious. Most of his friends had turned against him, and only three remained on his side.

It is clear that this boy's history showed signs of schizophrenic disorganization before he graduated from high school. That event, with separation from his circle of friends, dealt a setback to his adjustment and sharply increased his symptoms. He now began to lose track of the line between fantasy and fact, speaking of his fantasies of noble lineage as if they were true. The motive behind these fabrications was pathetically clear: if he could not go to college, he would at least have some form of distinction to keep him on a footing with his friends, and while he was at it he provided himself with a mother. Unfortunately his attempts at compensation only irritated his friends and their unsympathetic action constituted a second, more direct, and more personal rejec-

487

tion. This event threw him into deeper psychosis. His delusions about hostile friends and a hostile Third Element reflected the real feeling of hostility that he sensed in his accusers. Unfortunately the delusions now began to assume a generalized form that made him more and more inaccessible to friendly advance from others.

Arieti (1975) sees two primary patterns of preschizophrenic behavior that usually become distinct in later childhood. The *schizoid* pattern of aloofness, detachment, and lack of involvement with people is illustrated by the case just described. The second pattern, which he calls *stormy*, is characterized by explosive, antisocial, or unpredictable behavior. It is illustrated by the case of Walter Young, the youngest of two children whose father died in a car accident when the boy was only four. The loss was traumatic and matters became worse when his mother remarried, because he disliked his stepfather and disobeyed him, for which he was severely punished often. Early in school Walter was described as a rather shy, nervous child with a short attention span, who bothered other children. He often gave curt, hostile replies to teachers and was constantly in trouble, but, when questioned, he denied wrongdoing, became surly, and cried. His intelligence and scholastic performance were average, except in the academic subjects like reading and writing that did not interest him. Difficulties at home were noted in the school records as contributing to Walter's adjustment problems at school. He was referred for psychological evaluation and counseling in the sixth grade, though his teacher felt he was making good progress "for a nervous, erratic child."

In junior high school Walter developed an intense interest in golf, working during the summers as a caddy. This positive development was offset, however, by serious problems in his comportment at school. At first he was quiet and well behaved, though he had a quick temper that was kept well under control. In the eighth grade his absences increased substantially; he made friends with four other boys "of kindred spirit" and his grades dropped to a D average. Suddenly, he was "a *major* discipline problem who can't be trusted out of the teacher's sight . . . a despicable person!" Ninth grade brought more of the same and the teacher noted the danger Walter presented to peers: "For the safety of others in the group, the teacher *must watch* Walter at *all* times. Although quiet at times, he is gleeful about hurting others." Psychiatric help was urgently recommended, but not much help came forth.

In high school, teachers noted Walter's unresponsiveness, his uncaring, sometimes negative, attitude. He tried to improve in this regard, but failed. Citing that he was very odd or strange, he was referred to a guidance counselor. He was rated by teachers as lower than average on motivation, responsibility, and concern for others. He failed a course in the twelfth grade, but graduated nevertheless—in the bottom half of his class. The only bright spot was that his interest and ability in playing golf increased.

In the three years after his graduation from high school Walter suffered a traumatic broken romance, followed by enlistment in military service, hospitalization, and discharge with a diagnosis of paranoid schizophrenia. There followed a series of hirings and firings for menial jobs and two police arrests for criminal violations. At first he was judged not competent to stand trial because of his psychiatric condition, but after a period of observation and treatment at a state hospital, at last report he was being brought to trial at age twenty for two minor offenses.

Cases with gradual onset, as illustrated by Walter Young and the boy contending with the Third Element, are usually classified as process schizophrenics.

In general it can be said that steep downhill steps on the path to schizophrenia occur in connection with events that lower the already feeble self-esteem or challenge in some way the adequacy of the vulnerable person. Anything that contributes to the feeling of alienation or incompetence has a devastating effect on the person's contact with reality and sense of personal identity. The sexual changes of puberty, and such major challenges as engagement, marriage, childbirth, or heavy vocational responsibilities, often serve as precipitating events. Each step toward fuller independence and maturity stands like a threat and may deepen the schizophrenic reaction.

Early Identification of Vulnerability to Schizophrenia

A natural outgrowth of the increasing recognition that schizophrenia does not just happen all of a sudden is an expansion of efforts to identify children at risk for schizophrenia before the onset of psychosis. Retrospective studies based on records from child guidance clinics and schools have isolated a number of likely indications of vulnerability. Preschizophrenic children have been found to have lower intelligence, on the average, than their classmates (Watt & Lubensky, 1976) and siblings (Lane & Albee, 1965). They have an unusually high frequency of parental death during childhood, and there is some indication that the risk is more extreme if the death occurs before the child reaches eight years of age (Barry, 1949; Watt & Nicholi, 1979). Examining the cumulative school records of preschizophrenic children, Watt and Lubensky (1976) found sharp sex differences in social adjustment; teachers described the boys as abrasive, defiant, and emotionally unstable, corresponding to Arieti's *stormy* type, whereas the girls were primarily inhibited, sensitive, and introverted, showing the *aloof* pattern. Slight deviation was apparent during the primary school years, but the sharpest behavioral abnormalities were manifest in junior and senior high school (Watt, 1978), which suggests that the social maladjustments begin to accumulate in early adolescence for many preschizophrenics until they culminate in breakdown in young adulthood.

A major obstacle to studying children prior to the onset of schizophrenia is that the disorder occurs so rarely in a general population. However it is well

489

established that about 10 percent of the children of schizophrenic parents will become schizophrenic themselves. Therefore Mednick and Schulsinger (1968) seized on the ingenious idea of studying adolescent children of process schizophrenic mothers. Their group of 207 such children was considered to have a "high risk" for schizophrenia; "low risk" controls were 104 children of normal mothers. When initially tested around fifteen years of age in 1962 there were already pronounced differences between the groups. The high-risk children were more nervous, withdrawn, passive, easily upset, and poorly adjusted socially. Their performance was lower on arithmetic and coding subtests of intelligence, which required sustained concentration and effort, and their word associations tended to drift. On psychophysiological measures they were more easily and quickly aroused by mild stress, indicating highly labile autonomic responsivity. On follow-up five years later 20 of the high-risk children had already suffered psychiatric breakdown. These 20 (the "Sick" Group) were compared with 20 other high-risk children whose initial adjustment level was comparable but who were still functioning adequately (the "Well" Group). The Sick Group had been separated earlier from their mothers, who were rated more severely ill. The Sick Group were described by their teachers as more disturbing in class and more easily upset, which is remarkably consistent with the retrospective school record studies reported above. They also showed more associative drifting on a continuous word association test. Thus there are consistent early indications of associative disturbance, autonomic lability, and social maladjustment years before the onset of psychotic symptoms.

Ten-year follow-up interviews were conducted "blindly" (without knowing which children had schizophrenic parents) by a psychiatrist with more than 90 percent of the original sample in 1972 (Schulsinger, 1976). A consensus of three different diagnostic procedures based on the interviews yielded the following classifications:

	High-Risk Subjects		Normal Controls	
	(N = 181)		(N = 91)	
Schizophrenia	15	8%	1	1%
Borderline	55	30%	4	4%
Psychopathy	5	3%	4	4%
Other personality disturbance	22	12%	9	10%
Neurosis (anxiety disorder)	30	17%	33	36%
No mental disorder	25	14%	27	30%
Nonspecific disagreement	21	12%	13	14%
Deceased*	8	4%	0	0%
	181		91	

*The deceased included four suicides, two diagnosed schizophrenic posthumously.

The two index groups classified in 1967 as "Sick" and "Well" were diagnosed as follows in 1972:

	"Sick" Group		"Well" Group	
	(N = 20)		(N = 20)	
Schizophrenia	6*	30%	2	10%
Borderline	6	30%	3	15%
Paranoid	1	5%	0	0%
Other personality disturbance	6	30%	4	20%
Neurosis (anxiety disorder)	1	5%	5	25%
No mental disorder	0	0%	4	20%
Interview refused	0	0%	1	5%
Unavailable	0	0%	1	5%
	20		20	

*Three of the deceased schizophrenics in the "Sick" group committed suicide.

Mednick and Schulsinger had asked the teachers in 1962 to judge which children were most likely to have psychiatric breakdowns eventually; of those considered to be the most likely candidates 33 percent were diagnosed schizophrenic in 1972, 21 percent were borderline cases, and only 6 percent had no mental illness. Schulsinger (1976) compared retrospectively the 1962 teacher ratings of classroom behavior in the eventual schizophrenics and their classmates: the preschizophrenics were more prone to be angered and upset, disturbed class more with inappropriate behavior, were more violent and aggressive, and had more disciplinary problems than the other children. Clearly, these differences conform more to Arieti's (1975) characterization of the "stormy" prepsychotic personality than of the "schizoid" type.

Other studies of children with high genetic risk for schizophrenia confirm the evidence of early psychological deviance. Weintraub et al. (1975) investigated children of schizophrenic mothers, of depressed mothers, and of normal mothers. The two groups whose mothers were psychiatric patients disturbed their school classes more than the controls with their impatience, disrespect, defiance, inattentiveness, and withdrawal. Teachers also rated both index groups as low in comprehension and creative initiative, and remote in their relations to the teachers. Sociometric ratings were also obtained from peers; children of schizophrenic mothers were judged by classmates in grades two through nine more aggressive and more unhappy and withdrawn than the normal controls (Weintraub et al., 1978). Daughters of schizophrenics were also considered less likable than the controls. In general, the children of schizophrenic mothers were not different from the children of depressed mothers. Rolf and Garmezy (1974) likewise found lower peer acceptance for *sons* of schizophrenic mothers (though not for daughters) and no differences between children of schizophrenic and depressed mothers. Preliminary analysis in still another high risk project found that children of schizophrenic parents were less intelligent, less emotionally stable, and more introverted than children of normal parents, as judged by classroom teachers (Grubb & Watt, 1979). These investigations thus show evidence of both "stormy" and "schizoid" maladjustment in children at high genetic risk for schizophrenia, but raise questions as to whether they can be distinguished from children of depressed parents.

Most of these high risk projects are planned to follow the children for 20 years or more, through the period of maximum psychiatric risk. As the early results indicate, we can expect from these projects and others like them (Anthony, 1971; Cowen et al., 1973) important new leads in the etiology of schizophrenia.

DISORGANIZATION IN SCHIZOPHRENIC THINKING

From the descriptions already given it will be clear that the problem of schizophrenia can be approached from several directions. As in the anxiety disorders, emotional problems crop out at every turn: difficulties with sex and aggression, with love and hate, with competence and self-esteem are everywhere apparent in the case histories. This leads our thoughts toward the family circle and the interaction of parents and child during the early years. We notice also a weakening of social interest and a progressive failure of communication with others, suggesting unusual difficulties in the process of social adaptation. Thus far we might be dealing with another variety of anxiety disorder; but then we are confronted everywhere by signs of disorganization, a seeming breakdown in the very structure of thinking that has no counterpart in the anxiety disorders and is somewhat like what we will study in connection with brain injuries. Perhaps such fundamental disorganization can be understood in psychodynamic terms, though it is hard to conceive of it happening without some biochemical changes in the brain. Whatever the ultimate explanation turns out to be, we must try to understand this central aspect of the disorder.

It is extraordinarily difficult to follow the thought processes of a schizophrenic patient. With other types of patients the observer can usually establish empathy and follow the course of thought even though it appears somewhat strange. It is not difficult, for instance, to comprehend a deluded paretic who offers us a pleasant weekend at his country estate, or to understand a manic patient when she lays vast plans for humanitarian reform. These patients may be psychotic, but somehow the schizophrenic patients seem even more disturbed. Their thinking falls to pieces, it defies logic, it contains weird constructions like prestigitis, the Third Element, and the Strong Material Major

Body Resistance Force. Nevertheless it is not always impossible to understand what is going on in schizophrenic thought. What we have to realize is that the thought processes are autistic, like dreams and daydreams; more than that, they are full of conceptions that seem quite immature. We will try to learn why this should be so.

The Development of Paranoid Thinking

The study of schizophrenic thought is most easily begun at the point where it is least abnormal. We therefore start by considering delusions. A delusion is essentially a misinterpretation of experience. It does not, like an hallucination, entail a distorted registering of experience or a false perception of what is going on. Hallucinated patients hear voices in the ventilating system that loudly discuss their faults and denounce their sins. Merely deluded patients proceed with more respect for reality. They may correctly perceive a number of people talking and, without actually overhearing the conversation, *infer* that their faults are being discussed and their sins denounced. In delusions the disorder is localized at the point where inference or the interpretation of experience begins. Otherwise the contact with reality is correctly maintained.

Delusional thinking is primarily a disorder of communication. Children acquire an image of themselves by noticing how others react to them (Laing, 1960). Their criticism of their own behavior contains a distillation of the criticisms they have received from others. Gradually they learn to see themselves and their conduct in different perspectives: as mother sees them, or as brother or teacher or chum or rival sees them. By shifting perspectives they can take different attitudes toward their behavior. By taking the role of others, children incorporate alternative perspectives in their own behavior. Role taking is an acquired skill, and there are great individual differences in the extent to which it is acquired. "The adult who is especially vulnerable to paranoid developments is one in whom this process of socialization has been seriously defective" (Cameron, 1959). Like everyone else such vulnerable people draw inferences from what they observe, but unlike others they remain amateurs in realizing how these inferences might appear to someone else.

Now suppose that a person whose limited social experience deprives him or her of that flexibility of perspective becomes involved in emotional difficulties. More specifically, suppose that the internal economy of aggression, sense of competence, and self-esteem suffer a serious setback. The effect of this is to sensitize the person to any impressions about social image or reputation. Then, like the playwright on opening night, the individual scrutinizes the audience for clues to their reaction, selecting fragments of behavior, many of which may be totally irrelevant, and weaving them together into a fictitious critique. The problem is especially serious for the person whose self-esteem has been shattered. Everything that happens seems related to this consuming problem. In this condition the conclusions reached about other people's judg-

493

ments may be completely fictitious. They correspond only to what the person is thinking about him- or herself. As we saw earlier in the paranoid schizophrenic homosexual, everyone *else* had to think he was homosexual because he couldn't tolerate that repugnant thought himself.

The critical point in the development of delusions, however, is the *failure of correction*. Weak in habits of role taking, accustomed to puzzle and brood alone, the person becomes trapped in a single perspective and shares misgivings with no one. The result is cumulative misinterpretations; "the lone individual lacks the usual checking over with other persons which might modify and correct them." Before long he or she has built up what Cameron calls a "pseudo-community," ascribing imaginary attitudes and functions to the real people in the environment. They are detectives, gangsters, or pursuers who mean harm. The more organized this pseudo-community appears, the more it becomes necessary to take action in it. Eventually some protective maneuver or aggressive behavior is undertaken; the action takes place in the real social field, and other persons in that field judge it to be insane.

Despite these distortions of reality and the social withdrawal that follows, schizophrenics often attempt to regain contact with other people, reconstituting their social relations and laying a new basis for human contact. It is important to bear this general principle in mind in our study of schizophrenia. In many cases psychosis involves not only disorganization but also a peculiar or psychotic reorganization of experience.

Nature of the Intellectual Disorder

It is natural to suppose that the disorganization in schizophrenic thinking will be accompanied by a drop in level of intelligence. Actually the deficit on intelligence tests is smaller than might be expected. Schooler and Feldman (1967) have abstracted 28 studies published in this area between 1950 and 1965. They show a consistent but moderate deficit in over-all intelligence. The impairment is general rather than specific to any particular domain and seems to be related to understandable aspects of the patient's life situation, such as education, length of hospitalization, age, and severity of current distress. In most comparisons the schizophrenics were less impaired than patients with known brain damage. The conclusion is unmistakable that the poor performance of schizophrenics is as much attributable to social inaccessibility as to intrinsic (organic) pathological processes. Performance is worst on tasks requiring sustained attention and effort, and even these improve if the patient's clinical condition gets better.

In past years much attention was given to the concept of possible regression in schizophrenic thinking because of features that are reminiscent of children's thinking: simplicity, concreteness, overgeneralization, stimulus-boundness, distractibility, weak governance by principles of relevance. The general consensus now is that regression is neither an accurate description nor a good metaphor for schizophrenic thought (Brown, 1973). More significant is the clue provided by the weakness of sustained effort and attention (Oltmanns & Neale, 1978), as if schizophrenics could not regularly summon the mental energy necessary for the organization of thought of which they are still capable. Frankl (1955) has called attention to a very general characteristic of schizophrenic experience that he calls the "passivizing of the psychic functions." The patients feel helpless, observed, photographed, influenced, the passive object of things happening around them. They complain that the world has become shifting and kaleidoscopic; this perhaps signifies a kind of perceptual passivity in which all stimuli have a claim on attention and nothing can be excluded. They perform poorly on complex learning tasks with many alternatives because they cannot maintain the learner's active role of selecting the relevant and excluding the irrelevant, They fail in sustained abstract thinking because they do not muster the necessary degree of active control over intellectual processes. The passivizing of thought may be the most telling description of the change that characterizes schizophrenic mental operations. It is this that a biochemical or psychodynamic hypothesis must explain.

PSYCHOSES IN CHILDHOOD

Recently there has been a great deal of interest in childhood psychoses; much research has been conducted, mostly through the medium of attempts at psychotherapy. Considering the substantial difficulties of diagnosis, the many varieties of clinical picture, and the different ages of the children studied, it is not surprising that some rather different formulations have appeared in print. What is overwhelmingly clear, however, is that serious disorders having a resemblance to adult schizophrenias make their appearance early in life.

Infantile Autism

One fairly clear category, *infantile autism*, is seen as early as the first two years of life. It is readily distinguished from most forms of mental retardation because the infant has an intelligent and pensive expression and shows normal if not superior skill in dealing with the inanimate environment. The difficulty shows itself in a serious lack of contact with people, a backwardness in the use of language for communication, and an obsessive desire for the preservation of sameness. This last trait conveys the impression that the child cannot tolerate anything new; its sense of security depends on keeping the environment constant and free from surprises. If we imagine these traits as remaining throughout the course of development it is clear that the end result would correspond in many respects to the unassertive adult schizophrenic who faces hesitantly each new stage of growth, communicates poorly with other people, and has no strong affective bonds with anyone.

Infantile autism is a rare and relatively specific symptom syndrome with a prevalence of about 2 cases per 10,000 population (Treffert, 1970). It should not be confused with childhood psychosis as a whole. The distinguishing marks are early appearance and the central symptom of unresponsiveness to the human environment. The baby is usually unresponsive from the very beginning, even when attempts are made to mother, cuddle, and play with it. Observational studies confirm that autistic children relate more to objects than to peers, and they engage frequently in solitary, repetitious behavior (Black et al., 1975). More than simply not responding, they seem actively to resist the human environment, in a fashion not unlike what is seen in catatonic stupor. They look past or through adult would-be playmates, turn their backs, or occupy themselves with something else. The impairment is less marked when dealing with the inanimate environment. Here they seem to establish some of the sense of competence they are unable to feel with people. Almost all autistic children have serious difficulties acquiring and mastering language, and some never do. The quality of language mastery is closely related to the adequacy of later personal adjustment. A third of them appear to have neurological dysfunction, either seizures or abnormal EEG tracings (Lotter, 1974). In extreme cases there may be virtually total preoccupation with mechanical objects, repetitious rhythmic body movements, sensory deficits,

These autistic children are in a relatively small room together, but they behave as if they were alone, not interacting with each other. The attention of some of them is engaged by the toys, but several stare vacantly into space. Such extreme aloofness often diminishes somewhat as the children get older, but their social skills usually remain severely limited throughout their lives.

head-banging, and temper tantrums (Rutter, 1974). Not infrequently they are thought, at first, to be deaf because of their mutism and apparent inability to acquire language.

The parents of autistic children have been reported to have higher intelligence and socioeconomic status than average, although these reports have been challenged on the grounds that wealthier, better educated, and more intelligent parents are more likely to seek psychiatric help (Bettelheim, 1967). Initially, the parents were thought to be cold, distant, obsessive, and mechanical in their handling of their babies (Kanner, 1965). These unflattering descriptions have been countered, in interactional terms, with the argument that initial unresponsiveness on the infant's part would make the parents' roles unrewarding and at the same time fill them with anxiety. Recent investigations (Cox et al., 1975) have found that parents of autistic children are *not* less warm, emotionally demonstrative, responsive, or sociable than parents of aphasic children, who are known to suffer from organically based disorders that present similar communicational obstacles. This raises questions about the theoretical implications of the earlier observations.

Kanner (1973) reported a 30 year follow-up of 11 autistic children originally studied in 1943. Two developed epileptic seizures. One had died and another had been hospitalized. Four spent most of their lives in institutions. One remained mute but was able to work on a farm and in a nursing home. Two continued to live at home with their families but were employed and had developed some recreational interests. By coining the term *infantile autism*, Kanner had hoped to avoid a premature assumption that such children supplied recruits for later schizophrenia, but the outcomes for these 11 indicate a destiny that is hardly any better.

Childhood Schizophrenia

It is usual to reserve the term *childhood schizophrenia* for disorders that make their appearance after the first four or five years. There are various symptom pictures, but on the whole they cannot be interpreted simply as autism of later onset. This is most sharply shown in a pattern described by Margaret Mahler (1952) as *symbiotic psychosis*. In contrast to autism, where the child displays no attachment to the mother or anyone else, in this group of cases there is a tremendously strong relationship between mother and child. The term *symbiosis*, which is in general use in biology, refers to close mutual dependence between two organisms, each requiring the other for its continued existence, as bees require flowers for honey and flowers require bees for fertilization. The symbiotic psychosis may be said to exist when the mother-child relationship has been so close that the infant fails to differentiate mother from self and thus stumbles over the whole process of distinguishing itself and its thoughts from external realities. Any threat of separation throws the child into disorganized panic, which is the central aspect of numerous, more acute symptoms. Mahler's description is built on direct study of young child patients, but a moving

497

autobiography by a patient of Frieda Fromm-Reichmann shows how the underlying schizophrenic potential can remain latent until late childhood, when the new stresses of adolescence reactivate the earlier confusion in reality testing (Green, 1964).

At somewhat older ages, in the juvenile era and later childhood, the diagnosis of schizophrenia can usually be made on the strength of behavior that is more openly and obviously bizarre. A six-year-old boy described by Ross (1955), for example, rummaged through women's purses whenever he got a chance, entered rest rooms to examine the pipes under bathroom fixtures, got on his hands and knees to look at women's legs, hit other children on the head, was deeply preoccupied with the daily mail delivery, crawled under parked trucks to examine fender aprons, frequently swung his arms around in purposeless movements, was acutely anxious in games with other children, and tried to keep his mother at his side as much as possible. If we reduce these eccentricities to the formula of aggression, anxiety, dependence, and curiosity about anatomy, they are not different in kind from the interests of normal younger children and from continuing unconscious trends in older ones, but we do not expect them to be expressed so openly, controlled so poorly, or pursued with such repetitive intensity that no energy is left over for general enjoyment or constructive growth. A central characteristic in many cases is this lack of nuance and proportion; they react in extremes instead of in moderation. Their attacks of anxiety, for example, are as uncontrolled as those of very young children. There is usually a general retardation of ego development, with prominent impulsiveness, explosive behavior, overintense pursuit of certain goals, and also passivity and fear.

There are about 10,000 psychotic children in state hospitals, residential treatment, day care centers, and outpatient clinics; estimates of the total number of schizophrenic children in this country range from 100,000 to 500,000 (Wolman, 1970). One cannot help having the highest respect for professional workers who have addressed themselves to the task of treating autistic and schizophrenic children. Their work is slow and discouraging; it requires infinite patience and persistence, and it must often go unrewarded by responsiveness and improvement on the child's part. Substantial recovery is claimed for only 20 to 25 percent of child patients, and those who remain unchanged or deteriorate run from 23 to 33 percent (Eisenberg, 1957). Schizophrenias that are already crippling in childhood can be presumed to be unusually serious, so perhaps the thing we should emphasize in the figures is that something like a quarter of these severely disordered children can be rescued.

PSYCHODYNAMIC ASPECTS OF THE SCHIZOPHRENIC DISORDER

With these facts before us we can turn directly to a consideration of causes. In this section we look at things from the psychodynamic point of view, empha-

Psychological treatment of autistic and other severely disturbed children requires enormous emotional resources, and usually as many therapists as clients. The autistic child at the left may actually show considerable aptitude in playing the xylophone. Coping with extreme emotions, as shown on the right, is typically very difficult for autistic children.

sizing the child's experience in the family circle. It should be kept in mind that a fully adequate theory must account not only for emotional problems but also for schizophrenic disorganization.

Parent-Child Interactions

It is already clear that parents, especially mothers, play a vital part in those events of infancy that are assumed to be the starting point for schizophrenic developments. Therefore it is not surprising that the parents of schizophrenics have been the object of close psychological scrutiny. They have been mercilessly criticized by clinical researchers and there has been some name calling (e.g., "schizophrenogenic") that borders on scapegoating. Partisanship is understandable. Clinical work with schizophrenics requires exceptional capacity for empathy and it is extremely difficult to remain impartial to the anguish and hostility of the clients, much of which is bound up with, and directed at, their parent. Nevertheless, we will see that there is also objective evidence that parents may contribute to disturbance in their schizophrenic offspring.

The essence of the psychodynamic approach is that schizophrenic experience and behavior, which in adult clients usually appear to be senseless, often make more sense when they are examined in their original family context (Laing & Esterson, 1971). It is presumed that, even though schizophrenic *breakdown* may be quite abrupt, the unconventional patterns of thinking and relationship have a long and intelligible history of learning. Therefore this approach looks for characteristic patterns of socialization from which a child might acquire the mental and emotional habits exemplified in schizophrenic disorder. From this perspective, in this social context, psychotic behavior must be in some sense appropriate. Typically the focus of research is on faulty relationship or role learning, faulty thinking and communication, or both. Day and Semrad (1978) emphasize the varied patterns of early parenting of schizophrenics, which usually create uncertainty, emotional insecurity, identity confusion, and self-doubt either through overprotective, overbearing, authoritarian, or hostile-rejecting relationships. These authors trace much of the serious maladjustment of late childhood and adolescence to emotional residuals of these early childhood experiences.

Jacobs (1975) reviewed 57 family interaction studies, most of which included some families with a schizophrenic patient among the offspring. The review showed that research has generally centered on *interpersonal conflict, parental dominance, affective expression, and clarity and accuracy of communication*. With regard to *conflict*, schizophrenic families—especially those with a poor premorbid schizophrenic member—show more disagreement between the parents, though normal families interrupt one another more than schizophrenic families do. The latter result may reflect mainly that families of schizophrenics interact less actively than is usual, in effect modelling a pattern of distant relationship. Generally, normal children and their fathers have been found to be more *dominant* in family interactions than schizophrenic offspring and their fathers, respectively, but mothers of schizophrenics are more dominant than their normal counterparts. There are conflicting results regarding the amount or quality of *affective expression*, so no general conclusion could be drawn. It is interesting to note that disturbed families *without a schizophrenic offspring* express more negative than positive affect, and normal families express more positive than negative affect. One might infer that results for families of schizophrenics are inconclusive because there is more emotional ambivalence or ambiguity in their communications, which is consistent with the claim that parents of schizophrenics repeatedly disclaim or qualify their affective declarations toward their children (Watzlawick, Beavin, & Jackson, 1968). Families of schizophrenics *communicate with less clarity and accuracy* than normal families do, though the more objective measures for these findings are less compelling than those requiring more clinical inference (and hence subject to more potential bias in interpretation). The overall conclusion drawn by Jacobs was that family interaction studies, al-

500

though sound methodologically, *have not yet isolated family patterns that reliably differentiate families of schizophrenics from those of normals.*

The uncertainty in the literature about the quality of expressed emotion is surprising in one respect. Brown, Birley, and Wing (1972) confirmed in a replication study that schizophrenics released from the hospital to their own families were more likely to relapse—and to do so sooner—if their families expressed a high degree of emotion and hostility, especially toward the patient, than if the families expressed little negative affect. If such emotionality in the family dependably precipitates schizophrenic relapse, it might possibly contribute to schizophrenic breakdown in the first place.

Summers and Walsh (1977) found greater evidence in projective tests and interviews for symbiotic maternal relations in schizophrenic offspring than in other psychiatric patients or normal controls. This was manifest in four particular ways: (1) lack of differentiation between the desires, views, and interests of the mother and the child; (2) intrusively acting for the other, taking responsibility for solving the other's problems and taking action to prohibit the other's autonomy, including invasion of privacy; (3) reacting painfully to separations from the other and resisting relationships between the other and outsiders; and (4) requesting help, advice, or comfort in a dependent way and making subtle threats to the other's independence. Both the schizophrenics and their mothers concurred that the symbiotic needs of the mother were greater than those of the child. The authors distinguished their findings from the popular notion that mothers of schizophrenics are "domineering" or "overprotective"; the mother's concerns were not so much for the *child's* well-being or capacity for independence as for her own sense of security. Hence, the subtle maneuvers by the mother that stifled the child's independence or relations with others were primarily motivated out of self-defense. The dependency of the mother on the child generally predated the schizophrenic break, so the authors reasoned that the maternal relationship may have contributed to a lack of differentiation between self and world in the offspring, which makes understandable many of the cardinal features of schizophrenic disorder. For example, paranoid ideas, referential thinking, delusions, and hallucinations all attribute to the environment what belongs to the self.

The summary of this empirical investigation could almost be written as a case study of Kathi Hermann's mother, whose attitude toward her child combined "spoiling, protectiveness, intrusive dominance, and a need for close companionship." She interfered with Kathi's friendships, shared with Kathi the most intimate details of her romantic affairs, and "of course she always read Kathi's letters and diaries." And, like the subjects studied by Summers and Walsh, the symbiotic relationship clearly served the mother's needs more than Kathi's.

Waring and Ricks (1965) studied the parents of children treated at a child guidance clinic. Some of the children were subsequently hospitalized for schizophrenia and later released; some were hospitalized for schizophrenia and remained there permanently; the controls were never hospitalized for psychiatric disorder. On almost all counts there was greater parental pathology among the schizophrenics than the controls, and in most respects greater parental disturbance among the chronic than among the released schizophrenics. The chronics had more parents who were themselves psychotic or seriously disturbed, a finding of ambiguous significance for psychodynamic hypotheses because of the established genetic connection discussed earlier. Still we cannot dismiss the pathogenic potential of a close relationship with a seriously disturbed parent, especially in genetically predisposed offspring. There were more symbiotic unions involving the schizophrenic child in the families of the chronic patients, and more evidence of *emotional divorce*, an expression coined by Murray Bowen (1960) to characterize marriages in which the partners have grown so distant and hostile toward one another that they are divorced in reality, if not in fact, while continuing to live together. At first glance these two findings might appear to be contradictory, implying that the chronics were exposed both to too much and too little close relationship. But closer examination shows that the results may be complementary, depending on the constellation of alliances within the family. It is frequently found, for example, that as the parents grow further apart from one another, one of them (often the mother) compensates for this with an all too strong investment in the child. The child may then become an instrument for coping with the father or an overvalued and overprotected object of love. If such a relationship becomes a way of life for the child, this presents enormous obstacles to separating later and emerging at the appropriate stage of development to a sense of independent selfhood. As we have seen, a central problem for Kathi Hermann in later childhood was to protect herself from a demanding, interfering, oversolicitous mother.

Waring and Ricks also found that the released schizophrenics were more often openly rejected and forced to leave home and the control group families showed more open conflict. From this we can infer that open hostility and rejection are damaging for the child but temporary in their effects. Covert forms of emotional conflict seem to be more pernicious. Surprisingly, there were more "classic schizophrenogenic" mothers in the control and released families. Perhaps that singular creature is more ubiquitous than most people think. (And that, of course, is a major problem with the concept.)

The Double Bind

Probably the most stimulating and influential conception of the psychodynamic etiology of schizophrenia is the *double bind* hypothesis of Bateson et al. (1956). This work grew out of the earlier views of Sullivan on the significance of interpersonal communication. Basing their observations on the interactions of schizophrenics with their families, the Bateson group reasoned that ambiguous communication by the parents could be a primary cause of schizophrenia. A principal means of socialization is through communication with parents, first because it gives the child an orientation to language and thought, and, perhaps more importantly, because it establishes the child's basic approach to human relationships. The Bateson group observed that the parents of schizophrenics characteristically expressed double messages that disqualified or contradicted each other, often at different levels of abstraction. They offer the following illustration of the double bind.

> A young man who had fairly well recovered from an acute schizophrenic episode was visited in the hospital by his mother. He was glad to see her and impulsively put his arm around her shoulders, whereupon she stiffened. He withdrew his arm and she asked, "Don't you love me any more?" He then blushed, and she said, "Dear, you must not be so easily embarrassed and afraid of your feelings." The patient was able to stay with her only a few minutes more and following her departure he assaulted an aide and was put in the tubs.

The authors point out that this kind of treatment, extrapolated over many years of impressionable childhood, would teach the child a peculiar kind of intellectual deception ("What you say is not what you mean, at least not unequivocally"). More importantly, since interpersonal relations are based fundamentally on communications between people and you can't trust those unequivocally, the child learns to avoid a definite relationship with other people. It is safer than committing oneself to a particular kind of relationship and being whip-sawed in the middle. Given such a developmental history it is not surprising that schizophrenics would be confused or confusing in their thinking and abnormally cautious in their approach to relationships with other people.

A particularly insidious aspect of the double bind illustrated above is that the mother controls every aspect of their relationship, even the boy's thoughts about it. A natural reaction to her duplicity would be to point out the contradictions in her behavior, but the boy's intense dependency and previous training prevent him from doing this, though she interprets his behavior, even his unexpressed feelings, and forces him to accept them, on pain of losing her love. The boy's dilemma is clear: she expresses ambiguous or downright contradictory messages about their relationship. He is punished if he discriminates accurately what she means and responds appropriately to one of the messages, for example, withdrawing his arm when she stiffens. On the other hand, he is also chastised for not responding to the other message, of love. And finally it is the boy who is at fault for being uncertain of his feelings rather than the mother for being ambivalent. Is it any wonder that his thinking would be confused or his approach to other people cautious and supersensitive?

503

We saw elements of the double bind pattern in the case of Kathi Hermann. Her mother often boasted of her own nonconformity and tacitly supported her daughter's escapades, but she nagged incessantly when Kathi became a beatnik, dressed and acted in sexually provocative ways, and *really* let herself go. She was very proud and supportive of Kathi's wide social interests, but often interfered with her friendships, driving away the "wrong kind" of companions. Finally, she would not relinquish control of her daughter, even though she shipped her off to boarding schools and families in Europe. One has to wonder about the motives of a woman who needs such a close relationship with her daughter, spoils and protects her, and intrudes constantly in her life, but still chooses to have her reared somewhere else. Obviously Kathi had to fight for her independence, though perhaps not so literally as she did. Given this perspective, we can see the wisdom of the decision to release Kathi from the hospital to the custody of a responsible family friend. We may even indulge in a bit of optimism about her future prospects, once the War of Independence has been waged and won.

Limits of Psychodynamic Explanation

These analyses of emotional conflicts in the family, and of the subtle communication of irrationality to the child, represent a great advance over earlier studies of the "schizophrenogenic" mother. They are impressive, but they have by no means stilled the voices of controversy. It is prudent to remember that psychodynamic explanations of anxiety disorders and of delinquent behavior generally imply no small amount of emotional stress in the family, leading, however, to quite different outcomes in the child. When one tries to isolate what might be peculiar to the family of the schizophrenic—the irrational methods of dealing with conflict and the "double-bind" type of communication—one can hardly avoid misgivings about the specificity. It has certainly not been demonstrated that parental behavior is less pathological and communication less irrational in the families of other psychiatric patients. We may even suspect, listening to the average level of communication in the fast-moving daily events of family life, that a goodly portion of irrationality and "double-bind" is universal in childhood. It is important not to contrast the "schizophrenogenic" family with a wholly fanciful image of normal rationality. In addition it must be kept in mind that not every child in a family is likely to be schizophrenic. There is no reason to doubt that each child will be treated a little differently, but if we want the psychodynamic hypothesis to be completely adequate we must be prepared to show how the well children escaped the fate of the sick one.

A critic of the psychodynamic viewpoint developed here might argue that there is little empirical support for the claim that family interaction contributes causally to schizophrenic disorder; families of schizophrenic individuals are like most other families when, *because of something unusual about the child*, they must be different—better than average—if the child is to escape a schizophrenic fate. That interpretation remains an open possibility to keep in mind as we consider what progress has been made toward detecting a biological component that might account for "something unusual about the child."

BIOLOGICAL ASPECTS OF THE DISORDER

It seems clear that one cannot conceive of schizophrenia as a neurological disease that is analogous to general paresis. It does not follow a course nor have a character that is consistent with gross cerebral pathology, but the clinical symptoms and course of schizophrenia are consistent with such possibilities as a generalized vulnerability, an oversensitive disposition, or even a subtle biochemical deviation. Such psychodynamic processes as we have discussed may be significant causes of the disorder in most cases. However, for our explanation to be complete, other ingredients are required; there must be some element of biological disposition that might plausibly take the form of an innate temperamental peculiarity or neurophysiological abnormality. We turn our attention now to those possibilities.

Genetic Evidence

Certainly no other research area in schizophrenia has yielded more advance and refinement of knowledge than this one. Much of the refinement has consisted of moderating the early and overzealous estimates of the magnitude of the genetic contribution by such pioneers as Franz Kallmann (1938). For example, a prime focus of research has been the *concordance rates* of identical versus fraternal twins.* Higher concordance among identical twins would confirm a genetic factor in the disorder. A survey of such concordance studies from 1928 to 1967 shows that the median rates reported before 1954 were 68 percent for monozygotic (identical) and 18 percent for dizygotic (fraternal) twins (Dohrenwend & Dohrenwend, 1969). However, the studies after 1960, which were based on much improved experimental designs and better procedures for discerning zygosity, reported median rates of 38 percent, and 9 percent for MZ and DZ twins, respectively. The rate differential is still impressive and strongly implicates a genetic determinant; the overall reduction in the estimates indicates how much the recent work has improved on the methodology used in the earlier research.

Similar confirmation comes from studies of family histories. Heston (1966) followed up 47 children who had been permanently separated from their

*Twins are concordant if both share a particular physical or behavioral attribute or if neither manifests it. Twins are discordant for schizophrenia, for example, if one becomes schizophrenic but the other does not. Identical twins originate from the same union of egg and sperm, so they share all genetic characteristics. Fraternal twins originate from different unions of parental cells, so they are genetically no more alike than nontwin siblings.

schizophrenic mothers at birth. He found five (11%) who became schizophrenic, as contrasted with none of the control children of normal mothers. The recent cross-fostering studies in Denmark, one of which has been discussed already, show remarkably consistent results. Kety et al. (1975) studied the prevalence of schizophrenia in the biological relatives of adopted children who became schizophrenic: 14 percent of the relatives had psychiatric disorders "in the schizophrenic spectrum," although only 3 percent were chronic or true schizophrenics. This was contrasted with less than 3 percent of the *adoptive* relatives with schizophrenic spectrum disorders, and less than 1 percent with chronic schizophrenia. There was little evidence of schizophrenic illness in the biological relatives of acute schizophrenics, which suggests that the acute or episodic form of the disorder may *not* be genetically transmitted. Apparently, genetic vulnerability in chronic schizophrenia is transmitted via the germ cells at conception. That hypothesis is reinforced by the fact that the risk of schizophrenia in the offspring of two schizophrenic parents is 40 percent (Kety, 1978) and by the consistent finding from twin studies that concordance rates for identical twins are significantly higher than those for fraternal twins, which are the same as those for nontwin siblings (Gottesman & Shields, 1972). On the other hand, the relatively low concordance rates for identical twins (42% in Gottesman & Shields, 1972) indicates the importance of nongenetic factors in potentiating (augmenting) the genetic vulnerability and precipitating clinical breakdown.

Rosenthal et al. (1968) carried out a companion study, using the same basic pool of adopted Danish subjects, which essentially replicated Heston's study. Like Heston, they examined the prevalence of schizophrenia among adopted children whose biological parents had been schizophrenic: 11 (32%) had psychiatric disorders "in the schizophrenic spectrum." We can tell that these figures are unusually high because 15 percent of the control adoptees had diagnoses in the schizophrenic spectrum. These diagnoses were based on direct

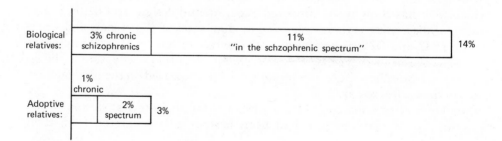

Figure 13.1

Prevalence of various types of schizophrenia in the biological and adoptive relatives of adopted Danish children who became schizophrenic. *Source:* Kety *et al.* (1975).

psychiatric interviews and the interviewers probably made their diagnoses liberally so as not to overlook any signs of pathology. Nevertheless, the large differential in the rates can be trusted because the interviews were conducted "blind": the interviewers did not know to which group the subjects belonged.

All these findings taken together mean that a schizophrenic psychosis is more likely to develop in individuals who carry a certain inherited predisposition. The risk of schizophrenia in first-degree relatives is not large, probably no more than one in five or ten. But the contribution of genetic determinants, even if it is a small one, is incontrovertible. Moreover, we can specify that the genetic disposition for schizophrenia is distinguishable from that for affective psychosis (Astrup & Noreik, 1966). There remains some ambiguity about genetic factors in the reactive or remitting schizophrenias, where the evidence for inheritance is either equivocal or nonexistent, as discussed before.

Modes of Genetic Transmission

Explaining the mode of genetic transmission has been devilishly difficult because the family pedigrees do not conform to simple Mendelian formulas. Many investigators are now turning to a *diathesis-stress* model of etiology for schizophrenia that presumes a *polygenic* mode of genetic inheritance (Rosenthal, 1970). This means that a constitutional defect determined by several genes is inherited by many people, whom Meehl (1962) calls *schizotypes*. They will have many of the schizoid traits, avoidance of others, inability to experience pleasure, and so on, but most of them will not become manifestly schizophrenic except under very unfavorable circumstances of personal history and psychological stress. If the mode of transmission is polygenic, then the person's genetic vulnerability would depend on the number of defective genes inherited. This model assumes a far larger number of *potential* schizophrenics in our society than most theories do, but it also assigns a much greater weight to the significance of personal history in bringing about the manifest disorder. This should make it a more acceptable vehicle for reconciling the genetic evidence with the clinical data on psychodynamic causes.

Biochemical and Neurophysiological Evidence

Kraepelin hoped that some day drugs would be available that produced temporarily the symptoms of schizophrenia in normal people; analysis of their properties might then point the way to the chemical secrets of the disorder. It has been discovered that a number of chemicals called psychotomimetics (because they mimic psychosis) come fairly close to having this effect. For example, lysergic acid (LSD-25), mescaline, and psilocybin all can produce states in normal subjects that are remarkably similar to psychotic episodes with considerable turmoil and confusion. There may be marked disturbances of thinking, perceiving, and feeling. Some people show catatonic reactions, others halluci-

507

nations, others paranoid suspiciousness and delusions. Sometimes they report losing their sense of personal identity and experiencing their bodies in peculiar ways, such as the legs walking of their own volition. People around them look different, sometimes hostile and sinister, sometimes changed in size, sometimes as if transparent or behind a glass partition. The subjects suffer a loss in sociability; more of their behavior than usual is avoidant, hostile, or dependent. In tests of intellectual processes they show an impairment in concentration and consecutive thinking. Attention wanders and is often caught by minute features of the physical environment. The psychotic-like episode usually lasts for only a few hours, and normal people recover their customary functioning after the brief visit to insanity.

It was soon discovered that mescaline, LSD-25, and most of the other hallucinogens are methylated compounds that are structurally similar to *dopamine* and *serotonin*, neurotransmitters known to be centrally involved in the normal functioning of the brain. Therefore it was hypothesized that some forms of schizophrenia might be caused by an alteration in the metabolic process of methylating normal neurochemicals so that abnormal compounds similar to mescaline were produced (Kety, 1967). This view was supported by the demonstration, several times replicated, that psychotic symptoms were made worse in some schizophrenics by administering methionine, which is known to stimulate the methylation process. It is plausible that methionine and the psychotomimetic drugs produce their abnormal effects by inhibiting or changing these necessary neurochemicals in some way.

Pursuit of these leads, however, has turned up a number of contradictory and puzzling findings, leaving investigators with the feeling that although serotonin and dopamine are essential for normal functioning, they have not yet fathomed the manner of their disturbance, if any, in schizophrenia. Schizophrenics also report noticeable differences between their natural symptoms and those induced by psychotomimetic drugs. So this important line of research has not yet quite solved the problem.

Angrist and Gershon (1970) administered progressively increasing doses of *d*-amphetamine to volunteer subjects who had no evidence of preexisting schizophrenia or schizoid tendencies. In one to four days virtually all of them became floridly psychotic; obviously, the drug was not simply precipitating latent schizophrenic tendencies. The subjects showed flattened affect and schizophrenic thinking patterns. Amphetamine is also known to exacerbate psychotic symptoms in schizophrenics (Snyder, 1974b). Snyder postulates a double effect of amphetamine. The first is a schizophrenic-like psychosis (flat affect, withdrawal, autism) that is mediated by *dopamine*, and the second is an alerting action mediated by *norepinephrine* that forces the person to strive for an intellectual framework to account for the strange feelings as the psychosis develops, which resolves into a paranoid delusional system. On the basis of this reasoning, Snyder hypothesized that dopamine excess may produce the pri-

508

mary schizophrenic symptoms, whereas norepinephrine excess causes accessory symptoms and "paranoid solutions."

The discovery of the antipsychotic drugs, such as *phenothiazines*, led to an important breakthrough in our understanding of the biochemistry of schizophrenic symptoms. The drugs that proved to be most effective in containing the psychotic symptoms also produced, as side effects, Parkinson's disease, a neurological illness known to result from deficient dopamine in the brain. As a result much research has been directed toward the hypothesis that schizophrenic symptoms may be caused by excess dopamine in the brain where it affects the efficiency of neural transmission (Kety, 1978). It is now established that antipsychotic drugs achieve their dramatic effects, in part, by blockade of dopamine receptors at those synapses. Overactivity of dopamine synapses may play a crucial role in causing some schizophrenic symptoms (e.g., stereotyped behavior, paranoid delusions, and auditory hallucinations) but would not account for others (e.g., anhedonia, withdrawal, autism, flatness of affect).

Both dopamine and norepinephrine are *catecholamines* that function in the body as *neurotransmitters*, either facilitating or inhibiting neural impulses, especially in the brain. Most of the biochemical processes just reviewed are subsumed under *the dopamine hypothesis*. Snyder (1974b) reports that the *fundamental* schizophrenic symptoms (thought disorder, blunted affect, withdrawal, and autistic behavior) are more responsive to phenothiazine treatment than the *accessory* symptoms are (hallucinations, paranoid ideation, grandiosity, hostile belligerence); anxiety and depression are not usually affected. The phenothiazines block catecholamine receptor sites in the brain, which homeostatically accelerates the synthesis or turnover of catecholamines, especially dopamine, and these effects are known to correlate with improvement in clinical symptoms. On the basis of these known effects, we may formulate the dopamine hypothesis as follows: schizophrenic disorder results, in part, from biochemical abnormalities in the brain involving catecholamine metabolism, with excess dopamine accounting for the fundamental symptoms and either too much or too little norepinephrine accounting for the accessory symptoms, depending upon the clinical picture.

Matthyse (1974) takes the reasoning a step further to speculate how such biochemical abnormalities might affect the afflicted person cognitively. He postulates that the emergence of pre- or semi- or unconscious ideas into full conscious awareness is normally resisted or inhibited by neurons in the brain, as an evolutionary means of controlling the volume of intellectual effort required for adaptation. Dopamine has the effect of disinhibiting or neutralizing that filter, which releases a larger volume of subliminal ideas into the stream of consciousness. Therefore, excess dopamine in schizophrenics leads to underactive thought filtration and the characteristic symptoms of disorganized associations, sensory "deluge," autistic preoccupation, and so on. By blockading dopamine receptors, antipsychotic drugs help to reestablish the

509

filtering mechanism and "repress" the barrage of distracting ideas, impulses, and feelings.

Limits of Biological Explanation

We must be careful to keep within legitimate bounds our ideas about the role of biological factors. Wonder-drug reasoning has led some enthusiasts to believe that once we find the magic substance, schizophrenia will be eliminated by the simple process of injection. Unfortunately, this is a little like supposing that a drug can blast a person out of lifelong habits and convictions. Wondrous as the effects of tranquilizing drugs have been, as we will see in the next section, they promise no such panacea. Let us say that a patient's nervous system has operated under a biochemical handicap; nevertheless, it has operated, and the resulting pattern of life cannot be undone in a moment. Whatever else it may be, schizophrenia is certainly a cumulative disorder, rooted in the habits and attitudes built up through a long individual history. It is not a temporary poisoning that clears up and leaves the patient in perfect health.

To illustrate the point let us imagine that the middle-aged spinster described earlier has been given a drug that cures schizophrenia. The medication could not greatly clarify her thinking processes, which are already quite normal except on the subject of her reputation and the assault on her brain. It could not remove her lifelong anxious feelings of inferiority, and it would therefore have little effect on her compensatory delusions of grandeur or her solitary way of life. This was, of course, an older woman whose disorder had become consolidated. If we take an example of incipient psychosis in a younger person whose life is still in the making, we can suppose that the imaginary drug would be more helpful though still not omnipotent. We saw how rapidly Kathi Hermann's acute psychotic symptoms responded to medication, but no drug can resolve her crises of identity and independence. One must earnestly hope that the biological mysteries will soon be solved, but this happy event would not eliminate the need for skilled personal treatment of schizophrenia.

TREATMENT OF SCHIZOPHRENIA

It may seem incongruous to report great improvements in the treatment of schizophrenia after depicting such bewilderment about the classification and causes of the disorder and citing the Hindoo fable about groping in the dark. But there is a good deal of precedent for this in medical history. In the Maternity Hospital of Vienna in 1858, medical students' maternity cases showed an average over a period of six years of 99 deaths per thousand from puerperal fever; almost one in ten mothers died in childbirth. Semmelweiss, who was the physician in charge of the hospital at that time, believed the cause to be something arising within the hospital and made his students wash their hands in a solution of chloride of lime. In one year the death rate in his wards tumbled from 18 percent to 3 percent and soon after to one percent. It was not until 1866 that Lister published his work on antisepsis, giving us the first knowledge of the causal *agents* of infection, but the treatment Semmelweiss devised on a hunch was no less effective because of his ignorance of specific etiology. We will see that the treatment of schizophrenia has proceeded historically by a series of similar trial-and-error experiments and a few accidents with far-reaching effects.

Before 1930 schizophrenic patients received only the most minimal treatment. For the most part they were committed to mental hospitals that were overcrowded and chronically understaffed. Nothing more was attempted than to keep them in good physical health and comfort. "Treatment" usually consisted of sedation, physical restraint, or ice packs to cool patients down if they got upset or assaultive, and plenty of latitude for them to do what they liked, which more often than not was nothing. It was not understood at that time that such purely custodial incarceration contributed in itself to the deterioration and regression that were considered prominent features of schizophrenic disorder.

The insulin coma method of shock treatment discovered by Manfred Sakel was one of those chance discoveries that seemed to promise a revolution in treatment. However it proved to be very expensive because of the amount of medical supervision and nursing care required. The treatment lasted several months and patients typically gained enormous amounts of weight because of the tampering with their sugar metabolism. Moreover the frequency of relapse after improvement proved to be high.

Insulin shock treatment soon gave way to electroconvulsive therapy (ECT) and is no longer used. Initially the procedures for administering ECT were primitive, but refinements have been made over the years. Nowadays a patient receives prior injections of a sedative to induce loss of consciousness, and curare or a similar drug to relax the muscles and inhibit the violence of the convulsive response. Before the introduction of this last precaution patients and even those attending them sometimes sustained serious injuries from the uncontrolled thrashing of the body and limbs. This violent convulsion is produced by passing a powerful jolt of electric current between electrodes attached to the head. When the seizure has run its course, the patient sleeps or rests for a few minutes until the head clears and the aroused somatic functions revert to normal, before returning to business as usual. The procedure has been so streamlined that some private physicians offer the treatment to outpatients in their offices.

ECT had many of the same effects as insulin shock (quieting, amnesia, social accessibility) but few of the unpleasant side effects, and was less expensive. It enjoyed a similar boom of enthusiasm and remained a primary mode of treating psychoses until largely displaced by antipsychotic drugs in the mid-1950s. The effectiveness of ECT treatment of schizophrenics has been dis-

511

puted for many years. It has a much better record in treating affective disorders, though even here its main benefit is to speed up the pace of recovery rather than to increase the number of recoveries (Szalita, 1966). ECT today occupies a minor place in treating schizophrenia. A recent survey of patients admitted from 1920-1971 suggests that it may be almost as effective as drugs for treating catatonics (Morrison, 1973). This may be explained, in part, by the fact that catatonic symptoms are quite similar to certain symptoms of affective psychosis.

Psychotropic Drugs

The most effective antipsychotic drugs proved to be a group of phenothiazine chemicals whose amazing effects were first discovered accidentally by Deschamps and Laborit in 1952 as they were trying to develop a powerful sedative for use in sleep therapy. Delay and Deniker (1952) capitalized on this happy accident by employing *chlorpromazine* as a therapeutic agent in schizophrenia and other psychoses with psychomotor agitation. The results were so dramatic that they initiated a revolutionary breakthrough in psychiatric treatment. The phenothiazines were called *tranquilizing* drugs because their most obvious effect was to reduce tension. However, it also became clear that they could directly affect perception, attention, and mood, so they are widely regarded now as antipsychotic drugs. To gain some impression of their impact, one need only consult the statistics on resident populations in U. S. public mental hospitals. There were annual increments of 2 percent in the resident patient population of state and county mental hospitals from 1946 to 1955, when it peaked at 558,922 (Kramer et al., 1972). Since then the census has declined steadily to about half of that number (Greenblatt & Glazier, 1975). Enlightened hospital management has also contributed to this trend.

Like most forms of treatment, antipsychotics are most successful with cases having a recent onset of relatively abrupt character. Results are poorer with patients who have made their peace, so to speak, with a psychotic condition. It is generally conceded that the drugs alleviate symptoms but that patients improved by drugs may relapse if treatment is discontinued. Here, however, the drugs have a practical advantage: patients can be kept on maintenance doses even after they have been discharged. In fact, more and more cases are being treated in Community Mental Health Centers and outpatient clinics without being hospitalized at all. The only hazard is that the drugs may have harmful side effects when taken in large doses or over a long period of time, a point that is under close scrutiny in pharmacological research.

The revolution in treatment has transformed patterns of hospital care for schizophrenics. The annual discharge rate rose from 3 percent to 9 percent from 1967 to 1970, with a resulting decrease of 27 percent in the resident population of schizophrenics (Gunderson et al., 1974). At the same time the annual readmission rates have doubled, creating a kind of revolving door at the portals of many institutions. The effect on the patients, even for those who remain in the community, is not entirely beneficial. "The locus of care has shifted from the isolated and neglected wards of the state hospital to newly created but not always adequate facilities in the community. There is growing evidence that some of the former hospital patients are not cared for by anyone; they live in single-room occupancy units, kinless and friendless, subsisting marginally on welfare allotments. Given what most state mental hospitals once were and what many still are, most patients are better off out of them than in them. This, however, does not excuse our failure to provide for the patients lost in the shuffle from one pattern of care to another" (Eisenberg, 1973).

Psychotherapy

The earliest attempts at psychotherapy encountered what seemed to be an insuperable obstacle. Try as they might, therapists could almost never break through the wall of the patient's reserve to establish a trustful working relationship. It has been pointed out that whereas nonpsychotics must learn to accept repressed *psychological* facts, the psychotic must learn to accept rejected *external* facts. This difference is vitally important when it comes to establishing the initial therapeutic relationship. The therapist can be the ally of the patient whose task it is to accept repressed psychological facts. It is much more difficult to occupy this role with a psychotic patient because the treatment agents may themselves be among the rejected external facts. Schizophrenics are often remarkably aware of their inner lives, so it may be of no great value to have them learn more about them. In fact, it may even do harm, deepening their preoccupation and increasing their disturbance. The therapeutic task is instead to help the patient discover that reality can be bearable and even rewarding. This fact may first be discovered in the relation to the therapist.

Fromm-Reichmann (1950) pointed out that schizophrenics enter a withdrawn state as a means of protection from the frustrations of reality, with its constant reminders of personal inadequacy. Being suspicious and mistrustful of everyone, they are particularly sensitive about any attempt to intrude into their isolated worlds and personal lives. For this reason she made it abundantly clear to her clients that they need not take her into their world or give up any part of their "sickness" until they were completely ready to do so on their own accord (Green, 1964). Yet she was convinced that all schizophrenics have some dim notion of the unreality and loneliness of their substitute delusionary world. A part of them still longs for contact and understanding, and once the therapist has managed to win their acceptance, the attachment may become unbelievably strong. They are so sensitive that almost anything that happens may wound their self-esteem. One patient responded twice with catatonic stupor when the hour of appointment had to be changed; both times it was immediately dispelled when the therapist explained the reasons for the

513

change. Nothing could show more clearly the nature of the schizophrenic disorder. Having been injured many times, the schizophrenic has learned the art of protective withdrawal, but retains the capacity to develop strong relationships of love and hatred toward the therapist.

In some cases, especially with the helpful adjunct of antipsychotic medication, it is possible to establish the necessary contact by daily conversation, expressions of consistent interest, and a tactful policy of waiting for the patient to build up confidence in the therapist. The patient is treated as an adult, though a very sensitive one. This process may take a long time, however, sometimes several months, and it may be quite impossible if the patient is much disturbed or extremely regressed. When treating an acute schizophrenic in the hospital, it is more important to accurately identify the central emotional impasse causing the extreme psychological condition than to formulate a formal psychiatric diagnosis (Day & Semrad, 1978). Usually the emotional precipitant is loss of someone highly valued, one of the normal but stressful stages of the life cycle, or chronic frustration.

Will (1967) stressed the importance of persistently defining the relationship with the patient, refusing the patient's desires to deny or evade it by withdrawing, protesting an inability to change, or claiming indifference. For this purpose it is essential to have regular meetings to engage the patient's senses and emotions as fully as possible. Sometimes it is necessary to enter directly into the patient's regressed world, gratifying infantile needs, expressing affection, and using the kind of language and symbols that dominate the patient's own disorganized thought processes. The ultimate purpose of all of this is to establish trust and a feeling of security that the therapist understands the patient. In this way the therapist becomes a model of parenthood, often a better one than the patient's own parents. Establishing an emotional bond with the therapist serves to bring the patient out of the acute psychosis and thus restores sufficient organization so that a more rational psychotherapy becomes possible. There are limits to the rescuing power of love, sympathy, and understanding; ultimately the patient must be able to function without depending on such a bounty of parental devotion.

Increasingly in recent years psychotherapy has been directed toward the adult instead of the infantile aspects of the personality. The purpose is to promote a sense of personal identity and enhance self-esteem. These more ego-oriented approaches concentrate on correcting evasive adjustment patterns, retreats in the face of difficulty and maneuvers to avoid making decisions and solving problems independently. However, conventional goals of social adjustment and extraversion are often uncongenial to former schizophrenics, and may even constitute a hazard for future health. It may be better for some to find their own sources of satisfaction and security, irrespective of the approval of their neighbors, of their families, and of public opinion. Toward this end it may be more helpful for the therapist to champion individuality, not conventionality. This may explain, in part, the great popularity, especially among young schizophrenics, of the views of R. D. Laing (1967), who lays the blame for much of madness squarely on the doorstep of the family home and encourages his patients to savor their acute psychotic experience as an inner voyage of personal discovery, from which one should expect to profit and grow.

The Hospital as Therapeutic Milieu

We examined in Chapter 8 the widespread changes that have occurred in transforming the mental hospital from a custodial institution to a therapeutic milieu. Schizophrenic patients are among the chief beneficiaries of this change. Withdrawal and regression, it is now realized, did not just happen in the custodial hospital as a result of disease; they were actively encouraged by an environment in which there was nothing for the patient to live for, nothing to do, nothing to arouse interest and create an atmosphere of rewarding participation. When a ward is organized as a therapeutic milieu every attempt is made to reverse these conditions, creating an environment designed to promote interest, friendly interaction, usefulness, and self-esteem. The appeal, as in individual therapy, is to the adult in the patient rather than to dependent needs. The reader should not imagine that milieu therapy quickly transforms the ward into a scene of merriment and lively social life. Schizophrenics become socially responsive, if at all, at their own very slow pace, and life on the ward would seem tame indeed to an extravert from the outside world. But it is a distinct forward step when a detached, confused schizophrenic dares to make a sympathetic remark to another patient, agrees to help make sandwiches for a ward party, gets dressed without reminder in time for a meal in the cafeteria, ventures to speak up in a patient government meeting—and these are steps that point in the direction of resuming a normal place in the world.

An Experimental Comparison of Treatment Methods

May (1968) and his associates carried out a very careful study comparing the effectiveness of five treatment programs at a large state hospital in California. They assigned randomly 228 first admission schizophrenics from the middle third of prognostic range to one of five treatment conditions: (1) individual psychotherapy alone, (2) antipsychotic drugs alone, (3) individual psychotherapy plus antipsychotic drugs, (4) electroshock, and (5) milieu. All patients were treated in one of these programs until release or one year after admission and then followed up for several years subsequently. In terms of release rates, drugs plus psychotherapy and drugs alone were the most effective methods, whereas milieu and psychotherapy alone were the least effective. The rates were 96 percent for drugs plus psychotherapy, 95 percent for drugs, 79 percent for ECT, 64 percent for psychotherapy, and 59 percent for milieu. Drugs reduced the length of hospital stay by 20 percent, whereas psychotherapy extended it by 14 percent, perhaps because of the complications of terminating

515

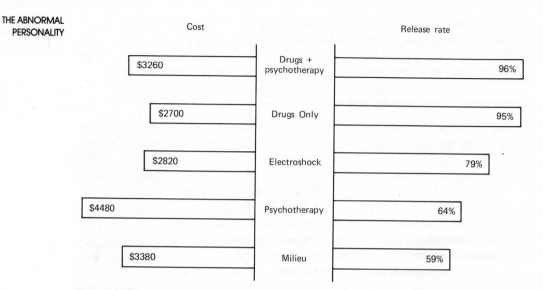

Cost		Release rate
$3260	Drugs + psychotherapy	96%
$2700	Drugs Only	95%
$2820	Electroshock	79%
$4480	Psychotherapy	64%
$3380	Milieu	59%

Figure 13.2

Summary of the effectiveness and cost of five alternative methods for treating hospitalized schizophrenics. *Source:* May *et al.* (1968).

the therapeutic relationship. By most of the clinical criteria drugs seemed to have the best effect, but drugs plus psychotherapy led to the most insight. From a practical point of view, the analysis of comparative cost was a matter of importance. The cost of treatment from admission to release was least for drugs alone ($2700) and most for psychotherapy alone ($4480). The costs for the other programs fell in between: ECT ($2820), drugs plus psychotherapy ($3260) and milieu ($3380).

The poor results for psychotherapy alone have been sharply challenged on the grounds that the therapists were inexperienced residents under supervision. Karon and Vandenbos (1970) report that psychotherapy with experienced clinicians in their project reduced length of hospitalization and improved psychiatric condition significantly regardless of whether drugs were used adjunctively. Therapy with inexperienced clinicians led to *longer* hospitalization without drugs but *shorter* hospitalization with drugs. They conclude that May's findings must be limited to treatment by inexperienced therapists. However an independent study by Hogarty et al. (1973) confirmed May's findings.

A similar question could logically be raised about the poor results of milieu treatment. If the milieu program was being run by inexperienced therapists, student nurses, and attendants in training, it might be expected to fare badly, for a ward can be run on a truly therapeutic basis only if there is a happy combination of training, talent, experience, and seasoned wisdom. The tribute to tranquilizing drugs that is implicit in these results is undoubtedly deserved, but it is worth noting that the surprising benefit attributed to ECT is out of line with other findings concerning its value in schizophrenia.

Long-term follow-up of the patients 2 to 5 years after first admission showed that drugs, ECT, and drugs plus psychotherapy still retained their advantage over psychotherapy and milieu treatment, in terms of time spent in the hospital after admission and after release (May et al., 1976). One explanation may be that the first three treatment regimes all led to rapid release from the hospital, thus avoiding the social disruption and "institutionalism" that often accompany prolonged hospital treatment. Psychotherapy and milieu treatment required much longer periods of initial hospitalization. ECT-treated patients had, as a group, fewer hospital readmissions than patients who had received any other treatment (May and Tuma, 1976). The authors concluded that ECT was equal to or better than any other treatment, including drug treatment, for patients in this study. That conclusion is bound to elicit controversy because the general consensus is that ECT may be useful in catatonic syndromes but not very useful in other, especially chronic, schizophrenics. The main problem with this finding is that there is no theoretical explanation for the effectiveness of ECT. One clue is worth exploring: ECT is known to affect drastically the level and turnover of dopamine, norepinephrine, and serotonin—the neurotransmitters many believe to be critical factors in the etiology of schizophrenic symptoms (Salzman, 1978). Conceivably, a sharp alteration in these chemicals early in the course of illness may have beneficial long-term effects.

It was suggested that early release from the hospital may be advantageous, in order to avoid extended social disruption and institutional dependency. This hypothesis receives support from cross-cultural investigation. The prognosis for schizophrenia in modern industrial societies seems to be worse than in nonindustrial societies like Nigeria, India, Sri Lanka, and Colombia, because expectations and beliefs about mental illness and treatment systems serve to alienate patients from their normal roles and to prolong illness (Waxler, 1979). In peasant societies treatment is always short-term; mental illness is usually attributed to external causes rather than to the person's character or social past; the family provides strong support throughout the illness and readily reassimiliates the patient after the crisis is past, facilitating the reestablishment of previous social and work roles. For all our scientific knowledge and advanced technology, it appears that we may still have some basic human lessons to learn from those peasant societies.

SUGGESTIONS FOR FURTHER READING

Probably the first thing that should be undertaken by a student who wants to read further about schizophrenia is to get a better idea of how things look to the patient.

Anton Boisen's book, *Out of the depths* (1960), offers penetrating schizophrenic's-eye hindsight on the disorder. Also ideal for this purpose is the collection of subjective excerpts edited by B. Kaplan, *The inner world of mental illness* (1964), and the one by C. Landis, edited by F. A. Mettler, *Varieties of psychopathological experience* (1964). A. A. Stone and S. S. Stone show the phenomenology of mental illness with literary excerpts written by disordered people in *The abnormal personality through literature* (1966). H. Green's *I never promised you a rose garden* (1964) is an extraordinarily lucid and moving autobiography of a schizophrenic girl who recovered without extravagant promises from her therapist, Frieda Fromm-Reichmann.

Collections of case studies are available by R. D. Laing and A. Esterson, *Sanity, madness and the family* (1971), and by C. G. Schulz and R. K. Kilgalen, *Case studies in schizophrenia* (1969). There isn't a better clinical introduction to the disorder than E. Bleuler's *Dementia praecox, or the group of schizophrenias* (1911). The important ideas of Harry Stack Sullivan can be gleaned from his posthumously published lectures, *Schizophrenia as a human process* (1962).

An excellent review of the process-reactive literature is available in N. Garmezy's article, *Process and reactive schizophrenia: Some conceptions and issues* (1970). L. Phillips presents a theoretical formulation of early psychological development in schizophrenia, *Human adaptation and its failures* (1968). C. Astrup and K. Noreik have written an exceptional monograph on prognosis in *Functional psychoses* (1966).

For a survey of research on schizophrenia and theories about its origin, *The etiology of schizophrenia*, edited by D.D. Jackson (1960), is recommended. A comprehensive collection of research papers based on the Second International Rochester Conference on Schizophrenia, *The nature of schizophrenia*, was edited by L.C. Wynne, R.L. Cromwell, and S. Matthyse (1978). A superb selection of research papers culled from the world literature on schizophrenia by a distinguished panel of international investigators is reprinted in R. Cancro's *The schizophrenic syndrome: An annual review* (1971); new volumes are published each year. J.C. Shershow has edited a series of lectures by distinguished experts that sample the whole field in *Schizophrenia: Science and practice* (1978). K.F. Bernheim and R.R.J. Lewine have written a readable paperback synopsis, *Schizophrenia: Symptoms, causes and treatments* (1979).

S. Arieti's book, *Interpretation of schizophrenia* (1975), contains a detailed consideration of the problems of schizophrenic thinking, as does the book by L.J. Chapman and J.P. Chapman, *Disordered thought in schizophrenia* (1973), from a more experimental point of view. A research scholar will find very useful a compilation of abstracts of published articles from 1950 to 1965 by C. Schooler and S.E. Feldman, *Experimental studies of schizophrenia* (1967). Increasing attention is being given to borderline syndromes, which is the exclusive subject in *The borderline patient* by R.R. Grinker and B. Werble (1977).

Comprehensive summaries of the literature on childhood schizophrenia and infantile autism are included in B. Rimland's *Infantile autism* (1964) and in M. Rutter and E. Schopler (eds.), *Autism: A reappraisal of concepts and treatment* (1978).

518 Collections of papers bearing on family communication and the double bind have been published by D.D. Jackson, *Communication, family and marriage* (1968) and

Therapy, communication and change (1969). T. Lidz, S. Flect, and A.R. Cornelison offer an alternative view in *Schizophrenia and the family* (1965). S.R. Hirsch and J.P. Leff present a critical review in *Abnormalities in parents of schizophrenics* (1975).

Papers with a longitudinal perspective are collected in a continuing series of volumes edited by M. Roff, D.F. Ricks, and others, *Life history research in psychopathology*, which have been published in 1970, 1972, 1974, 1975, 1977, and 1979. The first four volumes were published by the University of Minnesota Press, the fifth by Plenum Press and the sixth by Williams and Wilkins. D. Rosenthal and S.S. Kety (eds.), *The transmission of schizophrenia* (1968), contains papers mainly on genetic research from leading investigators throughout the world. A more systematic treatment is available in *The genetics of mental disorders* by E.T.O. Slater and V. Cowie (1971).

Everything you ever wanted to know about the biochemistry of schizophrenia is revealed by S. Matthyse and S.S. Kety (eds.) in *Catecholamines and schizophrenia* (1975) and by S.H. Snyder in *Madness and the brain* (1974). Snyder also provides an intelligible explanation of the chemical action of the prominent psychotropic drugs.

An unusually fine introduction to the topic of psychotherapy is L.B. Hill's *Psychotherapeutic intervention in schizophrenia* (1955). E. Goffman wrote a devastating critique of mental hospitals in *Asylums: Essays on the social situation of mental patients and other inmates* (1962). An experimental comparison of treatment methods is reported in P.R.A. May, *Treatment of schizophrenia* (1968).

519

A drawing by R. Högfeldr.

14
Affective Disorders

Melancholia and mania have been recognized as forms of psychological disorder for more than two thousand years. In some respects they seem to be opposites, but long before modern times it was observed that in certain patients mania and melancholia succeeded each other. On the whole the opinion prevailed that these were cases in which one disorder transformed itself into another. Toward the middle of the last century, however, there were frequent suggestions that mania and melancholia belonged together in a single disease process, both being exaggerations in the sphere of mood. Designations such as "cyclical insanity" were from time to time proposed. Finally, in 1899, Kraepelin introduced the term *manic-depressive insanity*, including under this heading not only the alternating forms but the simple manias and melancholias as well. "In the course of years," he wrote, "I have been more and more convinced that all of these pictures are but forms of a single disease process. Certain fundamental features recur in these morbid states notwithstanding manifold external differences" (Jelliffe, 1931). Thus the concept of *manic-depressive psychosis* became firmly established in psychiatric thought.

Whatever the ultimate nature of these disorders turns out to be, they rank as a profoundly serious form of affliction. Depressed states typically mean prolonged and seemingly senseless suffering for the person. Manic states, which appear excitedly happy, may lead to unwise decisions and to ultimate exhaustion, and they impose heavy burdens on the environment. When the variations in mood are quite extreme these disorders may be classified under *psychosis*. The distinguishing mark of psychosis is loss of contact with reality, which can be so severe that the person is unable to provide elementary self-care or is dangerous to others, or both. This occurs in severely depressed states and highly manic states, for both of which hospitalization may be necessary. On the other hand, people are seen constantly at clinics or in private practice who show marked mood changes, generally along with other symptoms, yet who are not disoriented, "out of their heads," or in need of hospital care (Beck, 1967). In fact, only about 10 percent of all depressed people show delusions, hallucinations, confusion, and other elements of impaired reality testing (Klerman, 1978). The rest have psychological disorders with a wide range of severity, roughly comparable to psychophysiologial and anxiety disorders.

Estimates of the lifetime prevalence of affective disorders range from 8 percent to 20 percent, which means that at least one of every 12 persons in the general population experiences depressive or manic episodes—often of moderate severity—at some point in life, but only one in five or ten of them seeks professional attention (Klerman, 1978). Only about 1 to 2 percent of the population ever suffers from *bipolar depression*, the modern term for manic-depressive psychosis, and these require the most professional service. Affective disorders accounted for 15 percent of all patient care episodes in U.S. psychiatric facilities in 1971, compared with 22 percent for schizophrenic disorders, 9 percent for alcoholic disorders, 5 percent for brain disorders, 3 percent for mental retardation, and 3 percent for drug disorders (Kramer, 1976). Affective disorders are about twice as common in women as in men, except for bipolar depression where there is no sex difference.

We begin our account at a descriptive level, considering depressed and manic states in their own right. Then we turn to the complicated question of classification before reviewing the evidence about etiology, pathology, and treatment.

DEPRESSED STATES

In a carefully designed factor analysis of the clinical symptoms of depression, as recorded by the hospital staff in daily observation of a series of 96 patients,

Grinker and associates (1961) found four partially independent clusters or patterns of behavior and feeling. The first pattern, in which the patient feels dismal, hopeless, and painfully low in self-esteem and in which action, speech, and thought are laboriously slow, corresponds fairly well to what has previously been called a *retarded depression*. The second factor, involving high anxiety, guilt feelings, and hopelessness together with agitated behavior and clinging demands for attention, sounds much like the older idea of an *agitated depression*. The other two patterns are less sharply distinguished. Both entail the typical depressive affects of gloom and hopelessness, but in both the behavior is more assertive, described by such terms as "demanding," "angry," and "provocative." These observable distinctions warn us not to oversimplify the problem of depression. The idea of a single "typical" form is a fiction.

Retarded Depressions

The typical symptoms of retarded depression can be grouped under the headings of underactivity and a dejected mood. In their mildest form they shade imperceptibly into a normal state of discouragement. The underactivity shows itself in slowness of movement and speech. Exertion is experienced as difficult; depressed people prefer to sit in one place with folded hands, and cannot summon the energy to perform the simplest errands. If questioned they speak slowly, in a low tone, with great economy of words, and they prefer not to speak at all. There is a similar retardation in the sphere of thought. Ideas do not come to mind and a great inertia seems to block problem solving. As one patient described it, "At these times my brain feels paralyzed; I have not the strength or ambition to do anything. . . . I have the impulse to act, but it seems as if something shuts down and prohibits action" (White, 1932, p. 161). Illustrative of the retardation in thought is the person's reaction to reading. What is read seems to call up no associations; it is not assimilated, and the whole business of keeping up continuous attention is felt as painfully exhausting.

The dejected mood may take the form simply of unrelieved sadness. Everything looks gloomy; if they talk about their troubles they paint a picture of utter hopelessness. Some concentrate their woes on bodily complaints, feeling sure that they have an incurable disease. Others concentrate on the theme of poverty and deprivation, believing that their money is gone and that there is no hope for the future. The one theme on which they have strength enough to converse is that of their worthlessness and wickedness. The mechanism of projection appears to be unavailable to depressed people. Their minds are full of self-blaming, and they do not lift this burden by transferring the blame to outside persecutors. If they think the tax collector or the police will come for them, this action is perceived as entirely justified. In severe cases the hopelessness is so profound that the possibility of suicide cannot be discounted. Indeed, death by suicide occurs in 1 percent of the cases during the year of the acute episode, and in 15 percent over the lifetime of people with recurrent depressions (Klerman, 1978).

523

It becomes clear how intractable this attitude is if any attempt is made to influence it. The obvious social response to declarations of despair and worthlessness is to try to cheer up such people, but these efforts are of no avail. There is no answering smile, no look of relief, if one tells them that they are loved and valued or reminds them of creditable past performances. The conviction of poverty does not yield even to such objective evidence as a bank statement. The depressed mood seems to be firmly in command, and nothing but frustration awaits the person who tries to bring about a more objective testing of reality.

Besides the symptoms of despondent mood and retardation in facial expressions, gestures, speech, and thinking, there is usually a loss of capacity to experience pleasure. Things that previously would evoke joy and interest now seem boring, tedious, or even burdensome. A triad of biological abnormalities is common: disturbance of sleep, fatigue that is disproportionate to the effort expended, and loss of appetite. Typically there are rhythmic daily patterns, with the most severe symptoms experienced on awakening and in the early morning hours (von Praag, 1977). Such *diurnal swings* imply biochemical aberrations which, as we will see later, probably occur in the metabolism of amino acids in the brain.

Example of Retarded Depression

In our historical chapter we mentioned the autobiography of Clifford W. Beers (1931), a book that did a great deal to establish the mental hygiene movement. Beers was in a psychotic condition with ups and downs for three years. The seriousness of his condition first became fully apparent when he tried to commit suicide by throwing himself out the window of his bedroom. For the next two years he was in a depressed state, complicated in various ways by hallucinations and other less usual features. At the end of this time he changed rather quickly to a manic condition. His account of his experiences will provide us with illustrations for both conditions.

Because of injuries sustained in his jump from the window, Beers was first taken to a general hospital in his home city. He conceived that he was under a criminal charge for attempted suicide, and that his crime must be known to everyone in the city. "The public believed me the most despicable member of my race. The papers were filled with accounts of my misdeeds." The hospital was located on the street that led to the university athletic field, and a crowd of students and graduates went by on their way to a class-day game. Beers was sure that every one of these people loathed him for having disgraced his alma mater. "When they approached the hospital on their way to the athletic field, I concluded that it was their intention to take me from my bed, drag me to the lawn, and there tear me limb from limb." Some time later he was taken to a sanatorium in another community. "The day was hot, and, as we drove to the railway station, the blinds on most of the houses in the streets through which we passed were seen to be closed. I thought I saw an unbroken line of deserted houses, and I imagined that their desertion had been deliberately planned as a sign of displeasure on the part of their former occupants. I supposed them bitterly ashamed of such a despicable townsman as myself."

Nearly two years later Beers was still convinced that he was to go on trial. His brother, who visited him often, was apt to comment favorably on his health and to add, "We shall straighten you out yet." To Beers this was an ambiguous phrase "which might refer to the end of the hangman's rope, or to a fatal electric shock." He interpreted his improving physical health as a sign that the doctors were fattening him for the slaughter after his trial which, of course, could have but one outcome. Suicide seemed a preferable fate, and for many weeks he devised a series of schemes to bring about this result. Everything that happened only served to remind him of his misery. He could take no pleasure in his daily walks with his attendant, for example, because he was sure that everyone knew his black record and impending punishment. "I wondered why passers-by did not revile and stone me. It was not surprising that a piece of rope, old and frayed, which someone had carelessly thrown on a hedge by a cemetery that I sometimes passed, had for me great significance."

These examples show the pervasive effect of the dejected mood. Even quite incidental impressions receive a distorted meaning that fits them into the person's depressed state of mind. The sense of sin and worthlessness is so dominating that experience can no longer be interpreted in any other terms. This characteristic has led to the description of depressive and manic conditions as *affective disorders* or disorders in the sphere of mood.

Agitated Depressions

The second clinical pattern disclosed in Grinker's research includes depressive affect without retardation of action or thought. There is the same mental content of hopelessness and worthlessness that appears in the retarded depressions, but there is likely to be a stronger emphasis on sin, guilt, responsibility for surrounding evils, and dire punishments that must be in store. Thoughts of death are prominent and suicide is a real danger. But instead of sitting silently in an attitude of despair, such people are extremely active and talkative. They cannot keep still, cannot sleep, but can only pace up and down with moans and sighs and wringing of the hands. The existence of this variant form of depression makes it clear that dejected mood and underactivity do not necessarily go together. As a matter of fact people are sometimes found who combine mood and activity in the reverse patterns: action and thought are seriously retarded, but the mood is one of exultation. In the case of agitated depressions the behavior reflects a combination of depressed mood and anxious tension.

The following example can be considered a fairly typical case (Strecker & Ebaugh, 1940). A fifty-three-year-old woman of apparently healthy ancestry and good educational background was admitted to the hospital in a highly agitated and deeply depressed condition. As a young woman she had been quiet, conscientious, and self-sacrificing, but distinctly sociable, well-liked by

525

her friends, and a capable manager of the house. At twenty-five she married a man who proved to be a hopeless alcoholic and drug addict. This was the beginning of a life that grew more and more difficult. The patient was constantly worried about her husband, her children, and the family finances. When the husband's deterioration made further home life impossible, she separated from him and took to running a rooming house to support herself and the children. For five years before her illness she had been unable to secure help and was constantly exhausted by the work of the house. As a result she had severe attacks of flu every winter and was in a badly run down condition. The depression came on suddenly. She began to moan, pace up and down, and wring her hands. She felt herself a wicked sinner for having left her husband; she ought never to have been born because she brought such trouble on the whole world.

In this condition she arrived at the hospital. She was in a state of almost ceaseless activity, squirming in her chair, walking rapidly about, pulling at her hair, pinching her cheeks, biting her fingers. Her deeply lined face bore an expression of unutterable woe. At times she was frankly terrified; at other times she shrank from the nurse's hand because she felt herself unworthy to be touched. She believed that all her family and been killed because of her wrongdoing. "Oh, what have I done!" she would exclaim. "Can't I be saved? What is in store for me?" Then she wuuld get started on her poverty: "Not a cent left, not a cent." She made one unsuccessful attempt at suicide. In spite of her miserable state and violent self-accusations, she was not disoriented or hallucinated nor were there any discernible gaps in her memory. At the end of a year she was well on the way to recovery, with the beginnings of insight into the distorted nature of her previous ideas.

MANIC STATES

Characteristics of Mania

In its mildest stages, often called hypomania or subacute mania, a manic state is difficult to distinguish from a normal state of good spirits and high efficiency. There is a certain amount of overactivity, expressing itself both in motor channels and in a free flow of ideas and speech. There is also a show of confidence and enterprise that may drift over into boastful self-assertion. Ordinary people are apt to envy people in this stage, and business offices consider them ready for promotion. The signs that all is not well do not show themselves in single actions but rather in the continuity of one action or idea with another. It will be apparent that the person flies from one idea to a different one, makes a plan one moment only to cancel it in the next, and is unduly irritated if the least frustration stands in the way. Subacute mania bears some resemblance to mild alcoholic intoxication. Such people are lively, witty, and jolly, free in speech and high in self-confidence. They are full of plans and not

526

bothered by the thought of difficulties or risks in carrying them out. Just as in alcoholic intoxication, efficiency may be lowered but the illusion of efficiency raised. They may be having a wonderful time and see not the slightest reason why anyone should be concerned about them.

The true hallmarks of the disorder can be more clearly perceived in acute mania. Outstanding is the stream of talk, which seems never to abate. Taken in short units, it is perfectly coherent, but change from topic to topic is constantly taking place. These changes reveal the person's distractibility. Whatever is seen or heard may divert attention completely, and may elicit personal remarks that take others aback: "My, how gray your hair is," or "Look at those holes in your sweater." In the motor sphere there is constant restlessness. The person is always busy, never tired, sleeps little at night and awakens eager for action long before sunrise. If he or she cannot find enough ways to use up the excess energy, the solution may be to burst into shouts and song, smash furniture, or do sitting-up exercises. The need for action amounts to an irresistible pressure. Continued over many days and through sleepless nights it presently begins to tell on the person's health. Physical restraint and continuous hot baths were formerly in frequent use to keep manic patients quiet. Tranquilizing drugs are now more commonly used for the same purpose, but fairly large supervised doses are usually needed to produce appreciable results.

The prevailing mood is one of joyous elation. The person is full of confidence and is quite willing to carry promising enterprises to the White House, to Wall Street, to Hollywood, or wherever they will be most rapidly dispatched to their splendid conclusions. The confident mood easily rises to domineering arrogance, especially toward those in authority. Very inconsiderate of other people, the person is easily aroused to anger and fury if these activities are in any way curbed. If thoughts take a sexual turn, these will show a similar lack of restraint. All impulses come to immediate expression in words and in acts insofar as these are permitted. Any kind of restraint is extremely uncomfortable because of the pressure to activity.

Disturbances of thought and loss of contact with reality are incidental results of the overactivity and overconfidence. The person is too distractible to perceive the environment with accuracy, too changeable to turn the flight of ideas into consecutive thinking, too elated to take account of facts that run counter to the expansive mood. Delusions of great wealth or accomplishment readily develop, but the distortion of reality sometimes extends to hallucination. In a way, a manic patient does not strike an observer as being as crazy as a schizophrenic or general paretic. The effect is instead of a person abnormally speeded up and thus seriously disorganized, but not unintelligible. Such patients are highly incompetent to carry on their own affairs and need to be hospitalized for their own good and for the sake of their health. But they do not seem as far away from the normal as other psychotics do.

Just as it is difficult to encourage a really depressed person, so it is difficult to discourage a manic one. There is the same implacable dominance of mood over the testing of reality. It is of no use to ask the person to sit still, take some rest, or stop talking and give others some rest. Attempts to sidetrack a proposed telephone call to the White House will be answered, "But I know the President is just waiting to hear from me." Well-meaning intervention is bounced off by the manic patient just as effectively as by the depressed.

Example of Manic Behavior

We turn to the third year of Clifford Beers' psychosis for a concrete example of the manic state. While there were many preliminary signs that Beers' depression was lifting, the decisive change of mood came quite suddenly. The sensation was like the lifting of a cloud, and at once his mind began to be flooded with ideas for a vast program of humanitarian reform. The following day he attended a church service. Instead of discovering gloomy forebodings and veiled threats in the service, he now heard every word as if it were a personal message from God. Phrases from the psalms clearly referred to the great projects that were coursing through his mind, and to his own role as the instrument chosen to carry them out. "My heart is inditing a good matter," he heard, "my tongue is the pen of a ready writer." This surely referred to his heart and his tongue, so he began writing letters about everything that had happened to him. Soon exhausting his supply of stationery, he arranged to secure large quantities of wrapping paper that he cut in strips a foot wide and pasted together into vast rolls. "More than once, letters twenty or thirty feet long were written, and on one occasion the accumulation of two or three days of excessive productivity, when spread upon the floor, reached from one end of the corridor to the other—a distance of about one hundred feet. My hourly output was something like twelve feet. . . . Under the pressure of elation one takes pride in doing everything in record time. Despite my speed my letters were not incoherent. They were simply digressive, which was to be expected, as elation befogs one's 'goal idea.'"

The writing of colossal letters soon proved an insufficient means of using up his energy. "I proceeded to assume entire charge of that portion of the hospital in which I happened at the moment to be confined. What I eventually issued as imperative orders were often presented at first as polite suggestions. But, if my suggestions were not accorded a respectful hearing, and my demands not acted upon at once, I invariably supplemented them with vituperative ultimatums." Beers soon determined to conduct a complete investigation of the hospital. This proved very trying to the staff and resulted in serious friction. It led to his being placed in a small cell in the violent ward where for want of paper he proceeded to write all over the walls. Angered at his treatment, he rigged up a fake scene of suicide to frighten the attendants—a striking contrast to his serious and persistent attempts to take his life when depressed. Before long his mind turned to inventions. Characteristically, these were not of a minor order; he decided "to overcome no less a force than gravity itself." Tearing a carpet into strips, he managed to suspend his bed with himself in it between the window and a transom over the door. "So epoch-making did this discovery appear to me that I noted the exact position of the bed so that a wondering posterity might ever afterward view and revere the exact spot on the earth's surface whence one of man's greatest thoughts had winged its way to immortality."

The successful overcoming of gravity seemed to open endless possibilities. Great wealth would soon be in his hands. And with this he planned to transform his home city into a veritable garden spot and center of learning. Scores of parks would be dotted with cathedrals, libraries, art galleries, theaters, and great mansions, the whole scene to be crowned by the most magnificient and efficient university in the world. But his mind was presently recalled from these splendid prospects by the more immediate problem of correcting the abuses in state hospitals. With great ingenuity he smuggled a long letter to the governor, who was sufficiently impressed by the tales of violent treatment to interrogate the staff of the institution.

It is interesting to observe the continuity between Beers' intentions at this time and his career following recovery. So lasting was the impression made on him by his treatment in mental hospitals that he dedicated his life to what presently became the mental hygiene movement. He became instrumental in bringing about reforms that were much needed and highly constructive. His scientific experiments were discontinued and his plans for improving his home city fell by the wayside, but at least one of the goals conceived at the height of his illness was capable of realistic fulfillment. Again one is impressed with the fact that the manic patient is less basically confused than other psychotics. He is overdriven, speeded up, and expansive, and this results in a distorted relation to reality, but the radical change of tempo takes place in a fundamentally sound mind. When normal tempo and normal mood are restored, mental function may not show the slightest trace of impairment.

NATURE OF AFFECTIVE DISORDERS

Most people can read descriptions of depressed and manic behavior with a feeling of at least partial empathic understanding. The emotions of joy and sadness are familiar in everyday experience; we all know what it is like to feel elated and to be plunged into discouragement. It is a fairly common experience, although there are large individual differences in this respect, to undergo changes of mood over short intervals of time, even in the course of the day. External demands coming in a steady stream often conceal our natural rhythms; we must go on whether or not we feel like it. But all of us are aware to some extent of our better and poorer times of day. For some, morning is the time when ideas flow freely, when many things seem possible, and when action is energetic and full of zest. With afternoon comes fatigue, drowsiness, a dulling of the bright morning prospects, a need to put everything aside. Others experience the diurnal rhythm in reverse, reaching their peak of zestfulness in the evening. We are no strangers to mood. If required to do so, as were groups of college students in a research by Wessman and Ricks (1966), we can keep a daily diary of our mood states, even rating ourselves by means of check lists on highly specific aspects of affective experience. The subjects in this research differed widely with respect to stability of mood. Everyone, however, was aware of some degree of variation between different self-rating periods.

Everyday experience of moods, however, does not quite prepare us for the extremes of manic and depressive behavior. Even if we recall our most vivid experiences—the joy of a hard-won triumph, the misery of a bereavement, the gloom of a far-reaching failure—our behavior does not fully correspond to that of a manic or depressed patient. Our extreme moods may seem to flood us, but not to the extent of subverting our judgment and making us impervious to the influence of others. Pathological depression and mania imply something more than sorrow and joy. Their onset, their duration, and their frequently spontaneous remission often bear no obvious relation to circumstances, and they interfere gravely with realistic judgment. The suffering of depressed patients is painfully real, yet disproportionate and senseless. Also real is the elation of manic patients, but unlike pure joy it is compulsive, overdriven, and again senseless.

Fortunately, the outcome is usually good, even in quite extreme cases: 70 to 85 percent have substantial or complete remission of acute episodes (Klerman, 1978). Recovery before the advent of electroshock and drug treatments usually occured within 6 to 8 months, but is now achieved in a few weeks. About 15 percent have depressions with a chronic course and do not regain previous levels of functioning, and 40 to 50 percent have at least one recurrence of the disorder. Manic episodes used to last about three months before modern treatments were available, but they too usually clear up in a few weeks at most now, especially in response to lithium treatment.

The Distinction between Unipolar and Bipolar Depression

Primary affective disorder is diagnosed when no other psychiatric illness predates the onset of the affective disturbance. The affective disorder is considered *secondary* if it accompanies or follows another illness, such as anxiety disorder, antisocial personality disorder, or drug abuse. Primary depressives are more likely than secondary despressives to die by suicide.

A useful distinction has been drawn in recent years between primary affective disorders with a *bipolar* course and those with a *unipolar* course. Bipolar depressives have recurrent depressive episodes interspersed with manic phases, whereas unipolar depressives display no manic phases at all. Unipolar manic disorders are extremely rare, and they appear to resemble in most essential respects bipolar disorders (except for the lack of depressive syptoms). Unipolar disorders usually start later (average age 36) than bipolar disorders (age 28), and bipolar patients become ill more often than unipolar patients, who typi-cally have only a single episode of depression (Winokur, Clayton, & Reich, 1969).

Cadoret and Winokur (1975) reviewed six studies with a cumulative total of 1700 patients, which showed that on the average 44 percent of the bipolar de-pressives had one or more relatives with affective illness, compared with only 27 percent of the unipolar depressives. A complementary study (Winokur & Clayton, 1967) found that depressed patients were more likely to be admitted to the hospital in a *manic* state if they had an affectively disordered parent or child than if there were no evidence of affective illness in the family. There is a greater frequency of suicide in the families of bipolar patients. First degree relatives of bipolar depressives tend toward bipolar illness, not unipolar ill-ness, but relatives of unipolar depressives tend toward unipolar illness (Perris, 1966). (See Table 14.1). There is a higher incidence of *postpartum* episodes (depression following childbirth) in bipolar patients and they are more inclined toward *retarded* depressions, whereas unipolar patients have agitated, as well as retarded depressions (Fieve & Dunner, 1975).

Table 14-1 The Relation between Type of Affective Illness in Hospitalized Patients and in Their First Degree Relatives

Illness in the Patients	Illness in the Relatives	
	Bipolar	Unipolar
Bipolar	11%	1%
Unipolar	1%	7%

Source: Perris (1966).

To summarize, bipolar depression is characterized by both mania and de-pression, and increased prevalence of affective illness in the family; unipolar depression is usually characterized by depressive illness only and less affective illness among relatives. Genetic factors appear to play a greater role in the eti-ology of bipolar disorders, which may relate to their earlier onset, and there seem to be different mechanisms of genetic transmission for unipolar and bi-polar illness.

Suicide

It has been estimated that primary affective disorder accounts for 12,900 sui-cides committed each year in the United States (Miles, 1977). That is about half the total suicides that are certified each year. About 15 percent of persons with primary affective disorder ultimately take their own lives (Motto, 1975). Suicide ranks among the ten leading causes of death in this country, and among the top five in the 15 to 24 age group; it is second only to accidents in ending the lives of college students. About 200,000 suicide *attempts* are es-timated to occur annually, so we can infer that more than 100,000 are attrib-

531

"THE ANSWER IS POLITICS. IN YOUR MANIC STATE YOU CAN GO OUT CAMPAIGNING, AND IN YOUR DEPRESSIVE STATE YOU CAN STAY IN THE OFFICE."

utable to clinical depression. Other motivations for suicide are to relieve pain, to make a symbolic gesture (which is sometimes psychotically distorted), or as a momentary impulse resulting from brain dysfunction, such as in toxic or delirious states.

In a sample of depressed psychiatric inpatients, suicide attempters were found to be younger than average (Crook, Raskin, & Davis, 1975), although the risk of *successful* suicide is greatest among older people, especially men with a history of prior suicide attempt or chronic self-destructive pattern, a recent severe loss (or threat of loss), or poor physical health (Motto, 1975). Suicide risk can be identified by a pattern of chronic interpersonal maladjustment, which is reflected clinically in withdrawal from social contact and display of hostility or irritability toward others (Crook, Raskin, & Davis, 1975). It is particularly ominous if the person has a detailed suicide plan and the contemplated method or instrument is at hand. The most likely candidate for suicide often refuses offers of assistance from friends or clinicians. Psychiatric complications that commonly contribute to accomplished suicides, besides depression, are psychotic thought disorder, alcoholism, and drug abuse (Motto, 1975).

Three patterns of suicide are among the most common according to Motto (1975):

1. *Stable prior pattern with forced change.* This is often seen in young adult women who have enjoyed a stable life pattern built around a sym-

SEVEN COMMON MISCONCEPTIONS ABOUT SUICIDE

Myth	*Reality*
1. People who talk about suicide don't commit suicide.	About 80 percent of suicides are indicated in advance by definite signs of warning, including verbal statements.
2. If someone wants to take his or her own life, there's nothing you can do to stop it.	Most suicidal people are ambivalent about seeking death, and respond favorably to therapeutic efforts.
3. Once a person is suicidal, the risk is always there.	Most suicidal states are definitely time-limited.
4. When improvement in mood occurs, the risk is over.	Most suicides occur within 90 days after the clinical picture begins to improve.
5. Suicide is more common among the rich (or among the poor).	Suicide occurs at about the same rate in all socioeconomic groups.
6. Suicide runs in families.	There are no specific genetic determinants of suicide.
7. A person must be mentally ill to want to commit suicide.	Most persons who commit suicide are not psychotic, and many are not psychiatrically ill.

Source: Adapted from *Facts about suicide* (1961).

biotic relationship that is seriously disrupted. Sudden divorce for a satisfied homemaker would be an example. Usually there is no history of prior suicide attempts, alcoholism, psychosis, or socially disruptive behavior, but rather a consistently stable pattern of schooling, residence, work, and marital and social relationships, which may insidiously have "trained" the person to be dependent, vulnerable, or brittle.

2. *Progressive constriction.* This occurs most often in men who display considerable strength and ability in many aspects of their life, but experience a gradual, relentless shrinkage in their sources of emotional support. A parent dies, children grow up and leave home, occupational horizons fade, financial losses occur, sexual capacity diminishes, friends drift away, separation or divorce is threatened. Any one of these stresses, though serious, might be handled effectively by itself, but as they accumulate the burden becomes unendurable, leading to suicide.

3. *Adolescent transition.* Everyone needs to feel worthy of love and secure in relationship with significant others in one's life. A common source of

emotional stress for adolescents occurs with the transition from childhood to young adulthood, as the focus of critical relationships is transferred from the primary family to peers. An adolescent is particularly vulnerable if the background includes family disruption, chronic unsatisfactory relationships, difficulty establishing close ties with peers, a "loner" pattern or excessive dependency on peer approval, and abuse of alcohol or drugs as a substitute for healthy relationships. For such an adolescent any crisis or setback may precipitate a suicide attempt. The proportion of accomplished suicides is relatively low in this group, but nevertheless suicide is one of the most common causes of death in adolescence.

PSYCHOLOGICAL ASPECTS OF AFFECTIVE DISORDERS

Melancholia and mania owe their age-long recognition as psychological disorders to emotional excessiveness, to something more beyond sorrow and joy. This has led many observers to believe that depressed and manic states are analogous to sedated and intoxicated conditions. Some peculiarity of metabolic regulation, it is argued, makes the person's mood shoot down or up as if in response to a strong sedative or a powerful drink. This is essentially the theory proposed by Kraepelin and favored by those with a biological orientation. We will see presently that the evidence for something of this kind is considerable, but this does not exempt us from searching for the psychological meaning of affective disorders. Even if we suppose that extreme moods result from autonomous fluctuations in the metabolic system, we must examine all the available evidence, including the person's subjective experiences and behavior, for clues as to the nature of this fluctuation. We therefore turn our attention first to the psychological aspects of the problem, and examine more closely the content of the two conditions as shown in behavior and conversation. Is it possible to discern in these disordered states an adaptive attempt, a struggle to cope with human difficulties? Can we perceive an intelligible relation between manic states and depressions?

Psychological Content of Manic States

The first thing to notice is that the two states are at opposite poles with respect to self-esteem. In depression there is an utter collapse of self-esteem. The person can hardly find words strong enough to express the depth of degradation and worthlessness that is felt. In manic states, on the other hand, self-esteem is joyfully boundless. All things seem possible, and the person's feeling of competence extends in every direction. There is often a sensation of being flooded by plans for today, tomorrow, and the distant future, yet the person is not bothered by the thought that time and resources may prove to be limited. To

534

an observer who does not share the manic mood there is something false about this high level of self-esteem. It is different from the expansive planning of a person whose self-confidence is founded on a record of real achievement. It is maintained by two devices: speed and change of direction. Like a good broken-field runner in football, the person's mind races forward at top speed and dodges sharply whenever it is in danger of being tackled by a hard fact. Records of manic conversation show that there is tremendous distractibility, but the distractions are not entirely at random. They achieve the purpose of avoiding thoughts that would be detrimental to self-esteem.

The deduction has been made from such observations that manic people make heavy use of the primitive mechanism of *denial*, "benignly neglecting" the existence of every fact and every thought that might cause depressed feeling (Lewin, 1950). This evasive behavior can be regarded as a defense against the possibility of being depressed. It is the heavy reliance on these two mechanisms that gives manic buoyancy its element of falseness. A similar pattern of behavior is sometimes seen in response to sudden tragedy. The reaction to a particularly tragic bereavement, for instance, may be sudden immersion at once in work, business plans, activities, even amusement; the whole pattern constitutes a daily assertion that the person is not deserted, grief-striken, or helpless. Occasionally it happens that a true manic attack develops as the first response to a situation that involves loss and a threat to self-esteem. In such instances manic behavior especially seems to have the character of an attempt to control and counteract depression and thus escape the pains of shattered self-esteem.

The Adaptive Attempt in Depressed States

On the face of it there is no parallel adjustive attempt in depressions. These states seem rather to represent breakdown and collapse with little sign of a struggle to rectify the situation. While it is true that certain extreme disorders—for example, the disorganization that goes with total panic—represent pure breakdown, we must always be on the watch for signs of attempted repair and restoration. Can we detect a purpose in depressed behavior, a struggle to accomplish something that will improve the person's situation and reduce the force of the distress experienced?

Much theorizing has viewed depression in terms of reaction to loss. Perhaps a loved one dies or deserts the person. Perhaps the moral support of a congenial group is lost. Perhaps the loss is of a more subtle and symbolic nature, such as perceiving a cooling of interest from one's spouse or a reduction of applause from audiences that were previously enthusiastic. Depressed behavior can be understood, in part, as a cry for love: a display of helplessness and a direct appeal for the affection and security that have been lost. But the whole reaction may be greatly complicated by the presence of angry hostility toward the deserting person and by guilty fear that this hostility has actually caused the desertion. Early attempts may be made to vent aggression directly and force some return of esteem, but these usually give way to repentance and the anger becomes directed against the self. Unending self-criticism is intended as an act of expiation. By fully accepting the blame for everything and confessing unworthiness, the person strives to win back lost esteem and affection, but the pain of self-punishment and the despair caused by the constant downgrading of self-esteem may become unbearable, even driving the person to suicide, before the attempted expiation brings any sense of restored love (Rado, 1954). There is a certain method in this madness: an attempt, however misguided, to repair the situation created by serious loss of support and respect.

Depressed behavior also contains essential hostility directed toward the environment as well as toward the self (Bonine, 1966; Weissman, Klerman, & Paykel, 1971). The effect of depression on the people with whom the person lives is in fact frustrating, even punishing. The stubborn refusal to be cheered up, the quick rejection of any hopeful suggestion as if it were utterly stupid, keeps putting those around the depressed person in a position of helpless incompetence. Behavior that contains in one package a cry for love, a plea for forgiveness, an expiatory but tiresome self-criticism, and an implacable rejection of attempts to be helpful, hardly constitutes a workable pattern, and the adaptive effort not surprisingly produces no coherent result.

Coping with Affect

These views on the adaptive attempt in manic and depressed states obviously do not point to rational and well-considered ways of dealing with human relations and problems of self-esteem. It is possible to view the behavior in a different light simply as an attempt to cope with extreme mood states. This is consistent with a biological interpretation of the moods: if they arise from internal biochemical events they simply flood the person with either positive or negative affect that has no intelligible relation to past or present experience. The mood developed in this way enjoys pre-emptive strength, so that every event and every thought is invested either with gloom or with exhuberant elation. The person naturally tries to account for these subjective changes. In a manic mood everything feels so wonderful that it must be happening to a wonderful person capable of doing anything that comes to mind. In a depressed mood everything feels so dreadful that it must be happening to a dreadful person, sinful and worthless, for whom there can be no hope. Depressed behavior and conversation fit this alternative explanation fairly well. Good cheer is out of the question because every supposedly hopeful communication from others is at once drowned in negative affect and thus interpreted as not really hopeful. Feeling so badly, the person accounts for it with self-blame and self-criticism, but it is not inconsistent that a cry for help, and anger because nothing does help, should be woven into the pattern.

The Theme of Loss

It would strengthen psychological accounts of affective disorders if a high frequency of serious losses were associated with them, but the evidence in this regard is ambiguous. Some studies have found that depression is not associated with parental death, divorce, broken engagements, and similar losses of significant relationship (Malmquist, 1970; Watt & Nicholi, 1979). On the other hand, Paykel (1974, 1975) found that depressed patients reliably experience more stressful life events—especially separations and interpersonal losses—prior to the onset of disorder than do general populations, medical patients, and most other psychiatric patients. Also more undesirable events than desirable ones are associated with depression. The evidence for an acquired vulnerability to loss in affective disorders is not conclusive, although it remains a hypothesis of keen interest and empirical study. Many clinical workers would identify loss as a major precipitating factor in most cases.

Personality Patterns and Premorbid Adjustment

According to Klerman (1978) is is widely believed that persons prone to depression have low self-esteem, strong superego, clinging and dependent interpersonal relations, and limited capacity for mature and enduring object relations. There is not very consistent evidence here, but it is generally true that antisocial, paranoid, and other types of individuals who employ projection and other externalizing modes of defense do *not* often become depressed. The psychiatric symptoms of depression imply internalizing modes of defense, which Phillips (1968) characterizes as "turning against the self." He reasons that the extremes of affect shown by these patients indicate a capacity for experiencing emotion deeply, feeling guilt, and coping with emotional difficulties by *internalizing* conflicts and stress. The experience of adaptive failure is more likely to elicit guilt and anxiety in patients who have incorporated high ideals, standards, and societal values. These patients would tend to be more competent and capable of coping with psychosocial stresses, and hence would have a better prognosis for speedy and permanent recovery than patients who evidenced little affective reactivity during the acute phase of the disorder.

The internalizing orientation is sharply contrasted with the externalizing or *extrapunitive* coping styles seen in sociopaths or delinquents ("turning against others") and with the evasive mechanisms that are prominent in schizophrenic disorders ("avoidance of others").

Phillips presented empirical evidence to support his theoretical formulations based on systematic studies of Worcester State Hospital records. Corroborative evidence has been published by other investigators. Lewine et al. (1978) found that, as children, psychotic depressives were described by school teachers as significantly more independent than their classmates, showing signs of leadership and scholastic maturity (though not interpersonal matur-

537

ity). Watt et al. (1979) replicated Phillips' finding that extreme emotionality and internalizing attitude toward stress during the acute breakdown are positively correlated with childhood social competence and with long-term favorable outcome. The reasoning here was that because of their high personal standards depressives recovered more rapidly than patients with other kinds of disorder, and their high level of competence served them well in their efforts for rapid rehabilitation and reintegration in society.

It has been noticed that in their periods of remission, and reportedly also before the first onset of their disorder, bipolar depressives show a characteristic pattern of traits. This pattern, known technically as the *cyclothymic* pattern, is not one that suggests weakness or maladjustment; on the contrary, it contains many elements that are generally associated with psychological health. Cyclothymic people are apt to be energetic, lively, and full of interests. They are warmly responsive to others and are often esteemed as delightful companions. In their closer relationships they are affectionate, loyal, and strongly attached. When in good health they function well, often leading rich and highly satisfying lives. Yet there is a vulnerable point in the organization of their personalities. Beneath the surface they are acutely dependent on their principal love-objects and cannot tolerate frustration or disappointment from this source. As Edith Jacobson (1971) expresses it, "What they require is a constant supply of love and moral support from a highly valued love-object." This love object is usually a person, "but it may be represented by a powerful symbol, a religious, political, or scientific cause, or an organization of which they feel a part." The weak spot in these otherwise healthy personalities is this specific overdependence on one principal person as a source both of love and of self-esteem.

Strong interpersonal needs may create a weak spot in a person's feeling of competence. Securing a central supply of supporting love is a problem that cannot be handled by direct, assertive measures, no matter how effective one is in achieving other aims. Love cannot be commanded; it has to be won. But this is an issue on which the cyclothymic individual cannot afford to lose, or even to be moderately frustrated. Consequently some cyclothymics resort to skillful manipulation of others, maneuvering them into positions where they either want or feel obliged to express devotion and give emotional support. However, this kind of maneuvering is at best an uncertain business, and if it fails the result may be a precipitous loss of self-esteem.

Because cyclothymic people are often highly productive people, extreme episodes of mania and depression place frustrating limits on their achievements and originality; an appreciable benefit of modern drug treatments, especially with lithium, has been to dampen their abnormal mood swings and increase their overall productivity (Fieve & Dunner, 1975).

The Theme of Guilt

Depressive states, as we have seen, often show a heavy content of guilt, expressed as feelings of sinfulness and a conviction that one deserves to be punished.

Such excessively conscientious behavior is understandable from the viewpoint of Phillips' account of their moral development, which we have just reviewed. The theme of guilt sometimes emerges clearly in depressions of men in military service following the death of a comrade. The soldier may constantly blame himself for the comrade's death even when he had not the least part in it. When it is possible to probe carefully into the meaning of the comrade's death a curious mixture of feelings may be uncovered. In one case, for example, that of a depressed airman, much was heard at first about the dead friend's virtues, his generosity, his wonderful qualities of companionship. Only later did it come out that there was another side to the relationship, less clearly conscious: the two men were also keen rivals in matters of prowess and had been competing intensely for the position of flight leader. On the mission which proved fatal to the friend, our airman had been designated flight leader. Near the target the friend had drawn his plane out of formation and tried to take the leader's position, but the patient refused to yield. It was at this point that the friend's plane had been struck by ground fire and had gone down in flames. Our airman's childhood history had left him with strong competitive feelings, behind which there is always a good deal of hostility toward rivals. His anger must have been unbounded when his friend on a dangerous mission refused to play fair and stay in formation. The outcome must have seemed a perfect piece of justice, but for a person in whom jealous hostility is repressed it is a terrific threat to have a death wish come true. The case of Bert Whipley has taught us how shattering this can be in early childhood. In the present case the airman berated himself for his friend's death and for many other incidents in which his conduct had actually been blameless. He was overwhelmed with guilt because the consequences were so devastating and so irreparable (Grinker & Spiegel, 1945).

Social Reinforcement and Learned Helplessness

Depressed behavior is not determined exclusively by intrapsychic events. Social learning theories have recently emphasized the importance of the social environment in shaping the behavior of depressed people. Lewinsohn (1974) has observed that depressed feelings and related symptoms, such as fatigue, may be elicited when behavior receives little reinforcement, which in turn tends to reduce activity and social participation even further. This results in still fewer reinforcements, and the cycle perpetuates itself. Three variables usually determine the amount of positive reinforcement a person receives: (a) personal characteristics such as age, sex, and attractiveness to others; (b) the environment in which the person behaves, for example, more reinforcement can usually be expected at home than in a prison or on the streets of a big city; (c) the person's repertoire of behavior that can gain reinforcement, for example, vocational and social skills. Depressed behavior, of course, elicits response from others. It is natural to react to it with sympathy, concern, or reassurance, which may reinforce the despondent mood, inactivity, and retraction of interest. Some treatment programs attempt to interrupt the vicious cycle of re-

539

inforcements for depression by *ignoring* the depressive "tactics" and by *rewarding* actions that break the negative pattern: taking initiative, speaking affirmatively about oneself, participating actively in social events, and the like.

Seligman (1975) has developed a cognitive model of depression as "learned helplessness," which is based on animal studies that show responses to frustration of coping efforts that are remarkably analogous to human depression. The experimental paradigm is familiar to students of experimental psychology: dogs are placed in a cage with an electric grid that is contiguous to an "escape chamber" where they can be safe from pain. When electric current is passed through the grid, the animals receive extremely painful electric shocks, precipitating frantic efforts to escape that ultimately succeed. The dogs learn very rapidly, usually after very few trials, that when a warning signal appears (a buzzer or a light) they must quickly run to the escape chamber in order to avoid the imminent shock. It is very simple avoidance learning that is quickly acquired and resistant to extinction.

The learning, however, can be impaired if the dogs have been subjected previously to "helplessness training,"—that is, *inescapable* shock in a similar setting. If such dogs are then placed in the avoidance apparatus and shocked, they soon stop running around frantically, and seem to give up and accept the painful shocks passively. They do not learn the avoidance response as efficiently as other dogs do. The psychological explanation is that the previous exposure to uncontrollable aversive stimulation creates a sense of learned helplessness, which later interferes with adaptation in stressful situations that *can* be controlled. Seligman points to many parallels between the helpless dogs and depressed humans: both respond to stress passively ("paralysis of will"), lose appetite and weight, show depletion of norepinephrine in the brain, and are impaired in adaptive learning by negative expectations for success.

Reasoning from this experimental analogy, Seligman argues that many humans become depressed, in part, because they come to believe that they are helpless to influence their fate. A wide-ranging program of research with humans has added some credence to the theory. In laboratory experiments nondepressed college students were exposed to unsolvable problems or to noise that was unpleasant but inescapable. Their reactions to these procedures and their performance on various experimental tasks were then measured. *Inducing* a sense of helplessness experimentally in this fashion was found to interfere with problem solving, slow down their adaptive responses to stress, cause depressed mood, and lead them to discount evidence of their own successful performance on tasks requiring skill. On the basis of these findings Seligman concluded that learned helplessness undermines the motivation to respond, retards the ability to learn that responding works, and contributes to emotional disturbance, mainly depression and anxiety. Unfortunately, depressed patients seem not to act in accord with Seligman's theory (Huesmann, 1978).

Seligman finds elements of helplessness in the well-known studies of hospitalism, of monkeys deprived of mothers, of the development of self-esteem, of the effects of overcrowding, and of failure in the classroom. *Ego strength* and *competence* are concepts that relate to mastery over events; both are surely learned primarily in childhood and deeply engrained in the structure of personality. Seligman suggests that the reverse kind of learning, of helplessness and uncontrollability, may insidiously lead to ego weakness, a sense of incompetence, and ultimately depression.

Why should depression occur twice as often in women as in men? Differences in the socialization of men and women for sex roles, family life, employment, and the development of social skills and self-concept may distinctively dispose women to depression as adults (Chesler, 1972). The mechanisms for this are not yet clear, but on the basis of a survey of 2500 men and women Radloff (1975) discounted some popular myths. The homemaker's role does *not*, by itself, account for the difference, because working wives were more depressed than working husbands but no less depressed than women without employment outside the home. Working wives were *not* more depressed because of having dual responsibilities, at home and on the job; although they did more housework than working husbands, this was not correlated with higher levels of depression. Radloff attributes the difference primarily to learned helplessness. Lack of personal and political power handicaps women in developing a sense of competence and worth. Childrearing customs train little girls

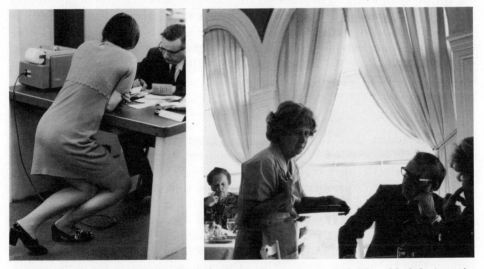

Socialization pressures in most modern societies foster an attitude of helplessness in women, which may indirectly dispose them to become depressed. In the office scene above, the woman seems to want to be close to the work at hand, but there appears to be implicit agreement that the man should do the work. The waitress in the restaurant exudes an impression of apology for ineffectuality and humility, which may or may not be called for in this situation. One's attitude toward life situations plays a significant part in causing affective disorders.

to be helpless, and encourage helpless young women to marry rather than seek a career. And occupational establishments have traditionally discriminated against women who try to build a career. It will be interesting to observe whether the changing roles of women in our society eventually lead to a change in the sex ratio for depression.

The theory of learned helplessness has a certain value, but it cannot be taken as a *specific* hypothesis to explain depression. Social helplessness is common in schizophrenia, especially in autistic children; inhibited effectiveness is often a feature of anxiety disorders, and violent delinquents are sometimes understood to be rebelling against the helplessness imposed by a depriving environment. To use learned helplessness as an explanation for depression we must link it with further factors that account for this specific outcome. The specific factor may lie among the hypotheses previously discussed, or it may consist of some biological vulnerability that converts discouragement into pathological depression.

BIOLOGICAL ASPECTS

Turning now to the biological side of the problem, the central task is to search for the biochemical and neurophysiological correlates of extreme moods and their fluctuations. If the hypothesis is correct that abnormal internal events take place that affect the functioning of the nervous system, then extreme moods should be correlated with erratic tendencies in biochemical regulation or in other physiological processes. Is it possible to detect such a biological tendency in affective disorders?

Genetic Factors

Statistical studies show that there is a significant tendency for affective disorders to run in families. While figures reported by different investigators do not agree perfectly, they regularly show a prevalence of disorder in the relatives of affectively disordered people that is well above chance. Klerman (1978) cites a morbidity risk for first degree relatives of 15 percent compared with a 1 to 2 percent prevalence for the general population. The prevalence of affective disorder in the parents of identified patients ranges from 7 to 25 percent in different studies, and similar figures for siblings run between 14 and 29 percent (Beck, 1967; Mendels, 1970). The concordance rate for monozygotic (identical) twins is 68 percent, contrasted with 23 percent for dizygotic (fraternal) twins (Klerman, 1978). These findings leave little doubt that genetic factors are involved in the occurrence of affective disorders. Recent advances in genetics improve the chances of eventually identifying these factors. Winokur and Reich (1970), for example, present evidence for the thesis that two different genes may be involved, one providing a tendency to depression and the other adding a predisposition to mania.

Genetic predisposition is certainly part of the picture, but it cannot stand alone as the cause of affective disorders. If its sway were absolute, as in the case of a dominant gene, then the concordance rate for identical twins would be 100 percent and the other figures would be higher than they are. What would we expect of children whose parents had suffered from affective disorder? Mendels (1970) calls attention to a European study in which the investigator found 20 married couples, both members of which had been diagnosed for affective disorders. Of the 47 adult offspring of these parents, 14 (30%) had developed a psychotic illness, 10 (21%) were classified as affective psychoses, but 33 (70%) appeared to be entirely normal. "This suggests that whatever the genetic mechanism may be," Mendels concludes, "it does not have 100% penetrance; that is, it does not operate invariably" (p. 92).

A very restricted interpretation must be applied to another line of evidence based on the study of physique. More than half a century ago Kretschmer (1925) pointed out an association between affective psychosis and the so-called *pyknic* physique. This meant that the disorder was more likely to occur in people of broad and solid frame, deep-chested and with relatively large trunk and viscera, and was less likely in small-muscled, small-boned, slender people. Kretschmer and later workers reported associations between the pyknic physical type and traits of personality that correspond to the cyclothymic pattern mentioned earlier in this chapter. This line of research has generally fallen into disrepute and neglect, but Rees (1961) published a highly detailed review of this topic up to 1960, and considered the correlation to be confirmed, although with much smaller figures than Kretschmer had supposed. The findings again point to a constitutional factor that may be associated with affective disorder, though the connection may be weak. Any investigator who pursues this inquiry should formulate a plausible rationale to explain the relation between body physique, which is known to be genetically transmitted to a significant extent, and the more established biological features of affective disorder.

Biochemical Factors

Both the activity and the sense of well-being shown by manic patients suggest a high rate of speed in vital processes, whereas the depressed mood and general retardation seem to imply that the whole bodily system has slowed down. This contrast has led many investigators to frame hypotheses around metabolic functions—the rate of vital activity in the tissues as a whole. It is clear now that mania and depression are not polar opposites in most aspects of bodily functioning. Measurements of basal metabolism, blood sugar level, blood pressure, rate of blood flow, and the like show few important differences between manic and depressed patients. Wherever significant differences have been found, they have proved to be more closely related to activity level than to mood. At the biological level, therefore, agitated depressions and manic states are very much alike, both differing significantly from retarded depressions.

Research on this problem is made difficult by the enormous complexity of biochemical processes. When the importance of the endocrine glands was first recognized, early in this century, the hope dawned that each gland controlled a particular function, the nature of which would quickly be discovered. Such reasoning soon proved to be far too simple. The glands constitute a regulatory system, constantly influencing one another and producing their results through elaborate teamwork. Complex systemic functioning seems to be characteristic of all biochemical processes, including those that affect the activity of the nervous system. Furthermore, events taking place in nervous tissue and in its biochemical milieu are not open to ready inspection; they must usually be inferred from indirect measures such as the concentration of particular substances in the blood or urine, measures which are not specific to brain physiology but to the body as a whole. It is not surprising tha the hypothesis of metabolic instability remained for many years indefinite and controversial. Even the discovery that treatment by electric shock could be helpful did not at first point to any plausible somatic mechanism. But the introduction of antidepressant drugs produced a sudden burst of research interest, and the decade of the 1960s was marked by striking progress in understanding and treating the affective disorders.

Research has moved forward along several lines. For a while it appeared that the adrenal glands might be major culprits. Among the many functions of those glands is the secretion of a number of steroid hormones whose concentration in the body can be measured in the urine. One of these hormones, *cortisol*, was shown to be overproduced in depressed patients; it was even possible to demonstrate a close connection in time between increased cortisol production and the onset of episodes of depression (Bunney, Mason, & Hamburg, 1965). Other work has shown, however, that increased cortisol production is not peculiar to depressions. It occurs in other disorders and in normal responses to stressful circumstances; it therefore seems best considered a nonspecific response to stress. This explanation is consistent with results obtained by Sachar (1967) in the course of psychotherapy with depressed clients. Cortisol levels, most of the time within normal range, became elevated on those days on which the client attained sudden upsetting insights into the aspects of his or her problems and experienced marked distress.

A second line of work, pointed more directly at the functioning of the nervous system, deals with *electrolyte metabolism*. Electrolytes, or electrically charged atoms, have a vital part in the activity of nerve cells and the transmission of neural impulses. They are unevenly distributed on either side of the cell's membrane; in particular, there is normally a higher concentration of sodium ions on the outside of the membrane and of potassium ions on the inside. This arrangement maintains an electrical balance or equilibrium that determines the cell's resting potential, and it is restored after the passage of a nervous impulse. Several investigations have turned up evidence that in depressed patients, and still more in manic patients, there is an abnormally high concentration of sodium ions inside the cell membrane, which changes the normal balance in the direction of greater excitability. In a paper reviewing the topic, Whybrow and Mendels (1969) propose the hypothesis that there is "an unstable state of central nervous system hyperexcitability in depression, and probably also in mania." It may seem paradoxical to invoke overexcitability for retarded depressions, though the concept seems appropriate for agitated depressions and manic states. But the research on electrolyte metabolism is still in its early stages, and the hypothesis of neural hyperexcitability needs considerably more confirmation.

A third line of research is directed toward *biogenic amine metabolism*. Biogenic amines are hormones that have important effects on the functioning of the central nervous system. Among them are the so-called catecholamines, which include dopamine and norepinephrine, known for some time to be produced by the adrenal glands in emergency reactions but now recognized as arising from other sites as well; and the *indole amines* of which serotonin and histamine are representative. Experiments with animals have shown that drugs that increase the level of amines in the brain produce alertness and overactivity, whereas those that deplete brain amines result in sedation and inactivity. The maintenance of effective amine concentrations is a constant metabolic process. Amines are used up, so to speak, by activity in nerve cells but are also steadily produced to make up for the loss, so that in normal circumstances homeostasis—a steady state—is maintained. It is conceivable, however, that the delicate balance might be upset, that precisely at this point there might be defects in regulation leading to episodes of underproduction and overproduction of brain amines and thus to sharp changes of activity and mood. It is even possible that such defects would manifest themselves chiefly in connection with life stress, with the upset in amine regulation occurring only when there were heavy demands upon the central nervous system. Biogenic amine metabolism now seems to be established as the most probable site of biochemical abnormality in affective disorders (Baldessarini, 1978), so we will devote special attention to it.

The Biogenic Amine Hypothesis. The first clues to the biochemical etiology of affective disorders were suggested by their responsiveness to two very different kinds of medication, *tricyclic antidepressants* and *monoamine oxidase (MAO) inhibitors*. These medications have two characteristics in common: they have a beneficial influence on vital (retarded) depression, and in the brain they behave like monoamine agonists, that is they augment the amount of biogenic amines available in the central nervous system (von Praag, 1977). Corroborative evidence was provided by the discovery that *reserpine*, an antipsychotic drug, provokes typical vital depressions while reducing the amount of amines available in the brain. In 1965 Schildkraut, surveying a large amount of evidence, proposed a catecholamine hypothesis to account for affective disorders, to the effect "that some, if not all, depressions are associated

545

with an absolute or relative deficiency of catecholamines, particularly norepinephrine, at functionally important receptor sites in the brain. Elation conversely may be associated with an excess of such amines." The hypothesis has since been broadened to include serotonin, which seems to play a somewhat similar part (Glassman, 1969). Recent evidence has supported the hypothesis. In bipolar depressives urinary excretion of metabolites of norepinephrine and dopamine is relatively *lower* during periods of depression than during mania or after recovery, and some patients with agitated or anxious depressions show increased excretion of catecholamine metabolites (Schildkraut, 1978). It is now believed that electroshock therapy may have its clinical effect by increasing the turnover of biogenic amines (norepinephrine, dopamine, and serotonin) in the brain. Lithium also affects the metabolism of biogenic amines but it is unclear how; for example, it appears to affect norepinephrine metabolism in a manner opposite to that of many antidepressant and stimulant drugs. Murphy et al. (1971) have found that large doses of L-dopa (a catecholamine precursor) induce manic symptoms in patients with previous episodes of spontaneous mania, but the effect could not be elicited in unipolar depressed patients, which indicates that mania and depression may involve different mechanisms instead of reflecting opposite poles of catecholamine activity.

It is not yet possible, of course, to account fully for the biochemical abnormality. Erratic regulation of amine metabolism might occur for a variety of reasons; the precise mechanism has by no means been laid bare. Kraines (1966) has put forward a theory, worked out in great detail, that pushes the explanation to a particular brain center, the hypothalamus, which is known to have a strong influence on emotional expression and is also an important source of norepinephrine. His thesis is that "a persistent, intensifying inhibition of hypothalamic function is the mechanism of a depressive syndrome and that a gradually increasing excitation of this area produces the manic state." Even so, we do not quite catch up with the initial abnormality; we are bound to ask what causes the unusual inhibition and excitation of the hypothalamus. Clearly the topic is not closed, but this should not obscure the progress that is being made in biochemical research nor the more optimistic attitude that has come to prevail regarding treatment.

METHODS OF TREATMENT

Affective disorders do not usually manifest themselves early in life, although a few cases of their occurrence in childhood have been reported. The most frequent period of onset is the decade of the thirties. In some cases, attacks recur, making repeated hospitalization necessary, but a single depressive episode with complete recovery is common. The expectation of at least temporary spontaneous recovery is so high that it is difficult to evaluate the effects of therapeutic measures. Most of the patients get well anyway, regardless of what is done. Therapeutic goals cannot be set up in terms simply of recovery, but most include considerations such as shortening the period of illness, reducing the recurrence, and freeing the patient's life from unnecessary psychological burdens.

Hospitalization

The specialized care provided by a mental hospital or other inpatient facility is clearly needed in severely depressed and manic states such as those described earlier in this chapter. Manic people are disturbing and exhausting to those around them, and with their indiscriminate self-confidence they may get themselves into a lot of trouble, including laying a trail of unpaid bills that far exceeds their actual financial resources. Depressed people are disturbing in a different way, and the danger of suicide hangs in the air even though taking one's life is talked about more often than it is tried. The decision to use the services of a hospital must rest on a weighing of relevant considerations: the extent of the person's disturbance and irrationality, the kinds of treatment probably needed, the risk of suicide, the amount of friction that is being generated within the family, the protection of children from a parent's irrationality. The hospital can often do a better job than would be possible by a grim attempt to ride out the storm at home.

Placement in a mental hospital is less quickly and less often recommended today than was the case in the recent past. There is growing reluctance to send people out of the community to institutions that may be some distance away. If community mental health agencies exist, such as an outpatient clinic or psychiatric services in the local hospital, adequate care can be provided for patients who continue to live at home. Most of the less severely depressed and manic states can be handled on an outpatient basis. Even the biological methods of treatment—electroconvulsive therapy and the use of drugs—do not necessarily call for hospitalization; they can be adapted to both office and outpatient practice. It is no longer the inevitable fate of manic or depressed people to be sent away.

Psychological Methods

People in severe depressions or manic states are usually not very responsive to psychological treatment. Suggestion and persuasion are dramatic failures in both states; the depressed person automatically considers them useless, the manic barely listens. Treatment that involves interpretation of psychological problems may make a depressed person perceive new grounds for feeling worthless; the manic person finds the interpretation brilliant and skips on to the next thought. Behavior therapists who undertake to reward and reinforce more desirable behavior may discover that they are not in possession of re-

547

wards of real value to the clients. The extreme moods seem to capture the reward mechanism itself, so that the depressed client feels little reward in the therapist's favorable attention, while the manic finds everything else that happens equally rewarding. The burden for some depressed people can be slightly lightened by calm assurance that the depression will ultimately pass. Beyond this, little can be accomplished while mood is in such complete command. For these reasons dynamic psychotherapy is not recommended as the primary treatment for bipolar depressions or severe recurrent psychotic depressions (Klerman, 1978). Fortunately, the physical treatments, with drugs and ECT, are most effective for severe disorders (Baldessarini, 1978).

In milder states and during periods of remission the situation is more favorable for psychological work. A minimum goal might be to assist clients in learning to live with their illness, adapting their lives to the possibility of recurrent episodes. Setting the sight a little higher, clients may be helped to cope with difficulties in living that cause stress, such as marital problems, family relations, and issues about childrearing. This is of value even if these difficulties are specific causes of the affective disorder. Whether anything more should be attempted depends on one's judgment of the relevance of psychodynamic problems in the particular case. In cases of long-standing depressive personality disorder or reactive depression, Klerman (1978) considers the most effective treatment combination to prescribe drugs to control the symptoms and offer dynamic psychotherapy to promote coping ability, social effectiveness, and personal functioning, although he finds the evidence inconclusive for changing deep-seated personality patterns. Undoing such profound vulnerabilities and defensive strategies is an inherently difficult therapeutic task, yet some success in dealing with it has been reported (Gibson, 1963; Bonine, 1965; Jacobson, 1971).

Antidepressant Drugs

Antipsychotic drugs, which as we saw in the last chapter produced something of a revolution in the care of schizophrenic disorders, have played a less dramatic part in the affective disorders. Though helpful in manic states and agitated depression, they are clearly inappropriate for dealing with depressed moods of the retarded type. Effective antidepressant drugs were developed a little later, but they were quickly adopted and to a considerable extent, though not entirely, have supplanted ECT. This does not necessarily imply that they work better. ECT has consistently outperformed the drugs by a small margin of effectiveness, both in the short term and in the long term (Baldessarini, 1978). But drugs are easier and more pleasant; moreover, doses can be regulated and changed, and combinations can be worked out to suit the client's individual needs. This flexibility has improved treatment "to the point where management of the affective disorders is among the most gratifying aspects of clinical practice" (Lipton, 1970). This is true not only for clinicians, but also for clients and their families because, unlike with many other disorders, the treatment usually works.

It might be supposed that a stimulant like amphetamine would be perfect for depressions, but this drug has proved to be of no value. Two other classes of drugs, however, have shown antidepressant properties: the *tricyclic* drugs, of which imipramine is the most studied representative, and the *monoamine oxidase inhibitors*. These two classes are significantly different in chemical structure and operate through different biochemical mechanisms, but both appear to produce the result of increasing the quantity of biogenic amines available for use in the central nervous system. The drugs, especially the tricyclics, are given in increasing doses for 2 to 4 weeks until the desired clinical response is obtained, then gradually reduced over a period of about three months until they are withdrawn entirely. They may produce unpleasant and potentially dangerous side effects, especially at high dosages and in older patients: dry mouth, increased sweating, memory difficulty, urinary retention, and cardiac arrhythmias. Psychotic depressions sometimes do not respond to antidepressant drugs alone, but may require a combination of antidepressants and phenothiazines or ECT, whereas nonpsychotic depressions respond well to antidepressants (Klerman, 1978).

Lithium is a salt that has been successful in treating 70 to 80 percent of manic cases within 10 to 14 days. In this case it is more plausible to assume that electrolyte metabolism is affected; lithium salts may play a part analogous to sodium and calcium, affecting the electrical balance on the two sides of the nerve cell membrane. Lithium is chiefly used to bring down manic attacks (National Institute of Mental Health, 1970), but it has also shown a prophylactic effect on both unipolar and bipolar depression, reducing the number and/or the severity of the phases (Schon, 1973). In prophylactic maintenance therapy for manics and bipolar depressives, 23 percent of the patients receiving lithium salt relapsed, compared with 68 percent of those given placebo in eight controlled studies (Davis, 1975). The capacity of lithium to prevent the recurrence of both manic and depressive episodes suggests that there are fundamental neurochemical processes common to both extremes of mood, even though the precise mechanisms through which they arise may differ (Klerman, 1978).

It is important to keep our perspective in evaluating the overall effectiveness of antidepressant drugs and of lithium. When administered carefully by experienced clinicians with appropriate attention to dosage levels and combinations, they can do a lot of good for most people with affective disorders. However, there are large individual differences in the response to different drugs, and it must be kept in mind that drugs powerful enough to relieve depression or mania also have other effects that can be harmful or even dangerous. Some preparations produce drowsiness and dizziness, some interfere with motor coordination, and some tend to have too great an effect on heart rate or liver function. Such consequences set limits to the dosage and especially to the con-

549

tinued use of antidepressant drugs on a maintenance basis. It has been estimated that perhaps 10 percent of the American population uses psychotropic drugs of all kinds by prescription, which is clearly excessive (Baldessarini, 1978). These limitations and hazards should be borne in mind even while we recognize the progress that has been made in lightening the burdens of affective disorders.

Electroshock

This method of treatment, already described in the last chapter, continues to be used conservatively for depressions, where it often produces definite improvement. It is sometimes reported to have a calming influence in manic disorders, but lithium and tranquilizing drugs have largely supplanted it for this purpose. ECT has been widely used for more than 30 years, which has made it possible to accumulate a good deal of information about results. There is diversity in the reported figures, but complete remission seems to be obtained in from 40 to 80 percent of patients in depressed states, with the higher figure achieved in carefully selected patients (Klerman, 1978). Success is somewhat less in manic attacks. The involutional depressions (occurring in middle age and beyond) generally show the highest rate of improvement. Of course, the rate of spontaneous remission is high in the affective disorders, but ECT serves to hasten the remission and spare the patient many unpleasant and expensive weeks of hospitalization.

An early study (Bond, 1954) compared the recovery rates for 567 depressed and manic patients in the years 1925 to 1934, before ECT was available, and for 563 patients in the years 1940 to 1946, when ECT was regularly available but psychotrophic drugs were not yet in use. The later group showed a definite though not very large advantage in recovery rate, 72 percent as against 59 percent. At five-year follow-up the difference largely disappeared, as the lasting recovery figures were 66 percent and 65 percent. Most striking was the difference found for average length of stay in the hospital: 4.5 months in the earlier period, 2.3 months in the years after the introduction of ECT. Recurrence of disorder occurred more often in the later period. At the end of one year, 16 percent of the earlier cases had relapsed, with 28 percent of the later group, and this difference seemed to be sustained through several more years.

It is clear from these figures that ECT performs its greatest service in reducing the length of attacks. Particularly with depressions, where its benefit is largest, it can spare the patient many days of despair, acute suffering, and expense. On the other hand, it does not seem to reduce the likelihood of future attacks and it may protect the patients even less than spontaneous recovery. There have always been misgivings about its use. Even considering the modern improvements in its implementation, with anesthetics and muscle relaxants administered prior to the convulsive shock, there is no way to eliminate altogether the hazards of absorbing a powerful jolt of electric current. Some

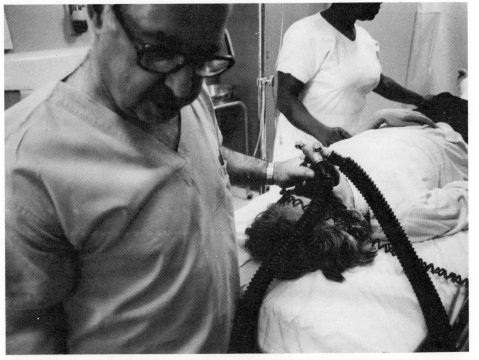

Electroshock therapy remains one of the most effective methods for treating affective disorders, especially intractable depression. However, it is usually the treatment of last resort because chemical treatments can achieve the same objectives usually at modest cost and with somewhat less risk. The woman being treated here has already received injections to induce sleep and relax her muscles. The doctor holds an apparatus that covers her mouth and nose to ensure adequate oxygen supply for the brain when the electric current is passed through the temples to induce a convulsive seizure.

patients dislike it and often become anxious about it, mainly because of unpleasant immediate after-effects: confusion, headache, muscular pains, and partial memory loss for as much as a week or two. The very efficiency of the treatment has led to some indiscriminate use. Earlier there were objections to its use because its mode of action was a mystery, but now it is generally believed that ECT causes rapid turnover of catecholamines in the brain and leaves more norepinephrine available at neural synapses (von Praag, 1977). Because the same objectives can be achieved at modest cost and with less risk by means of antidepressant drugs, ECT has generally become the treatment of last resort. However, it is still used for severe, acutely symptomatic, retarded depressions (Carney & Sheffield, 1974), for actively suicidal patients, and when tricyclics fail to work within a month or so, as happens in as many as 30 percent of severe depressions (Baldessarini, 1978).

SUGGESTIONS FOR FURTHER READING

Ideal as a first step toward increasing one's knowledge of depression is a small but clear and well-balanced survey by J. Mendels, *Concepts of depression* (1970). The literature on the same subject is gathered up in considerable detail by A.T. Beck in *Depression: Clinical, experimental and theoretical aspects* (1967), with possibly an overemphasis on how little of our knowledge has actually been proved. F.F. Flach and S.C. Draghi have brought together an excellent collection by leading experts in the field, titled *The nature and treatment of depression* (1977). G. Klerman presents a general up-to-date synopsis in his chapter on "Affective Disorders" in *The Harvard guide to modern psychiatry* (1978). Excellent for its clinical descriptions is E. Kraepelin's *Manic-depressive insanity and paranoia* (1921).

The epidemiology of depression (1968) by C. Silverman is devoted almost exclusively to actuarial facts about the affective disorders. In a small book, *Anxiety and depression* (1976), C. G. Costello offers a concise review of research and theory, with some emphasis on psychological considerations. E. Jacobson's *Depression: Comparative studies of normal, neurotic and psychotic conditions* (1971) gathers together her many influential papers on the subject from a psychoanalytic viewpoint. M.E.P. Seligman formulates a systematic psychological account of depression from a learning theory perspective in *Helplessness: On depression, development and death* (1975). An authoritative volume on the subject of suicide is E. S. Schneidman, N. Farberow, and R. Litman, *The psychology of suicide* (1970).

In addition to C. W. Beers' A mind that found itself (1931), which is used in the text to provide illustrations of depressed and manic states, there are other interesting inside accounts of affective disorders; for instance, *Reluctantly told* (1927) by J. Hillyer. Some cases of this kind are contained in a collection edited by B. Kaplan, *The inner world of mental illness* (1964); other firsthand accounts will be found in C. Landis and F. A. Mettler, *Varieties of psychopathological experience* (1964), Chapters 12 and 13.

A strong genetic orientation is prominent in *Manic-depressive illness* (1969) by G. Winokur, P. Clayton, and T. Reich. *Lithium: Its role in psychiatric research and treatment* (1973), edited by S. Gershon and B. Shopsin, brings together a collection of reports on one of the most important means of somatic treatment for affective disorders. An extremely thorough and authoritative review of biochemical treatment methods is contained in R. J. Baldessarini's chapter on "Chemotherapy" in *The Harvard guide to modern psychiatry* (1978).

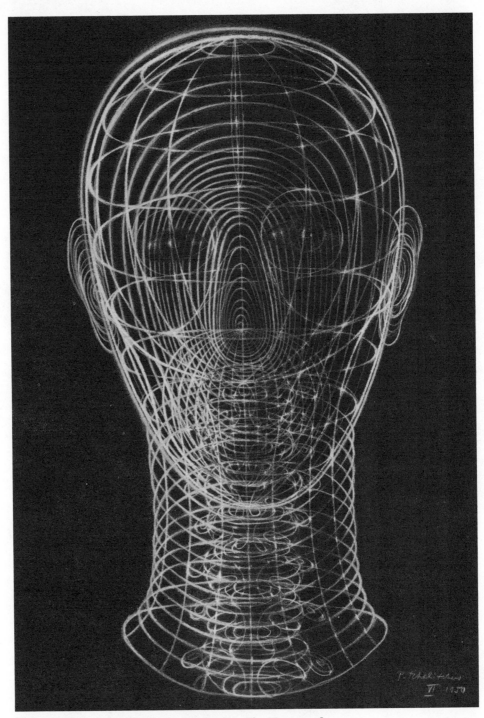

Head, VI (1950) by Pavil Tchlitchew. Collection, The Museum of
Modern Art, New York. Gift of Edgar Kaufman, Jr.

15
Brain Disorders

In our clinical introduction we made the acquaintance of a woman with a severe brain disorder. The case of Martha Ottenby formed a contrast with those people whose disorders arose from personal difficulties in living. She was the victim of a disease, an impersonal affliction that struck her without the slightest discernible relation to current life stress or to changes in her economy of happiness. In studying psychophysiological disorders we saw emotional problems. With the disorders now to be examined the situation is chronologically reversed. The trouble starts in neural tissue or in biochemical abnormalities that directly affect neural tissue. Disorders of behavior, feeling, and cognition follow, but as consequences of pathological influences on the operation of the nervous system.

The study of brain disorders lies by no means outside of the province of abnormal psychology. Historically this province has always included the mental and behavioral changes that result from injuries or other unusual conditions in the nervous system. How the brain works has been for many years the object of intensive research in laboratories all over the world. A review confined to the topic of recovery of function following brain injury included no less than 223 references (Rosner, 1970). Most research, of course, is done with animals, and therefore cannot include certain peculiarly human capacities such as speech and sustained thought. But diseases and accidental injuries in the human brain have added to the store of knowledge and given us fascinating insights into what is involved in complex activities like speaking, writing, linguistic understanding, planning, and the organization of behavior. One is likely to end with great respect for the infinitely complex organ that at its best manages such striking accomplishments, not the least of which is the study of itself.

VARIETIES OF PATHOLOGICAL PROCESS

What mishaps can befall the central nervous system, especially the brain? Encased within bony walls, the brain, like the spinal cord, is protected against certain obvious hazards. But it is by no means immune to injury or to internal conditions that impair its proper functioning. By way of initial orientation we survey the pathological processes that affect brain activity, citing illustrative syndromes for each.

Congenital Malformation

The first possibility is an inadequate development of brain tissue, technically called *aplasia*. Occasionally a child is born with almost no development of the cerebral cortex, a truly rudimentary brain. In cases of less severe defect the brain may be completely formed but of smaller than average size and with less well-marked convolutions, suggesting a primitiveness of structure. One variety of severe mental defect, microcephaly, is characterized by a greatly diminished size of the upper skull; within this constricted space the brain is small and poorly developed. In Down's syndrome the abnormality in the shape of the head is less marked, though still destructive, and the brain shows few obvious structural defects, but mental performance is sluggish and seriously deficient. These and several other types of congenital malformation, most of them accompanied by mental retardation, are examined in Chapter 16.

Traumatic Injury

Next on the list of cerebral mishaps is *trauma*, some direct physical injury to brain tissue. The head and the underlying cerebral tissue may be traumatized at the time of birth if the labor is extremely prolonged and difficult, so that the head is exposed to severe pressure. Any severe blow on the head may produce swelling and injury of brain tissue. Most children, of course, fall on their heads from time to time without damage, but occasionally one of these accidents produces temporary or even permanent brain injury. If the skull is fractured, and especially if brain tissue is penetrated as is the case in bullet or shrapnel wounds, a marked change in mental performance may result. Even when the wounds heal there may be atrophy and scar formation in the brain that impair its normal functioning.

Vehicular accidents alone account for three million head injuries every year in the United States, including 750,000 concussions, 150,000 skull fractures, and 150,000 significant brain injuries (Tuerk, Fish, & Ransohoff, 1975). Loss of consciousness commonly occurs in brain injuries, and the length of the period of unconsciousness is positively correlated with the extent of brain damage. It is believed that the loss of consciousness is attributable to changes in the reticular formation of the brain-stem. There is usually some temporary amnesia, which disappears with improvement. Damage may take the form of bruises, lacerations, or blood-filled swelling of the brain. Neurological symptoms may reflect either damage from the original trauma or various consequences of it, such as swelling, inflammation, infection, or seizures.

Brain Tumors

Another form of direct injury is caused by *brain tumors*. They account for less than 1 percent of new cases in general psychiatric practice, but mental hospitals find them present in 1.5 to 4.0 percent of their autopsies (Benson & Geschwind, 1975). As a tumor grows, it crowds and distorts the surrounding brain tissue. Up to a certain point, especially if the growth is slow, the brain can adapt itself to the change without functional impairment, but eventually the crowding prevents normal metabolism in the nerve cells.

Common symptoms are headache, vomiting, cranial pressure, seizures, paralysis, and visual defects. Behavioral changes usually occur before neurological symptoms appear, so that most tumor cases are seen first by psychiatrists. A simple test, the copying of line drawings, may often be diagnostic because the presence of the tumor interferes with the visual-motor coordination underlying geometric construction.

A Dramatic Example.   Charles Whitman was an honor student in architectural engineering at the University of Texas and a past Eagle Scout and scout leader. In a short space of time he developed tremendous headaches that caused him to worry about his health. Suddenly one day in 1966, with seemingly little provocation, he shot and killed his mother and wife. Then he took six guns and provisions to the top of a tower on the university campus, from where he shot 46 persons, killing 16. Police marksmen finally killed him. He left a note

557

complaining about the headaches and requesting an autopsy to determine whether he had a mental disorder. The autopsy revealed a large brain tumor. Quite possibly the tumor affected sections of his brain that control aggressive responses, and contributed to his bizarre rampage (McCaghy, 1976).

Infection

The nervous system may become the seat of *infection* by microorganisms. Certain not very common forms of illness such as "sleeping sickness" represent an inflammation of cerebral tissue resulting from infection. Some forms are benign, leading to full recovery, but others are malignant or even fatal, involving devastating memory loss and striking personality changes that mimic functional psychoses (Seltzer & Frazier, 1978). Other infectious conditions are pneumonia, typhoid fever, meningitis, and malaria, which sometimes cause acute inflammation of the brain and its coverings, with fever, delirium, and confusional state. Although resistant to most varieties of infection, brain tissue is susceptible to all of these.

In Chapter 1 we considered the best known infectious disease, *general paresis*. It has been recognized since 1798 but not well understood until early in this century. In 1877 von Krafft-Ebing suggested the following possible causes: heredity, dissipation (Bacchus and Venus), smoking of 10 to 20 Virginia cigars, excessive heat and cold, trauma to the head, exhaustive efforts to make a living, weak nerves, and fright. Actually, it had been suspected by others since 1857 that syphilis causes paresis. Half a century later syphilitic spirochetes were definitively located in the cortex of general paretics, forestalling the demise of the tobacco industry in Virginia (Bruetsch, 1975)! Before the discovery of penicillin, syphilis was one of the most common causes of dementia (insanity), accounting for 20 to 32 percent of psychiatric hospitalizations throughout the world, but by 1970 that figure had dropped to less than 1 percent. The incubation period ranges from three to forty years, averaging about fifteen years. The symptoms may include memory loss, apathy, anxiety, emotional instability, euphoria, loss of judgment, irritability, slovenliness, and sudden violence. One afflicted man drove through a red light at high speed, killing a pedestrian; when arrested, he didn't comprehend the seriousness of the charge against him and told police in an excited manner that he was King Herod. Another paretic came home with a six-foot maple tree and tried to plant it on the windowsill! Such gross loss of judgment is a basic symptom, from which delusions originate. Grandiose delusions are the most common, the victims claiming to be kings, czars, great inventors, war heroes, or other great personages. In the final stages, general paresis presents the most extreme form of dementia that is known. On autopsy, there is general atrophy of brain tissues with obvious shrinkage of the cerebral cortex.

The Wasserman test of the blood, a diagnostic procedure for syphilis, is positive in 95 percent of general paretics, and EEG tracings are abnormal in

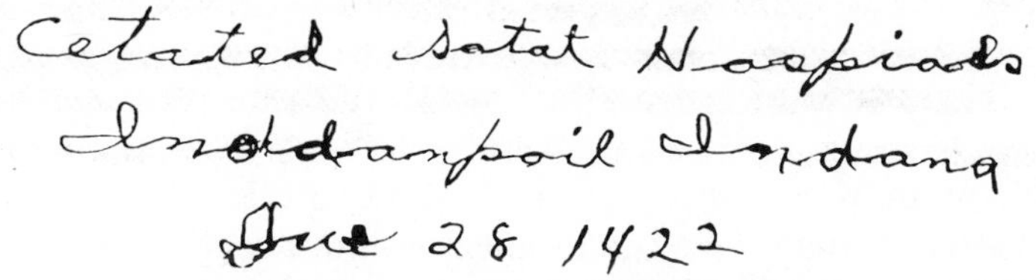

Cetated satat Haspiads
Inodranpoil Iordang
Aue 28 1422

Figure 15.1.
Physical symptoms of general paresis develop gradually: speech becomes slurred; abnormalities appear in the pupils of the eyes; there are changes in tendon reflexes; and handwriting becomes distorted. Here is a sample of handwriting in general paresis. The patient was asked to write Central State Hospital, Indianapolis, Indiana, and the date, which was June 28, 1952. *Source:* Arieti (1975).

most cases, usually those that develop seizures. Treatment at first employed various compounds like mercury. Later a popular method was to induce malaria, allowing the fever to reach 103 to 105 degrees several times, and then terminating the malaria with quinine. This procedure earned Dr. Wagner-Jauregg, a Viennese psychiatrist, the Nobel prize for medicine in 1927 (Bruetsch, 1975). In 1943 it was discovered that penicillin kills the spirochetes, and since then antibiotics have been the preferred method of treatment. More than 80 percent of the victims of syphilis can be cured when treated early with penicillin (Sherwin & Geschwind, 1978). General paresis only develops when syphilis remains untreated for several years. It should be remembered that, although paresis can be prevented with timely treatment, venereal diseases (including syphilis) have not been eliminated.

Metabolic Abnormalities

The functioning of the brain can be disturbed by unfavorable alterations in its internal environment. The maintenance of an internal condition that is optimal for cerebral functioning is part of the general process of homeostasis. *Metabolic disorders* may throw out the balance in one way or another so that optimal functioning is impaired. Certain endocrine disorders, for instance, especially those affecting the thyroid gland, bear a direct relation to mood, initiative, and intelligence. Furthermore, recent research has shown that vitamin deficiency plays a part in certain kinds of mental disorder. For example, deficiency of vitamin B_1 (thiamine) in the diet leads to *Wernicke's encephalopathy*, an acute confusional state that features apathy, eye movement paralysis, and memory impairment. The disorder responds well to improved nutrition, but without treatment it may lead to chronic and permanent *Korsakoff's syndrome*, with fixed memory deficit (Seltzer & Frazier, 1978). In this condition there is loss of recent memory but relative preservation of immediate and remote memory—that is, the person can recall clearly events from

559

childhood or repeat a series of numbers just recited, but may not remember his or her telephone number or the name of the doctor just introduced twenty minutes earlier. *Confabulation* is a dramatic feature of the disorder: the person replaces forgotten facts with fantasies and elaborate fabrications. In normal conversation we are often aware of rounding out a detail or two to make the story better; patients who can't remember most of the story do this in a big way. The condition was first observed by Korsakoff in 1887 among alcoholics with advanced brain damage, and also by Wernicke in patients following acute inflammation of the brain. It is known to result from malnutrition, which is common in alcoholics, but also from vascular disease and from trauma, often in the limbic region of the brain. The importance of this knowledge lies in locating the control and disturbance of recent memory in the limbic structures of the temporal lobe (Sherwin & Geschwind, 1978).

Parkinson's disease is a relatively common syndrome, with tremor, rigidity, expressionless facial appearance, shuffling gait, and "pill rolling" movements of the hands. Reduced intellectual capacity is observed in almost half of the cases and depression is found in most, probably owing to dopamine deficiency, the primary cause of the disorder. Some symptoms respond well to *levodopa*, a drug precursor of dopamine (Seltzer & Frazier, 1978).

Cerebral vascular accidents (CVAs) or strokes may be caused by blood clots or other obstructions of blood vessels (such as an air bubble), expansion or other distortion of a blood vessel because of weakness in the wall of the vessel, or hemorrhage. These produce acute disorders that cause *focal* brain damage (located in one place). Sometimes a series of minor CVAs may occur in hypertensive people, resulting in gradual progression of general dementia (Seltzer & Frazier, 1978).

Two other metabolic disorders, *shortage of oxygen* and *cerebral arteriosclerosis*, will be reviewed in detail later in this chapter.

Intoxication

In the last chapter we learned of the importance of electrolyte metabolism and of biogenic amines in nervous activity, especially in relation to mood level. The internal environment can also be altered by the action of *toxins* or poisons. The toxic effects of excessive alcohol come under most frequent observation, but analogous changes result from other drugs, certain metals like lead, and certain gases like carbon monoxide. Intoxication typically produces an acute confusional state with inattentiveness, hallucinations, and sometimes depression in the level of consciousness (from sedatives and hypnotic drugs) or hyperactive agitation (from stimulants). In addition to the nutritional deficiencies already discussed, alcohol addiction can cause brain damage through acute metabolic changes from the toxic effects of the alcohol itself.

Not infrequently, the most extreme aberrations may be seen on withdrawal of an intoxicating drug. For example, *delirium tremens* (DTs) may start three or four days after the cessation of heavy drinking and last 2 to 3 days or as long as a week. The person becomes sweaty, tremulous, hyperactive, restless, and shows quickened pulse, dilated pupils, and acute visual and auditory hallucinations (Seltzer & Frazier, 1978). The mortality rate for people suffering from the DTs may run as high as 15 percent (Victor, 1975).

Degenerative Disease

Finally, the central nervous system is subject to *degenerative changes*. Usually these are associated with old age, but sometimes, as in *Pick's disease* (from which Martha Ottenby suffered) and the rather similar *Alzheimer's disease*, changes of an apparently degenerative character begin in middle life. An invariable feature of Alzheimer's disease is the development of senile *plaques* (patches of deteriorated tissue) in the brain, especially in those structures located near the center of the brain and in the association areas of the cortex. These plaques are very similar to those found in very aged normals, and in Alzheimer's disease their quantity is directly correlated with the severity of clinical symptoms (Ferraro, 1975). The onset of the disease is usually in the fifth decade of life; progressive deterioration lasts for about four to seven years until death occurs. It accounts for 4 percent of the deaths studied by autopsy in psychiatric institutions. Slightly more than half of those affected are women (Busse, 1978). In the initial stages people with the affliction are neat, socially appropriate, and withdrawn, indicating that the frontal lobes are the last to be affected by the disease. The principal symptoms are memory impairment, illogical reasoning, empty or stereotyped speech, difficulty in putting things together, disorientation, and emotional volatility. Patients have trouble finding words, for example, identifying the lenses of spectacles as "the inside of glasses" or the frames as "the outer part." Getting dressed when a sleeve is turned inside out may cause a desperate struggle, with perplexity and ultimately failure. Insight is generally well preserved. In the final stages there are seizures, rigidity, and involuntary movements of the arms and legs, meaningless grasping and sucking responses, and invariably death (Seltzer & Frazier, 1978). Autopsy reveals gross cerebral atrophy, stringy filaments in the neurons, and the distinctive senile plaques.

Pick's disease likewise causes presenile dementia with onset in the middle fifties, and it affects twice as many women as men, but characteristically it affects the frontal and temporal lobes of the brain first (Corsellis, 1976), so that apathy and asocial behavior are prominent but intellect is relatively well preserved (Sherwin & Geschwind, 1978).

Some families have a high prevalence of Alzheimer's disease (Pratt, 1970). It appears that both Pick's and Alzheimer's diseases may be transmitted genetically, though the precise genetic mechanism is unclear (Busse, 1978). There is no treatment known for either disease.

Huntington's chorea is another degenerative disease that strikes about five people in 100,000 (Ball, Heaton, & Reitan, 1974). It is transmitted in classical Mendelian fashion as a dominant gene with almost complete penetrance, so

561

that 50 percent of the offspring of an affected person receive the gene and any-one who carries the gene and lives to the fourth or fifth decade of life will ulti-mately develop the disease. Onset occasionally occurs in childhood or adoles-cence, leading rapidly to death, but usually the symptoms appear between 30 and 50 years of age and progress gradually over 10 to 15 years until death oc-curs (Whittier, 1975). There is a slowly progressive dilapidation of all cogni-tive powers with apathy and inertia, ultimately leading to a mute, motionless state, but aphasia (language impairment), cortical blindness, or amnesia are seldom found (McHugh & Folstein, 1975). There are brief, quick, aimless mo-tions called chorea or choreiform movements, incoordination, and difficulty articulating speech. Many of the psychiatric symptoms are hard to distinguish from those of functional psychosis: depression, hallucinations, irritability, hostility, fits of rage and assaultiveness, sloppy indifference, and paranoid fea-tures (Seltzer & Frazier, 1978). Memory defects, disorientation, and loss of judgment are also common. Huntington's patients are highly disposed to alco-holism, drug abuse, and sexual promiscuity, partly because of the disinhibi-tion caused by atrophy of the brain. The degenerative changes affect primar-ily the cerebral cortex and the lower part of the brain, leading ultimately to total dementia, ceaseless choreiform movements, and death.

The Committee to Combat Huntington's Disease was formed in 1967 at the initiative of Marjorie Guthrie, the wife of singer Woodie Guthrie, who died from the affliction. Now there are chapters in most states in this country and elsewhere in the world that seek to promote research on the disease, genetic counseling, and clinical assistance for afflicted people and their families (Whittier, 1975).

Multiple sclerosis is a remitting and relapsing disease of the central nervous system accompanied by damage to the *myelin sheath* that covers CNS struc-tures, which causes paralysis, awkward speech, painful spasms, and numb-ness. Euphoria occasionally accompanies these painful and depressing afflic-tions, which indicates damage in the frontal lobes of the brain. In the later stages there is blindness, irritability, poor judgment, incontinence, and intel-lectual deterioration (Seltzer & Frazier, 1978). The cause of this disease is un-known, although there is some evidence that humans may acquire it by viral infection from small house-bound dogs with distemper (Jotkowitz, 1977).

EVALUATION OF ORGANIC BRAIN DISEASE

It is estimated that organic brain disorders account for one in five first admis-sions to mental hospitals (Seltzer & Frazier, 1978). The task of evaluating these disorders is extremely complex, involving both neurological and psychi-atric assessments. Lipowski (1975) argues that the neurological basis of psy-chopathology has been neglected recently, partly in reaction against the old-fashioned neuropsychiatry, which attempted to account for all of mental illness in terms of neuropathology. Since most of our attention to this point has been directed to psychological processes, we concentrate here mainly on the neurological assessments.

Psychiatric evaluation focuses on the content and process of thinking, judgment, reasoning, and ability to evaluate reality. Without neurological damage, disturbance in these functions suggests psychological disorder. Our ability to assess them is crude, however, and does not help to distinguish organic disorders from "functional" ones very well. Hence, for purposes of *differential diagnosis*, more emphasis is placed on other cognitive functions that primarily reflect organic damage: attention, short- and long-term memory, language, orientation, and construction ability (such as drawing, stick design, and maze learning). Disturbances in comprehension, calculation, knowledge, behavior, plus lability or shallowness of emotion may indicate organic syndromes if they reveal morbid *change* in subjective experience or objective performance, but they are somewhat more ambiguous because they can also occur in extreme psychological disorders (Seltzer & Frazier, 1978). Diagnosis of older people is further complicated by the fact that degenerative, vascular, toxic, and other brain diseases increase sharply with advanced age. For example, more than a third of all patients 65 or older who are discharged from general hospital psychiatric units in this country are given the diagnosis of organic brain disease (Lipowski, 1975). It is extremely difficult to discriminate normal and probably irreversible processes of aging from abnormal and potentially treatable organic processes.

There are several aspects of the evaluation to be considered. The first requirement is to classify the organic brain disease itself, which results from neurological damage or temporary metabolic derangement in the brain or one of its parts. One must also evaluate the reactive syndromes (psychoses, anxiety reactions, personality and behavioral disorders) that represent maladaptive ways of coping with organic (including cerebral) disease and its psychological and social consequences, which are subjectively distressing. Finally one must consider deviant illness behavior, such as self-destructive resistance to medical management, massive denial of illness, extreme dependency on doctors or family members, and the like, which may result in psychological invalidism or even death. In the first instance above, the organic structures for thinking are damaged or disturbed and require direct, usually medical, intervention. In the other instances the main problems concern the *interpretation* and *meaning* of information, distress related to the illness, and the attempts to cope with disability, symptoms, and stigma (Lipowski, 1975). These typically call for psychologically oriented treatment.

Diagnostic tests of blood or cerebrospinal fluid can detect many metabolic disturbances, syphilis, and other infections. Various radiological procedures can locate tumors, *subdural hematomas* (bruises in the brain), and vascular disease. Computerized axial tomography (CAT scan) is one of the most recently developed of these, which employs a sequence of cross-sectional X rays

563

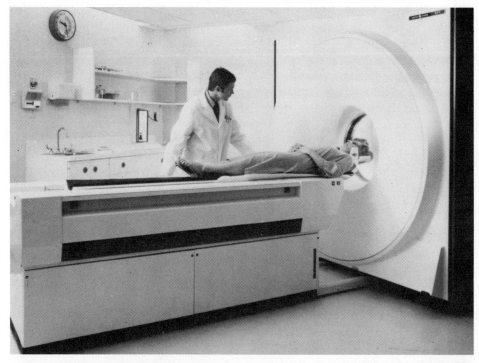

Computerized axial tomography or CAT scan represents one of the greatest technological advances for the diagnosis of brain damage. This Total Body Scanner system can complete an entire scan of any portion of the head and body in as little as 4.8 seconds. By compiling a sequence of cross-sectional X rays taken from different angles, it forms a composite picture that is multidimensional, locating precisely areas of injury or degeneration.

of the brain taken from different angles to arrive at a composite picture that is multidimensional. (Diagnosis of Martha Ottenby's brain disease with a CAT scan, had it been available, would probably have been immediate and definitive.) Psychological tests are useful for assessing dementia because of the general deterioration in intellectual abilities usually found in dementia. They can also be used to assess the type and amount of language deficit in aphasia, to evaluate sensory and memory loss, and to determine the location of focal brain damage.

In the remainder of the chapter we examine in some detail the effects of *localized* brain injury, especially in those areas that seem to serve fairly complex functions. Although local brain injuries are not especially common, they have been investigated with unusual care, and the use of brain surgery for certain types of disorder has yielded further information. Then we turn to the *general* consequences of abnormal conditions in the brain, examining the effects of oxygen deprivation, the mental state of delirium, and the intellectual changes believed to result from a diffuse lowering of cerebral efficiency. Next we give attention to brain injury in children, considering especially the overall effects on behavior and the problems inherent in training and schooling. One special form of disorder, epilepsy, will repay examination as a problem both of cerebral function and of adaptation to the fact of illness. Finally we survey the disorders of old age, placed against the background of the changed abilities and psychological situation of older people.

EFFECTS OF LOCALIZED CORTICAL INJURY

In war and in civilian accidents the brain is sometimes the site of direct physical injury. This injury is chiefly to the cerebral cortex, which lies directly beneath the skull, although it may reach the thalamus and lower brain centers as well. Occasionally the cortex is the site of disease such as brain tumor or a degenerative process, so that parts of the tissue have to be surgically removed. These accidents and interventions have contributed a good deal to our knowledge of the human brain.

One possible idea about the cerebral cortex would be that each bit of it governed some particular process or activity. We know that in the spinal cord there is clear localization of this kind, and that in lower brain structures such as medulla, cerebellum, and thalamus it has been possible to find centers for fairly specific functions. In 1861 the French surgeon Broca made a discovery that suggested precise localization in the cortex itself. He had the opportunity to examine carefully and later to do an autopsy on a patient who for many years had been unable to speak. There were no defects in the muscles involved in speech, and the patient could communicate by signs in a way that indicated unimpaired intelligence. The autopsy showed a small circumscribed lesion, apparently of long standing, in the left cerebral hemisphere. This led Broca to conclude that he had located the center for speech. His discovery inspired subsequent investigators to try to map the functions of the rest of the cortex. Most of the research was done with animals, but there were occasional opportunities to make parallel observations with human subjects. On the whole the results have not been what Broca would have expected. Some areas, to be sure, have a certain specificity. It can be predicted, for instance, that injury to the occipital poles, at the very back of the head, will cause an interference with visual functions but not affect auditory or motor processes; similarly, that injury to the temporal lobes, in the temples, is likely to affect auditory functions but leave vision undisturbed. The largest part of the cortex, however, seems to have very little specificity of function; and its injury has often produced fewer identifiable consequences than might have been expected.

Findings of this kind have led some workers to believe that the functions of the cerebral cortex are of a highly general nature. In the most radical form of this theory, it is claimed that the various parts are largely equipotential: defects will be in proportion to the amount of tissue that is damaged, more or less regardless of its location. In effect this assigns to the cortex a generalized organizing power, leaving to lower centers the specifics of what is to be organized. Comparing the two views, the student will recognize one of those situations where the truth is more likely to lie somewhere in the middle than at either extreme. There is certainly some localization in the cortex, but it is equally certain that we would miss important information if we were not alert to the general consequences of abnormal conditions in the brain.

We consider first the effects that seem to be closely connected with location. The cortex has been mapped by Brodmann into forty-six areas distinguished by the architecture of the cell layers. Part of this scheme is represented by the numbers on the accompanying figure (Figure 15-2), which shows the left cerebral hemisphere as it would be seen from the left side. These structurally different areas, however, correspond in only a few cases to areas having known specific functions. The diversity of architecture is not matched by diversity of functions.

The main sensory receiving stations in the cortex occupy a relatively small space. Area 17 is the center for vision, area 41 for hearing, areas 1, 2, 3, and 5 for touch and pressure from skin and deep end organs. The areas immediately surrounding these centers probably have a somewhat restricted function; area 18, for instance, is believed to be limited to the perceptual elaboration of visual impressions. Area 4 is the motor area, which when stimulated gives rise to specific muscular movements, and area 6 seems closely related to the motor sphere. This is about as far as one can go with specific localizations. Of the remaining parts of the cortex, two large zones are of particular interest. One of these is the *frontal* area, represented by the numbers 9, 10, 11, and possibly

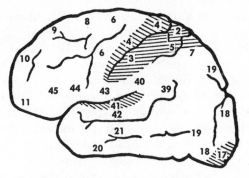

Figure 15.2

Schematic drawing of the left lateral aspect of the human cortex. The numbers are those assigned by Brodmann on the basis of cellular architecture. The shaded areas are those having fairly definite functions, as described in the text. Areas 9, 10, 11, and 45 together constitute the prefrontal area. The parietotemporal area is represented by the numbers 39, 40, 42, 43, and 44. (From Cobb, 1941, p. 72.)

45. It is the elaborate development of the frontal cortex that gives humans their high forehead and intelligent appearance in comparison with chimpanzees and monkeys, so that in popular thought the frontal areas are associated with the distinctively human attainments. The other area, the *parietotemporal*, represented on the diagram by the numbers 39, 40, 42, 43, and 44, turns out in fact to bear a special relation to the distinctively human attainments of language and the meaning of symbols. Curiously enough, this complex array of skills is dependent only on the leading or dominant hemisphere, the left in right-handed people. (It is unclear which hemisphere is dominant in left-handed people [Sherwin & Geschwind, 1978].) Injury to the parietotemporal area in the dominant hemisphere is a disaster. Injury to the corresponding area in the other hemisphere has somewhat less serious consequences, having no effect, for instance, on language. To this extent there is localization of function between the two hemispheres. Research on penetrating head wounds indicates that the areas in the left hemisphere governing the right hand do not exactly correspond to the areas in the right hemisphere controlling the left hand, which suggests that the organization of the two sides of the brain may be different (Semmes et al., 1960).

Many difficulties beset the investigator of localized injuries. Even when lesions can be fairly precisely located, account must be taken of the character of the injury. It has been shown that focal and diffuse lesions on the same site produce detectably different effects; that static and progressive lesions have different results; and even that it is possible to discern different consequences of lesions resulting from tumor, vascular disease, inflammation, and degenerative disorders (Reitan, 1962). Furthermore, the same kind of lesion in the same place will produce effects that differ from one person to another. The results of individual learning are represented in the brain, but since no two histories of personal experience are exactly alike we cannot expect that they will be registered in a standard manner in standard locations. Each brain becomes unique through the process of learning (Penfield & Perot, 1963). The effect of an injury is also influenced by the time of life at which the lesion occurs. Younger and older brains, differing in the amount and organization of experience, are differently affected by the same disease.

Injury in the Parietotemporal Area

Injury to the parietotemporal area in the dominant hemisphere produces an effect chiefly on language. This area lies between the centers for vision, the centers for hearing, and the motor centers. The use of language involves vision (apprehending the written word), hearing (apprehending the spoken word), and the motor acts of speaking and writing. It is not surprising, therefore, that injury to the parietotemporal cortex disturbs the language function in one way or another. The resulting conditions are known by the general name of *aphasia*.

567

The results of injury are extremely complex. At first sight the disorders seem highly selective and highly restricted. Thus one patient may display only an inability to read, with the understanding of spoken language and speech and writing being uninjured. Another may have a specific inability to find words, especially nouns, to express thoughts. Such a patient may show by gestures and fragments of speech perfect memory for the details of a walk just taken, but be unable to bring out the proper words to describe the objects seen along the way. A patient described by Hollingworth (1930) used almost no substantives, but inserted the automatisms "seriat" and "feriat" in their place. When asked where he lived, he said, "I come from seriat." When asked his occupation, he said, "I am a feriat." He drew a picture of an anvil, which he called a "seriat," and remarked that he worked at it. When the examiner called it an anvil he brightened and said, "That's it, you said it, it's a seriat." When he tried to read aloud he pronounced practically every word "seriat." Sometimes the disorder is even more narrowly selective. A foreign language is lost but the native tongue is unaffected. The extreme is represented in the case of a patient formerly able to read music who after his injury could read music in the key of C, with some difficulty in the key of G, and not at all in other keys. In all these cases it is apparent that general understanding is not greatly injured. The person seems to grasp much more than the injured language function is able to represent.

The high specificity of some of these losses has tempted many workers to think that the different aspects of language are localized in small specific parts of the cortex. Injury at one spot causes word blindness, at another spot word deafness, at another spot the comprehension of sentences, at still another spot the speaking of nouns, and so on. The parietotemporal cortex has even been compared to a typewriter keyboard, to a complex piece of electrical wiring, and to a computer. There may be something to these analogies, though they seem a little too metallic to explain the workings of an organ made up of living cells. The work of Penfield and his associates (1959) certainly indicates that there is some specialization among the cortical areas that subserve language. These workers have investigated the cortex very carefully in the course of brain surgery conducted with local anaesthesia of the scalp. The patients were comfortable and fully conscious, hence able to report on their experiences. Electrical stimulation somewhere in the region of areas 43 and 44 produced an arrest of speech: the patients knew what they wanted to say but could not say it. A little further back the effect of stimulation was to prevent the finding of names and nouns as in the case mentioned above. Such findings leave no doubt that there is an appreciable division of labor within the area responsible for language.

Two points are of especial importance here for the understanding of aphasic disorders. In the first place, the effect of electrical stimulation in the parietotemporal area appears to be inhibitory instead of excitatory. It does not, like stimulation in the motor area, produce involuntary overt movement. It does not cause the person to speak aphasically or to make incorrect writing movements. The person must be engaged in conversation and must take the initiative to speak in order to reveal the consequences of the stimulation. These consequences can be understood only as a suppression of accustomed behavior patterns. In the second place, what is suppressed can best be considered not as specific elements of speech but as larger linguistic functions such as the finding of words appropriate to express one's thoughts and the placing of words in grammatical arrangement. Penfield's experimental findings on speech are therefore consistent with the ideas of Hughlings Jackson, who in the nineteenth century conceived of the aphasias as disturbances of "propositional thinking," and of Henry Head, who after much experience with brain injuries in World War I reached the conclusion that the central disorder was of "symbolic formulation and expression." It is not parts of speech that are lost through injury; it is rather some part of the symbolizing activity that goes on in the understanding and use of language (Osgood & Miron, 1963).

These reflections make it possible to grasp more clearly the process of recovery from aphasia. Good results are often obtained by a process of retraining. Most, though not all, aphasias involve focal lesions. The language disorder results from organic disconnection between parts of the brain that control perception or expression from those that control thinking and memory. If the neural obstructions do not recover or cannot be circumvented by using other neural pathways, then the impairment becomes permanent (Sherwin & Geschwind, 1978). Retraining in such cases is directed toward finding some roundabout method of overcoming the defect. For example, if the person is neurologically incapable of recognizing objects through the visual medium, it may nevertheless be possible to learn to read again by a combination of eye movements and finger movements, tracing the letters with the fingers and following them with the eyes in order to provide the cues necessary for recognition. More typically, however, retraining does not involve new learning; it involves the reappearance of old learning that had been suppressed by the injury (Goodglass & Blumstein, 1973). It may take a long time to bring about some use of the suppressed function, but once it has begun to operate again it may soon be wholly restored. If our aphasic ironworker, for example, could be brought to use a few appropriate nouns instead of "seriat" and "feriat," he might presently recover the complete use of substantives. Some total aphasics have recovered virtually full use of language after a year or more of retraining in northern parts of the country, but resumed their speaking without impairment of their southern accents. This shows that resurgence of old learning is taking place, not new learning.

Injury to the Frontal Areas

It was long supposed that the frontal lobes were the seat of the highest intellectual functions, but research has demonstrated conclusively that this is not true. Removal of either frontal lobe may produce deficits in memory, concentration, and speed of thought, or it may cause an exaggerated sense of well-being (euphoria), restlessness, loss of initiative, or depression. These changes are distinctly nonintellectual in character and, by and large, not extensive ones. Neither does there appear to be much localization of specific functions there (Meyer, 1961).

This does not imply that the frontal lobes are a mere luxury without functions. It means that the functions are general, hard to measure, and not mainly intellectual. A clue to their nature is suggested in a case studied with great care and reported in a book by Brickner (1936). The patient, a successful broker, was operated on for cerebral tumor. The growth was extensive so that it proved necessary to remove from the left side most of area 8 and all of areas 9, 10, 11, and 45; from the right side a slightly larger area was excised. At the time of operation the patient was forty years old. Prior to his illness he had been an energetic, intelligent businessman, but in other respects a rather mild and submissive individual. As a child he was quiet and shy, dependent on his mother. When he married, following a courtship in which the girl took the active part, he expressed the desire to continue living in his parents' home. He rarely displayed aggression except in the form of facetious and somewhat boastful stories. Such was the man on whom the operation was performed. The effect of removing the frontal lobes was so great that the patient was never able to go back to work. Initiative was impaired, memory was imperfect, distractibility was increased, and the patient showed a clear deficit in judgment and logical reason. More striking, however, was the change in his self-criticism and self-restraint. After the operation he experienced considerable euphoria and appeared to lose all restraint over his previous mild boastfulness. He proclaimed himself the best of all businessmen, the man whom nobody could fool, and he told stories of youthful sexual exploits and of playground fights in which he knocked down all comers. Along with boastfulness and aggression his dependent tendencies were also exaggerated. He allowed others to bathe and dress him and care for all his wants. The constructive organization of personality was more markedly injured than the intellectual processes.

Prefrontal Lobotomy

It was this general picture of frontal lobe functions that prompted the Portuguese surgeon Moniz in 1935 to make the bold experiment of trying to relieve certain serious mental symptoms by brain surgery. He reasoned that patients who showed a tremendous excess of control, with constant tension, anxiety, and anguish, might be relieved and placed in a more relaxed frame of mind by deliberate interference with the frontal lobes. Prefrontal lobotomy does not involve the removal of nervous tissue, and the cerebral cortex is touched only to the extent that may be required for introducing the instrument. The purpose of prefrontal lobotomy is to sever some of the neural connections between the frontal lobes and other parts of the brain, particularly the thalamus and

570

hypothalamus. It might be described as an attempt to reduce the action of the frontal lobes upon the rest of the system, and it actually effects a partial isolation of the prefrontal cortex—areas 9, 10, 11, and 45. Although surgery of any kind is naturally frightening, the operation itself is not unusually difficult for the patient. It can be carried out under local anaesthesia with the patient fully conscious and able to talk.

The immediate effect of the operation is a stuporous and mildly confused state, but this passes in the course of time. Given standard intelligence tests after recovery, the patients perform nearly as well as they did before surgery. There is some impairment in accuracy, generalizing, profiting from past mistakes, and planning ahead. The main changes in behavior are similar to those described in Brickner's patient, although less extreme. There is a reduction in drive and self-concern, a superficial or shallow affect, and stimulus-bound responses to environmental cues—in short, the same sort of changes observed in frontal lobe syndromes of natural origin (Sherwin & Geschwind, 1978). Even Freeman (1955), the controversial enthusiast for psychosurgery, conceded that lobotomized patients become a little obtuse to the impression that they make on others and less capable of foresight. During the period between 1935 and 1952 many thousands of patients the world over received prefrontal lobotomy, many at the hands of Freeman himself, and there was widespread support for the procedure because of the emotional relief it brought for patients and hospital staff members, though empirical evaluations of its effectiveness showed that the operation was considerably less than miraculous (Tooth & Newton, 1961).

Not surprisingly, in view of the kind of results produced and the finality of a surgical procedure, there was a good deal of opposition to prefrontal lobotomy on both practical and ethical grounds. Was the brain surgeon justified in deliberately lowering a person's capacity for judgment, foresight, and self-criticism? The operation, of course, was used only as a last resort in cases that entailed great suffering. Then suddenly the surgical method was displaced by tranquilizing drugs, which put into the physician's hands a quicker, safer, far less expensive means of quieting patients who were tense, agitated, and anguished. The decline of prefrontal lobotomy as a therapeutic method was even more rapid than its rise, and it is used today only very rarely (Holden, Itil, & Hofstatter, 1970). Its chief legacy is an increase of knowledge about the functions of the frontal cortex, and the findings support in a general way what had previously been inferred from more gross forms of surgery.

GENERAL EFFECTS OF ABNORMAL CONDITIONS IN THE BRAIN

Research on abnormal functioning in the human brain often has to be done without knowing which localities are most affected. It is only through localized injuries, accidental or surgical, that the somewhat different functions of the parietotemporal cortex and the frontal cortex have come to light. The abnormal conditions created by oxygen lack, fever, and drugs may not affect all nervous tissue alike, but so far we have no direct evidence of such selectivity. Furthermore, many workers believe that brain impairment, whatever its locus, produces a weakening of certain over-all functions having to do with the organization of behavior. It is worthwhile to study these postulated general changes, partly for what they suggest about cerebral functions, partly for what they disclose about the normal organization of behavior, a subject about which we know all too little.

Effects of Anoxia

Nervous tissue is highly dependent on oxygen. Complete deprivation of oxygen, even for a few seconds, causes irreparable damage to nerve cells, especially to those in the brain. Oxygen deprivation can occur when the body is functioning normally if the supply of oxygen for breathing is sharply reduced or eliminated, for example, in drowning or inhaling carbon monoxide from auto exhaust fumes. It can also result from interference with the blood supply to the brain, as happens with some tumors, during heart attacks, or following vascular accidents or diseases.

Partial deprivation produces less drastic effects that are nevertheless of great practical importance to mountain climbers and flight personnel who operate at altitudes where the supply of oxygen is markedly reduced. Experiments on the effects of anoxia have been conducted at high altitudes and, more conveniently, in specially built chambers in which the concentration of oxygen can be controlled. As the oxygen content of inspired air is diminished, a fairly regular sequence of changes takes place. First comes a loss of self-criticism and judgment. Sometimes this is accompanied by feelings of exhilaration similar to those produced by mild alcoholic intoxication. Attention and concentration then begin to show impairment, and the speed and accuracy of mental work decline; scores of mental tests fall off. Motor and sensory performances resist somewhat longer, but as the anoxia increases there is a loss in such skilled acts as handwriting and an impairment of visual and auditory perception. Ultimately there is loss of consciousness (Posner, 1971).

The effects of long-continued low-grade anoxia are less clearly established. People who live for a long time at high altitudes usually become acclimatized, but there are individual differences in this compensation. Certain individuals become irritable, get along badly with their companions, suffer mild feelings of depression, and experience difficulty in concentrating on mental tasks. With a return to lower altitude the symptoms disappear. These changes have a familiar ring. They have much in common with the effects of alcoholic intoxication, as described in Chapter 11, and of injuries to the frontal lobes. The early vulnerability of self-criticism and judgment, and the lowering of attention and concentration, are alike in all three abnormal conditions.

Delirium

There are many common features in delirious behavior no matter what its cause (Heller & Kornfeld, 1975). A delirious person is typically restless, confused, and disoriented, misidentifying people and things, showing marked defects of recent memory, and appearing to be at the mercy of dreamlike and often terrifying images. It is difficult to catch and hold the person's attention, and sometimes even a simple question is answered in groping, rambling speech that quickly drifts away from the point. *Incoordination* is illustrated in the staggering gait, fumbling manipulation, and slurred speech. *Interpenetration* occurs when one sequential act invades another, as in the case of a man who starts to change his clothes for dinner and ends up in pajamas. Thinking is often *fragmented* and *overinclusive*, being constantly influenced by momentary impulses and surrounding impressions. These defects come from disturbances of attitude and orientation. Delirious people seem to be unable to maintain habitual attitudes of anticipation and intellectual pursuit in the presence of competing distractions.

This description should give us a new respect for what the normal intact brain accomplishes even in the ordinary affairs of life. A tremendous task of ordering, selecting, and excluding goes on throughout our waking hours. The necessary control and direction is provided by certain attitudes, the nature of which can be made clear by an illustration. When interviewing a patient a physician gives selective attention to the story of the illness, the symptoms, the probable cause and probable remedy, excluding all stimuli that are not relevant to this purpose. The guiding principle is provided by an anticipant attitude—to try to understand this particular case—behind which lies a general set of supporting attitudes—to fulfill the role of physician, to be of service, and so on. The delirious brain seems unable to maintain these orienting attitudes. Without them, behavior simply falls to pieces and loses its organized plan. Memory depends on organization, and it is therefore easy to understand how little a person can recall of the events of delirium (Cameron & Magaret, 1951).

It is possible to detect certain similarities between the general impairments in brain injury and those seen in delirium, although brain injury tends to produce apathy instead of excitement. Overinclusion, distractibility, and fragmentation are common consequences of brain injury, and we can probably assume that there is a similar difficulty in maintaining orienting attitudes, but the wild disorder of delirious behavior is counterbalanced in the brain-injured by a tendency toward rigid perseveration. Attention sometimes becomes riveted on some object of interest, and if a solution is managed for some difficult problem it is tried repeatedly for other new tasks.

Perceptual Peculiarities

Abnormalities in perception are often associated with local injury, for example, the changes in the apprehension of language that go with parietotem-

573

poral injuries. Many clinicians, however, attach importance to a perceptual peculiarity that seems to be a consequence of many forms of cerebral dysfunction. This is described as a blurring of the boundaries between figure and ground. It is very obvious in normal perception, especially visual perception, that a certain portion of what is perceived constitutes a clearly defined figure, with the remainder a less clearly defined ground. In certain ambiguously drawn pictures it is possible to make figure and ground reverse themselves in rapid succession, but ordinarily the two can be clearly discriminated. This characteristic of perception applies also to any complex process in the nervous system. An action such as raising the arm constitutes figure, but is accompanied by a ground of readjustments in other muscles that keep the body in equilibrium. In brain injury, especially in injury to the cortex, the relation of figure and ground is disturbed and leveled.

Partly because of this handicap, children with neurological injury take more time than normals and make twice as many errors when given the task of copying geometric designs with sticks (Wise, 1968). Brain-injured adults are

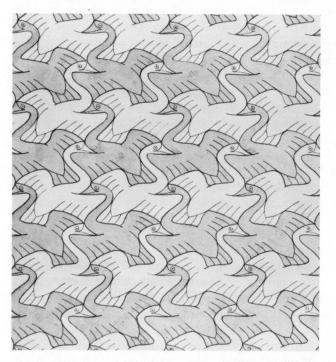

This classical art work from the Escher collection in The Hague shows a perceptual illusion in which the discrimination between figure and background is ambiguous. Some people may see white geese flying to the right; others may see dark geese flying to the left. Everyone is somewhat susceptible to such figure-ground illusions, but brain injury sometimes accentuates susceptibility.

also more sharply disrupted than other psychiatric patients when required to copy figures on paper that already has a background design (Canter, 1966). Brain injury makes it difficult to keep the figure from getting mixed up with the ground.

Loss of the Abstract Attitude

Goldstein attempted to conceptualize an important general consequence of brain injury as a loss of the abstract attitude. With this notion we are already somewhat familiar because it was well illustrated in the case of Martha Ottenby. In describing how she got lost when returning from the hospital workroom, how she determined whether it was winter or summer, and how she ran into the street to talk with her brother who was actually dead, we reached the conclusion that her behavior was bound by immediate and concrete impressions. She was unable to detach herself from these impressions or to think about her behavior in abstract terms. Even in test performances she was blocked by the simplest abstraction, although she could perform quite well with concrete problems.

Goldstein conceived of the abstract attitude broadly as a capacity of the total personality rather than as an acquired mental set or a specific aptitude (Goldstein & Scheerer, 1941). In contrast to the concrete attitude, which is realistic, immediate, and unreflective, the abstract attitude includes in its scope more than the immediately given situation. The real stimulus is transcended and dealt with in a conceptual fashion. Objects before us are seen as members of a class or category, or they are apprehended in a framework of wider implications. To take a very simple example: patients show great skill in throwing balls into boxes that are located at different distances from them, but they are unable to say which box is farthest away or how they manage to aim differently. They are able to function concretely but not to manage the abstract idea of distance, and they can give no account of throwing harder or less hard. The importance of loss of the abstract attitude becomes even clearer when we consider the following limitations: the patients cannot keep in mind several aspects of a situation at one time, cannot readily grasp the essentials of a given whole, cannot plan their actions ahead in ideational fashion. Even with so simple a task as copying a clear, unambiguous figure in reverse, the patients are blocked by the abstraction that is involved (Haydn & Rutsky, 1966).

Shortcomings in the capacity for abstraction make themselves apparent in tests that require sorting and classification, for example, in picture arrangement tests that measure capacity to develop a logically coherent story about a social situation. Many elements of their stories will be appropriate and understandable because most brain-damaged patients are not primarily out of touch with reality, but some elements of their perceptions may be far-fetched and implausible, being based on Klang associations (associations based on

575

sound), peculiar uses of implements, tangential explanations of purpose, and literal interpretations of metaphors. It is evident that the world might become at times a little confusing to a mind that is slightly off-target in these ways.

Not all workers agree with Goldstein that the described changes are best interpreted in terms of concreteness and abstractness. There is little doubt, however, that we are dealing with a loss of organization, a kind of flattening of mental activity that makes it hard to exclude the irrelevant, to subordinate associative processes to consecutive thought, and to govern behavior in the direction of steadily imagined future goals. Though less dramatically exaggerated, the picture overlaps a good deal with the loss of habitual anticipant and supporting attitudes noticed in delirium.

Symptoms Expressing the Struggle with Defect

Whatever the merits of the concept of abstract attitude, we owe to Goldstein an illuminating recognition that the brain-damaged patient is a person who is trying to adapt to the limitations imposed by injury. Many curious forms of behavior become explicable as adaptive attempts of this kind. In various ways patients try to find or make an environment in which demands that are beyond their resources will not occur. Brain injury makes it difficult to deal with anything that is unexpected. It is sometimes observed that patients start violently when they are addressed. One means of protection against the unexpected is excessive orderliness. All the patient's belongings are kept in the most meticulous arrangement, so that everything can be found and used with a minimum of mental exertion. Another means of protection is to be constantly busy. By concentrating on a particular activity, even one that is not important in itself, protection may be obtained from dreaded social stimulation and surprise. At certain points in their convalescence some patients immerse themselves in housecleaning activities around the hospital, seemingly oblivious to everything around them for hours, but becoming upset when interrupted by other patients. Such useful activity may win a certain amount of recognition and gratitude, but its main benefit is to shield the patients from continual harassment by external stimulation. Orderliness and persistent work are clearly not direct consequences of brain damage. They are adaptive strategies designed to prevent confusion, distraction, and surprise.

BRAIN DYSFUNCTION IN CHILDREN

Until recently it was assumed that brain disorders in children were of relatively rare occurrence. They were chiefly known through examples in which there was gross impairment of behavior or severe limitation in mental capacity. As we will see in the next chapter, some forms of mental retardation are associated with visible physical abnormalities and have been shown to depend on structural defects in the brain. Other disorders that clearly imply dysfunction in the central nervous system are known by dramatic behavioral manifestations like the convulsions of epilepsy or the jerky spastic movements of cerebral palsy. Brain disorder thus occupied the position of a rare but drastic affliction that was expected to show itself in marked behavioral disorder. Neurological examination, consisting of a systematic series of small behavioral tests, would clinch the diagnosis by revealing a large number of abnormal signs such as tremor, poor motor control, perceptual irregularities, and changes in reflex patterns. Little could be done to correct the failings of the nervous system, and treatment consisted of training to get around the handicaps and live with them.

Cerebral Palsy

An example of a disorder that fits this conception is provided by cerebral palsy. This term refers to a group of disorders that depend on injuries to lower brain centers rather than the cortex, injuries that are presumed to occur either prenatally or as a consequence of difficult birth. The effects appear most prominently in motor control; intelligence is typically spared and is superior in a proportionate number of cases. The motor handicaps may be severe and are of such a nature as to attract unfavorable notice. Locomotion may be extremely slow and awkward, the arms may jerk and the hands twitch uncontrollably, and frequent involuntary grimaces may sweep across the face. Obviously a child thus handicapped is unlikely to profit from indiscriminate interaction with other children, who tend to find a "spastic's" behavior either terrifying or hilarious until they become fully accustomed to it. Much can be accomplished through special programs of training during childhood. Signs of disability are likely to remain, but the person can learn to some degree how to get around the handicap and lead a relatively normal life. There are many "spastic" adults who lead normal and even highly productive lives in spite of a permanent disorder of motor control. These are, however, the relatively fortunate ones. About a third of the children born with cerebral palsy are so handicapped that they require permanent custodial care, and another third become trained and minimally educated only through close personal supervision (Denhoff & Robinault, 1963).

Brain Injury

Sometimes following a severe head injury, and sometimes following an attack of encephalitis (which is known to injure brain tissue at least temporarily), the behavior of a previously well-adjusted child will undergo a sharp change. There is a conspicuous rise in the level of motor activity. The child seems to be constantly restless, continually in motion, unable to sit still, creating annoyance by getting into everything. The restraint of sitting still at table or in the school classroom becomes suddenly more difficult; the teacher complains

577

about the pupils leaving their desks and wandering around the room. Attention is unfavorably affected; there is great distractibility, and power to stick to a task is damagingly reduced. There is also loss of control over impulse and temper. Delay of gratification cannot be brooked, and outbursts of emotion and irritation occur with increased frequency. Probably the symptom of hyperactivity is more prominent in children; otherwise, this pattern differs hardly at all from what we have seen to be characteristic of adult brain dysfunctions.

It is fair to ask whether children with brain damage are capable of listening and trying, because some of them show an almost total disregard for the rights and feelings of others. On what does consideration for others depend? Studies of moral development have shown that it depends to a large extent on being able to see things from another person's point of view (Staub, 1975). It calls for multiple perspectives. One of the components of the abstract attitude is the ability to hold simultaneously in mind various aspects of a situation. If brain injury impairs the abstract attitude, it also handicaps the child in learning to be considerate of others. The failure to become a socialized member of groups comes partly from an intellectual inability to grasp what it means to be a considerate group member.

Training programs have to be adapted to the limitations imposed by injury (Strauss & Kephart, 1955). Everything possible must be done to minimize distraction. The schoolroom must be undecorated, bare, removed from outdoor noises, its windows painted so that the children cannot see out. Desks should be far apart, perhaps even facing the walls, so that the children will not distract each other. Gloomy as this sounds, it is often welcomed with great appreciation by the children themselves, who suddenly find themselves able to keep their minds on their tasks. Restlessness and hypermotility must be met by a program that includes many activities, and by devices that link learning with motor action. To overcome the leveling of figure and ground it is often necessary to prepare the teaching materials with a sharp outlining of the essential figures in color. All these devices are used only to get the children started on a better educational performance; as rapidly as possible they are trained to participate in a more traditional school routine.

Minimal Brain Dysfunction

During the 1960s two developments took place that put certain childhood disorders in a new light and at the same time held out greater hope of improvement for children with brain dysfunction. In the first place, the expansion of clinical facilities for children made it possible to document the fact that the pattern of traits hitherto attributed to brain damage and encephalitis was relatively common. One of the most frequent reasons for referring a child, especially a boy, to a mental health clinic is the familiar combination of restless hyperactivity, inconsiderate and aggressive behavior, low attention span, and poor performance in school work (Renshaw, 1974). In the second place, experiments were tried with some of the new drugs that had proved helpful with other types of disorder, and the startling discovery was made that this pattern of symptoms responded favorably to amphetamine. This drug is a stimulant, and it seemed paradoxical that it should benefit behavior already so overactive and impulsive. (Similar "paradoxical" drug reactions occur in some elderly persons who presumably have some degree of cerebral dysfunction: sedative effects result from stimulants and agitation can be produced by tranquilizers.)

We must first notice the diagnostic dilemma resulting from these discoveries. Many of the young patients referred for the brain-damage behavior patterns have no histories of birth injury, head trauma, or encephalitis; furthermore, when given a neurological examination they do not necessarily reveal a sufficient number of abnormal signs to justify a traditional positive diagnosis. In such cases the evidence for cerebral dysfunction is wholly indirect, an inference from the over-all pattern of behavior. Classification might be made, of course, on the basis of the effects of amphetamine, but this principle fits no better with neurological signs. The drug is not effective in all cases. It works well in some cases with clear signs of brain damage, but fails in others; it works well in some cases with no direct evidence of brain damage, but fails in others. The reason behind such findings has yet to disclose itself.

As a best guess, however, a good many child psychiatrists have agreed on a diagnostic category called *minimal brain dysfunction*. It is applied to children who show all or most of the hyperactive, impulsive, distractible pattern of behavior and to children with special difficulties in school learning. Readers who find this solution arbitrary should bear in mind that the classification of disorders is not an emanation of pure reason but serves practical purposes in clinical work. To talk of minimal brain dysfunction, instead of concentrating on human relations and attitudes, suggests at once that treatment should be somatic rather than psychological. Prior to the use of amphetamine the hyperactive, distractible, impulsive pattern in children with no direct signs of brain damage was considered to be caused psychologically. The child was seen as a victim of parental rejection who because of anxiety and resentment had failed to acquire the internal controls needed for socialized living either at home or at school. This suggested psychological treatment, sometimes on a one-to-one basis with the child, more often in some joint form involving the parents. The results were poor; the children all too often made scant progress in developing the desired controls. The diagnosis of minimal brain dysfunction announces the physician's preference for a somatic approach. The child's behavior may resist influence because it proceeds from some condition in the brain that makes anything else impossible. The first step in treatment should therefore be biochemical, designed to alter the cerebral abnormality that makes the child's behavior so difficult.

When amphetamine produces a good result, it often does so in a surprisingly short time. Instances are cited by Wender (1971) in which substantial change of behavior occurs in a matter of weeks. One boy of seven, who in ad-

579

dition to the typical pattern had been steadily stealing and had twice set fire to the house, changed so during the first week that his mother wrote: "He is behaving like an angel . . . he is a different child." A week later she specified in detail his accomplishments, which included reading and drawing quietly by himself , helping around the house without being asked, and complete cessation of tantrums, stealing, and fire-setting; she added, "For the first time in four years he is enjoying life instead of fighting it." In another case two weeks was enough to bring about a sharp change of behavior at home, and at three weeks the mother reported with surprise: "He has friends. . . . Children come to the house for him. . . . He does what he is told. . . . He's never been so good for so long in his whole life before." Of a third case, a boy of eight, his teacher wrote after three months: "Mike has improved considerably. . . . He feels he's taking the 'magic' pill and so he can do no wrong while under the influence of it. Consequently his whole self-image appears to have changed. He is now considered by *himself* and his *classmates* to be the *new* Mike, a 'good' Mike, the Mike who helps everyone." Formerly a bully, he now stopped other children from bullying. Simultaneously, his reading comprehension score took a remarkable upward jump and his schoolwork as a whole became satisfactory.

Dramatic results of this kind are not, of course, obtained in every case. Sometimes amphetamine is ineffective and in rare instances it seems to make things worse. But the good results, especially when they occur quickly, make a strong case for a neurological basis of the disorder. It is hard to understand the rapid emergence of the good new Mike if we think of the bad old one as frozen by resentment or as stamped in by a long history of reinforcement in an unfortunate family situation. The boy had little trouble understanding and enacting a different pattern of behavior; he seemed only too glad to try it once he could slow down and keep his attention from chasing every stimulus. Children with this syndrome often report bewilderment at their own bad behavior and inability to control it. They describe the effects of amphetamine in such phrases as "I am a lot more relaxed," "my head feels clearer," and "I can concentrate better." The assumption seems justified that the drug corrects a biochemical condition that reduces optimal cerebral efficiency in a way analogous to brain damage. Seen in this light, the paradox vanishes that amphetamine, a stimulant, should produce behavior that is outwardly more tranquil. Control and organization are important cerebral functions, and it is perhaps these, perhaps specifically the frontal cortex, that are especially stimulated. Clear-headedness and better reasoning are reported by adults who have used amphetamine, along with a kind of alertness that makes them respond with more interest to other people. The good new Mike was ready to emerge as soon as the cerebral basis was made right.

There is an air of magic about dramatic good results, and a broader clinical view is needed to restore balance. Wender, a strong advocate of amphetamine medication, makes clear in the following words the limits of its action.

Drug treatment is of great importance, but it must be emphasized that there are several things medication cannot accomplish. Once the syndrome has remained untreated for any length of time, psychological deficits accumulate. Obviously, medication cannot compensate for educational and experiential deficits. Medication can facilitate learning, not provide compensation for several years in which a child may have been severely handicapped in learning. It can help a child learn to read, but it cannot teach him. Drugs can make the child more amenable to discipline and more lovable, but they cannot provide the experience of having been loved, trusted, admired, and accepted in the past. . . . New experience will be necessary for the child to learn that which he has not learned and to experience that which he has been prevented from experiencing (p. 109).

In order to improve the chances that this new experience will be constructive, Wender advocates a program of "psychological management" that includes explanations to parents, advice on how to make the home environment more predictable and appropriately rewarding, help in softening parental attitudes built up by the child's past annoying behavior, explanation to the child in terms not injurious to self-esteem why he or she needs pills when others do not, and other practical advice as occasion may require. More than this, however, may often be necessary. The parents may find it difficult to change the attitudes engendered by months and years of mingled anxiety and frustration in trying to manage an unmanageable child. The child's peers may be slow to accept a new version of the pest who has so often spoiled their fun. The teachers may view with distrust the unaccustomed calm and expect at every moment a renewal of restless mischief. Change in one person's behavior spreads its influence widely. To produce a new set of interactions with others, and to develop an expectation that these interactions will continue, may require more than a little psychological help.

As now used, the category of minimal brain dysfunction applies to cases of unusual learning difficulty even when hyperactivity is not part of the problem. That this classification is justified is indicated in a study by Hertzig, Bortner, and Birch (1969), who conducted neurological examinations on 90 children aged ten to twelve with conspicuous learning disabilities. These children were classed as "brain-damaged" merely on educational grounds; the problem was to see whether or not independent evidence of cerebral dysfunction could be obtained. The results were clear: in contrast to educationally normal controls, this group of children showed a substantial number of signs indicative of cerebral abnormality. These included abnormal reflex responses, motor discoordination as shown in a certain clumsiness of gait and balance, difficulties in executing fine motor processes, mild disorders of speech, and tremor and small involuntary movements. Only 5 percent of the 90 cases were wholly free from such signs, compared to 67 percent of the controls. These findings, the authors conclude, justify the label of brain dysfunction in severe learning difficulties. There is "primary atypicality in the organization of the central nervous system," a basic handicap that affects many other aspects of behavior (p. 445). These research findings were corroborated by a similar study (Wikler, Dixon, & Parker, 1970).

581

The most likely point of origin for minimal brain dysfunction is shortly before, during, or after birth. Two studies (Pasamanick & Knobloch, 1966; Knobloch & Pasamanick, 1966) have shown a significant association between this type of disorder and a number of unfavorable circumstances surrounding birth, such as toxemia, infection, premature birth, or anoxia during long and difficult labor. These complications, writes Eisenberg (1969), occur more frequently "among the poor, the black, the unmarried, the underaged, and the overaged mothers" and appear to result "from an interaction between inadequate diet, poor prenatal care, poor housing, and gross stress, each of which is associated with pregnancy outcome." Steps that might be taken to prevent minimal brain dysfunction thus belong in the broad realm of public health and environmental betterment.

Treatment of children with amphetamine has aroused considerable opposition both within and outside the mental health professions. This drug, once widely used in low dosages as a "pep pill" and a means of keeping awake while cramming for examinations, has recently been classified as dangerous, and its prescription by physicians is strictly limited to certain disorders, one of which, however, is minimal brain dysfunction. Taken in large doses for "kicks," amphetamine is undoubtedly dangerous, leading occasionally to psychotic episodes, possibly to brain damage, and often to a bad subsequent let-down. This is the usage that justifies stricter legal control, but small doses taken even over long periods of time have not been shown to produce harmful side-effects. The trouble is that the drug produces no permanent alteration in brain chemistry and must therefore be taken every day. Does this imply that medication must go on forever and that the brain-damage syndrome will immediately reappear if the pills are stopped? Two arguments are advanced by those who favor drug treatment. (1) There is evidence that some symptoms, especially overactivity, tend to fade out as puberty approaches, making possible a tapering off of medication. (2) Educational and interpersonal gains made during the period of treatment are not abruptly wiped out if medication is stopped. There may be some loss of efficiency and concentration, but their effects will be far less damaging if in the meantime behavior has become more habitually mature and stably organized. These two points, however, still require research confirmation, as does the nature of the biochemical reaction produced by amphetamine.

Many workers object both to the use of drugs, with their never quite known side effects, and to the designation "minimal brain damage." They prefer to call the described condition *hyperactivity* or *hyperkinetic behavior*, sticking to what is observable and avoiding assumptions about a damaged brain when the neurological evidence so often does not demand it. Recently behavior therapists have been especially active in devising methods to reduce the hyperactive behavior pattern. These methods use systematic rewards much in the manner of token economies, administered by parents and teachers as well as therapists. Rewards are given selectively for slowing down, sitting still, paying steady attention to tasks, and controlling impulsiveness. Schaefer and Millman (1977), reviewing a number of reports, believe it confirmed "that, regardless of the cause of hyperactivity or restlessness, children can learn to slow down" (p. 324). There is growing support for the position that behavioral treatment or psychotherapy should be the preferred method of treatment. Use of drugs, in this view, should be reserved for cases that do not make good progress—those cases, perhaps, in which brain dysfunction is really of serious proportions.

EPILEPSY

Epilepsy is based on a disordered condition of the brain that leads to periodic seizures. The name derives from a Greek word meaning "a taking hold of or a seizing." The most distinctive feature is a temporary loss of consciousness, but this may be accompanied by varying degrees of motor and autonomic disturbance. Many parts of the brain, especially those in the limbic region that control motor and autonomic functions, are extremely sensitive to stimulation by electrical activity, metabolic changes, or excitatory drugs. Seizures may be triggered by any of these, as well as by oxygen deprivation or focal brain injuries. They occur with wide variation in periodicity, some as often as several times a day, others once every year or two. They may be precipitated reflexively, for example, by flickering lights or patterns of sound (Glaser, 1975).

One in 20 persons has a seizure at some time in life, and about one in 160 develops chronic seizures, though this prevalence is difficult to assess accurately because many forms involve attacks without motor convulsions and may go unrecognized as seizures (Pincus & Tucker, 1974). The prevalence figure may seem small, but it means that about 1,300,000 persons in the United States are afflicted with epilepsy. It is more common in men than in women. Although the disorder is not continuous, and the person is in a perfectly normal state between attacks, it constitutes even in its milder forms a serious handicap in living.

Seizure disorders are sometimes classified etiologically: *primary* or *idiopathic* epilepsy has no discernible precipitating cause, although it may be associated with genetic factors; in *secondary* or *acquired* epilepsy some extrinsic precipitating cause or causes can be identified. The age at onset gives important clues to etiology. If the seizures commence before six months of age, the disorder is likely to be secondary epilepsy resulting from congenital malformations, such as Down's syndrome or microcephaly, birth injury at delivery, metabolic error, infection, or accidental brain damage. If onset occurs between two and twenty years of age, it is likely to be idiopathic epilepsy with traceable genetic predisposition. Onset after age thirty-five indicates secondary epilepsy that stems from vascular insufficiency, brain tumor, or degenerative disease. Seizures seldom begin between twenty and thirty-five except as a

583

result of trauma, drug abuse (especially alcoholism), or infection; these would be classified also as secondary or acquired disorders (Pincus & Tucker, 1974). It will be noticed that seizures may be symptomatic of *any* brain disorder.

Varieties of Epileptic Attack

There are three main types of epileptic seizure. Most dramatic and most frequent of occurrence are the *grand mal* attacks, which correspond to the idea most people have of an epileptic seizure. The second variety, *petit mal,* is not badly described as a smaller seizure limited to a brief loss of consciousness with few motor accompaniments. The third variety, the least common of the three, has not yet been stably christened. It is variously known as *psychic seizures, psychic equivalents, psychic variants*, or *psychomotor seizures*. The reader will easily deduce from this fumbling with names that the third class of epileptic phenomena is still only little understood. The condition is an interesting one, however, and it may prove ultimately to be very instructive.

Grand Mal. Warning symptoms called the *aura* often precede grand mal attacks. These may consist of dizziness, tingling, numbness, peculiar sensations in the head, discomfort in the abdomen. They last for a few seconds and often do not give the patient time enough to prepare for the fit. The seizure itself is introduced by sudden muscular rigidity. Respiration is suspended so that the face turns dark, and if not supported the victim falls heavily to the ground. Almost at once the tonic phase (with muscular rigidity) gives place to the clonic phase of the seizure, characterized by rapid jerking movements of the muscles. The jaws are included in the jerking movements so that the tongue is often bitten and frothy saliva gathers on the lips. Autonomic disorganization is shown in involuntary urination and sometimes defecation. Within a few minutes the clonic phase gives place to coma. Consciousness may be regained almost at once or only after a matter of hours. Some people have grand mal attacks very infrequently, perhaps once or twice a year. Usually the attacks occur more frequently, and in severe cases there may be several convulsions a day.

Petit Mal. The excitation in the brain remains more limited in petit mal seizures. It rarely occurs in anyone over fifteen and most have no other type of seizures (Robinson & Robinson, 1976). The petit mal attack is of short duration and is limited to loss of consciousness, perhaps with a few small twitchings of the eye and face muscles. No mental confusion attends these attacks; there is simply a "mental black-out," starting and stopping suddenly and lasting from a few seconds to a minute or two. The effect may be so transient that other people set it down to a mere moment of absent-mindedness. Petit mal attacks may occur with great frequency, many times a day. While not as disturbing either to those afflicted or their families, they may constitute almost as

584

Some victims of epilepsy have seizures so frequently that it is necessary to wear a protective helmet, to prevent head injuries from falling to the ground when a convulsion begins. This man obviously maintains a full life while wearing the helmet.

severe a handicap as the grand mal attacks. Childhood petit mal epilepsy of subcortical origin appears to be transmitted genetically by a dominant gene, since half of first-degree relatives show typical EEG epileptic patterns, although a much lower proportion have actual seizures (Metrakos & Metrakos, 1969).

Psychomotor Attack. The third variety of seizure is characterized by at least a partial loss of consciousness without suspension of organized motor activity. There may be slight signs of tonic rigidity for a moment, but thereafter the person continues to perform purposeful acts. During these periods consciousness is dramatically altered so the person may appear to pay no attention to the environment, but organized actions that require vision, coordination and thinking may be carried out, after which the person returns to normal consciousness with no recollection of the attack. Psychomotor seizures may last for as much as an hour or even longer. Some people commit acts of a violent and criminal nature during the course of an extended psychomotor epileptic attack. This possibility has to be considered when there is genuine confusion and amnesia for the period during which the offense was committed. This form of epilepsy, sometimes referred to as focal or partial epilepsy, accounts

585

for 25 percent of childhood seizure disorders and more than half of those in adult life. Most of these cases present a definite, focal brain lesion, usually in the temporal lobe (Glaser, 1975).

About one half of the victims of epilepsy have only one type of seizure. The other half have two and even three types, sometimes mixed in the same seizure. The three varieties of attack are thus not three different kinds of disease. They can be assumed to spring from similar conditions in the brain.

The Electroencephalogram in Epileptics

Spontaneous, wave-like electrical activity in the brain has been observed and measured systematically since 1929 (Sherwin & Geschwind, 1978). Nowhere has electroencephalography proved of greater value than in the study of epilepsy. Whatever the nature of the underlying neural disturbance, it reflects itself with extraordinary clearness in the electrical activity of the cortex. The *electroencephalogram* (EEG) is a graphic recording of the electrical activity of the cortex. When electrodes are attached to the scalp and connected with an amplifier it is possible to record fluctuations in voltage, popularly known as "brain waves," which arise from activity in cerebral tissue. Under basic conditions—that is, with the person awake but resting quietly with closed eyes—the normal adult record shows a predominance of slow waves, *alpha rhythms*, averaging about 10 cycles per second. Superimposed on these waves are the faster *beta rhythms* with a frequency anywhere up to 40 cycles per second. Waves of four to six cycles per second are called *theta rhythms*. Rhythms of less than four cycles per second, called *delta waves*, are rare in the records of normal adults. They are typical of infants in the first year of life, and their frequency of occurrence decreases with age. In persons with known brain damage and in minimal brain dysfunction there may be a distinctly greater frequency of very slow waves than is characteristic for the person's age, but that is not very helpful for diagnostic purposes because many people with no signs of disordered behavior also show the same EEG pattern.

During epileptic seizures, however, the EEG becomes abnormal in an entirely different way, and the pattern of abnormality is different for each of the three varieties of attack. Figure 15-3 shows four tracings that are typical for grand mal, petit mal, a variant form of petit mal, and the psychomotor seizure. Each tracing begins with a section of normal record, affording a sharp contrast with the record during seizure. The tonic phase of grand mal is accompanied by very fast waves of high voltage. These give place in the clonic phase to waves still of high voltage having a characteristically erratic form. In petit mal attacks there is a typical association of slow waves with spikes, with each pair coming at the rate of three a second. Sometimes the rate is even slower: at two a second it is called petit mal variant and is not usually associated with an overt seizure. The waves are shaped quite differently in psychomotor attacks. Voltage is abnormally high, and the waves frequently have square tops. They occur at the rate of between four and eight a second.

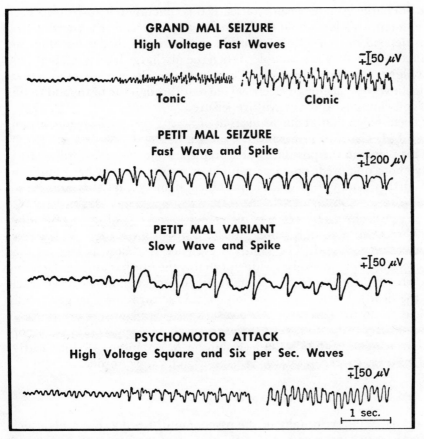

GRAND MAL SEIZURE
High Voltage Fast Waves

$\mp$I50 μV

Tonic   Clonic

PETIT MAL SEIZURE
Fast Wave and Spike

$\mp$I200 μV

PETIT MAL VARIANT
Slow Wave and Spike

$\mp$I50 μV

PSYCHOMOTOR ATTACK
High Voltage Square and Six per Sec. Waves

$\mp$I50 μV

1 sec.

Figure 15.3
Representative electroencephalograms of four patients show records taken before and during four different types of seizures; grand mal, two forms of petit mal, and a psychomotor attack. At the right is the perpendicular deflection made by a 50-millionth or 200-millionth volt potential, and at the bottom the time marked by one second. The left of each tracing is a portion of the person's normal record. The rest of the tracing was made during a seizure. The uppermost record is the tonic, and then after an interval, the clonic phase of a grand mal convulsion. The second tracing is the three-second alternate wave and spike of petit mal. The third tracing is of the relatively rare two-a-second wave and spike called petit mal variant. The fourth tracing was taken during two phases of a psychomotor seizure. The tracings are about one third their natural size. (From Gibbs, Gibbs, and Lennox, 1939, p. 1112.)

Virtually all epileptics show abnormal EEGs between seizures. These abnormalities consist of short bursts of waves having higher than normal voltage and taking a form similar to those recorded during seizures. The evidence suggests that what is going on during the attacks is an abnormal discharge of energy by the neurones of the brain, and that the epileptic's brain has a tendency toward

587

excessive discharge even between attacks. If this conclusion is correct we learn a new and interesting fact about the brain: consciousness and the coordinating functions depend on a level of activity in the neurones that is less than the maximum of which they are capable. When the discharge level is too high, the so-called higher functions disappear. They disappear also in electroshock therapy, which involves passing an electrical current through the brain and results in loss of consciousness and a convulsive seizure.

It has been shown that about 10 percent of normal people have abnormalities in the EEG that are similar to those found in epileptic patients (Kolb, 1968). This points to the possibility of a predisposition toward overdischarge, with only about one predisposed person out of twenty actually becoming epileptic. A further finding is of great importance, namely, that abnormal EEG's are found with great frequency in the relatives of epileptics. Among first-degree relatives (parents, siblings, and offspring) of individuals with idiopathic epilepsy, the risk of chronic seizure disorder is about seven times higher than in the general population. The family prevalence is almost as high as that among secondary epileptics also, which probably means that among the many children who endure traumatic events (birth injury, childhood fever, accidents to the head), the few that develop chronic seizures must be genetically predisposed to do so. Far more relatives of epileptics have abnormal EEGs than have seizures, suggesting that environmental experience plays an important part in triggering the disorder (Robinson & Robinson, 1976). Clearly, most epileptics carry an hereditary predisposition for the disorder.

A Special Problem: Temporal Lobe Seizures

Temporal lobe epilepsy, usually of the psychomotor variety, has a high incidence, is resistant to treatment, and difficult to diagnose; hence it is the most troublesome variety of seizure disorder. In contrast to the jerking movements and tingling sensations of most seizures, these show complex sensorimotor and autonomic disturbances with alterations of consciousness. Victims usually appear completely normal on neurological examination. The disorder is believed to result often from oxygen deprivation during gestation or in childhood. The seizures range from momentary absence (like petit mal) to major motor seizures of the grand mal type. They often involve vivid hallucinations with subsequent amnesia, and *deja vu* experiences. Feelings of anger may be accompanied by aggressive acts that are a serious feature, leading to unpredictable violence precipitated by seemingly minor provocation. Long-winded excuses are typical, in contrast to the blatant aggressiveness of frontal lobe epileptics or the obliviousness of sociopaths.

A personality pattern observed with some frequency in this syndrome is characterized by religious fervor, cosmic concerns, day-to-day variability in temperament, aggression alternating with unctuous good-naturedness, overly detailed analysis of trivial events, and verboseness. There is frequently a loss of

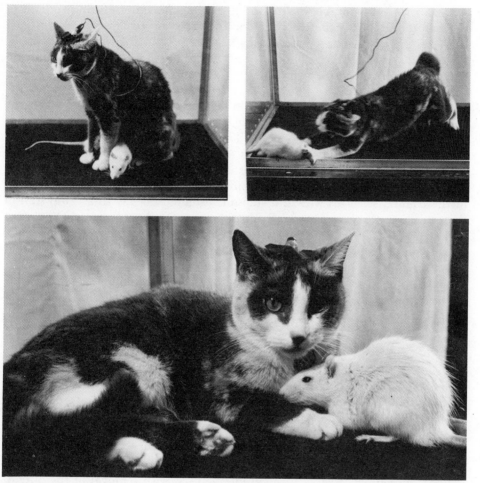

Research with animals demonstrates what probably occurs in psychomotor epileptic seizures in which violent behavior is expressed. Under anesthesia, thin wires were placed in this cat's hypothalamus, a section of the brain that controls, among other things, emotional response, temperature and blood pressure. The wired cat was caged with a rat and accepted it as a friendly companion until an electric current was passed through the wires to the brain. A slight electric impulse caused the cat to see the rat as an enemy and attack it. But a stronger stimulus caused the cat to try to flee from the rat. By shifting the placement of the wires around, researchers learned that the zone in the cat's brain where current caused flight was much larger than the area where it caused a fight. Similar electrical aberrations may account for the violent behavior that occasionally occurs in a few people afflicted with epilepsy.

sexual drive and a notable inclination toward a schizophreniform psychosis of the paranoid type. If the disorder does not respond to anticonvulsant drug therapy, surgery has had encouraging success in reducing the seizures themselves, but it is less likely to eliminate aggressive behavior or schizophreniform psychosis (Sherwin & Geschwind, 1978).

An Illustrative Case. A forty-year-old man had suffered from temporal lobe seizures since puberty. When he finally married, he showed no sexual interest but became increasingly religious, and every few weeks he suffered periods of marked moodiness lasting several days. As gentle, friendly, and deferent as he usually was, he could be sarcastic, hostile, and arrogant during his bad days. The following incident led to his first hospitalization: He had spent a weekend in the country with his wife and stepson, listening all day to a radio station that continuously transmitted religious sermons. On the way home he debated with his wife, arguing that she was not saved, while his soul was saved. When his stepson asked him how this was possible, he slapped both the youngster and his wife, shouting, "For a nickel, I will kill you both!" His angry outbursts, although limited usually to verbal threats and hostile glares, were always frightening, but within days he would revert, without explicit apologies, to his usual self (Blumer, 1975).

Facts Bearing on the Causes of Epilepsy

There is an unmistakable relation between convulsive seizures and brain injuries. The way in which brain injuries lead to convulsions has been the object of special study by Penfield and Erickson (1941). In certain cases of epilepsy it can be shown that the attacks always begin with excessive neuronal discharge in a particular region of the brain, spreading from there to involve the cerebrum as a whole. This form of the disorder is called "focal epilepsy" in contrast to the many cases in which no local point of origin can be detected. Focal epilepsy sometimes permits surgical intervention with removal of the offending tissues, an operation for which Penfield and his associates became famous. The first step in locating the focal point is to make a careful study of the aura, which is actually a part of the attack even though it precedes the loss of consciousness. If the aura always contains certain sensations or motor actions, this constitutes presumptive evidence for a focus in the corresponding sensory or motor area of the cortex. If there are repetitive dream-like images in the aura the temporal lobes are likely to be involved. The second step in the search is to refine the location by means of the EEG. The electrodes are placed on different parts of the head until the spot is found that most regularly yields an abnormal record. If these steps point to a fairly circumscribed area — which is by no means always the case — a direct investigation of the cortex is made. Under local anaesthesia a flap of bone and skin is cut and turned back, exposing the suspected area. It is then possible to explore by means of electrical stimulation until the precise spot is found that produces an aura, if not actually a convulsion, and the pathological tissues can be examined and removed.

In these focal cases there is pretty certain to be evidence of an old injury, very likely the consequence of some internal mishap such as a hemorrhage instead of a trauma from outside. In the area of injury part of the tissues will be dead, but dead tissues are not responsible for seizures. Penfield and Erickson often found that the crucial tissues were those on the edge of a dead area, alive but insufficiently supplied with blood to permit normal functioning. They proposed the hypothesis that these nerve cells suffered from anemia "due to periodic impairment of blood flow through one or other of the small local blood vessels," and that a certain degree of anemia is "irritative in the sense that greater activity occurs in local neurones". Perhaps there is an analogy here to the frantic struggle of a person that is drowning or partly asphyxiated; the deprived cells, struggling to stay live, fire with everything they have. However this may be, the hypothesis has virtue in explaining the facts discovered about epilepsies with a highly focalized point of origin in the cortex. Excessive discharge in one area can eventually overload the whole system and provoke the generalized overdischarge that constitutes the seizure.

What we do not know, of course, is whether this hypothesis can be extended to encompass the more common cases in which no local starting point for the convulsive seizures can be detected. Evidence suggests that there may be widespread small areas of injury with constricted blood supply, but the possibility remains open that dysrhythmic overdischarge by cerebral neurones can also result from other conditions (Redlich & Freedman, 1966).

Psychological Aspects

The influence of psychological factors seems to be distinctly secondary in epilepsy. It is true that the individual attack is often precipitated by a situation involving emotional stress, but stress cannot be considered a primary cause. The claim once advanced that there is a characteristic epileptic personality type has not received convincing research support (Glaser, 1975). Furthermore, some of the traits often mentioned in this connection, such as distractibility and inattentiveness, sound like those of minimal brain dysfunction, while others can be readily understood as reactions to handicapping illness. The peculiarity of the disorder has led to restrictive actions by society and to general stigmatization. It now appears that most of the severe emotional problems and disturbances develop as reactions to the restrictions, the stigmatization, and the personal rejection by family members. Having an affliction so overwhelming and meaningless is, after all, not conducive to taking life in a calm and joyous spirit. Especially if the disorder includes grand mal attacks, one must anticipate passing into a state of unconsciousness that is terrifying to others, leads to avoidance and ostracism by others, precludes holding most jobs and such activities as driving a car—in short, that amounts to a severe

591

handicap in leading a satisfactory life. If a person should become morose and oversensitive under such circumstances, appear self-centered, emotionally shallow, and a little antagonistic toward others, this is a most natural outcome of an epileptic's psychological situation.

A significant number of epileptics with frequent, recurrent generalized seizures, especially *status epilepticus* (continuous seizures), may develop cognitive disturbances affecting memory, learning, attention, language, and perception. In the rare instances when continuous seizures cannot be brought under control, radical surgery to separate the two hemispheres by removing the corpus callosum may be necessary to save the life of the victim. Fortunately, the majority of epileptics with adequate control of the seizures show no such difficulties and retain normal intellectual function (Glaser, 1975).

Treatment of Epilepsy

Although the surgical procedures used by Penfield and others are often successful when there is a highly focalized cortical lesion, it is obvious that they cannot be used with the majority of epileptic patients. Early efforts at treatment took the form of diets and medication that had been shown to reduce the frequency of seizures. Starting about forty years ago, good results began to be obtained with phenobarbital, with dilantin sodium, and with a combination of the two. Very great improvement can often be obtained by means of these drugs, and the recently burgeoning research with new drugs now gives the physician a considerable choice of medications that can be adapted to individual needs, including bromides, amphetamines, steroids, and barbiturates (Kolb, 1968). All the anticonvulsant drugs have potential toxic effects that must be monitored carefully. Most of them have a depressant action on neurons, thus counteracting the spread of electrical discharge throughout the brain, although the exact mechanism for their effectiveness is not fully understood.

Seizures in most epileptic disorders can be controlled with the proper drug; control is adequate for more than 60 percent of the cases and partial for 25 to 30 percent more. Selecting the appropriate drug for an individual case is usually a matter of trial and error. No single drug can totally eliminate all seizures in all cases or even in a particular type of seizure disorder.

Unfortunately, most adult epileptics must continue using the drugs throughout their lives, as the seizures will usually recur if the drugs are withdrawn, even after several years of treatment. Some children with petit mal disorders may outgrow the disorder with age and maturity, so careful experimentation with gradual drug withdrawal may be attempted when they reach adolescence or young adult age (Glaser, 1975).

Psychological treatment can be an important adjunct, though obviously not with the goal of curing the brain condition. In the first place, it can be helpful in reducing conflicts and tensions in general, and this in itself is sometimes found to diminish the frequency and severity of seizures. In the second place, it can help the person to work out the worst anxieties and resentments over the fact of being handicapped and provide some support to meet the frustrations with something closer to equanimity. In the third place, it can help to overcome the warping that may have occurred developmentally through the bewilderment and anxiety of the parents (Bagley, 1967).

MENTAL CHANGES AND DISORDERS OF OLD AGE

One person out of five entering a mental hospital suffers from a disorder associated with old age. The frequency of such disorders is steadily increasing. This is an indirect consequence of the general advance of medical science. As fewer people die of such diseases as tuberculosis, diptheria, and pneumonia, more survive into their sixties and seventies when senile changes begin to take place. It is to be expected that this trend will continue. If medicine succeeds in conquering such enemies as cancer and heart disease, an even greater part of the population will live into their seventies. In 1870 only 2.9 percent of the population lived beyond 65; in 1970, 9.9 percent exceeded that age (Busse, 1978). Whether this will mean a steadily increasing incidence of senile mental disorders depends on our ability to understand and alleviate these afflictions of later life. The senile psychoses can be regarded as exaggerated forms of the changes that are inseparable from aging. Some of these changes are bodily, others are psychological. We first consider the normal course of change with advancing years, thus establishing a background for the understanding of senile disorders.

The Decline of Abilities

As age advances, there is a marked decline of physical energy. One after another the more vigorous forms of physical exertion have to be avoided. Even for people who take their physical limitations goodnaturedly, it is hard to avoid a feeling of growing helplessness. The decrease in motor capacity is matched by a weakening of sensory acuity. Less sharpness both in vision and hearing is characteristic of the older years. There is also a decline in the speed of response. Studies of reaction time show a steady decrease, beginning in the second or third decades of life, and proceeding at a faster rate in the later decades. There are wide individual differences, but the general trend is clear. Older people register the environment less keenly, respond to it less quickly, and are able to respond in less varied and energetic ways.

A similar decline is observed in those functions that are measured by intelligence tests. This is partly but not wholly a function of speed. In tests where speed is not important the decrease is less marked but still present. Not all types of performance are equally affected. Tests of vocabulary and tests of

593

general information show the smallest losses with advancing years, whereas tests requiring ingenuity in new performances are particularly vulnerable. The effects of age may be markedly resisted in the case of knowledge and skills that continue in active use. Thus elderly scholars who keep steadily at work may show a minimum of impairment in their special field of expertness, remembering details in a way that startles younger people who do not share their interest in the field. There are also great individual differences in the amount of loss; plenty of people in their eighties, and a few in their nineties, remain keen and productive. Nevertheless, intellectual competence undergoes on the average a definite decline comparable to the falling off of sensory and physical prowess. There is evidence that the decline is associated with a variety of more direct signs of impairment in cerebral function (Wang, Obrist, & Busse, 1970).

Failing memory is one of the most obvious symptoms of aging. The inability to remember names is often extremely frustrating. Although tests of rote memory do not show much impairment until after the age of eighty, the assimilation of memories and the power to act on them appear to decline somewhat earlier. It is a generally observed fact that the memory loss of older people is greatest regarding recent events. They may remember current happenings so poorly that they seem almost disoriented, yet remain completely clear about the earlier events of their lives, even of their childhood. There is no fully satisfactory explanation for this fact, which is also found in cases of brain deterioration caused by general paresis and chronic alcoholism. It is possible that attention and initial registration are more at fault than recall. In any event the net result is a weakening of memory, especially for recent and current happenings.

The decline of abilities can be measured at even more basic levels than those just discussed. Behind the weakening physical and mental capacity it is possible to conceive of a more generalized impairment that affects the cells of all tissues, including those in the central nervous system. In old tissues there is an increase of inert material, chiefly fibrin and collagen. This inert material surrounds many cells and simply by mechanical blocking impairs the delivery of oxygen and nutrient materials to the still active or metabolizing cells. There is, furthermore, a diminution of the number of functioning cells in older tissues. In addition, the flow of blood may be less adequate and regular, especially if the artery walls have hardened and thickened. The result of these changes is to interfere with normal cellular metabolism. Changes of this kind probably affect the cells of the body but are especially important for those in the central nervous system. Reviewing a large amount of evidence from research, Hicks and Birren (1970) conclude that deterioration in lower brain centers, rather than in the cortex itself, best explains at least the psychomotor slowing that occurs in old age.

The effect of this general lowering of cellular efficiency is an increasing difficulty in maintaining homeostasis. The body becomes less capable of maintaining the constancy of its internal environment and has to work harder to achieve this goal. Reserve capacities and emergency reactions must be drawn on more freely, leaving less surplus energy for other activities. Stress continues to occur, and a greater proportion of available energy has to be devoted to restoring equilibrium. If we consider the maintaining of homeostasis as the first demand on any organism, it becomes clear that a general restriction will necessarily be felt in all activities not directly concerned with that central demand.

Psychosocial Situation of the Aged

When family units are large, as is still the case in some societies and perhaps in rural areas generally, older people remain in the family circle. Grandparents continue to play an essential though reduced part in the life of the family. The situation is different in the small urban family unit which at least in the United States is rapidly becoming the standard pattern. The family unit typically consists of one pair of parents and their children, and a grandparent living in the home is quite generally felt to be a burdensome intrusion. Many older people face the alternative of being an unwelcome visitor in the household of one of their children or of living by themselves in restricted or lonely circumstances. In either case they are likely to feel useless and superfluous. Whereas in simpler times grandfather might putter around the farm with relatively useful results, he is now more likely to be distinctly retired and out of a job. If grandmother wants to help in the kitchen or with the children, she is likely to be told that her ideas on psychology are old-fashioned and that she must be careful not to break the kitchen appliances. The fact that our times are rapidly changing has the effect of decreasing the utility of older people. The wisdom of the aged is less wise in a time of rapid change.

A second feature of our society that tends to create problems for older people is its powerful "accent on youth." The young do not want to look middle-aged, but the middle-aged want to look young, and they spend millions of dollars every year trying to create this illusion. In this cultural climate the old tend to be pushed aside much as used to be the case with mentally defective children. For reasons both technological and cultural, old people have thus dropped out of a position of significance in their society. They are likely to be treated with condescension, even by youthful psychologists and social workers bent on helping them to adjust. Small wonder that senior citizens, when asked what they want, say that they would like a voice in their own retirement and that they want somehow to remain an active part of the community, doing some kind of purposeful and productive work. They do not want to be put away on a shelf.

Old age thus involves for many people a variety of serious threats. Sometimes it is necessary to move to a new home in a new neighborhood, producing a sense of isolation from friends and old associations. If the older people re-

Elderly people that are not welcome to live with their children's families may be placed in nursing homes, where the group living situation may resemble a mental institution. Here many of the residents hardly pay any attention to the musical concert being played for them. Senile changes in the brain and the stultifying effects of institutional living both may contribute to such loss of interest.

main in the same home, the situation is only relatively better. They are likely to experience loss of friends by death, and they are not in a good position to make new ones. For those who have had regular outside employment, retirement may bring a shrinking of both agreeable interactions with others and a sense of personal significance. The desire to be loved and valued may encounter the further frustration that younger people are often impatient with the limitations of the elderly. The difference in tempo alone can be irritating. To wait for slow movement, slow speech, slow comprehension can indeed be frustrating, and such surface irritations may obstruct the expression of liking and esteem. Failure of communication between young and old can be caused also by the difference in time perspective. In youth, most of life lies ahead; the future may be unformulated, but many splendid achievements are within the range of possibility. Young people have little interest in hearing how things used to be before they were born, especially if there is some suggestion that things ever since have been going to the dogs. Older people's lives are mostly behind them. What they have achieved and what they have become as persons are both matters of history, capable of no further change. What sometimes appears to be an obstinate conservatism can represent a determined effort to preserve self-respect by reaffirming the worth of what one has done and valued.

Cumming and Henry (1961) have described the overall direction of change in later life as a process of disengagement. Older people deal with their own diminished resources by disengaging themselves from the commitments and social activities that were central earlier in their lives. Inner events take on greater importance than outer events, and older people resist being shaped by social expectations. The challenge for aging individuals is to find meaning and satisfaction in life as their capacities and their connections with other people decline (Kastenbaum, 1965).

Many people succeed in growing old gracefully, usefully, and happily. In a study of men close to and after retirement, the pattern rated most successful by the observers, who labelled it *mature*, represented a nice balance between maintaining an active, interested life and accepting inevitable limitations (Reichard, Livson, & Peterson, 1962). Characteristically, self-respect was not shaken by becoming old; the men participated appropriately in the life around them and enjoyed having more time to see friends and pursue hobbies. For another group of men contentment was reached quite differently. The *rocking-chair* pattern was favored by relatively passive, dependent men who tended to lean on others. For the most part these were unambitious men who found little satisfaction in work, and they were glad to take it easy when retirement came. For this group, happiness was found in the opportunity to sit and talk and enjoy freedom from pressure. A third group, which the observers chose to call *armored*, found their contentment in continuing, perhaps a little strenuously, to be active after retirement. There was latent anxiety in these men about becoming helpless and dependent, but this was successfully counteracted by finding a part-time job or by self-initiated projects such as repairing the house, continuing the satisfaction derived from being busy. Thus the men in this study dealt with aging not in standard fashion, but in their own particular ways.

Maladaptive Patterns

Sometimes the inherent threats connected with aging give rise to disordered personal reactions. The two most common forms are *hypochondria* and *reactive depression* (Busse, 1961). The realistic basis for hypochondria lies in the actual aches, pains, and ailments that become more frequent in later years. Concern with health is natural, but when it becomes preoccupying, so that the person thinks and talks of little else, imposes undue self-restrictions, and cannot stop pestering the family doctor, the behavior has the overdriven character that suggests maladaptive anxiety and defense. Conceivably, worry about health in such cases acts to divert and conceal worries about isolation, boredom, dependence, and crumbling self-esteem. Fancied ill health can also serve as an excuse for not taking initiatives that come harder as the years go

Many people grow old gracefully and usefully. The retired man on the left is reading to elementary school pupils, as part of a foster grandparent program. Such limited activity is clearly within his current work capacity and it provides a valuable cost-saving service, while promoting individualized human contact that is mutually beneficial for the children and the "grandparent." The enterprising old lady on the right has a more ambitious work role: she is a free-lance photo-journalist covering a national political convention at age 72.

by. Depressions in older people are often rather clearly connected with events that entail loss. They are doubtless made more common by the time perspective of the later years: losses are final, unlikely to be compensated, and improved conditions are hardly to be expected. Therapeutic goals in treating such cases must be modest, but the therapist's interest may somewhat repair self-esteem and encouragement may help the client to resume interest and participation in whatever is still possible.

Senile Dementia

When a chronic mental disorder occurs in an elderly person and is accompanied by signs of mental deterioration, it is called senile dementia. This condition is really a combination of senile deterioration with special reactions that still further increase the loss of contact with reality. Depressed states, agitated states, delirious and confused states, or paranoid reactions may add themselves to the general picture of impairment. The onset is gradual, sometimes almost imperceptible. The person becomes a little more egocentric and conservative, inefficient and forgetful, sad, disturbed, or suspicious, until it seems to everyone that he or she can no longer get along outside the hospital. Perhaps forgetfulness crosses the line into confusion, taking a walk and not finding the way home. Perhaps querulous complaints about food and digestion slip over into delusions of being poisoned by a daughter-in-law. Sometimes a physical illness or some situational stress marks the boundary a little more sharply. Perhaps the family home has to be sold and the old person moved to new surroundings. Sickness or ailments of a lasting sort may suddenly restrict the range of available activities. In all such cases the person is called on rather suddenly to make a whole series of readjustments, and proves unequal to the strain. But deterioration has been in progress and the onset is never really sudden.

Senile people are apt to be restless and sleepless. Often they wander in the night and at such times are likely to be particularly confused. Irritation is frequent, judgment is poor, attention is erratic, and the registration of impressions decidedly irregular. On top of this general picture of impairment go the depressed, agitated, or paranoid reactions. As the disorder advances, intellectual deficit increasingly dominates the picture. Speech becomes rambling and incoherent, and failing memory may be pieced out with fabrications. The person may fail to recognize close relatives. In the course of time, episodes of confusion, occasionally with hallucinations, occur with greater frequency. Social amenities and courtesy are preserved almost to the last, but the end point is a state of helplessness and vegetation in which the person becomes oblivious of surroundings. It is obvious that not much can be done for senile people except to make them comfortable, keep them in physical health, provide occupations that are within their powers, and protect them from unnecessary difficulties.

The changes in the brain that underlie senile dementia are of a degenerative character whose causes are not fully understood. Autopsy findings include a general shrinkage of brain tissue, a reduction in the number of nerve cells, and a thickening in the intercellular tissues. All the changes are diffuse; they are not concentrated in any one spot sufficiently to alter the cortical architecture. The signs of degeneration are not peculiar to senile dementia; they are found with lesser severity in normal older people and with greater severity in those with Alzheimer's and Pick's diseases (Birren, 1964).

Psychoses with Cerebral Arteriosclerosis

When there is a considerable degree of arteriosclerosis, the changes in the brain are of a more devastating character. Hardening and thickening of the walls of the blood vessels, including not only the large arteries but also the small arterioles and capillaries, reduce the supply of blood to all tissues. The effect of this reduction is especially serious in the brain, where the tissues are peculiarly dependent on an adequate supply of oxygen and nutrient materials. The brains of arteriosclerotic patients at autopsy show a variety of severe focal lesions in which the cerebral structure is completely destroyed, although surrounding nervous tissue may be in a state of good preservation. Softened and disintegrated tissue is found at the points of lesion. The temporal and occipital areas seem to be particularly vulnerable. While the cause of these focal softenings is not definitely known, the best hypothesis seems to be that they occur as a result of restricted blood supply.

Like all arterial diseases, this one is much more common in men, occurring three times as often as in women. Women are believed to receive extra protection from female hormones. There are usually various premonitory symptoms prior to the development of full psychosis. Physical letdown may be noticed, along with headaches and dizziness. There is a gradual decline of intellectual functions: memory, judgment, and attention. Insight is generally preserved fairly well. Many become irritable, aggressive, and quarrelsome. Depression and suicide are common. Some slowing of EEG frequencies is observed in elderly people who have the disease. There is known to be a correlation between EEG frequency and blood flow, so the slower EEGs may indicate a decrease in oxygen consumption and cerebral metabolism with aging (Busse, 1978).

In more than half the cases the onset of the acute psychosis is sudden, differing in this respect from senile dementia. It takes the form of an attack of confusion with clouding of consciousness, incoherence, great restlessness, and complete loss of contact with the environment. The confused state may last for weeks or months. In about half the cases it subsides, leaving the person with considerable senile impairment but in a much less confused condition. Later attacks are the rule, however, and cure is not to be expected.

It is logical to direct treatment efforts at the suspected cause of the mental changes of aging, namely at oxygen deprivation of the brain that is attributed to arteriosclerotic vascular changes, high concentration of carbon dioxide, and various minor clots and obstructions that interfere with the distribution of blood throughout the brain. Some improvements in cognitive functioning of elderly people with chronic brain syndromes have been achieved with repeated exposure to "hyperbaric" oxygen. The treatment entails inhaling 100 percent oxygen for 90-minute sessions, with periodic repetitions (Busse, 1978).

The condition of the brain caused by cerebral arteriosclerosis is fairly similar to the condition found in general paresis. The mental changes are of a somewhat similar order. It is therefore interesting to notice certain differences in the content of the symptoms and the psychological processes which they imply. Occasionally there are delusions of grandeur and persecution in psychoses with cerebral arteriosclerosis, but these are far less characteristic and less extravagantly developed than is the case in general paresis. This difference seems to be attributable to the age of the people, or more directly, to the general level of vitality at which they are living. An old person already physically handicapped and living within shrunken horizons having no perspective toward the future typically becomes confused, perhaps with a touch of depression or agitation, when the brain reaches a point of damage that is no longer consistent with integrated action. A person in middle life, still relatively vigorous, ambitious, with considerable strength of drive, reacts to brain damage with symptoms of a more compensatory kind. Thoughts may be delusional, but they are delusions that place the person in satisfying and glorious situations or that use the mechanism of projection to evade any sense of personal shortcoming. Thus it is essential to consider psychological factors in the study of brain diseases, even though these are not responsible for initiating the disorder. Disease happens to a person, and the person places an individualized stamp on the symptoms that result from the disease. In this respect older people are like everyone else: we all contribute to our own diseases and to our own health, each in our own way.

SUGGESTIONS FOR FURTHER READING

For the student interested in brain disorders, a certain amount of immersion in medical literature is necessary to understand the anatomy and functions of the nervous system. For this purpose two books on clinical neurology are recommended: D. F. Benson and D. Blumer (eds.), *Psychiatric aspects of neurological disease* (1975) and W. Blackwood and J.A.N. Corsellis (eds.), *Greenfield's neuropathology*, 3rd ed. (1976). Most of the disorders taken up in this chapter are described in more technical detail in A. M. Nicholi, Jr. (ed.), *The Harvard guide to modern psychiatry* (1978) and in S. Arieti (chief ed.), *American handbook of psychiatry*, 2nd ed. (1975), the fourth volume of which is devoted exclusively to organic disorders and includes Kurt Goldstein's important contributions to the study of brain injury in his chapter, "Functional disturbances in brain damage."

P. H. Wender's *Minimal brain dysfunction in children* (1971) is a thorough review marked by an enthusiasm for biochemical methods of treatment. Another perspective on the same general area is provided by D. Renshaw's *The hyperactive child* (1974).

601

The human problems encountered by epileptic children are discussed by C. Bagley, *The social psychology of the epileptic child* (1967). Penfield's work and reflections appear in a large work entitled *Epilepsy and the functional anatomy of the human brain* by W. Penfield and H. H. Jasper (1954). A more recent compilation of research in this area is available in H. H. Jasper, A. A. Ward, Jr., and A. Pope (eds.), *Basic mechanisms of the epilepsies* (1969).

A standard informative work on the problems and disorders of the older years is J. E. Birren, *The psychology of aging* (1964). Commendable for its descriptions of different adaptive patterns is the report by S. Reichard, F. Livson, and P. G. Petersen, *Aging and personality: A study of eighty-seven older men* (1962). Degenerative disorders of aging are discussed from a medical viewpoint by A. E. Slaby and R. J. Wyatt in *Dementia in the presenium* (1974).

A. R. Luria presents an intensive case study of traumatic head injury and the efforts to cope with it in an intelligent Russian soldier, *The man with a shattered world* (1972). *Psycholinguistics and aphasia* by H. Goodglass and S. Blumstein (1973) reviews language disorders associated with brain dysfunction. The first volume of a series, *Advances in neurology*, is devoted exclusively to one of the most enigmatic diseases known, *Huntington's chorea, 1872–1972*, edited by A. Barbeau, T. N. Chase, and G. W. Paulson (1973).

The Secret of Life (1936) by Harry Sternberg. The Philadelphia Museum of Art. SmithKline Corporation Collection.

16
Mental
Retardation

A first visit to a home for mentally retarded children is likely to be full of surprises. Those who are unfamiliar with the subject have in mind a dismal scene with children sitting around like vegetables, lethargic, expressionless, peculiar looking, and destined to stay there forever. Visitors who in their personal lives have attached great importance to intellectual brilliance may even imagine that the children must be dreadfully unhappy because of their handicap. So it is startling to be greeted at the door by a self-appointed receptionist who, though short of stature, odd of countenance, and husky of voice, takes evident pleasure in making the visitors welcome and showing them around. Looking out the window toward the play yard, the visitors may be further surprised to see three healthy look-

605

ing youngsters vigorously engaged in the cooperative task of building a snow fort. Presently a child will be encountered who is not only physically perfect but almost incredibly beautiful; the visitors will be astonished when they learn that this Adonis is incapable of any kind of restraint and happily destroys everything within reach. Elsewhere the face of a somber child may light up responsively with a beatific smile that the visitors will remember with delight for many days. Of course some of the sights are sadder. Some of the children are lethargic, some are unattractive and even deformed, a few give the impression of taking in little of what goes on around them. But the visitors are likely to come away with a far less dismal conception of life at the home, and they will have stored up another valuable lesson about the vast range of human individual differences, which show so dramatically even among the mentally retarded.

There are now increasing opportunities to make such observations in public places, private residences, schools, and the byways of the community. Programs and services are coming to be guided by a *principle of normalization*: mentally retarded citizens are entitled to services and experiences that are as "culturally normative" as possible, in order to establish and maintain personal behaviors and characteristics that are normal, adaptive, and integrated, within the limitations of their handicaps (Robinson & Robinson, 1976). The result is that many special classes are being replaced by programs that allow retarded children to spend most of each day in regular classrooms, and various forms of placement in the community are being substituted for institutional care. More and more of us will therefore be rubbing elbows with mentally retarded people, taking part in what amounts to an important therapeutic experiment.

Having a retarded child is almost inevitably a tragedy for the parents, but it need not be seen in this light for the children. Retardation by no means necessarily interferes with being happy and affectionate or with enjoying life, and one can well argue in our time that a mental horizon too limited to understand the state of the world qualifies as something of a blessing. In the recent past mental retardation, like mental illness, carried undertones of shame and was mentioned as little as possible. It has shared, however, in the recent revolutionary change of attitude. Parents have organized to secure better educational opportunities for their children, and services for the retarded have won a place in community mental health programs. Retarded children thus stand a better chance than ever before to develop their full potential and make the most of their lives, even though the scale of these lives may be small.

Measurement and Varieties of Retardation

A milestone in the history of psychology was established early in this century when Binet devised his first test for the measurement of intelligence. The practical request that prompted this venture was to find some way of sorting

out beforehand those school children who could not keep up with their classes.
The unprecedented success of Binet's scales led to a close association between
intelligence tests and the whole concept of mental retardation. In some places
mental retardation was even legally defined as a Binet intelligence quotient of
less than 75, and the criterion of the IQ was considered sufficient for placement in special classes or in state schools for the feeble minded. The same
basis was used in making the division of mental retardation into three grades:
mild subnormality (moron) with IQ from 69 to 50 and adult mentality on the
level of children of eight to twelve years; moderate subnormality (imbecile)
with IQ from 49 to 20 and mental age of three to seven years; and severe subnormality (idiot) with IQ of 19 or less and mental age no higher than two
years.

Eventually the flood tide of enthusiasm for the IQ began to recede, making
possible a more balanced and realistic conception of intelligence. The tests
were too much like school tasks and placed too much emphasis on verbal and
intellectual skills. They were not always successful in predicting the adequacy
of behavior in the practical concerns of everyday life. It was in order to meet
this difficulty that Edgar Doll (1953) worked for many years to perfect the
Vineland Social Maturity Scale. This is a scale to be filled out by observers of
the child's daily behavior, and it includes motor performances and social adjustments as well as linguistic development. The criterion of social incapacity
can thus be added to the result of tests, and mental retardation comes to have
the more reasonable meaning of a lack of "common sense" or of general
adaptability. This is reflected in the recent definition of mental retardation by
the American Association on Mental Deficiency as "significant subaverage
general intellectual functioning which originates during the developmental
period and is associated with impairment in adaptive behavior" (Grossman,
1973). Nowadays it is preferred to classify retarded children more practically
in terms of general adaptive potential, as "educable," "trainable," or "totally
dependent" (Report of the American Medical Association Conference on
Mental Retardation, 1965). An educable child may achieve a fourth- or fifth-
grade scholastic level, a moderate level of social adjustment, and a satisfactory
degree of self-support through occupations not requiring abstract thought. A
trainable child may attain an acceptable level of self-care, social adjustment
to home and neighborhood, and a degree of economic usefulness in a home,
residential facility, or sheltered workshop. A totally dependent child needs assistance in personal care, makes little adaptation to the environment, and
usually requires permanent institutionalization.

It has been estimated that over six million people in the United States, that
is, about 3 percent, are mentally subnormal (Robinson & Robinson, 1976).
This proportion corresponds roughly to the percentage of individuals with IQs
below 70. However, 4 percent of the eighteen to twenty-seven-year-old men
screened for military service in World War II were rejected for intellectual inadequacy (Ginzberg & Bray, 1953). The actual prevalence of subnormality

may be even higher than that. By far the largest part, about 85 percent of those called mentally subnormal are only mildly retarded, as contrasted with about 1 percent who are profoundly retarded (Bernstein, 1978). The mildly retarded are clearly educable and capable of leading productive lives. Most of them are classified as *socioculturally* retarded because they typically come from families and cultural backgrounds where retardation is common.

About 200,000 retarded individuals reside in institutions, 82 percent of which are designed for people below the educable or mildly retarded level of intelligence (Klaber, 1969). It has been proposed to reserve the term *mental deficiency* for these more extremely retarded children because their handicaps are more pronounced and are presumably related to brain damage. In such cases there is almost always clear evidence of gross developmental abnormality. Structural defects are apparent both in the nervous system and in other organs. For most of these disorders there is strong evidence against simple inheritance of low intelligence, as in sociocultural retardation; they commonly occur in families of average intelligence and sometimes in the offspring of highly gifted parents. There are several recognized varieties of severe mental deficiency, but most of them occur quite rarely.

In this chapter we describe in some detail three illustrative forms of retardation and mention briefly several others to give some impression of the variety of possible causes for mental retardation. The principal illustrations are *Down's syndrome*, a chromosomal disorder; *phenylketonuria*, a metabolic disorder; and *sociocultural* retardation, which will introduce us to the effect of environmental influences in the development of intelligence.

DOWN'S SYNDROME

Nearly a century ago Langdon Down, a British physician, gave the name of *mongolism* to a form of mental deficiency in which it struck him that the child had the facial characteristics of the Mongolian races. The alleged resemblance is actually found only in the eyes, which especially during the first few years are almost almond shaped and slope upward toward their outer corners. *Down's syndrome*, as it is now called, is a severe form of mental deficiency in which the trainable level is usually not surpassed. But it is more than a mental deficiency; in view of the many associated physical symptoms, it must be considered a form of general developmental arrest. The whole head is peculiarly shaped, quite flat on the back, and with depression of the nasal bridge. The tongue is large and coarsely fissured; in many cases it protrudes from the mouth a good deal of the time. The hands and feet are stubby and square, and there is often a wide separation between the big toe and the other toes. Stature is small for age, the musculature tends to be hypotonic or rubbery, and gait is awkward and shambling. The physical appearance is decidedly

608

odd and becomes only more so if these children grow to adulthood. Their adjustment to society would be no easy matter even if intelligence were normal.

On post-mortem study, the brain is found to be clearly abnormal, showing signs of widespread interference with the growth of neural cells. Investigators differ as to how to characterize and explain this defect, but Benda (1969) believes that asphyxiation of nerve cells is one of the most important features. He speculates that a metabolic deficiency may prevent the brain cells, as well as other tissues, from developing normally.

Down's syndrome accounts for 10 percent of the cases institutionalized for mental subnormality (Benda, 1969). The proportion is undoubtedly smaller among retardates who live at home since Down's syndrome children usually fall in the lower ranges of ability and are therefore less readily managed at home. A few children with Down's syndrome advance to the point of mastering simple speech and doing simple chores. One study rated only 4 percent of those living at home as educable (Wunsch, 1957), but Rynders, Spiker, and Horrobin (1978) argue that the educability of Down's syndrome children has been seriously underestimated; they reviewed 15 studies and concluded that a third to a half are educable, especially those with the *mosaic* form of the disorder (which we describe later). Typically, speech is absent or confined to a few hoarsely spoken sounds, and activities consist of rather repetitive play. Despite their limited equipment, these children are not usually sluggish or unhappy. Institutional workers find them more friendly, happy, and affectionate than other severely handicapped children. A small minority are aggressive and hostile. However, the frequency of emotional disturbance is no greater than in other groups, even of normal children. Menolascino (1965) found abnormal EEG tracings in half of his disturbed cases, suggesting that additional cerebral abnormalities may be responsible for their deviation from the "sunny disposition" stereotype.

Physical health in Down's syndrome is poor. It has been found that 30 percent die before one month, 53 percent by one year, and 60 percent by ten years (Kirman, 1964). Few live very far into adulthood. The most common causes of death are bronchopneumonia and congenital heart disease. Noting the high frequency of death by tuberculosis, Down (1866) attributed the cause of mongolism to an inherited disposition to tuberculosis. It now appears that having a large tongue protruding from a small mouth induces mouth breathing and susceptibility to all sorts of upper respiratory infections. With the recent discovery of the true cause of the disorder, a basic genetic flaw that is reproduced throughout the body, it is now understandable that such children would be exceptionally vulnerable to physical disease.

The birth rate for Down's syndrome is approximately one in 650 live births (Kirman & Bicknell, 1975). However the rate increases sharply as the age of the mother goes up. For mothers under 25 the risk is less than one in 1500 births, but it increases to one in 150 births for mothers over 35 and to one in 38 for

609

mothers over 45 (Robinson & Robinson, 1976). A study in Sweden yielded even more extreme results, with higher rates at every age interval and one in 16 Down's syndrome babies born to women over 45 (Lindsjö, 1974)! There is as yet no certain explanation for this correlation with maternal age. Some workers have pointed out that the diverse physical symptoms of Down's syndrome make a certain sense when one considers them as lying in those organs which undergo crucial differentiation during the second and third months of embryonic life. The fetus with Down's syndrome shows during this period a deceleration of normal development which is not compensated in the later months before birth. It is noteworthy that at precisely this period there is a fairly radical readjustment in the maternal hormone pattern in order to sustain the further development of the fetus. Conceivably in older mothers, near the end of reproductive capacity, hormonal changes give rise to the genetic fault that initiates the general developmental deviation.

Sensorimotor and mental development usually follow a course of relative decline during the first year or two of life, followed by a slower decline in the developmental quotient to age three or four, and then a relative leveling off. The modal IQ of those living at home is 40 to 54, but those in institutions usually have IQs lower than 35 (Robinson & Robinson, 1976). The principal intellectual limitations are in higher-level integrative abilities, such as concept

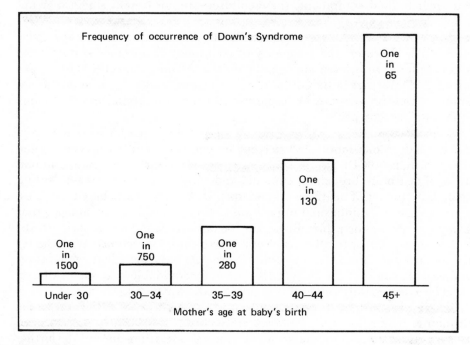

Figure 16.1
(From Smith and Wilson, 1973, p. 17.)

formation, abstraction, and expressive language (Cornwell, 1974). With supervision, many adults can do productive work: driving a tractor, housework, simple carpentry.

Genetic Fault

Because of the striking physical abnormalities it has been suspected for a long time that genetic aberrations might cause Down's syndrome. Only recently have the technical means been developed to discern this aberration specifically. One of the great breakthroughs in modern mental health was the discovery in 1959 that the body cells of Down's syndrome children contain 47 chromosomes instead of the normal 46. In the course of normal reproduction the egg cell from the mother and the sperm cells from the father separately undergo cell division to reduce the chromosome count in each from 46 to 23, so that when the two unite during fertilization the offspring will possess the normal complement of 46 chromosomes, half from each parent. Lejeune and his colleagues (1959) found that affected children have three, rather than two, number 21 chromosomes, and labelled this pattern *trisomy 21*. They inferred that the fault lay in the failure of the two chromosomes of pair number 21 to separate *(nondisjunction)* in the egg cell prior to ovulation. If such an ovum with 24 chromosomes is fertilized by a normal sperm with 23 chromosomes, the offspring with 47 chromosomes will have Down's syndrome. It is possible that the extra chromosome could come from the father, but the vastly larger number of sperm cells favors the selection of normal sperms for conception. Because the total number of egg cells produced is much smaller, the likelihood of an abnormal one being selected for conception is far greater. In the fruit fly nondisjunction is greatly influenced by maternal aging, and considering the correlation between maternal age and Down's syndrome birth rate, it seems most likely that the egg bears the extra chromosome. It is still not known precisely what causes the faulty maturation of the egg.

Down's syndrome caused by nondisjunction is very rarely familial. It is a *genetic* disorder but not an *inherited* one, because the reproductive error produces a genetic makeup unlike that of the parents. There is a rare form of Down's syndrome, about 4 percent of all cases, that can be inherited. In the preparation for reproduction a piece of one chromosome may break off and become attached to another chromosome, producing the *translocation* syndrome. Parents may be phenotypically normal carriers of the syndrome, though males are less often carriers than females. The offspring of a carrier have a 10 percent risk of the disorder, and the translocation syndrome carries a much higher risk of recurrence in future siblings of an affected child (Kirman & Bicknell, 1975).

Nondisjunction can also occur during cell division in the fetus *after* conception is complete. In this case, one of the daughter cells would receive three chromosomes, rendering it trisomic, and the other would receive only one

611

chromosome, causing it probably to die. This produces a *mosaic* pattern whereby individuals display varying proportions of normal and trisomic cells, depending on how soon the abnormal cell division occurred following fertilization. Down's syndrome mosaics are less affected mentally and physically than those with classical trisomy 21 (Melnyk & Koch, 1976). About 2 to 3 percent of all Down's syndrome cases show the mosaic pattern and, like the translocation syndrome, mosaicism can be transmitted genetically from one generation to the next. In the great majority of cases, parents with one Down's syndrome child need not fear passing on a genetic liability through their normal children, and if they are still young and want to have more children they are usually advised to do so.

Over a dozen cases have been recorded of women with Down's syndrome giving birth, but there are no known instances of men with the disorder fathering children. Five of 13 babies on record had Down's syndrome, two were otherwise mentally retarded, four were normal, and three were stillborn (Kirman & Bicknell, 1975). Nature's disapproval of this flagrant genetic mutation is clear to see.

Early Detection

Amniocentesis, a simple and reasonably safe diagnostic procedure, is now recommended during pregnancy when the risk for Down's syndrome is known to be high, for example, if one parent is known to be a carrier for the translocation or mosaic syndrome, if the couple already has a child with Down's syndrome, or if the mother is older than thirty-five. Women over thirty-five account for about 6 percent of all births, but about a third of all Down's syndrome infants are born to them. However, only 5 percent of women in this age range now obtain the test. At about 14 to 16 weeks of pregnancy a small amount of amniotic fluid is extracted through the mother's abdomen with a long needle, exercising care to avoid injuring the fetus. The procedure requires only a few minutes in a doctor's office. Many of the early hazards encountered have now been brought under control, so that it is relatively safe, carrying a risk of less than 1 percent for spontaneous abortion. Three weeks are required to culture enough of the cells for the necessary laboratory studies, but the accuracy of assessment is very high for Down's syndrome and many other gestational abnormalities. For instance, almost all spinal column defects (spina bifida, anencephaly) can be detected by a large volume of a distinctive protein in the amniotic fluid (Crandall, 1978).

If the laboratory cultures indicate that the fetus is abnormal, abortion can be performed while it is still safe to do so. The incidence of Down's syndrome has begun to decline because older mothers are having fewer children and with the increasing availability of amniocentesis the termination of high-risk pregnancies has reduced the overall level of mortality at birth (Collmann & Stoller, 1969).

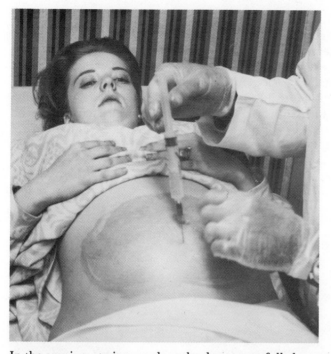

In the amniocentesis procedure the doctor carefully locates the fetus first, then inserts a long needle through the mother's abdomen to extract a small amount of amniotic fluid from a spot that is not occupied by the fetus. The accuracy of diagnostic assessment for reproductive abnormalities is extremely high.

Treatment

Children with Down's syndrome are not destined for substantial improvements in intelligence. No drug treatments have proven to reduce their handicaps (Share, 1976), which is understandable in the light of the irreversible genetic etiology. In most cases the children are placed in institutions at an early age and live out the remainder of their lives there. However, Sarason and Doris (1969) offer a spirited critique of "instant institutionalization" unless it is medically necessary (e.g., when the child has congenital heart defects) or otherwise required by social considerations. In increasing numbers families have decided to raise the children at home. The decision is fraught with difficulty. Probably it is better for the child to be at home, but the parents may overestimate their own capacity to be tied down by continuous intensive care, and the effects on their normal children may be far from desirable. If they decide for home rearing, they will do well to seek such help as can be obtained from community mental health agencies.

Parents who do decide to raise the children at home can take encouragement from some early education programs designed to maximize the intellec-

613

tual and adaptive potential in Down's syndrome children. Rynders and Hor-robin (1975) described such a program with tutoring carried out by *parents*, aimed especially at accelerating deficient communication skills. This was aug-mented through itinerant teaching by specialists in a mobile camper, to pro-vide variety in their learning experience and important social exposure to adults outside the family. The children were enrolled at 3 to 9 months of age and continued through 30 months in infancy training by the parents in the home. From 30 months to five years of age they attended a preschool program staffed by professionals. The project was organized with 20 experimental and 20 control children. At five years of age the experimental group was not signif-icantly ahead of the controls on the two targeted intellectual abilities (concept

There once was a time when virtually all children with Down's syndrome were institu-tionalized at an early age and never returned to the community. Now many of them live at home or in sheltered environments in the community, and develop active lives—within limits—just like other people. This dance pupil may never match the graceful-ness and skill of her teacher, but she may surprise her parents and many skeptics with her progress.

utilization and expressive language) but the experimental group advanced significantly more in IQ scores and motor functioning.

A similar program reported by Hayden and Dmitriev (1975) has produced encouraging initial results. They enrolled 44 children in four sequential programs. The infancy learning unit from five weeks to 18 months concentrated on developing sensorimotor skills; the early preschool program from 18 months to three years focused on gross motor development, concept learning, and language; the advanced preschoolers from three to five years of age learned cognitive skills and social interaction. The Kindergarten program from four and one-half to six years was still to be designed. The infancy learning unit resulted in scores on the Gesell Preliminary Behavior Inventory one month below their chronological age at 18 months, whereas the norm for Down's syndrome children is one year below chronological age. The early preschool results showed the greatest progress in gross motor development and concept learning, but least progress in language. By age three, after 6 to 12 months in the program, the children had a mean deficit of about six months in mental age, as compared with a deficit of 21 months for youngsters just starting the program. After one year in the advanced preschool program, the mean IQ for the group increased from 75 to 83, which is high enough to expect that some of them will be able to succeed in regular public school programs.

PHENYLKETONURIA (PKU)

Phenylketonuria is a rare form of mental retardation. It occurs about once in 13,000 to 20,000 live births (Robinson & Robinson, 1976) and accounts for about one percent of the cases in institutions for the retarded (Heber, 1970). However, it has great theoretical significance because it is one of the most thoroughly understood forms of retardation, it can be effectively treated if discovered early, and it serves as a prototype for investigating a whole class of metabolic disorders that have been discovered recently.

PKU was first recognized in 1934 by Asbjorn Følling, a Norwegian biochemist and physician, when the parents of two retarded children brought to his attention a musty odor in the urine of both children. On chemical analysis he ascertained that the odor was caused by phenylpyruvic acid, which was excreted in the urine because the children lacked a basic enzyme that is necessary to metabolize *phenylalanine*, an amino acid. Surveys of institutions for the retarded in several countries turned up many other cases and quickly made it clear that the disorder is transmitted genetically in recessive Mendelian fashion. It has been estimated that one person in 100 carries the gene (Penrose, 1963), but more recent prevalence figures would indicate that carriers may number twice that many. A retarded child results only when one carrier mates with another carrier, which accounts for the fortunately low prevalence of the disorder. However, the risk increases considerably when relatives marry because if one mate carries the gene the other is more likely to carry it also. The danger is highest, of course, in any family which already has a phenylketonuric child; this constitutes clear evidence that the gene is carried on both sides of the family. One in four siblings of a child with PKU will also predictably have the disorder.

Now it is known that the missing enzyme is *phenylalanine hydroxylase*, which is produced normally in the liver for the purpose of converting phenylalanine to tyrosine. Tyrosine is important for the formation of skin pigmentation, among other things, so most affected children are blond and blue-eyed with fair skin that is susceptible to eczema. They usually are of small stature and have rather small heads. Their teeth are broad and widely spaced. Their reflexes are accentuated and they may be somewhat humpbacked, which causes them to move and walk peculiarly. Sometimes they sweat excessively. About 90 percent of untreated cases develop severe or moderate mental retardation, which is probably associated with the degenerative changes in the brain found on autopsy; very few achieve an IQ above 50, about two-thirds cannot talk and a third cannot walk or control excretion. They are restless, jerky, fearful, hyperactive, irritable, and given to uncontrollable temper tantrums (Knox, 1972). Other common symptoms are vomiting, epileptic seizures, and unpredictable behavior, such as rocking movements, grinding of teeth, arm waving, and overall aimless movements; several of these lead to occasional misdiagnosis as early childhood schizophrenia (Koch, Acosta, & Dobson, 1976). Paradoxically, PKU children usually enjoy good physical health and many are quite attractive in facial appearance, which is unusual in severe forms of retardation.

The presence of phenylpyruvic acid in the urine is revealed by very simple tests with ferric chloride, usually in the first few weeks of life. However, in some cases the acid may not build up to detectable levels in the urine until as late as five weeks. Prompt detection is vital to early treatment and to genetic counseling regarding future pregnancies. More complicated and expensive tests can be made for excessive phenylalanine in the blood serum after the fifth or sixth day of life, even before the infant leaves the newborn nursery (Guthrie & Susi, 1963). In this way siblings of known PKU victims or the offspring of two known carriers of the gene can be monitored carefully from birth onward for signs of the disease. Most states in this country now require massive screening programs in hospitals and thorough routine pediatric follow-up. It is possible (though not yet foolproof) to identify carriers of the recessive gene by feeding them very large amounts of phenylalanine and measuring how fast it disappears from the blood (Hsia et al., 1956; Berry, Sutherland, & Guest, 1957).

Dietary Control

616   The reason so much attention has been concentrated on diagnosing PKU early is that proper dietary control may greatly lessen or prevent altogether the

damaging effects of the metabolic error. Special diet preparations are now available that contain all the necessary nutrients and the minimum essential amount of phenylalanine. The synthetic foods are supplemented with natural foods of low phenylalanine content and sufficient milk to prevent blood levels of phenylalanine from falling too low; if that happens the child's growth and neurological development are impaired in another way. Like most amino acids, some phenylalanine is vital for growth.

Dietary treatment should begin as early as possible because the ultimate IQ a child attains is very highly correlated (r = .67) with age at which treatment is begun. Knox (1960) estimated an average loss of nearly five IQ points for each ten weeks' delay in treatment. The protection against intellectual impairment is dramatic for most children if treatment begins early, and many attain normal IQs. Berman and Ford (1970) found that successfully treated PKU children performed intellectually in the average range (M = 96) but 12 points below the average for their own families, showing a mild deficit. Kirman and Bicknell (1975) reported that even with timely dietary treatment IQs remain 20 to 25 points below the mean for unaffected siblings, which presumably reflects excesses in the diet, either too little or too much phenylalanine. The Collaborative Study of Children Treated for Phenylketonuria (1975) is a cooperative venture among treatment teams throughout the country that are currently following a total of 150 true PKU cases treated initially before four months of age. (The mean starting time was 19 days of age.) The children were divided into two subgroups that are being maintained at different levels of blood phenylalanine—neither low enough to prove damaging—in order to determine which is the optimum level for healthy development. The early results to age four show no IQ differences between the two groups (M = 91 and 92) and a low but significant deficit as compared to unaffected siblings (M = 97). The fact that this deficit is so small, by comparison to earlier studies, underlines how necessary it is to monitor carefully the phenylalanine levels after dietary treatment has begun, in order to prevent imbalance in *either* direction. This is especially important for infants that show high levels shortly after birth for other reasons than phenylketonuria, because phenylalanine starvation also results in impairment of the central nervous system. It is apparently not the phenylalanine itself that has adverse effects on the brain, but rather the total disturbance of metabolism that results from its accumulation, presumably because it competes with other essential processes, such as those that facilitate *myelination* (the development of a protective sheath around organs in the central nervous system).

If phenylketonuria is untreated, most of the intellectual damage is done during the first two or three years of life, when brain development is most rapid. For this reason it was believed until recently that dietary treatment could be discontinued after about six years of age (Sarason & Doris, 1969). The rationale was that, after that point, the central nervous system was sufficiently mature to tolerate the elevated phenylalanine levels without further

A brother and sister, both of whom have phenylketonuria. The girl's diet was restricted early to reduce the serious consequences of the disease. Not having had the treatment, the boy is not only intellectually retarded, but has some difficulty sitting up straight in the chair.

damage or intellectual deterioration. However, Brown and Warner (1976) have found that PKU children taken off the diet after six lost 9 to 10 IQ points by age sixteen, while those on the diet remained about the same. The special diet may also result in behavioral improvement for older children without previous treatment, but IQ gains are very limited. Phenylketonuric mothers who are untreated during their pregnancies have a large number of children that are retarded; about 25 percent have congenital malformations, such as microcephaly (Perry et al., 1973). Unless the father also carries the recessive gene for PKU, the baby is not phenylketonuric, which indicates that the retardation is caused by the high phenylalanine in the intrauterine environment, rather than by the genes inherited. All of this speaks for continuing the diet in affected people at least throughout childhood and during pregnancy. Perry et al. (1973) also recommend giving ferric chloride urine tests routinely for all pregnant women.

An Ethical Problem for Genetic Disorders

Finding ways to limit the transmission of a recessive gene would meet enormous practical and ethical obstacles. First it would be necessary to identify all the unaffected carriers of the gene, who may number over four million in the United States alone. Naturally such screening could omit all people over or under the childbearing age, but that would still leave tens of millions of Americans to be tested. With present techniques that would be exorbitantly expensive. However it is conceivable that in the next few years the screening procedures will be streamlined enough to permit a PKU carrier test for all couples who apply for a marriage license, in the same way that the Wasserman test for syphilis is now required. How would the knowledge of those results be utilized to help eliminate PKU? Presumably, a couple that learned they were both carriers of the recessive gene might find the 25 percent risk of conceiving a defective child was too great and decide to adopt children instead. But by what logic would society impose that decision on them if they were unwilling? Or consider the less threatening case of a carrier marrying a noncarrier. Could society justify prohibiting that couple from procreating, merely on the ground that this would perpetuate a latent potential for the disorder in subsequent generations?

It seems clear that such a eugenic program would not be tolerated. We are left with the prospect of living with the latent threat. But fortunately we are not without some tools to cope with phenylketonuria in its manifest form. It is already feasible now to identify most infants with the disorder, at modest cost, by means of the ferric chloride urine test and/or the Guthrie blood serum test. Once identified, the severe effects of the disorder can be limited in most cases by careful dietary treatment during childhood. And in the not too distant future, with improved actuarial and technical procedures, it may be possible to carry out the pedigree studies necessary to pinpoint the matings and the childbirths that require the closest surveillance.

Many other metabolic disorders are now better understood because of the early screening programs with infant blood tests for PKU. A good example is *galactosemia*, a recessive genetic disorder in which an enzyme required to metabolize the lactose in milk and milk products is missing, causing a buildup of toxic galactose and its derivatives; this causes damage to the lens of the eye, brain, liver, and other tissues, and results in mild mental retardation if not promptly treated dietetically by eliminating milk from the diet (Kalckar, Kinoshito, & Donnell, 1973). A partial solution to the ethical problem just raised may be provided by amniocentesis, which can already identify more than 30 of these metabolic errors *in utero* (Kirman & Bicknell, 1975). The practical problem that remains is to identify for further evaluation those pregnancies with the highest risk of infant abnormality, which depends primarily on locating the potential parents that are most disposed to faulty reproduction.

SOCIOCULTURAL RETARDATION

Only 4 percent of the retarded reside in institutions; the rest live at home (Report of the American Medical Association Conference on Mental Retardation, 1965). By far the largest part of these are only mildly retarded. Most are educable and able to work. There is seldom evidence for gross structural defect in the brain. The majority do not have an abnormal electroencephalogram

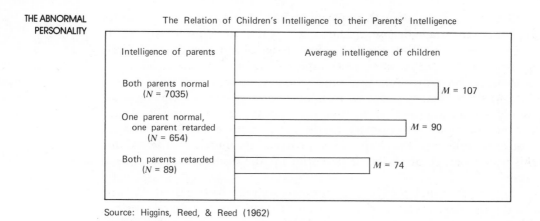

Source: Higgins, Reed, & Reed (1962)

Figure 16.2

The relation of children's intelligence to their parents' intelligence. *Source:* Higgins, Reed, & Reed (1962).

(EEG) and do not, if they come to autopsy, show distinctive peculiarities in cerebral tissues. On psychological tests they do not make the sort of performance errors that are characteristic of brain-injured people. In contrast to Down's syndrome and phenylketonuria, no single physical agent is presumed to cause this sort of retardation. Affected children are normal in physical appearance, health, and longevity. We use here the term *sociocultural retardation* to cover this milder form of backwardness. The diagnosis is usually made when the child enters school and often is dropped on leaving school, suggesting that intellectual retardation is more conspicuous than deficiencies in social adaptation. The real trouble is that the child is slow in schoolwork and seems perhaps a little dull in general understanding.

These children usually do not differ much from their parents in IQ. Higgins, Reed, and Reed (1962) studied 7778 families with varying levels of parental intelligence (see Figure 16-2). Among 7035 children with neither parent retarded the average IQ was 107; among 654 with one retarded parent the average was 90; if both parents were retarded, as in 89 cases studied, the child's IQ averaged 74. The risk of retardation was somewhat higher if the retarded parent was the mother (Reed & Anderson, 1973), which suggests that her contribution to the child's upbringing may be pivotal. This is consistent with the results of Clarke-Stewart (1973), who observed the interactions of 36 mothers with their first-born infants, ages 9 to 18 months. The overall competence of the child was highly related to the quality of mothering behavior: expressions of affection, provision of social stimulation, contingent responsiveness to and acceptance of the child's behavior, effectiveness in using materials to stimulate the child's play, and the appropriateness of the mother's behavior for the child's age and ability. Language development was strongly related to the mother's verbal stimulation.

On the other hand, we might infer that children simply inherit limited intellectual capacities genetically, a possibility no more startling than that the children of gifted intellectual people tend to inherit superior intellectual gifts. The fact that retardation is most prevalent among the nearest relatives of retarded persons (Reed & Reed, 1965) could signify that the milder forms of retardation are a consequence of polygenic inheritance. Although no single dominant or recessive gene accounts for the inheritance of intelligence in general, it is now believed that a number of related genes in combination do so. This conception of the genetic aspect would lead us to expect that if two itinerant farm hands or two slum dwellers of limited intelligence produce offspring, their children will likewise be of limited intelligence (Jensen, 1969). Just as bright parents have bright children, dull parents have dull children—so goes the strictly genetic reasoning.

Recent studies of intelligence, however, put the question of nature versus nurture in a somewhat different light. These studies show that intelligence, as measured at any point, depends significantly on past experience and past stimulation; whatever the natural potential, it has to be developed by exercise (Hunt, 1961, 1969). This means that environment plays a part in what we refer to as level of intelligence. New significance at once appears in the fact that mildly retarded children come so often from families with poor education and living in depressed neighborhoods. Illiteracy rates in this country are three times the national average among youths from families with incomes below $3000 per year, and twice the national average if family income is between $3000 and $5000 (Vogt, 1973). To quote from a national report on retardation:

> Epidemiological data from many reliable studies show a remarkably heavy correlation between the incidence of mental retardation, particularly in its milder manifestations, and the adverse social, economic, and cultural status of families and groups of our population. These are for the most part the low income groups—who often live in the slums and are frequently minority groups—where the mother and the children receive inadequate medical care, where family breakdown is common, where individuals are without motivation and opportunity and without adequate education. In short, the conditions which spawn many other health and social problems are to a large extent the same ones which generate the problems of mental retardation. To be successful in preventing mental retardation on a large scale, a broad attack on the fundamental adverse conditions will be necessary (The President's Panel on Mental Retardation, 1962, pp. 9-10).

Sociocultural Deprivation

The adverse social conditions mentioned above are those commonly associated with poverty as Miller (1970) lists them: "economic privation, social and economic discrimination, inadequate and overcrowded housing, substandard nutrition, low parental education attainment, unskilled laboring vocations,

621

usually large families, and often, minority group membership" (p. 457). That they are related to mental retardation is shown in estimates of retarded intelligence at various socioeconomic class levels. Over 11 percent of children in the lowest class (of five) have IQ's below 75, as compared with 4 percent in the middle class and less than one percent in the highest class (Heber, 1970). Similarly, over 25 percent of black men were excused from military service in World War II because of deficient intelligence, compared with less than 3 percent of white men (Ginzberg & Bray, 1953).

Sociocultural deprivation contributes to mental retardation in two physical ways: birth complications and malnutrition. Obstetrical mishaps are disproportionately frequent among the economically disadvantaged, and the incidence of mental retardation is significantly greater when pregnancy or delivery is complicated. Consider, for example, some facts concerning premature births. Substantially more premature babies are born to lower-class parents than to middle- or upper-class parents (Heber, 1970). Incidence of physical and mental abnormalities increases as birth weight decreases. On Gesell developmental examinations at forty weeks after birth, 17.6 percent of very small babies were judged to be retarded or borderline in intellectual potential, as compared with 1.8 percent of the moderately small babies and 1.6 percent of the control babies with average birth weight (Knobloch et al., 1956). It is clear that mental retardation is more common among deprived classes because they have more premature births, which in turn is explained by a number of interrelated circumstances. They have more pregnancies at a very early age, inadequate and tardy prenatal medical care, small maternal stature, and poor nutrition and general health.

Malnutrition is a common condition in the large rural areas of the southeastern United States, in crowded urban slums, and especially where minority populations are large (Reschly & Jipson, 1977). Women in these areas have diets that are poor, especially in the proteins that are essential for the development of the central nervous system. They also have the highest rates of congenital malformations in their children, particularly those affecting the central nervous system. It is well known that malnutrition can impair mental development. Beginning six months before birth and lasting until six months after birth, cell division causes rapid growth of brain tissue. Nutritional deprivation during this period can severely retard that growth, and this may be irreversible unless treatment begins before cell division ends. From six months through the second year of life, the rate of brain growth is still very rapid, mainly through protein synthesis, but nutritional rehabilitation still can be partially effective. Beyond this point the rate of brain growth is much slower so the effects of treatment on IQ scores are negligible after the age of four (Kaplan, 1972). Harrell, Woodyard, and Gates demonstrated convincingly the effect of good nutrition on intelligence by giving daily dietary supplements to pregnant mothers of poor socioeconomic status in Virginia. Children whose mothers had received supplements of thiamine, riboflavin, niacin, and iron during pregnancy had significantly higher IQ's at three years of age than those whose mothers had been given only inert material. Such results are encouraging because they indicate that inexpensive and expedient intervention *can* increase the intellectual potential of large numbers of deprived children.

Sociocultural deprivation affects mental retardation by another route. Disadvantaged children make a poor start in school. Initially they score substantially lower on intelligence tests and the gap increases with age (Heber & Dever, 1970). They come to school without the skills necessary to profit from first grade work. In their language skills, both written and spoken, they are less advanced than other children. Visual discrimination is poorly developed.

Poverty is often associated with poor nutrition and large families, and unfortunately with poor mental health. Retarded intelligence, for example, is most prevalent among the lowest social classes.

They fall two years behind in scholastic achievement by the sixth grade and almost three years behind by the eighth grade. Not surprisingly, they are more likely to drop out of school before completing a secondary education. Even those socioculturally deprived children who have adequate ability are less likely to go to college (Hess & Shipman, 1965). As a result of abortive schooling the employment prospects for such children are bleak, and getting worse. Advances in technology displace mostly people from unskilled jobs while creating new positions for people with high levels of education and technical skill. Over-all employment in this country expanded steadily from 1953 to 1963 but jobs for those without high school education declined by 25 percent. Two-thirds of the unemployed in 1963 had failed to complete high school. Meanwhile jobs for registered nurses, auto mechanics, carpenters, computer operators, and machinists went begging (Tizard, 1970). When culturally deprived children grow up, their horizons remain limited because their lack of education and skills leaves them no leverage for economic and social advancement. Consequently their children enter school with the same cultural handicaps that their parents had, and the cycle begins again.

Finally, physical abuse of children is more prevalent among lower social classes and minority groups, and it is significantly associated with intellectual deficit. One study found that 25 percent of children with major head injuries attributed to child abuse achieved IQs below 70, compared with only 3 percent for a control group of similar economic background (Sandgrund, Gaines, & Green, 1974).

Stimulation and Motivation

Two important reasons for the scholastic and social limitations of deprived children are their lack of early intellectual stimulation and their failure to acquire the values and motives of the dominant culture in our society. Numerous studies have shown that their parents read less to them in the preschool years; they have less variety of visual and other sensory exposure; and verbal interchanges with their parents are restricted. Their physical and social environments are relatively unresponsive to their natural urges to explore and "do things" because they live in drab settings with few novel objects and their parents are too preoccupied with managing daily life to return a smile or to engage in entertaining play. Behavior patterns that produce a result tend to be repeated, and getting results, as we have seen, is prerequisite to acquiring a sense of competence and mastery over the environment. It seems reasonable to infer that discouraging exploratory behavior through nonresponse leads to the apathy and incompetence so often seen in these children. Similarly, deprived children receive less parental encouragement for their natural efforts in self-care and independence. There are fewer rewards to make them strive for achievement in school, learn aesthetic and technical skills, develop personal control, or delay gratification (Uzgiris, 1970). These are obvious handicaps to success in school and later in the job market.

Orphanages, hospitals, and schools for the retarded are special kinds of deprived environments and, unfortunately, they have the same adverse effects on intelligence and social adaptation (Bowlby, 1966; Spitz, 1945). Skeels and Dye (1939) measured substantial rises in the IQ's of retarded children after transfer from a dull orphanage to an institution where they became the objects of much affection and encouragement. After two years in the new setting the children gained more than 28 IQ points on the average while a control group that remained in the orphanage lost 26 IQ points. Most of the experimental group were placed in adoptive homes and maintained their earlier gains in intelligence. Follow-up study 21 years later showed that the two groups maintained their divergent patterns of ability as adults. All of the experimental group were self-supporting; their average education was through twelfth grade and their average income was $5220; almost all of them had married and their children had an average IQ of 104. By contrast, a third of the control children remained wards of institutions and one had died during adolescence in an institution; their average education was through third grade and their average income was only $1200; only two had married, one having four normal children and the other having a retarded child (Skeels, 1966). Had the experimental children remained in the orphanage or similar institutions, it seems clear they would not have approached their full intellectual and social potential, and quite possibly that constriction might have extended to their children and beyond.

Some public schools resemble these custodial institutions in their effects on children's growth. It is well known that the quality of education is poorest in "racially imbalanced" school systems (where there are few or no white children), in isolated rural areas like Appalachia, in urban slum areas, and in other places where poverty is extensive. There are obvious reasons for this. Good teachers, equipment, and school buildings are expensive commodities, and competing demands for public service have a claim on tax dollars. The quality of public education is determined in part by the pressure for improvement exerted by citizens and parents. Here again the effects of deprivation are self-perpetuating. Well-educated parents place a high value on their children's education and readily translate that desire into political and social action. Should their efforts be frustrated, they resort to private education. Less educated parents, on the other hand, typically exert less pressure to improve schools, perhaps because they are less aware of their value or because they doubt the efficacy of their efforts to bring about change. Finally, teachers and parents and the children themselves tend to *expect* poor scholastic performance from culturally deprived youngsters. Early belief that a child is untalented is likely to drain the teacher's attention and interest to pupils who seem more gifted, and who thus unwittingly receive a better education. It may well be that lower-class children are prevented from reaching their full potential by the discouraging attitudes of their teachers. The happy counterpoint to that is that changing attitudes toward their capacity to learn may pay off handsomely.

Learned Passivity and Incompetence

Harter and Zigler (1974) tested the effects of mental retardation and of institutionalization on *effectance motivation* by comparing the performance of normal children, institutionalized retarded children, and retarded children living at home. They devised four measures that tapped variety-seeking, curiosity, mastery for the sake of competence, and preference for challenging tasks. On every measure the nonretarded children demonstrated the highest degree of effective motivation, followed by the noninstitutionalized retardates and then those in institutions. Apparently the retarded children were "shaped" by a long history of defeats to take a passive orientation toward life, and institutionalization may extend the process through its pressures for conformity and passivity. That demoralizing pattern can be reversed in retarded children of all levels of capability. Even profoundly retarded children can learn elementary self-help and work responsibilities, such as sweeping the floor or feeding younger children. These responsibilities can become the focus of their sense of competence, for they, like everyone, seek to be the masters of their own environment.

The Milwaukee Project

One of the most ambitious ventures of social engineering ever undertaken in the field of mental health is the Milwaukee Project (Heber & Garber, 1975; Heber, 1978). It began with a survey of the most impoverished neighborhood in the city. Mothers with IQs below 80 comprised less than half of the survey sample but produced four-fifths of the children with IQs below 80. These children also showed progressive intellectual decline with age. The neighborhood included 2.5 percent of the population of Milwaukee but yielded about a third of the city's educable retarded public school children. The area was placed in the lowest census categories for educational level and income, and in the highest categories for population density, housing delapidation, and unemployment.

An experimental intervention program was designed with a sample of 40 families, all black, with mothers whose IQs were less than 75. Half the sample was randomly assigned to the experimental treatment condition, and the other half served as controls. At the time of birth there were no known differences in weight, height, abnormality of delivery, or infant condition between the two groups, nor any difference in the economic status of the families or the number of siblings.

The program began with rehabilitation training for the experimental mothers, which consisted of a one-month course of adult education to provide the basic academic tools necessary for vocational adaptation and six months of occupational training for special skills in health services, for example, nursing assistance, dietetics, housekeeping, and laundry. Group counseling was provided at the end of each day of training. All but one of the 20 mothers were rated employable at the end of the training program. On securing employment, the training focus shifted to family and home care: budgeting, nutrition and food preparation, family hygiene, and the mother's role in child growth and development. Fathers were marginally involved in the training for the mothers. The employment training was generally found to be successful, but the training in homemaking and child care did not succeed well in many cases.

The child training program began at 3 to 6 months and continued — all day, five days a week, 12 months each year — through six years of age, when the children would start first grade in public schools. The child was transported each day to and from the training center by project staff, and received intensive educational training in perceptual-motor skills, language and cognitive skills, and social-emotional development. Except for one professional teacher, the education was provided by paraprofessionals, with special emphasis on mathematics and problem solving, reading readiness, and language. Each preschool day lasted from 9 o'clock to 4 o'clock and was divided into half-hour periods of small-group learning, activity, and play, with two hours around noon for lunch and a long nap. Scholastic learning was centered on specific cognitive skills: classification, association, generalization, integration, and interpretation. Achievement motivation was fostered by creating an atmosphere that was interesting, providing success experiences with supportive and corrective feedback from responsive adults, and gradually increasing the child's responsibility for completing tasks. It was hoped that the children would develop a positive, confident self-image through these successful, pleasant learning experiences, reinforcement from adults, positive peer interactions, and opportunities for self-expression.

Both the experimental and control children entered public schools at six, and they have been followed for three years since then without further intervention. The results of the experiment have been dramatic. Early development was measured with the Gesell Developmental schedule at six months and every four months after that. There were no group differences at 6, 10, and 14 months, but significant differences at 18 months and thereafter, with the controls falling below national norms and the experimental children advancing well beyond them. By four-and-a-half years of age the experimental group tested at nine months *above* their chronological age on psycholinguistic development, whereas the controls were nine months *below*, so that the apparent effect of the training amounted to a one-and-one-half year gain.

Intelligence was regularly measured, from 12 to 21 months with the Gesell schedules, from 24 to 66 months with the Cattell and Binet tests, and thereafter with the Wechsler Preschool and Primary Scale of Intelligence (WPPSI) and the Wechsler Intelligence Scale for Children (WISC). Figure 16-3 plots the IQ development of the two groups as measured by the various tests through age nine. Obviously there are appreciable measurement differences among the five tests used, but all are consistent in showing a difference be-

627

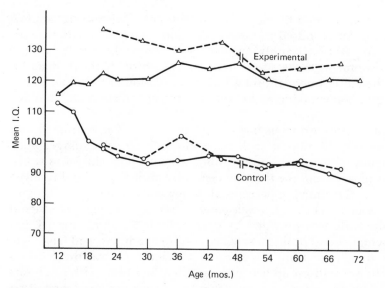

Figure 16.3
Mean IQ performance for experimental (A) and control (O) children in the Milwaukee Project from one to nine years of age. Intelligence was measured with the Gesell,
Cattell, and Binet tests from one to six years and with the WPPSI and WISC tests from
four to nine years. Measurement differences between the tests account for the fact that
the IQ estimates are not identical from four to six years. The Wechsler tests are more
difficult. *Source:* Heber (1978), pp. 58-59.

tween the groups of 20 to 30 IQ points, lasting until three years after the treatment program ended. By contrast, the nontreated older siblings of *both*
groups showed a steady decline from a mean of 88 at two years of age to 77 at
13 years of age. This trend is consistent with an earlier survey finding that the
mother's IQ is a better predictor of the child's IQ at 18 than is the child's own
IQ at two.

Heber and Garber (1975) concluded that negative experiences can seriously
interfere with the learning process. The failure of many children to learn
seems to be due, at least in part, to the restricted learning environments
created for them by mothers who are incapable of providing better ones. Children thus learn behavioral systems that are antagonistic to the learning required for successful school performance. Sociocultural retardation *can* be
mitigated by intensive intervention during pregnancy and early development
of the offspring of retarded mothers.

What about changes in the rest of the family? The IQs of the mothers in the
two groups did not change in eight years, but the vocational training greatly
benefited the experimental group mothers: salaries earned favored them by
an average of $40 per week. There were also "diffusion effects" of the treat-

ment on the untreated siblings: there was a small but significant IQ difference in favor of the experimental group's siblings, and twice as many of the control group siblings (29%) as experimental group siblings (13%) have been placed in special classes for the mentally retarded.

Teacher comments in the school records indicate that about a third of the treated children are having some social and behavioral difficulties in the school setting. Often these can be translated to mean that "the child talks too much." They are able to confront the teachers and their classmates verbally, in part because they were trained to have confidence, skill, and practice in using language as an effective tool for interacting with adults in their lives. An example will illustrate:

> . . . one little girl of the experimental group tested at the 96th percentile in reading on a pre-first-grade achievement test. During her first two months of school she decided that she did not want to speak. Possibly she was angry about no longer being with her preschool teachers. Her teacher had decided to place her back in kindergarten because her parents offered no support for the first grade adjustment problem she was having. Luckily, just before the change was to be made, the child walked up to the teacher's desk, opened a book and fluently read from it. A shocked teacher called in her supervisors to witness the event. From then on she has been a model student (Heber, 1978, p. 61).

The Milwaukee Project is not without critics or controversy. Page (1975) has strongly condemned the research evaluation for the project on three counts: biased selection of treatment groups, contamination of criterion tests, and failure to specify the treatments employed. He claims that the experimental children were very highly *trained* in IQ test-related performance skills, but there was no demonstration yet of *generalization* to other intelligence measures. On this basis he questions whether the dramatic IQ gains shown are decisively grounded in broad *educational growth*. That particular challenge seems to be effectively countered by the continuing success of the treated children after three years in the public schools. Nevertheless, Heber is circumspect about the gains achieved, while still optimistic about the prospects for future intervention efforts:

> It is our subjective judgment that continuing parent-school incompatibilities and disrupted family living environments will continue to erode the high hopes engendered by our experimental children's performance at the terminal point of our intervention effort. Nevertheless, the performance of our experimental children three years into follow-up is such that it is difficult to conceive of their ever approaching the performance standards of the control group. Those of us who have participated in this experience have witnessed a capacity for learning on the part of these children dramatically in excess of their epidemiologically-based expectations. And, at the same time, we are rapidly approaching the view that intervention and support for children reared with the intellectually inadequate parent and living in a dis-

rupted family environment must continue throughout the child's school as well as preschool years. Nevertheless, our data to this point in time do nothing to inhibit the hope that it may indeed prove possible to prevent the high frequency of mental retardation among children reared by parents of limited intellectual competence under circumstances of severe economic deprivation (Heber, 1978, pp. 61-62).

Summary

Sociocultural retardation is by far the most common form of mental retardation. Typically such retardates are only mildly impaired and have no obvious organic pathology. They usually come, however, from families of low intelligence and from social classes that are poor and underprivileged. It is plausible to presume that genetic endowment may set some upper limit on their intellectual and social capacities. But it is also clear that a variety of environmental circumstances can contribute to that impairment. Mental development can be limited by sociocultural deprivation through inadequate prenatal and infant medical care, malnutrition, lack of intellectual stimulation and parental encouragement, and the discouraging attitudes of teachers and others. Deprivation is perpetuated from one generation to the next in insidious ways, making it extremely difficult to break into the vicious cycle of retarded parents begetting retarded offspring. Custodial institutions and even some public schools contribute to the problem through lack of stimulation, challenge, and personal encouragement.

Fortunately, intervention works. The progressive retardation associated with lower-class or institutional living can be substantially offset by early removal from the depriving environment, by improved nutrition and medical care, and through carefully constructed preschool and elementary school programs aimed at scholastic and social enrichment. Encouragement can be found in the apparent success of *Sesame Street*, the public television program, in teaching culturally deprived preschoolers (and privileged children, too) how to read, spell, and count.

Recent evidence indicates that the earliest years of life may be critical for determining ultimate intellectual capacity, which prompts Kirk (1970) to urge that special educational programs be initiated as early as possible, preferably at one or two years of age. Many educational programs have not produced sustained improvement in academic achievement, perhaps because they started too late in the child's development. Intensive stimulation in infancy and early childhood initially produces impressive advancement in intellectual development, but much of the gain from enrichment is lost when the child leaves the intervention program, unless steps are taken to provide continued educational support to maintain the advantage (Lally & Honig, 1975).

Among the many programs in the War on Poverty, Project Headstart was by far the largest compensatory education program. There was great optimism at the outset, followed by discouragement and pessimism when results

630

did not measure up to the initial hopes. Most group programs had immediate impact that was favorable, but the long-term effects of brief or partial intervention were negligible. It is clear that compensatory activities must begin early and be continued; otherwise early gains achieved at preschool age wash out in the first three grades at public school. The continuing effects of home and school environments typical of poor neighborhoods cannot be prevented by an "inoculation" of preschool experience. Thus far, only small intensive programs—such as the Milwaukee Project—have managed to achieve and sustain superior achievement in disadvantaged children. Bronfenbrenner (1974) questions whether compensatory programs can help such children. They typically profit least from them, presumably because their *parents* are so overburdened with tasks and frustrations of sheer survival to participate fully in programs for their children. The parents are the key to success.

In later childhood and early adulthood, vocational habilitation is a valuable method of treatment. Many retardates can now find employment and job

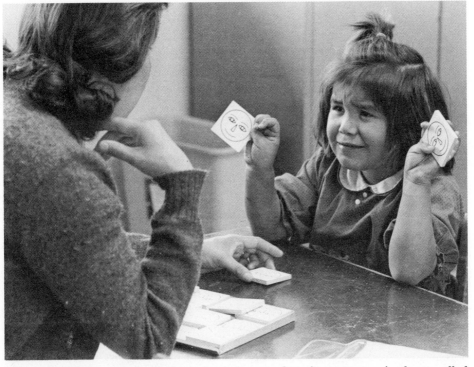

Project Headstart was the largest compensatory education program in the so-called War on Poverty. This little girl at the Muckleshoot Indian Reservation is taking instruction in identifying emotions. She appears to have some dramatic talent. It has generally been found that such special educational programs as this must be maintained for several years if they are to have lasting impact.

631

success if their attitudes and other personal qualities are favorable. Though most of these jobs are unskilled (thus offering little opportunity for economic advancement) people of limited IQ can perform and hold them about as well as nonretarded persons doing the same work (Heber & Dever, 1970); even for more skilled positions, job success is only *partly* related to intelligence (Jencks, 1969). A great deal more is required to prevent sociocultural factors from having their deleterious effects. As recommended by the President's Panel on Mental Retardation, this will require a broad attack on the adverse social conditions that tend to keep intelligence depressed: poverty, ignorance, and discrimination. This is an ambitious undertaking, and success depends on the willingness of the public to make it possible.

OTHER FORMS OF RETARDATION

The brief synopses that follow might lead to some confusion about how various forms of mental retardation are classified. The labels for some refer to a cardinal symptom of the disorder, as microcephaly, for example, denotes small head size. Other labels designate the persons who discovered or publicized the disorder, for example, Tay and Sachs. Still others name the cause: maternal rubella. This inconsistency is partly to be understood by considering how we come to know about disorders historically. Ideally in medicine disorders are classified according to fundamental causes that thus at once suggest the methods of treatment. Initially, however, and in the early stages of investigation of a newly discovered disorder, enough may not be known to single out the fundamental causes. In that case the disorder may be labeled and classified according to a particular theory, as Langdon Down did with *mongolism* because of a quaint theory about racial evolution. Or it might be called *Down's syndrome* by others who accept Down's description but doubt his theory. Finally, as our knowledge about it increases we may classify it as a genetic disorder of specifiable origin, and we may possibly relabel it as *trisomy 21* to indicate what went wrong and where.

In part the inconsistencies in classification reflect real irregularities in the disorders themselves. It would be difficult to classify microcephaly according to causes because it has been shown to result from a variety of causes. On the other hand it could be misleading to classify maternal rubella (German measles) by its symptoms because it may cause a number of different symptoms or no damage at all, depending on the stage of fetal development when the infection occurs. We must tolerate a certain amount of ambiguity in classification until our knowledge of these disorders is as advanced as our knowledge about Down's syndrome and phenylketonuria.

Maternal Rubella (German Measles)

According to the Collaborative Perinatal Study (Hellman & Pritchard, 1971), about 5 percent of pregnancies are complicated by clinically apparent viral infections, including measles, chickenpox, smallpox, polio, hepatitis, encephalitis, mumps, and others. Of these the most dangerous is German measles or rubella. Following an Australian epidemic of rubella in 1941 it was discovered that many defective babies were born to mothers who had the disease during the first three months of pregnancy (Penrose, 1963). The virus destroys some cells and changes the growth rate of others; it may interfere with the blood supply to the developing fetal tissues, causing permanent growth deficiency, deafness, blindness from cataracts, heart malformation, microcephaly, glaucoma and other eye defects, and mental retardation. These congenital defects occur in about 10 percent of such pregnancies, although almost half the infants are abnormal if the infection occurs in the *first month* of pregnancy. When retardation occurs it is usually moderate to severe and is frequently accompanied by cataracts or deafness. In the most recent rubella epidemic of 1964, mental retardation was more common than in previous epidemics. Chess, Korn, and Fernandez (1971) found mild to moderate retardation in a quarter of a group of 153 affected children, and dull-normal intelligence or borderline retardation in another quarter of them. Mothers of a substantial proportion of deaf-mutes report rubella in pregnancy. Many of the pregnancies affected are complicated or aborted and many of the babies die. The risk of defect diminishes greatly if the infection occurs after the first trimester of pregnancy. The fetus is protected from many infections during pregnancy, but rubella is obviously one of those that can cross the placental barrier via the blood supply. A vaccine to prevent rubella infection has been developed that may eliminate the disorder altogether as a pregnancy complication. Ideally, all girls will be vaccinated before they reach childbearing age.

Congenital defects can also be caused by other maternal infections, such as syphilis and Asian flu, and by drugs taken during pregnancy. The latter possibility was illustrated in 1962 by the shocking example of thalidomide, a seemingly innocent tranquilizer, which when taken during pregnancy produced the side-effect of gross abnormality in the developing fetus. Although some symptoms of these disorders can be treated after the baby is born, there is no known antidote for structural damage occurring *in utero*. However, they can be prevented by shielding expectant mothers from exposure early in pregnancy. Effective prevention requires widespread dissemination of information about the dangers of infection and drugs in pregnancy.

Microcephaly

This disorder is diagnosed when the head circumference is very small. In rare cases it is carried by a single recessive gene, but more commonly it results from maternal infections, massive irradiation in pregnancy, or birth complications. In the inherited form the skull is small and conically shaped. The back of the head is flattened and the jaw and forehead recede, which makes the scalp wrinkle as though it were too big for the skull. The face and ears are about normal in size, so they stand out prominently, giving the head a bird-like appearance. The child is short and has a curved spine and apparently long ex-

633

tremities, which cause him or her to walk in a stooped position or hop rather like a monkey. The majority are severely retarded, never develop speech, and are completely dependent on others for feeding and toilet care. Visual defects and convulsions are common.

In the secondary form of microcephaly, which is acquired after conception, the clinical picture is more variable. Any of the above symptoms may be present in varying degrees, with a markedly reduced head circumference as the critical sign. The best documented cause is radiation exposure in pregnancy. There were seven microcephalics among eleven children born to mothers who in the first 20 weeks of pregnancy were exposed at close hand to the atomic blast at Hiroshima (Plummer, 1952). The proportion of defective children was much smaller for pregnant women who were some distance from the center of the blast. Massive therapeutic X rays during pregnancy have also been found to produce serious abnormalities in half of the babies born, with microcephaly the most frequent.

It is obvious why microcephalic children are mentally retarded. The small size of the skull indicates small size of the brain, especially in the upper cortical regions that are essential to the higher intellectual processes. In fact, an estimate of the weight of the cortex provides a reasonably accurate approximation to the degree of intellectual retardation to be expected in adulthood. Some microcephalics have virtually no cortex at all, which renders them entirely helpless. As might be expected in such a severe structural deficiency, there is little that can be done to recapture the lost intellectual potential once the initial damage has occurred. If microcephalics survive infancy they do not usually have poor health, although they seldom live to very old age and almost never can have children of their own. Most are institutionalized although some could be kept at home if the family had the resources to provide the extensive personal care required (Robinson & Robinson, 1976).

A promising new procedure for early detection of microcephaly has been reported by Karp et al. (1975). They made a prenatal test for microcephaly using *ultrasound* during the third pregnancy in a family with two previous affected children. (Ultrasound techniques can be used like X rays to obtain a profile of the baby by projecting sound waves toward the womb and recording their reflections from the baby's body, without danger to the baby.) Fortunately, the third child was normal.

Hydrocephaly

This is another skull malformation that occurs approximately once in 2000 live births. It may be caused by a sex-linked recessive gene, maternal infection, birth injury, tumor, and a number of other factors that influence the amount of cerebrospinal fluid within the skull. In some cases the normal channels for draining fluid from the brain are blocked, causing fluid to accumulate in the skull and pressure to increase within the brain. In other cases

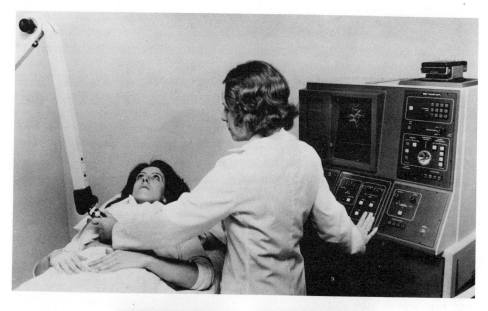

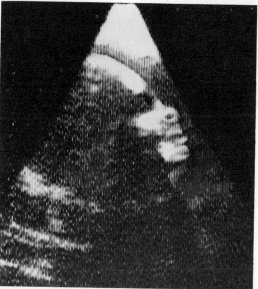

With *ultrasound*, the physician can determine the exact placement of the fetus, the size of the head, and the location of the placenta—all vital information for predicting complications in labor and delivery—without the risks involved in X-ray techniques. Ultrasound can also guide the physician's needle in performing amniocentesis, helping to avoid harming the fetus. The expectant mother above is undergoing ultrasound assessment, which will yield a picture scan on the screen at the left similar to the one of a five-month fetus shown below.

635

the accumulation is caused by overproduction or underabsorption of the fluid. As fluid accumulates, the cerebral cortex may be stretched until it is paper thin and the skull may expand in a globular shape, often to prodigious size. The head of one seven-year-old child weighed 27 pounds. The upper part of the face expands so that the eyes become widespread and the bridge of the nose flattened. In advanced cases one often finds visual impairment, deafness, epilepsy, and spastic paralysis of the lower limbs. In such cases body growth is severely limited; the child is bedridden and usually dies before adulthood. However the severity of symptoms varies widely. In mild cases the child may participate in normal activities and be only slightly retarded. If the condition is arrested before the cortex is permanently damaged, there may be no intellectual deficit at all.

Like Down's syndrome and other malformations of the central nervous system, the incidence of hydrocephaly increases dramatically with maternal age; the reasons for this are unknown. Mothers over forty have five times as many hydrocephalic babies as those between twenty and thirty-five (Masland, 1958). Perhaps 5 percent of male hydrocephalics have sex-linked inherited disorders (Kirman & Bicknell, 1975). Allan et al. (1973) have developed a new prenatal test for neural tube defects, of which spina bifida (gaps in the spine) and hydrocephaly are two of the most important. By amniocentesis a sample of amniotic fluid is obtained about the 16th week of pregnancy and tested for the presence of *alpha-fetoprotein*, a fetal circulating serum protein that seems to escape in significant amounts into the amniotic fluid only when neural tube defect is present. If the test is positive, there is still time to terminate the pregnancy safely, and thus prevent the birth of a defective child.

Blockage of the drainage channels can sometimes be corrected by surgically inserting drainage tubes at the base of the brain to *shunt* the excess fluid directly into the heart for recirculation. If the operation is performed early enough, brain damage and the accompanying retardation can be prevented or mitigated, but there is some mortality risk from the operation itself. Drug treatment has had some success in slowing the accumulation of the fluid. Without treatment about half of the hydrocephalics die, usually quite young, but arrest of the disorder is now possible in 90 percent of the shunt operations attempted (Kirman & Bicknell, 1975).

Blood-Type Incompatibility

Many jokes are told about man's unconscious desire to return to the womb, where all earthly needs were met and life was uncomplicated. It must have been quite a shock for many to learn around 1941 that in some rare instances the womb is the most dangerous place for a baby to be. At that time it was discovered that blood-type incompatibilities of mother and fetus may be harmful, even lethal, to the fetus. There are several types of incompatibility possible, but the one that is best known and most frequently associated with mental retardation is *Rh incompatibility*. Blood type is inherited. The *Rhesus factor*

is transmitted as a dominant characteristic, so that 87 percent of white persons are classified as *Rh-positive*. When a baby inherits both recessive genes, it has the *Rh-negative* blood type. If an Rh-negative mother conceives an Rh-positive child, the conditions are set for a dangerous clash between the blood systems of the two, which are separate but connected. Components of the child's blood may be absorbed through the placental barrier into the mother's bloodstream, causing the mother's blood to become sensitized to the Rh factor. Her body retaliates by producing an antibody to combat the foreign intruder, and that antibody can enter the baby's bloodstream and destroy its red blood cells. This results in oxygen deprivation in the fetus and death or abortion. In less extreme cases the child may be born with severe anemia and jaundice, permanent brain damage, paralysis of limbs, deafness, and mental retardation.

The danger to the baby is greatest if the mother has already developed antibodies in her blood. For this reason first-born children are less likely to be affected than later children. Maternal sensitization used to occur in about one in 200 pregnancies, making Rh incompatibility a common major threat in pregnancy. Popular reaction to the danger was so extreme that many believed Rh-incompatible mates should not conceive any children at all, but now it is known that only about 5 percent of Rh-negative mothers become sensitized during pregnancy.

Even more reassuring has been the great success of treatments. The first techniques developed involved *exchange transfusions* (complete replacement of the entire blood supply) during the first day or two of life. By replacing all the baby's blood with new blood free of the antibodies, the threat to the baby's health was terminated. Follow-up studies showed that such children retain a slight intellectual handicap (5 to 10 IQ points) compared to their own unaffected siblings, which is probably attributable to the damage done *in utero*. Severely affected children, by contrast, have a handicap of more than 20 IQ points. In 1944 it was estimated that blood-type incompatibility accounted for 3 to 4 percent of institutionalized retarded cases, but by 1963 that figure was less than one percent (Heber, 1970). Now maternal sensitization can be avoided altogether by administering antibodies against the Rh factor to the mother just after she gives birth to an Rh-incompatible infant, thereby destroying the Rh-positive fetal cells in the mother's circulatory system before her immune system has been stimulated to produce its own antibodies. The result is that nowadays fewer and fewer women are becoming Rh-sensitized (Clarke, 1973). Given our advanced knowledge, it is now routine practice to monitor carefully the pregnancies of Rh-incompatible parents and, if need be, to induce early labor should maternal sensitization become so extreme as seriously to threaten the baby (Robinson & Robinson, 1976).

Cretinism

All forms of cretinism stem from a lack of the thyroid hormone *thyroxin*, which stimulates metabolic processes throughout the body. In about a third of the cases the disorder is inherited through receipt of one of several recessive genes that interfere with the production and metabolism of thyroxin. The genetic forms usually produce an enlargement of the thyroid gland, known as *goiter*, which distinguishes them from the more common nongenetic forms, where atrophy of the thyroid gland usually precludes goitrous growth. *Endemic* cretinism occurs mainly in the mountainous regions like the Rocky Mountain area because the soil, water, and air contain unusually low concentrations of iodine, which is essential for the production of thyroid hormone. The incidence of endemic cretinism has been effectively reduced by the addition of iodine to table salt and by careful regulation of maternal diet during pregnancy.

The typical clinical features are severe mental retardation, sluggish behavior, dwarfed stature, coarse dry skin and hair, a large protruding tongue, and not infrequently deafness. In some respects cretins resemble Down's syndrome children, but it is easy and important to distinguish between them because prompt, controlled thyroid medication works wonders in cretinism. The physical symptoms respond favorably to thyroid medication in almost all cases. Mental retardation is also moderated, although normal intelligence is seldom achieved. Damage done to the central nervous system before birth is, of course, irreparable. Cretinism has always been relatively rare in institutional populations, and with improved diet and medical treatment its prevalence has been greatly reduced (Penrose, 1963).

Tay-Sachs Disease

This is the best known of several disorders of fat metabolism that are caused by a recessively inherited enzyme deficiency. Tay-Sachs is the infantile form of a group of such disorders that used to be called *amaurotic familial idiocy* because of the profound retardation and total blindness (amaurosis) that was invariably present. Due to the faulty enzyme, fatty substances accumulate in the central nervous system and cause progressive deterioration of the brain and optic nerve. The child usually appears normal until six months of age, when motor coordination begins to decline, vision deteriorates, and apathy sets in. Spastic paralysis, convulsions, and death ensue, usually within one to three years. Similar forms of the disorder that have onset later in childhood have different names but very similar features, course, and outcome (Robinson & Robinson, 1976).

Tay-Sachs disease is more prevalent among Ashkenazic Jewish families, where one in 30 is a carrier, than in the general population, where one in 300 is a carrier. The historical ostracism of Jews has probably led to a disproportionately large number of marriages between blood relatives, which tends to increase the frequency with which a recessive genetic disease becomes manifest. An ambitious project is currently underway in the Baltimore–Washington area, aimed at blood-testing thousands of Jews of childbearing age. This and other large screening programs in metropolitan areas have identified more than 50 pregnancies in which both prospective parents are carriers. In such cases one in four offspring will predictably have the disease. It is now possible, by amniocentesis, to test sample extracts from the amniotic fluid during pregnancy for evidence of the critical enzyme. If it is missing, the baby will almost certainly have the disease, and therapeutic abortion can be performed, there being no known treatment for the Tay-Sachs syndrome. This project is an exciting experiment in mass education and genetic counseling. Surely it will prove useful for all the carriers to know this fact about themselves, and the information gathered from such large numbers should provide valuable knowledge about the disorder (Kaback & O'Brien, 1973).

CONCLUSION

There has been much tangible progress during the last thirty years in understanding and treating mental retardation. It is worth pointing out that most of the breakthroughs in knowledge concern etiology and prevention as well as pathology and remediation. Most severe types of retardation are first of all physical disorders of the brain that secondarily entail disruptions of mental processes. The causes are frequently genetic or biological, centering around the processes of reproduction and early development. Prevention or treatment may be as simple as changing a diet or having a routine blood test. There are indications throughout that severe mental retardation is a field of abnormality about which we can *do* something. In this respect it is gratifying to tie together the lessons to be learned from our study. Indeed it is tempting to write such a summary in a humorous vein, as *A Layman's Guide to Having Healthy Babies or Prescriptions for Amateur Parents (As If There Were Any Other Kind)*. But there are too many sober sides to mental retardation to allow for such amusement: physical deformities, wasted human potential, parental anguish and guilt, and enormous social cost. In part, though, these tragic undercurrents create a zeal in research workers to keep on pressing their search.

Family Planning

Planning a family actually begins with selecting a mate. It is clear that much genetic mischief has resulted from relatives marrying. The majority of the forms of retardation reviewed in this chapter *may* be inherited recessively, and the pairing of recessive genes is much more frequent in consanguineous marriages. If relatives do marry, they should at least be aware of the measure of danger to their offspring. Penrose (1963) has found that more than 18 percent of their children are retarded, as compared with a norm of 4 percent. Simple blood and urine tests can determine the risk of the most common forms of defect, but this is not at all foolproof. There may be recessive disorders that are still unknown. Stern (1960) estimates that each of us carries more than 10 re-

639

cessive genes that are potentially detrimental. All these potential threats are more likely to be actualized in consanguineous marriages. It would be unusual but by no means frivolous for *any* enlightened couple to request thorough medical and laboratory examinations before conceiving children. This is especially recommended if defective children have previously been born in either family.

There is a decided correlation between maternal age and maldevelopment of the central nervous system in babies. This is particularly significant for women over thirty-five although the risk is reduced if they have had babies previously. Risk is also greater for very young mothers. For this reason Penrose (1960) encourages prospective mothers to have their offspring between the ages of twenty-two and thirty. Many individuals and religious groups remain opposed to birth control and abortion on moral grounds, and these objections must be respected. There is no question, however, that the improvements in these procedures and their increased availability have made family planning more feasible and more effective. The means for birth control are now legally available in most states in the United States. Abortion is an accepted practice in many countries and has recently been offered on request, at modest cost, in most states in this country. Liberalized abortion has been seized as a major objective of Women's Liberation campaigns, which will probably help to produce wider acceptance of the practice.

Prenatal and Early Childhood Care

In the field of mental retardation an ounce of prevention is worth *several* pounds of cure. Anyone who has planted seeds knows that the most crucial period for survival and healthy development is the very first period of life. The situation is no different with human beings. Neither is the sort of care very different. Like plants, human seedlings require a balanced diet with adequate amounts of necessary nutrients, minerals, and vitamins. They must be shielded from unnecessary exposure to infection, extreme irradiation, and drugs, especially in the first three months of prenatal life. For human beings the mother's body provides the first environment for growth. For this reason competent prenatal medical supervision is extremely important, starting as soon as conception is suspected, in order to regulate the mother's diet, monitor the baby's development, and handle any emergencies that may arise.

Regular medical supervision is also essential from birth until school age. As we have pointed out, many of the initial signs of mental retardation are apparent to the trained observer or laboratory technician during the first week after birth. Others can be picked up in routine pediatric follow-up through blood tests and periodic charting of the developmental milestones. Most of the special treatments for retardation must be prescribed, executed, or monitored by physicians. But many of the childhood needs of retardates are the same as other children's: security, discipline, stimulation and challenge, good example, and affectionate care. If the family is not too burdened by poverty, ignorance, and cultural deprivation, and if the parents are capable of psychological generativity (Erikson, 1963), much can be done to lighten the effects of intellectual handicap.

Attitudes Toward Mental Retardation

Not so long ago the public attitude toward mental retardation was one of looking away and forgetting. Institutions were poorly financed, research was weakly supported, special training opportunities were provided on a most inadequate scale. Even the parents of severely retarded children sometimes fell in with this attitude, placing children in institutions and pretending that they did not exist. The problem for parents, however, was always much complicated by the inadequacies of institutions. Some state training schools do not admit children under five years, and sometimes waiting lists delay admittance even longer. Furthermore, financial and emotional considerations often conspire to favor rearing even severely retarded children at home, sometimes against professional advice and at considerable cost to the happiness and adjustment of normal siblings.

Today there are signs of a decided change in the public attitude. For this change the parents of retarded children are largely responsible. They have formed influential organizations all over the world that work for improvement of state institutions, cooperative nursery schools, more and better special classes in the public schools, and informational and group therapy programs for themselves. By 1974 the National Association for Retarded Citizens included 213,000 members (Robinson & Robinson, 1976). The members provide moral support for one another in that they share a common plight, either the frustration and disturbance of having a retarded child at home or the guilt they feel for having placed their child in an institution. Their morale is further strengthened by the discovery that something can be accomplished through joint effort. Similar developments have occurred with respect to cerebral palsy and epilepsy. In the long run it may prove to be not the least of the services rendered by these movements that they awakened interest in research and stimulated financial support for it.

Rights of Retarded Citizens

The decade of the 1970s brought forward many champions for the rights of retarded citizens. In the first place, there were increasing challenges to the practices for defining and classifying mental retardation, which stem from the growing recognition of the destructive potential in labelling people of borderline intelligence as retarded. Mercer (1974) has criticized the practice of classifying children solely on the basis of performance on standardized intelligence tests, because it results in labelling as mentally retarded a disproportionately

641

large number of ethnic minority children. As an alternative, she proposes that we add supplementary evaluations of competencies outside of school. She would place in special education classes for retarded children only those who score in the lowest 3 percent on standardized IQ tests and on adaptive behavior evaluations, excluding those children who meet the social expectations in their own cultural group.

National attention has been drawn to the civil rights of citizens who are declared to be retarded, including those in institutions. In response to the scandalous news of involuntary sterilization of retarded adolescent girls in Alabama and elsewhere, the American Association of Mental Deficiency (1974) published the following strong declaration:

> Mentally retarded persons have the same basic rights as other citizens. Among these . . . are the rights . . . to marry, to engage in sexual activity, to have children, and to control one's own fertility by any legal means available. . . .
>
> However, recent reports on cases involving the sterilization of mentally retarded individuals without even the most elementary legal and procedural safeguards raise serious questions concerning the adequacy of current efforts to protect the human and constitutional rights of such citizens (p. 59).

In line with the principle of normalization mentioned at the beginning of this chapter, significant efforts have been directed at "mainstreaming" retarded children and adults, bringing them out of institutions and special training programs into the community, regular public schools, and private homes to whatever extent is possible and practical. The concept of mainstreaming is based on several premises: (1) regular classroom experience breaks down the isolation inherent in special classes; (2) retarded children can learn more, both academically and socially, when exposed to models whose achievement is more expert than their own; (3) regular classrooms bear greater resemblance to the "real world" than special classrooms do; (4) exposure to handicapped children helps other children to understand and accept them. The initial effects of the mainstreaming movement were meager: more than half of all mentally retarded children attending public schools were in special classes all day, nearly a quarter were receiving no specialized services, and the rest were involved in a variety of other arrangements (Borginsky, 1974). Research evaluating the effects of mainstreaming is rather equivocal thus far. It is certainly not a panacea, but the early results show that at least mildly retarded children may function better in regular classrooms, whereas more profoundly retarded children may do better in special classes (Robinson & Robinson, 1976). Considering that the vast majority of retarded children have only mild intellectual handicaps, this can be taken as an encouraging sign.

Some older retardates are now able to live in sheltered community placements, sometimes working part-time in occupations of limited challenge. Public funds have energetically supported these programs; in fiscal 1973, 39

"Mainstreaming" programs follow the principle of normalization, bringing retarded people out of institutions and into the community. The boys above are learning wood-working skills in a public junior high school class for children with special needs. The young man below has obviously just struck it rich in a counting class at a rehabilitation center. Learning such elementary skills as counting, telling time, making change, and learning bus routes is necessary for these handicapped people to make the transition from a dependent existence in institutions to independence in the community.

percent of all spending for mental retardation by the United States Govern-ment went into income maintenance payments to support the efforts of retarded citizens to remain in the community (Robinson & Robinson, 1976). Another aspect of this trend is more troubling. With the recent attempts to de-institutionalize retarded people by providing alternative facilities in the com-

643

The Special Olympics program recognizes some simple truths: retarded or not, children love to play, need to be recognized, and thrive when they develop their bodies and their skills to the fullest extent possible.

munity, institutional populations are tending to become younger and more profoundly retarded. At one institution the proportion of profoundly retarded patients (with IQs below 20) has increased from 27 to 53 percent from 1950 to 1974, while the proportion of mildly retarded patients (with IQs above 50) has dropped from 24 to 7 percent (Tarjan et al., 1973). That trend is bound to make the task and the morale of both patients and staff at those institutions more bleak.

The cumulative impact of the progressive movements for the retarded has been encouraging, one might even say exhilarating. As a nation we are learning how malleable are the intelligence and adaptive potential of our children. The Special Olympics, which are now televised nationally, have brought home to most of us the athletic abilities and the human qualities of handicapped youngsters. Raising *our* consciousness about the untapped potential of retarded people appears to be just the first step toward raising *theirs*.

SUGGESTIONS FOR FURTHER READING

To gain some perspective on the recent advances in mental retardation the reader might skim through A.F. Tredgold's *A textbook of mental deficiency*, 6th ed. (1937).

For decades this text, in various editions, was consistently the most authoritative source. The sixth edition was published before most of the important breakthroughs in genetics, blood chemistry, epidemiology, and the psychological effects of deprivation. Although an excellent book, it illustrates nicely the state of our ignorance less than half a century ago. There have been several more recent editions, the latest being M. Craft (Ed.), *Tredgold's mental retardation*, 12th edition (1979).

For thoroughness and readability the best modern textbook is N.M. Robinson and H.B. Robinson, *The mentally retarded child: A psychological approach*, 2nd ed. (1976). In addition to treatments of all the major syndromes, on which the present chapter relied heavily, it includes a basic introduction to the concepts and theories of intelligence, retardation, and human genetics. A third of the book is devoted to the practical clinical problems of diagnosis and treatment, which clinicians will find useful. Almost as useful is a comprehensive textbook by B. Kirman and J. Bicknell, *Mental handicap* (1975).

One cannot read very far in this field before discovering the immense influence of L.S. Penrose, *The biology of mental defect*, 3rd ed. (1963). For four decades Penrose was the leading authority on genetic aspects of birth defects. American readers may find a certain archaic quality in his thinking about retardation, giving rather short shrift to the social and psychological aspects, but there is nowhere a more comprehensive account of the genetic and biological aspects. V.A. McKusick and R. Claiborne have edited a more recent volume along the same lines, *Medical genetics* (1973).

Balance for the biological viewpoint can be found in a book edited by H.C. Haywood, *Socio-cultural aspects of mental retardation* (1970), a report of the proceedings of a major conference at George Peabody College, with contributions from 38 leading investigators from throughout the world. J. Bowlby's *Maternal care and mental health* (1966) emphasizes the psychological aspects of maternity.

B.Z. Friedlander, G.M. Sterritt, and G.E. Kirk (Eds.), *Exceptional infant*, volume 3 (1975) is part of a series that features especially reports of treatment and early intervention programs. R. Heber, *Epidemiology of mental retardation* (1970) is a small book (99 pages) that compiles succinctly, though not very systematically, a wealth of quantitative facts about mental retardation and birth defects. W.K. Estes presents a systematic review of literature on mental retardation from a learning theory perspective in *Learning theory and mental development* (1970). Recommended for parents of retarded children as well as those interested in work with the retarded is E.L. French and J.C. Scott, *Children in the shadows* (1960). A complete treatment of the subject of Down's syndrome is available in D.W. Smith and A.A. Wilson, *The child with Down's syndrome* (1973), and in D. Gibson, *Down's syndrome: The psychology of mongolism* (1978).

The Sunday Afternoon on the Island of La Grande Jatte (1884–86) by
Georges Seurat. Courtesy of The Art Institute of Chicago.

17
Community Mental Health

The problems created by maladaptive personal reactions cannot be solved without reference to the society in which they occur. Treating and caring for
people whose behavior is disturbed, investigating
the causes of this disturbance, and possibly preventing these troubles from occurring in the first
place—all imply a high level of social effort and social organization. In this chapter we ask what it
takes to deal effectively with the problems of mental
health. How great are those problems, what institutions and what methods of intervention are needed
to cope with them, what forms of training and varieties of skill are required, and how much will it all
cost? Clearly the huge task of improving mental
health cannot be borne by professional mental
health workers alone. We therefore also consider

the contributions that can come from citizens who care to make their behavior as parents and members of the community count in this direction.

In the historical introduction we took note of a major revolution in the public attitude toward mental health. Until the 1950s it was possible to think of professional mental health workers and their civilian supporters as a tiny band struggling for existence, unable to attract interest or financial support, working almost in vain to overcome a public tendency to look away from the problems rather than confronting them. But the time was evidently ripe for a drastic change. Within a few years mental health came to be regarded as a concern of the whole community and a suitable object for community action.

SIZE OF THE PROBLEM

In 1955 an act of Congress called the Mental Health Study Act ordered the formation of a Joint Commission on Mental Health and Illness that was charged with the task of evaluating needs and making recommendations for a national mental health program. The Commission took the charge seriously and made its report only after five years of solid work. Reading today the short version intended for the general public, *Action for Mental Health* (Joint Commission, 1961), it is hard to realize the profound stir created by this monumental investigation. The Commission demonstrated, as people had only begun to suspect, that mental health was a huge problem calling for a vastly increased allocation of resources. Historically, the report marked the turning point in the acceptance of mental health as a community and national responsibility.

The Problem of Numbers

The Joint Commission in 1961 made an estimate that 17 million people in the United States suffer at one time or another from relatively serious mental disorder. At any given moment the number of sufferers was guessed to be around 700,000. Half the nation's hospital beds in 1960, the report further pointed out, were occupied by mental patients—a vivid reminder of the relative size of this medical and social problem. Expressing these facts a little differently, Weinberg (1952) estimated that mental illness in a form serious enough to require hospital care "strikes about 1 in 5 families and 1 in 13 people in the course of a lifetime." These gloomy estimates were slightly brightened by the statement that in 1950 about 340,000 patients were discharged, not all fully recovered but at least in an improved condition. Furthermore, the long continued rise in mental hospital populations seemed to have passed its peak, with a decline of 3 percent between 1956 and 1960. But these figures did little to soften the disturbing main finding that mental disorders are so common.

Hospital patients are easy to count, but the true extent of mental health needs can be uncovered only through community surveys. In the Midtown Manhattan Study, for instance, needs were esimated through extensive interviews with 1660 people, a carefully chosen representative sample from a circumscribed population of 110,000 in New York City (Srole et al., 1962) Only 18 percent of the sample were rated as really "well," that is, free from psychiatric symptoms, whereas 23 percent were judged to be seriously impaired by their symptoms. The latter group stood in real need of mental health care, but in fact only a quarter of these people had received any kind of treatment. Large as the current demand for mental health services is, the *potential* demand would seem to be still larger by a considerable margin.

Mental health services do not mean simply those provided by mental hospitals. During the 1950s there had been guesses by specialists that chronic alcoholics might number 1,600,000, people with anxiety disorders 2,500,000, epileptics 650,000, the mentally retarded 2,500,000; no one dared even guess at the number of delinquents. Only a small proportion of these people needed the mental hospital, but all needed services of some kind. The Joint Commission's most striking recommendation was that services should be organized around community mental health centers. These would gradually take over many of the functions of hospitals and would offer help close at hand to all who needed it.

In 1977 President Carter appointed a commission instructed to report on how the nation's mental health needs were being met. The first volume of this report is in print as the *Report of the President's Commission on Mental Health* (1978). The Commission reported a sharp decline in the population of state mental hospitals, from 550,000 in 1955 to 200,000 in 1975. During the same period there was a steep rise in the number of community mental health centers; by 1978 these numbered 647, with more on the way. The transfer of care from hospital to community had indeed gone well forward, but the number of community centers fell far short of the Joint Commission's recommendation in 1961. These centers, moreover, were not well distributed to meet everyone's needs. They had started where local intitiative and support were strongest, not where need might be greatest. The President's Commission, much concerned about this problem, reported at length on the underserved or inappropriately served, especially rural dwellers, minority ethnic groups, and the urban poor. Special services available to troubled children and adolescents and to the elderly were deemed insufficient, and chronic patients set loose by the closing of hospitals had not always found suitable alternatives in the community. In short, the job of providing local mental health services to all who needed them was well begun but no more than half done. The Commission recommended a large increase in Federal appropriations to carry it forward. Ironically, this was the year in which cutting down government expenses became a widely popular political issue.

The Financial Problem

In 1974 the total cost of mental and emotional disorders was 36 billion dollars a year (Levine & Willner, 1976). It is hard to make figures in billions convey

Chronic patients set loose by the closing of mental hospitals did not always find suitable alternatives in the community. The job was no more than half done because Federal appropriations fell short of what was needed.

more than a sense of vast magnitude, but that is the right impression in this case. Mental and emotional disorders are by all odds the most costly of the nation's health problems. The figure just quoted breaks down into roughly 14.5 billion for direct care and 21.5 billion in indirect costs, which include the maintaining of institutions, the support of training and research, and, very important, the loss of income due to disability or death. Loss of wages and other income as a consequence of becoming psychologically disabled accounts for more than 10 billion of the total figure. If we said nothing about the loss of happiness and effectiveness that result from maladaptive personal behavior, we would still have a serious problem of financial loss.

COMMUNITY MENTAL HEALTH CENTERS

Early in 1963 President Kennedy, influenced by the Joint Commission's report, sent a special message to Congress in which he urged the establishment of community mental health centers. While part of the aim was to reduce the number of patients under custodial care in mental hospitals, the purpose was much broader. The President envisioned community centers as providing comprehensive service for all mental health needs, with special emphasis on prevention. Congress passed the necessary legislation the same year, and federal funds became available to assist the establishment of community mental health centers.

The Ideal

The stated goal of the national program was to set up a fully staffed community mental health center for every 100,000 people, obviously a goal that could be realized only over many years. The legislation states that a center must provide, at a minimum, these services: (1) inpatient care, (2) outpatient care, (3) partial hospitalization including especially day care, (4) 24-hour emergency service, and (5) consultation and education with agencies in the community. Other services are encouraged, including aftercare of patients discharged from mental hospitals, services for the mentally retarded, and special classes for children with unusual disabilities. Occasionally, a community mental health center has been started from scratch, with a complex of buildings providing for the whole array of services. But this is expensive; more often, the attempt is made to utilize or enlarge existing facilities, and, if they were previously separate, to join them in a single comprehensive organization. In one community, for instance, there already existed, in widely scattered buildings, a psychiatric outpatient clinic for children and adults, a family counseling service, an association for retarded children, and a mental health society doing educational work. These separate enterprises turned into a mental health center when the general hospital opened a psychiatric ward capable of meeting the inpatient and emergency requirements, when the four existing agencies moved to a building on the hospital grounds, and when an administrator was appointed to see that they all operated in reasonable concert.

We can most quickly understand the potential value of a community mental health center by imagining how it might work in a particular case. John and Mary Doe's family, let us suppose, labors under a series of handicaps. There is John's elderly father living in the home, who is beginning to have difficult episodes suggesting senile psychosis. Their son, always a disciplinary problem, is now, in early adolescence, experimenting with drugs and delinquent adventures. Their daughter performs badly at school, seems socially inept, and may possibly be mentally retarded. Mary, overwhelmed by so much trouble, has fits of weeping and is becoming too lethargic to manage the housework and her part time job. And John, clinging desperately to his ill-paid job, feels mounting resentment and recognizes that his marital relation is deteriorating. If the date is 1940 there is a strong chance that this situation will simply go from bad to worse. The old father will be committed to a mental hospital fifty miles away. The son will be caught by the police and sent to a reform school forty miles in another direction. The daughter will drift along, become an early dropout, and perhaps land in an institution for the retarded sixty miles in a third direction. Mary will be told that she needs psychoanalysis, but no one will take her for the small amount she could pay. She and John become further estranged and reach emotional if not actual divorce.

651

If we shift the date to 1980 and place the family in a community with a well-organized mental health center, there is a chance of a better outcome. In the first place, the problems will be seen not as individual disorders but as part of family relations; in the second place, there will be facilities at hand for each special need. Partial hospitalization or short periods in the local psychiatric ward may keep father at home without his being in everybody's hair. The adolescent son can receive individual or group treatment at the outpatient clinic. The daughter's attitude in school may be helped through talks between the teacher and a mental health consultant. If her difficulties appear to be emotional, the center can provide both individual counseling and special classes for the emotionally disturbed; if retardation proves to be genuine, there is a sheltered workshop for the handicapped. Mary can receive psychotherapy regardless of capacity to pay, and John can be drawn into family treatment that may put the marital relation on a firmer footing. Neighbors may notice that the Doe family, in spite of its multiple problems, seems to be getting along rather well.

To tell the story in this fashion no doubt makes the whole thing sound easy. In actuality, nothing of the kind could happen without long preparation and an extensive deployment of human resources. If the Doe's are going to commit their family to the center's care, they must have formed a favorable opinion of what it can accomplish. Such an opinion is not inborn. Even today, even in relatively advantaged communities, it may take five years or so of educational work to produce confidence in "this psychology stuff" and conviction that there is a real local need. Then there is the question of expense. A good deal of professional time is being devoted to the Doe family. Implicit in the story is a large corps of trained experts: psychiatrists, psychotherapists, nurses and occupational therapists on the psychiatric ward, a consultant to the schools, a teacher of special classes, a supervisor of the sheltered workshop, a family counselor. All of this is costly, as is the general staff required to run such an organization and keep the necessary records. As a public service the center must be open to rich and poor alike, and clients' fees can never be expected to meet more than a small fraction—perhaps 10 or 15 percent—of the costs. Those in charge thus find themselves constantly scrounging to balance the budget, continually involved in appeals to a reluctant community, an economy-minded legislature, and federal granting agencies whose funds are not unlimited. Even those citizens who are most convinced of the value of a community mental health center may sometimes wonder, as taxpayers, whether they can afford to pay for it.

Few communities can expect to pay for a center from local resources. Local health departments can contribute only a little from their already pinched budgets; private donations and charitable trusts in most communities can add only a little more. Mental health care is such a large operation—a "major American industry," as David Mechanic (1969) has called it—that financial support must come mainly from state and federal sources. Federal start-up funds have been essential in creating community mental health centers, but when these temporary boosters run out, the centers, thrown on state and local resources, must sometimes restrict their operations in order to survive. Financial crisis is part of their way of life.

The Actuality

Opening a mental health center does not solve all problems. The imaginary case of the Doe family stands as an ideal that cannot always be met in actuality. First enthusiasms have waned, difficulties have had time to appear, and the community experiment has received a good measure of critical scrutiny.

One of the most insistent themes in the criticism is that professional workers have failed to adapt to the new conditions implicit in community centers. They have tended to perceive these centers as opening new slots in which to continue their traditional activity. Thus they may initiate prolonged one-to-one treatment even though this seriously limits the number of clients who can be served. Continuing the familiar procedures of office practice, workers have failed to look outward at the community, to see their clients as members of a society, and to utilize or develop community resources that might extend the effects of their own therapeutic endeavors. Every professional person who has been obliged in the course of his or her life to work under radically changed conditions will realize that it is no small matter to shift one's style, redirect one's skills, and risk one's habituated sense of competence. But community mental health has somewhat the character of a new deal. Many more clients must be served in many more ways, using a variety of new resources. Flexibility and a spirit of innovation are much needed, and those always seem to be in short supply.

A second point of criticism is the one so strongly emphasized in the report of the President's Commission (1978): the failure of community mental health centers to reach the wider population for which they were intended. Ryan (1969) early called attention to this problem in a survey made in Boston, a city unusually rich in mental health personnel. Ryan's list of unmet needs was long. He mentioned in particular the needs of multi-problem families, one of whose troubles is likely to be poverty. He further specified, as the President's Commission was presently to confirm for the country as a whole, a shortage of service to seriously disturbed children and adolescents, the aged, and people returning to the community from mental hospitals. Only a small part of Boston's mental health workers was engaged in community work; most of the effort was still directed to patients seen in private practice. Commenting on this study, Albee (1970) remarked: "The settlement houses are helping more disturbed children than the child psychiatry clinics, and the clergy are seeing

653

more disturbed people for counseling than are psychiatrists." But the difficulty
is not wholly on the side of the professionals. When a mental health center is established in the middle of a poverty area, its existence may be scarcely noticed
by the surrounding population. Social workers visiting homes may recommend using the service, but perhaps in no more than one case in four will this
advice be followed. The very concept of mental health may be foreign to people of limited education and outlook. Thus one can have the spectacle of a
costly mental health center, set down by legislative fiat in a city slum, which
for some time does not draw enough clients to keep its staff busy.

These troubles can be viewed as the growing pains of a new movement.
Community mental health is a more drastic innovation than was at first realized. The central problem of reaching out into the community, however,
has prompted many workers to advocate a distinction between *community
mental health* and *community psychology*. The first expression refers to the
work done by community mental health centers, which consists primarily of
making psychological services available to those in the community who seek
them. Community psychology implies something different. It aims to change
the community itself in order to provide a better environment for human
growth. An improved environment would presumably reduce the occurrence
of maladaptive behavior, but the goal is larger: to give all the inhabitants better
opportunities to realize their potential. The two kinds of activity are different;
as Goodstein and Sandler (1978) point out, they require different knowledge,
training, and skills. Mental health centers are mainly staffed by psychiatrists,
clinical psychologists, and social workers, whose skills lie in dealing with
troubled people. Community psychology tries to intervene in existing institutions to make them more responsive to growth needs. This brings contact with
schools, courts, police, family services, recreation programs, and many other
community institutions. Essential is a thorough knowledge of social systems,
experience with program design, and above all great skill in dealing with those
who already run the institutions. It is work in which the therapist-patient relation is unsuitable and for which clinical training may not be especially
helpful.

Even if this division of labor becomes general, changes are necessary within
the community mental health centers. Trying to do for many people what has
been done with less than perfect success for a few requires, and is receiving,
radical rethinking. Three questions in particular deserve the most careful
scrutiny.

1. What changes in methods of *intervention* are needed to make
   community mental health care more effective?
2. What *human resources* must be drawn upon and what new methods of
   training must be devised to meet the expanding need?
3. What expectations are reasonable and realistic with respect to the
   prevention of maladaptive personal behavior?

DEVELOPING NEW FORMS OF INTERVENTION

Community mental health centers, designed to serve large numbers of clients, must be economical with time. Most methods of psychological treatment, as we saw in Chapters 7 and 8, require a lot of time. Even behavioral methods, praised at first for their relative brevity, often stretch out over several months. No one can seriously advocate shortcuts that would make treatment superficial and ineffective, perhaps even harmful, but community work has stimulated interest in methods that can produce useful results in a fairly short time. Short methods are most applicable to troubles that arise suddenly, perhaps in a crisis, where a limited goal can be set even if it is no more than restoring the client to a previous level of equanimity. There will not be time for such tools as exploring the past, constructing the existential situation, learning through an extended relation with the therapist, or programs of desensitization and conditioning. But there are many clients who are hardly ready for such sophisticated procedures, and they are well served if immediate discomfort and anxiety can be reduced and if confidence can be increased to deal with problems in the future.

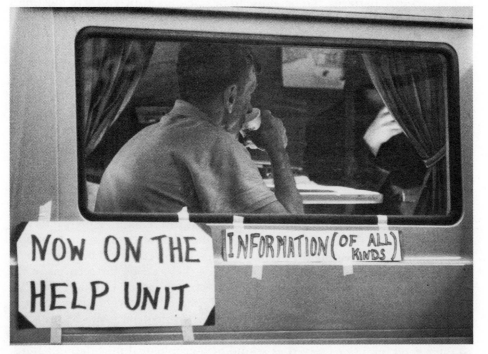

A skid row inhabitant drinks coffee and finds comfort aboard the Mobile Help Unit, founded through the Central City Health and Social Agency in San Francisco. Community outreach programs of this kind bring services to the place where they are needed.

Crisis Intervention

Crisis intervention as a planned tool of psychological treatment had its origin following a disaster in Boston in 1943, when nearly five hundred people were killed in a fire at the Coconut Grove nightclub. Local hospitals were crowded with survivors recovering from burns or other injuries, many had lost spouses and close friends in the fire. Erich Lindemann, staff psychiatrist at the Massachusetts General Hospital, interviewed a large number of these shocked and bereaved people. He found it possible to help them struggle with their grief, and presently he wrote what has become a classic paper (Lindemann, 1944) on the nature of grief, showing that timely intervention might give this reaction a more favorable course. Crisis intervention was subsequently developed by Lindemann himself and by Caplan (1964); its range and varieties are described in a collection of papers edited by Parad (1965).

Bereavement is only one of the life crises that can sometimes be benefited by intervention. Accident and injury, sickness, childbirth, recognition of severe handicaps or abnormalities in one's children, divorce, sudden financial pressure, being mugged or robbed or turned out of one's home—all these situations cause shock and put a person under stress that may badly upset established adaptive patterns. To be of use to people thus afflicted there must be a mental health service close at hand. Its staff must be willing to reach out to those in trouble instead of waiting for them to come in with their complaints. This puts the mental health professional in a somewhat unfamiliar role, but the client, who is in an unfamiliar state of disturbance, may be unusually open to help. Obviously, the topic of conversation will be the crisis and the feelings it has engendered. To a person overwhelmed by despair, anxiety, anger, or guilt it is valuable simply to have these feelings recognized by a sympathetic listener. It is still more valuable to learn that they are common, that they will not go on forever, and that there may be competent ways of dealing with the altered life situation. People recover from crises spontaneously, but not always in good ways. The bereaved may deny their loss completely, or freeze themselves into a permanent pattern of mourning. Those permanently damaged by accident or illness may continue to imagine a renewed normal life and thus fail to develop the more limited possibilities that still remain. Timely intervention may head off the less constructive ways of dealing with crisis, thus not only helping now but increasing the probability that future crises will be better met.

Most crises occur unpredictably, but when they can be foreseen, as in the case of childbirth, preventive intervention can be useful. Caplan (1964) reports favorable results from a program with Peace Corps volunteers about to start assignments in cultures widely different from their own. Being made aware beforehand of culture shock, personal isolation, and possible resistance to their good intentions served as a kind of psychological inoculation against emotions that might otherwise have proved overwhelming.

Crisis intervention has become an important function of community mental health centers. Before we add "successful" we should heed the warning of

Auerback and Kilmann (1977) that the difficulty of evaluating outcomes still stands in the way of decisive quantitative findings. Most clinical workers are not deterred by this from trying their best to deal with crises.

Consultation

Consultation has emerged as another important activity of community mental health centers. When called on to serve as a consultant, the mental health professional does not work directly with clients but gives advice to those who are already doing so. Consultation may be sought, for example, by a playground director whose program is being injured by a stubbornly rebellious and destructive child. What can be done differently to bring this black sheep into the fold? The consultant's role is not to see the child but to make suggestions for the playground director to carry out. As Korchin (1976) expresses it, "The consultant is said to provide an *indirect* service to the person or organization in need, for he works through someone who continues to provide *direct* services" (p. 511).

Consultation has the virtue of spreading more widely the influence of the highly skilled professional consultant. Help can be conveyed to more clients than would be possible through direct service alone. Another advantage is a gain in understanding and skill by those who receive the consultant's advice and apply it in work with their clients. As Caplan (1970) points out, people seeking consultation sometimes already suspect that their own difficulties in dealing with certain types of behavior may be as much of a problem as the client's troubles. There is double gain when a worker discovers through consultation that a certain type of aggression has been irrationally infuriating, and the client then learns that this aggression no longer infuriates the worker.

School systems are among the community institutions that can benefit from mental health consultation. Schools today generally consider their services to pupils incomplete if counseling is not included. The main functions of a school guidance department are typically educational counseling, the appraisal of abilities, and vocational advice, but maladaptive patterns of personal behavior often come to the counselors' attention. Usually the guidance staff lacks training to deal with these difficulties if they do not respond to nondirective counseling, and it is at this point that the community mental health center can make a useful contribution. This help may take the form of a consultation service for members of the school staff. A psychiatrist, social worker, or psychologist holds regular conference hours each week at which teachers or counselors can discuss problems they may be having with particular children. Under this arrangement the mental health worker does not see the disturbed child, but can often assist a teacher by pointing out the possible significance of some of the behavior and suggesting how the teacher, without trying to play psychiatrist, can best be helpful to the trouble-giving child. If these measures prove to be unsuccessful it may be necessary, of course, for the child to be seen at the mental health center. But sometimes this step, a little upsetting in itself,

657

can be avoided, and the mental health consultant will hear the good news that the problem child is doing much better and that the teacher is feeling more competent.

Mental health consultation in the schools has expanded widely in recent years, as shown in a comprehensive survey by Meyers, Parsons, and Martin (1979).

Services for Children

Services offered to children are perhaps the most quickly appreciated functions of a community mental health center. Many adults are more willing to seek help for their children's problems than for their own; furthermore, there is the hope that timely ministering to the needs of children will prevent the evolution of more serious disorders.

Child Guidance Clinics.

These are not new; the National Committee for Mental Hygiene, founded in 1909, assisted in the opening of children's clinics especially during the 1920s. Much was learned from these clinics, but there were not nearly enough of them to meet growing needs. All too often a child recommended for treatment went on a waiting list and was not seen for many months. The starting of community mental health centers quickly bettered this situation. As soon as their doors opened their services for children were likely to be in much demand. Children could now be seen and their treatment started with a minimum of delay.

In their original form, child guidance clinics were customarily staffed by psychiatrists, clinical psychologists, and psychiatric social workers. There was a rough division of functions according to which the psychiatrist was responsible for diagnosis and treatment, the psychologist for diagnostic testing and appraisal of the child's capacities, the social worker for securing the parents' version of the history and carrying out such measures as advising the parents and changing the child's activities. These functions became blurred as thinking developed in the direction of family psychotherapy. The whole team became co-therapists in attempting to deal with the complex of family relations that usually lies behind a child's problems. A children's service often proves to be the means whereby adult emotional problems and mental disorders are brought to the surface for treatment.

Services for the Mentally Retarded.

In recent years it has been increasingly recognized that children's mental health needs often require more than can be provided through individual and family psychotherapy. This is clearly apparent when *mental retardation* is part, or perhaps all, of a child's difficulty. Separate training schools for the retarded still perform an essential function when the disability is large, but for those children classed as "educable" it is an advantage for all concerned to have facilities in the community. These may well consist of kindergartens, special classes in the public schools, and sheltered workshops for those who have finished their formal education. The first and third facilities gain something by proximity to the community mental health center: they need from time to time the diagnostic and appraisal services and the family counseling resources that are to be found there.

Services for Emotionally Disturbed Children. Benefiting also from close contact with other services are special classes for *emotionally disturbed* children. These are children who cannot prosper in the ordinary school system because they are too anxious, too impulsive, too excitable, or too lethargic and withdrawn; they can learn only in a very small group where instruction can be individualized and wide latitude allowed for idiosyncrasies. Such classes require specially trained teachers and readily available consultation with a child psychiatrist.

Day Centers. Another desirable and appropriate form of service is the *day center* especially for disturbed adolescents. A day center makes it possible to take upset adolescents out of their homes, where they are usually experiencing great friction, and put them in quarters pleasantly furnished where there are opportunities for crafts, reading, music, games, preparing snacks, and perhaps a bit of group psychotherapy, all under the supervision of skilled leaders. The treatment of adolescent patients in mental hospitals has been shown to have rather poor outcomes (Hartman et al., 1968). The day center is certainly a better way to start, even if its results are less than magical.

Partial Hospitalization

One of the services that must be offered by a mental health center in order to qualify for federal support goes under the name of partial hospitalization. The image that springs to mind of a patient standing in the door with one foot in and one foot out is not correct: the patient's time is divided between hospital and home. Under certain conditions the patient may spend nights in the hospital and days at home or at work. This is especially appropriate with older patients who sleep badly and become confused during the night, and with those given to nocturnal attacks of anxiety. Generally, however, partial hospitalization signifies care during the day, with the patient returning home for the night.

The day hospital plan is unsuitable for patients who are highly disturbed or too apathetic to follow the routine, but it is entirely practicable with many whose condition is less severe. An early experiment carried on for several years at the Massachusetts Mental Health Center in Boston led to half of the patients being on day care, and many of these were admitted directly to it, without any period of full-time residence in the hospital (Kramer, 1962). The rationale and problems of partial hospitalization are discussed by Glasscote

659

(1969) who includes a number of "case studies" of particular programs. The saving in beds, space, and night care commends the experiment on financial grounds, but the strongest arguments in its favor are psychological. Provided there is a hospital or psychiatric ward in the community—otherwise the experiment is unworkable—the patient is not taken wholly out of the neighborhood, the relatives are not wholly relieved of their responsibility, the role of the sick person is not sharply established, and the regressive attractions of bed care are not added to the patient's other difficulties in facing the conditions of his or her life. When the time comes to end daily visits to the hospital, the transition does not have the character of an abrupt shock.

The Mental Hospital in Relation to Community Centers

The movement for community mental health has put traditional mental hospitals on the defensive. Emphasizing services near at hand, including psychiatric wards in general hospitals, the community movement makes a virtue of keeping patients out of mental hospitals; this goal was explicit in the original act of Congress. In historical perspective this can be seen as an injustice to a type of institution to which we owe most of our knowledge of the more serious mental disorders. The leading mental hospitals have unquestionably played an outstanding part in the advancement of knowledge and in the training of professional workers. Why have they been so suddenly given the role of villain in the mental health drama?

The shortest answer is that over the years they turned in a poor therapeutic record. Originally called asylums, they gave shelter and protection to mental patients but accomplished too little in the way of rehabilitation. They served the custodial function demanded by the public but put too little effort into sending patients home again in an improved condition. Considering how little was known about treatment for so long, and considering also the meager financial support provided by the taxpayers, it is not remarkable that many hospitals did not go beyond their custodial functions. Furthermore, we should remember that the better ones were pioneers in the development of shock treatments, drug therapy, group psychotherapy, and therapeutic milieux, and recovery rates have been steadily moving up. Even so, the mental hospital, often remote from the community and exhibiting some of the rigidity of a long-established institution, has become the target of a great deal of criticism.

This does not mean that mental hospitals should be wholly abandoned. "The psychiatric hospital need not be a social anachronism," says a report prepared by a committee of the Group for the Advancement of Psychiatry (1970-71); "it has unique functions that can complement community mental health programs." There are always cases in which constant observation and supervision are necessary, in which community resources have proved unequal to the strain, or in which hospitalization can serve as a useful retreat permit-

Recapturing self-esteem is an important part of making the transition from the traditional mental hospital to a community placement. This patient is being fitted for a part of her new image at a store in a state hospital.

ting the patient to "remarshall his forces." Five definite indications for hospitalization are specified in the report:

1. When supportive measures have been unsuccessful in halting or reversing the regressive process.
2. When the magnitude of regressive, depressive, or aggressive behavior is no longer tolerable to the patient and/or society.
3. When the management of special treatments, somatic procedures, and psychopharmacologic drugs requires continuous observation.
4. When a controlled environment is essential for the use of psychotherapy.

5. When medication or drugs on which the patient has become dependent
    must be withdrawn (p. 569).

The authors of the report further urge that when any of these conditions are
found to prevail, hospitalization should be recommended as a positive step
rather than as a reluctant last resort. They caution against haste in sending
the patient home. Returning to the community is a difficult step, and it is no
service to bring pressure to take it before careful preparations have been made
both at home and in the patient's own expectations.

The Patient's Return to the Community

When patients are discharged from a mental hospital, they do not return to
an unchanged situation at home. The behavior that led up to hospitalization
may have been disturbingly noticeable in the community and at places of
work. It is certain to have been seriously upsetting to the members of the family.
The family has probably been under great strain during the course of the
breakdown and has felt no small sense of relief when responsibility could be
turned over to doctors and nurses. In many ways the homecoming may be joyful, but we cannot be surprised that there are misgivings about returning patients. Will they be able to resume their former places and take up their usual
activities? Must they be treated in a special way? Will they break down again?

Cure does not end at the hospital. Patients' chances of continued improvement depend to some extent on their reception in the community. To a degree
the community has lost confidence in the patient, just as the patient may have
lost self-confidence. Thus the return to the community is bound to require adjustments. An important function of community mental health centers is to
provide services that will assist these readjustments.

Halfway Houses.   For patients who have been severely ill, whose confidence
has been deeply shaken, and whose contact with other people is still painfully
fragile, it is helpful to ease the return by introducing an intermediate step.
This is sometimes accomplished by foster family care. Another method is the
so-called "halfway house," a boarding house whose occupants ideally include
patients, a certain number of understanding people who are not patients, and
a trained person in charge or at least supervising the operation. In such a setting the former patient can go out to work every day but return to the house
either to mingle with the others or not; and the step of adapting again to family and old acquaintances is postponed to a later time. Raush and Raush
(1968) have drawn a composite portrait of both halfway houses and their residents.

The modal resident of the modal halfway house is an ex-hospital patient, at one
time diagnosed as schizophrenic. Directly or shortly after leaving the hospital, he
came to the house, perhaps after some visiting. He finds the house very different

from the hospital ward. For one thing, it is in a residential area of the city. It is a many-roomed place, dating from the twenties or thirties, in town rather than in the suburbs. It is a house, and it looks like a house and not like a hospital. Aside from staff, there are only about ten other residents. The resident has his own room or he shares a room with just one other person; also, unlike the hospital, the house has no locked rooms. While there are lots of things to do at the house, he has to go outside for any special entertainment. Moreover, he pays for his room and board.

At the modal house the resident receives no written rules. Still, he finds out that there are some things he must not do, such as drink on the premises, and some things that he must do, such as tell staff when he goes out, come to meals promptly, keep himself and the premises clean and obey his doctor's orders. He must care for his own room and he is usually expected to do some extra work of his own choice around the house. If he doesn't live up to these requirements, considerable social pressure will be placed on him and he may even be threatened with having to leave the house. In some ways, then, it isn't like living independently at a boarding house; it is much more closely supervised, and there is much more interaction with staff and other residents. . . .

The modal resident will stay at the house from four to eight months (pp. 190–91).

The halfway house differs also from a boarding house in its provision of services. Conspicuous among these is helping ex-patients to find jobs and to manage their own finances. In a true sense these houses are halfway between the hospital and independent living, and they seem to serve as a valuable stepping stone for patients unable to make the transition in one stride.

Former Patients' Associations.   Another scheme to ease the return is the establishment of community centers or clubs for former patients. These might be nicknamed "three-quarters houses" on the ground that the ex-patients have returned to their usual residence but still need certain periods of extra social support. With the help of initiative by the staff, these centers can become scenes of great activity, with regular meetings, amateur shows, dances, concerts, outings, even a weekly newsletter, all of which implies planning and committee work that in the end is mostly accomplished by the former patients. The fact that all the members are familiar with mental illness creates a feeling of unusual comradeship and understanding. Somewhat different in emphasis is a scheme reported by Fairweather and associates (1969) whereby a group of mental patients was removed from an open hospital ward, established in a disused motel, and set to operate, at first under supervision, a private, commercially competitive janitorial service. Conditions being favorable, the experiment was successful; the small subsociety implanted in the community took root, the service prospered, and the former patients progressively took over the management, with great benefit to their self-respect.

All these facilities perform a valuable service and show that by careful management it is possible to do a better job in restoring mental patients to normal existence. Optimism, however, should be tempered. Research done under relatively favorable conditions showed that six months after discharge from a mental hospital 21.6 percent of the patients had been readmitted; at the end of a year the percentage was 37.4 (Michaux et al., 1969). Further, it appears that readmission is not closely correlated with adverse external factors such as uneasy employers, unsympathetic neighbors, and destructive attitudes on the part of family members (Angrist et al., 1968). An ex-patient's behavior can continue to be difficult even when circumstances seem favorable. Mental disorders, after all, entail deeply rooted maladaptive tendencies that interfere with flexible response to the environment immediately present. When these tendencies persist after discharge, as happens all too often, there are bound to be disappointing failures in even the most skillful work of rehabilitation.

SHORTAGE OF PROFESSIONALLY TRAINED WORKERS

A close look at the unmet needs in mental health shows that the difficulty is not wholly financial. There is a shortage of trained people in the related professions. This was already true before the Joint Commission in 1961 issued its call for community mental health centers and federal funds became available to start them. In a survey of state and county mental hospitals Albee (1959) reported that 25 percent of the positions budgeted for psychiatrists and psychologists, and 20 percent of those budgeted for social workers and nurses, remained unfilled because nobody could be found to take them. Budgeted positions, of course, do not necessarily reflect the number needed for high quality service. As against the standards formulated by the American Psychiatric Association for the adequate staffing of mental hospitals and clinics, a survey in 1958 (Joint Commission, 1961) showed that these institutions had in fact only 57 percent of the physicians needed, 75 percent of the psychologists, 40 percent of the social workers, and 23 percent of the registered nurses. The shortage contributed to a most unequal distribution of mental health work throughout the nation, which to some extent still remains (Richards & Gottfredson, 1978). With most workers having choices of jobs, there was a high concentration in large cities of the North, East Coast, and West Coast; and the problem of staffing services in smaller communities and rural areas was already severe.

The movement for community mental health centers was bound to increase these shortages. To meet the goal of a fully staffed center for every 100,000 people it would be necessary to open hundreds of new centers and to increase the staffs of many more that were in operation on a part-time basis. The demand for trained professionals was clearly going into a steep upward curve. How could such a demand be met?

The answer that first springs to mind is that training institutions should have drastically increased their output, trebling or quadrupling it if necessary to meet the rising need. The National Institute for Mental Health put its weight behind increased output by providing federal training stipends for graduate students preparing for the mental health professions. At the height of its policy in the late 1960s NIMH was granting 10,000 stipends a year, though this rate has since declined somewhat as pressures increased for economy in federal welfare agencies. There has been in fact a substantial increase of numbers in the mental health professions, but it is not sufficient to meet current demands (Bloom, 1977; President's Comission, 1978), and it is by no means easy to eliminate the discrepancy. Why this is so will become clear if we consider what is involved in training of this kind.

Professional Training

Psychiatry.   The complexity of the problem comes out clearly in the case of psychiatry. A psychiatrist is first of all a physician. This means going through medical school, taking whatever training in psychiatry is offered during the four-year course, receiving the M.D. degree, and specializing in psychiatry in subsequent internships. It is incorrect to call anyone a psychiatrist who does not have the M.D. degree. Psychiatry is a medical specialty.

Implicit in this training is a huge institutional backing. To the facilities of the medical school itself are added those of teaching hospitals and clinics where first-hand experience has to be found. Much of the learning of one's specialty takes place during internships and residencies, and it may be several years beyond the M.D. degree before board examinations are taken to be qualified as a certified specialist. If psychoanalytic training is sought, which is offered by independent psychoanalytic institutes, the young doctor may remain partly in the status of a trainee for three or four more years. Of course, interns and resident physicians start giving service as well as being trained, but they still make demands on the time of older doctors to teach and supervise them. A crash program designed to increase the output of physicians would put impossible demands on the personnel and institutions now responsible for training. There is no way to increase quickly the number of senior physicians and other seasoned experts who would have to teach the enlarged group of new students. It looks as if the complaints from outlying community mental health centers that they cannot find medical directors will continue to be heard for some time.

Clinical Psychology.   Stepping up numbers is only a little less difficult in the case of clinical psychologists. The ranks of this professional group have swelled considerably during the last quarter-century, though not yet enough to meet the current need. Fully trained clinical psychologists typically hold a Ph.D. degree granted by a university faculty of arts and sciences. Their training is thus somewhat more academically oriented than that of psychiatrists. It includes supervised practice and a year's clinical internship, but it also includes training in research and a doctoral dissertation that is intended to make a contribution to scientific knowledge. In practice today, clinical psychologists are likely to perform a variety of duties including psychotherapy, counseling, consultation, and the appraisal of abilities, but they can be of special value in planning and guiding research on, among other things, the effectiveness of different clinical procedures. Again the necessary training is of a character that does not permit doubling the output overnight. It requires the support of clinical and research facilities, both notably expensive, and it makes large demands on senior staff for individual supervision.

There is active debate among clinical psychologists about training and the future shape of their profession. Attachment to academic departments of psychology, with their single-minded scientific ideals and lack of interest in application, has caused a great deal of friction. In several states independent schools of professional psychology have been established and are well patronized. Some of these have been authorized to grant the degree of Doctor of Psychology (Psych. D.). Their courses of study, which include abundant clinical training, are designed to prepare students specifically for the clinical positions they are likely to occupy.

Clinical Social Work.   The professional group that has grown most rapidly is that of psychiatric social worker, now coming to be called clinical social worker. Originally a social worker was a person who visited homes and brought helpful advice and services to needy inhabitants. The role had no connection with psychiatry until certain psychiatrists began to see that their work with office patients could be helped by direct knowledge of the social and family background. In due course the psychiatric social worker evolved from being the psychiatrist's social investigator to being a co-therapist in work with the whole family. This professional group is taking an increasingly important part in community mental health.

The clinical social worker typically completes a course of training that leads to a Master's degree. The academic side of the training consists of courses in psychiatry and psychology, child development, community organization, and social statistics. Emphasis is placed on supervised field training, which occupies at least half of the two-year program. The students are placed at clinics or hospitals where they participate increasingly in the work and thus learn their trade at first hand under careful supervision. Direct experience with research has gradually been given greater emphasis. Increasingly the social worker takes part in institutional research programs and needs familiarity with the impersonal rigors of research method. The output of clinical social workers can be more easily increased merely because the training takes a shorter time. Supporting institutions and senior supervisors, whose number rises slowly, play a large part in that training.

A number of social work schools have developed doctoral programs that offer research and theoretical training in addition to clinical skills. As a consequence of current shortages, some community agencies are directed and staffed entirely by social workers, using psychiatrists and clinical psychologists only as occasional consultants (Korchin, 1976).

Psychiatric Nursing. Anyone who has been a patient in a hospital, for whatever reason, knows the importance of the nurses. Some patients have been heard to say that it was the nurses more than the doctors who got them well. Nurses with additional psychiatric training carry many responsibilities and play a vital part in mental hospital care. Their role is increasing in community mental health centers. As visiting nurses they can be important points of anchorage in the lives of former patients returned to the community. Their place in mental health work seems likely to grow.

Shortage of personnel in the chief mental health professions is real, severe, and not subject to rapid correction. Does this mean that the movement for community mental health will have to stop short of its goals, leaving many communities without this type of service?

Nonprofessional Aides

Instead of accepting such a frustrating conclusion, mental health leaders have considered the possibility of using larger numbers of people not trained to the professional level. Such a move always produces anxiety, raising direful images of well-meaning blunders making clients worse rather than better. Nevertheless, when the question is examined closely it seems sensible that some of the work of community mental health might be done by interested nonprofessionals, provided they are carefully chosen, receive practical training, recognize limits in what they attempt, and work under close professional supervision. These provisos are of the utmost importance. If they are not met, the nonprofessional worker is indeed a well meaning blunderer who would be wiser not to tinker with mental health.

Beginning in the mid-1950s, college students began volunteering to serve as aides in mental hospitals. Experience with these volunteers, now quite extensive, illustrates both the possibilities and the problems of lay helpers in mental health work. Students were drawn to this work partly because of the glaring need: many patients in hospitals that had a custodial orientation were badly neglected, receiving no treatment and minimal attention from the overworked staff. In what are called Companion Programs each volunteer is assigned to a particular patient who is visited at least once a week. At these meetings the volunteer tries to engage the patient in conversation, which may not be easy, and seeks to be friendly and helpful. Perhaps the patient has wants or grievances that can be called to the attention of the staff; perhaps communication with relatives has broken down and can be restored through the efforts of the volunteer; perhaps the patient can be sent home if the volunteer takes initiative and helps in making the necessary arrangements. Even if none of these is possible, the patient may be pleased and perceptibly brightened by the attention.

The program can work, however, only if it is supervised by someone who selects and knows the students, who knows and selects the patients, who runs a weekly group meeting for the volunteers, and who is available for individual conferences and advice. Sometimes the volunteers become bewildered by the peculiarities of psychotic conversation. Sometimes they try to push the patient too fast toward behavior that takes confidence and initiative. Sometimes they become discouraged when there are no signs of improvement, perhaps piqued that their own good intentions are ineffective. Sometimes they feel hurt and rejected by behavior that a more seasoned observer would attribute to mood changes or internal dramas having little to do with the actual visitor. The supervisor's help is constantly needed to sustain the volunteer's morale and to interpret the interactions with the patient. The students' work may be harder than expected, the gain smaller than was hoped. Yet the enterprise is worthwhile on both sides. Several reports strongly suggest that visited patients, compared to others in the same hospital, are more likely to show improvement, and more of them reach the point of discharge (Gruver, 1971). The students, on their part, report valuable changes in themselves. They believe that "they learned a great deal from the case-aide experience," that they "gained insight into their own personalities and problems through their relationships with the patients and their own group," and that identity formation and vocational choice were often favorably affected (Umbarger et al., 1962; Holzberg, Knapp, & Turner, 1966).

Homemakers constitute another source of nonprofessional help in mental health work. In one program, for instance, it proved possible after fairly brief training to use homemakers as mental health counselors working directly with clients (Rioch et al., 1963). The women chosen for such programs are generally well-educated, and their activities are circumscribed in the sense that they work with assigned clients and report frequently to their professional supervisor. In another program, at the University of Rochester, homemakers are trained to serve as teacher aides in public schools (Zax & Cowen, 1969). The women chosen may be of any age and often have limited education, but are judged to have been effective mothers, genuinely interested in young children, and potentially capable of relating to them warmly and comfortably. Their job is to work with children screened from regular classes because of emotional difficulties. The training of these women is limited to five weeks; it consists of orientation to basic aspects of mental health, personality development, behavior problems, and the nature of the school system. They are paid for their work, but not at a rate that would attract fortune hunters. Ministering to the emotional needs of children and fostering their educational development can be construed as both currently therapeutic and preventive of later disorders. The homemakers are well suited to this work; indeed, their experience as effective mothers may be a more relevant credential than a formal certificate of professional training.

By 1970 it was possible to speak of a "nonprofessional revolution in mental health" (Sobey, 1970). A large variety of programs for training, service, and supervision could presently be surveyed (Gershon & Biller, 1977). It is still too soon to assess the results systematically, but there is confidence that nonprofessional aides can be of great value in forwarding community mental health. But we must be careful not to exaggerate the part that can be taken by those who are not professionally trained. What must especially be avoided is lack of communication with professional experts. Unexpected problems are always likely to crop up for which only a broad professional experience can provide answers. A well-organized community mental health center offers the best possibility that communication will stay open among all those who are cooperating in the work.

PREVENTION

Sensible readers, familiar with the adage that an ounce of prevention is worth a pound of cure, should now be asking how much we can expect of community mental health in forestalling maladaptive personal behavior. If mental health services are made widely available in the community, can we hope that preventive programs, early recognition of risks, prompt treatment, and the spread of information will decisively lower the future incidence of mental disorders and maladaptive behavior?

Prevention is, of course, a recognized goal of community mental health centers. But if we let our minds run over the many topics discussed in this book it will be apparent that prevention means a great many different things. Much of the needed effort does not lie within the traditional field of mental health. As we have seen, schizophrenic disorders occur with highest frequency at low socioeconomic levels. There is a clear relation between poverty and such troubles as juvenile delinquency and drug abuse. Even mental retardation, once thought to be wholly a matter of inheritance, turns out to be influenced by cultural deprivation. We would presumably have a lower incidence of schizophrenia, juvenile delinquency, crime, drug abuse, and socio-cultural retardation if poverty were ameliorated and society more humanely organized. Keniston (1977), reporting on a five-year study by The Carnegie Council on Children, argues that the needs of children require extensive economic reorganization leading to better distribution of jobs, income, and security in society as a whole. He urges child advocates to become public advocates in a major effort to improve the climate for human growth. Such a task is clearly outside the scope of a community mental health center. It calls for political action that has effective support among citizens of voting age.

Another important part of prevention has its locus in general medical care. One of the most obvious ways of reducing later maladaptive behavior, according to Huessy (1971) is "to see to it that no pregnant mother does without an adequate protein diet, that no expectant mother does without adequate prenatal and perinatal care, and that no infant goes through its first year with inadequate nutrition." We would certainly have a lower incidence of disorders such as cerebral palsy, minimal brain damage, and several forms of severe mental retardation if these public health measures were more effectively performed. This again is not the usual sphere of direct mental health intervention, but Huessy urges that "a mental health program worth its salt should be turning heaven and earth to see to it that whoever is responsible or able to do this job gets it done. One must give them all the support possible."

Still another part of prevention rests with neurological and biochemical research. Previous chapters have shown that some of the more serious mental disorders, including affective disorders and schizophrenia, are related to biochemical peculiarities that may be open to correction. Perhaps the already valuable results of drug medication can be substantially improved as increasing knowledge yields increasing powers of control.

Social and economic change, public health measures, and biochemical and neurological research thus form part of the concerted effort needed for better prevention of maladaptive personal behavior. Closer to the activities of community mental health centers are problems that have their origin in the personal history of learning. For prevention in this sphere, the psychological model must be kept in mind even though it makes the task look more difficult.

Preventing Psychological Disorders

The most obvious contribution that a community mental health center can make to prevention is to intervene more promptly in the lives of troubled people. Providing local services, at low cost if necessary, is a step in this direction. Services for children and consultations in the schools are designed to locate maladaptive behavior early and provide such redirection as may be possible. Especially when family psychotherapy has a successful result, the hope seems justified that a situation otherwise destined to go from bad to worse has been turned around to permit further growth. We will not be able for some time, of course, to assess the results of earlier intervention, but the policy certainly deserves a thorough trial.

Strictly speaking, however, early intervention is still corrective instead of preventive. It occurs only after maladaptive behavior has begun to show itself. More fundamental prevention would mean trying to keep such behavior from happening in the first place. Is it possible to detect in advance those children who are likely to have difficulties? Is it possible, having detected them, to help these children avoid future trouble or cope with it better? In imagination we can picture a universal screening process whereby all children likely to become psychological casualties are ticketed in advance and given the benefit of immediate professional help. Reality quickly dissipates this dream. Psychologists do not claim that their tests are equal to such a sensitive early screening process. Mental health workers do not feel confident about effective intervention. Nobody is certain that what we now consider ominous signs are regularly followed by later breakdown. Parents do not look kindly on meddling with children who outwardly are doing all right. Prevention on a giant scale is an idea whose time has decidedly not come.

The problem must be approached in smaller steps. Progress has been made in recent years by selecting "high risk" children, following their development closely, and in some cases intervening to improve their general development. Garmezy (1971, 1979), a pioneer in this kind of research, used four groups of children considered to be at risk: (1) children of schizophrenic mothers, (2) children of depressive or personality-disordered mothers, (3) antisocial aggressive children. Rolf and Hasazi (1977) added physical and mental disabilities, developmental lag, and severe economic disadvantage as contributing to risk. While these factors are derived from certain conceptions about what is harmful for development, the research method, as Mednick and Witkin-Lanoil (1977) point out, yields the bonus of making these conceptions more exact—of refining our ideas about etiology. Children of schizophrenic mothers, for instance, may develop schizophrenia, but they may develop instead a different form of disorder, and they may turn out normally competent if not superior. The knowledge gained from carefully studying their lives over time can lead to much more refined ideas of the precise antecedents of different kinds of disorder. It can also illuminate the adaptive tactics and strategies whereby some children deal competently with highly unfavorable conditions.

In the studies reported by Rolf and Hasazi (1977) a variety of interventions was explored. These included consultations with classroom teachers, coaching in speech and language when these were deficient, special practice in private of skills the child dared not attempt in public, small play groups to improve a shy child's chances of social participation, and meetings with parents either individually or in parent education classes. These interventions can be described as attempts to encourage development wherever it is lagging. Seen in this way, as forms of education, they cannot fairly be characterized as psychiatric meddling. It is too soon to decide on the value of these programs, but most workers believe they achieve at least a modest success.

Parent Education

To the extent that parents' behavior and attitudes influence children's development, parent education is a promising route toward the prevention of maladaptive learning. During the 1930s and 1940s, when psychoanalysis was describing parents as agents of repression and subsequent neurosis, parent education became a popular mental health goal. Unfortunately, the early messages reached parents in a form more alarming than helpful. Children could be ruined by their parents early in life, ruined by attitudes of which the

671

parents were not fully conscious, after which only the expert could save them. This was all that many parents could make of what they were told at that time.

The educative task was naturally assumed by psychiatrists, social workers, and psychologists, who seem to have approached it at first without much imagination. Through books, lectures, and magazine articles parents were warned of the dreadful things that would happen if they did not shape up and start exuding warmth and acceptance. Undoubtedly a factor in this difficulty was the tendency of professional workers to side with patients against parents and to perceive parents, either in the present or through their past influence, as the chief obstacles to therapeutic success. It is small wonder that parents sometimes felt they were being berated rather than helped.

After a while it was recognized that parent education was producing unfortunate consequences. Some of these were examined in a paper by Bruch (1954), who pointed out that "the enumeration of all the possible acts and attitudes that might injure a child creates an atmosphere of uncertainty and apprehension." Instead of being helpfully informed, parents and future parents were in too many cases simply intimidated. Clearly the production of anxiety in parents defeats the purpose of reducing it in their children. Teaching that makes parents hesitant, self-conscious, and fearful cannot be expected to bring children a feeling of security. Bruch pointed out another undertone in parent education that might be considered even more sinister. The parents are given an illusion of omnipotence, a supposedly scientific reason for believing that their influence upon the child is paramount, so that they can set "the goal of manipulating him into becoming a perfect adult." This opens the way for the parent to feel not only guilt and anxiety over the child's faults but also a most unbecoming vainglory over excellencies. Sometimes when a child does something particularly well one hears the parents receiving congratulations for having done a fine job of upbringing. Can we be surprised that the product of this fine job shows resentment "when he senses that he is supposed," as Bruch puts it, "to prove something about the parents, and not about himself?" Bruch's work was symptomatic of a change of heart that presently steered parent education into new channels.

Newer Trends in Parent Education

Parents do not select their attitudes voluntarily, nor do they assume them simply out of ignorance. Attitudes toward children are deeply embedded in the personalities of parents and may be complexly involved with the parents' own problems. The only way to have a beneficial effect on unfortunate attitudes is to provide corrective experiences for parents such as those intended as the goal of psychotherapy. They must themselves be motivated to change, they must go at their own pace, they must not be made resistant by untimely interpretations, they must feel that the atmosphere is one of understanding and respect. If these conditions prevail, parents can reach real working insights into how they interact with their young, but at the same time not lose their sense of the child's part in the interaction. They can become better parents without sacrificing the naturalness and individuality of their behavior at home.

This goal can best be accomplished not by the lecture method but by group discussion. Success seems to be greatest when the discussion is conducted with a minimum of direction, so that the topics introduced come straight from the actual problems of individual parents. There is a certain advantage in keeping the experts out of sight. Parent groups can be successfully conducted by volunteers from the community provided these lay workers have received brief training in mental health concepts and in methods of facilitating group discussion. The absence of an expert encourages the participants to go further in seeking their own solutions to the problems that have brought them together.

The new spirit is well represented in a program described by Gordon (1977) called Parent Effectiveness Training. This is an educational program conducted as a series of three-hour classes, one each week for eight weeks. Meetings are held at some convenient community center and are scheduled in the evening so that working parents can attend. There is always a trained leader, but free discussion and exchange of experiences are encouraged. Whatever knowledge and skills the parents acquire are immediately applied at home with the children. The results, good or bad, are reported and discussed at subsequent meetings and are likely to improve over time. The parents learn how to listen better to their children. They become more aware of their feelings toward the children, and more courageous in acting on these feelings. They learn to steer between arbitrary punishment and indiscriminate permissiveness. Of course, the results are not miraculous, but from parents' comments afterwards we can conclude that in some cases family life has moved in better directions. Parents describe themselves as "more relaxed, less uptight," as more aware of the feelings on both sides, as "less judgmental." "We're not afraid any more to talk about feelings," one parent reported, and another said, "I am closer to my sons in an intimate way I never would have dreamed of, and at the same time I am happier about their independence." Change is perceived by the children; one son said, "I really think you love me more than you used to." Parent education can be botched, as it was at first, but when it is done with sympathy and skill it seems capable of contributing importantly to family well-being.

Programs of this kind, however, work best with relatively educated people. Like so much that is being done today about mental health, parent education does not easily reach less favored levels of the population. There is much still to be done.

THE CITIZEN'S CONTRIBUTION

Many readers of this book will not be planning a professional career in which knowledge of abnormal psychology is generally deemed essential. Their relation to public health, mental hospitals, and community mental health centers will be no closer than that of an intelligent citizen. They will properly ask themselves what part the citizen can play in alleviating the burden of maladaptive personal reactions. They will want to know whether abnormal psychology, in addition to its special professional uses, adds anything to the leaven of thought by which the world is changed for the better. The subject is, to be sure, a relatively specialized field of knowledge. In one respect, nevertheless, the knowledge and insight that can be most readily gained by studying it reaches out beyond the bounds of a specialty and becomes significant for anyone who wants to play an enlightened part in human betterment. For the task of preventing maladaptive personal reactions penetrates deeply, as we have seen, into public and private life.

The most direct form of service consists of volunteering as a nonprofessional aide. Earlier this meant what we might call civilian duty in a mental hospital, analogous to the volunteer service that has proved so valuable in operating general hospitals. The community mental health movement has greatly expanded the opportunities for civilian duty and stands in great need, as we saw, of varied nonprofessional assistance. Another form of service, decidedly challenging to those who like to take part in community affairs, is the civilian management of mental health facilities. Although public funds and professional direction play a large part in the community centers, citizens' boards have a role in securing additional monies, providing buildings and equipment, supervising the practical side of the operation, and enlarging community contacts. A mental health center that does not have this kind of community cooperation can hardly operate at all.

The citizen's contribution can be of a less direct but hardly less important kind. In our personal lives we interact with many other people, and our effects on them may or may not be conducive to mutual adjustment. We are all familiar with people who have a gift for stirring up trouble. They cannot enter the most harmonious group without throwing it into violent discord, and they seem adept at making the anxious people more anxious, the guilty more guilty, the angry more angry. Other people seem generally to have the opposite effect; things go better when they are around. This desirable effect is not achieved simply by being a peacemaker. There may be strong partisanship and a vehement espousal of ideas, but the person is able to do this without rancor, without implying that every other viewpoint is stupid, without anger when others disagree, without resentment when outvoted. This is one aspect of the many-sided quality generally called emotional maturity. We can often improve our maturity if we become interested in reflecting on our feelings and noticing our interactions with others. We are not likely to change overnight, but it is part of our contribution as citizens to do what we can in the direction of personal maturity.

To complete the list, the citizen as parent can contribute importantly toward mental health. The fallacy of parental omnipotence should be avoided, but the parent is still a significant item in the child's environment. Interest plays an important part in the success of parent-child relationships. When parents are interested in their children and can regard them in a spirit that combines affection with a humorous sense of perspective, many excellencies follow as a matter of course. Interest guarantees that they will at least not ride roughshod over the child's strivings and preoccupations. Then there is the matter of respect. While realizing the child's inexperience and immaturity, parents should recognize accomplishments as they appear and let the child know that they appreciate initiative and growing competence.

A contemporary hazard for healthy development is the confusion so many people feel about values. The recent fast rate of change in the conditions of life and a generally critical attitude toward the values of the past have combined to produce a widespread state of uncertainty. Many parents today are badly muddled about their own values. Others find it hard to translate adult beliefs into clear "do's" and "don'ts" comprehensible to children. These uncertainties make it difficult to be consistent models of adult maturity. They also interfere seriously with giving children a structured cognitive outlook. Adaptation is a process of learning, and learning cannot take place advantageously when the cognitive field is not clear. Permissiveness as a childrearing doctrine lost repute when parents began to realize, professionals began to notice, and research began to show that children were more secure and confident when they grew up in households with explicit rules and expectations (White, 1976, pp. 48-50). These regulations gave them needed guidance and enabled them to feel competent when they met standards of mature behavior. Parents or future parents who seriously try to think out their values, deciding what they really want to stand for, may be making an important contribution to mental health in themselves, their children, and the people around them.

The task of preventing abnormal behavior is one in which every citizen can participate. To the extent that such behavior arises out of the process of socialization, everyone can be of some help in its prevention. As parent and as teacher, everyone can learn to guide more wisely the steps by which children adapt themselves to the requirements of living together. As voter and citizen, everyone can throw their influence in favor of a social and moral order intelligently fashioned to encourage the best possibilities in human nature.

SUGGESTIONS FOR FURTHER READING

A pivotal point in the history of mental health care is occupied by *Action for mental health* (1961), the final report of the Joint Commission on Mental Health and Illness. This report, covering finances, facilities, programs, and personnel, was the document that set in motion the national policy of establishing community mental health centers. For an official updating of this report there is the *Report of the President's Commission on Mental Health*, Volume 1 (1978), which stresses the still unmet needs.

There is now an outpouring of publications on community mental health. A judicious overview is provided by S. Korchin in Part V of his *Modern clinical psychology* (1976). B. L. Bloom's *Community mental health: A general introduction* (1977) is a fine survey in a style that is easy to read. These works are relatively optimistic; controversy is provided by the severely critical work, *The mental health industry: A cultural phenomenon* (1978), by P. A. Magaro, R. Gripp, and D. J. McDowell, which questions whether the job is being well done.

The basic book on crisis intervention is G. Caplan's *Principles of preventive psychiatry* (1964). The same author has written *The theory and practice of mental health consultation* (1970). A comprehensive guide to school consultation, directed especially to professionals and future professionals, is *Mental health consultation in the schools* (1979) by R. D. Meyers, J. Parsons, and M. Martin.

For readers who are curious about innovations in the care of mental patients there is an interesting book by H. L. Raush with C. L. Raush, *The halfway house movement: A search for sanity* (1968). Valuable also is R. M. Glasscote *et al., Partial hospitalization for the mentally ill* (1969). A valuable and straightforward guide toward helping former patients back into the family is the book by K. R. Beutner and N. G. Hale, Jr., *Emotional illness: How families can help* (1957).

An experiment in the use of college students as group leaders to help in the treatment of chronic hospitalized mental patients is reported by J. Rappaport, J. M. Chinsky, and E. L. Cowen, *Innovations in helping chronic patients: College students in a mental institution* (1971). A companion program of college students with troubled fifth- and sixth-grade boys is reported by Gerald Goodman, *Companionship therapy: Studies in structured intimacy* (1972). The use and training of nonprofessionals in mental health work is surveyed by M. Gershon and H. B. Biller in *The other helpers: Paraprofessionals and nonprofessionals in mental health* (1977).

Current work on preventing psychological disorders can be followed in an annual publication, based on conferences held at the University of Vermont, entitled *Primary prevention of psychopathology*; three volumes (1977–1979) have thus far been published.

References

Abrams, R., & Taylor, M. A. Catatonia: A prospective clinical study. *Archives of General Psychiatry*, 1976, *33*, 579–581.

Abse, D. W., Wilkins, N. M., van de Castle, R. L., Buxton, W. D., DeMars, J. P., Brown, R. S., & Kirschner, L. G. Personality and behavioral characteristics of lung cancer patients. *Journal of Psychosomatic Research*, 1974, *18*, 101–113.

Ackerman, N. W. *The psychodynamics of family life*. New York: Basic Books, 1958.

Ackerman, N. W. Further comments on family psychotherapy. In M. I. Stein (Ed.), *Contemporary psychotherapies*. New York: The Free Press of Glencoe, 1961, pp. 245–255.

Ackerman, N. W. Family psychotherapy today: Some areas of controversy. *Comprehensive Psychiatry*, 1966, *7*, 375–388.

Adams, H. E., & Sturgis, E. T. Status of behavioral reorientation techniques in the modification of homosexuality: A review. *Psychological Bulletin*, 1977, *84*, 1171–1188.

Ader, R. Experimentally induced gastric lesions. Results and implications of studies in animals. In H. Weiner (Ed.), *Advances in psychosomatic medicine*. Basel: Kruger, 1971.

Adler, A. *The practice and theory of individual psychology*. New York: Harcourt Brace Jovanovich, 1929.

Adorno, T. W., Frenkel-Brunswick, E., Levinson, D. J., & Sanford, R. N. *The authoritarian personality*. New York: Harper & Row, 1950.

Agras, S., Sylvester, D., & Oliveau, D. The epidemiology of common fears and phobia. *Comprehensive Psychiatry*, 1969, *10*, 151–156.

Ainsworth, M. D., Andry, R. G., Harlow, R. G., Lebovici, S., Mead, M., Prugh, D. G., & Wootton, B. *Deprivation of maternal care: A reassessment of its effects* (Public Health Papers). Geneva: World Health Organization, 1962.

677

Albee, G. W. *Mental health manpower trends*. New York: Basic Books, 1959.

Albee, G. W. Through the looking glass. *International Journal of Psychiatry*, 1970–71, *9*, 293–298.

Alcoholics Anonymous. New York: A. A. World Service, 1955.

Alexander, A. B., Miklich, D. R., & Hershkoff, H. The immediate effects of systematic relaxation training on peak expiratory flow rates in asthmatic children. *Psychosomatic Medicine*, 1972, *34*, 388–394.

Alexander, F. *The medical value of psychoanalysis*. New York: Norton, 1937.

Alexander, F. *Psychosomatic medicine: Its principles and applications*. New York: Norton, 1950.

Alexander, F. Educative influence of personality factors in the environment. In C. Kluckhohn, H. A. Murray, & D. M. Schneider (Eds.), *Personality in nature, society and culture* (2nd ed.). New York: Alfred A. Knopf, 1953, pp. 421–435.

Alexander, F., French, T. M., Bacon, C. L., Benedek, T., Fuerst, R. A., Gerard, M. W., Grinker, R. R., Grotjahn, M., Johnson, A. M., McLean, H. V., & Weiss, E. *Psychoanalytic therapy*. New York: Ronald Press, 1946.

Alexander, F., French, T. M., & Pollack, G. H. *Psychosomatic specificity: Experimental study and results*. Chicago: University of Chicago Press, 1968.

Allan, L. D., Ferguson-Smith, M. A., Donald, I., Sweet, E. M., & Gibson, A. A. M. Amniotic fluid alpha-feto-protein in the antenatal diagnosis of spina bifida. *Lancet*, 1973, *2*, 522–525.

Allen, F. H. *Psychotherapy with children*. New York: Norton, 1942.

Allport, G. W. The ego in contemporary psychology. *Psychological Review*, 1943, *50*, 451–478.

American Association on Mental Deficiency. Sterilization of persons who are mentally retarded: A statement. *Mental Retardation*, 1974, *12*, 59–60.

American Psychiatric Association. *Diagnostic and statistical manual of mental disorders* (Preliminary draft—3rd ed.). Washington, D.C.: American Psychiatric Association, 1978.

American Psychiatric Association. *Diagnostic and statistical manual of mental disorders* (3rd ed.). Washington, D.C.: American Psychiatric Association, 1980.

Amir, M. *Patterns in forcible rape*. Chicago: University of Illinois Press, 1971.

Angrist, B., & Gershon, S. The phenomenology of experimentally-induced amphetamine psychosis. Preliminary observations. *American Journal of Psychiatry*, 1970, *126*, 95–107.

Angrist, B., & Gershon, S. Possible dose-response relationships in amphetamine psychosis. In C. J. D. Zarafonetis (Ed.), *Drug abuse: Proceedings of the international conference*. Philadelphia: Lea & Febiger, 1972, pp. 263–269.

Angrist, S. S., Dinitz, S., Lefton, M., & Pasamanick, B. *Women after treatment: A study of former mental patients and their normal neighbors*. New York: Appleton-Century-Crofts, 1968.

Angyal, A. *Neurosis and treatment: A holistic theory*. New York: Wiley, 1965.

Ansbacher, H. L., & Ansbacher, R. R. *The individual psychology of Alfred Adler*. New York: Basic Books, 1956.

Anthony, E. J. A clinical evaluation of children with psychotic parents. In R. Cancro (Ed.), *The schizophrenic syndrome*. New York: Brunner/Mazel, 1971, pp. 244–256.

Argyris, C. *Interpersonal competence and organizational effectiveness*. Homewood, Ill.: Dorsey Press, 1962.

Arieti, S. *The intrapsychic self*. New York: Basic Books, 1967.

Arieti, S. *Interpretation of schizophrenia*. New York: Basic Books, 1975.

Aronfreed, J. *Conduct and conscience*. New York: Academic Press, 1968.

Arthurs, R. G. S., & Cahoon, E. B. A clinical and electroencephalographic survey of psychopathic personality. *American Journal of Psychiatry*, 1964, *120*, 875–882.

Asch, S. E. *Social psychology*. Englewood Cliffs, N.J.: Prentice-Hall, 1952.

Astrup, C., & Noreik, K. *Functional psychoses*. Springfield, Ill.: Charles C. Thomas, 1966.

Auerbach, S. M., & Kilmann, P. R. Crisis intervention: A review of outcome research. *Psychological Bulletin*, 1977, *84*, 1189–1217.

Averill, J. R. Grief: Its nature and significance. *Psychological Bulletin*, 1968, *70*, 721–748.

Ayllon, T., & Haughton, E. Modification of symptomatic verbal behaviour of mental patients. *Behaviour Research and Therapy*, 1964, *2*, 87–97.

Bach, G. R. *Intensive group psychotherapy*. New York: Ronald Press, 1954, p. 213.

Bagley, C. *The social psychology of the epileptic child*. Coral Gables, Fla.: University of Miami Press, 1967.

Baker, B. L., & Ward, M. H. Reinforcement therapy for behavior problems in severely retarded children. *American Journal of Orthopsychiatry*, 1971, *61*, 124–135.

Bakewell, W. E., & Wikler, A. Symposium: Non-narcotic addiction. Incidence in a university hospital psychiatric ward. *Journal of the American Medical Association*, 1966, *196*, 710–713.

Baldessarini, R. J. Chemotherapy. In A. M. Nicholi, Jr. (Ed.), *The Harvard guide to modern psychiatry*. Cambridge, Mass.: Harvard University Press, 1978, pp. 387–432.

Baldwin, J. *Notes of a native son*. Boston: Beacon Press, 1955.

Ball, J. C., & Chambers, C. D. *The epidemiology of opiate addiction in the United States*. Springfield, Ill.: Charles C. Thomas, 1970.

Ban, T. A. *Conditioning and psychiatry*. Chicago: Aldine, 1964.

Bandura, A. *Social learning theory*. Englewood Cliffs, N.J.: Prentice-Hall, 1977.

Bandura, A., Ross, D., & Ross, S. A. Vicarious reinforcement and imitative learning. *Journal of Abnormal Social Psychology*, 1963, *67*, 601–607.

Bandura, A., & Walters, R. H. *Adolescent aggression*. New York: Ronald Press, 1959.

Bandura, A., & Walters, R. H. *Social learning and personality development*. New York: Holt, Rinehart & Winston, 1963.

Barbeau, A., Chase, T. N., & Paulson, G. W. (Eds.). *Advances in neurology (Vol. 1—Huntington's chorea, 1872–1972)*. New York: Raven, 1973.

Bardill, D. Behavior contracting and group therapy with preadolescent males in a residential treatment setting. *International Journal of Group Psychotherapy*, 1972, *22*, 333–342.

Baron, J. H. Gastric secretion in relation to subsequent duodenal ulcer and family history. *Gut*, 1962, *3*, 158–161.

Barry, H., Jr. Significance of maternal bereavement before age eight in psychiatric patients. *Archives of General Psychiatry*, 1949, *62*, 630–637.

Bateson, G., Jackson, D. D., Haley, J., & Weakland, J. H. Toward a theory of schizophrenia. *Behavioral Science*, 1956, *1*, 251–264. Reprinted in D. D. Jackson (Ed.), *Communication, family and marriage*. Palo Alto: Science and Behavior Books, 1968, pp. 31–54.

Bay-Rakal, S. The significance of EEG abnormality in behavior problem children. *Canadian Psychiatric Association Journal*, 1965, *10*, 387–391.

Beach, F. A. Hormonal control of sex-related behavior. In F. A. Beach (Ed.), *Human sexuality in four perspectives*. Baltimore: Johns Hopkins University Press, 1977, pp. 247–267. (a)

Beach, F. A. (Ed.). *Human sexuality in four perspectives*. Baltimore: Johns Hopkins University Press, 1977. (b)

Beall, L. The corrupt contract: Problems in conjoint therapy with parents and children. *American Journal of Orthopsychiatry*, 1972, *42*, 77–81.

Beaubrun, M., & Knight, F. Psychiatric assessment of 30 chronic users of cannabis and 30 matched controls. *American Journal of Psychiatry*, 1973, *130*, 309–311.

Beck, A. T. *Depression: Clinical, experimental and theoretical aspects*. New York: Harper & Row, 1967.

Beck, A. T. *Cognitive therapy and the emotional disorders*. New York: International Universities Press, 1976.

Becker, W. C. Consequences of different kinds of parental discipline. In M. L. Hoffman & L. W. Hoffman (Eds.), *Review of child development research* (Vol. 1). New York: Russell Sage Foundation, 1964.

Beers, C. W. *A mind that found itself*. Garden City, N.Y.: Doubleday, 1931. (Originally published, 1908).

Bell, A. P. Research in homosexuality: Back to the drawing board. In E. A. Rubinstein, R. Green, & E. Brecher (Eds.), *New directions in sex research*. New York: Plenum Press, 1975, pp. 99–109.

Bellack, A. S., & Hersen, M. *Behavior modification: An introductory textbook*. New York: Oxford University Press, 1977.

Benda, C. E. *Down's syndrome*. New York: Grune & Stratton, 1969.

Benson, D. F. The hydrocephalic dementias. In D. F. Benson & D. Blumer (Eds.), *Psychiatric aspects of neurological disease*. New York: Grune & Stratton, 1975, pp. 83–98.

Benson, D. F., & Blumer, D. (Eds.). *Psychiatric aspects of neurological disease*. New York: Grune & Stratton, 1975.

Benson, D. F., & Geschwind, N. Psychiatric conditions associated with focal lesions of the central nervous system. In S. Arieti (Chief Ed.), *American handbook of psychiatry* (2nd ed. — Vol. 4). New York: Basic Books, 1975, pp. 208–243.

Bergin, A. E., & Lambert, M. J. The evaluation of therapeutic outcomes. In S. L. Garfield & A. E. Bergin (Eds.), *Handbook of psychotherapy and behavior change* (2nd ed.). New York: Wiley, 1978, pp. 139–189.

Berlyne, D. E. Behavior theory as personality theory. In E. F. Borgatta & W. W. Lambert (Eds.), *Handbook of personality theory and research*. Chicago: Rand McNally, 1968, pp. 630–682.

Berman, J. L., & Ford, R. Intelligence quotients and intelligence loss in patients with phenylketonuria and some variant states. *Journal of Pediatrics*, 1970, *77*, 764–770.

Berne, E. *Principles of group treatment*. New York: Oxford University Press, 1966, pp. 254–256.

Bernheim, K. F., & Lewine, R. R. J. *Schizophrenia: Symptoms, causes and treatments*. New York: Norton, 1979.

Bernstein, N. R. Mental retardation. In A. M. Nicholi, Jr. (Ed.), *The Harvard guide to modern psychiatry*. Cambridge, Mass.: Harvard University Press, 1978, pp. 551–566.

Berry, H., Sutherland, B., & Guest, G. M. Phenylalanine tolerance tests on relatives of phenylketonuric children. *American Journal of Human Genetics*, 1957, *9*, 310–316.

Bettelheim, B. *The empty fortress*. New York: The Free Press of Glencoe, 1967.

Beutner, K. R., & Hale, N. G., Jr. *Emotional illness: How families can help*. New York: G. P. Putnam's Sons, 1957.

Bieber, I., Dain, H. J., Dince, P. R., Drellich, M. G., Grand, H. C., Gundlach, R. H., Kremer, M. W., Rifkin, A. H., Wilbur, C. B., & Bieber, T. B. *Homosexuality: A psychoanalytical study*. New York: Random House, 1962.

Binet, A. Le fetichisme dans l'amour. *Revue Philosophique*, 1887, *24*, 143–167; 252–274.

Binswanger, L. Existential analysis and psychotherapy. In F. Fromm-Reichmann & J. L. Moreno (Eds.), *Progress in psychotherapy*. New York: Grune & Stratton, 1956.

Birren, J. E. *The psychology of aging*. Englewood Cliffs, N.J.: Prentice-Hall, 1964.

Black, M., Freeman, B. J., & Montgomery, J. Systematic observation of play behavior in autistic children. *Journal of Autism and Childhood Schizophrenia*, 1975, *5*, 363–371.

Black, S. Inhibition of immediate-type hypersensitivity response by direct suggestion under hypnosis. *British Medical Journal*, 1963, *1*, 925–929.

Bleuler, E. *Dementia praecox or the group of schizophrenias* (J. Zinkin, trans.). New York: International Universitities Press, 1911. Reprinted 1950.

Bleuler, E. *Textbook of psychiatry*. New York: Macmillan, 1924.

Bloom, B. L. *Community mental health: A general introduction*. Monterey, Calif.: Brooks/Cole, 1977.

Blumer, D. Temporal lobe epilepsy and its psychiatric significance. In D. F. Benson & D. Blumer (Eds.), *Psychiatric aspects of neurological disease*. New York: Grune & Stratton, 1975, pp. 171–198.

Blumer, D., & Benson, D. F. Personality changes with frontal and temporal lobe lesions. In D. F. Benson & D. Blumer (Eds.), *Psychiatric aspects of neurological disease*. New York: Grune & Stratton, 1975, pp. 151–170.

Bockoven, J. S. *Moral treatment in American psychiatry*. New York: Springer, 1963.

Bockoven, J. S. *Moral treatment in community mental health*. New York: Springer, 1972.

Boisen, A. T. *Out of the depths*. New York: Harper & Row, 1960.

Boll, T. J., Heaton, R., & Reitan, R. M. Neuropsychological and emotional correlates of Huntington's chorea. *Journal of Nervous and Mental Disease*, 1974, *158*, 61–69.

Bond, E. D. Results of treatment in psychoses—with a control series. *American Journal of Psychiatry*, 1954, *110*, 881–887.

Bond, I. K., & Hutchinson, H. C. Application of reciprocal inhibition therapy to exhibitionism. In L. P. Ullman & L. Krasner (Eds.), *Case studies in behavior modification*. New York: Holt, Rinehart & Winston, 1965, Chap. 24.

Bonine, W. A psychotherapeutic approach to depression. *Contemporary Psychoanalysis*, 1965, *2*, 48–53.

Bonine, W. The psychodynamics of neurotic depression. In S. Arieti (Ed.), *American handbook of psychiatry* (Vol. 3). New York: Basic Books, 1966.

Borgatta, E. F., & Evans, R. R. (Eds.). *Smoking, health, and behavior*. Chicago: Aldine, 1968.

Borginsky, M. E. *Provision of instruction to handicapped pupils in local public schools, Spring, 1970*. Washington, D.C.: Office of Education, 1974.

Bortner, R. W., Rosenman, R. H., & Friedman, M. Familial similarity in Pattern A behavior: Father and sons. *Journal of Chronic Diseases*, 1970, *23*, 39–43.

Boss, M. *Daseinsanalyse and psychoanalysis*. New York: Basic Books, 1963.

Bossard, J. H. S. *Parent and child*. Philadelphia: University of Pennsylvania Press, 1953.

Botwinick, J. *Cognitive processes in maturity and old age*. New York: Spring-er, 1967.

Bowen, M. A family concept of schizophrenia. In D. D. Jackson (Ed.), *The etiology of schizophrenia*. New York: Basic Books, 1960.

Bowlby, J. *Maternal care and mental health, Monograph Series No. 2*. Gene-va: World Health Organization, 1951.

Bowlby, J. *Maternal care and mental health*. New York: Schocken Books, 1966.

Brady, J. V. Ulcers in executive monkeys. *Scientific American*, 1958, *199*, 95-104.

Breger, L., & McGaugh, J. L. Critique and reformulation of "learning the-ory" approaches to psychotherapy and neurosis. *Psychological Bulletin*, 1965, *63*, 338-358.

Brenner, J. H. Drugs and society. In C. J. D. Zarafonetis (Ed.), *Drug abuse: Proceedings of the international conference*. Philadelphia: Lea & Febiger, 1972, pp. 115-126.

Breuer, J., & Freud, S. *Studies in hysteria* (A. A. Brill, Trans.). New York: Nervous and Mental Disease Publishing Co., 1926.

Brickner, R. M. *The intellectual functions of the frontal lobes*. New York: Macmillan, 1936.

Bromberg, W. *The mind of man: The story of man's conquest of mental ill-ness*. New York: Harper & Row, 1937.

Bronfenbrenner, U. Freudian theories of identification and their derivatives. *Child Development*, 1960, *31*, 15-40.

Bronfenbrenner, U. Is early intervention effective? In S. Ryan (Ed.), *A report on longitudinal evaluations of preschool programs* (Vol. 2). Washington, D.C.: Office of Child Development, 1974.

Brown, C. *Manchild in the promised land*. New York: Macmillan, 1965.

Brown, E. S., & Warner, R. Mental development of phenylketonuric children on or off diet after the age of six. *Psychological Medicine*, 1976, *6*, 287-296.

Brown, G. W., Birley, J. L. T., & Wing, J. K. Influence of family life on the course of schizophrenic disorders: A replication. *British Journal of Psy-chiatry*, 1972, *121*, 241-258.

Brown, R. *Social psychology*. New York: The Free Press of Glencoe, 1965.

Brown, R. Schizophrenia, language, and reality. *American Psychologist*, 1973, *28*, 395-403.

Bruch, H. Parent education or the illusion of omnipotence. *American Journal of Orthopsychiatry*, 1954, *24*, 723-732.

Bruch, H. *Eating disorders: Obesity, anorexia nervosa, and the person within*. New York: Basic Books, 1973.

Bruetsch, W. L. Neurosyphilitic conditions: General paralysis, general pare-sis, dementia paralytica. In S. Arieti (Chief Ed.), *American handbook of psychiatry* (Vol. 4—2nd ed.). New York: Basic Books, 1975, pp. 134-151.

683

Bryant, T. E. Recent history of drug use and abuse. In C. Kryder & S. P. Stickland (Eds.), *Americans and drug abuse: Report from the Aspen Conference*. New York: Aspen Institute for Humanistic Studies, 1977, pp. 9–13.

Bugental, J. F. T. *The search for existential identity*. San Francisco: Jossey-Bass, 1976.

Bunney, W. E., Jr., Mason, J. W., & Hamburg, D. A. Correlations between behavioral variables and urinary 17-hydroxycorticosteroids in depressed patients. *Psychomatic Medicine*, 1965, *27*, 299–308.

Burchard, J. Systematic socialization: A programmed environment for the habilitation of antisocial retardates. *Psychological Record*, 1967, *17*, 461–476.

Bureau of the Census. *Expectation of life, Statistical abstract of the United States, Life table values No. 69*, p. 53. Washington, D.C.: Bureau of the Census, 1971.

Burton, A. *Case studies in counseling and psychotherapy*. Englewood Cliffs, N.J.: Prentice-Hall, 1959.

Burton, A., & Harris, R. E. *Case histories in clinical and abnormal psychology*. New York: Harper & Row, 1947.

Burton, A., & Harris, R. E. *Clinical studies of personality*. New York: Harper & Row, 1955.

Busse, E. W. Psychoneurotic reactions and defense mechanisms in the aged. In P. H. Hoch & J. Zubin (Eds.), *Psychopathology of aging*. New York: Grune & Stratton, 1961, Chap. 16.

Busse, E. W. Aging and psychiatric diseases of late life. In S. Arieti (Chief Ed.), *American handbook of psychiatry* (Vol. 4—2nd ed.). New York: Basic Books, 1975, pp. 67–89.

Butcher, J. N., & Koss, M. P. Research on brief and crisis-oriented psychotherapies. In S. L. Garfield & A. E. Bergin (Eds.), *Handbook of psychotherapy and behavior change* (2nd ed.). New York: Wiley, 1978, pp. 725–767.

Cadoret, R., & Winokur, G. Genetic studies of affective disorders. In F. F. Flach & S. C. Draghi (Eds.), *The nature and treatment of depression*. New York: Wiley, 1975, pp. 335–346.

Cameron, D. C. The many faces of deviant drug use. In C. J. D. Zarafonetis (Ed.), *Drug abuse: Proceedings of the international conference*. Philadelphia: Lea & Febiger, 1972, pp. 17–26.

Cameron, N. The paranoid pseudo-community revisited. *American Journal of Sociology*, 1959, *65*, 52–58.

Cameron, N., & Magaret, A. *Behavior pathology*. Boston: Houghton Mifflin, 1951.

Cancro, R. *The schizophrenic syndrome: An annual review*. New York: Brunner/Mazel, 1971.

Cannon, W. B. *Bodily changes in pain, hunger, fear and rage* (2nd ed.). New York: Appleton-Century-Crofts, 1929.

Canter, A. A background interference procedure to increase sensitivity of the Bender-Gestalt Test to organic brain disorders. *Journal of Consulting Psychology*, 1966, *30*, 91–97.

Caplan, G. (Ed.). *Prevention of mental disorders in children*. New York: Basic Books, 1961.

Caplan, G. *Principles of preventive psychiatry*. New York: Basic Books, 1964.

Caplan, G. *The theory and practice of mental health consultation*. New York: Basic Books, 1970.

Capote, T. *In cold blood*. New York: Random House, 1965.

Carney, M. W. P., & Sheffield, B. F. The effects of pulse ECT in neurotic and endogeneous depression. *British Journal of Psychiatry*, 1974, *125*, 91–94.

Carr, A. T. Compulsive neurosis: Two psychophysiological studies. *Bulletin of the British Psychological Society*, 1971, *24*, 256–257.

Carr, A. T. Compulsion neurosis: A review of the literature. *Psychological Bulletin*, 1974, *81*, 311–318.

Cautela, J. R. Covert sensitization. *Psychological Record*, 1967, *20*, 459–468.

The challenge of crime in a free society. Report of the President's Commission on Law Enforcement and Administration of Justice. New York: E. P. Dutton, 1968.

Chapman, L. J., & Chapman, J. P. *Disordered thought in schizophrenia*. New York: Appleton-Century-Crofts, 1973.

Charcot, J. M. *Oeuvres complètes*. Paris: Lecrosnier & Babé, 1890.

Chesler, P. *Women and madness*. Garden City, N.Y.: Doubleday, 1972.

Chess, S., Korn, S. J., & Fernandez, P. B. *Psychiatric disorders of children with rubella*. New York: Brunner/Mazel, 1971.

Chess, S., Thomas, A., & Birch, H. Characteristics of the individual child's behavioral responses to the environment. *American Journal of Orthopsychiatry*, 1959, *29*, 791–802.

Cimino, J. A., Doud, R. M., Andima, H. S., & West, S. A. Narcotic addiction in the United States: A nationwide survey. *Contemporary Drug Problems*, 1973, *2*, 401–415.

Clarke, A. M., & Clarke, A. D. B. *Early experience: Myth and evidence*. Riverside, N.J.: The Free Press, 1976.

Clarke, C. A. The prevention of Rh isoimmunization. In V. A. McKusick & R. Claiborne (Eds.), *Medical genetics*. New York: Hospital Practice Publishing Co., 1973.

Clarke-Stewart, K. A. Interactions between mothers and their young children: Characteristics and consequences. *Monographs of the Society for Research in Child Development*, 1973, *38*, (6–7, Serial No. 153).

Cleckley, H. *The mask of sanity* (5th ed.). St. Louis: Mosby, 1976.

Clinard, M. B., & Abbott, D. J. Crime in developing countries. In L. Radzinowicz & M. E. Wolfgang (Eds.), *Crime and justice* (2nd ed.). New York: Basic Books, 1977, pp. 25–52.

Cobb, S. *Foundations of neuropsychiatry*. Baltimore: Williams & Wilkins, 1941.

Cobb, S. *Emotions and clinical medicine*. New York: Norton, 1950.

Cobb, S., & Rose, R. M. Hypertension, peptic ulcer and diabetes in air traffic controllers. *Journal of the American Medical Association*, 1973, *224*, 489–492.

Coehlo, G. V., Hamburg, D. A., & Adams, J. E. (Eds.). *Coping and adaptation*. New York: Basic Books, 1974.

Cohen, A. K. *Delinquent boys: The culture of the gang*. New York: The Free Press of Glencoe, 1955.

Cohen, S. Information and misinformation about drugs. In J. R. Wittenborn, J. P. Smith, & S. A. Wittenborn (Eds.), *Communication and drug abuse*. Springfield, Ill.: Charles C Thomas, 1970.

Cohen, S. Patterns of drug abuse—1970. In C. J. D. Zarafonetis (Ed.), *Drug abuse: Proceedings of the international conference*. Philadelphia: Lea & Febiger, 1972, pp. 333–337.

Collaborative study of children treated for phenylketonuria, Preliminary report No. 8. Principal investigator: Richard Koch. Presented at the Eleventh General Medical Conference, Stateline, Nevada, 1975.

Collmann, R. D., & Stoller, A. Shift of childbirth to younger mothers, and its effect on the incidence of mongolism in Victoria, Australia, 1959–1964. *Journal of Mental Deficiency Research*, 1969, *13*, 13–19.

Connolly, K. J., & Bruner, J. S. (Eds.). *The growth of competence*. New York: Academic Press, 1974.

Cornwell, A. C. Development of language, abstraction, and numerical concept formation in Down's syndrome children. *American Journal of Mental Deficiency*, 1974, *79*, 179–190.

Corsellis, J. A. N. Aging and the dementias. In N. Blackwood & J. A. N. Corsellis (Eds.), *Greenfield's neuropathology* (3rd ed.). Chicago: Year Book, 1976.

Costello, C. G. *Symptoms of psychopathology*. New York: Wiley, 1970.

Costello, C. G. *Anxiety and depression*. Montreal: McGill-Queen's University Press, 1976.

Cowen, E. L., Pedersen, A., Babigian, H., Izzo, L. D., & Trost, M. A. Long-term follow-up of early detected vulnerable children. *Journal of Consulting and Clinical Psychology*, 1973, *41*, 438–446.

Cowen, E. L., Zax, M., Klein, R., Izzo, L. D., & Trost, M. A. The relation of anxiety in school children to school record, achievement, and behavioral measures. *Child Development*, 1965, *36*, 685–695.

Cox, A., Rutter, M., Newman, S., & Bartak, L. A comparative study of infantile autism and specific developmental language disorders: II. Parental characteristics. *British Journal of Psychiatry*, 1975, *126*, 146–159.

Craft, M. (Ed.). *Tredgold's mental retardation* (12th ed.). New York: Macmillan, 1979.

Craft, M., Stephenson, G., & Granger, C. A controlled trial of authoritarian and self-governing regimes with adolescent psychopaths. *American Journal of Orthopsychiatry*, 1964, *34*, 543–554.

Crandall, B. F. Genetic disorders and mental retardation. In S. Chess & A. Thomas (Eds.), *Annual progress in child psychiatry and child development, 1978*. New York: Brunner/Mazel, 1978, pp. 395-416.

Cressey, D. R. The respectable criminal. In J. F. Short (Ed.), *Modern criminals*. Chicago: Aldine, 1970, pp. 111-114.

Crook, T., Raskin, A., & Davis, D. Factors associated with attempted suicide among hospitalized depressed patients. *Psychological Medicine*, 1975, *5*, 381-388.

Cumming, E., & Henry, W. *Growing old*. New York: Basic Books, 1961.

Curtis, L. A. *Criminal violence*. Lexington, Mass.: Lexington Books, 1974.

Damon, W. *The social world of the child*. San Francisco: Jossey-Bass, 1977.

Davis, J. B. Neurotic illness in the families of children with asthma and wheezy bronchitis: A general practice population study. *Psychological Medicine*, 1977, *7*, 305-310.

Davis, J. M. Overview: Maintenance therapy in psychiatry. *American Journal of Psychiatry*, 1975, *133*, 1-13.

Davis, R. C., & Berry, F. Gastrointestinal reactions during a noise avoidance task. *Psychological Reports*, 1963, *12*, 135-137.

Day, M., & Semrad, E. V. Schizophrenic reactions. In A. M. Nicholi, Jr. (Ed.), *The Harvard guide to modern psychiatry*. Cambridge, Mass.: Harvard University Press, 1978, pp. 199-243.

Death in the afternoon. *Time*, July 23, 1979, p. 41.

Delay, J., & Deniker, P. Le traitement des psychoses par une methode neurolytique derivee de l'hibernotherapie. In Congres de medecins alienistes et neurologistes de France et des pays de langues francaise. Luxembourg, 1952.

DeLeon, G., & Sacks, S. Conditioning functional enuresis: A four year follow-up. *Journal of Consulting and Clinical Psychology*, 1972, *39*, 299-300.

Denhoff, E., & Robinault, I. P. *Cerebral palsy and related disorders*. New York: McGraw-Hill, 1963.

The Denver Post. Parole chief: Sentences may be lighter. Friday, July 20, 1979.

Deutsch, A. *The mentally ill in America*. Garden City, N.Y.: Doubleday, 1937.

Deutsch, H. *The psychology of women: A psychoanalytic interpretation* (Vol. 1). New York: Grune & Stratton, 1944.

Diagnostic and statistical manual of mental disorders (2nd ed.). Washington, D.C.: American Psychiatric Association, 1968.

Diamond, M. Human sexual development: Biological foundations for social development. In F. A. Beach (Ed.), *Human sexuality in four perspectives*. Baltimore: Johns Hopkins University Press, 1977, pp. 22-61.

DiCara, L. V. (Ed.). *Limbic and autonomic nervous systems research*. New York: Plenum Press, 1974.

Dicks, H. V. Experiences with marital tensions seen in the psychological clinic. *British Journal of Medical Psychology*, 1953, *26*, 181-196.

687

Diven, K. Certain determinants in the conditioning of anxiety reactions. *Journal of Psychology*, 1937, *3*, 291–308.

Dix, D. L. *Memorial in behalf of the pauper insane and idiots in jails and poorhouses throughout the Commonwealth.* Boston: Monroe & Francis, 1843.

Dohrenwend, B. P., & Dohrenwend, B. S. *Social status and psychological disorder.* New York: Wiley, 1969.

Dohrenwend, B. S., & Dohrenwend, B. P. (Eds.). *Stressful life events: Their nature and effects.* New York: Wiley, 1974.

Doll, E. A. *Measurement of social competence.* Vineland, N.J.: Educational Publishers, 1953.

Domino, E. R. Panel discussion: Hallucinogens and marihuana. In C. J. D. Zarafonetis (Ed.), *Drug Abuse: Proceedings of the international conference.* Philadelphia: Lea & Febiger, 1972, pp. 347–358.

Down, J. L. Observations on an ethnic classification of idiots. *London Hospital Reports*, 1866.

Drury, T. F., & Howie, L. J. Prevalence of selected chronic digestive conditions, United States, 1975. *National Health Survey* (Series 10, Number 123), July, 1979.

Eisenberg, L. The course of childhood schizophrenia. *A. M. A. Archives of Neurology and Psychiatry*, 1957, *78*, 69–83.

Eisenberg, L. School phobia: A study in the communication of anxiety. *American Journal of Psychiatry*, 1958, *114*, 712–718.

Eisenberg, L. Child psychiatry: The past quarter century. *American Journal of Orthopsychiatry*, 1969, *39*, 389–401.

Eisenberg, L. Psychiatric intervention. *Scientific American*, 1973, *229*, 116–127.

Eisenberg, M. M. *Ulcers.* New York: Random House, 1978.

Eissler, K. R. Remarks on the psychoanalysis of schizophrenia. In E. B. Brody & F. C. Redlich (Eds.), *Psychotherapy with schizophrenics.* New York: International Universities Press, 1952.

Ellis, A. *Reason and emotion in psychotherapy.* New York: Lyle Stuart Press, 1962.

Emrick, C. D. A review of psychologically oriented treatment of alcoholism. *Quarterly Journal of Studies of Alcohol*, 1974, *35*, 523–549.

Emrick, C. D. A review of psychologically oriented treatment of alcoholism. II. The relative effectiveness of different treatment approaches and the effectiveness of treatment versus no treatment. *Quarterly Journal of Studies of Alcohol*, 1975, *36*, 88–108.

Engel, G. L., & Schmale, A. H. Psychoanalytic theory of somatic disorder: Conversion, specificity and the disease onset situation. *Journal of the American Psychoanalytic Association*, 1967, *15*, 344–365.

Engel, G. L., & Schmale, A. H. Conservation-withdrawal: A primary regulatory process for organismic homeostatis. In Ciba Foundation Symposium 8

(new series), *Physiology, emotion and psychosomatic illness.* Amsterdam:
Elsevier, 1972, pp. 57–87.

Erikson, E. H. The problem of ego identity. *Psychological Issues*, 1959, *1*, No. 1.

Erikson, E. H. *Childhood and society* (2nd ed.). New York: Norton, 1963.

Erikson, E. H. *Youth: Identity and crisis.* New York: Norton, 1968.

Escalona, S. K. *The roots of individuality: Normal patterns of development in infancy.* Chicago: Aldine, 1968.

Estes, W. K. *Learning theory and mental development.* New York: Academic Press, 1970.

Evans, J. *Three men: An experiment in the biography of emotion.* New York: Alfred A. Knopf, 1954.

Evans, R. Childhood parental relationships of homosexual men. *Journal of Consulting and Clinical Psychology*, 1969, *33*, 129–135.

Eysenck, H. J. (Ed.). *Handbook of abnormal psychology: An experimental approach.* New York: Basic Books, 1961.

Eysenck, H. J. *Crime and personality.* London: Methuen, 1964.

Eysenck, H. J. *The structure of human personality*, (3rd ed.). London: Methuen, 1970.

Eysenck, H. J., & Rachman, S. *The causes and cures of neurosis.* San Diego: Robert Knapp, 1965.

Ezriel, H. A psychoanalytic approach to group treatment. *British Journal of Medical Psychology*, 1950, *23*, 59–74.

Facts about suicide: Causes and prevention. U.S. Public Health Service Publication 852, Health Information Series 101, 1961.

Fairbairn, W. R. D. Observations on the nature of hysterical states. *British Journal of Medical Psychology*, 1954, *27*, 105–115.

Fairweather, G. W., Sanders, D. H., Cressler, D. L., & Maynard, H. *Community life for the mentally ill: An alternative to institutional care.* Chicago: Aldine-Atherton, 1969.

Fancher, R. E. *Pioneers of psychology.* New York: Norton, 1979.

Feldman, M. P., & MacCulloch, M. J. *Homosexual behavior: Therapy and assessment.* Oxford: Pergamon Press, 1971.

Fenichel, O. *Outline of clinical psychoanalysis.* New York: Norton, 1934.

Fenichel, O. *The psychoanalytic theory of neurosis.* New York: Norton, 1945.

Ferraro, A. The neuropathology associated with the psychoses of aging. In S. Arieti (Chief Ed.), *American handbook of psychiatry* (Vol. 4—2nd ed.). New York: Basic Books, 1975, pp. 90–133.

Ferreira, A. J. Family myth and homeostatis. *Archives of General Psychiatry*, 1963, *9*, 457–463. Reprinted in J. G. Howells, *Theory and practice of family psychiatry.* New York: Brunner/Mazel, 1971, Chap. 14.

Fieve, R. R., & Dunner, D. L. Unipolar and bipolar affective states. In F. F. Flach & S. C. Draghi (Eds.), *The nature and treatment of depression.* New York: Wiley, 1975, pp. 145–160.

Fischer, W. E. *Theories of anxiety*. New York: Harper & Row, 1970.

Flavell, J. H. *Cognitive development*. Englewood Cliffs, N.J.: Prentice-Hall, 1977.

Ford, D. H., & Urban, H. B. *Systems of psychotherapy: A comparative study*. New York: Wiley, 1963.

Forisha, B. L. *Sex roles and personal awareness*. Morristown, N.J.: General Learning Press, 1978.

Foulkes, S. H. Concerning leadership in group-analytic psychotherapy. *International Journal of Group Psychotherapy*, 1951, *1*, 319.

Fowler, R. C., McCabe, M. S., Cadoret, R. J., & Winokur, G. The validity of good prognosis schizophrenia. *Archives of General Psychiatry*, 1972, *26*, 182–185.

Fox, B., & DiScipio, W. J. An exploratory study in the treatment of homosexuality by combining principles from psychoanalytical theory and conditioning. *British Journal of Medical Psychology*, 1968, *41*, 273–282.

Frank, J. D. *Persuasion and healing: A comparative study of psychotherapy*. Baltimore, Johns Hopkins Press, 1961.

Frank, J. D. Psychotherapy and the sense of mastery. In R. L. Spitzer & D. F. Klein (Eds.), *Evaluation of psychological therapies*. Baltimore: Johns Hopkins University Press, 1976.

Frankl, V. E. *The doctor and the soul*. New York: Alfred A. Knopf, 1955.

Fraser, H. F. Patterns of abuse of narcotics: An historical review. In C. J. D. Zarafonetis (Ed.), *Drug abuse: Proceedings of the international conference*. Philadelphia: Lea & Febiger, 1972, pp. 141–151.

Freedman, D. X. Treatment. In C. Kryder & S. P. Strickland (Eds.), *Americans and drug abuse: Report from the Aspen Conference*. New York: Aspen Institute for Humanistic Studies, 1977, pp. 29–36.

Freeman, L. *Before I kill more: The William Heirens story*. New York: Crown Publishers, 1955.

Freeman, W. Psychosurgery. *American Journal of Psychiatry*, 1955, *111*, 518–520.

French, T. M., & Alexander, F. Psychogenic factors of bronchial asthma. *Psychosomatic Medicine Monographs*, 1941, *4*, No. 1.

Freud, A. *The ego and the mechanisms of defence*. London: Hogarth Press, 1937.

Freud, A. *The psycho-analytic treatment of children*. New York: International Universities Press, 1959.

Freud, S. *A general introduction to psychoanalysis*. New York: Liveright, 1920.

Freud, S. *Collected papers* (Vol. 1—J. Tiviere, Trans.). London: International Psychoanalytic Press, 1924.

Freud, S. *The problem of lay-analyses*. New York: Brentano's, 1927.

Freud, S. *The problem of anxiety* (H. A. Bunker, Trans.). New York: Norton, 1936.

Freud, S. The origin and development of psychoanalysis. In *The standard edi-*

tion of the complete psychological works of Sigmund Freud. London: Hogarth Press, 1953. (Originally published, 1910.)

Freud, S. Three essays on the theory of sexuality. In *The standard edition of the complete psychological works of Sigmund Freud* (Vol. 7). London: Hogarth Press, 1953, pp. 130–243.

Freud, S. Repression. In *The standard edition of Freud's works* (Vol. 14). London: Hogarth Press, 1957. (Originally published, 1915.)

Freud, S. Inhibition, symptom and anxiety. In *The standard edition of Freud's works* (Vol. 20). London: Hogarth Press, 1959. (Originally published, 1926.)

Friedlander, B. Z., Sterritt, G. M., & Kirk, G. E. (Eds.). *Exceptional infant* (Vol. 3). New York: Brunner/Mazel, 1975.

Friedman, A. S. Interaction of drug therapy with marital therapy in depressive patients. *Archives of General Psychiatry*, 1975, *32*, 619–637.

Friedman, G. D., Ury, H. K., Klatsky, A. L., & Siegelaub, A. B. A psychological questionnaire predictive of myocardial infarction: Results from the Kaiser-Permanente epidemiologic study of myocardial infarction. *Psychosomatic Medicine*, 1974, *36*, 327–343.

Friedman, M. *Pathogenesis of coronary heart disease*. New York: McGraw-Hill, 1969.

Friedman, M., & Rosenman, R. H. *Type A behavior and your heart*. New York: Alfred A. Knopf, 1974.

Friedman, R., & Iwai, J. Genetic predisposition and stress-induced hypertension. *Science*, 1976, *193*, 161–162.

Fromm-Reichmann, F. *Principles of intensive psychotherapy*. Chicago: University of Chicago Press, 1950.

Gagnon, J. H. *Human sexualities*. Glenview, Ill.: Scott, Foresman, 1977.

Gardner, G. E. (Ed.). *Case studies in chidhood emotional disabilities* (Vol. 1). New York: American Orthopsychiatric Association, 1953.

Gardner, G. E. (Ed.). *Case studies in childhood emotional disabilities* (Vol. 2). New York: American Orthopsychiatric Association, 1956.

Garmezy, N. Process and reactive schizophrenia: Some conceptions and issues. *Schizophrenia Bulletin*, 1970, *2*, 30–74.

Garmezy, N. Vulnerability research and the issue of primary prevention. *American Journal of Orthopsychiatry*, 1971, *41*, 101–116.

Garmezy, N. But is it good for children? *The Clinical Psychologist*, 1977, *31*, 3–4.

Garmezy, N., Masten, A., Nordstrom, L., & Ferrarese, M. The nature of competence in normal and deviant children. In M. W. Kent & J. E. Rolf (Eds.), *Primary prevention of psychopathology* (Vol. 3 — Social competence in children). Hanover, N. H.: The University Press of New England, 1979.

Gaudry, E., & Spielberger, C. D. *Anxiety and educational achievement*. New York: Wiley, 1971.

Gebhard, P. H. Incidence of overt homosexuality in the United States and western Europe. In J. M. Livingood (Ed.), *National Institute of Mental*

691

Health Task Force on Homosexuality: Final report and background papers. Rockville, Md.: National Institute of Mental Health, 1972.

Gellhorn, E. Motion and emotion. *Psychological Review*, 1964, *71*, 457–472.

Gellhorn, E., & Loufbourrow, G. N. *Emotions and emotional disorders.* New York: Hoeber-Harper, 1963.

Gendlin, E. T. Research in psychotherapy with schizophrenic patients and the nature of that "illness." *American Journal of Psychotherapy*, 1966, *20*, 4–16.

Gendlin, E. T. A short summary and some long predicitons. In J. T. Hart & T. M. Tomlinson (Eds.), *New directions in client-centered therapy.* Boston: Houghton Mifflin, 1970, pp. 544–562.

Gergen, K. J. *The concept of self.* New York: Holt, Rinehart & Winston, 1971.

Gershon, M., & Biller, H. B. *The other helpers: Paraprofessionals and non-professionals in mental health.* Lexington, Mass.: Lexington Books, 1977.

Geschwind, N. The borderland of neurology and psychiatry: Some common misconceptions. In D. F. Benson & D. Blumer (Eds.), *Psychiatric aspects of neurological disease.* New York: Grune & Stratton, 1975, pp. 1–9.

Gibbens, T. C. N., Briscoe, O., & Dell, S. Psychopathic and neurotic offenders in mental hospitals. In A. V. S. de Reuck & R. Porter (Eds.), *The mentally abnormal offender.* London: J. & A. Churchill, 1968, pp. 143–149.

Gibbs, F. A., Gibbs, E. L., & Lennox, W. G. Cerebral dysrythmias of epilepsy. Measures for their control. *Archives of Neurology and Psychiatry*, 1938, *39*, 298–314.

Gibson, D. *Down's syndrome: The psychology of mongolism.* New York: Cambridge University Press, 1978.

Gibson, R. W. Psychotherapy of manic-depressive states. *Psychiatric Research Reports, American Psychiatric Association*, 1963, *17*, 91–102.

Ginzberg, E., & Bray, D. W. *The uneducated.* New York: Columbia University Press, 1953.

Glaser, D. *Adult crime and social policy.* Englewood Cliffs, N.J.: Prentice-Hall, 1972.

Glaser, G. H. Epilepsy: Neuropsychological aspects. In S. Arieti (Chief Ed.), *American handbook of psychiatry* (Vol. 4—2nd ed.). New York: Basic Books, 1975, pp. 314–355.

Glasscote, R. M., Kraft, A. M., Glasman, S. M., & Jepson, W. W. *Partial hospitalization for the mentally ill.* London: Garamond Pridemark, Ltd., 1969.

Glassman, A. H. Indoleamines and affective disorders. *Psychosomatic Medicine*, 1969, *31*, 107–114.

Goetz, P. L., Succop, R. A., Reinhart, J. B., & Miller, A. Anorexia nervosa in children: A follow-up study. *American Journal of Orthopsychiatry*, 1977, *47*, 597–603.

Goffman, E. *Asylums: Essays on the social situation of mental patients and other inmates.* Chicago: Aldine, 1962.

Gold, W. M. Asthma. *American Thoracic Society News*, 1976, *1*, 12-20.

Goldberg, C. Group sensitivity training. *International Journal of Psychiatry*, 1970, *9*, 165-192.

Goldberg, E. L., & Comstock, G. W. Life events and subsequent illness. *American Journal of Epidemiology*, 1976, *104*, 146-158.

Goldfarb, W. Emotional and intellectual consequences of psychologic deprivation in infancy: A revaluation. In P. H. Hoch & J. Zubin, *Psychopathology of childhood*. New York: Grune & Stratton, 1955.

Goldfried, M. R., & Davison, G. C. *Clinical behavior therapy*. New York: Holt, Rinehart & Winston, 1976.

Goldman, H., Kleinman, K. M., & Snow, M. Y. Relationship between essential hypertension and cognitive functioning: Effects of biofeedback. *Psychophysiology*, 1975, *12*, 569-573.

Goldstein, A. Current research in narcotics addiction. In C. Kryder & S. P. Strickland (Eds.), *Americans and drug abuse: Report from the Aspen Conference*. New York: Aspen Institute for Humanistic Studies, 1977, pp. 23-28.

Goldstein, J. H. *Aggression and crimes of violence*. New York: Oxford University Press, 1975.

Goldstein, K., & Katz, S. The psychopathology of Pick's disease. *Archives of Neurology and Psychiatry*, 1937, *38*, 473-490.

Goldstein, K., & Scheerer, M. Abstract and concrete behavior: An experimental study with special tests. *Psychological Monographs*, 1941, *53*, 1-31.

Golumbiewski, R. T., & Blumberg, A. (Eds.). *Sensitivity training and the laboratory approach: Readings about concepts and applications* (3rd ed.). Itaska, Ill.: Peacock Publishing, 1977.

Gonen, J. Y. The use of psychodrama combined with videotape playback on an inpatient floor. *Psychiatry*, 1971, *34*, 198-213.

Goodglass, H., & Blumstein, S. *Psycholinguistics and aphasia*. Baltimore: John Hopkins University Press, 1973.

Goodman, G. *Companionship therapy: Studies in structured intimacy*. San Francisco: Jossey-Bass, 1972.

Goodstein, L. D., & Sandler, I. Using psychology to promote human welfare: A conceptual analysis of the role of community psychology. *American Psychologist*, 1978, *33*, 882-892.

Goodwin, D. W., Schulsinger, F., Knop, J., Mednick, S. A., & Guze, S. B. Alcoholism and depression in adopted-out daughters of alcoholics. *Archives of General Psychiatry*, 1977, *34*, 751-755.

Gordon, T. Parent Effectiveness Training. A preventive program and its delivery system. In G. W. Albee & J. M. Joffe (Eds.), *Primary prevention of psychopathology* (Vol. 1—The issues). Hanover, N. H.: The University Press of New England, 1977.

Gottesman, I. I., & Shields, J. *Schizophrenia and genetics: A twin study vantage point*. New York: Academic Press, 1972.

Grace, W. J., & Graham, D. T. Relationship of specific attitudes and emotions to certain bodily diseases. *Psychosomatic Medicine*, 1952, *14*, 243-251.

Graham, D. L., & Cross, W. C. Values and attitudes of high school drug users. *Journal of Drug Education*, 1975, *5*, 97-107.

Graham, D. T. Psychosomatic medicine. In N. S. Greenfield & R. A. Sternbach (Eds.), *Handbook of psychophysiology*. New York: Holt, Rinehart & Winston, 1972, pp. 839-924.

Graham, D. T., Kabler, J. D., & Graham, F. K. Physiological responses to the suggestion of attitudes: Specificity of attitude hypothesis in psychosomatic disease. *Psychosomatic Medicine*, 1962, *24*, 159-169.

Graham, D. T., Stern, J. A., & Winokur, G. Experimental investigation of the specificity of attitude hypothesis in psychosomatic disease. *Psychosomatic Medicine*, 1958, *20*, 446-457.

Grant, V. W. A fetishistic theory of amorous fixation. *Journal of Social Psychology*, 1949, *30*, 17-37.

Grant, V. W. Preface to a psychology of sexual attachment. *Journal of Social Psychology*, 1951, *33*, 187-208.

Grant, V. W. *This is mental illness*. Boston: Beacon Press, 1963.

Greden, J. F. Anxiety or caffeinism: A diagnostic dilemma. *American Journal of Psychiatry*, 1974, *131*, 1089-1092.

Greden, J. F., Fontaine, P., Lubetsky, M., & Chambelin, K. Anxiety and depression associated with caffeinism among psychiatric inpatients. *American Journal of Psychiatry*, 1978, *135*, 963-966.

Green, H. *I never promised you a rose garden*. New York: Holt, Rinehart & Winston, 1964.

Greenberg, I. *Psychodrama*. New York: Human Sciences Press, 1974.

Greenblatt, M., & Glazier, E. The phasing out of mental hospitals in the United States. *American Journal of Psychiatry*, 1975, *132*, 1135-1140.

Greenblatt, M., Levinson, D. J., & Williams, R. H. (Eds). *The patient and the mental hospital*. New York: The Free Press, 1957.

Greene, B. *A clinical approach to marital problems: Evaluation and management*. Springfield, Ill.: Charles C. Thomas, 1971.

Greer, S., & Morriss, T. Psychologic attributes of women who develop breast cancer: A controlled study. *Journal of Psychosomatic Research*, 1975, *19*, 147-153.

Grier, W. H., & Cobbs, P. M. *Black rage*. New York: Basic Books, 1968.

Grinker, R. R., & Holzman, P. S. Schizophrenic pathology in young adults. *Archives of General Psychiatry*, 1973, *28*, 168-175.

Grinker, R. R., Miller, J., Nunn, R., & Nunnally, J. C. *The phenomena of depressions*. New York: Harper & Row, 1961.

Grinkler, R. R., & Spiegel, J. P. *Men under stress*. Philadelphia: Blakiston, 1945, pp. 281-288.

Grinker, R. R., & Werble, B. *The borderline patient*. New York: Jason Aronson, 1977.

Grinspoon, L. *Marihuana reconsidered.* Cambridge, Mass.: Harvard University Press, 1971.

Grossman, H. (Ed.). *Manual on terminology and classification in mental retardation, 1973 revision.* Washington, D.C.: American Association on Mental Deficiency, 1973.

Group for the Advancement of Psychiatry. *Sex and the college student.* Greenwich, Conn.: Fawcett Publications, 1968.

Group for the Advancement of Psychiatry. The crisis in psychiatric hospitalization. *International Journal of Psychiatry,* 1970-71, *9,* 565-603.

Grubb, T., & Watt, N. F. Longitudinal approaches to promoting social adjustment through public school programs. Paper presented at the meeting of the Society for Research in Child Development, San Francisco, March, 1979.

Gruver, G. G. College students as therapeutic agents. *Psychological Bulletin,* 1971, *76,* 111-127.

Gunderson, E. K. E., & Rahe, R. H. (Eds.). *Life stress and illness.* Springfield, Ill.: Charles C. Thomas, 1974.

Gunderson, J. G., Autry, J. H., Mosher, L. R., & Buchsbaum, S. Special report: Schizophrenia, 1972. *Schizophrenia Bulletin,* 1974, *9,* 15-54.

Gunderson, J. G., & Mosher, L. R. The cost of schizophrenia. *American Journal of Psychiatry,* 1975, *132,* 901-906.

Gunn, J., & Robertson, G. Psychopathic personality: A conceptual problem. *Psychological Medicine,* 1976, *6,* 631-634.

Gurman, A. S., & Kniskern, D. P. Research on marital and family therapy: Progress, perspective, and prospect. In S. L. Garfield & A. E. Bergin (Eds.), *Handbook of psychotherapy and behavior change: An empirical analysis* (2nd ed.). New York: Wiley, 1978, pp. 817-902.

Guthrie, R., & Susi, A. A simple phenylalanine method for detecting phenylketonuria in large populations of newborn infants. *Pediatrics,* 1963, *32,* 338-343.

Guttmacher, J. A., & Birk, L. Group therapy: What specific therapeutic advantages? *Comprehensive Psychiatry,* 1971, *21,* 546-556.

Guze, S. B. The role of follow-up studies: Their contribution to diagnostic classification as applied to hysteria. *Seminars in Psychiatry,* 1970, *2,* 392-402.

Haan, N. *Coping and defending.* New York: Academic Press, 1977.

Hackett, T. P., & Cassem, N. H. Psychological effects of acute coronary care. In L. E. Meltzer (Ed.), *Textbook of coronary care.* Amsterdam: Excerpta Medica, 1973.

Haley, J. Family therapy. *International Journal of Psychiatry,* 1970-71, *9,* 233-248.

Haley, J. *Problem-solving therapy.* San Francisco: Jossey-Bass, 1978.

Hall, C. S., & Lindzey, G. *Theories of personality* (3rd ed.). New York: Wiley, 1978.

Hamburg, D. A., & Adams, J. E. A perspective on coping behavior: Seeking and utilizing information in major transitions. *Archives of General Psychiatry*, 1967, *17*, 277–284.

Hare, R. D. *Psychopathy: Theory and research.* New York: Wiley, 1970.

Harlow, H. F. The nature of love. *American Psychologist,* 1958, *13*, 673–685.

Harlow, H. F., & Harlow, M. K. A study of animal affection. *Journal of the American Museum of Natural History,* 1961, *70*, No. 10.

Harlow, H. F., & Harlow, M. K. Social deprivation in monkeys. *Scientific American*, 1962, *207*, 2–10.

Harrell, R. F., Woodyard, E., & Gates, A. I. *The effects of mothers' diet on the intelligence of offspring.* New York: Teachers College, 1955.

Harris, G. G. (Ed.). *The group treatment of human problems: A social learning approach.* New York: Grune & Stratton, 1977.

Harter, S. Effectance motivation reconsidered: Toward a developmental model. *Human Development*, 1978, *1*, 34–64.

Harter, S., & Zigler, E. The assessment of effectance motivation in normal and retarded children. *Developmental Psychology*, 1974, *10*, 169–180.

Hartley, D., Roback, H., & Abramowitz, S. Deterioration effects in encounter groups. *American Psychologist*, 1976, *31*, 247–255.

Hartman, E., Glasser, B. A., Greenblatt, M., Solomon, M. H., & Levinson, D. J. *Adolescents in a mental hospital.* New York: Grune & Stratton, 1968.

Haslam, J. *Observations on insanity.* London: F. & C. Rivington, 1798.

Hatcher, C., & Brooks, B. S. (Eds.). *Innovations in counseling psychology.* San Francisco: Jossey-Bass, 1977.

Hawk, A. B., Carpenter, W. T., & Strauss, J. S. Diagnostic criteria and five-year outcome in schizophrenia. *Archives of General Psychiatry*, 1975, *32*, 343–347.

Hayden, A. H., & Dmitriev, V. The multidisciplinary preschool program for Down's Syndrome children at the University of Washington Model Preschool Center. In B. Z. Friedlander, G. M. Sterritt, & G. E. Kirk (Eds.), *Exceptional infant* (Vol. 3). New York: Brunner/Mazel, 1975, pp. 193–221.

Haydn, G. G., & Rutsky, A. Figure-reversing ability in chronic brain syndrome and controls. *Journal of Nervous and Mental Disease*, 1966, *142*, 168–171.

Healy, W. *Mental conflicts and misconduct.* Boston: Little, Brown, 1917.

Heath, R. G., Fitzjarell, A. T., Carey, R. E., & Myers, W. A. Chronic marihuana smoking: Its effects on function and structure of the primate brain. In G. G. Nahas and W. D. M. Paton (Eds.), *Marihuana: Biological effects.* New York: Pergamon Press, 1979.

Heber, R. F. *Epidemiology of mental retardation.* Springfield, Ill.: Charles C. Thomas, 1970.

Heber, R. F. Sociocultural mental retardation—A longitudinal study. In D.

Forgays (Ed.), *Primary prevention of psychopathology, Vol. II, Environmental influences.* Hanover, N. H.: University Press of New England, 1978, pp. 39-62.

Heber, R. F., & Dever, R. B. Research on education and rehabilitation of the mentally retarded. In H. C. Haywood (Ed.), *Socio-cultural aspects of mental retardation.* New York: Appleton-Century-Crofts, 1970, pp. 419-424.

Heber, R. F., & Garber, H. The Milwaukee Project: A study of the use of family intervention to prevent cultural-familial mental retardation. In B. Z. Friedlander, G. M. Sterritt, & G. E. Kirk (Eds.), *Exceptional infant* (Vol. 3). New York: Brunner/Mazel, 1975, pp. 399-433.

Heine, R. W. *Psychotherapy.* Englewood Cliffs, N.J.: Prentice-Hall, 1971.

Heller, S. S., & Kornfeld, D. S. Delirium and related problems. In S. Arieti (Chief Ed.), *American handbook of psychiatry* (2nd ed.-vol. 4). New York: Basic Books, 1975, pp. 43-66.

Hellman, L. M., & Pritchard, J. A. *Williams' obstetrics* (14th ed.). New York: Appleton-Century-Crofts, 1971.

Hendrick, I. *Facts and theories of psychoanalysis* (2nd ed.). New York: Alfred A. Knopf, 1939.

Henry, H. P. The induction of acute and chronic cardiovascular disease in animals by psychosocial stimulation. *International Journal of Psychiatry in Medicine*, 1975, *6*, 145-158.

Herling, J. *The great price conspiracy.* New York: Van Rees Press, 1962.

Hermann, H. J. M., Rassek, M., Schafer, N., Schmidt, T., & von Uexkull, T. Essential hypertension: Problems, concepts, and an attempted synthesis. In O. Hill (Ed.), *Modern trends in psychosomatic medicine* (Vol. 3.). London: Butterworths, 1976, pp. 260-287.

Hertzig, M. E., Bortner, M., & Birch, H. G. Neurologic findings in children educationally designated as "brain damaged." *American Journal of Orthopsychiatry*, 1969, *39*, 437-446.

Hess, R. D., & Shipman, V. C. Early experience and socialization of cognitive modes in children. *Child Development*, 1965, *36*, 869-870.

Heston, L. L. Psychiatric disorders in foster home reared children of schizophrenic mothers. *British Journal of Psychiatry*, 1966, *112*, 819-825.

Hicks, L. H., & Birren, J. E. Aging, brain damage, and psychomotor slowing. *Psychological Bulletin*, 1970, *74*, 377-396.

Higgins, J. V., Reed, E. W., & Reed, S. C. Intelligence and family size: A paradox resolved. *Eugenics Quarterly,* 1962, *9*, 84-90.

Hill, L. B. *Psychotherapeutic intervention in schizophrenia.* Chicago: University of Chicago Press, 1955.

Hill, O. (Ed.). *Modern trends in psychosomatic medicine* (Vol. 3). London: Butterworths, 1976.

Hillyer, J. *Reluctantly told.* New York: Macmillan, 1927.

Hine, F. R. *Introduction to psychodynamics: A conflict-adaptational approach.* Durham, N. C.: Duke University Press, 1971.

Hirsch, S. J., & Keniston, K. Psychological issues in talented college dropouts. *Psychiatry,* 1970, *33,* 1–20.

Hirsch, S. R., & Leff, J. P. *Abnormalities in parents of schizophrenics.* London: Oxford University Press, 1975.

Hobbs, N. H. Group-centered psychotherapy. In C. R. Rogers, *Client-centered therapy.* Boston: Houghton Mifflin, 1951, pp. 278–319.

Hoff, E. C. The use of pharmacological adjuncts in the comprehensive therapy of alcoholics. In E. D. Whitney (Ed.), *World dialogue on alcohol and drug dependence.* Boston: Beacon Press, 1970, pp. 248–252.

Hogan, B. K. The new sex therapy: An interim report on a changing discipline. In H. H. Grayson & C. Loew (Eds.), *Changing approaches to the psychotherapies.* New York: Spectrum Publications, 1978.

Hogarty, G. E., Goldberg, S. C., & the Collaborative Study Group. Drugs and sociotherapy in the aftercare of schizophrenic patients. *Archives of General Psychiatry,* 1973, *28,* 54–62.

Hokanson, J. E., & Burgess, M. The effects of three types of aggression on vascular processes. *Journal of Abnormal and Social Psychology,* 1962, *65,* 232–237.

Hokanson, J. E., & Shetler, S. The effect of overt aggression on physiological tension level. *Journal of Abnormal and Social Psychology,* 1961, *63,* 446–448.

Holden, J. M. C., Itil, T. H., & Hofstatter, L. Prefrontal lobotomy: Stepping-stone or pitfall? *American Journal of Psychiatry,* 1970, *127,* 591–598.

Hollingworth, H. L. *Abnormal psychology.* New York: Ronald, 1930.

Holmes, T. H., & Masuda, M. Psychosomatic syndrome: When mothers-in-law or other disasters visit, a person can develop a bad, bad cold. Or worse. *Psychology Today,* 1972, *5,* 71–72; 106.

Holmes, T. H., & Masuda, M. Life change and illness susceptibility. In B. S. Dohrenwend & B. P. Dohrenwend (Eds.), *Stressful life events: Their nature and effects.* New York: Wiley, 1974, pp. 45–72.

Holmes, T. H., & Rahe, R. H. The Social Readjustment Rating Scale. *Journal of Psychosomatic Research,* 1967, *11,* 213–218.

Holzberg, J. D., Knapp, R. H., & Turner, J. L. Companionship with the mentally ill: Effects on the personalities of college student volunteers. *Psychiatry,* 1966, *29,* 395–405.

Hook, E. B. Behavioral implications of the human XYY genotype. *Science,* 1973, *179,* 139–150.

Hooker, E. The adjustment of the male overt homosexual. *Journal of Projective Techniques,* 1957, *21,* 18–26.

Hooker, E. Parental relationships and male homosexuality. *Journal of Consulting and Clinical Psychology,* 1969, *33,* 140–142.

Horn, D. The health consequences of smoking. In E. F. Borgatta & R. R. Evans (Eds.), *Smoking, health and behavior.* Chicago: Aldine, 1968.

698

Horney, K. *The neurotic personality of our time.* New York: Norton, 1937.

Horney, K. *New ways in psychoanalysis.* New York: Norton, 1939.

Horney, K. *Self-analysis.* New York: Norton, 1942.

Horney, K. *Our inner conflicts: A constructive theory of neurosis.* New York: Norton, 1945.

Hornstein, H. A. *Cruelty and kindness: A new look at aggression and altruism.* Englewood Cliffs, N. J.: Prentice-Hall, 1976.

Horton, P., & Miller, D. The etiology of multiple personality. *Comprehensive Psychiatry*, 1972, *13*, 151–159.

Hsia, D. Y., Driscoll, K. W., Troll, W., & Knox, W. E. Detection by phenylalanine tolerance tests of heterozygous carriers of phenylketonuria. *Nature*, 1956, *178*, 1239–1240.

Huesmann, L. R. (Ed.). Special issue: Learned helplessness as a model of depression. *Journal of Abnormal Psychology*, 1978, *87*, 1–198.

Huessy, H. Community mental health: Fact and fiction. *Mental health in western Massachusetts: Issues in training.* Amherst, Mass.: Department of Psychology, University of Massachusetts, 1971, pp. 7–23.

Hughes, J. R. A review of the positive spike phenomenon. In W. Wilson (Ed.), *Applications of electroencephalography.* Durham, N.C.: Duke University Press, 1965, pp. 54–101.

Hunt, J. McV. *Intelligence and experience.* New York: Ronald, 1961.

Hunt, J. McV. *The challenge of incompetence and poverty.* Urbana: University of Illinois Press, 1969.

Ianni, F. A. J. *A family business.* New York: Russell Sage Foundation, 1972.

Jackson, D. D. (Ed.). *Communication, family and marriage.* Palo Alto: Science and Behavior Books, 1968.

Jackson, D. D. (Ed.). *Therapy, communication and change.* Palo Alto: Science and Behavior Books, 1969.

Jacobs, T. Family interaction in disturbed and normal families: A methodological and substantive review. *Psychological Bulletin*, 1975, *82*, 33–65.

Jacobson, E. *Depression: Comparative studies of normal, neurotic and psychotic conditions.* New York: International Universities Press, 1971.

Jaffe, J. H. The maintenance approach to the management of opioid dependence. In C. J. D. Zarafonetis (Ed.), *Drug abuse: Proceedings of the international conference.* Philadelphia: Lea & Febiger, 1972, pp. 161–169.

Janet, P. *The major symptoms of hysteria.* New York: Macmillan, 1907.

Janet P. *Major symptoms of hysteria* (2nd ed.). New York: Macmillan, 1920.

Janet, P. *Psychological healing: A historical and clinical study* (E. Paul & C. Paul, Trans.). London: Allen & Unwin, 1925.

Jelliffe, S. Some historical phases of the manic-depressive synthesis. *Journal of Nervous and Mental Disease*, 1931, *73*, 353–374; 499–521.

Jencks, C. What color is IQ? *The New Republic,* 1969, *161*(10-11), 25–29.

Jenkins, C. D., Zyzanski, S. J., Ryan, T. J., Flessas, A., & Tannenbaum, S. I.

Social insecurity and coronary-prone Type A responses as identifiers of severe atherosclerosis. *Journal of Consulting and Clinical Psychology*, 1977, *45*, 1060–1067.

Jenkins, R. L. Psychiatric syndromes in children and their relation to family background. *American Journal of Orthopsychiatry*, 1966, *36*, 450–457.

Jensen, A. How much can we boost IQ and scholastic achievement? *Harvard Educational Review*, 1969, *39*, 1–123.

Johns, J. H., & Quay, H. C. The effect of social reward on verbal conditioning in psychopathic and neurotic military offenders. *Journal of Consulting Psychology*, 1962, *26*, 217–220.

Johnson, R. N. *Aggression in man and animals*. Philadelphia: W. B. Saunders, 1972.

Joint Commission on Mental Illness and Health. *Action for mental health*. New York: Science Editions, 1961.

Jones, H. E. *Development in adolescence*. New York: Appleton-Century-Crofts, 1943.

Jones, M. *The therapeutic community*. New York: Basic Books, 1953.

Jones, M. C. A laboratory study of fear: the case of Peter. *Journal of Genetic Psychology*, 1924, *31*, 308–315.

Jotkowitz, S. J. Multiple Sclerosis and exposure to house pets. *Journal of the American Medical Assoc.*, 1977, *238*, 854.

Kaback, M. M., & O'Brien, J. S. Tay-Sachs prototype for prevention of genetic disease. In V. A. McKusick & R. Claiborne (Eds.), *Medical genetics*. New York: Hospital Practice Publishing, 1973.

Kagan, J. Information processing in the child. In P. H. Mussen, J. J. Conger, & J. Kagan (Eds.), *Readings in child development and personality*. New York: Harper & Row, 1965, pp. 313–323.

Kagan, S. G., & Weiss, J. H. Allergic potential and emotional precipitants of asthma in children. *Journal of Psychosomatic Research*, 1976, *20*, 135–139.

Kalckar, H. M., Kinoshita, J. H., & Donnell, G. N. Galactosemia: Biochemistry, genetics, pathophysiology, and developmental aspects. *Biology of Brain Dysfunction*, 1973, *1*, 31–88.

Kallman, F. J. *The genetics of schizophrenia*. New York: Augustine, 1938.

Kanfer, F. H., & Phillips, J. S. *Learning foundations of behavior therapy*. New York: Wiley, 1970.

Kanner, L. Follow-up of eleven autistic children originally reported in 1943. In L. Kanner (Ed.), *Childhood psychosis: Initial studies and new insights*. Washington, D.C.: Winston-Wiley, 1973.

Kanner, L. Infantile autism and the schizophrenias. *Behavioral Science*, 1965, *10*, 412–20.

Kaplan, B. (Ed.). *The inner world of mental illness*. New York: Harper & Row, 1964.

Kaplan, B. Malnutrition and mental deficiency. *Psychological Bulletin*, 1972, *78*, 321–334.

Kaplan, H. S. *The new sex therapy.* New York: Brunner/Mazel, 1974.

Karon, B. P., & Vandenbos, G. R. Experience, medication and the effectivenss of psychotherapy with schizophrenics. *British Journal of Psychiatry*, 1970, *116*, 427–428.

Karp, L., Smith, D. W., Omenn, G. S., Johnson, S., & Jones, K. The use of ultrasound in the prenatal exclusion of primary microcephaly. *Gynecologic Investigation*, 1974, *5*, 316.

Kastenbaum, R. (Ed.). *Contributions to the psychobiology of aging.* New York: Springer, 1965.

Katz, J. L., Weiner, H., Gallagher, T. F., & Hellman, L. Stress, distress and ego defenses: The psychoendocrine response to impending tumor. *Archives of General Psychiatry*, 1970, *23*, 131–142.

Kay, E. J., Lyons, A., Newman, W., Mankin, D., & Loeb, R. C. A longitudinal study of the personality correlates of marihuana use. *Journal of Consulting and Clinical Psychology*, 1978, *46*, 470–477.

Kaye, H. E., Berl, S., Clare, J., Eleston, M., Gerschwin, B., Gerschwin, P., Kagan, L., Torda, C., & Wilber, C. Homosexuality in women. *Archives of General Psychiatry,* 1967, *17*, 626–634.

Kazdin, A. E. *The token economy: A review and evaluation.* New York: Plenum Press, 1977.

Kazdin, A. E. *History of behavior modification.* Baltimore: University Park Press, 1978.

Kellner, R. Psychotherapy in psychosomatic disorders: A survey of controlled studies. *Archives of General Psychiatry,* 1975, *32*, 1021–1028.

Keniston, K., & The Carnegie Council on Children. *All our children: The American family under pressure.* New York: Harcourt Brace Jovanovich, 1977.

Kesey, K. *One flew over the cuckoo's nest.* New York: Viking Press, 1962.

Kety, S. S. The hypothetical relationships between amines and mental illness: A critical synthesis. In H. E. Himwich, S. S. Kety, & J. R. Smythies (Eds.), *Amines and schizophrenia.* Oxford: Pergamon Press, 1967.

Kety, S. S. Genetic and biochemical aspects of schizophrenia. In A. M. Nicholi, Jr. (Ed.), *The Harvard guide to modern psychiatry.* Cambridge, Mass.: Harvard University Press, 1978, pp. 93–102. (a)

Kety, S. S. Heredity and environment. In J. C. Shershow (Ed.), *Schizophrenia: Science and practice.* Cambridge, Mass.: Harvard University Press, 1978, pp. 47–68. (b)

Kety, S. S., Rosenthal, D., Wender, P. H., Schulsinger, F., & Jacobsen, B. Mental illness in the biological and adoptive families of adopted individuals who have become schizophrenic: A preliminary report based upon psychiatric interviews. In R. Fieve, D. Rosenthal, & H. Brill (Eds.), *Genetic research in psychiatry.* Baltimore: John Hopkins University Press, 1975.

Kinsey, A. C., Pomeroy, W. B., & Martin, C. E. *Sexual behavior in the human male.* Philadelphia: W. B. Saunders, 1948.

701

Kinsey, A. C., Pomeroy, W.B., Martin, C. E., & Gebhard, P. H. *Sexual behavior in the human female*. Philadelphia: W. B. Saunders, 1953.

Kirk, S. A. The effects of early intervention. In H. C. Haywood (Ed.), *Sociocultural aspects of mental retardation*. New York: Appleton-Century-Crofts, 1970, pp. 490–495.

Kirman, B. H. The patient with Down's Syndrome in the community. *Lancet*, 1964, *2*, 705–714.

Kirman, B. H., & Bicknell, J. *Mental handicap*. Edinburgh: Churchill Livingstone, 1975.

Kirshner, L. A. Dissociative reactions: An historical review and clinical study. *Acta Psychiatrica Scandinavica*, 1973, *49*, 498–711.

Kirsner, J. B. Ulcerative colitis: Mysterious, multiplex and menacing. *Journal of Chronic Diseases*, 1971, *23*, 681–684.

Klaber, M. M. The retarded and institutions for the retarded — A preliminary research report. In S. B. Sarason & J. Doris, *Psychological problems in mental deficiency*. New York: Harper & Row, 1969, pp. 148–185.

Klapman, J. W. *Group psychotherapy: Theory and practice*. New York: Grune & Stratton, 1946.

Klerman, G. L. Affective disorders. In A. M. Nicholi, Jr. (Ed.), *The Harvard guide to modern psychiatry*. Cambridge, Mass.: Harvard University Press, 1978, pp. 253–281.

Klerman, G. L. The evolution of a scientific nosology. In J. C. Shershow (Ed.), *Schizophrenia: Science and practice*. Cambridge, Mass.: Harvard University Press, 1978.

Knapp, P. H. Psychosomatic aspects of bronchial asthma. In M. F. Reiser (Ed.), *Organic disorders and psychosomatic medicine* (Vol. 4) in S. Arieti (Ed.-in-Chief), *American handbook of psychiatry* (2nd ed.). New York: Basic Books, 1975, pp. 693–708.

Knapp, P. H., & Nemetz, S. J. Acute bronchial asthma: I. Concomitant depression and excitement, and varied antecedent patterns in 406 attacks. *Psychosomatic Medicine*, 1960, *22,* 42–56.

Knapp, R. P., & Shostrom, E. L. POI outcomes in studies of growth groups: A selected review. *Group and Organization Studies,* 1976, *1*, 187–202.

Knobloch, H., & Pasamanick, B. Prospective studies on the epidemiology of reproductive casualty: Methods, findings and some implications. *Merrill-Palmer Quarterly of Behavior and Development*, 1966, *12*, 27–43.

Knobloch, H., Rider, R., Harper, P., & Pasamanick, B. Neuropsychiatric sequalae of prematurity: A longitudinal study. *Journal of the American Medical Association*, 1956, *161*, 581–585.

Knox, W. E. An evaluation of the treatment of phenylketonuria with diets low in phenylalanine. *Journal of Pediatrics*, 1960, *26*, 1–11.

Knox, W. E. Phenylketonuria. In J. B. Stanbury, J. B. Wyngaarden, & D. S. Frederickson (Eds.), *The metabolic basis of inherited disease*. New York: McGraw-Hill, 1972.

Koch, R., Acosta, P. B., & Dobson, J. C. Two metabolic factors in causation.

In R. Koch & J. C. Dobson (Eds.), *The mentally retarded child and his* *family*. New York: Brunner/Mazel, 1976, pp. 100-115.

Kohl, R. N. Pathological reactions of marital partners to improvement of patients. *American Journal of Psychiatry*, 1962, *118*, 1036-1041. Reprinted in J. G. Howells (Ed.), *Theory and practice of family psychiatry*. New York: Brunner/Mazel, 1971, Chap. 50.

Kohler, W. *The mentality of apes*. New York: Harcourt Brace Jovanovich, 1925.

Kolb, L. C. *Noyes' modern clinical psychiatry* (9th ed.). Philadelphia: W. B. Saunders, 1977.

Kolodny, R., Masters, W., Hendryx, J., & Toro, G. Plasma testosterone and semen analysis in male homosexuals. *New England Journal of Medicine*, 1971, *285*, 1170-1174.

Korchin, S. J. *Modern clinical psychology: Principles of intervention in the clinic and community*. New York: Basic Books, 1976.

Korner, A. F. Individual differences at birth: Implications for early experience and later development. *American Journal of Orthopsychiatry*, 1971, *41*, 608-619.

Kraepelin, E. *Manic-depressive insanity and paranoia* (R. M. Barclay, Trans.). Edinburgh: Livingstone, 1921.

Kraepelin, E. *One hundred years of psychiatry* (1917) (W. Baskin, Trans.). New York: Citadel Press, 1962.

Kraepelin, E. Dementia praecox and paraphrenia (R. M. Barclay, Trans.). New York: Robert E. Krieger, 1919. Reprinted with an historical introduction, 1971.

Kraines, S. H. Manic-depressive syndrome: A physiologic disease. *Diseases of the Nervous System*, 1966, *27*, 573-582; 670-676.

Kramer, B. M. *Day hospital: A study of partial hospitalization in psychiatry*. New York: Grune & Stratton, 1962.

Kramer, J. C. Some observations on and a review of the effect of high-dose use of amphetamines. In C. J. D. Zarafonetis (Ed.), *Drug abuse: Proceedings of the international conference*. Philadelphia: Lea & Febiger, 1972, pp. 253-261.

Kramer, M. Issues in the development of statistical and epidemiological data for mental health services research. *Psychological Medicine*, 1976, *6*, 185-215.

Krasner, L. The operant approach in behavior therapy. In A. E. Bergin & S. L. Garfield (Eds.), *Handbook of psychotherapy and behavior change: An empirical analysis*. New York: Wiley, 1971.

Kremer, M. W. & Rifkin, A. H. The early development of homosexuality: A study of adolescent lesbians. *American Journal of Psychiatry*, 1969, *126*, 91-96.

Kretschmer, E. *Physique and character* (W. J. H. Sprott, Trans.). London: Routledge & Kegan Paul, 1925, Chap. 2.

Kroeber, T. C. The coping functions of the ego mechanisms. In R. W. White (Ed.), *The study of lives*. New York: Atherton Press, 1963, Chap. 8.

Krohn, A. *Hysteria: The elusive neurosis.* New York: International Universities Press, 1978.

Kurtz, G. N. Putting people in the communications process: A national drug abuse education campaign. In J. R. Wittenborn, J. P. Smith, & S. A. Wittenborn (Eds.), *Communication and drug abuse.* Springfield, Ill.: Charles C. Thomas, 1970, pp. 335–356.

Lacey, J. Somatic response patterning and stress: Some revisions of activation theory. In M. H. Appley & R. Trumbull (Eds.), *Psychological stress.* New York: Appleton-Century-Crofts, 1967.

Lacey, J. I., & Van Lehn, R. Differential emphasis in somatic response to stress. *Psychosomatic Medicine*, 1952, *14*, 71–81.

Lacey, J. R., Smith, R. L., & Green, A. Use of conditioned autonomic responses in the study of anxiety. *Psychosomatic Medicine*, 1955, *17*, 208–227.

Lader, M., & Marks, I. *Clinical anxiety.* London: William Heinemann, 1971.

Laing, R. D. *The divided self.* London: Tavistock Publications, 1960.

Laing, R. D. *The politics of experience.* New York: Pantheon Books, 1967.

Laing, R. D., & Esterson, A. *Sanity, madness and the family* (2nd ed.), New York: Basic Books, 1971.

Lally, J. R., & Honig, A. S. Education of infants and toddlers from low-income and low-education backgrounds: Support for the family's role and identity. In B. Z. Friedlander, G. M. Sterritt, & G. E. Kirk (Eds.), *Exceptional infant* (Vol. 3). New York: Brunner/Mazel, 1975, pp. 285–303.

Lamberd, W. G. The treatment of homosexuality as a monosymptomatic phobia. *American Journal of Psychiatry*, 1969, *126*, 512–518.

Landis, C., & Mettler, F. A. *Varieties of psychopathological experience.* New York: Holt, Rinehart & Winston, 1964.

Lane, E., & Albee, G. Childhood intellectual differences between schizophrenic adults and their siblings. *American Journal of Orthopsychiatry*, 1965, *35*, 747–753.

Lanyon, R. I., & Lanyon, B. P. *Behavior therapy: A clinical introduction.* Reading, Mass.: Addison-Wesley, 1978.

Lazarus, A. A. The treatment of a sexually inadequate man. In L. P. Ullmann & L. Krasner (Eds.), *Case studies in behavior modification.* New York: Holt, Rinehart & Winston, 1965.

Lazarus, A. A. *Behavior therapy and beyond.* New York: McGraw-Hill, 1971.

Lazarus, R. S. Cognitive and coping processes in emotion. In A. Monat & R. S. Lazarus (Eds.). *Stress and coping: An anthology.* New York: Columbia University Press, 1977.

Lebovitz, P. S. Feminine behavior in boys: Aspects of its outcome. *American Journal of Psychiatry*, 1972, *128*, 1283–1289.

Lefcourt, H. M. *Locus of control: Current trends in theory and research.* Hillsdale, N. J.: Lawrence Erlbaum, 1976.

Lehmann, H. E. Schizophrenia: Clinical features. In A. M. Freedman, H. I. Kaplan, & B. J. Sadock, (Eds.), *Comprehensive textbook of psychiatry* (2nd ed.). Baltimore: Williams & Wilkins, 1975.

Lejeune, J., Gautier, M., & Turpin, R. Le mongolisme: Premier exemple d'aberration autosomique humaine. *Annales de Genetiques*, 1959, *1*, 41–49.

Leon, G. R. *Case histories of deviant behavior* (2nd ed.). Boston: Holbrook Press, 1977.

Leonard, W. E. *The locomotive-God.* New York: Appleton-Century-Crofts, 1927.

Lester, D. *Unusual sexual behavior: The standard deviations.* Springfield, Ill.: Charles C. Thomas, 1975.

Leventhal, H. Experimental studies of anti-smoking communications. In E. F. Borgatta & R. R. Evans (Eds.), *Smoking, health and behavior.* Chicago: Aldine, 1968.

Levine, D. S., & Willner, S. G. The cost of mental illness, 1974. *Mental Health Statistical Note No. 125.* Bethesda, Md.: National Institute of Mental Health, 1976.

Levy, D. M. Oppositional syndromes and oppositional behavior. In P. H. Hoch & J. Zubin (Eds.), *Psychopathology of childhood.* New York: Grune & Stratton, 1955.

Lewin, B. D. *The psychoanalysis of elation.* New York: Norton, 1950.

Lewine, R. R. J., Watt, N. F., Prentky, R. A., & Fryer, J. H. Childhood behavior in schizophrenia, personality disorder, depression, and neurosis. *British Journal of Psychiatry*, 1978, *132*, 347–357. (a)

Lewine, R. R. J., Watt, N. F., & Fryer, J. H. A study of childhood social competence, adult premorbid competence, and psychiatric outcome in three schizophrenic subtypes. *Journal of Abnormal Psychology,* 1978, *87*, 294–302. (b)

Lewinsohn, P. H. A behavioral approach to depression. In R. J. Friedman & M. M. Katz (Eds.), *The psychology of depression: Contemporary theory and research.* Washington, D. C.: Winston-Wiley, 1974.

Lewis, O. *The children of Sanchez: Autobiography of a Mexican family.* New York: Random House, 1961.

Liberman, B. L. The role of mastery in psychotherapy: Maintenance of improvement and prescriptive change. In J. D. Frank, R. Hoehn-Saric, S. D. Imber, B. L. Liberman, & A. R. Stone, (Eds.), *Effective ingredients of successful psychotherapy.* New York: Brunner/Mazel, 1978.

Lidz, T., Fleck, S., & Cornelison, A. R. *Schizophrenia and the family.* New York: International Universities Press, 1965.

Lieberman, M. A., Yalom, I. D., & Miles, M. B. *Encounter groups: First facts.* New York: Basic Books, 1973.

Lindemann, E. Symptomatology and management of acute grief. *American Journal of Psychiatry*, 1944, *101*, 141–148.

Lindemann, E. Symptomatology and management of acute grief. In H. G.

Parad (Ed.), *Crisis intervention*. New York: Family Service Association of America, 1965.

Lindsjö, A. Down's syndrome in Sweden: An epidemiological study of a three-year material. *Acta Paediatrica Scandinavica*, 1974, *63*, 571–576.

Lipowski, Z. J. Organic brain syndromes: Overview and classification. In D. F. Benson & D. Blumer (Eds.), *Psychiatric aspects of neurological disease.* New York: Grune & Stratton, 1975, pp. 11–35.

Lipowski, Z. J. Psychophysiological cardiovascular disorders. In A. M. Freedman, H. I. Kaplan, & B. J. Sadock (Eds.), *Comprehensive textbook of psychiatry—II*. Baltimore: Williams & Wilkins, 1975, pp. 1660–1668.

Lipowski, Z. J. Psychosomatic medicine in the 70's: An overview. *American Journal of Psychiatry*, 1977, *134*, 233–244.

Lipton, E. L., Steinschneider, A., & Richmond, J. B. Autonomic function in the neonate. II. Physiological effects of motor restraint. *Psychosomatic Medicine*, 1960, *22*, 57–65.

Lipton, M. A. Affective disorders: Progress, but some unresolved questions remain. *American Journal of Psychiatry*, 1970, *127*, 357–358.

Liss, J. L., Alpers, D., & Woodruff, R. A. The irritable colon syndrome and psychiatric illness. *Diseases of the Nervous System*, 1973, *34*, 151–157.

Little, W. A., Honour, A. J., & Sleight, P. Direct arterial pressure and electrocardiogram during motor car driving. *British Medical Journal,* 1973, *2*, 273–277.

Locke, E. A. Is "behavior therapy" behavioristic? (An analysis of Wolpe's psychotherapeutic methods.) *Psychological Bulletin*, 1971, *76*, 318–327.

Lotter, V. Factors related to outcome in autistic children. *Journal of Autism and Childhood Schizophrenia*, 1974, *4*, 263–277.

Louria, D. B. Medical complications of illicit drug use. In C. J. D. Zarafonetis (Ed.), *Drug abuse: Proceedings of the international conference.* Philadelphia: Lea & Febiger, 1972, pp. 585–596.

Lovibond, S. H. *Conditioning and enuresis.* New York: Macmillan, 1964.

Lowe, G. Alcoholism and psychology—Some recent trends and methods. In J. S. Madden, R. Walker, & W. H. Kenyon (Eds.), *Alcoholism and drug dependence: A multidisciplinary approach.* New York: Plenum Press, 1977, pp. 105–113.

Luborsky, L. New directions in research on neurotic and psychosomatic symptoms. *American Scientist*, 1970, *58*, 661–668.

Luborsky, L., & Auerbach, A. H. The symptom-context method: Quantitative studies of symptom formation in psychotherapy. *Journal of the American Psychoanalytic Association*, 1969, *17*, 68–99.

Luparello, T. J., Leist, N., Lourie, C. N., & Sweet, P. The interaction of psychologic stimuli and pharmacologic agents on airway reactivity in asthmatic subjects. *Psychosomatic Medicine*, 1970, *32*, 509–513.

Luria, A. R. *The man with a shattered world.* New York: Basic Books, 1972.

706

Luria, Z., & Rose, M. D. *Psychology of human sexuality.* New York: Wiley,
1979.

Maccoby, E. E., & Jacklin, C. M. *The psychology of sex differences.* Stanford, Calif.: Stanford University Press, 1974.

MacKinnon, D. W., & Dukes, W. F. Repression. In L. Postman (Ed.), *Psychology in the making: Histories of selected research problems.* New York: Alfred A. Knopf, 1962, Chap. 11.

Madden, J. S., Walker, R., & Kenyon, W. H. (Eds.), *Alcoholism and drug dependence: A multidisciplinary approach.* New York: Plenum Press, 1977.

Magaro, P. A., Gripp, R., & McDowell, D. J. *The mental health industry; A cultural phenomenon.* New York: Wiley, 1978.

Maher, B. A. *Principles of psychopathology.* New York: McGraw-Hill, 1966.

Maher, B. A., & Maher, W. B. Abnormal psychology: From the seventeenth century to modern times. In G. Kimble & K. Schlesinger (Eds.), *History of modern psychology.* New York: Wiley, 1980.

Maher, W. B., & Maher, B. A. Abnormal psychology: To the sixteenth century. In G. Kimble & K. Schlesinger (Eds.), *History of modern psychology.* New York: Wiley, in press.

Mahler, M. On child psychosis and schizophrenia. In *The psychoanalytic study of the child* (Vol. 7). New York: International Universities Press, 1952, pp. 286-305.

Main, T. I. Mutual projection in a marriage. *Comprehensive Psychiatry,* 1966, *7,* 432-449.

Malamud, W. The psychoneuroses. In J. McV. Hunt (Ed.), *Personality and the behavior disorders* (Vol. 2). New York: Ronald Press, 1944.

Malinowski, B. *Sex and repression in savage society.* New York: Harcourt Brace Jovanovich, 1927.

Malmo, R. B., Shagass, C., & Davis, F. H. Specificity of bodily reactions under stress. A physiological study of somatic symptom mechanisms in psychiatric patients. In *Proceedings of the Association for Research in Nervous Diseases* (Vol. 29, *Life stress and bodily disease*). Baltimore: Williams & Wilkins, 1950, pp. 231-262.

Malmquist, C. P. Depression and object loss in acute psychiatric admissions. *American Journal of Psychiatry,* 1970, *126,* 1782-1787.

Manning, B. A. Criminal justice. In C. Kryder & S. P. Strickland (Eds.), *Americans and drug abuse: Report from the Aspen Conference.* New York: Institute for Humanistic Studies, 1977, pp. 37-42.

Marcia, J. E. Development and validation of ego identity status. *Journal of Personality and Social Psychology,* 1966, *3,* 551-559.

Mark, V. H., & Ervin, F. R. *Violence and the brain.* New York: Harper & Row, 1970.

Marks, I. M. Research in neurosis: A selective review. I. Causes and courses. *Psychological Medicine,* 1973, *3,* 436-454.

Marks, I. M., & Lader, M. Anxiety states (anxiety neurosis): A review. *Journal of Nervous and Mental Disease*, 1973, *156*, 3–18.

Masland, R. L. The prevention of mental subnormality. In R. L. Masland, S. B. Sarason, & T. Gladwin, *Mental subnormality*. New York: Basic Books, 1958.

Maslow, A. H. *Motivation and personality* (2nd ed.). New York: Harper & Row, 1970.

Masserman, J. H. *Principles of dynamic psychiatry*. Philadelphia: W. B. Saunders, 1946.

Masserman, J. H. Presidential address: The future of psychiatry as a scientific and humanitarian discipline in a changing world. *American Journal of Psychiatry*, 1979, *136*, 1013–1019.

Masters, W. H., & Johnson, V. E. *Human sexual inadequacy*. Boston: Little, Brown, 1970.

Mathe, A. A., & Knapp, P. H. Emotional and adrenal reactions to stress in bronchial asthma. *Psychosomatic Medicine,* 1971, *33*, 323–340.

Matthyse, S. Schizophrenia: Relationships to dopamine transmission, motor control, and feature extraction. In F. O. Schmitt & F. G. Worden (Eds.), *The Neurosciences: Third study program*. Cambridge, Mass.: MIT Press, 1974, pp. 733–737.

Matthyse, S., & Kety, S. S. (Eds.). *Catecholamines and schizophrenia*. Oxford: Pergamon Press, 1975.

Maurice, W. L., & Guze, S. B. Sexual dysfunction and associated psychiatric disorders. *Comprehensive Psychiatry*, 1970, *11*, 539–543.

Mausner, B., & Platt, E. S. *Smoking: A behavioral analysis*. New York: Pergamon Press, 1971.

Mawson, A. R. Anorexia nervosa and the regulation of intake: A review. *Psychological Medicine,* 1974, *4*, 289–308.

May, P. R. A. *Treatment of schizophrenia*. New York: Science House, 1968.

May, P. R. A., & Tuma, A. H. A follow-up study of the results of treatment of schizophrenia: Hospital stay and readmission. In R. L. Spitzer & D. F. Klein (Eds.), *Evaluation of psychological therapies*. Baltimore: Johns Hopkins University Press, 1976.

May, P. R. A., Tuma, H., Yale, C., Potepan, P., & Dixon, W. J. Schizophrenia: A follow-up study of results of treatment. *Archives of General Psychiatry*, 1976, *33*, 481–486.

May, R. *The meaning of anxiety* (Rev. ed.). New York: Norton, 1977.

May, R., Angel, E., & Ellenberger, H. F. (Eds.). *Existence: A new dimension in psychiatry and psychology*. New York: Basic Books, 1958.

McCabe, M. S., Fowler, R. C., Cadoret, R. J., & Winokur, G. Familial differences in schizophrenia with good and poor prognosis. *Psychological Medicine*, 1971, *1*, 326–332.

McCaghy, C. H. *Deviant behavior: Crime, conflict and interest groups*. New York: Macmillan, 1976.

McCleary, R. A. Response-modulating functions of the limbic system: Initiation and suppression. In E. Stellar & J. Sprague (Eds.), *Progress in physiological psychology* (Vol. 1.) New York: Academic Press, 1966, pp. 209–272.

McClelland, D. C., Davis, W. N., Kalin, R., & Wanner, E. *The drinking man.* New York: The Free Press of Glencoe, 1972.

McClelland, D. C. Testing for competence rather than for "intelligence." *American Psychologist*, 1973, *28*, 1–14.

McCord, W., & McCord, J. *The psychopath: An essay on the criminal mind.* Princeton, N. J.: Van Nostrand Reinhold, 1964.

McCord, W., & McCord, J. *Origins of alcoholism.* Stanford, Calif.: Stanford University Press, 1960.

McCord, W., McCord, J., & Zola, I. K. *Origins of crime.* New York: Columbia University Press, 1959.

McDougall, W. *An introduction to social psychology* (1908) (16th ed.). Boston: John W. Luce, 1923.

McDougall, W. *Outline of abnormal psychology.* New York: Charles Scribner's Sons, 1926.

McHugh, P. R., & Folstein, M. F. Psychiatric syndromes of Huntington's Chorea: A clinical and phenomenologic study. In D. F. Benson & D. Blumer (Eds.), *Psychiatric aspects of neurological disease.* New York: Grune & Stratton, 1975, pp. 267–286.

McNichol, K. N., & Williams, H. E. Asthma in children. *British Medical Journal*, 1973, *4*, 7–20.

Mechanic, D. *Mental health and social policy.* Englewood Cliffs, N.J.: Prentice-Hall, 1969.

Mechanic, D. Social psychologic factors affecting the presentation of bodily complaints. *New England Journal of Medicine*, 1972, *286*, 1132–1139.

Mednick, S. A., & Witkin-Lanoil, G. H. Intervention in children at high risk for schizophrenia. In G. W. Albee & J. M. Joffe (Eds.), *Primary prevention of psychopathology* (Vol. 1—The issues). Hanover, N. H.: The University Press of New England, 1977.

Meehl, P. E. Schizotaxia, schizotypy, schizophrenia. *American Psychologist*, 1962, *17*, 827–838.

Meichenbaum, D. *Cognitive-behavior modification: An integrative approach.* New York: Plenum Press, 1977.

Melnyk, J., & Koch, R. Genetic factors in causation. In R. Koch & J. C. Dobson, *The mentally retarded child and his family.* New York: Brunner/Mazel, 1976, pp. 49–64.

Mendels, J. *Concepts of depression.* New York: Wiley, 1970.

Menolascino, F. J. Psychiatric aspects of mongolism. *American Journal of Mental Deficiency*, 1965, *69*, 653–660.

Mercer, J. R. A policy statement on assessment procedures and the rights of children. *Harvard Educational Review*, 1974, *44*, 125–141.

Merrill, M. A. *Problems of child delinquency.* Boston: Houghton Mifflin, 1947.

709

Meserve, W. G. Congressional action on smoking and health. In E. F. Borgatta, & R. R. Evans (Eds.), *Smoking, health and behavior*. Chicago: Aldine, 1968.

Metcalfe, M. Demonstration of a psychosomatic relationship. *British Journal of Medical Psychology*, 1956, *29*, 63–66.

Metrakos, J. D., & Metrakos, K. Genetic studies in clinical epilepsy. In H. H. Jasper, A. A. Ward, Jr., & A. Pope (Eds.), *Basic mechanisms of the epilepsies*. Boston: Little, Brown, 1969.

Meyer, A. Fundamental conceptions of dementia praecox. *British Medical Journal*, 1906, *2*, 757–760.

Meyer, J. E. Personal communication, 1967.

Meyer, J. E. Anorexia nervosa of adolescence. *British Journal of Psychiatry*, 1971, *118*, 539–542.

Meyer, V. Psychological effects of brain damage. In H. J. Eysenck (Ed.), *Handbook of abnormal psychology: An experimental approach*. New York: Basic Books, 1961.

Meyers, J., Parsons, R. D., & Martin, M. *Mental health consultation in the schools*. San Francisco: Jossey-Bass, 1979.

Miall, W. E., & Oldham, P. D. The hereditary factor in arterial blood pressure. *British Medical Journal*, 1963, *1*, 75–80.

Michaux, W. M., Katz, M. M., Kurland, A. A., & Gansereit, K. H. *The first year out: Mental patients after hospitalization*. Baltimore: The John Hopkins Press, 1969.

Miles, C. P. Conditions predisposing to suicide: A review. *Journal of Nervous and Mental Disease*, 1977, *164*, 231–246.

Miles, H. H. W., Cobb, S., & Shands, H. C. *Case histories in psychosomatic medicine*. New York: Norton, 1952.

Miller, G. A., Galanter, E., & Pribram, K. H. *Plans and the structure of behavior*. New York: Holt, Rinehart & Winston, 1960.

Miller, D. R. *A construct validity study of the Interpersonal Maturity Level Classification System*. Unpublished doctoral dissertation, University of Massachusetts, 1972.

Miller, J. O. Cultural deprivation and its modification: Effect of intervention. In H. C. Haywood (Ed.), *Sociocultural aspects of mental retardation*. New York: Appleton-Century-Crofts, 1970.

Miller, W. B. American youth gangs: A reassessment. In L. Radzinowicz & M. E. Wolfgang (Eds.), *Crime and justice* (2nd ed.). New York: Basic Books, 1977.

Miller, W. B. White gangs. In J. F. Short, Jr. (Ed.), *Modern criminals*. Chicago: Aldine, 1970.

Mintz, E. E. *Marathon groups: Reality and symbol*. New York: Appleton-Century-Crofts, 1971.

Minuchin, S. *Families and family therapy*. Cambridge, Mass.: Harvard University Press, 1974.

Minuchin, S., Baker, L., Rosman, B. L., Liebman, R., Milman, L., & Todd,
T. C. A conceptual model of psychosomatic illness in children. *Archives of General Psychiatry*, 1975, *32*, 1031–1038.

Mira, E. *Psychiatry in war.* New York: Norton, 1943.

Mirsky, A. Neurophysiological basis of schizophrenia. *Annual Review of Psychology*, 1969, *20*, 321–348.

Mittelmann, B. Motility in infants, children, and adults. *Psychoanalytic Study of the Child*, 1954, *9*, 158–170.

Moment, D., & Zalesznik, A. *Role development and interpersonal competence.* Boston: Harvard Business School, Division of Research, 1963.

Monat, A., & Lazarus, R. S. (Eds.). *Stress and coping: An anthology.* New York: Columbia University Press, 1977.

Money, J. *Sex errors of the body.* Baltimore: Johns Hopkins Press, 1968.

Money, J. Sexual dimorphism and homosexual gender identity. *Psychological Bulletin*, 1970, *74*, 425–440.

Money, J. Differentiation of gender identity and gender role. *Psychiatric Annals*, 1971, *1*, 44–49.

Money, J. Human hermaphroditism. In F. A. Beach (Ed.), *Human sexuality in four perspectives.* Baltimore: Johns Hopkins University Press, 1977, pp. 62–86.

Money, J., Hampson, J. G., & Hampson, J. L. Hermaphroditism: Recommendations concerning assignment of sex, change of sex, and psychologic management. *Bulletin of Johns Hopkins Hospital*, 1955, *97*, 284–300.

Money, J., & Pollitt, E. Cytogenetic and psychosexual ambiguity. *Archives of General Psychiatry*, 1964, *11*, 589–595.

Moore, D. J., & Shiek, D. A. Toward a theory of early infantile autism. *Psychological Review*, 1971, *78*, 451–456.

Mordkoff, A., & Parsons, D. The coronary personality: A critique. *International Journal of Psychiatry*, 1968, *5*, 413–426.

Moreno, J. L. *Psychodrama.* Beacon, N. Y.: Beacon House, 1946.

Morgan, H. G., & Russell, G. F. M. Value of family background and clinical features as predictors of long-term outcome in anorexia nervosa: Four-year follow-up study of 41 patients. *Psychological Mediciine*, 1975, *5*, 355–371.

Morrison, J. R. The syndrome of catatonia: Results of treatment. In M. Roff, D. F. Ricks, & A. Thomas (Eds.), *Life history research in psychopathology* (Vol. III). Minneapolis: University of Minnesota Press, 1973.

Morrison, J. R. Catatonia: Prediction of outcome. *Comprehensive Psychiatry*, 1974, *15*, 317–324.

Motto, J. A. The recognition and management of the suicidal patient. In F. F. Flach & S. C. Draghi (Eds.), *The nature and treatment of depression.* New York: Wiley, 1975, pp. 229–254.

Mowrer, O. H. *Learning theory and personality dynamics.* New York: Ronald Press, 1950.

Mowrer, O. H., & Mowrer, W. M. Enuresis: A method for its study and treatment. *American Journal of Orthopsychiatry,* 1938, *8,* 436–459.

Mucha, T. F., & Reinhardt, R. F. Conversion reactions in student aviators. *American Journal of Psychiatry,* 1970, *127,* 493–497.

Mulvihill, D. J., & Tumin, M. M. *Crimes of violence,* Staff report submitted to the National Commission on the causes and prevention of violence (Vol. 11). Washington, D. C.: U. S. Government Printing Office, 1969.

Murphy, D. L., Brodie, H. K. H., Goodwin, F. K., & Bunney, W. E., Jr. Regular induction of hypomania by L-dopa in "bipolar" manic-depressive patients. *Nature,* 1971, *229,* 135–136.

Murphy, G. *Personality: A biosocial approach to origins and structure.* New York: Harper & Row, 1947.

Murphy, L. B. *Personality in young children* (Vol. 2). New York: Basic Books, 1956.

Murphy, L. B. *The widening world of childhood.* New York: Basic Books, 1962.

Murray, H. A. The effect of fear upon estimates of the maliciousness of other personalities. *Journal of Social Psychology,* 1933, *4,* 310–329.

Murray, H. A. *Explorations in personality.* New York: Oxford University Press, 1938.

Murray, H. A. A conception of personality. In C. Kluckhohn, H. A. Murray, & D. Schneider (Eds.)., *Personality in nature, society, and culture* (2nd ed.). New York: Alfred A. Knopf, 1953.

Mussen, P., Conger, J. J., & Kagan, J. *Child development and personality* (5th ed.). New York: Harper & Row, 1979.

Mussen, P., & Eisenberg-Berg, N. *Roots of caring, sharing, and helping: The development of prosocial behavior in children.* San Francisco: Freeman, 1977.

Nahas, G. G. *Marihuana—deceptive weed.* New York: Raven Press, 1973.

Nahas, G. G. *Keep off the grass.* New York: Pergamon Press, 1979.

Nahas, G. G., Sucin-Foca, N., Armand, J. P., & Morishima, A. Inhibition of cell-mediated immunity in marihuana smokers. *Science,* 1974, *183,* 419–420.

Nameche, G., Waring, M., & Ricks, D. F. Early indicators of outcome in schizophrenia. *Journal of Nervous and Mental Disease,* 1964, *139,* 232–240.

National Advisory Commission on Criminal Justice Standards and Goals. *Report on corrections.* Washington, D. C.: U. S. Government Printing Office, 1973.

National Institute of Mental Health. *Lithium in the treatment of mood disorders.* Washington, D. C.: Government Printing Office, 1970.

Nemiah, J. C. Psychoneurotic disorders. In A. M. Nicholi, Jr. (Ed.), *The Harvard guide to modern psychiatry.* Cambridge, Mass.: Harvard University Press, 1978, pp. 173–197.

Neuberger, M. B. *Smoke screen: Tobacco and the public welfare.* Englewood Cliffs, N.J.: Prentice-Hall, 1963.

Nichols, W. W. Genetic hazards of drugs of abuse. In C. J. D. Zarafonetis (Ed.), *Drug abuse: Proceedings of the international conference.* Philadelphia: Lea & Febiger, 1972, pp. 93-100.

Nielsen, J., & Christensen, A. L. Thirty-five males with double Y chromosome. *Psychological Medicine*, 1974, *4*, 28-37.

Nodine, J. H., & Moyer, J. H. (Eds.). *Psychosomatic medicine.* Philadelphia: Lea & Febiger, 1962.

Offer, D. *The psychological world of the teenager.* New York: Basic Books, 1969.

Ofman, W. V. *Affirmation and reality: Fundamentals of humanistic existential therapy and counseling.* Los Angeles: Western Psychological Services, 1976.

Ohlin, L. E. The effect of social change on crime and law enforcement. In H. S. Ruth, et al., *The challenge of crime in a free society: Perspectives on the report of the President's Commission on Law Enforcement and the Administration of Justice.* New York: Da Capo Press, 1971.

Oltman, J., & Friedman, S. Parental deprivation in psychiatric conditions. *Diseases of the Nervous System*, 1967, *28*, 298-303.

Oltmanns, T. F., & Neale, J. M. Abstraction and schizophrenia: Problems in psychological deficit research. In B. A. Maher (Ed.), *Progress in experimental personality research* (Vol. 8). New York: Academic Press, 1978.

Orlinsky, D. E., & Howard, K. J. The relation of process to outcome in psychotherapy. In S. L. Garfield & A. E. Bergin (Eds.), *Handbook of psychotherapy and behavior change* (2nd ed.). New York: Wiley, 1978, pp. 283-330.

Osgood, C. E., & Miron, M. S. *Approaches to the study of aphasia.* Urbana, Ill.: University of Illinois Press, 1963.

Ovesey, L. *Homosexuality and pseudohomosexuality.* New York: Science House, 1969, pp. 126-137.

Page, E. B. Miracle in Milwaukee: Raising the IQ. In B. Z. Friedlander, G. M. Sterritt, & G. E. Kirk (Eds.), *Exceptional infant* (Vol. 3). New York: Brunner/Mazel, 1975, pp. 434-446.

Papp, P. (Ed.). *Family therapy: Full-length case studies.* New York: Gardner Press, 1977.

Parad, H. (Ed.). *Crisis intervention.* New York: Family Service Association of America, 1965.

Parens, H., & Saul, L. J. *Dependence in man: A psychoanalytic study.* New York: International Universities Press, 1971.

Parkes, C. M., Benjamin, B., & Fitzgerald, R. G. Broken heart: A statistical study of increased mortality among widowers. *British Medical Journal*, 1969, *1*, 740-743.

713

Pasamanick, B., & Knobloch, H. Retrospective studies on the epidemiology of reproductive casualty: Old and new. *Merrill-Palmer Quarterly of Behavior and Development*, 1966, *12*, 7-26.

Pattison, E. M. Nonabstinent drinking goals in the treatment of alcoholism. *Archives of General Psychiatry*, 1976, *33*, 923-930.

Paul, G. L. *Psychosocial treatment of chronic mental patients.* Cambridge, Mass.: Harvard University Press, 1978.

Paykel, E. A. Recent life events and clinical depression. In E. K. Gunderson & R. H. Rahe (Eds.), *Life stress and illness.* Springfield, Ill.: Charles C. Thomas, 1974.

Paykel, E. S. Environmental variables in the etiology of depression. In F. F. Flach & S. C. Draghi (Eds.), *The nature and treatment of depression.* New York: Wiley, 1975, pp. 57-72.

Penfield, W., & Erickson, T. C. *Epilepsy and cerebral localization.* Springfield, Ill.: Charles C. Thomas, 1941.

Penfield, W., & Perot, P. The brain's record of auditory and visual experience. *Brain*, 1963, *86*, 595-696.

Penfield, W., & Roberts, L. *Speech and brain mechanisms.* Princeton, N.J.: Princeton University Press, 1959.

Penrose, L. S. *The biology of mental defect* (3rd ed.). New York: Grune & Stratton, 1963.

Perls, F. S. *Gestalt therapy verbatim.* Lafayette, Calif.: Real People Press, 1969.

Perls, F. S. Four lectures. In J. Fagan & I. L. Sheperd (Eds.), *Gestalt therapy now.* Palo Alto, Calif.: Science and Behavior Books, 1970.

Perris, C. A study of bipolar (manic-depressive) and unipolar recurrent depressive psychoses. *Acta Psychiatrica Scandinavica*, 1966, *42* (Supplement 194).

Perry, T. L., Hansen, S., Tischler, B., Richards, F. M., & Sokol, M. Unrecognized adult phenylketonuria. *New England Journal of Medicine*, 1973, *289*, 395-398.

Perry, W. G., Jr. *Forms of intellectual and ethical development during the college years.* New York: Holt, Rinehart & Winston, 1970.

Peters, J. E., & Stern, R. M. Specificity of attitudes hypothesis in psychosomatic medicine: A re-examination. *Journal of Psychosomatic Research*, 1971, *15*, 129-135.

Peterson, D. R. *The clinical study of social behavior.* New York: Appleton-Century-Crofts, 1968.

Peterson, D. R., Quay, H. C., & Tiffany, T. L. Personality factors related to juvenile delinquency. *Child Development*, 1961, *32*, 355-372.

Phares, E. J. *Locus of control in personality.* Morristown, N. J.: General Learning Press, 1976.

Philip, A. E., & Cay, E. L. Psychiatric symptoms and personality traits in patients suffering from gastro-intestinal illness. *Journal of Psychosomatic Research*, 1972, *16*, 47–51.

Phillips, L. *Human adaptation and its failures*. New York: Academic Press, 1968.

Phillipson, R. V. (Ed.). *Modern trends in drug dependence and alcoholism*. New York: Appleton-Century-Crofts, 1970.

Piaget, J. *The construction of reality by the child*. (M. Cook, Trans.). New York: Basic Books, 1954.

Pickens, R., & Harris, W. C. Self-administration of D-amphetamine by rats. *Psychopharmacologia*, 1968, *12*, 158–163.

Pickens, R., Weisch, R., & McGuire, L. E. Methamphetamine reinforcement in rats. *Psychonomic Science*, 1967, *8*, 361–372.

Pickering, G. Hyperpiesis: High blood pressure without evident cause—essential hypertension. *British Medical Journal*, 1965, *2*, 959–968; 1021–1026.

Pilowsky, I., Spalding, D., Shaw, J., & Korner, P. I. Hypertension and personality. *Psychosomatic Medicine*, 1973, *35*, 50–56.

Pincus, J. G., & Tucker, G. *Behavioral neurology*. New York: Oxford University Press, 1974.

Pinel, P. *Traité médico-philosophique sur l'alienation mentale*. Paris: J. A. Brosson, 1801.

Plaut, T. F. A. *Alcohol problems, A report to the nation by the Cooperative Commission on the Study of Alcoholism*. New York: Oxford University Press, 1967.

Platt, J. J., & Labate, C. *Heroin addiction: Theory, research and treatment*. New York: Wiley, 1976.

Plummer, G. Anomalies occurring in children exposed *in utero* to the atomic bomb in Hiroshima. *Pediatrics*, 1952, *10*, 687–693.

Polansky, N. A., & Harkins, E. B. Psychodrama as an element in hospital treatment. *Psychiatry*, 1969, *32*, 74–87.

Posner, J. B. Delirium and exogenous metabolic brain disease. In P. Beeson & W. McDermott (Eds.), *Cecil and Loeb textbook of medicine*. Philadelphia: Saunders, 1971, pp. 88–95.

Powers, E., & Witmer, H. L. *Experiments in the prevention of delinquency: The Cambridge-Somerville Youth Study*. New York: Columbia University Press, 1951.

Pratt, R. T. C. The genetics of Alzheimer's disease. In G. E. W. Wolstenholme & M. O'Connor (Eds.), *Alzheimer's disease and related conditions*. London: Churchill, 1970.

The President's Commission on Mental Health. *Report to the President* (Vol. 1). Washington, D. C.: U. S. Government Printing Office, 1978.

The President's Panel on Mental Retardation. *A proposed program for national action to combat mental retardation*. Washington, D.C.: Government Printing Office, 1962.

715

Prince, M. *The dissociation of personality*. London: Longmans, Green, 1905.

Prince, M. Miss Beauchamp: The psychogenesis of multiple personality. *Journal of Abnormal Psychology*, 1920, *16*(1). Reprinted in M. Prince *Clinical and experimental studies in personality*. Cambridge, Mass.: Sci-Art Publishers, 1939, pp. 185–268.

Pritchard, J. C. *Treatise on insanity*. London: Gilbert & Piper, 1835.

Provence, S., & Lipton, R. C. *Infants in institutions*. New York: International Universities Press, 1962.

Purcell, K. Critical appraisal of psychosomatic studies of asthma. *New York State Journal of Medicine*, 1965, *65*, 2103–2109.

Purcell, K., & Weiss, J. H. Asthma. In C. G. Costello (Ed.). *Symptoms of psychopathology*. New York: Wiley, 1970, pp. 597–623.

Rachman, S. The treatment of anxiety and phobic reactions by systematic desensitization psychotherapy. *Journal of Abnormal and Social Psychology*, 1959, *63*, 259–263.

Rada, R. T., Meyer, G. G., & Kellner, R. Visual conversion reaction in children and adults. *Journal of Nervous and Mental Disease*, 1978, *166*, 580–587.

Radloff, L. Sex differences in depression: The effects of occupation and marital status. *Sex Roles*, 1975, *1*, 249–265.

Rado, S. Hedonic control, action-self, and the depressive spell. In P. H. Hoch & J. Zubin (Eds.), *Depression*. New York: Grune & Stratton, 1954, Chapter 11.

Radzinowicz, L., & Wolfgang, M. E. (Eds.). *Crime and justice* (2nd ed.). New York: Basic Books, 1977.

Rappaport, J., Chimsky, J. M., & Cowen, E. L. *Innovations in helping chronic patients: College students in a mental institution*. New York: Academic Press, 1971.

Raush, H. L., & Raush, C. L. *The halfway house movement: A search for sanity*. New York: Appleton-Century-Crofts, 1968.

Redlich, F. C., & Freedman, D. X. *The theory and practice of psychiatry*. New York: Basic Books, 1966.

Reed, E. W., & Reed, S. C. *Mental retardation*. Philadelphia: W. B. Saunders, 1965.

Reed, J. L. The diagnosis of "hysteria." *Psychological Medicine*, 1975, *5*, 13–17.

Reed, S. C., & Anderson, V. E. Effects of changing sexuality on the gene pool. In F. F. de la Cruz & G. D. LaVeck (Eds.), *Human sexuality and the mentally retarded*. New York: Brunner/Mazel, 1973.

Rees, L. Constitutional factors and abnormal behavior. In H. J. Eysenck (Ed.), *Handbook of abnormal psychology: An experimental approach*. New York: Basic Books, 1961, Chap. 9.

Reeves, C. *The psychology of Rollo May*. San Francisco: Jossey-Bass, 1977.

Reich, W. *Character-analysis* (T. P. Wolfe, Trans.) (3rd ed.). New York: Orgone Institute Press, 1949.

Reichard, S., Livson, F., & Petersen, P. G. *Aging and personality.* New York: Wiley, 1962.

Reiser, M. F. Changing theoretical concepts in psychosomatic medicine. In M. F. Reiser (Ed.), *Organic disorders and psychosomatic medicine*, Vol. 4 in S. Arieti (Ed.-in-Chief), *American handbook of psychiatry* (2nd ed.). New York: Basic Books, 1975, pp. 477–500. (a)

Reiser, M. F. (Ed.). *Organic disorders and psychosomatic medicine*, Vol. 4 in S. Arieti (Ed.-in-Chief), *American handbook of psychiatry* (2nd ed.). New York: Basic Books, 1975. (b)

Reisman, J. M. *Toward the integration of psychotherapy.* New York: Wiley, 1971.

Reitan, R. M. Psychological deficit. *Annual Review of Psychology*, 1962, *13*, 415–444.

Remington, F. J. The limits and possibilities of the criminal law. In H. S. Ruth et al., *The challenge of crime in a free society: Perspectives on the report of the President's Commission on Law Enforcement and the Administration of Justice.* New York: Da Capo Press, 1971.

Renshaw, D. *The hyperactive child.* Chicago: Hall, 1974.

Report of the American Medical Association conference on mental retardation. *Journal of the American Medical Association*, 1965, *191*, 183–232.

Reppucci, N. D. Individual differences in the consideration of information among two-year-old children. *Developmental Psychology*, 1970, *2*, 240–246.

Reschly, D. J., & Jipson, F. J. Ethnicity, geographical locale, age, sex, and urban-rural residence as variables in the prevalence of mild retardation. In S. Chess & A. Thomas (Eds.), *Annual progress in child psychiatry and child development, 1977.* New York: Brunner/Mazel, 1977, pp. 612–624.

Ribble, M. A. Disorganizing factors of infant personality. *American Journal of Psychiatry*, 1941, *98*, 459–463.

Ribble, M. A. *The rights of infants.* New York: Columbia University Press, 1943.

Richard, R. Alcoholism. *Boston Sunday Globe*, February 2, 1969.

Richards, J. M., Jr., & Gottfredson, G. D. Geographic distribution of U. S. psychologists. *American Psychologist*, 1978, *33*, 1–9.

Ricks, D. F., & Nameche, G. Symbiosis, sacrifice and schizophrenia. *Mental Hygiene*, 1966, *50*, 541–551.

Riesman, D. *The lonely crowd: A study of the changing American character.* New Haven: Yale University Press, 1950.

Riley, V. Mouse mammary tumors: Alteration of incidence as apparent function of stress. *Science*, 1975, *189*, 465–467.

Rimland, B. *Infantile autism.* New York: Appleton-Century-Crofts, 1964.

Rioch, M. J., Elkes, C., Flint, A. A., Usdansky, B. S., Newman, R. G., & Silber, E. National Institute of Mental Health pilot study in training of mental health counselors. *American Journal of Orthopsychiatry*, 1963, *33*, 678–689.

Robins, E., & Guze, S. B. Establishment of diagnostic validity in psychiatric illness: Its application to schizophrenia. *American Journal of Psychiatry*, 1970, *126*, 983–987.

Robins, L. N. *Deviant children grown up*. Baltimore: Williams & Wilkins, 1966.

Robinson, N. M., & Robinson, H. B. *The mentally retarded child: A psychological approach* (2nd ed.). New York: McGraw-Hill, 1976.

Rodale, J. I. *If you must smoke*. Emmaus, Penn.: Rodale Books, 1970.

Rodin, S. S. Psychodynamic aspects of school phobia. *Comprehensive Psychiatry*, 1967, *8*, 119–128.

Rogers, C. R. *Counseling and psychotherapy*. Boston: Houghton Mifflin, 1942.

Rogers, C. R. *Client-centered therapy*. Boston: Houghton Mifflin, 1951.

Rogers, C. R. The necessary and sufficient conditions of therapeutic personality change. *Journal of Consulting Psychology*, 1957, *21*, 95–103.

Rogers, C. R., & Dymond, R. F. *Psychotherapy and personality change*. Chicago: University of Chicago Press, 1954.

Rolf, J. E., & Garmezy, N. The school performance of children vulnerable to behavior pathology. In D. F. Ricks, A. Thomas, & M. Roff (Eds.), *Life history research in psychopathology* (Vol. 3). Minneapolis: University of Minnesota Press, 1974.

Rolf, J. E., & Hasazi, J. E. Identification of preschool children at risk and some guidelines for primary intervention. In G. W. Albee & J. M. Joffe (Eds.), *Primary prevention of psychopathology* (Vol. 1 — The issues). Hanover, N.H.: The University Press of New England, 1977.

Rose, S. D. *Group therapy: A behavioral approach*. Englewood Cliffs, N.J.: Prentice-Hall, 1977.

Rosenman, R. H., Brand, R. J., Jenkins, D., Friedman, M., Straus, R., & Wurm, H. Coronary heart disease in the Western Collaborative Group study. *Journal of the American Medical Association*, 1975, *223*, 872–877.

Rosenthal, D. Genetic research in the schizophrenic syndrome. In R. Cancro (Ed.), *The schizophrenic reactions*. New York: Brunner/Mazel, 1970, pp. 245–258.

Rosenthal, D. Wender, P. H., Kety, S. S., Schulsinger, F., Welner, J., & Ostergaard, L. Schizophrenics' offspring reared in adoptive homes. In D. Rosenthal & S. S. Kety (Eds.), *The transmission of schizophrenia*. Oxford: Pergamon Press, 1968, pp. 377–391.

Rosner, B. S. Brain functions. *Annual Review of Psychology*, 1970, *21*, 555–594.

Ross, A. B. A schizophrenic child and his mother. *Journal of Abnormal and Social Psychology*, 1955, *51*, 133–139.

Rotter, J. B. Generalized expectancies for internal versus external control of reinforcement. *Psychology Monographs*, 1966, *80*, No. 1.

Royal College of Physicians of London. *Smoking and health now.* London: Pitman Medical, 1971.

Ruitenbeek, H. M. *The new group therapies.* New York: Avon Books, 1970.

Rush, B. *Medical inquiries and observations upon the diseases of the mind.* Philadelphia: Kimber & Richardson, 1812.

Russell, G. K. *Marihuana today: A compilation of medical findings for the layman.* New York: The Myrin Institute, 1978.

Rutter, M. Sex differences in children's responses to family stress. In E. J. Anthony & C. Koupernick (Eds.), *The child in his family* (Vol. 1). New York: Wiley, 1970.

Rutter, M. The development of infantile autism. *Psychological Medicine*, 1974, *4*, 147–163.

Rutter, M. *Helping troubled children.* New York: Plenum Press, 1975.

Rutter, M., & Schopler, E. (Eds.). *Autism: A reappraisal of concepts and treatment.* New York: Plenum, 1978.

Ryan, W. *Distress in the city.* Cleveland: Case Western Reserve University Press, 1969.

Rychlak, J. F. *The psychology of rigorous humanism.* New York: Wiley, 1977.

Rynders, J. E., & Horrobin, J. M. Project EDGE: The University of Minnesota's communication stimulation program for Down's Syndrome infants. In B. Z. Friedlander, G. M. Sterritt, & G. E. Kirk (Eds.), *Exceptional infant* (Vol. 3). New York: Brunner/Mazel, 1975, pp. 173–192.

Rynders, J. E., Spiker, D., & Horrobin, J. M. Underestimating the educability of Down's Syndrome children: Examination of methodological problems in recent literature. *American Journal of Mental Deficiency*, 1978, *82*, 440–448.

Sachar, E. J. Corticosteroid responses to psychotherapy of depressives. *Archives of General Psychiatry*, 1967, *16*, 461–470.

Saghir, M. T., & Robins, E. Male and female homosexuality: Natural history. *Comprehensive Psychiatry*, 1971, *12*, 503–510.

Salzman, C. Electroconvulsive therapy. In A. M. Nicholi, Jr. (Ed.), *The Harvard guide to modern psychiatry.* Cambridge, Mass.: Harvard University Press, 1978, pp. 471–479.

Salzman, L. Obsessions and phobias. *International Journal of Psychiatry*, 1968, *6*, 451–476.

Sampson, A. *The sovereign state of ITT.* New York: Stein & Day, 1973.

Sandgrund, A., Gaines, R. W., & Green, A. H. Child abuse and mental retardation: A problem of cause and effect. *American Journal of Mental Deficiency*, 1974, *79*, 327–330.

Sanford, N., & Comstock, C. (Eds.). *Sanctions for evil.* San Francisco: Jossey-Bass, 1971.

Sarason, I. G., Johnson, J. H., & Siegel, J. M. Assessing the impact of life changes: Development of the Life Experiences Survey. *Journal of Consulting and Clinical Psychology*, 1978, *46*, 932–946.

Sarason, S. B., Davidson, K. S., Lighthall, F. F., Waite, R. R., & Ruebush, B. K. *Anxiety in elementary school children.* New York: Wiley, 1960.

Sarason, S. B., & Doris, J. *Psychological problems in mental deficiency* (4th ed.). New York: Harper & Row, 1969.

Sarbin, T. R. The concept of role-taking. *Sociometry*, 1943, *6*, 273–285.

Sargent, J. D., Green, E. E., & Walters, E. D. The use of autogenic feedback training in a pilot study of migraine and tension headaches. *Headache*, 1970, *12*, 120–124.

Sassenrath, E. N., Golub, M. S., Soo, G. P., & Chapman, L. F. Long-term chronic exposure to delta-9-THC: Reproductive deficit and offspring responsiveness in primates. In G. G. Nahas & W. D. M. Paton (Eds.), *Marihuana: Biological effects.* New York: Pergamon Press, 1979.

Satir, V. *Conjoint family therapy: A guide to theory and technique* (Rev. ed.). Palo Alto, Calif.: Science and Behavior Books, 1967.

Savin, H. A. Multi-media group treatment with socially inept adolescents. *The Clinical Psychologist*, 1976, *29*, 14–17.

Saxe, J. G. The blind men and the elephant: A Hindoo fable. In *The poems of John Godfrey Saxe.* Boston: James R. Osgood, 1873.

Schacht, T., & Nathan, P. E. But is it good for the psychologists? Appraisal and status of DSM-III. *American Psychologist*, 1977, *32*, 1017–1025.

Schachter, J. Pain, fear and anger in hypertensives and normatensives. *Psychosomatic Medicine*, 1957, *19*, 17–29.

Schachter, S. Nicotine regulation in heavy and light smokers. *Journal of Experimental Psychology: General*, 1977, *106*, 5–12.

Schachter, S., Silverstein, B., & Perlik, D. Psychological and pharmacological explanations of smoking under stress. *Journal of Experimental Psychology: General*, 1977, *106*, 31–40.

Schaefer, C. E., & Millman, H. L. *Therapies for children: A handbook of effective treatments for problem behaviors.* San Francisco: Jossey-Bass, 1977.

Schaffer, H. R. *The growth of sociability.* Baltimore: Penguin Books, 1971.

Schildkraut, J. J. The catecholamine hypothesis of affective disorders: A review of supporting evidence. *American Journal of Psychiatry*, 1965, *122*, 509–522.

Schildkraut, J. J. The biochemistry of affective disorders: A brief summary. In A. M. Nicholi, Jr. (Ed.), *The Harvard guide to modern psychiatry.* Cambridge, Mass.: Harvard University Press, 1978, pp. 81–91.

Schneidman, E. S., Farberow, N., & Litman, R. *The psychology of suicide.* New York: Science House, 1970.

Schon, M. Prophylactic lithium maintenance treatment in recurrent endogenous affective disorders. In S. Gershon & B. Shopsin (Eds.), *Lithium: Its role in psychiatric research and treatment.* New York: Plenum Press, 1973.

Schooler, C., & Feldman, S. E. *Experimental studies of schizophrenia.* Goleta, Calif.: Psychonomic Press, 1967.

Schreiber, D. (Ed.). *Profile of the school dropout.* New York: Alfred A. Knopf, 1968.

Schulsinger, H. A 10-year follow-up of children of schizophrenic mothers: Clinical assessment. *Acta Psychiatrica Scandinavica*, 1976, *53*, 371–386.

Schulz, C. G., & Kilgalen, R. K. *Case studies in schizophrenia.* New York: Basic Books, 1969.

Schutz, W. D. *Joy: Expanding human awareness.* New York: Grove Press, 1967.

Schwab, J. J., Fennell, E. B., & Warheit, G. J. The epidemiology of psychosomatic disorders. *Psychosomatics*, 1974, *15*, 88–93.

Schwab, J. J., McGinnis, N. H., Norris, L. B., & Schwab, R. B. Psychosomatic medicine and the contemporary social scene. *American Journal of Psychiatry*, 1970, *126*, 1632–1642.

Schwartz, G. E. Biofeedback as therapy: Some theoretical and practical issues. *American Psychologist,* 1973, 28, 666–672.

Schwitzgebel, R. Short-term operant conditioning of adolescent offenders on socially relevant variables. *Journal of Abnormal Psychology*, 1967, *72*, 134–142.

Scott, D., & Goldberg, H. L. The phenomenon of self-perpetuation in Synanon-type drug treatment programs. *Hospital and Community Psychiatry*, 1973, *24*, 231–233.

Scott, J. C. *Children in the shadows.* Philadelphia: J. B. Lippincott, 1960.

Scott, J. E., & Vandiver, R. D. The use of discretion in punishing convicted adult offenders. In M. Riedel & T. P. Thornberg (Eds.), *Crime and delinquency: Dimensions of deviance.* New York: Praeger, 1974, pp. 191–208.

Sears, R. R. Experimental studies of projection: I. Attribution of traits. *Journal of Social Psychology*, 1936, *7*, 151–163.

Seevers, M. H. Drug dependence and drug abuse: A world problem. *The Pharmacologist*, 1970, *12*, 172–181.

Seligman, M. E. P. *Helplessness: On depression, development and death.* San Francisco: Freeman, 1975.

Seltzer, B., & Frazier, S. H. Organic mental disorders. In A. M. Nicholi, Jr. (Ed.), *The Harvard guide to modern psychiatry.* Cambridge, Mass.: Harvard University Press, 1978, pp. 297–318.

Selye, H. *The stress of life.* New York: McGraw-Hill, 1956.

Selye, H. *Stress without distress.* New York: Lippincott, 1975.

Semelaigne, R. *Les grands aliénistes francais* (Vol. 1). Paris: 1930.

721

Semmes, J., Weinstein, S., Ghent, L., & Teuber, H. L. *Somatosensory changes after penetrating brain wounds in man.* Cambridge, Mass.: Harvard University Press, 1960.

Seward, G. H. *Sex and the social order.* New York: McGraw-Hill, 1946.

Seymour, W. N., Jr. *Why justice fails.* New York: William Morrow, 1973.

Shakow, D. Segmental set: The adaptive process in schizophrenia. *American Psychologist,* 1977, *32,* 129-139.

Shapiro, A. P. Essential hypertension—why idiopathic? *American Journal of Medicine,* 1973, *54,* 1-5.

Shapiro, D. *Neurotic styles.* New York: Basic Books, 1965.

Share, J. B. Review of drug treatment for Down's Syndrome persons. *American Journal of Mental Deficiency,* 1976, *80,* 388-393.

Shaw, C. R. *The jack roller.* Chicago: University of Chicago Press, 1930.

Sheehan, D. V., & Hackett, T. P. Psychosomatic disorders. In A. M. Nicholi, Jr. (Ed.), *The Harvard guide to modern psychiatry.* Cambridge, Mass.: Belknap Press, 1978, pp. 319-353.

Shershow, J. C. (Ed.). *Schizophrenia: Science and practice.* Cambridge, Mass.: Harvard University Press, 1978.

Sherwin, I., & Geschwind, N. Neural substrates of behavior. In A. M. Nicholi, Jr. (Ed.), *The Harvard guide to modern psychiatry.* Cambridge, Mass.: Harvard University Press, 1978, pp. 59-80.

Short, J. F. (Ed.). *Modern criminals.* Chicago, Aldine, 1970.

Short, J. F., & Strodtbeck, F. L. *Group process and gang delinquency.* Chicago: University of Chicago Press, 1965.

Siegelman, M. Parental background of male homosexuals and heterosexuals. *Archives of Sexual Behavior,* 1974, *3,* 3-18.

Silber, E., Hamburg, D. A., Coehlo, G. V., Murphy, E. B., Rosenberg, M., & Pearlin, L. D. Adaptive behavior in competent adolescents: Coping with the anticipation of college. *Archives of General Psychiatry,* 1961, *5,* 354-365.

Silverberg, W. V. *Childhood experience and personal destiny.* New York: Springer, 1952.

Silverman, C. *The epidemiology of depression.* Baltimore: Johns Hopkins Press, 1968.

Simeons, A. T. W. *Man's presumptuous brain.* New York: E. P. Dutton, 1962.

Skeels, H. M. Adult status of children with contrasting early life expectancies. *Monographs of the Society for Research in Child Development,* 1966, *31,* 3, Ser. No. 5.

Skeels, H. M., & Dye, H. B. A study of the effects of differential stimulation on mentally retarded children. *Proceedings of the American Association on Mental Deficiency,* 1939, *44,* 114-136.

Skinner, B. F. *Walden two.* New York: Macmillan, 1952.

Skinner, B. F. *Science and human behavior.* New York: Macmillan, 1953.

Skinner, W. I. *Tobacco and health: The other side of the coin.* New York: Vantage Press, 1970.

Slaby, A. E., & Wyatt, R. J. *Dementia in the presenium.* Springfield, Ill.: Charles C. Thomas, 1974.

Slack, C. W. Experimenter-subject psychotherapy: A new method of introducing office treatment for unreachable cases. *Mental Hygiene,* 1960, *44,* 238–256.

Slater, E. T. O. Diagnosis of "hysteria." *British Medical Journal,* 1965, *1,* 1395–1399.

Slater, E. T. O., & Cowie, V. *The genetics of mental disorders.* London: Pergamon Press, 1971.

Slater, E. T. O., & Glithero, E. A follow-up of patients diagnosed as suffering from "hysteria." *Journal of Psychosomatic Research,* 1965, *9,* 9–13.

Slavson, S. R. *An introduction to group therapy.* New York: Commonwealth Fund, 1943.

Slavson, S. R. Group psychotherapies. In J. L. McCary & D. E. Sheer, *Six approaches to psychotherapy.* New York: The Dryden Press, 1955, Chapter 3.

Sloane, R. B. The converging paths of behavior therapy and psychotherapy. *International Journal of Psychiatry,* 1969, *7,* 493–503.

Smart, R. G., & Fejer, D. Drug use among adolescents and their parents: Closing the generation gap in mood modification. *Journal of Abnormal Psychology,* 1972, *79,* 153–160.

Smith, D. C., Jr. *The Mafia mystique.* New York: Basic Books, 1975.

Smith, D. E. A physician's view of the adolescent drug scene. In C. J. D. Zarafonetis (Ed.), *Drug abuse: Proceedings of the international conference.* Philadelphia: Lea & Febiger, 1972, pp. 271–275.

Smith, D. W., & Wilson, A. A. *The child with Down's Syndrome (mongolism).* Philadelphia: Saunders, 1973.

Smith, R. C. Speed and violence: Compulsive methamphetamine abuse and criminality in the Haight-Asbury district. In C. J. D. Zarafonetis (Ed.), *Drug abuse: Proceedings of the international conference.* Philadelphia: Lea & Febiger, 1972, pp. 435–448.

Snyder, S. H. *Madness and the brain.* New York: McGraw-Hill, 1974. (a)

Snyder, S. H. Catecholamines as mediations of drug effects in schizophrenia. In F. O. Schmitt & F. G. Worden (Eds.), *The neurosciences: Third study program.* Cambridge, Mass.: M.I.T. Press, 1974. (b)

Sobey, F. *The non-professional revolution in mental health.* New York: Columbia University Press, 1970.

Sollod, R. N. Behavioral and psychodynamic dimension of the new sex therapy. *Journal of Sex and Marital Therapy,* 1975, *4,* 335–340.

Solomon, R. L., Turner, L. H., & Lessac, M. S. Some effects of delay of punishment on resistance to temptation in dogs. *Journal of Personality and Social Psychology,* 1968, *8,* 233–238.

Spanos, N. Witchcraft in histories of psychiatry: A critical analysis and an alternative conceptualization. *Psychological Bulletin*, 1978, *85*, 417–439.

Spaulding, W. B. The psychosomatic approach in the practice of medicine. *International Journal of Psychiatry in Medicine*, 1975, *6*, 169–181.

Spitz, R. A. Hospitalism: An inquiry into the genesis of psychiatric conditions in early childhood. *Psychoanalytic Study of the Child*, 1945, *1*, 53–74.

Srole, L., Langner, T. S., Michael, S. T., Opler, M. K., & Rennie, T. A. C. *Mental health in the metropolis: The Midtown study* (Vol. 1). New York: McGraw-Hill, 1962.

Stachnik, T. J. The case against criminal penalties for illicit drug use. *American Psychologist*, 1972, *27*, 637–642.

Stallibrass, A. *The self-respecting child*. New York: Warner Books, 1979.

Stampfl, T. G., & Levis, D. J. Essentials of implosive therapy: A learning theory based on psychodynamic behavioral therapy. *Journal of Abnormal Psychology*, 1967, *72*, 496–503.

Stanton, A. H., & Schwartz, M. S. *The mental hospital*. New York: Basic Books, 1954.

Starr, A. *Psychodrama: Rehearsal for living*. Chicago: Nelson-Hall, 1977.

Steadman, H. J., & Braff, J. Incompetency to stand trial: The easy way in? In M. Riedel & T. P. Thornberry (Eds.), *Crime and delinquency: Dimensions of deviance*. New York: Praeger, 1974, pp. 178–190.

Steen, E. B., & Price, J. H. *Human sex and sexuality*. New York: Wiley, 1977.

Stefanis, C. N., & Issidorides, M. R. Cellular effects of chronic cannabis use in man. In G. G. Nahas, W. D. M. Paton, & J. E. Idanpaan-Heikkila (Eds.), *Marihuana: Chemistry, biochemistry and cellular effects*. New York: Springer, 1976, pp. 533–550.

Stein, M. Etiology and mechanisms in the development of asthma. In J. H. Nodine & J. H. Moyer (Eds.), *Psychosomatic Medicine*. Philadelphia: Lea & Febriger, 1962, pp. 149–156.

Steiner, J. A questionnaire study of risk-taking in psychiatric patients. *British Journal of Medical Psychology*, 1972, *45*, 365–374.

Stekel, W. *Sexual aberrations*. New York: Liveright Publishing Co., 1930.

Stephan, W. Parental relationships and early social experiences of activist male homosexuals and male heterosexuals. *Journal of Abnormal Psychology*, 1973, *82*, 506–513.

Stephánsson, J. G., Messina, J. A., & Meyerowitz, S. Hysterical neurosis, conversion type: Clinical and epidemiological considerations. *Acta Psychiatrica Scandinavica*, 1976, *53*, 119–138.

Stephens, J. H., & Astrup, C. Prognosis in "process" and "non-process" schizophrenia. *American Journal of Psychiatry*, 1963, *119*, 945–954.

Stern, C. *Principles of human genetics* (2nd ed.). San Francisco: W. H. Freeman, 1960.

Stern, W. *Psychology of early childhood*. New York: Holt, Rinehart & Winston, 1930.

724

Stevenson, H. W. *Children's learning*. New York: Appleton-Century-Crofts, 1972.

Stieper, D. R., & Wiener, D. N. *Dimensions of psychotherapy: An experimental and clinical approach*. Chicago: Aldine, 1965.

Stoller, R. J. Sexual deviations. In F. A. Beach (Ed.), *Human sexuality in four perspectives*. Baltimore: Johns Hopkins University Press, 1977, pp. 190-214.

Stoller, R. P. *Sex and gender*. New York: Science House, 1968.

Stone, A. A., & Stone, S. S. (Eds.). *The abnormal personality through literature*. New York: Prentice-Hall, 1966.

Stone, R. A., & DeLeo, J. Psycotherapeutic control of hypertension. *New England Journal of Medicine*, 1976, *294*, 80-84.

Straub, E. *The development of prosocial behavior in children*. Morristown, N.J.: General Learning Press, 1975.

Strauss, A. A., & Kephart, N. C. *Psychopathology and education of the brain-injured child*. New York: Grune & Stratton, 1955.

Strauss, J. S., & Carpenter, W. T. Characteristic symptoms and outcome in schizophrenia. *Archives of General Psychiatry*, 1974, *30*, 429-434.

Strecker, E. A., & Ebaugh, F. G. *Practical clinical psychiatry* (5th ed.). Philadelphia: Blakiston, 1940.

Strupp, H. H., Fox, R. E., & Lessler, K. *Patients view their psychotherapy*. Baltimore: The Johns Hopkins Press, 1969.

Strupp, H. H., Hadley, S. W., & Gomes-Schwartz, B. *Psychotherapy for better or worse: The problem of negative effects*. New York: Jason Aronson, 1977.

Subotnik, L. Spontaneous remission: Fact or artifact? *Psychological Bulletin*, 1972, *77*, 32-48.

Sullivan, C. E., Grant, M. Q., & Grant, J. D. The development of interpersonal maturity: Application to delinquency. *Psychiatry*, 1957, *20*, 373-385.

Sullivan, H. S. *The interpersonal theory of psychiatry*. New York: Norton, 1953.

Sullivan, H. S. *Schizophrenia as a human process*. New York: Norton, 1962.

Summers, F., & Walsh, F. The nature of the symbiotic bond between mother and schizophrenic. *American Journal of Orthopsychiatry*, 1977, *47*, 484-494.

Sutherland, E. H. *White collar crime*. New York: Holt, Rinehart & Winston, 1961.

Sutherland, E. H., & Cressey, D. R. *Criminology* (9th ed.). Philadelphia: J. B. Lippincott, 1974.

Sutherland, E. H., & Cressey, D. Learning and transmitting criminal behavior. In L. Radzinowicz & M. E. Wolfgang (Eds.), *Crime and justice* (2nd ed.). New York: Basic Books, 1977, pp. 521-527.

Sutherland, J. D. Notes on psychoanalytic group therapy: I. Therapy and training. *Psychiatry*, 1952, *15*, 111-117.

725

Swinehart, J. W. Changes over time in student reactions to the Surgeon General's Report on Smoking and Health. *American Journal of Public Health*, 1966, *56*, 2023-2027.

Switzer, A. *Drug abuse and drug treatment.* California Youth Authority, 1974.

Szalita, A. B. Psychodynamics of disorders of the involutional age. In S. Arieti (Ed.), *American handbook of psychiatry.* New York: Basic Books, 1966.

Szasz, T. S. The psychiatric classification of behavior: A strategy of personal constraint. In L. D. Eron (Ed.), *The classification of behavior disorders.* Chicago: Aldine, 1966.

Taggart, P., Carruthers, M., & Somerville, W. Electrocardiogram, plasma catecholamines and lipids, and their modification by oxprenolol when speaking before an audience. *Lancet*, 1973, *2*, 341-346.

Tarjan, G., Wright, S. W., Eyman, R. K., & Keeran, C. V. Natural history of mental retardation: Some aspects of epidemiology. *American Journal of Mental Deficiency*, 1973, *77*, 369-379.

Taub, E. Self-regulation of human tissue temperature. In G. E. Schwartz & J. Beatty (Eds.), *Biofeedback: Theory and research.* New York: Academic Press, 1977, pp. 265-300.

Taylor, J. A. A personality scale of manifest anxiety. *Journal of Abnormal and Social Psychology*, 1953, *48*, 285-290.

Templer, D. I., & Lester, D. Conversion disorders: A review of research findings. *Comprehensive Psychiatry*, 1974, *15*, 285-294.

Thomas, A., Chess, S., Birch, H., & Hertzig, M. E. A longitudinal study of primary reaction patterns in children. *Comprehensive Psychiatry,* 1960, *1*, 103-112.

Thomas, A., Chess, S., Birch, H. G., Hertzig, M. E., & Korn, S. *Behavioral individuality in early childhood.* New York: New York University Press, 1963.

Thomas, L. The health care system. *New England Journal of Medicine*, 1975, *293*, 1245-1246.

Thompson, N., Schwartz, D., McCandless, B., & Edwards, D. Parent-child relationships and sexual identity in male and female homosexuals and heterosexuals. *Journal of Consulting and Clinical Psychology*, 1973, *41*, 120-127.

Thompson, T., & Grabowski, J. (Eds.). *Behavior modification of the mentally retarded* (2nd ed.). New York: Oxford University Press, 1977.

Thorne, F. C. A critique of non-directive methods of psychotherapy. *Journal of Abnormal and Social Psychology*, 1944, *39*, 459-470.

Tizard, J. The role of social institutions in the causation, prevention and alleviation of mental retardation. In H. C. Haywood (Ed.), *Socio-cultural aspects of mental retardation.* New York: Appleton-Century-Crofts, 1970.

Tolman, E. C. *Purposive behavior in animals and men.* New York: Appleton-Century-Crofts, 1932.

Tolman, E. C. Cognitive maps in rats and men. *Psychological Review,* 1948, *55,* 189-208.

Tooth, G. C., & Newton, M. A. Leucotomy in England and Wales, 1942-1954. *Ministry of Health reports on public and medical subjects.* London: H. M. Stationery Office, 1961, No. 104.

Tredgold, A. F. *A textbook of mental deficiency* (6th ed.). Baltimore: Wm. Wood, 1937.

Treisman, M. Mind, body and behavior: Control systems and their disturbances. In P. London & D. Rosenhan (Eds.), *Foundations of abnormal psychology.* New York: Holt, Rinehart & Winston, 1968, pp. 460-518.

Trieschman, A. E., Whittaker, J. K., & Brendtro, L. K. *The other 23 hours.* Chicago: Aldine, 1969.

Tuerk, K., Fish, I., & Ransohoff, J. Head injury. In S. Arieti (Chief Ed.), *American handbook of psychiatry* (2nd ed.-vol. 4). New York: Basic Books, 1975, pp. 166-181.

Ullmann, L. P., & Krasner, L. (Eds.). *Case studies in behavior modification.* New York: Holt, Rinehart & Winston, 1965.

Ullmann, L. P., & Krasner, L. *A psychological approach to abnormal behavior* (2nd ed.). Englewood Cliffs, N.J.: Prentice-Hall, 1975.

Umbarger, C. C., Dalsimer, J. S., Morrison, A. P., & Breggin, P. R. *College students in a mental hospital.* New York: Grune & Stratton, 1962.

U. S. Bureau of the Census. *Statistical abstracts of the United States: 1970* (91st ed.). Washington, D. C., 1970.

U. S. Chamber of Commerce. *A handbook on white collar crime.* Washington, D. C.: U. S. Chamber of Commerce, 1974.

U. S. Department of Health, Education and Welfare. *Health, education and welfare trends,* 1966-67 ed., Part 1. Washington, D.C.: Government Printing Office, 1968.

U. S. Department of Health, Education, and Welfare. *Asthma.* NIH Publication No. 79-525. Washington, D.C.: Government Printing Office, 1979.

U. S. Department of Justice. *Uniform crime reprts for the United States—1977.* Washington, D. C.: U. S. Government Printing Office, 1978.

U. S. Department of Justice, LEAA. *Criminal victimization surveys in the nation's five largest cities.* Washington, D. C.: U.S. Government Printing Office, 1975.

U. S. Public Health Service. *Smoking and health,* Report of the Advisory Committee to the Surgeon General of the Public Health Service. Washington, D. C.: U. S. Department of Health, Education and Welfare, 1964.

U. S. Public Health Service. *Students and drug abuse.* Washington, D. C.: Government Printing Office, 1969.

U. S. Department of Justice. *Fact sheets.* Washington, D. C.: Government Printing Office, 1970. (a)

U. S. Public Health Service. *LSD: Some questions and answers.* Washington, D. C.: U. S. Department of Health, Education and Welfare, 1970. (b)

U. S. Public Health Service. *Alcohol and health, First special report from the Secretary of Health, Education and Welfare.* Washington, D. C.: Government Printing Office, 1971.

U. S. Public Health Service. *Marihuana and health, Second annual report to Congress from the Secretary of Health, Education and Welfare.* Washington, D.C.: Government Printing Office, 1972.

Uzgiris, I. C. Sociocultural factors in cognitive development. In H. C. Haywood (Ed.), *Socio-cultural aspects of mental retardation.* New York: Appleton-Century-Crofts, 1970, pp. 39-46.

Vachon, L., & Rich, E. S., Jr. Visceral learning and asthma. *Psychosomatic Medicine,* 1976, *38,* 122-130.

Vaillant, G. E. The prediction of recovery in schizophrenia. *Journal of Nervous and Mental Disease,* 1962, *135,* 534-543.

Vaillant, G. E. Prospective prediction of schizophrenic remission. *Archives of General Psychiatry,* 1964, *11,* 509-519.

Vaillant, G. E. Sociopathy as a human process. *Archives of General Psychiatry,* 1975, *32,* 178-183.

Van Buskirk, S. S. A two-phase perspective on the treatment of anorexia nervosa. *Psychological Bulletin,* 1977, *84,* 529-538.

van Praag, H. M. *Depression and schizophrenia: A contribution on their chemical pathologies.* New York: Spectrum Publications, 1977.

Victor, M. Alcoholism. In A. B. Baker & L. H. Baker (Eds.), *Clinical neurology* (Vol. 2). Hagerstown, Maryland: Harper & Row, 1975.

Vogt, D. K. *Literacy among youths 12-17 years.* U.S. Department of Health, Education and Welfare Publication No. (HRA) 74-1613. Washington, D. C.: U. S. Government Printing Office, 1973.

von Mering, O., & King, S. H. *Remotivating the mental patient.* New York: Russell Sage Foundation, 1957.

Wachtel, P. L. *Psychoanalysis and behavior therapy: Toward an integration.* New York: Basic Books, 1977.

Wagner, N. N. (Ed.). *Perspectives on human sexuality: Psychological, social and cultural research findings.* New York: Behavioral Publications, 1974.

Wakefield, J. (Ed.). *Influencing smoking behavior,* Report of the Committee for Research in Smoking Habits to the Norwegian Cancer Society. Geneva: International Union Against Cancer, 1969.

Waldfogel, S., Coolidge, J. C., & Hahn, P. B. The development, meaning and management of school phobia. *American Journal of Orthopsychiatry,* 1957, *27,* 754-780.

Wang, H. S., Obrist, W. D., & Busse, E. W. Neurophysiological correlates of the intellectual function of elderly persons living in the community. *American Journal of Psychiatry,* 1970, *126,* 1205-1212.

Waring, M., & Ricks, D. F. Family patterns of children who became adult schizophrenics. *Journal of Nervous and Mental Disease,* 1965, *140,* 351-364.

Watson, J. B., & Rayner, R. Conditioned emotional reactions. *Journal of Experimental Psychology*, 1920, *3*, 1–14.

Watson, R. I. *The clinical method in psychology*. New York: Harper & Row, 1951.

Watt, N. F. Patterns of childhood social development in adult schizophrenics. *Archives of General Psychiatry*, 1978, *35*, 160–165.

Watt, N. F., Fryer, J. H., Lewine, R. R. J., & Prentky, R. A. Toward longitudinal conceptions of psychiatric disorder. In B. A. Maher (Ed.), *Progress in experimental personality research* (Vol. 9). New York: Academic Press, 1979, pp. 199–283.

Watt, N. F., & Lubensky, A. W. Chilhood roots of schizophrenia. *Journal of Consulting and Clinical Psychology*, 1976, *44*, 363–375.

Watt, N. F., & Nicholi, A. M., Jr. Early death of a parent as an etiological factor in schizophrenia. *American Journal of Orthopsychiatry*, 1979, *49*, 465–473.

Watzlawick, P., Beavin, J. H., & Jackson, D. D. *Pragmatics of human communication*. New York: Norton, 1967.

Waxler, N. E. Is outcome for schizophrenia better in non-industrial societies? The Case of Sri Lanka. *Journal of Nervous and Mental Disease*, 1979, *167*, 144–158.

Weinberg, H., & Hire, A. W. *A casebook in abnormal psychology*. New York: Alfred A. Knopf, 1956.

Weiner, H. *Psychobiology and human disease*. New York: Elsevier North-Holland, 1977.

Weiner, H., Thaler, M., Reiser, M. F., & Mirsky, I. A. Etiology of duodenal ulcer: I. Relation of specific psychological characteristics to rate of gastric secretion (serum pepsinogen). *Psychosomatic Medicine*, 1957, *19*, 1–10.

Weinstein, E. A., Eck, R. A., & Lyerly, O. G. Conversion hysteria in Appalachia. *Psychiatry*, 1969, *32*, 334–341.

Weintraub, S., Liebert, D., & Neale, J. M. Teacher ratings of children vulnerable to psychopathology. *American Journal of Orthopsychiatry*, 1975, *45*, 838–845.

Weintraub, S., Prinz, R. J., & Neale, J. M. Peer evaluations of the competence of children vulnerable to psychopathology. *Journal of Abnormal Child Psychology*, 1978, *6*, 461–473.

Weiss, E., & English, O. S. *Psychosomatic Medicine* (3rd ed.). Philadelphia: W. B. Saunders, 1957, pp. 246–249.

Weiss, J. M. Influence of psychological variables on stress-induced pathology. In R. Porter & J. Knight (Eds.), *Psychology, emotion and psychosomatic illness*. New York: Associated Scientific Publishers, 1972, pp. 253–265.

Weissman, M. M., Klerman, G. L., & Paykel, E. S. Clinical evaluation of hostility in depression. *American Journal of Psychiatry*, 1971, *128*, 261–266.

Weissman, M. M., Klerman, G. L., Paykel, E. S., Prusoff, B., & Hanson, B.

Treatment effects on the social adjustment of depressed patients. *Archives of General Psychiatry*, 1974, *30*, 771–778.

Wender, P. H. *Minimal brain dysfunction in children.* New York: Wiley, 1971.

Wessman, A. E., & Ricks, D. F. *Mood and personality.* New York: Holt, Rinehart & Winston, 1966.

Whalen, R. E. Brain mechanisms controlling sexual behavior. In F. A. Beach (Ed.), *Human sexuality in four perspectives.* Baltimore: Johns Hopkins University Press, 1977, pp. 215–246.

Wheeler, S., Cottrell, L. S., Jr., & Romasco, A. Juvenile delinquency: Its prevention and control. *Task Force Report: Juvenile Delinquency and Youth Crime*, Report to the President's Commission on Law Enforcement and Administration of Justice. Washington, D. C.: Government Printing Office, 1967.

White, R. W. Motivation reconsidered: The concept of competence. *Psychological Review*, 1959, *66*, 297–333.

White, R. W. Competence and the psychosexual stages of development. In M. Jones (Ed.), *Nebraska symposium on motivation.* Lincoln: University of Nebraska Press, 1960.

White, R. W. *The enterprise of living: Growth and organization of personality.* New York: Holt, Rinehart & Winston, 1972.

White, R. W. Strategies of adaptation: An attempt at systematic description. In G. V. Coehlo, D. A. Hamburg, & J. E. Adams (Eds.), *Coping and adaptation.* New York: Basic Books, 1974, Chapter 4.

White, R. W. *Lives in progress* (3rd ed.). New York: Holt, Rinehart & Winston, 1975.

White, R. W. *The enterprise of living: A view of personal growth* (2nd ed.). New York: Holt, Rinehart & Winston, 1976.

White, W. A. *Outlines of psychiatry* (13th ed.). New York: Nervous and Mental Disease Publishing Co., 1932.

Whitney, E. D. (Ed.). *World dialogue on alcohol and drug dependence.* Boston: Beacon Press, 1970.

Whitney, G., McClearn, G. E., & DeFries, J. C. Heritability of alcohol preference in laboratory mice and rats. *Journal of Heredity*, 1970, *61*, 165–169.

Whitten, P., & Robertson, I. A way to control heroin addiction. *Boston Sunday Globe*, May 21, 1972.

Whittier, J. R. Mental disorders with Huntington's chorea. In S. Arieti (Chief Ed.), *American handbook of psychiatry* (2nd ed.-vol 4). New York: Basic Books, 1975, pp. 412–417.

Whybrow, P. C., & Mendels, J. Toward a biology of depression: Some suggestions from neurophysiology. *American Journal of Psychiatry*, 1969, *125*, 1491–1500.

Wikler, A., Dixon, J. F., & Parker, J. B., Jr. Brain function in problem children and controls: Psychometric, neurological and electroencephalographic comparisons. *American Journal of Psychiatry*, 1970, *127*, 634–645.

Wilkins, W. Desensitization: Social and cognitive factors underlying the effectiveness of Wolpe's procedure. *Psychological Bulletin*, 1971, *76*, 311–317.

Will, O. A. Schizophrenia: Psychological treatment. In A. M. Freedman, H. I. Kaplan, & B. J. Sadock (Eds.), *Comprehensive textbook of psychiatry*. Baltimore: Williams & Wilkins, 1967.

Winokur, G., Clayton, P., & Reich, T. *Manic depressive illness*. St. Louis: C. V. Mosby, 1969.

Winokur, G., & Reich, T. Two genetic factors in manic-depressive disease. *Comprehensive Psychiatry*, 1970, *11*, 93–99.

Winslow, R. W. (Ed.). *Crime in a free society*. Selections from the Report of the President's Commission on Law Enforcement and Administration of Justice. Belmont, Calif.: Dickenson, 1968.

Winstead, D. K. Coffee consumption among psychiatric inpatients. *American Journal of Psychiatry*, 1976, *133*, 1447–1450.

Wise, J. H. Performance of neurologically impaired children copying geometric designs with sticks. *Perceptual and Motor Skills*, 1968, *26*, 763–772.

Wittenborn, J. R., Smith, J. P., & Wittenborn, S. A. (Eds.). *Communication and drug abuse*. Springfield, Ill.: Charles C. Thomas, 1970.

Wolf, S., & Wolff, H. G. *Human gastric function*. New York: Oxford University Press, 1947.

Wolman, B. B. *Children without childhood*. New York: Grune & Stratton, 1970.

Wolpe, J. *Psychotherapy by reciprocal inhibition*. Stanford, Calif.: Stanford University Press, 1958.

Wolpe, J. *The practice of behavior therapy*. New York: Pergamon Press, 1969.

Woodruff, R. A., Guze, S. B., & Clayton, P. J. Anxiety neurosis among psychiatric outpatients. *Comprehensive Psychiatry*, 1972, *13*, 165–170.

Woodworth, R. S. *Dynamics of behavior*. New York: Holt, Rinehart & Winston, 1958.

World Health Organization. *Seventh report by the Expert Committee on Addiction-Producing Drugs*. Technical Report Series No. 116, 1957.

Wright, R. *Black boy: A record of childhood and youth*. New York: Harper & Row, 1945.

Wright, S. *Applied physiology* (8th ed.). New York: Oxford University Press, 1945.

Wunsch, W. L. Some characteristics of mongoloids evaluated at a clinic for children with retarded mental development. *American Journal of Mental Deficiency*, 1957, *62*, 122–130.

Wynne, L. C., Cromwell, R. L., & Matthyse, S. (Eds.). *The nature of schizophrenia: New approaches to research and treatment*. New York: Wiley, 1978.

Yablonsky, L. *The violent gang*. New York: Macmillan, 1962.

Yablonsky, L. *The tunnel back: Synanon*. New York: Macmillan, 1965.

Yablonsky, L., & Enneis, J. M. Psychodrama theory and practice. In F.

731

Fromm-Reichmann & J. L. Moreno (Eds.), *Progress in psychotherapy* (Vol. 1). New York: Grune & Stratton, 1956.

Yalom, I. D. *The theory and practice of group psychotherapy* (2nd ed.). New York: Basic Books, 1975.

Yando, R., Seitz, V., & Zigler, E. *Imitation: A developmental perspective.* New York: Halsted Press, 1978.

Yolles, S. F., & Kramer, M. Vital statistics. In L. Bellak & L. Loeb (Eds.), *The schizophrenic syndrome.* New York: Grune & Stratton, 1969.

Zagona, S. V. (Ed.). *Studies and issues in smoking behavior.* Tucson: University of Arizona Press, 1967.

Zarafonetis, C. J. D. (Ed.). *Drug abuse: Proceedings of the international conference.* Philadelphia: Lea & Febiger, 1972.

Zax, M., & Cowen, E. L. Research on early detection and prevention of emotional dysfunction in young school children. In C. D. Spielberger, *Current topics in clinical and community psychology.* New York: Academic Press, 1969, pp. 67–108.

Zeithin, B. B. The therapeutic community: Fact or fantasy? *International Journal of Psychiatry,* 1969, 7, 195–212.

Zelson, C. Infant of the addicted mother. *New England Journal of Medicine,* 1973, *288,* 1393–1395.

Ziegler, F. J., & Imboden, J. B. Contemporary conversion reactions: II. A conceptual model. *Archives of General Psychiatry,* 1962, *6,* 279–287.

Zilborg, G., & Henry, G. W. *A history of medical psychology.* New York: Norton, 1941.

Glossary

Abortion The termination of a pregnancy.

Abreaction A full and dramatic release of suppressed emotion associated with some drastic incident in the past; presumed to result in the permanent disappearance of the symptom that had been laid down on that occasion.

Abstinence Voluntarily refraining from something, especially drug or alcohol use.

Abstract attitude A capacity of the total personality to transcend immediately given stimuli, to synthesize conceptually, and to engage in long-term planning.

Accessory symptoms Secondary symptoms of a disorder.

Acting out Overt action (e.g., stealing, lying, or sexual promiscuity) that represents an individual's problems or maladjustment; as used in a psychoanalytic sense, acting out refers to the overt expression in action of underlying repressed conflict.

Adaptive behavior An individual's interaction with the environment that maximizes the benefit and minimizes the harm for the individual.

Adaptive strategy A successful strategy for handling problems in living; an adaptive strategy is characterized by: (1) adequate, relevant information, (2) affect that is supportive instead of disorganizing, and (3) competent action that is discerned and attempted.

Addiction A state of drug use in which a person desires to continue taking a drug and to obtain it at all costs, shows a tendency to increase the dose and/or frequency, manifests some degree of physical dependence and abstinence syndrome, and often carries behavior to a point that is detrimental to society.

Adrenalin A proprietary name for epinephrine, a hormone secreted by the adrenal medulla; a powerful neurochemical, it functionally increases blood pressure, heart rate, and cardiac output.

Affect The subjective part of an emotion often accompanied by physical reactions.

Aggression   The tendency to aim at injury and destruction.

Agitated depression   A form of depression in which a person exhibits agitated behavior, demands a great deal of attention, and experiences high anxiety and guilt.

Agraphia   A type of aphasia characterized by an inability to write.

Alexia   A type of aphasia characterized by an inability to understand written language.

Alienation   Feeling of apartness or lack of relationships.

Alkaline   Any substance having a high pH factor. Opposite of acid.

Allergen   Any substance which causes an allergy.

Ambivalence   The simultaneous existence of two contradictory emotions (such as love and hate).

Amines   A group of organic compounds containing nitrogen; some amines (e.g., norepinephrine, dopamine, serotonin, and histamine) have an important role in central nervous system functioning.

Amnesia   Any kind of pathological forgetting, whether caused by drugs, brain injury, old age, or psychological factors.

Amniocentesis   A simple and reasonably safe diagnostic procedure in which a small amount of amniotic fluid is extracted through the mother's abdomen. The process is highly accurate in the assessment of Down's syndrome and many other gestational abnormalities.

Amphetamine   A synthetic central nervous system stimulant with two popular isomers, dextroamphetamine and methamphetamine; called in slang "pep pills," "bennies," or "speed." When used chronically, amphetamines can lead to irreversible brain damage or paranoid psychosis.

Anencephaly   A developmental anomaly in which the skull is missing and the cerebral hemispheres either are completely missing or reduced to small masses.

Anesthesia   A disorder of sensory processing marked by a complete or partial loss of sensitivity to external stimuli; may be caused by organic or psychological factors.

Angina   A condition in which a person chokes or suffers from suffocative pain in spasms.

Angiograph   An X ray of the blood vessels, requiring the introduction of a dye into the blood stream.

Anhedonic   Lacking a pleasant emotional tone in the appropriate situation.

Animal magnetism   A now-debunked concept (introduced by Mesmer) that referred to a presumed ability of one person to influence another through an invisible fluid; the process was thought to be analogous to that of physical magnetism. (See **Hypnotism**)

Anorexia nervosa   A functional disorder characterized by active refusal of food, extreme loss of body weight, distortion in body image, amenorrhea in women and impotence in men, and occasionally death by starvation.

Anoxia   Deprivation of oxygen in the brain which can cause irreparable damage to nerve cells.

Antibody   Part of the body's defense system which destroys foreign particles in the bloodstream.

Antigen   Protein or carbohydrate which causes the body to make antibodies.

Antihistamine   A substance used to counteract the effects of histamines.

734

Antipsychotic drug Any drug used to treat psychosis.

Antisocial personality disorder Introduced in DSM-III to describe people engaged in asocial or antisocial activity; having failed to respond adequately to the process of socialization, these peoples' activities may range from the flaunting of social mores to murder.

Anxiety A state of apprehension or fear often accompanied by autonomic response such as heart palpitations, difficulty in breathing, sweating, and nausea.

Anxiety disorders A group of disorders in which anxiety is the primary disturbance; anxiety may be actually present (as in panic attacks) or avoided as when one tries to stop or resist one's symptom (e.g., trying to resist a hand-washing compulsion).

Apathy Lack of emotions or an indifference to the surroundings.

Aphasia Partial or complete inability to use language appropriately due to brain damage; aphasia subsumes a number of specific language use disorders, such as alexia and agraphia.

Aphonia The loss of speech or the inability to speak above a whisper resulting from laryngeal dysfunction or from psychological variables.

Aplasia Inadequate development of brain tissue.

Apraxia Inability to engage in a sequence of purposeful movements; the result of a lesion in the motor region of the cortex.

Arteriosclerosis A hardening and thickening of the walls of the blood vessels which reduces the supply of blood to all tissues.

Asocial behavior Behavior without regard to social customs or norms.

Assertiveness training The use of learning principles to teach an individual when and how to express one's feelings and opinions.

Autism Thinking characterized by extreme preoccupation with one's self and motivated by personal needs and desires.

Autohypnosis Self-induction of a hypnotic state.

Autonomic activity Involuntary bodily activity such as heart beat.

Autonomic nervous system One of the major divisions of the nervous system that regulates glandular and visceral processes; it is made up of the sympathetic system, largely mediating emergency responses, and the parasympathetic system, largely mediating restorative processes.

Autopsy An examination to determine the cause of death or the extent of the disease which caused death.

Aversive treatment method A behavioral treatment to reduce the frequency of an unwanted behavior by pairing it with an aversive stimulus.

Avoidance Behavior that allows an individual to prevent the occurrence of some physically or psychologically aversive event; distinguished from escape in which the aversive event occurs and the individual either terminates the aversive event or leaves the aversive situation.

Axon Long fibers connecting neurons.

Barbiturate One of the major narcotics that acts as a central nervous system depressant and produces sedative effects.

Baroreceptor A sensory nerve sensitive to changes in pressure.

735

Basal metabolism The minimum heat production of an organism during rest as measured after fasting.

Behavior therapy A form of psychological intervention that relies on laboratory-demonstrated principles of learning.

Bereavement A complex emotional response (including depression, anger, and guilt) to the loss of an important other.

Biofeedback The use of conditioning techniques to bring previously involuntary processes under voluntary control, for example, heart rate.

Biogenic amine Hormones that have important effects on the functioning of the central nervous system.

Bipolar depression A current term largely replacing the older term "manic-depressive psychosis"; bipolar depression is marked by both mania and depression, increased family risk for psychosis, early onset, and a greater role of genetic factors in etiology than in unipolar depression.

"Blind" research procedure Research method in which the experimenter is "blind" as to which subjects have received the treatment and which subjects did not; also used with reference to knowledge of the hypotheses of a study.

Blocking The subjective experience of having one's thoughts totally disappear while in the midst of ongoing thinking; this is not the same as having a "blank" mind, for blocking occurs as a disruption of ongoing thought.

Blunting A severe reduction in the intensity of affect; also referred to as flattened affect; most frequently associated with chronic schizophrenia.

Borderline An increasingly well-delineated clinical syndrome, the borderline individual is characterized by excessive anger, as the main (or only) affect, disturbances in self-identity, serious difficulties in interpersonal relations, and difficulty in social communication.

Brain tumor An abnormal growth in the brain which has no functional purpose and can cause physical impairment and death.

Bronchial constriction Constriction of the air passage to the lungs.

Caffeine A water and alcohol soluble substance (found most commonly in tea, coffee, and soft drinks) that acts as a central nervous system stimulant.

Cardiac disorder Disease or malfunction of the heart.

Cardiology The study of the heart and its diseases.

Cardiovascular disorders A disease or malfunction of the heart or blood vessels.

Catalepsy A state, commonly found in catatonic schizophrenia, characterized by a trance-like stupor and the maintenance of muscles in a rigid position.

Catatonic schizophrenia A form of schizophrenia in which the individual exhibits peculiar postures and gestures, curious grimaces, and engages in repetitive, stereotyped actions; the most commonly cited symptom of this subtype is "flexibilitas cerea"—"waxy flexibility."

Catecholamines A group of biochemical neurotransmitters (including epinephrine, norepinephrine, and dopamine) implicated in the etiology of psychiatric disorders.

Catharsis The purging of emotions or tensions.

Cerebellum Located at the rear base of the cortex, this brain structure is phylogenetically old and probably the first to be specialized for sensory-motor coordination.

Cerebral cortex The surface layer of the brain (cortex) in which the motor, sensory, and other higher brain function areas are found.

Cerebral hemispheres Refers to the two halves of the brain, each of which mediates different functions.

Cerebral palsy A group of disorders that depend upon injuries to lower brain centers rather than the cortex. The injuries are presumed to appear at birth.

Cerebral pathology An abnormality or disorder in the upper part of the brain.

Cervix The outer end of the uterus.

Character armor A term introduced by Reich to describe rigid and extreme control over one's emotions and behavior.

Charlatan A fraud or fake.

Child abuse Excessive chronic physical or psychological punishment that is dangerous to the child's health; often associated with physical harm.

Child guidance center (clinic) A clinic specifically serving the needs of children, child guidance centers provide both assessment and therapy. Families are often involved with child guidance centers because of the importance of family relations to the child's problems.

Childhood schizophrenia Usually appearing after the age of four or five, childhood schizophrenia often is associated with a symbiotic psychosis between child and parent (usually the mother), inappropriate emotional responses, general impulsiveness, explosive behavior, overly intensive pursuit of goals, and general "immaturity."

Cholesterol A fatty-like alcohol, found in all animal oils and fats, milk, egg yolks, cheese, etc.; cholesterol is important in the formation of cysts, carcinomatous tissue, and gall stones; recently implicated in cardiovascular disorders.

Chromosome The biochemical bodies carrying genes, the elementary units of heredity; in humans there are 22 pairs of chromosomes, in addition to the two chromosomes that determine sex.

Chronicity The duration and recurrence of a disorder.

Circulatory system The heart, blood vessels, and lymph network.

Clang association The association of one word to another on the basis of similar sound; for example, "dog" and "log."

Client centered therapy A form of humanistic, existential psychotherapy that emphasizes self-direction in individual growth; the primary task of the therapist is to facilitate this growth through paraphrasing, reflection of feeling, and provision of unconditional positive regard.

Climax Orgasm.

Clinical psychologist Usually refers to someone who has a doctoral degree in clinical psychology and has had supervised therapy experience; increasing numbers of states now require some form of certification for clinical psychologists.

Clitoris Female organ located above the vaginal opening which is very sensitive to sexual stimulation.

737

Cognition The act of knowing, including awareness, reasoning and judgment.

Cognitive map A term introduced by Tolman to describe the internal cognitive map of the environment that organisms build up on the basis of incoming impressions.

Cold turkey To abruptly and completely quit using a drug.

Colitis Inflammation of the large intestine (colon).

Community mental health A concept of mental health treatment largely arising during the 1950s, that emphasizes the treatment of individuals in the community; ideally, community mental health centers provide a wide range of services from emergency inpatient care to consultation and education.

Community psychology In contrast to the traditional services provided by community mental health services, community psychology seeks to change the community itself in order to provide a better environment for human growth.

Competence The sense or general experience of being a competent person who can produce desired effects.

Compulsion A recurrent or persistent thought, image, impulse, or action that is accompanied by sense of subjective compulsion and a desire to resist it; compulsion frequently has been used to refer to the irresistible impulse for action.

Concordance Rate The percent of relatives who have the same trait as the index individual.

Concrete attitude A capacity of the total personality characterized by a realistic, immediate, and unreflective stance toward the environment.

Conditioned response A response, given to a previously unconditioned stimulus (for example, salivation to the presence of food), now elicited by the conditioned stimulus (for example, a bell); established through repeated pairing of unconditioned and conditioned stimuli.

Conditioned stimulus A stimulus that, though previously neutral, has come to take on the signalling properties of an unconditioned stimulus through continuous pairing; in the classic example of conditioned salivation in dogs, the bell (previously a neutral stimulus) came to elicit salivation in the dogs through continued pairing with the presentation of food.

Confabulation Fantasies and elaborate fabrications provided in place of forgotten facts; often found in organic brain disorders.

Congenital malformation A malformation which originates at birth or during fetal development.

Conglomerate A corporation with many diverse activities.

Conjoint sexual therapy The simultaneous treatment of a couple for an identified sexual problem; as is true for marital therapy, conjoint therapy is based on the belief that the identified problem of an individual is the result of an interaction between partners.

Constructional apraxia A disability characterized by a difficulty in copying and manipulating spatial patterns.

Consultation A form of mental health intervention in which a psychologist or other mental health professional provides advice to those giving direct service to clients.

Consummatory response The last response in a series of responses that brings a state of adjustment. (See **Appetitive Response**.)

Contiguity Closeness in time, space, or meaning of two or more objects or events.

Contingencies of reinforcement The formal relationship between the schedule of reward and responding; in the laboratory, for example, rewards may be given on fixed or variable schedules.

Continuum Something which is continuous and has no definite boundaries.

Conversion hysteria A form of hysteria in which an underlying conflict is transformed into a sensory or motor expression; that is, the form of the physical symptom (e.g., hysterical blindness or anesthesia) is thought to represent the underlying psychic conflict; this term is currently being replaced by "somatoform disorders" (DSM-III).

Corpus callosum The bank of fibers which connects the two hemispheres of the brain.

Cortical blindness Blindness caused by a problem in the cerebral cortex.

Counter-conditioning The elimination of an old response by learning a new incompatible response to a stimulus.

Cranial pressure Pressure on the brain which can be caused by tumors or excess fluids.

Cretinism A condition caused by a lack of the thyroid hormone thyroxin which stimulates metabolic processes throughout the body. Clinical features of the condition are severe mental retardation, sluggish behavior, dwarfed stature, course dry skin and hair, a large protruding tongue, and deafness.

Crisis intervention The provision of psychological services to people in the midst of a specific crisis, for example, a natural disaster or death of a loved one.

Custodial care Minimal care of patients which does not include treatment.

Cyclothymic personality An otherwise healthy personality pattern that is marked by extreme variations of mood, thought to predispose an individual to depression.

Day center A mental health facility that provides therapy and activities only during the day; frequently popular for work with adolescents.

Defense mechanism An inferred psychodynamic process that protects the individual from anxiety, shame, or guilt; an inflexible behavioral pattern.

Degenerative disease Any disease which causes deterioration of the central nervous system.

Delay of gratification The ability to put off some behavior in order to obtain greater future satisfaction.

Delirium A mental state in which a person is confused, has disordered speech, hallucinations and delusions.

Delirium tremens (DTs) Symptoms of withdrawal from heavy drinking, characterized by sweatiness, tremulousness, hyperactivity, restlessness, hallucinations, and extreme anxiety.

Delusion A false belief that cannot be modified by reasoning or external information; a delusion is a belief, while hallucinations and illusions are perceptual phenomena.

Delusions of control (passivity) The belief that one's feelings, impulses, thoughts, actions, indeed one's very will, are imposed from without by an external force or agent; these thoughts, feelings, etc. are experienced as ego-alien, that is, as not belonging to the person.

Dementia A state of mind in which a person's thoughts are disorganized, abstract reasoning is difficult or impossible, and general reasoning ability has been lost; results from both organic and functional disorders.

Dementia praecox A precursor in name and concept (first coined by Morel and popularized by Kraepelin) to schizophrenia, dementia praecox is early mental deterioration; thought to be organically based and resulting in inevitable poor outcome.

Deoxyribonucleic acid (DNA) A complex molecular structure that mediates the transfer of genetic information and regulates metabolism.

Dependency conflict The tension created between the need to depend on others and the desire to be independent.

Depression A state of sadness, despondency, and unhappiness often accompanied by disturbances in sleeping, eating, and the ability to experience pleasure, loss of hope, and a lowered sense of self-esteem.

Derailment A metaphor used to characterize loosening of associations; often found in schizophrenia.

Designated or identified patient The person or persons who need therapy or change.

Detumescennce The resolution stage of sexual intercourse.

Diabetes A group of disorders characterized by the body's inability to properly utilize sugar; diabetes mellitus is a metabolic disorder in which the body's ability to oxidize carbohydrates is lost.

Diagnostic and Statistical Manual of Mental Disorders (DSM) The official classification of mental disorders used in the United States; this manual, prepared under the sponsorship of the American Psychiatric Association, represents a major shift to an empirically based diagnostic scheme.

Diathesis-stress model A model for the development of psychopathology that assumes a genetically transmitted predisposition (diathesis) that interacts with environmental stress to produce the clinical disorder.

Differential diagnosis The use of symptoms, family history, response to treatment, course, or response to testing to distinguish between similar disorders.

Diphtheria A disease which produces a false membrane in the throat and inflammation of the heart and nervous system.

Displacement A defense mechanism in which emotions are displaced from a more threatening to a less threatening object.

Dissociation A concept introduced by Janet to describe what appeared to be a split between various processes of a person in hysteria; for example, there was "la belle indifference" that depicted the hysterics' apparent lack of emotional concern over what they described as serious bodily symptoms; splitting off of ideas that serve to prevent unbearable psychological pain or conflict involving irreconcilable motives.

Dissociative disorders These functional disorders are characterized by a sudden and temporary change in normally integrated processes of consciousness and identity; people with dissociative disorders may suffer from amnesia, a loss of the usual sense of self, and a feeling of unreality.

Distemper A viral infection in dogs.

Diurnal swing A rhythmic daily pattern of physical or emotional changes.

DNA See *Deoxyribonucleic acid*.

Double-bind This concept from communications theory describes a situation in which contradictory messages at different levels of communication are expressed; the effect of this contradictory double message is to make it impossible for the responder to give a "correct" response.

Dominant gene A gene which carries the dominant genetic character or information. The characteristic of a dominant gene will mask the characteristic of a recessive gene.

Dominant hemisphere The side of the brain, left in right-handed people, which exerts the most control over skills such as language and understanding symbols.

Dopamine A neurotransmitter thought to play an important role in schizophrenia; dopamine precursors are used in the treatment of Parkinson's disease and depression.

Down's syndrome A general form of developmental arrest accompanied by severe mental deficiency; caused by one of three forms of chromosomal aberration: trisomy 21, translocation syndrome, and a mosaic pattern.

Drug dependence A state in which a person relies either physically or psychologically on some drug.

Duodenal ulcer An ulcer of the duodenum (the small intestine); often associated with stress.

Economy of happiness A metaphor used to describe a person's transactions that maintain an overall level of pleasurable affect.

ECT Electroshock therapy.

Ectomorphic body build A thin, lean body type. (See **Endo-** and **Mesomorphs**).

EEG See **Electroencephalograph**.

Efficacy The feeling that is produced when an individual performs an act that comes out as intended; a feeling of having effectively influenced the environment.

Ego Commonly used to refer to the sense of self or "I"; in psychoanalytic theory, ego is one of the three portions of the mind that serves reality functions, in contrast to the id which serves pleasure and the superego that represents a heightened sense of conscience.

Ego-alien behavior Behavior which is uncharacteristic of a person or seems to be out of one's control.

Egocentric Popularly used to describe selfishness or preoccupation with oneself; when used in a cognitive developmental sense, egocentric refers to thinking that is characterized by the lack of ability to take another's perspective.

Ego functions Any of the presumed activities of the ego, such as mediation between the id and superego and mediation between the individual and external reality.

Ejaculation The expulsion of semen during orgasm.

741

EKG   See **Electrocardiogram**.

Electra complex   The girl's counterpart to the Oedipus complex, this term reflects the young girl's love of father and jealous fear of mother.

Electrocardiogram (EKG)   A visual record of the electrical activity of the heart obtained by recording via electrodes from the chest; used primarily in diagnostic work.

Electroencephalograph (EEG)   A pictorial representation of the electrical activity of the brain obtained from electrodes placed on the outside of the skull and attached to a recording device.

Electroshock therapy   Treatment in which electric shocks are used to produce convulsions. Used primarily in depression and thought to speed up natural recovery.

Embezzlement   To divert entrusted funds to one's personal use.

Embryonic development   Development of the embryo in the uterus.

Emotional blunting   A presumed decrease or absence in emotional response; differentiated from depression in which there is feeling, but one of sadness.

Emotional divorce   A marriage in which the partners have grown so distant and hostile toward one another that they are "divorced" emotionally, if not legally.

Emphysema   A disease of the lungs which can also impair heart action.

Encephalitis   Inflammation of brain tissue.

Encounter groups   Encompassing a wide range of groups (such as EST, T-groups, marathon groups, nude encounters, etc.), this form of gathering seeks either to train or extend personal awareness and growth, rather than treating for disorder.

Endocrine disorder   A metabolic disorder which may affect mood, initiative and intelligence especially when the thyroid gland is affected.

Endomorphic body build   Characterized by heavy or fat body structure. (See **ecto-** and **mesomorph**.)

Enmeshed family system   A family in which boundaries among individuals are not clearly defined and attempts to establish oneself as independent from the family are actively discouraged.

Enuresis   Bed-wetting.

Epidemiology   The study of disease distributions in the population.

Epileptic seizure   A nervous disorder characterized by convulsions.

Epinephrine   A powerful hormone causing increased blood pressure, stimulation of the heart, accelerated heart rate, and cardiac output; used pharmaceutically to stimulate the heart.

Erogenous zones   Areas of the body which are sensitive to sexual stimulation.

Ethnic minority   Any minority based on cultural ties.

Etiology   The study of the causes of disorder or disease.

Etymology   The study of derivation.

Euphoria   A state of extreme optimism and elevated motor activity.

Excitatory process   An inferred state of the cortex in which there is increased or ongoing cortical activity.

Exhibitionism   A disorder of sexual aim in which sexual gratification comes primarily from the public exposure of one's genitals; almost exclusively a disorder of males.

Experimental neurosis   An "abnormal" behavioral state (such as stereotyped behavior, emotional display, or loss of motivation) produced by subjecting an animal to very difficult learning tasks often with severe punishment for failure.

Expressed emotion   The quality of emotional interaction.

Extrapunitive coping style Coping with frustration by placing blame outside of oneself. Opposite of intropunitive coping style.

Extrasensory perception Perception without using any of the five senses.

Externalization   A process by which internal conflicts are played out with environmental or external objects.

Extinction   The removal or suppression of behavior by withholding rewards, through punishment or through counterconditioning.

Factitious disorder Introduced in DSM-III, a disorder in which the psychological or physical symptoms appear to be under the patient's control; in contrast to malingering, factitious disorder has no obvious goal other than to adopt the patient role.

Family therapy   A form of group psychotherapy in which the entire family is perceived as having a psychological problem; based on systems theory, the family therapy perspective views the "sick" individual as a victim of the larger disorder of the family.

Fee-splitting   Giving part of an earned fee to the person who made the referral. This is often unethical or illegal.

Felony   A major crime punishable by imprisonment of one year or more.

Fertilization   The joining of the sperm and egg in reproduction.

Fetishism   A sexual practice in which some small part of the sex object, for example, a hand, a shoe, or a lock of hair, captures special power of sexual arousal.

Fetus   The developing, unborn offspring; commonly thought to be "alive" from the third month of pregnancy.

Flat affect Having little or no emotional response to any stimulus.

Florid symptoms Colorful, dramatic clinical symptoms.

Focal brain damage Brain damage limited to only one part of the brain; usually produces circumscribed behavioral effects.

Foreplay   Mutual stimulation by partners as a prelude to sexual intercourse.

Fragmented thinking   The breaking up of normal cognitive entities into pieces.

Free association   A psychoanalytic technique first introduced or coined by Freud that requires the client (analysand) to say everything that comes into his or her mind, no matter how silly or irrelevant it may seem.

Frigidity   A psychosexual condition in which the female fails to gain pleasure from sexual intercourse and to reach orgasm.

Frontal lobes   An area of the cortex associated with voluntary behavior, abstract thought, and problem solving.

Fugue   The sudden assumption of a new identity, amnesia for one's prior identity, and unexpectedly leaving one's customary workplace or home.

Ganglia   Plural of ganglion, a group of nerve cells lying outside the central nervous system.

Gastritis   Inflammation of the stomach.

Gastrointestinal tract The stomach and intestines.

Gay lifestyle Homosexual lifestyle.

743

Gender identity The subjective and consistent experience of one's own sex role.

General paresis (dementia paralytica or general paralysis) The end state of a degenerative process caused by syphilitic infection; characterized by defective speech, involuntary movement, disorientation, disordered thinking, confusion, dementia, and physical weakness.

Generalization In learning, the process by which the power of a stimulus to elicit or reinforce a response is shared by other stimuli that are similar to it.

Generativity A sense of wanting to help, establish, and guide the next generation; frequently occurring in middle age.

Genital organ Sexual or reproductive organs.

Genotype The underlying genetic or hereditary traits of a species or biological group; contrasted with phenotype, which is the overt behavioral expression of both genetic and environmental contributions.

Gesell developmental scale Behavioral inventories that assess the development of motor functioning, adaptation, language, and interpersonal behavior.

Gestalt therapy A form of psychotherapy broadly based on the principles of Gestalt psychology (roughly captured by the principle that "the whole is greater than the sum of its parts"); with respect to personality, this orientation emphasizes the person as a total functioning being; emphasis in therapy is placed on an individual's perceptions, feelings, and immediate awareness.

Gestation Period of fetal development in the uterus between conception and birth.

Glaucoma A disease of the eye in which liquids or humors cause an increase in pressure within the eyeball. Glaucoma can cause blindness.

Glove anesthesia An hysterical symptom characterized by the loss of sensation in one or both hands in the area that would roughly be covered by a glove (hence its name); there is no anatomic or physiological condition that could account for this pattern of sensory loss.

Gonadotrophin hormone A hormone that mediates the regulation of ovaries and testes.

Grandiose delusion An extreme, irrational belief in the supremacy of one's power, wealth, or fame.

Grief Intense sadness or depression, often with sobbing, that accompanies loss.

Group psychotherapy A generic term describing psychotherapy practiced in groups of six clients or more; theoretical orientation can vary considerably from one group leader to the next.

Habituation With reference to drug use, a state in which a person desires to continue taking a drug but has no overwhelming compulsion to obtain it at all costs, shows little or no tendency to increase the dose, manifests some degree of psychic dependence on the effects of the drug but no physical dependence, and does not carry drug related behavior to a point that is detrimental to society.

Halfway house A residence in the community that serves to ease an ex-patient's reentry into the community; some supervision is provided and the ex-patient can have the support of both staff and other patients.

Hallucination A marked perceptual

744

distortion in which someone perceives something for which there is no external stimulus; distinguished from illusions, which are the distortions of externally based perceptions.

Hallucinogens A class of drugs, such as LSD, characterized by their extreme effects on perception and information processing.

Heart palpitation A strong, rapid heartbeat.

Hebephrenic schizophrenia A subtype of schizophrenia that is rarely seen today; characterized by silliness, inappropriate smiling and laughter, bizarre disorganized ideas, and an incoherent stream of talk.

Hepatitis A disorder in which the liver becomes inflamed; presenting symptoms may include fever, headache, loss of appetite, jaundice, and gastrointestinal distress.

Hermaphrodite An individual who has the sexual organs of both sexes; generally one set is slightly more developed than the other.

High risk A term used to designate groups of people at statistically elevated risk for some disorder; with respect to schizophrenia high risk usually has been defined on the basis of parental diagnosis.

Histamine An amine, common to all animal and vegetable tissue, that causes expansion or swelling of the capillaries and stimulates gastric secretion.

Histrionic Extremely emotional or theatrical actions.

Hives A generic term for any number of skin disorders marked by swelling, itching, and redness.

Homeostatic mechanism A mechanism which keeps bodily functions at a stable level.

Homosexuality The sexual attraction to or engagement of sexual intercourse with members of one's own sex; for many years considered a formal psychiatric disorder, homosexuality recently has been deleted from psychiatric diagnoses.

Hormone A chemical substance made in the endocrine glands that elicits or controls bodily functions or behavior.

Hydrocephaly A developmental skull malformation caused by the accumulation of cerebral spinal fluid in the skull; this disorder may sometimes be treated by a shunt operation in which the excess cerebral spinal fluid is drained from the brain.

Hyperactivity A high degree of activity or restlessness in children; thought by some to be caused by some form of brain damage.

Hypo-activity Below normal motor activity and restlessness.

Hyper-activity Above normal motor activity and restlessness.

Hyperbaric oxygen A treatment for those suffering from inadequate oxygen in the brain in which 100% oxygen is inhaled for 90-minute sessions with periodic repetitions.

Hypertension A state of abnormally high blood pressure; essential hypertension occurs in the absence of any known organic cause, while secondary hypertension is a result of some primary medical condition.

Hypnotism The induction of an altered state of consciousness marked by relaxation, suspension of criticism, and trustful compliance; controversy continues regarding the extent to which a

745

hypnotist can influence the person hypnotized.

Hypochondriasis   An excessive concern over one's physical health.

Hypoglycemia   Abnormally low blood sugar sometimes resulting in cognitive and emotional disturbances, indistinguishable from functional psychiatric disorders.

Hypomania   A mild version or subacute form of mania, often indistinguishable from a normal state of good spirits and high efficiency.

Hypothalamus   Found at the junction of the midbrain and thalamus, this brain structure is an important mediator of autonomic nervous system reactions, emotions, feeding, etc.

Hysteria   Most prominent in the nineteenth century, this maladaptive behavior is characterized by emotional excitement, altered consciousness, and changes in sensory functioning that often have an organic-like quality to them; however, the "organic" symptoms do not conform to known organic processes.

Ideas of reference   Finding personal significance in trivial and unimportant events. A type of delusional thinking. (See **Referential Thinking**.)

Identification   The process by which a person comes to resemble a specific other person in thinking, feeling, and behavior.

Identity crisis   Recurring periods in the life cycle (though most often associated with adolescence) when one questions one's values, the meaning of life, and who one is.

Identity diffusion   An inability to define clearly who one is.

Idiosyncratic shift   An odd or unusual change in thought.

746

Illiteracy   The lack of reading and writing skills due to poor education and not mental deficiency.

Implosive therapy   A behavioral therapy characterized by the immediate presentation of the primary anxiety-provoking stimulus, while preventing the individual for escaping; contrasts with systematic desensitization, which relies on the presentation of increasingly more anxiety-provoking situations.

Impotence   Either the male's inability to engage successfully in sexual intercourse or infertility.

Incarceration   Confinement or imprisonment.

Incipient schizophrenia   A form of schizophrenia in which the person is keenly aware of outside stimulation even without overtly responding to it and in which the florid symptoms of schizophrenia are absent.

Incoherence   Having minimal organization or integration especially in speech.

Incontinence   An inability to control bodily excrements.

Infantile autism   A psychiatric disorder of childhood (frequently occurring as early as the first two years of life) characterized by a serious lack of contact with people, a backwardness in the communicative function of language, and an obsessive desire for the preservation of sameness.

Inferiority complex   A term introduced by Adler to refer to intense, unconscious feelings of insignificance, insecurity, or inability to cope with life; a persistent maladaptive pattern of functioning in which a person continually makes unfavorable comparisons between self and others.

Inflammation A local response to an injury characterized by swelling and redness.

Inhibition The conscious restraint of a behavior.

Inhibitory process An inferred state of the cortex in which cortical activity is decreased or stopped.

Innate A characteristic or trait of a person from birth.

Innocuous Harmless or inoffensive.

Insane A legal term used to describe an individual suffering from a mental disorder that is sufficiently severe to make informed and competent judgments impossible.

Insanity Largely of historical interest, insanity is the extreme disruption in behavior that causes people to be out of touch with reality; the term "mental disability" has been used more recently in reference to these behaviors.

Insight An individual's self-understanding; with respect to psychotherapy, insight describes the bringing into awareness of previously unconscious motives, feelings, conflicts, etc., and their effect on current functioning.

Insomnia An inability to sleep.

Instrumental response A behavior which becomes a means to an end such as a response to reduce anxiety.

Intellectualization A defense mechanism in which feelings and emotions are ignored and problems are analyzed in purely intellectual (metaphysical, religious, or political) terms, devoid of the original affect.

Intercourse Sexual mating or coitus.

Internalization Taking on as one's own the attitudes, behaviors, opinions, and feelings of others in the environment; different from imitation in that imitation is an intentional copying of others' behaviors.

Interpenetration The invasion of one sequential act with another, as in the case of man who starts to change his clothes for dinner and ends up in pajamas.

Interpretation A technique in psychodynamic therapy in which the therapist calls attention to something the client has said or points out relations among past experiences.

Involutional depression Post-menopausal depression characterized by depressive mood, worry, hypochondriasis, agitation, and delusions; current controversy exists regarding its etiology (hormonal or social).

Isolation A defense mechanism by which a person separates a memory or wish from the rest of the conscious psyche; this is in contrast to repression, which occurs at an unconscious level.

Juvenile delinquency—A term describing a regular pattern of antisocial, asocial, or criminal activity among juveniles; three types of juvenile delinquency have been suggested: socialized or subcultural is typically characterized by association with bad companions or gang membership; overanxious juvenile delinquency is characterized by shyness, apathy, sensitivity, and submission, but without impulsive and aggressive tendencies; and unsocialized aggressive delinquency is characterized by starting fights, being assaultive, cruel, defiant, and malicious.

Kaleidoscopic A constantly changing pattern.

Kickback Illegal payment in order to obtain business.

Klinefelter's syndrome An anomaly of the sex chromosomes (found only in

747

males) that results in tallness, leanness, breast enlargement, and smallness of undeveloped testes; mental defects occur in about a quarter of the men with this syndrome.

Lability Instability; rapid change; usually refers to mood or affect.

Laceration A jagged or torn wound.

Latency A psychosexual stage (from about four years of age to the onset of puberty) during which a child presumably shows no manifest interest in sexual activity; the potential for sexual activity exists, however, throughout this period.

Law of Effect Formulated by Thorndike, the Law of Effect states that the pleasure or satisfaction of a reward, for example, eating food, strengthens the responses immediately preceding the attainment of that goal.

Learned helplessness An empirically derived concept of depression as the learned belief that the outcomes (rewards and punishments) in one's life are unaffected by one's behavior; i.e., one learns that outcome is not contingent on behavior.

Learning As used in the text, learning may be conceived as the intergradation of signals that have predictive value for social interaction.

Lesion Damage to body tissue caused by injury or disease.

Lethargy Indifference or abnormal drowsiness.

Limbic system A group of structures in the brain believed to control emotional patterns.

Lithium A drug used in the treatment of affective psychosis.

Litigious patient A patient who is prone to engage in lawsuits. Often as-

sociated with paranoid personality or paranoid schizophrenia.

Lobotomy A surgical procedure to change behavior by cutting the nerve pathway between the frontal lobe and the thalamus.

Locus of control A social learning theory that describes the extent to which people attribute their behavior to forces within themselves (internal locus of control) versus those outside themselves (external locus of control).

LSD See **Lysergic acid diethylamide.**

Lysergic acid diethylamide (LSD) One of the more common hallucinogens, this synthetically produced drug was first discovered by Dr. Albert Hofmann, a Swiss chemist. LSD produces dramatic changes in perception, information processing, and beliefs, all of which are characterized in common parlance as "tripping."

Mainstreaming The placement of mentally retarded children in regular classrooms.

Major tranquilizers A class of potent drugs including chlorpromazine (Thorazine) that depress central nervous system functioning; used most often in the treatment of psychotic disorders, especially schizophrenia.

Maladaptive behavior Behavior that causes people's lives to go astray, so that they find themselves frustrated, unhappy, anxious, baffled in their deepest desires, or misfits in their society; in the most serious instances maladaptive behavior refers to behavior that gets so badly out of touch with surrounding life that we call this behavior insane.

Malaria A disease transmitted by mosquitoes, which causes fever, chills, and inflammation of the brain and its coverings.

Malingering A self-conscious production of psychological and/or physical symptoms by a person to obtain a specific goal (for example, an inmate in a prison "acting crazy" in order to be hospitalized in a psychiatric hospital rather than imprisoned).

Mania Derived from a Greek word meaning madness, this term refers to a state of overactivity, talkativeness, little sleep, energy, happy thoughts, and grandiose, flamboyant plans; differentiated from normal good spirits and productivity by its intensity, lack of control, and impulsiveness.

Manic-depressive psychosis First conceived by Kraepelin as a single mental disease entity, this disorder is a severe affective disorder in which extreme states of agitation, grandeur, and overexcitement (mania) and/or depression (very slow motor movement, lack of motivation to do anything, extreme low spirits, and poor self-esteem) occur.

Marathon groups A form of encounter group primarily characterized by its intensity and duration, meeting continuously for two or more days with only minimal time out for eating, sleeping, and other essentials.

Marital counseling Often referred to as conjugal therapy, a form of psychotherapy based on the belief that the marital complaints of the given individual are the result of interaction with the individual's mate; therapy focuses on communication between the partners.

Masochism Attainment of sexual gratification through the infliction of pain to one's own body.

Maternal sensitization The process of an Rh-negative mother's blood being exposed to her Rh-positive child's blood during pregnancy. This causes the mother's system to form antibodies against the child's blood.

McNaghten rules A legal guideline to determine insanity based on whether the defendant knew what he was doing or whether he knew it was wrong.

Medulla oblongata A continuation of the spinal cord, it is the innermost part of the brain containing the fibers that connect the brain with the spinal cord.

Melancholia A state of extremely low spirits, depression, excessive brooding, slow movements, very little motivation, and a great difficulty in experiencing pleasure.

Meningitis A disease caused by bacteria and characterized by the inflammation of the meninges surrounding the brain and spinal cord.

Mental deficiency Pronounced retardation presumably related to brain damage. Structural defects are apparent in the nervous system and other organs.

Mental retardation Sub-normal intelligence. May be divided into three categories, mild subnormality with I.Q. from 69 to 50, moderate subnormality with I.Q. from 49 to 20 and severe subnormality with I.Q. of less than 19.

Mescaline A psychoactive drug derived from the peyote cactus plant, producing vivid hallucinations and alterations in perception; mescaline also can be manufactured synthetically.

Mesomorphic body build A sturdy body structure type, falling midway between endo- and ectomorphs.

Metabolic function All those chemical

processes taking place in a living organism.

Metabolic disorders Disorders which produce a biochemical imbalance so that optimal functioning is impaired.

Metabolite Product of vital chemical process in the body.

Methadone A synthetic drug used as a substitute for heroin in the pharmacological treatment of drug addiction; unlike heroin, methadone is thought not to produce euphoria.

Microcephaly A developmental anomaly that retards the growth of the skull; results in severe mental retardation.

Microorganism Small organisms which are often the cause of infection and disease.

Midbrain Technically known as the mesencephalon, this part of the spinal cord merges into the hypothalamus and thalamus.

Minimal brain dysfunction A diagnostic term applied to children who show either hyperactive, impulsive, and distractible patterns of behavior or to children with special difficulties in learning (learning disabilities).

Minor tranquilizer A group of drugs including meprobamate (Milltown, Equanil), chlordiazepoxide (Librium), and diazepam (Valium) that depress central nervous system functioning and are used generally to reduce anxiety; in contrast to major tranquilizers, the dose necessary for clinical effectiveness of minor tranquilizers seems to produce less sleepiness.

Misdemeanor Minor crime punishable by less than one year imprisonment or a fine.

Modal IQ The most frequently occurring I.Q. in the given distribution.

Modeling Learning behavior through the observation of another.

Mongolism An old term used to describe Down's syndrome; a genetic disorder resulting in mental retardation.

Monoamine oxidase (MAO) inhibitors A group of drugs used in the treatment of depression which work by inhibiting the action of the monamine oxidase enzyme.

Monozygotic (identical) twins Twins who develop from the same fertilized egg. Contrast with dizygotic or fraternal twins.

Moral treatment A treatment started by Pinel in which mental patients were treated with kindness and understanding and released from restraints.

Morbidity rate Prevalence of persons with some designated disease in a defined locality or group.

Morphology The study of the form and structure of organisms.

Mortality ratio Death rate calculated by taking the ratio of the total number of deaths within a given category to the total population.

Motivation A drive or incentive which moves an organism towards a goal.

Multiple personality The coexistence of two or more complete personalities, each with its own set of memories, interpersonal relationships, and behavior patterns; the individual typically is dominated by only one of the personalities at any given time and transition from one personality to another is usually sudden and frequently is precipitated by stress.

Mutism An inability to speak caused by the lack of development of the necessary organs, deafness, physical disorder, or psychological disorder; "elective mutism" is the voluntary choice to not speak.

Myelin sheath The layer of fatty substance which surrounds and protects nerve fibers.

Narcotic A class of drugs acting primarily on the central nervous system; used medically to relieve pain, tranquilize, sedate, induce sleep, and relieve coughing and diarrhea; euphoria is often reported by narcotic addicts; narcotics can be natural (e.g., opium) or synthetic (e.g., methadone).

Negativism An inferred attitude characterized by the individual's resistance to suggestions; often an act that is opposite to that desired; this may take the form of behavioral, thinking, or emotional resistance.

Neologism Any word that is made up or coined; in a psychiatric context, neologisms are frequently associated with schizophrenia.

Neurasthenia A disorder characterized by fatigue and anxiety.

Neurology The study of the function and structure of the nervous system.

Neuron A nerve cell body with all of its connecting fibers.

Neurosis Literally meaning "abnormal or diseased condition of the nerves," this term came to represent a group of functional disorders having in common the presence of or ineffectual defense against anxiety; in contrast to people with psychotic disorders, neurotics maintain insight and are less affected in their everyday living. This term has been officially deleted from DSM-III and has been broken up into several new categories, most of which are subsumed under Anxiety Disorders.

Neurotic paradox Behavior that appears to be simultaneously self-perpet-uating and self-defeating; sometimes explained in terms of secondary gain, the advantages accruing to the "sick" or "patient" role.

Neurotransmitter Chemical compounds such as norepinephrine, which carry nerve impulses across a synapse.

Nicotine The active ingredient in tobacco on which cigarette smokers become dependent.

N,N-dimethyltryptamine The active ingredient in "yurema," a hallucinogen made from a Brazilian root of the Mimosa hostilis and used by Brazilian Indians to facilitate visions of the spirit world.

Norepinephrine A hormone which stimulates the sympathetic nervous system.

Nuclear conflict A primary psychological conflict that involves the child's relation to its mother. Dynamic psychologies see this as the main problem in infancy.

Obsession A persistent, frequently irrational idea that is outside the individual's control; when the individual tries to stop the obsessive thought, anxiety is experienced.

Oedipal complex One sign of the early, genital phase of psychosexual development, this term refers to a young boy's repressed desire for sexual intercourse with his mother and a corresponding jealousy and fear of the father.

Onset Age and way in which symptoms of a disorder appear.

Ontogenesis The history of the development of the individual organism.

Operant A term used by Skinner to describe classes of behavior that exist in an animal's repertory and act on (or operate on) the environment.

Operant conditioning A type of learning in which behaviors that already exist in an organism's repertoire are strengthened or weakened through the use of rewards and punishments; the administration of rewards and punishments is contingent on the organism's responses; this is in contrast to the classical conditioning paradigm in which stimuli are paired irrespective of the organism's response.

Oral impregnation The association between food and impregnation.

Orgasm Involuntary, pleasurable climax to sexual intercourse.

Outpatient A patient who comes to the clinic or hospital for therapy instead of staying at the hospital as does an inpatient.

Overinclusive thinking Thinking in which normally accepted conceptual boundaries overlap substantially with one another.

Panacea A cure for all problems or ills.

Panic attack The sudden, intense breakthrough of anxiety; represents the momentary failure of defense mechanisms that usually keep the person reasonably serene.

Paranoia A psychotic condition in which an individual persists in maintaining delusional beliefs of persecution or grandeur, but with no deterioration in other areas of functioning.

Paranoid schizophrenia One of several forms of schizophrenia characterized by the maintenance of delusional beliefs about persecution or grandeur in association with typical symptoms of schizophrenic personality disorganization and emotional response.

Parasympathetic nervous system One of two divisions of the autonomic nervous system; concerned primarily with conserving and restoring the body resources.

Parental Care The medical care of mother and child during pregnancy in order to regulate the mother's diet, monitor the baby's development, and handle any emergencies that may arise.

Parietotemporal area An area of the brain which bears a special relation to the human attainments of language and meaning of symbols.

Parkinson's disease A paralytic disorder characterized by muscle tremors, stiff gait and an expressionless face.

Partial hospitalization Hospitalization for specific periods during the day, e.g., for purposes of evening meals and sleeping overnight; one of the services required at community mental health centers.

Passive-aggressive A term used to characterize either a personality or defensive style marked by the passive expression of hostility or anger; for example, becoming extremely quiet in response to anger.

Pediatric medicine The area of medicine concerned with the care of children.

Pedophile A person who is sexually attracted to immature, young children.

Pepsinogen A precursor of pepsin, an important enzyme in digestion.

Peptic ulcer Ulceration, found in the esophagus, stomach, or duodenum, caused by overactivity of the stomach (or the oversecretion of acid gastric juice).

Peripheral nerves Nerves that fall outside the spinal cord.

Perseveration The persistent repetition

of an act, thought, or feeling, frequently associated with brain damage.

Personality disorders A characterological style that causes social conflict; may be accompanied by cognitive, emotional, or motivational disturbances.

Peyote A cactus plant from which mescaline is derived.

Phenotype The overt behavioral expression of underlying genetic (genotypic) traits; phenotypic behavior is a product of both genetic and environmental factors.

Phenylalanine An amino acid which is not properly metabolized in cases of phenylketonuria (PKU).

Phenylketonuria (PKU) A recessively transmitted metabolic disorder resulting from an absence of a basic enzyme, leading to the accumulation of phenyl alanine, an amino acid; left untreated PKU can result in severe motor and intellectual dysfunction; however, immediate institution of low phenylalanine diet prevents the more extreme abnormality.

Phobia An irrational dread of an object, act, or situation.

Phyletic program Development based on natural evolutionary patterns.

Physiology The study of processes and mechanisms of living organisms (especially those that allow the organisms to live under varied conditions, e.g., temperature regulation, food intake control, hormonal functioning).

Pituitary gland A small gland found at the base of the brain that is responsible for the production of numerous hormones important for growth, metabolism, and other body functions.

Placebo An inactive treatment (usually a drug) given to a patient who believes that he is being given actual treatment.

Pornography Material which is considered erotic, causes sexual arousal, and violates the tastes of a given society.

Possession A state in which some malignant demon presumably inhabits the body of the victim or directs the disordered behavior from without; a belief largely popular during the fifteenth and sixteenth centuries, it has had a small resurgence during the last decade.

Postpartum depression Depression which occurs after childbirth.

Precipating factor or precipitating stresses The factor or stress which causes a disorder to begin.

Precursor A forerunner or something which procedes.

Premature ejaculation The early discharge of semen during orgasm; it may occur either before insertion or soon afterwards.

Premorbid adjustment The psychological, social, and work adjustment of an individual before the onset of a disorder; usually predictive of outcome.

Prescriptive penology A concept in which society's response to a criminal act varies as a function of the offender's potential for reform.

Prevalence Percent of a population with a given disorder at a given time.

Prevention Intervention designed to either stop a disorder from developing (primary prevention) or to identify and intervene early in the disorder to reduce the impact of the illness (secondary and tertiary prevention).

Primary affective disorder An affective disorder that is apparently unaccompanied by other disorders and oc-

753

curs in the absence of a history of any other psychiatric illness.

Primary gain   The control or better management of anxiety.

Primordial   Primary or first.

Proaction   Behavior that is steered by the anticipation of future goals and satisfaction, proaction includes making plans, imagining future possibilities, and executing serial steps that lead to distant goals.

Process schizophrenia   An empirically based subtype of schizophrenia characterized by poor premorbid adjustment, insidious onset of symptoms, a deteriorating course of disorder, and generally poor outcome. (See **Reactive schizophrenia.**)

Prognosis   The predicted outcome of a disorder.

Prohibition   Period in U.S. history when the distillation and sale of alcohol were illegal.

Projection   A defense mechanism in which one's own traits, conflicts, or attributes are attributed to others in the environment.

Prophylactic   maintenance   therapy   Therapy aimed at prevention.

Protein   Part of the cell made up of strings of amino acids.

Pseudocommunity   Coined by Cameron, this term refers to the imaginary attitudes and functions attributed to real people in the environment by the paranoid person.

Pseudoneurotic schizophrenia   An old term used to describe a "borderline" form of schizophrenia midway between schizophrenic psychosis and neurosis.

Psilocybin   A hallucinogenic drug derived from a Mexican mushroom.

Psychasthenia   An obsolete term for a form of neurosis whose symptoms in-

clude fixed ideas, obsessions and anxiety reactions.

Psychedelic   Intensified or distorted sensory perception.

Psychiatric social worker   Originally someone who visited homes and offered practical advice, the social worker now engages in therapy as well as the immediately practical tasks of finding living arrangements, financial resources, etc.

Psychiatrist   A person with a degree in medicine who specializes in psychiatric (emotional, thinking, and behavioral) disorders; one of the major differences between the psychiatrist and all other mental health professionals is the former's right to prescribe medication.

Psychoactive drug   A drug that affects mental process primarily.

Psychodrama   Originated by Moreno, this psychotherapy uses play acting or small dramatizations of psychological conflicts; it is thought that having patients "act" through various conflicts facilitates emotional expression.

Psychodynamic   An orientation of psychology that emphasizes forces, motives, and wishes, largely unconscious.

Psychogenic   Processes arising from psychological origins, i.e., originating from emotional, mental, or behavioral sources; psychogenic processes arise out of the adaptive process.

Psychological treatment   An inclusive term that designates all forms of intervention in maladaptive and abnormal behavior that work fundamentally through the learning process.

Psychologist   A person trained in behavioral sciences, usually with a Master's, PhD, or PsyD degree.

Psychology   Originating as a study of the mind and behavior, psychology has expanded to include all aspects of individual functioning as well as social interactions.

Psychopathic personality (psychopath) An individual who engages in criminal or marginally criminal activity, does not seem able to plan for the future, seems to lack guilt and anxiety over the criminal activity, and has shallow interpersonal relations.

Psychopathology The study of maladaptive behavior presumably caused by ideas or other psychological processes.

Psychophysiological disorders A current term used to characterize organ system dysfunction in which emotional stress plays an important causal role.

Psychosis A generic term including all serious mental disturbances in which there is an extreme loss of contact with reality, an inability to function in the environment, and for which no organic basis can be found.

Psychosocial stressors Stressors which are dependent on symbolic activity and emotions.

Psychotherapy Any of a number of psychological treatments for mental disorders.

Psychotomimetic A drug, such as LSD, which produces a state similar to psychosis.

Psychotropic drug Any of a number of mind altering drugs.

Puberty The stage of sexual development during which the sexual organs fully mature and become completely functional; starting around the ages of twelve to fourteen, this period is marked by much physical growth and psychological turmoil.

Rape Forced sexual relations.

Raynaud's Syndrome The intermittent loss of blood to extremities, especially the fingers or toes and occasionally the ears and nose; known as Raynaud's disease when there is no known organic cause for the phenomenon; in some cases, it can lead to gangrene.

Reaction A response to existing and past stimuli or events; distinguished from proaction, which is behavior motivated by the anticipation of future stimuli or events.

Reaction formation A defense mechanism characterized by the expression of thoughts, feelings, and behavior that are opposite to the "true," underlying ones (e.g., compulsive tidiness as a reaction formation against destructive, messy tendencies).

Reactive depression A depressive response to some external, environmental life change; distinguished from endogenous depression that appears to arise in the absence of any obvious environmental stress.

Reactive schizophrenia An empirically based subtype of schizophrenia characterized by good prognosis, acute symptom onset, and presence of precipitating stresses.

Recessive Mendelian trait Any trait which is not expressed unless a person has both recessive genes.

Recidivist One who relapses or returns to an old habit, often applied to criminal activity.

Reciprocal inhibition A conditioning principle which states that learning one behavior inhibits another that is incompatible with it; for example, learning to relax is incompatible with feeling anxious.

Referential thinking Beliefs and interpretations of the environment in which unrelated events are given personal sig-

755

nificance, often with a negative or perjorative implication.

Refractory patients Patients who are unmanageable and obstinate or resistant to treatment.

Regression A return to earlier modes of thinking, feeling, and acting; formal regression is the return to identical behaviors found in earlier stages of psychosexual behavior.

Rehabilitation The process of returning one to productive activity.

Remediation The process of relieving or curing a disease through treatment.

Remission Temporary disappearance of the symptoms of a disorder.

Rumination The uncontrollable and unpleasant persistence of thoughts or ideas.

Replicate To produce the same results.

Repression The most primitive of defense mechanisms characterized by the exclusion from thoughts of memories, images, and impulses involving severe anxiety; repression occurs most frequently in early childhood in response to instinctual urges that would lead to disastrous consequences if expressed.

Resistance A postulated defense mechanism which keeps threatening thoughts out of the conscious mind.

Respiratory system Lungs and air passages.

Retarded depression A depressive state in which a person feels hopeless, dismal, and has extremely low self-esteem; speech, thought and action are extremely slow; and the person experiences extreme lethargy and lack of motivation.

Reticular formation (reticular activating system) A system of cells starting at the top of the spinal cord and ascending through the medulla to the brain stem; thought to be especially important in the mediation of attention, awareness, sleeping, and selective perception.

Rhesus factor incompatibility A condition occurring when an Rh-negative mother conceives an Rh-positive child. If components of the child's blood enter the mother's bloodstream the mother's system will produce antibodies to destroy the child's red blood cells. Rh incompatibility can cause mental retardation.

Rheumatoid arthritis Chronic inflammation of the joints, accompanied by swelling, redness, and pain.

Ribonucleic acid (RNA) Large protein molecules found in some nuclei that are believed to act as "messengers" in genetic information and possibly mediate memory.

RNA See **Ribonucleic acid.**

Rorschach Developer of the Rorschach Inkblot Test. A projective personality assessment.

Sadism The attainment of sexual gratification through the infliction of pain to one's partner.

Schizoaffective schizophrenia A subtype of schizophrenia in which the individual, in addition to the common thought disturbances, exhibits a great deal of emotional disorder as well; usually associated with good premorbid history, acute onset, and good prognosis.

Schizoid A detached, withdrawn personality with a lack of involvement with others.

Schizophrenia Literally meaning "spilt mind," schizophrenia is a functional disorder characterized by thinking disorder, social withdrawal, flat or inappropriate affect, and ambivalence;

sometimes confused with the far rarer disorder "split personality."

Schizophrenic spectrum A term coined to describe the nonpsychotic, but clearly deviant personalities of some relatives of schizophrenics.

Schizophrenogenic mother A type of mother, characterized by dominance, aloofness, and emotional overinvolvement with her child, that was presumed to play a significant role in the etiology of schizophrenia; now generally believed to be untrue.

Secondary affective disorder An affective disorder that occurs with another illness, such as anxiety disorder, antisocial personality, or drug use.

Secondary gain The advantages accruing from the existence of symptoms; gains from illness and other effects on the person's environment.

Sedative-hypnotics A general term including a wide range of drugs that have in common a generally depressing and tranquilizing effect on the user; includes alcohol, barbiturates, and minor tranquilizers.

Seizure A sudden attack of convulsions.

Self-actualization The development of one's own talents and capacities.

Self-esteem The affective component of a self-concept that reflects how "good" or "bad" an individual feels about him- or herself.

Semantic dementia A tendency towards verbalizations devoid of emotional meaning.

Sensory deficit A deficiency in any of the senses.

Sensory overload A state of excessive sensory information input.

Serology The study of blood and its properties.

Serotonin A compound in the brain believed to regulate emotion and sleep.

Service-connected The status of veterans who are suffering from various disorders, both medical and psychological; a disorder is service-connected if it developed while the individual was in active military service.

Sex role The public expression of gender identity.

Sexual promiscuity Indiscriminate sexual behavior.

Shunt operation Surgical procedure used to correct the build up of brain fluid in hydrocephalics. Drainage tubes are inserted at the base of the brain to divert the excess fluid directly to the heart for recirculation.

Simple schizophrenia One of the schizophrenias in which onset is gradual, individuals are "quietly" disturbed, and withdrawn, and affective life is outwardly shallow and uneventful.

Simulate Having only the outward appearances of something.

Social amenities Acts or customs conventionally observed in social intercourse.

Social class Groups based on economic level, education, and family background.

Social competence Having the necessary abilities to function in society.

Social conditioning Behavioral learning mediated by social factors.

Socialization The process of fitting one into the social environment by teaching social customs and cultures.

Social learning theory An area or perspective of psychology emphasizing the importance of social interaction in the learning process (for example, imitation, identification, and modeling).

Sociocultural retardation A mild form

757

of mental backwardness attributable to familial, cultural, or social factors; this group makes up by far the largest portion of the mentally retarded in this country.

Sociometric ratings The measurement of an individual in a group, usually by peers.

Sociopathic personality A person characterized by maladjustment in the area of social relations, especially sexual, or whose behavior can be said to be asocial. (Also, see **Psychopathic personality**.)

Somatoform disorder Functional disorders in which physical symptoms suggesting physical disorder predominate; these are presumed functional disorders because specific physiological and/or anatomical dysfunction cannot be demonstrated by any known laboratory procedures; in contrast to factitious disorders or malingering, somatoform disorders are not under the voluntary or conscious control of the person exhibiting the symptoms.

Somnambulism Sleepwalking.

Spastic Uncontrollable motor behavior.

Specificity hypothesis A theory of psychophysiological disorders in which practical attitudes are believed to contribute to the clinical symptoms observed.

Speech articulation The manner in which one pronounces.

Sphincters Muscles which open and close body openings. The anal and urethral sphincters contract during orgasm.

Spina bifida A developmental disease marked by a defect in the bony encasement of the spinal cord.

Spinal cord Tracts of fibers running the length of the body that carry sensory information to the brain and commands for motor movement from the brain.

Spontaneous recovery or remission Any recovery or remission of symptoms with little or no treatment.

Stimulant Any drug which increases motor activity and reduces fatigue; a central nervous system arouser.

STP An LSD-like drug frequently mixed with it.

Stress A state of psychological or physical strain; psychological stress often occurs in situations in which one is unable to produce relevant and expectably effective actions.

Stupor Condition in which a person is unoriented and does not respond to stimuli.

Subliminal idea Unconscious idea.

Suggestion The process of influencing behavior or feelings through hypnosis or direct commands.

Symbiotic psychosis A psychotic condition in which the child and parent (usually the mother) are engaged in an extremely intense relationship marked by very weak ego boundaries between parent and child; separation of child from parent produces disorganization and panic in the child.

Sympathetic autonomic nervous system One of two divisions of the autonomic nervous system concerned primarily with the mobilization of resources of the body for use in work or emergency.

Synapse A connection between nerve cells; a nerve impulse is transmitted from one nerve cell through the synapse to the next nerve cell via neurochemical transmitters.

Syndrome A group of symptoms which

occur together and characterize a disorder.

Syphilis A contagious venereal disease including symptoms of memory loss, apathy, anxiety, emotional instability, euphoria, loss of judgment, irritability, slovenliness, and sudden violence.

Systematic desensitization The presentation of increasingly anxiety-provoking stimuli in conjunction with relaxation techniques; this allows an individual to cope gradually with higher levels of anxiety via the incompatible response of relaxation.

Tay-Sachs disease A recessively inherited enzyme deficiency, most prevalent among Ashkenazic Jews, that results in profound retardation and total blindness, and premature death.

Temporal lobe An area of the brain important in the mediation of recent memory.

Testes Male reproductive gland.

Testosterone A hormone, produced by the male's testes, responsible for the development of masculine sex characteristics.

Tetrahydrocannibol (THC) The active ingredient producing psychological effects in hashish and marijuana; also produced synthetically.

T-groups (training groups) The earliest form of encounter group, T-Groups were developed shortly after World War II to train people to better understand human relations.

THC See **Tetrahydrocannibol.**

Therapeutic alliance The interpersonal relationship between therapist and client on which the work of therapy is based; this relationship is characterized by trust, respect, empathy, warmth, and genuineness.

Therapeutic milieu A concept of group psychotherapy in which everyone in a client's environment is incorporated into the treatment program; milieu therapy originated in hospitals and included the training of attendants and other hospital staff, as well as the organization of patients into groups to provide a therapeutic atmosphere.

Thought broadcasting The belief that private thoughts are actually transmitted across space and perceived by the external world; a Schneiderian first rank symptom thought by some to be pathognomic of schizophrenia.

Thought insertion A belief that thoughts are actually inserted into the mind; this is not the same as believing that one's thoughts are influenced by external sources, but rather that thoughts not belonging to the person have replaced the person's own.

Thought withdrawal A delusional explanation for thought blocking in which it is believed that an external agent has physically removed the thought from one's mind.

Tic Involuntary, spasmodic jerking in a small coordinated group of muscles.

Token economy A system based on secondary reinforcement used to shape behavior; as used in hospitals, a token economy may require that a patient work for tokens that may then be exchanged for privileges such as watching television or going to the canteen.

Tolerance A change in physiological state, resulting from drug use, in which increasingly large doses are required to produce a given subjective state.

Toxemia A condition in which poison is present in the blood.

Trait A measurable characteristic of an individual.

759

Tranquilizer Any drug which reduces tension and anxiety.

Transference A psychoanalytic concept describing a client's displacement of his or her affective relationship with the parent onto the therapist.

Transsexual An individual whose psychological gender identity is contrary to his or her biological sex.

Transvestism A condition in which sexual excitement is obtained by wearing clothes of the opposite sex.

Trauma Usually a direct physical injury; also used in reference to psychological impact.

Tremor The shaking or trembling of the body or limbs; tremor occurs in two forms: intentional tremor that occurs only when a person begins to perform a voluntary movement and tremor of rest that occurs more or less constantly.

Tricyclic antidepressant Drug used in the treatment of some forms of depression.

Tuberculosis A highly communicable disease which mainly affects the lungs.

Tunnel vision Used to describe a state of restricted vision in which a person can only see things directly in front; may be caused by either psychological or physical factors.

Twilight states Confusion, distress, and a sense of unreality and dream-like state.

Typhoid fever A communicable disease caused by bacteria and characterized by fever, diarrhea and inflammation of the brain.

Ulcer Loss of skin or mucuous surface substance leading to disintegration and death of cells.

Ultrasound Frequencies which are above the range of human hearing.

Unconscious motivation A drive or motivation of which the individual is not consciously aware.

Undoing A defense mechanism in which one engages in ritualistic behavior designed to counteract or negate the effects of previous behavior.

Unipolar depression A form of depression which displays no manic phase. There is usually only one episode of depression.

Uterus The saclike organ where the fetus develops.

Vacillation Indecision or an inability to act.

Vagina Female genital organ leading from the uterus to the exterior of the body.

Vasoconstriction Constriction of the blood vessels.

Vigilance Alertness and watchfulness.

Viral infection Any one of a number of diseases which is caused by a virus.

Visual-motor coordination An ability often impaired by brain tumors, refers to the successful interaction of visual input to guide motor output.

Volition Will; the act of making a choice or decision.

Voyeurism A disorder of sexual aim in which a person derives sexual gratification from watching others undress or engage in sexual relations.

Withdrawal symptoms The physical symptoms, suchas irritability, nervousness, and sweating, which occur when a drug on which a person has become physically dependent is withdrawn.

Word association test An assessment procedure designed to measure an individual's association to a series of words; the responses presumably reflect unconcious conflict or motivation;

there are two types of association tests: a free association test in which a person is instructed to give the first response that comes to mind and a controlled association test in which a person is to give the first response in a specified category.

Word salad A descriptive term referring to what appears to be strings of unconnected words, sometimes appearing in the speech of seriously disturbed schizophrenics.

Chapter 16

613: Leonard McCombe/Time-Magazine, Time Inc. 614: Rick Windsor/Woodfin Camp. 618: Courtesy Williard R. Centerwall, M.D. from *Phenylkentonuria*, Frank L. Lyman, ed;, Charles C. Thomas, 1963. 623(top): Ken Heyman. 631: Karen R. Preuss/Jeroboam. 635(top): Courtesy, Hamot Medical Center. 635(bottom): Copyright 1976, by Newsweek, Inc. All rights reserved. Reprinted by permission. 643(top): Rick Freidman/Picture Cube. 643(bottom): Robert Foothorap/Jeroboam. 644: Bruce Kliewe/Jeroboam.

Chapter 17

650: Jean-Marie Simon. 655: B. Kliewe/Jeroboam. 661: Paul Fusco/Magnum.

Name Index

767

Levis, D. J., 249
Levy, D. M., 119
Lewin, B. D., 187, 535
Lewine, R. R. J., 476, 537
Lewinsohn, P. H., 539
Lewis, O., 130
Liberman, B. L., 267
Lieberman, M. A., 295
Lindmann, E., 91, 237, 310, 656
Lindsjö, A., 610
Lindzey, G., 111
Lipowski, Z. J., 310, 312, 326, 336, 337, 340, 562, 563
Lipton, E. L., 338
Lipton, M. A., 548
Lipton, R. C., 117
Liss, J. L., 326
Little, W. A., 328
Livson, F., 597
Locke, E. A., 252
Lotter, V., 496
Louria, D. B., 407, 410
Lowe, G., 418
Lubensky, A. W., 489
Luborsky, L., 210
Luparello, T. J., 335
Lyerly, O. G., 216

McCabe, M. S., 480, 484
McCaghy, C. H., 348, 350, 353, 378, 558
Maccoby, E. E., 431
McCelland, D. C., 420
McCord, J., 369, 373
McCord, W., 360, 369, 373
MacCulloch, M. J., 453
McDougall, W., 160, 209
McGaugh, J. L., 252
McGuire, L. E., 405
McHugh, P. R., 562
MacKinnon, D. W., 170
McLeary, R. A., 373
McNichol, K. N., 332
Maher, B., 5, 6
Maher, B. A., 370, 374
Maher, W. B., 5, 6
Mahler, M., 497
Main, T. I., 281
Malamud, W., 214

Malinowski, B., 428
Malmquist, C. P., 537
Malmo, R. B., 338
Mannig, B. A., 393
Marcia, J. E., 149
Margaret, A., 573
Marks, I., 190, 195, 196
Marks, I. M., 213
Martin, C. E., 449
Martin, M., 658
Masland, R. L., 636
Maslow, A. H., 252
Mason, J. W., 544
Masserman, J. H., 36, 165, 168
Masters, W. H., 282, 436, 442, 444
Masuda, M., 307, 308, 309, 312
Mathe, A. A., 335
Matthyse, S., 509
Maurice, W. L., 442
Mausner, B., 387, 389
Mawson, A. R., 324, 325
May, R., 253, 259, 515, 516, 517
Maynard, H., 663
Mechanic, D., 213, 652
Mednick, S. A., 671
Meehl, P. E., 507
Meichenbaum, D., 251
Melnyk, J., 612
Mendels, J., 542
Menolascino, F. J., 609
Mercer, J. R., 641
Merrill, M. A., 356
Meserve, W. G., 388
Messina, J. A., 214, 217
Metcalfe, M., 334
Metrakos, J. D., 585
Metrakos, K., 585
Meyer, A., 482
Meyer, G. G., 214
Meyerowitz, S., 214, 217
Meyer, J. E., 324, 325, 482
Meyer, V., 570
Meyers, J., 658
Miall, W. E., 328
Michaux, W. M., 664
Micheal, S. T., 649
Miklich, D. R., 341
Miles, C. P., 531
Miles, M. B., 295

771

775

Subject Index

return of patients to the community, 662-664
prevention and, 669-673
shortage of professionally trained
workers, 664-669
Community psychology, 654
Companion programs, 667
Compensation, 34
Competence:
adaptive process and, 92
aggression and, 128-129
early growth of, 119-123
psychological treatment and, 266-267
during school years, 131-133
self-esteem and, 120-122
Comprehensive Alcohol Abuse and
Alcoholism Prevention, Treatment, and Rehabilitation Act of
1970, 424
Compulsions (compulsive anxiety
disorders), 200-208
distinctive features of, 202-203
illustrative case of, 205-208
symptoms of, 201-202
Compulsive personality types, 200, 217
Compulsive promiscuity, 147-148
Compulsive self-sufficiency, 118
Computerized axial tomography (CAT
scan), 563-564
Conditioned response, 97-98
extinction of, 100-101
phobia as, 196-197
see also Aversive conditioning
Confabulation, 560
Conformity:
anxious, 125
cannabis (marihuana) use and, 396
excessive, 140-141
mental retardation and institutionalization and, 626
Congenital malformation of brain
tissue, 556
Constitutional factors (or vulnerability),
27-28
in affective disorders, 542-546
in alcoholism, 420-421
in anxiety disorders, 220
in hypertension, 328-329
in peptic ulcers, 322-323

in psychophysiological disorders,
336-340
in schizophrenia, 484, 489-492,
505-510
biochemical and neurophysiological
evidence, 507-510
genetic evidence, 505-507
modes of genetic transmission, 507
see also Genetic factors
Consultation, 657-658
Contraceptives, 435
Control, 7
compulsive disorders and, 203
locus of, 108-109
see also Self-control
Conversion symptoms, 212-217
illustrative case of, 214-216
placement of, 216-217
Coping strategies, psychophysiological
disorders and, 339-340
Coronary heart disease, 329-331
Correctional institutions, therapeutic
milieu in, 297-299
Corrective emotional experience,
psychological treatment and,
227-228
Cortisol, depression and, 544
Cretinism, 637-638
Crime (criminal behavior), 346-355
case of Bert Whipley, 75-83, 109,
110, 128, 165, 363, 539
organized, 354-355
professional, 349-355
society's response to, 374-380
balancing effectiveness against
fairness in law enforcement, 378
prescriptive penology, 378-380
prognosis of different criminal
types, 376-378
revenge motive versus prevention
motive, 374-376
street, 346-349
white collar, 350-355, 377-378
see also Delinquency; Sociopathic
personality disorder
Crisis intervention, 656-657
Crisis-oriented therapy, 237
Cultural deviance, delinquency and,
356-357

784

Headstart project, 630–631
Hebephrenia (disorganized form of
     schizophrenia), 472–475
Hereditary predisposition, *see* Constitu-
     tional factors; Genetic factors
Hermann, Kathi, case of adolescent
     mental breakdown, 53–60, 474,
     501, 502, 504
Hermaphrodites, 448
Heroin, 409–411
Hickock, Dick, case of sociopathic per-
     sonality disorder, 366–371, 377
Histrionic personality traits, 212, 217
Hives, 311
Homeostasis, old age and, 594–595
Homosexuality, 445–457
     biological aspects of, 445–446, 448
     changing homosexual orientation,
          452–457
Hospitalism, 115
Hospitalization:
     for affective disorders, 547
     indications for, 661–662
     partial, 659–660
     see also Mental hospitals
Hospitals, 5
     see also Mental hospitals
Hostility, *see* Aggression
Humanistic-existential psychotherapy,
     252–259
     client-centered therapy, 253–257
     existential psychotherapy, 252–253
     meaning and, 257–259
Huntington's chorea, 561–562
Hydrocephaly, 634, 636
Hyperactivity (hyperkinetic behavior),
     582–583
     see also Minimal brain dysfunction
Hypertension, 305, 327–329
Hypnotism:
     hysteria and, 22–25, 28–30
     psychophysiological research using,
          310–312
Hypochondria, in old people, 597
Hypothalamus:
     affective disorders and, 546
     anorexia and, 325
     peptic ulcers and, 322–323

Hysteria, 22–30, 42
     Breuer and Freud's theory of, 28–30
     case of Irene, 27
     Charcot's study of, 24–26
     constitutional vulnerability to, 27–28
     dissociation and, 27
     hypnotism and, 22–25, 28–30
     as inadequate term, 212
     Janet's view of, 26–28
     memory and, 27
     see also Conversion symptoms

Identification, 108
     ego identity and, 149
     with therapist, 233
Identity, ego, 149–151
Identity achievement, 150
Identity diffusion, 150–151
Identity foreclosure, 149–150
Ideo-motor action, 24
Imitation:
     conversion symptoms and, 217
     sex roles and, 145–147
     see also Modeling
Immaturity, delinquency and, 358–359
Impotence, 438–440, 443
Incompetency to stand trial, 376
Incoordination, 573
Independence, 117–118
Indeterminate sentencing, 379–380
Individual psychology, 236–237
Indole amines, 545
Infantile autism, 495–497
Infection, brain disorders caused by,
     558–559
     see also General paresis
Inferiority, feelings of, 34
Inferiority complex, 122–123
Information, adaptive strategy and, 89
Insanity and the insane:
     criminal behavior and legal defense
          of, 375–377
     evolution of attitudes toward, 3–14
          charity, 4–5
          community mental health, 12–14
          mental hygiene movement, 11–12
          Pinel's reforms, 7–9
          possession by evil spirits, 6

785

793